STOW-ON-THE-WOLD
WAR MEMORIAL

STOW-ON-THE-WOLD WAR MEMORIAL

A HISTORY OF THE MEMORIAL AND ITS MEN

SUSAN BRATTIN

Copyright © 2015 Susan Brattin

The moral right of the author has been asserted.

Apart from any fair dealing for the purposes of research or private study, or criticism or review, as permitted under the Copyright, Designs and Patents Act 1988, this publication may only be reproduced, stored or transmitted, in any form or by any means, with the prior permission in writing of the publishers, or in the case of reprographic reproduction in accordance with the terms of licences issued by the Copyright Licensing Agency. Enquiries concerning reproduction outside those terms should be sent to the publishers.

Matador
9 Priory Business Park,
Wistow Road, Kibworth Beauchamp,
Leicestershire. LE8 0RX
Tel: 0116 279 2299
Email: books@troubador.co.uk
Web: www.troubador.co.uk/matador
Twitter: @matadorbooks

ISBN 978 1784622 770

British Library Cataloguing in Publication Data.
A catalogue record for this book is available from the British Library.

Typeset in 11pt Aldine401 BT Roman by Troubador Publishing Ltd, Leicester, UK

Matador is an imprint of Troubador Publishing Ltd

Lest We Forget…

In Memory of the Men who died in the First and Second World Wars and whose names are commemorated on the tower wall of St Edward's Church, Stow-on-the-Wold, Gloucestershire

Acknowledgements

Commonwealth War Graves Commission, Maidenhead
Churchill Archive Trust, Cambridge
National Archives, Kew
Evesham Journal
Gloucestershire Echo
Birmingham Central Library
Gloucester County Library
Stow-on-the-Wold Library
Gloucestershire Record Office
Warwickshire Record Office
Bedfordshire & Luton Archives, Bedford
The Royal Logistic Corps Museum, Deepcut
Soldiers of Gloucestershire Museum, Gloucester
Redcoats in the Wardrobe, Salisbury
Royal Regiment of Fusiliers (Warwickshire) Museum, Warwick
The Worcestershire Regiment Museum Trust, Worcester

Contents

Introduction — xv
The War Memorial — xvii

The First World War Men — 3

Their Home Addresses in Stow & District — 7
Their Service In The Royal Navy, Army, Royal Air Force, Australian and Canadian Forces — 11
Their Memorials and The Cemeteries Where They Are Buried — 17
Their Deaths In Chronological Order — 21

The Individuals

ARTHURS, John Thomas	22
BUTTERS, Henry Augustus	30
CAMPIN, Leonard Thomas	42
CAMPIN, Walter Edward	44
CASTLE, Edward William	48
CHAMBERLAYNE, Rupert Henry INGLES-	54
CLARK, William Hylton	62
CLIFFORD, Cecil Raymond	66
CLIFFORD, Eustace George	72
CLIFFORD, Horace	78
CLIFFORD, Tom Bernard Gregory	82
COOKE, William	86
CURTIS, Charles	92
DANCE, Philip	96
EATON, Arthur Ernest Wilson	100
ELLENS, Alfred	108
FRANCIS, Richard John	112
HATHAWAY, George	116
HEMMINGS, George	120
HIATT, Tom	124

STOW-ON-THE-WOLD WAR MEMORIAL

The war memorial was designed in two parts, the first part was the erection of the rood beam.

HICKS, Francis Alfred John	128
HICKS, Percy	134
HILLIER, John Henry	138
HODGKINS, Percy	142
HOOKHAM, Robert	146
KING, Leonard	154
MINCHIN, Richard Edward	160
MURRAY, John James	164
NEWCOMBE, Hubert Conroy	170
PHIPPS, Harold	174
PRATLEY, Frank	176
PULHAM, Benjamin William Thomas	178
PULHAM, Frank	182
RAILSTON, Spencer Julian Wilfred	184
ROBBINS, George	190
SANSOM, Alfred Charles	194
STEPHENS, Fred Albert	200
SUMMERSBEE, Austin Philip	204
TAYLOR, William George	212
TIMMS, John William	218
WEBB, Frank	220
WEBB, William	222
WEBLEY, John Robert	226
WEBLEY, Robert	230
YOUNG, Ernest Albert	234

The Second World War Men   *239*

Their Home Addresses in Stow & District	241
Their Service In The Royal Navy, Army & Royal Air Force	243
The Cemeteries Where They Are Buried	245
Their Deaths In Chronological Order	247

The Individuals:

BAILEY, Anthony	248
BAILEY, Christopher Sidney	250
BANNING, Frederick Anthony	256

STOW-ON-THE-WOLD WAR MEMORIAL

Carving the names of the fallen on the tower wall was the second part of the design of the war memorial.

COLDICOTT, Keith John	260
FOSTER, Richard Norman	262
JONES, Maurice Edwin	266
JOSLIN, Frank	270
KING, Frederick Harold	274
LOFF, Victor Charles	278
MILLER, Frederick	282
MILLER, George	288
ROSE, Joseph	290
SMITH, Henry Toomer	292
SUMPTION, John Barnett	296

STOW-ON-THE-WOLD WAR MEMORIAL

The Reverend John Evans, Rector of Stow from 1899 to 1935

Let us therefore make every effort to do what leads to peace and to mutual edification.
Romans 14:19

Introduction

It is said old soldiers never die but the fifty nine men whose names are listed on this war memorial did not have the opportunity to grow old. They died, the oldest aged 42 and the youngest only 17. One man had been in the army for only eighteen days, some of the others were regular soldiers and had served for several years. Between them they belonged to all three services. Five are buried in Stow, the others are buried or commemorated all over the world.

Inevitably as the years have passed, memories of these men and the details of their lives have faded. I set out to gather as much information as possible about them and to compile this book so that we might honour them and they were not just names on the tower wall. Most of them knew and loved St Edward's and I have shown such connections where known. The Rectors during both wars knew these men and grieved with and supported their families. The Rev John Evans was the incumbent at St Edward's from 1899 to 1935 and the Rev Christian Hare from 1935 to 1952.

The population of Stow was about 1750 in 1914 and the majority of people who lived here had never travelled very far. More than 200 of them went off to the war. The families left behind did what they could to help in many different ways such as aiding Belgian refugees in this country or by sending fresh eggs to nourish the wounded in clearing hospitals at the front. Some people wrote letters to young soldiers. The children grew vegetables in plots in their school garden. On one occasion they gave sixty cabbages to Mrs Chamberlayne at Hyde House who collected and sent vegetables each week by rail (carriage free) to Aberdeen for use on navy vessels.

Today in the Stow area there are still a few families and friends of the Second World War men but sixty years have now passed since the end of that conflict. It is indeed time to write down their stories. In World War One 45 Stow men died, including four pairs of brothers. Happily, in World War Two there were only about a third of that number – 14 deaths including two pairs of brothers. Finding out about them all has been like a treasure hunt or trying to complete a complex jigsaw puzzle. It has involved visits to the National Archive at Kew, Gloucester and Warwick Record Offices, Gloucester and Birmingham Central Libraries, several Regimental Museums and of course the internet has been invaluable. However, there are still gaps in the information. More than two thirds of the service records of soldiers covering the period 1914-1920 were destroyed or damaged by enemy action in World War Two and the service records of troops of the 1939-1945 conflict are not yet available for public scrutiny. To my very great disappointment, I have been totally unable to trace any record whatsoever which would indicate why Joseph Rose and John Sumption warranted inclusion in the World War Two names. Therefore, I should be delighted if any visitor reading this could provide me with further details. My sincere thanks go to all those people, and especially my husband, who have helped me with their time, information and suggestions. I have found the search enthralling and the stories fascinating. I hope you do too.

Susan F M Brattin, Stow-on-the-Wold, August 2005

STOW-ON-THE-WOLD WAR MEMORIAL

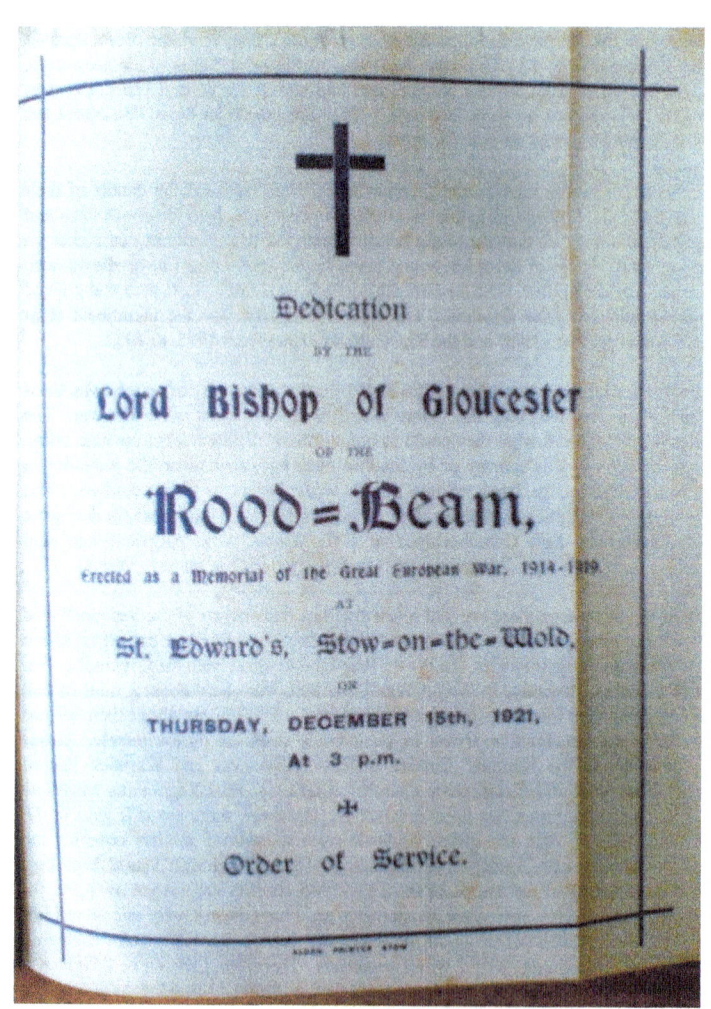

Order of Service – 15 December 1921

The War Memorial

The Rector, the Rev John Evans, presiding at the Easter Vestry meeting held in the Choir Vestry on 6 April 1915, said: "When the war is over (God grant it may be soon), we people of Stow will see that a lasting and fitting monument is erected in the parish church to perpetuate the memory of these heroic young Englishmen. Meanwhile we ask those who have been so sadly bereaved to accept our heartfelt sympathy. May God comfort them all in their bitter sorrow."

At the end of the war discussion ranged over various possible memorials until at a meeting of the PCC on 16 June 1920 it was finally agreed that a Rood Beam with the figures of Christ, the Virgin Mary and St John should be erected. Although the Armistice commenced at the eleventh hour on the eleventh day of November 1918, the Treaty of Versailles between the Allies and Germany was not signed until 28 June 1919, hence the dates shown on the memorial of 1914-1919. The design had been submitted by Messrs Healing & Overbury, architects in Cheltenham, at an approximate cost of £500. Mr Edward Francis, one of the Churchwardens, pledged £50, an anonymous donor gave £25 and there was already a balance at credit of £95 to start the fund off. By 20 October 1920 at a subsequent meeting of the PCC, matters had progressed. The Archdeacon of Cheltenham had suggested some modifications, which were agreed, and the architects proposed recording the names of the fallen by carving them on the tower wall. Although the full amount required had not yet been raised, it had been ascertained that payment would not be pressed for and therefore Messrs R L Boulton & Son, sculptors of Cheltenham, were requested to put the work in hand at once from the designs drawn up by Messrs Healing & Overbury.

A year later on 29 November 1921, arrangements for the dedication of the War Memorial were discussed and a committee formed of the Rector, the Churchwardens, Mrs Ingles-Chamberlayne and Mr McMurdie to deal with seating plans etc.

The Service of Dedication by the Lord Bishop of Gloucester took place on Thursday 15 December 1921. The PCC contributed to buy a wreath on the occasion of the dedication and the balance was given towards the erection of a permanent shelf under the Roll of Names for flowers to be placed thereon from time to time.

On 7 February 1922 in the Treasurer's statement on the War Memorial Fund, the total cost was £603 15s 3d against donations given and promised, plus bank interest to 31 December 1921, a total of £590 16s 3d. Contributions were invited to pay off the balance.

After the Second World War, in June 1946 the PCC unanimously agreed that the names of parishioners who had lost their lives in that war should also be inscribed on the tower wall, irrespective of what else was done as a war memorial in the parish. However, the war memorial in St Edward's to this day remains the principal war memorial in Stow. In February 1948 it was again unanimously agreed that plans from Messrs R L Boulton & Son be accepted and they were duly instructed to carry out the work immediately.

WORLD WAR ONE

Declaration of War – 4 August 1914

Armistice – 11 November 1918

Treaty of Versailles – 28 June 1919

The Memorial – The First World War Men

Note:

The ages shown on the memorial are not always correct. I have amended this on each individual's page.

THE ROOD BEAM IN THIS CHURCH WAS ERECTED IN MEMORY OF THE FOLLOWING WHO LAID DOWN THEIR LIVES IN THE GREAT EUROPEAN WAR 1914-1919

		Date of Death	Age
1.	ARTHURS, John Thomas	30.03.1915	42
2.	BUTTERS, Henry Augustus	31.08.1916	24
3.	CAMPIN, Leonard Thomas	03.07.1916	32
4.	CAMPIN, Walter Edward	21.03.1918	36
5.	CASTLE, Edward William	24.08.1918	31
6.	CHAMBERLAYNE, Rupert Henry INGLES-	15.10.1914	17
7.	CLARK, William Hylton	12.02.1919	32
8.	CLIFFORD, Cecil Raymond	01.04.1915	19
9.	CLIFFORD, Eustace George	05.10.1917	25
10.	CLIFFORD, Horace	29.11.1917	36
11.	CLIFFORD, Tom Bernard Gregory	01.03.1916	34
12.	COOKE, William	24.02.1917	27
13.	CURTIS, Charles	06.02.1915	39
14.	DANCE, Philip	28.06.1918	26
15.	EATON, Arthur Ernest Wilson	01.08.1915	23
16.	ELLENS, Alfred	01.12.1918	33
17.	FRANCIS, Richard John	31.03.1915	21
18.	HATHAWAY, George	09.05.1915	21
19.	HEMMINGS, George	02.05.1916	42
20.	HIATT, Tom	26.02.1919	31
21.	HICKS, Francis Alfred John	25.10.1918	39

STOW-ON-THE-WOLD WAR MEMORIAL

British Service Medals of the First World War

1914 Star   **1914-15 Star**   **Victory Medal 1914-1919**   **British War Medal 1914-1920**

1914 Star

The 1914 Star was awarded to members of the British Expeditionary Force who served in France or Flanders between 5 August 1914 and midnight on 22/23 November 1914.

1914-15 Star

The 1914-15 Star was awarded to those who saw service in any theatre of war against the central powers between 5 August 1914 and 31 December 1915 except those eligible for the 1914 Star.

Victory Medal

The Victory Medal 1914-19 was issued in commemoration of the Allied victory, mostly to those who served in a theatre of war between 5 August 1914 and 11 November 1918.

British War Medal

The British War Medal 1914-1920 was issued to commemorate the successful conclusion of the war and awarded to those who had served in a theatre of war up to and including the official end of the war in 1920.

22.	HICKS, Percy	06.04.1918	22
23.	HILLIER, John Henry	04.10.1917	41
24.	HODGKINS, Percy	25.05.1916	20
25.	HOOKHAM, Robert	03.07.1918	42
26.	KING, Leonard	18.11.1916	19
27.	MINCHIN, Richard Edward	07.09.1916	20
28.	MURRAY, John James	17.12.1919	29
29.	NEWCOMBE, Hubert Conroy	25.04.1918	33
30.	PHIPPS, Harold	16.08.1916	24
31.	PRATLEY, Frank	07.08.1916	21
32.	PULHAM, Benjamin William Thomas	28.10.1918	25
35.	ROBBINS, George	20.05.1917	25
36.	SANSOM, Alfred Charles	07.11.1918	36
37.	STEPHENS, Fred Albert	08.08.1915	20
38.	SUMMERSBEE, Austin Philip	25.04.1915	22
39.	TAYLOR, William George	24.05.1919	31
40.	TIMMS, John William	28.03.1918	19
41.	WEBB, Frank	26.07.1916	23
42.	WEBB, William	22.09.1917	22
43.	WEBLEY, John Robert	14.11.1918	30
44.	WEBLEY, Robert	10.08.1916	32
45.	YOUNG, Ernest Albert	02.10.1915	37

STOW-ON-THE-WOLD WAR MEMORIAL

Stow Towards the End of the 19th Century

Their Home Addresses in Stow and District

Many of the families were tenants of rented houses and moved house on several occasions over the years. The addresses shown here are their last address before the First World War started.

Back Walls	-	Richard Minchin
	-	Benjamin Pulham
Camp Gardens	- Ivy Cottage	Julian Railston
Cemetery Walk	- Wraggs Row	Fred Stephens
Chapel Street	- Hope Cottage	Eustace Clifford
	-	Philip Dance
	-	George Hemmings
	-	Robert Webley
Church Street	-	Frank Webb
	-	William Webb
Enoch's Row	-	John Murray
	-	William Taylor
Evesham Road	- no. 9	Horace Clifford
Fosseway	- The Rectory (now Bretton House)	Harry Butters
High Street	-	Tom Clifford
Oddfellows Row	-	George Hathaway
Park Street	-	John Arthurs
	-	Leonard Campin
	-	Walter Campin
	-	Cecil Clifford
	- Park Lodge	Charles Curtis
	-	Arthur Eaton
	-	Percy Hicks
	-	Francis Hicks
	-	Harold Phipps
	-	Frank Pulham
	-	John Timms
	-	Ernest Young

The Fosse Way at the Unicorn Hotel around 1900

Their Home Addresses in Stow and District

Sheep Street	-	William Clark
	-	John Hillier
	-	Philip Summersbee
Station Road	- South Hill Cottage	Robert Hookham
	-	George Robbins
The Square	-	Tom Hiatt
Union Street	-	Alfred Sansom
Well Lane	-	William Cooke
	- no. 20	Alfred Ellens
	-	Frank Pratley
Little Rissington	-	John Webley
Lower Oddington	- Parkers Cottages	Percy Hodgkins
Lower Swell	- Hyde House (now Fosse Manor Hotel)	Rupert Ingles-Chamberlayne
	- Beechwood	John Francis
Maugersbury	- Wyck Hill Lodge	Edward Castle
	- Half Moon House	Leonard King
	-	Hubert Newcombe

In 1914 Lord Kitchener of Khartoum was Secretary of State for War with responsibility for recruitment. A hastily drafted recruiting leaflet (probably written by Kitchener himself) appeared within days of the declaration of war on 4 August 1914. The famous poster was produced a few weeks later.

Their Service In The Royal Navy, Army, Royal Air Force, Canadian And Australian Forces

ROYAL NAVY

HMS Hawke
    Midshipman Rupert Ingles-Chamberlayne

ARMY

CAVALRY
4th (Royal Irish) Dragoon Guards
    Lieut Julian Railston – seconded from 18th King George's Own Lancers (Indian Army)

INFANTRY
Grenadier Guards

L/Cpl Frank Pratley	- 4th Battalion
Pte John Timms	- 2nd Battalion

Royal Warwickshire Regiment (6th of Foot)

Cpl John Murray	- 1st Battalion
Pte Richard Minchin	- 2nd Battalion

Norfolk Regiment (9th of Foot) – awarded prefix 'Royal' 1935

Pte Leonard Campin	- 2/4th Battalion

Somerset Light Infantry (13th of Foot)

L/Sgt Cecil Clifford	- 1st Battalion

Bedfordshire Regiment (16th of Foot)

Sgt Eustace Clifford	- 1/5th Battalion
L/Cpl John Hillier	- 8th Battalion

Gloucestershire Regiment (28th of Foot)

L/Cpl Alfred Ellens	- 8th Battalion
Pte John Arthurs	-1st Battalion
Pte George Hathaway	- 2nd Battalion

STOW-ON-THE-WOLD WAR MEMORIAL

Recruits for the Gloucestershire Regiment at Stow – 14 August 1914

From the Evesham Journal – Saturday May 15 1915

RECRUITING MEETING
On Stow Fair evening (Wednesday) a recruiting meeting was held in the Market place, when addresses were delivered by Mr T Spink and Mr R W Birkett, their remarks being illustrated by a series of views shown by an acetylene lantern on a sheet arranged in front of Lloyds Bank. Sergeants Smart and Terrell were present and the latter also spoke. In response to the appeal for recruits six men presented themselves.

Pte Percy Hicks — 13th Battalion
Pte (Sig) Leonard King — 8th Battalion
Pte Frederick Stephens — 7th Battalion
Pte William Taylor — 8th Battalion
Pte Robert Webley — 7th Battalion
Pte Ernest Young — 10th Battalion

Worcestershire Regiment (29th of Foot)
Pte Francis Hicks — 2nd Battalion
Pte Alfred Sansom — 14th Battalion (Severn Valley Rangers)

South Staffordshire Regiment (38th/80th of Foot)
L/Cpl Tom Clifford — 1st Battalion

Oxfordshire & Buckinghamshire Light Infantry (43rd/52nd of Foot)
L/Cpl Harold Phipps — 3rd Battalion
Pte George Hemmings — 1st Battalion

Sherwood Foresters (Nottinghamshire & Derbyshire) Regiment (45th/95th of Foot)
Pte Frank Webb — 1/6th Battalion

The Queen's Own Royal West Kent Regiment (50th of Foot)
Pte Walter Campin — 7th Battalion

King's Royal Rifle Corps (60th of Foot)
Rifleman George Robbins — 16th Battalion

London Regiment (The Rangers) – amalgamated with King's Royal Rifle Corps
Rifleman William Webb — 12th Battalion

York & Lancaster Regiment (65th of Foot)
Lieut John Francis — 2nd Battalion

ARTILLERY

Royal Field Artillery
2nd Lieut Harry Butters — 109th Brigade

Royal Garrison Artillery
2nd Lieut Edward Castle — 126th Siege Battery
Cpl William Cooke — 195th Siege Battery

STOW-ON-THE-WOLD WAR MEMORIAL

Silk embroidered postcards from World War One. They were mostly produced by Belgian and French women refugees and were hand embroidered on strips of silk mesh. The cards were mailed home at no charge to the sender in Military Mail pouches.

Gunner Horace Clifford   - 342nd Siege Battery
Gunner Hubert Newcombe - 263rd Siege Battery

CORPS

Army Service Corps – awarded prefix 'Royal' 1918
Pte Charles Curtis

Army Veterinary Corps – awarded prefix 'Royal' 1918
Pte Benjamin Pulham

Royal Army Ordnance Corps – awarded prefix 'Royal' 1918
Pte William Clark

Royal Defence Corps
Pte Frank Pulham

Labour Corps
Pte Philip Dance
Pte Robert Hookham
Pte John Webley

ROYAL AIR FORCE

Aircraft Supply
Aircraftsman 1st Class Tom Hiatt

CANADA

Canadian Infantry (Quebec Regiment)
Pte Percy Hodgkins

AUSTRALIA

Australian Infantry AIF
Pte Arthur Eaton   - 11th Battalion
Pte (Bugler) Philip Summersbee - 12th Battalion

Europe 1914

Their Memorials Or The Cemeteries Where They Are Buried

Belgium

La Clytte Military Cemetery	Hubert Newcombe
Lijssenthoek Military Cemetery	Percy Hodgkins
Steenkerke Belgian Military Cemetery	Horace Clifford
Ypres, Menin Gate Memorial	George Hathaway
	Julian Railston

England

Bradford, Scholemoor Cemetery	Benjamin Pulham
Chatham Naval Memorial	Rupert Ingles-Chamberlayne
Devonport, Weston Mill Cemetery	Tom Clifford
Stow-on-the-Wold Cemetery	Leonard Campin
	Philip Dance
	John Murray
	Frank Pulham
	William Taylor

France

Abbeville Communal Cemetery	Harold Phipps
Abbeville Communal Cemetery Extension	Percy Hicks
Armentieres, Cite Bonjean Military Cemetery	John Francis
Arras Memorial	George Robbins
	John Timms
	Frank Webb
Boulogne Eastern Cemetery	Frank Pratley
Bully-Grenay Communal Cemetery, British Extension	William Cooke
Etaples Military Cemetery	Ernest Young

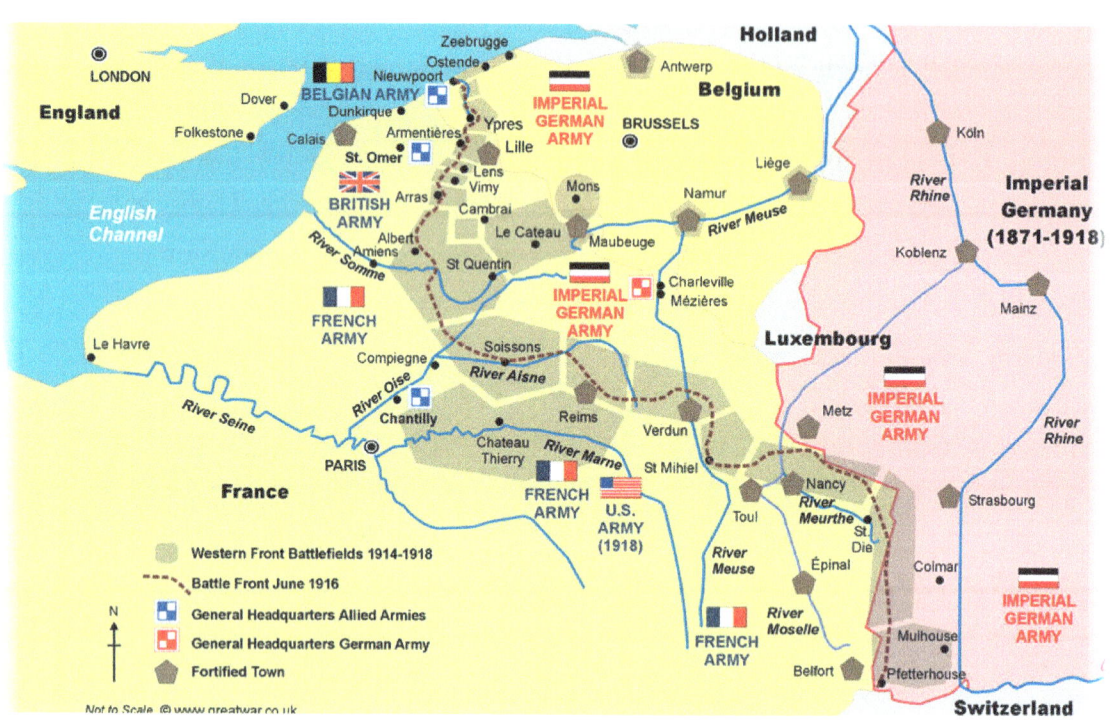

The Western Front

Their Memorials Or The Cemeteries Where They Are Buried

Loos British Cemetery	John Hillier
Manancourt, Rocquigny-Equancourt Road British Extension	Francis Hicks
Maricourt, Peronne Road Cemetery	Richard Minchin
Meaulte Military Cemetery	Harry Butters
Morchies Military Cemetery	William Webb
Neuve Chapelle British Cemetery	John Arthurs
Pozieres Memorial	Walter Campin
Querenaing Communal Cemetery	Alfred Sansom
Rouen, St Sever Cemetery	Charles Curtis
St Sever Cemetery Extension	Alfred Ellens
Sangatte, Les Baraques Military Cemetery	William Clark
St Omer, Longuenesse Souvenir Cemetery	Tom Hiatt
Thiepval Memorial	Leonard King
Villers-Bretonneux Military Cemetery	Edward Castle
Wimereux Communal Cemetery	Cecil Clifford
Wimille, Terlincthun British Cemetery	Robert Hookham

Gallipoli

Helles Memorial	Frederick Stephens
Lone Pine Memorial	Philip Summersbee
Shell Green Cemetery	Arthur Eaton

India

Trimulgherry Cantonment Cemetery	George Hemmings
(also Madras 1914-1918 War Memorial, Chennai)	

Iraq

Basra War Cemetery	Robert Webley

Israel

Gaza War Cemetery	Eustace Clifford

Republic Of Ireland

Grangegorman Military Cemetery	John Webley

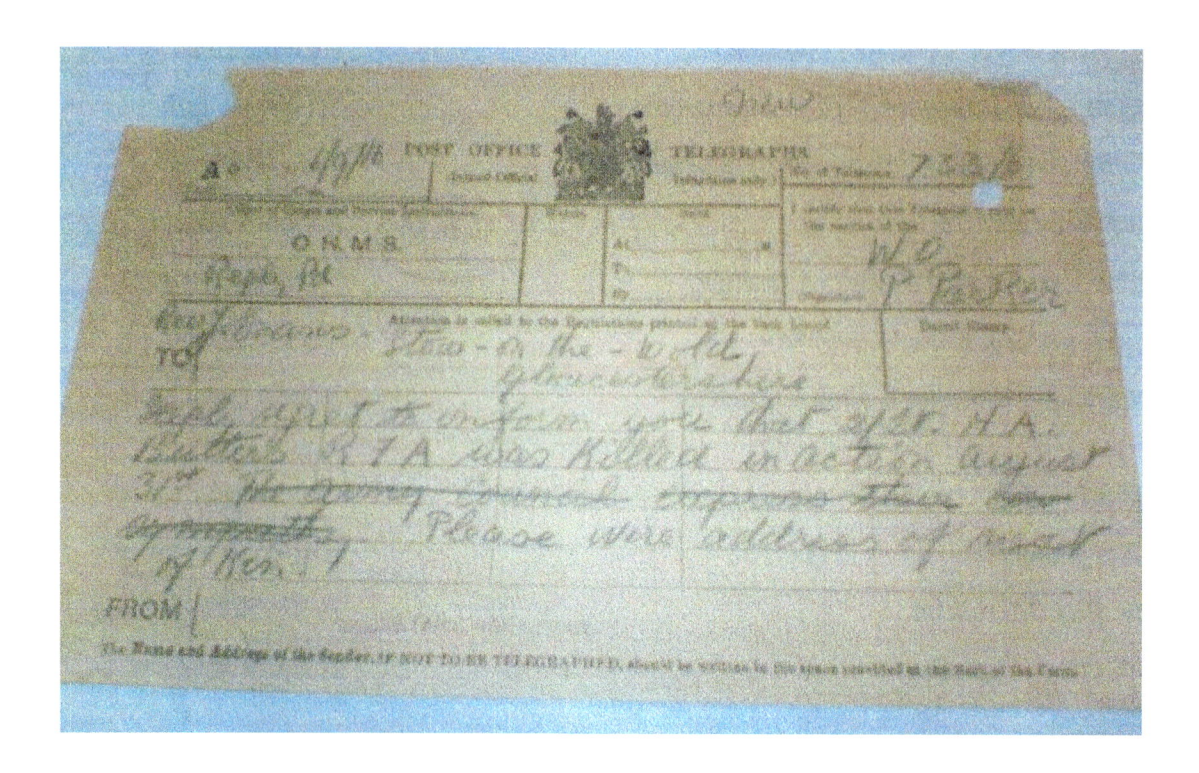

File copy of the telegram sent to the Rector, the Rev J Evans, advising of the death of Second Lieut Harry Butters

"6/9/16 To: Rev J Evans, Stow-on-the-Wold, Gloucestershire. Deeply regret to inform you that 2/Lt H A Butters was killed in action August 31st. Please wire address of next of kin. From: Secretary, War Office"

First World War Deaths Chronologically And Cause Of Death

1914
15 Oct	Rupert Ingles-Chamberlayne	KIA
30 Oct	Julian Railston	KIA

1915
06 Feb	Charles Curtis	I
30 Mar	John Arthurs	KIA
31 Mar	John Francis	DOW
01 Apr	Cecil Clifford	DOW
25 Apr	Philip Summersbee	KIA
09 May	George Hathaway	KIA
01 Aug	Arthur Eaton	KIA
08 Aug	Fred Stephens	KIA
01 Oct	Ernest Young	DOW

1916
01 Mar	Tom Clifford	I
02 May	George Hemmings	A
25 May	Percy Hodgkins	DOW
26 July	Frank Webb	DOW
07 Aug	Frank Pratley	DOW
10 Aug	Robert Webley	I
16 Aug	Harold Phipps	DOW
31 Aug	Harry Butters	KIA
07 Sept	Richard Minchin	DOW
18 Nov	Leonard King	KIA
16 Dec	Leonard Campin	I

1917
24 Apr	William Cooke	KIA
20 May	George Robbins	KIA
22 Sept	William Webb	KIA
04 Oct	John Hillier	KIA
05 Oct	Eustace Clifford	DOW
29 Nov	Horace Clifford	KIA

1918
21 Mar	Walter Campin	KIA
28 Mar	John Timms	KIA
06 Apr	Percy Hicks	DOW
25 Apr	Hubert Newcombe	DOW
28 June	Philip Dance	A
03 July	Robert Hookham	I
24 Aug	Edward Castle	DOW
25 Oct	Frank Hicks	DOW
28 Oct	Benjamin Pulham	I
07 Nov	Alfred Sansom	DOW
14 Nov	John Webley	I
01 Dec	Alfred Ellens	I
01 Dec	Frank Pulham	I

1919
12 Feb	William Clark	I
26 Feb	Tom Hiatt	I
24 May	William Taylor	I
17 Dec	John Murray	I

KIA – Killed In Action   DOW – Died Of Wounds   A – Accident   I – Illness

STOW-ON-THE-WOLD WAR MEMORIAL

*Cap badge of the
Grenadier Guards*

*Front and back cap badges of the
Gloucestershire Regiment*

Private John Arthurs

John Thomas Arthurs

Date of Birth	30 March 1873 – Little Rissington
Service	3691 Grenadier Guards (1892 -1904)
	2908 Private, 1st Battalion, Gloucestershire
Date of Death	Killed in action on 30 March 1915 – age 42P
Stow Address	Sheep Street (1901), Park Street (1907), Digbeth Street (1909)
Parents	Frederick Arthurs b. 1835 Fifield
	Harriet Arthurs b. 1836, d. 1879
Siblings	Alice b. 1864 Little Rissington – mother of Arthur Eaton, *(see page 100)*
	Frederick b. 1865 Little Rissington
	Harriet b. 1866 Little Rissington
	Emily b. 1868 Little Rissington
	Daniel b. 1869 Little Rissington
	Mary b. 1870 Little Rissington
	Edward b. 1872 Little Rissington
	George b. 1876 Little Rissington
Wife	Miriam Sarah Arthurs (nee Peach) b.1875 Chalk Hill Farm, Lower Swell. John and Miriam were married by the Revd F E Blacksby in the Methodist Chapel in Stow on 5 August 1896.
Children	Charles Albert b. 1896 Stow – Private, Glos Regt. – *see page 29*
	Thomas Frederick b. 1898 Stow
	Gladys b. 1903 Stow
	Leslie b. 1904 Stow
	Stuart b. 1906 Stow
	Harold b. 1908 Stow
	Daniel b. 1913 Stow
	Dorothy b. 1915 Stow
	The children were all christened in the Methodist Chapel, Stow.
Cemetery	Neuve Chapelle British Cemetery, Pas de Calais, France. Neuve Chapelle is a village fifteen kilometres south east of Armentieres. The cemetery was begun during the battle in March 1915 and there are over 50 1914-18 war casualties commemorated at this site.

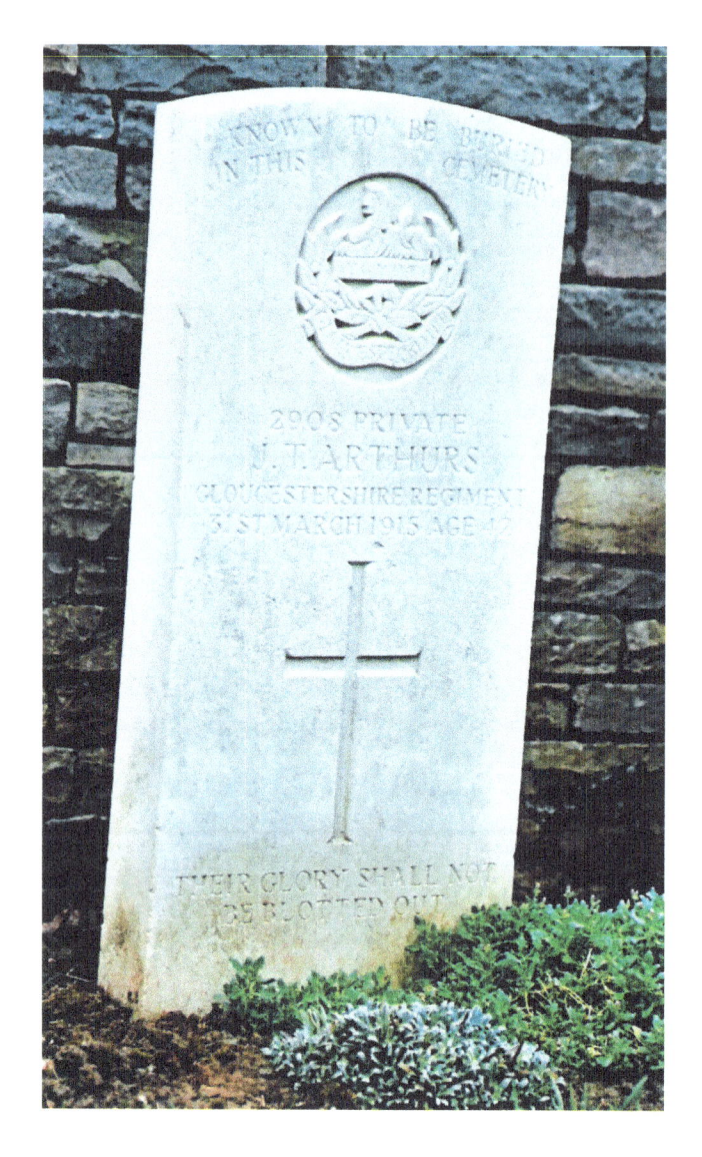

John's headstone in Neuve Chapelle British Cemetery, France

Notes

In 1871 John's father was the Miller at Little Rissington. John's mother had died in 1879. By 1891 the family had moved to Stow. John's father, brother George and John himself were listed as General Labourers in the census of 1891 while brother Edward was a Butcher. On 9 May 1982, aged 18, John enlisted in the Grenadier Guards in London having sworn his Oath of Allegiance to Queen Victoria four days previously in Oxford.

John's contract was for three years with the Colours and nine years in the Reserve. He was 5 feet 7 inches tall and weighed 9 stone 8lbs. He served in England for three years and was then transferred to the Army Reserve in May 1895. He was recalled to Army Service under Special Army order of 20 December 1899 and sent to South Africa on Boxing Day 1899 to fight in the Boer War. On demobilization on 13 March 1903 John was transferred again to the Reserve and he was finally discharged in May 1904.

On 11 March 1896, John's father, Frederick Arthurs, widower, married Mrs Ann Maria Hillier, widow, mother of John Henry Hillier *(see page 138)* in St Edward's. In the 1901 census John's wife Miriam is noted as Head of the household in Sheep Street comprising herself, her two small sons plus her brother-in-law, George Arthurs, as a Boarder.

Some years later John enlisted in Bristol as a Private in 1st Battalion, Gloucestershire Regiment. The battalion was under canvas on annual training at Rushmoor Bottom near Aldershot on 1 August 1914 when orders were received to march back to barracks at Bordon in Hampshire, a distance of 15 miles, and prepare for war. Further orders arrived – including "All ranks will carry 3 days rations per person" – then they left by train for Southampton on 12 August, sailing at 12.10pm that day on the *Gloucester Castle*. They landed at Le Havre the next morning, part of 3rd Brigade, 1st Division of the British Expeditionary Force, described by the Kaiser on 23 September 1914 as "General French's contemptible little army", a name adopted with pride by the survivors of the war as The Old Centemptibles. During the next month the Battalion marched over 200 miles, withdrawing and advancing, until on 16 September they dug in facing the Germans and trench warfare began. A move to Flanders followed where they took part in the First Battle of Ypres in October. They left the Ypres Salient the following month by which time only 2 officers and 100 men remained of the original Battalion. By Christmas they were at Givenchy. Periods in and out of the front line followed. The weather was so terrible that the troops were actually issued with fur coats made from goat skins. The Battle of Neuve Chapelle was the first British offensive of the war and was fought between 10 and 13 March 1915 with the object of recapturing Neuve Chapelle on 30 March. The Battalion Diary shows that only one man was killed on that day. It was John Arthurs, most likely killed by a sniper. It was his 42nd birthday. He was buried in the British Cemetery at Neuve Chapelle but later in the war a German shell destroyed six graves there, one of which was John's. New headstones for these six men are now lined up beside the wall, each bearing the text "Known to have been buried in this cemetery."

The six headstones commemorate six soldiers who were buried at Neuve Chapelle and whose graves were later destroyed by a German shell.
John's headstone is third from the left.

*This picture is of the actual campaign medals awarded to John Arthurs.
They are:-*

Queen Victoria

Queen's South Africa Medal with the clasps Wittebergen, Cape Colony and Transvaal.

King Edward VII

King's South Africa Medal with the clasps South Africa 1901 and 1902

King George V

1914 Star

British War Medal

Victory Medal

Two views of Neuve Chapelle British Cemetery, Framce

*Private Charles Arthurs, MM, eldest
son of John Thomas Arthurs*

Extract from a letter from Corporal Harry Cox in December 1915 to a friend in Stow:
"Some of our men have the fur coats but we are keeping off them as long as possible because they are generally a nuisance in the trenches, getting clogged with mud. Then again there is carrying them. Our load of that which is absolutely necessary is somewhere about three quarters of a hundredweight and you can imagine that we want no extras."

John's son, Private Charles Arthurs, followed his father into the Gloucestershire Regiment and in 1919 was decorated for bravery.

From the Evesham Journal – Saturday January 11 1919
MILITARY MEDAL FOR STOW MAN
The Military Medal has been awarded to Pte C Arthurs of the Gloucestershire Regt, of Stow-on-the-Wold, for bravery in the field on November 1 last. He was invalided home from Salonika and has served in France and Italy. He was home on furlough in October last. His father (*John Thomas Arthurs*) was killed in action in France and he has a brother serving with the colours. Private C Arthurs joined up in May 1916.

Cap Badge of the Royal Regiment of Artillery

Second Lieutenant Harry Butters

Henry Augustus Butters: An American Citizen

Date of Birth	28 April 1892 – San Francisco
Service	2nd Lieutenant, 11th Battalion Royal Warwickshire Regiment. Transferred to B Battery, 109th Brigade, Royal Field Artillery
Date of Death	Killed in action on 31 August 1916 – age 24
Stow Address	The Rectory (Bretton House), Fosseway
Parents	Henry Augustus Butters — b. Andover, Massachusetts
	Lucy Woodworth Butters (nee Beebee) — b. New York
Siblings	Harry's mother was a twice-married widow with seven children when she married Harry's father. Mrs Lucile Bray and David Edwards, two of those children, became Harry's co-guardians after both his parents died while he was still a minor.
Cemetery	Meaulte Military Cemetery, Department of the Somme, France. Meaulte is a village near Albert. The cemetery was begun in December 1915 and used until February 1917. Designed by Sir Edwin Lutyens, it contains 312 burials from the First World War.

Notes

As a child Harry travelled widely with his parents in the United States and to Europe and South Africa where Tom Evans, brother of the Rector of Stow, became a business associate of his father's and a close friend of Harry. From October 1906 he spent a year in England at Beaumont College, Old Windsor, a Jesuit College founded in 1861. His father died in October 1908 and his mother in June 1909. In February 1915, dismayed that the United States had not entered the war, he left his home in Oakland, California and travelled to England intent on joining the British Army. Father Tim Carey, his headmaster from Beaumont College days, endorsed his application for a commission, which included the incorrect statement that he was born in South Africa. The Rector of Stow was named as the person to be contacted in the event of his death.

Harry first visited the Rectory in Stow on 19 February 1915 when he stayed for four days. He later wrote to his sister Lucile: "Tom *(the Rector's brother)* and Jack *(the Rector)* met me and made me

Harry on horseback

Ploegsteert

Extract from a description of a visit to Ploegsteert War Cemetery during the 1930s, not very different from how it is today. Ploegsteert is a village in Belgium about ten miles south of Ypres, close to the border with France.

> It is a particularly pretty sylvan spot especially in the spring and the cemetery with its noble memorial was a glorious sight with beautiful double Japanese flowering cherries at their loveliest and, at the foot of the headstones to the fallen, the ground was gay with springtime flowers, lovingly tended by our ex-Servicemen gardeners. Then, when the twilight shadows steal over the landscape, from the adjacent wood comes, as on the Worcestershire plain, the melodious note of the cock pheasant calling to his mate. If one waits a little later in the evening, a veritable cascade of nightingale song echoing down the glades of the wood makes such patience very worthwhile.

most welcome. Jack is quite fatherly, very much interested, and Mrs Evans shows a decided inclination to take me under her wing. As for their daughter Alice, she is *all right … (Alice was 17)*. On the afternoon of 6th March I returned to Stow. All the family, including the maid, were really and truly delighted to have me back and Mrs Evans immediately began to spoil me again so for two days I had a very jolly time indeed." On 11 March 1915 Harry was granted a commission as a 2nd Lieutenant in the Royal Warwickshire Regiment and he was ordered to join the Warwickshires for duty at Brighton.

On 21 March he was again in Stow on leave for a few days. Back in camp he wrote to Lucile: "I can't tell you how frightfully good Jack and Mrs Evans and Alice are to me. I have my room there set up all the time that I am away to come back to, and Stow is really a home on this side. Alice and Mrs Evans are knitting sox for me and otherwise looking after me." In another letter he commented on the "altruistic attitude so dear to the heart of the Welsh dreamer *(Jack Evans)* that leads him to plant quaint and rare nuts that they may grow into stately trees to shade the future playground of his friends' grandchildren."

On 5 May to his delight Harry transferred to the Royal Field Artillery and was sent to Happy Valley Camp at Shoreham. Following three days leave in Stow, he went on a month's course at the School of Gunnery at Lark Hill on Salisbury Plain. In August he got away for three days to Newport Castle in Pembrokeshire with the Evans family. Then on 31 August as a section commander in D Battery in charge of 2 guns, 4 wagons, 50 horses and 70 men, he left for France. The Battery landed the next day to join the BEF. He took part in the Battle of Loos later that month when that village was captured from the Germans at a huge cost in casualties. Christmas was spent in rest camp, then back to the front until in February 1916 he had a week's home leave. He spent a night in London before heading to Stow for peace and a warm welcome at the Rectory.

In April at his observation post in a field close to Ploegsteert, just over the Belgian border from Lille, Harry first met Winston Churchill, commanding officer of the 6th Royal Scots Fusiliers, and his second-in-command, Major Archie Sinclair, later Lord Thurso. Winston took an immediate liking to the young American and invited him to join them for dinner at Battalion Headquarters a few days later. In May Harry's observation post took a direct hit and he had to spend several days in hospital suffering from concussion and shell shock. He was sent on leave to recuperate and stayed in London with Californian friends, the O'Sullivans. Tom Evans came up to town to be with him for four days, the American consul, Clarence Carrigan, helped to entertain him, he was introduced to Jim Garvin, the Editor of The Observer newspaper, and one evening he dined and went to the theatre with Winston Churchill, who had by then left the army and returned to politics. However, news arrived of the horrors of the first days of the Battle of the Somme and Harry felt compelled to rejoin his unit. He was put in charge of the Ammunition Column at the rear of the trenches until on 21 August he was sent forward to the front line to replace a casualty. Ten days later, on 31 August 1916, as he stood talking to his commanding officer outside his observation post, both men were killed by a direct hit from a gas shell. On 6 September the telegram with the awful news of Harry's death arrived at the Rectory in Stow *(see page 20)*.

Harry's arrival at the Rectory, Stow
This photograph was taken by Alice Evans, the Rector's daughter.

Captain Zambra, Harry's Section Commander, wrote to Harry's sister Lucile: "A Roman Catholic Chaplain buried him beneath the Union Jack (we tried to get an American flag but one was not procurable or he should have been honoured by both countries) in a military cemetery just outside Meaulte. There were many officers at the funeral, as many as could be spared from duty, including the Staff Captain, representing the General, and Colonel Talbot, a detachment from his battery and my section. A trumpeter sounded the Last Post."

From the Evesham Journal – Saturday September 23 1916
AMERICAN HERO'S ASSOCIATION WITH STOW
Last Sunday evening the church bells of Stow-on-the-Wold rang out a muffled peal for the young American hero, 2nd Lieut Henry Augustus Butters, RFA, of San Francisco, California, of whose association with their parish the Stow people may well be proud. Many of the English papers, including "The Observer" and "Public Opinions", have sung the praises in most eulogistic terms of this gallant young officer who has laid down his life for Britain, the country he loved next to his own, and for the cause of the Allies.

At the age of 24 he was killed on the night of August 31 by the same shell that killed his commander. His captain writes: "He was with his guns and no one could have died in a nobler way. He was one of the brightest, cheeriest boys I have ever known, and always the life and soul of the mess. We all realised his nobility in coming to the help of another country entirely of his own free will, and understood what a big heart he had. He was loved by all."

His temporary home in England was at the Rectory, Stow-on-the-Wold, and at the services in the parish church his name has been read with those of the Stow boys at the front ever since he left for the Continent a year ago. He loved Stow, its church, and everything and everybody about Stow. More than once he expressed the hope that if he fell, his name would be included on the Stow war memorial but that, if possible, a word might be added to denote his American nationality.

He was the only son of the late H A Butters, of Alta Vista, San Francisco, and nephew and heir of Mr Charles Butters, the well-known mining engineer and American millionaire. He had sailed round the world and, accompanied by his Ukelele, he could sing most of the quaint songs and melodies of the Pacific Islanders. He knew all about horses and motor cars. He was a crack shot and a fine polo player. His business ability was shown as soon as he took over the management of his father's estates.

He arrived in England early in 1915 when he came to Stow-on-the-Wold, whose Rector had known his family for many years. He got his first commission in the 11th Royal Warwickshire Regiment and was afterwards transferred to the Royal Field Artillery. He left Newport Castle, Pembrokeshire, where the Rector was spending his holiday on 1 September, 1915. "He was," wrote the Rector in the "Times" obituary notice, "a warm-hearted, fearless young officer – as fine an American gentleman as ever crossed the Atlantic." "It is much to say," said Mr Garvin *(the Editor)* in the "Observer", "but it is true."

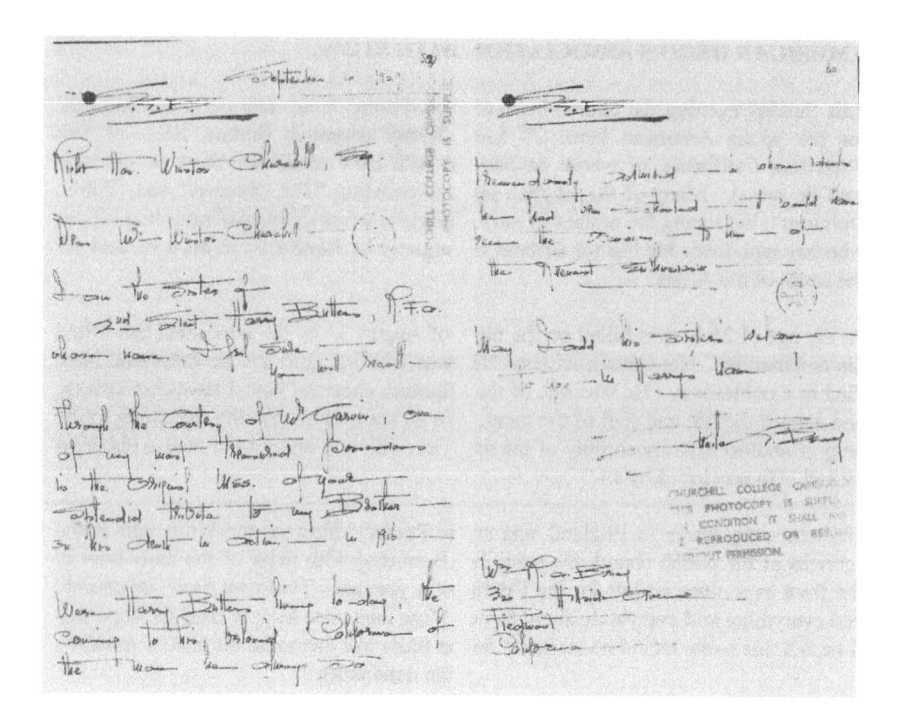

Letter from Lucile Bray, Harry's sister, to Winston Churchill

My thanks to the Churchill Archives Centre, Churchill Papers, for permission to use this letter – CHAR 1/207.

Writing to his sister Lucile in 1915, Henry said: "Father Carey *(of Beaumont College)* is a dear friend – and very much fascinated by your handwriting." Many years later, on 10 September 1929, Lucile wrote the following letter to Winston Churchill.

L.G.B. *September 10 1929*

Right Honourable Winston Churchill Esq

Dear Mr Winston Churchill

I am the sister of 2nd Lieut Harry Butters, RFA, whose name, I feel sure, you will recall. Through the courtesy of Mr Garvin, one of my most treasured possessions is the original Mss. of your splendid tribute to my Brother on his death in action in 1916. Were Harry Butters living today, the coming to his beloved California of the man he always so tremendously admired – in whose ideals he had been schooled – it would have been the occasion to him of the keenest enthusiasm.

May I add his sister's welcome to you in Harry's name?

Lucile G Bray -

Mrs R A Bray, 320 Hillside Avenue, Piedmont, California

Winston Churchill's tribute to his young friend was published ten days after Harry's death.

From The Observer, London, September 10 1916.
Death of 2nd Lieutenant Harry Butters
"The death in action of this young American gentleman is a blow to the many friends he had made for himself in the British Army. I met him quite by chance at his observation post near Ploegsteert and was charmed by his extraordinary fund of wit and gaiety. His conversation was delightful, full at once of fun and good sense and continually lighted by original reflections and captivating Americanisms. A whole table could sit and listen to him with the utmost interest and pleasure. He was a great 'character' and had he lived to enjoy his bright worldly prospects he could not have failed to make his mark.

He was a very good soldier and competent artillery officer, very well thought of by his comrades and trusted by his superiors. He had seen much service in the front line, including the battle of Loos, and came through unscathed until in May last a bouquet of 5.9 shells destroyed his observation post and stunned him with shell shock and concussion. Leave was pressed upon him but he could only be induced to take a few days' rest. In little more than a week he was back at the front – disdainful as ever of the continual threats of death. And thus quite simply he met his fate. "No, sir, I have taken no oath of allegiance but I am just as loyal."

I venture to put these few lines on paper not because his sacrifice and story differ from those of so many others in these hard days but because, coming of his own free will, with no national call or obligation, a stranger from across the ocean, to fight and die in our ranks, he had it in his power to pay a tribute to our cause of exceptional value. He did not come all the way from San Francisco only out of affection for the ancient home of his forbears or in a spirit of mere adventure. He was in sentiment a thorough American. All his ordinary loyalties rested with his own country but he had a very firm and clear conception of the issues which are at stake in this struggle. He had minutely studied the official documents bearing upon the origin of the war and he conceived that not merely national causes but international causes of the highest importance were involved and must now be decided by arms. And to these he thought it his duty to testify 'till a right peace was signed.' Such testimony cannot be impeached."

Winston S Churchill

Harry's grave in Meaulte Military Cemetery, France

Two views of Meaulte Military Cemetery, France

American volunteer ambulance drivers

The American Field Service in France 1914-1917

The American Field Service contributed appreciably to the enlightenment of American opinion in regard to the crucial meaning of the war. The little group of American volunteers numbered no more than two thousand and for the first three years of the Great War formed the most considerable organised representation which the United States had on the battle front. This volunteer service was organised on the pattern of the regular ambulance sections of the French Army.

At the outbreak of hostilities the American Hospital at Neuilly-sur-Seine had become the rallying centre for Americans and initiated American war relief work in France. The efforts of American residents in France were supplemented by men and funds from America. In the winter of 1914-15 many of the donated ambulances were lent with volunteer drivers to the French and British hospitals. The role of this service was to get the wounded as rapidly and comfortably as possible from the battle-line to a field hospital. A light small car seemed preferable and approximately 1200 Ford motor chassis were imported into France and the ambulance bodies were constructed there. The bodies projected far beyond the rear wheels and gradually it was developed by the Field Service so that it could comfortably accommodate three lying or five sitting cases or, at a pinch, seven or eight.

There was no sector in which French troops served where the ambulances were not known. In 1915 the little American ambulances scurried everywhere over the flat plains of Flanders. In 1916 throughout the terrible and prolonged Battle of Verdun, they were in evidence everywhere. The year 1917 also found Field Service Sections in every great engagement from the April battle in Champagne to the October battle of the Chemin des Dames. The English poet John Masefield, after visiting a number of the Field Service Sections in the summer of 1916, described them as including "the very pick and flower of American youth." Many hundreds of the members were graduates or students of American colleges and universities, not willing any longer to remain distant onlookers in the great world struggle.

When at last America joined forces with the Allies in 1917, the American government found the ambulance and transport branches of the American Field Service thoroughly established and functioning as useful parts of the French Army. The French authorities were anxious that the entry of the United States into the war should not result in any interruption of these services. Accordingly, during the autumn of 1917 the ambulance sections were incorporated into the United States Army Ambulance Service. The majority of the Field Service volunteer drivers willingly enlisted in the United States Army.

There is a very long list of donors of ambulances to the American Field Service in France. Each ambulance was given a name and one of these vehicles was:- "*Harry Butters, RFA, an American Citizen, killed on the Somme, August 31 1916. From those to whom he was dearest.*" It was donated through the Darrach Ambulance Fund.

Cap Badge of the Norfolk Regiment
Formed in 1685 as Cromwell's Regiment, it became the 9th Regiment of Foot in 1751.

Leonard's grave in Stow-On-The-Wold Cemetery

Leonard Thomas Campin

Date of Birth	3 July 1884 – Stow
Service	7832 Private, 2/4th Battalion, Norfolk Regiment
Date of Death	16 December 1916 – age 32
Stow Address	Sheep Street (1898)
	Park Street – next door to the Summersbee family (1901)
Parents	John Edward Campin — b. 1855 Lower Swell
	Margaret Ellen Campin (nee Luker) — b. 1860 Lower Swell
	They were married in St Edward's on 29 October 1879.
Siblings	Walter Edward — b. 1881 Stow – *see page 44*
Cemetery	Family grave in Stow-on-the-Wold cemetery

Notes

Leonard and Walter were christened in St Edward's on 28 January 1898 by the Rev E Lyon Harrison, Assistant Curate. Their father's occupation was given as Mason in the Baptism Register.

Leonard started work as an apprentice grocer in Sheep Street and later moved to a similar job in Evesham. He enlisted in Bristol and was posted to the Norfolk Regiment, who were in training in Yorkshire. One month later he died of pneumonia in Wheatley Hall Hospital, Doncaster.

From the Evesham Journal – Saturday December 23 1916

SAD DEATH OF A STOW-ON-THE-WOLD SOLDIER

Private L T Campin of the Norfolks, who was training at Doncaster, was taken ill with pneumonia at the end of last week. His parents were notified of the fact and his mother journeyed to Doncaster on Saturday. She arrived only a few hours before he died, which event occurred early on Sunday morning, just one month after he went into training. The mother and her deceased son's body arrived at Stow station on Wednesday evening and the funeral took place on Thursday, the Rector (the Rev J T Evans) officiating. Deep sympathy is extended to the parents, the brother and the young woman who was to have been the deceased's wife. Our Evesham readers will remember that Mr Campin lived in the town of Evesham for several years as a grocer's assistant. For the past two years he has carried on a grocery business in this town and it was a hard case that he should give it up and go into the army.

Cap Badge of the Queen's Own Royal West Kent Regiment
In 1831 the Regiment became "The Queen's Own" in honour of Queen Adelaide, wife of King William IV

British troops after landing at Le Havre

Walter Edward Campin

Date of Birth	11 October 1881 – Stow
Service	G/24591 Private, 7th Battalion, The Queen's Own Royal West Kent Regiment
Date of Death	Killed in action on 21 March 1918 – age 36
Stow Address	Sheep Street (1898)
	Park Street – next door to the Summersbee family (1901)
Parents	John Edward Campin b. 1855 Lower Swell
	Margaret Ellen Campin b. 1860 Lower Swell
	(nee Luker)
	They were married in St Edward's on 29 October 1879.
Siblings	Leonard Thomas b. 1884 – Stow – *see page 42*
Cemetery	Pozieres Memorial, Somme, France. Pozieres is a village six kilometres north west of Albert. The Memorial commemorates over 14,000 British casualties. It was designed by W H Cowlinshaw. Also commemorated on the family grave in Stow-on-the-Wold Cemetery.

Notes

Walter and Leonard were christened in St Edward's on 28 January 1898 by the Rev E Lyon Harrison, Assistant Curate. Their father's occupation was given as Mason in the Baptism Register.

In 1901 Walter's father was working as a Painter, his mother as a Dressmaker and Walter himself as a Painter's apprentice. Later Walter had a chinaware business in Sheep Street.

Walter enlisted in Stow and was posted initially to the Somerset Light Infantry and then transferred to 7th (Service) Battalion, The Queen's Own Royal West Kent Regiment, which was formed in September 1914 as part of 55th Brigade, 18th Division. The Battalion moved to France in 1915, landing at Le Havre on 27 July. As part of the Third Army, the Battalion was initiated into trench warfare on the right bank of the Somme in August and continued in the same area until the end of 1915.

After two spells in the trenches in January 1916, the Battalion then enjoyed a couple of months' employment on other duties, which included railway construction, before returning to the trenches at the end of March, again on the banks of the Somme. The Battalion was heavily engaged from 1 July during the Battle of the Somme where, on the night of 13/14 July, they beat off numerous German attacks and held on until relieved. At the end of July, they were transferred to the quieter Flanders front.

In June 1917 they were deployed at Poperinghe before undergoing further training in

Walter's name carved on the Pozieres Memorial, France

Two views of the Pozieres Memorial

preparation for a big offensive at Ypres, which was launched on 31 July with the intention of breaking through the German line. They endured a wet and uncomfortable four days in the front line with heavy and continuous rain. The trenches were in an appalling condition. However, because of their losses, the Division was withdrawn for nearly six weeks while waiting to be brought up to strength.

Early in October they returned to the Ypres Salient and at Poelcapelle were again in action. There mud was the chief obstacle. Not only did they suffer very heavy losses during the action but they also had a further 40 casualties as the result of an attack by a German aeroplane as they were preparing to withdraw.

The following spring on 21 March 1918 the Germans launched a massive offensive intended to end the war before the Americans joined the Allies in great numbers. In the attack against the British in the Arras area, 7th Battalion was overwhelmed in the defence of Durham Post and 18th Division retreated back across the Somme battlefields.

Walter was killed on 21 March 1918. He was awarded the Victory Medal and the British War Medal.

Walter's name on the Family Memorial in Stow Cemetery

Cap Badge of the Royal Garrison Artillery

Second Lieutenant Edward Castle

Edward William Castle

Date of Birth	February 1887 – Moreton-in-Marsh
Service	30073 Sergeant Royal Garrison Artillery, promoted to 2nd Lieutenant, 126th Siege Battery, Royal Garrison Artillery on 05 June 1918
Date of Death	Died of wounds on 24 August 1918 – age 31
Stow Address	Wyck Hill Lodge, Maugersbury
Parents	Edwin Castle — b. 1863 Ettington, Warwickshire
	Mary Ann Castle (nee Freeman) — b. 1865 Honington, Warwickshire
	Their marriage was registered in Shipston-on-Stour in 1883.
Siblings	Sidney — b. 1883 Ettington, Warwickshire
	Sarah Ellen Kate — b. 1885 Moreton-in-Marsh, d. 1911 Wyck Hill
	Elsie Emmaline — b. 1886 Moreton-in-Marsh
	Emma Mary — b. 1889 Moreton-in-Marsh – *mother of Henry Toomer Smith – see page 292*
	Edwin — b. 1891 Moreton-in-Marsh
Cemetery	Originally buried at Sailly Laurette Military Cemetery near Albert, France and later re-interred at Villers-Bretonneux Military Cemetery. Villers-Bretonneux is a village about 16 kilometres east of Amiens. The military cemetery was made after the Armistice when graves were brought in from other burial grounds in the area and from the battlefields. There are now 2141 Commonwealth servicemen commemorated or buried in this cemetery.
	Within the cemetery stands the Villers-Bretonneux Memorial, the Australian national memorial erected to commemorate all Australian soldiers who fought in France and Belgium during the First World War. The memorial was unveiled by King George VI in July 1938. Both cemetery and memorial were designed by Sir Edwin Lutyens.

Notes

In 1891 Edward's father was employed as a Coachman and his mother as a Laundress and the family lived in Oxford Street, Moreton-in-Marsh. Ten years later his father was working there as a Groom. By the time of Edward's death his father had become a Gardener, working at Wyck Hill House and the family was living at Wyck Hill Lodge.

Edward joined the Army at Banbury on 17 October 1908 and signed up for eight years with

Wyck Hill Lodge

Villers–Bretonneux Military Cemetery, France

the Colours and four years in reserve in the Royal Regiment of Artillery. Until that time he had been working as a Porter with the Great Western Railway at Stow Station, just down the hill from his home at Wyck Hill Lodge.

In October 1912 Edward was posted to Fort Connaught, Singapore. He was described as a steady, reliable NCO. In 1913 whilst playing football at Blakan Mati he tackled another player, fell and could not get up. He was carried off the field, his leg was bandaged and next day he reported sick – he had fractured his right tibia. The ensuing Court of Inquiry reported nothing untoward and that he had been perfectly sober at the time of the accident.

In February 1915 he was involved in operations against the Singapore mutineers. 815 men of the 5th Native Light Infantry and 100 men of the Malay States Guides mutinied. Some fired on a group of British officers, others went to Keppel Harbour where many men and women were killed and another group laid siege to the bungalow of the British commander. By Saturday 20 February the last of the mutineers had been rounded up and tried. Many were executed the following week.

In June 1915 Edward returned from Singapore to take part in the European war and was in France from 2 March 1916. In September 1917 he was granted sixpence a day extra pay as Battery Accountant. On 5 June 1918 he was granted a permanent commission in the field and took up his duties after 14 days leave.

He died in 11th Australian Field Ambulance on 25 August as the result of wounds from enemy aircraft action. Messrs Francis & Son of Stow-on-the-Wold administered his estate. His mother was his residuary legatee.

He was awarded the Victory Medal and the British War Medal.

From the Evesham Journal – Saturday September 21 1918
DEATH OF LIEUT CASTLE
Mr and Mrs E Castle of Wyck Hill Lodge, near Stow-on-the-Wold, have received the sad intelligence of the death of their son, Lieut Castle of the RGA. The circumstances are set forth in the letter which we reproduce below. Lieut Castle had served ten years in the Royal Garrison Artillery. His age was 31. He received his commission on May 5 last. His parents will receive the most sincere sympathy of a wide circle of friends. Mrs Castle has received the following letter from Major Russell:- "Dear Mrs Castle, You will have heard already of the death of your son. He was forward with his section in an advanced position and was helping his men to build dug-outs when a bomb was dropped by a German aeroplane and wounded him in the head. He was taken to a field dressing station at once but died without recovering consciousness. He had done most excellent work in the battery and I and all the rest of the officers miss him as a friend more than I can express. I miss him too as a most excellent officer. He was the best subaltern in the battery and I told him shortly before that he had been marked down for promotion. His hard work and unfailing cheerfulness endeared him to everyone who came in contact with him. The officers of the battery wish me to convey to you their deepest sympathy to which I add my own. Yours very sincerely, A Russell, Major 126 SB, RGA."

Edward's grave in Villers-Brettonneux Military Cemetery, France

Edward William Castle

Two views of Villers-Brettonneux Military Cemetery, France

Insignia of the Royal Navy

Midshipman Rupert Ingles-Chamberlayne

Rupert Henry Ingles-Chamberlayne

Date of Birth	4 July 1897 – Maugersbury Manor	
Service	Midshipman, Royal Navy	
Date of Death	Killed in action on 15 October 1914 – age 17	
Stow Address	Maugersbury Manor (1897)	
	Stow Lodge (1901)	
	Hyde House	
Parents	Henry Ingles-Chamberlayne	b. 1819 Nova Scotia, Canada
	Louise Grace Ingles-Chamberlayne (nee Marston)	b. 1855 Tonbridge, Kent
Siblings	Emily Hermione Grace	b. 1896 Maugersbury
Half-brothers and sisters:	Alice	b. 1847 Cape Breton, Nova Scotia
	Walter	b. 1850 Nova Scotia. Became a Barrister. On 1913 Electoral Roll listed as the Rev Walter Ingles-Chamberlayne of Shorwell, Newport, Isle of Wight.
	Laura	b. 1858 Woodstock, Ontario
	Charles	died young
Memorial	Chatham Naval Memorial. After the First World War to commemorate those members of the Royal Navy who had no known grave, an Admiralty committee recommended that the three manning ports in Great Britain – Chatham, Plymouth and Portsmouth – should each have an identical memorial, an obelisk, which would serve as a leading mark for shipping. The memorials were designed by Sir Robert Lorimer with sculpture by Henry Poole. Chatham Naval Memorial commemorates more than 8,500 sailors of the First World War and over 10,000 from the Second World War.	
	Also commemorated on the Lower Swell War Memorial.	

Notes

Rupert was educated at Winton House, Winchester and at Osborne and Dartmouth Royal Naval Colleges. On 4 August 1914 he was posted as Midshipman to HMS Hawke. After his death only ten weeks later, his tutor at Dartmouth wrote to Rupert's mother: "His pleasant, open, smiling

STOW-ON-THE-WOLD WAR MEMORIAL

The Chamberlayne Family

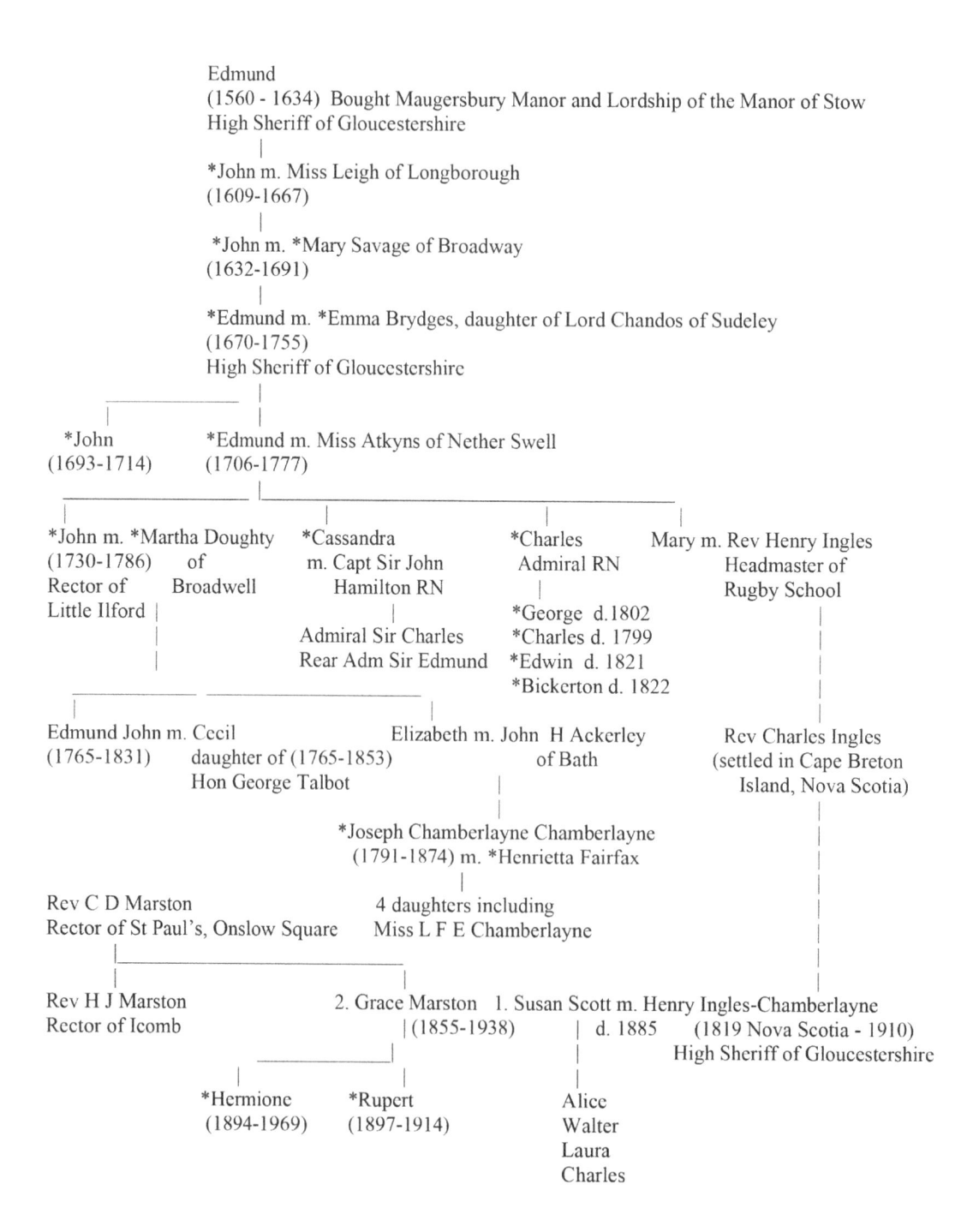

Edmund
(1560 - 1634) Bought Maugersbury Manor and Lordship of the Manor of Stow
High Sheriff of Gloucestershire
|
*John m. Miss Leigh of Longborough
(1609-1667)
|
*John m. *Mary Savage of Broadway
(1632-1691)
|
*Edmund m. *Emma Brydges, daughter of Lord Chandos of Sudeley
(1670-1755)
High Sheriff of Gloucestershire
|
```
    |                          |
*John              *Edmund m. Miss Atkyns of Nether Swell
(1693-1714)        (1706-1777)
                         |
    |                    |                    |                 |
*John m. *Martha Doughty   *Cassandra       *Charles       Mary m. Rev Henry Ingles
(1730-1786)    of         m. Capt Sir John   Admiral RN         Headmaster of
Rector of   Broadwell     Hamilton RN           |               Rugby School
Little Ilford |                |            *George  d.1802         |
              |           Admiral Sir Charles *Charles d. 1799       |
              |           Rear Adm Sir Edmund *Edwin   d. 1821       |
              |                              *Bickerton d. 1822      |
    |                              |                                 |
Edmund John m. Cecil         Elizabeth m. John H Ackerley      Rev Charles Ingles
(1765-1831)   daughter of (1765-1853)   of Bath              (settled in Cape Breton
              Hon George Talbot                               Island, Nova Scotia)
                                       |                             |
                       *Joseph Chamberlayne Chamberlayne              |
                          (1791-1874) m. *Henrietta Fairfax           |
                                       |                             |
Rev C D Marston               4 daughters including                   |
Rector of St Paul's, Onslow Square    Miss L F E Chamberlayne         |
    |                                                                 |
    |                          |                  |                   |
Rev H J Marston            2. Grace Marston   1. Susan Scott m. Henry Ingles-Chamberlayne
Rector of Icomb              | (1855-1938)     |  d. 1885    (1819 Nova Scotia - 1910)
    |                                                       High Sheriff of Gloucestershire
                    |              |                  |
                *Hermione       *Rupert             Alice
                (1894-1969)    (1897-1914)          Walter
                                                    Laura
                                                    Charles
```

face was so very attractive. The first glance I had of it left no doubt in my mind of his character and upbringing and all that I ever saw or heard of him merely strengthened my first impression. He was a clean-hearted English gentleman and worthy of the great service to which you so generously gave him." Lieut-Commander R R Rosoman, RN, HMS Hawke, wrote: "I feel certain the boy stuck to his post to the very last because he was a splendid fellow."

The Chamberlayne Family

Rupert's father, Henry Ingles, was born in Nova Scotia, Canada in 1819. He was educated at King's College, London, Ontario and later for some time was an active officer in a Canadian company of volunteers. On the death of Joseph Chamberlayne Chamberlayne of Maugersbury Manor in 1874, Henry Ingles (his second cousin) succeeded to the estate and added the name of Chamberlayne to his own. Prior to that, he had lived in Surrey for several years. His first wife died in 1885 and was buried at Oddington. His second wife, Rupert's mother, was the eldest daughter of the Rev C D Marston, Rector of St Paul's, Onslow Square, London, and her brother was the Rev H J Marston, Rector of Icomb.

In the 1891 census, while the family still lived at Maugersbury Manor, the household comprised the Ingles-Chamberlayne family plus a staff of a housekeeper, a cook, a housemaid and a footman. The Maugersbury Manor estate was sold in 1900 to John H Hewitt, a retired brewer and JP from Nottinghamshire. In the same year the building of Hyde House (now the Fosse Manor Hotel) was begun and work was completed the following year. In the interim the family lived at Stow Lodge, the property of the Hippisley family, although the Rev R W Hippisley had died in January 1901. The Chamberlaynes were still there when they completed the census in April 1901. Rupert's father was described in the census as a JP of independent means. As Lord of the Manor, Mr Henry Ingles-Chamberlayne had presented Stow-on-the-Wold with the land on which St Edward's Hall now stands. His coat of arms is depicted in a stained glass window in the hall.

In 1955 Rupert's sister, Miss Hermione Ingles-Chamberlayne, moved from Hyde Cottage in Station Road on the Fosseway to St Edward's Cottage in the Square next to St Edward's Hall where she lived until her death on 6 November 1969.

On the facing page:
★ = commemorated on a memorial in either the chancel or the sanctuary in St Edward's.

HMS Hawke

Otto Weddigen, Commander of the U9

German submarine U9

HMS Hawke And The German Submarine U9

HMS Hawke was launched at Chatham in 1891, an Edgar first class cruiser with a displacement of 7350 tons and a speed of 20 knots. The *Hawke* was well known for an unfortunate collision in thick fog with the White Star liner *Olympic* (sister ship of the *Titanic*) in the Solent on 20 September 1911, when she rammed into *Olympic's* starboard side. Although both vessels were damaged, no one was killed. At the outbreak of hostilities *HMS Hawke* was converted into a depot ship for destroyers and submarines.

The most famous German submarine of the First World War was launched on 22 September 1910 in the KWD naval yard at Danzig. It was the U9, fifth vessel of eight of the U5 series.

At dawn on 22 September 1914, off the Dutch coast, the U9 commanded by Otto Weddigen sighted a convoy of three English vessels: the battleship *Aboukir* and the cruisers *Hogue* and *Cressy*. *Aboukir* was hit by the first torpedo and sank quickly. The commanders of the other two ships stopped and lowered lifeboats to pick up survivors. U9 manoeuvred between the two and launched two bow and two stern torpedoes: *Hogue* was hit amidships and sank in ten minutes. The damage to *Cressy* was not fatal but U9 turned and fired its last torpedo at *Cressy* sinking her within a quarter of an hour. Survivors were picked up by several nearby merchant ships including the *Dutch Flora* and *Titan* and the British trawlers *JGC* and *Coriander*. In all, 1459 men died but 837 men were rescued amongst whom was Arthur John Dowler, a sailor on the *Hogue* and son of the Stationmaster at Stow. The Kaiser himself personally presented Otto Weddigen with the Iron Cross First Class after this action.

On 3 October 1914, the U9 began its third patrol in the Atlantic, ranging between the Shetland Islands, the Orkneys and Norway. At dawn on 15 October off Aberdeen it intercepted a convoy of three cruisers. Otto Weddigen was amazed to observe through his periscope that an English ship had stopped 100 metres from his submarine: *HMS Hawke*, under the command of Captain HPE Williams, was delivering mail to *HMS Endymion*. U9 launched a single torpedo and *HMS Hawke* sank almost immediately with a loss of 534 men and only 70 survivors. The men who died are commemorated on the Chatham Naval Memorial.

Otto Weddigen went on to command the U29 which in the Pentland Firth on 18 March 1915 was rammed by *HMS Dreadnought*, broken in two and sank in a few seconds with all hands. *Dreadnought* remains the only battleship to have sunk a submarine. The U9 survived the war and in November 1918 was ordered to surrender to the Royal Navy. It went first to Harwich, then in March 1919 it was ordered to sail to Morecambe but ran aground near Dover. After a month it was refloated and reached Morecambe in May where it was broken up.

STOW-ON-THE-WOLD WAR MEMORIAL

Chatham Naval Memorial

From the Evesham Journal – Saturday April 10 1915
STOW-ON-THE-WOLD
MEMORIAL TO MR RUPERT HENRY INGLES-CHAMBERLAYNE
A memorial tablet has recently been erected in the parish church to the memory of the first local man to fall in connection with the war. It reads as follows:- "Rupert Henry Ingles-Chamberlayne, midshipman, *HMS Hawke*. He was killed in action in the North Sea, October 15, 1914, aged 17 years. Numbered with Thy Saints in glory everlasting." A tablet recording the deaths in years long gone by,* which was formerly erected over the south door, has been restored and removed to a more conspicuous position (the new tablet referred to above is immediately underneath it). This tablet was sliced off an old sundial which was brought to this country by a former member of the Chamberlayne family and it is said that the sundial came from the Temple of Artemis at Ephesus. The Rector refers to it as the most interesting object in the church and thinks it is very probable that St Paul's eyes have looked upon it.

* (of Admiral Charles Chamberlayne and his four sons)

Charles Chamberlayne was captain of the *Bombay Castle* in the Mediterranean fleet under the command of Admiral Hotham in 1795. It is likely that he was the person who acquired the section of the pillar from the temple of Artemis from which the sundial was created.

Admiral Charles Chamberlayne and the sundial, made from a pillar from the temple of Artemis at Ephesus, now in the garden of the Fosse Manor Hotel, former home of the Ingles-Chamberlayne family

STOW-ON-THE-WOLD WAR MEMORIAL

Cap Badge of the Royal Army Ordnance Corps

Entries in the baptism register of St Edward's for the seven Clark children – 3 July 1898

William Hylton Clark

Date of Birth	11 September 1886 – Stow
Service	011888 Private, Calais Depot, Royal Army Ordnance Corps
Date of Death	12 February 1919 – age 32
Stow Address	Sheep Street
Parents	William Robert Clark — b. 1854 Coventry
	Annie Elizabeth Clark (nee Clifford) — b. 1861 Stow
Siblings	Gertrude Mary — b. 1884 Stow
	Annie Elizabeth — b. 1888 Stow
	Daisy Louisa — b. 1892 Stow
	Edith Dorothy — b. 1894 Stow
	Lily Kathleen — b. 1896 Stow
	Ronald Arthur — b. 1898 Stow, d. 1899
	Reuben Percy — b. 1903 Stow
Wife	Mrs M W Clark, 52 Balloch Road, Balloch, Dunbartonshire
Child	William — b. 27.05.1909
Cemetery	Les Baraques Military Cemetery, Sangatte, Pas de Calais, France. The cemetery is on the west of Calais. The first burials took place there in September 1917 and it continued in use until 1921. It now contains 1303 Commonwealth burials of the First World War. The cemetery was designed by Sir Herbert Baker.

Notes

On 3 July 1898 the Rev E Lyon Harrison, Curate in Charge, christened seven Clark children – William, Mary, Annie, Daisy, Edith, Lily and Ronald at St Edward's. William's father's occupation was given as Carpenter in the Baptism Register.

William was educated at Beale Brown Infants School and then at Stow Boys School. He left in 1896. In 1901 William was working as a Coachbuilder's apprentice.

Reuben Clifford was William's uncle, his mother's brother. He was a Colour Sergeant in 1st Battalion, Coldstream Guards and died at Deelfontein in South Africa during the Boer War on 9 May 1901 *(see the Boer War Memorial in St Edward's on the wall behind the pulpit)*. Reuben's two

STOW-ON-THE-WOLD WAR MEMORIAL

Les Baraques Military Cemetery, Sangatte, France

sons, Harry (b. 1890 in London) and Lewis (b. 1894 in Windsor) came to live with the Clark family and were enrolled at Stow Boys School on 27 March 1900. They had previously been at school at "Towers, London Military". They are listed with the Clark family in the 1901 census. The school register shows that they left Stow in 1902.

William's son, another William like his father and grandfather, was admitted to Stow Boys School on 23 October 1916 when he was seven. The register was marked "Previous school Barlock (Balloch?), Scotland" and then on 19 February 1917 "Gone to Scotland".

In April 1915 No 6 Base Supply Depot was started at Calais to help relieve the pressure on Boulogne and to provide a base nearer to the front than Le Havre or Rouen. The base remained open until the last Commonwealth forces left France in March 1921. There were also several hospitals stationed in the town, providing about 2500 beds. The unit in which William served was based at Calais and he died of influenza in hospital there.

Cap Badge of the Somerset Light Infantry

Lance Sergeant Cecil Clifford

The Clifford Family

There are four Cliffords named in the list of the dead of World War One and two other men on that list whose mothers' maiden name was Clifford.

* **Cecil** and **Horace** Clifford were brothers, sons of Henry and Hannah Clifford, Henry being the son of Charles and Charlotte Clifford of Stow.
* **Eustace** Clifford's father Edward was the son of Thomas and Elizabeth Clifford of Maugersbury.
* **Tom** Clifford's father William was also the son of Thomas and Elizabeth Clifford of Maugersbury. Tom and Eustace were cousins.
* William Clark's mother **Ann** was the daughter of Charles and Sarah Clifford of Stow.
* William Taylor's mother **Sarah** was the daughter of William and Hannah Clifford of Broadwell.

Cecil Raymond Clifford

Date of Birth	19 October 1894 – Stow
Service	9579 Lance Sergeant, 1st Battalion, Somerset Light Infantry (Prince Albert's)
Date of Death	Died of wounds on 1 April 1915 – age 20
Stow Address	Park Street – the cottage, now demolished, was on the site of Parkland Mews
Parents	Henry Clifford — b. 1858 Stow
	Hannah Clifford (nee Tidmarsh) — b. 1863 Little Compton
	They were married in Stow in the spring of 1880.
Siblings	Ernest Lee — b. 1880 Lower Swell
	Horace — b. 1881 Stow – *see page 78*
	Henry Lambert — b. 1883 Stow
	Frank — b. 1885 Stow
	Sydney — b. 1887 Stow
	Mabel — b. 1889 Stow
	Edith — b. 1892 Stow
	Oswald Eric) twins — b. 1897 Stow
	Myra Helen) — b. 1897 Stow
	Nora Olwen — b. 1901 Stow
	Gilbert Leslie — b. 1903 Stow
Cemetery	Wimereux Communal Cemetery, Pas de Calais, France. Wimereux is a small town situated about five kilometres north of Boulogne. The cemetery contains 2847 Commonwealth burials of the First World War and because of the sandy nature of the soil, the headstones lie flat. Buried among them is Lt Col John McRae, author of the poem "In Flanders Fields". The Commonwealth section of the cemetery was designed by Charles Holden.

Notes

Cecil was baptised by the Rev R W Hippisley in St Edward's on 17 February 1895. In later years he was a choirboy there. In 1901 his father was working as a Slater, his brothers Ernest as a Blacksmith, Horace as a Slater & Plasterer, Lambert as a Groom and Frank as a Page Domestic at Maugersbury Manor for Mr John Hewitt.

STOW-ON-THE-WOLD WAR MEMORIAL

Wimereux Communal Cemetery, France

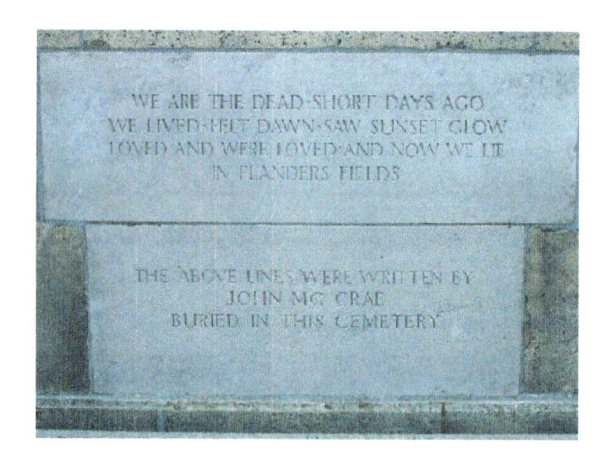

In Flanders fields the poppies blow
Between the crosses, row on row,
That mark our place; and in the sky
The larks, still bravely singing, fly
Scarce heard amid the guns below.

The poem was written by a Canadian military doctor, Lt Col John McCrae, who is also buried in Wimereux Communal Cemetery. The first draft was composed in May 1915 following the death of one of his friends.

Cecil enlisted in Bristol and was posted to the Somerset Light Infantry, which raised nineteen Battalions during the First World War. When war broke out, 1st Battalion was at Colchester and was in France by 21 August 1914 as part of 11th Brigade, 4th Division of the British Expeditionary Force.

11th Brigade also included 1st Battalion, East Lancashire Regiment, 1st Battalion, Hampshire Regiment, and 1st Battalion, Rifle Brigade.

German troops entered Brussels on 20 August and engaged the British Expeditionary Force at Mons three days later. The BEF retreated to Le Cateau where they stood and fought on 26 August 1914. 4th Division held their ground though heavily shelled but by afternoon it was evident the British would have to withdraw again. This time the front line was set at the River Marne and the British and French armies counter-attacked from that base to prevent a German breakthrough to Paris, which was only 30 miles away. The German forces were repulsed and the battle expanded north and westwards as the Germans fought to seize ports to prevent more British troops from arriving.

Antwerp surrendered to the Germans on 10 October. On 27 October the Belgians opened the sluices that held back the sea and flooded the plain along a twenty mile strip of land between Dixmude and Nieuwpoort, creating a two mile wide barrier between their position and the Germans. Both sides dug in at Ypres. During this First Battle of Ypres, fighting ebbed back and forth from 31 October to 17 November. Winter saved the Allies from total collapse and the lines remained stabilised until the following year. However, less than half of the 160,000 men of the BEF who took part in this battle came out unscathed.

Cecil was wounded on 31 October 1914 and died five months later in the British Hospital at Wimereux. He was awarded the 1914 Star, the Victory Medal and the British War Medal.

STOW-ON-THE-WOLD WAR MEMORIAL

D. C/68293/1   68/143986/15-16   English

The document attached hereto dated

and signed

C. R. Clifford L/C

9549 Somerset L. I.

appears to have been written or executed by

Testator died at   9549 L/Sergt. ~~Corporal~~

Boulogne   Cecil Raymond Clifford

from wounds   1st Battn.

received in Action   Somerset Light Infantry

on

1/4/15

while he was "in actual military service" within the meaning of the Wills Act, 1837, and has been recognised by the War Department as constituting a valid Will.

A. W. Crawley.

for the Assistant Financial Secretary.

WAR OFFICE,

Date 7th September 1915.

Facing page of Cecil Clifford's will

WILL.

In the event of my death I give the whole of my property and effects to my mother
Mrs H Clifford
No 1 Park Street
Stow on the Wold
Glos

Signed C. R. Clifford
9579 Somerset

Cecil Clifford's will

STOW-ON-THE-WOLD WAR MEMORIAL

Cap Badge of the Bedfordshire Regiment
16th Regiment of Foot

Eustace Clifford

Hope Cottage

Eustace George Clifford

Date of Birth	5 December 1891 – Stow
Service	3352 Private, Bedfordshire Regiment, Territorial Army
	200195 Sergeant, 1/5th Battalion, Bedfordshire Regiment
Date of Death	Died of wounds on Friday 5 October 1917 – age 25
Stow Address	High Street (1888)
	Well Lane (1891)
	Hope Cottage, Chapel Street (1892)

Parents

Edward John Clifford	b. 20 October 1849 Maugersbury
Emily Minnie Clifford (nee Mills)	b. 21 October 1858, d. 1901 Stow

They were married in St Edward's on 3 March 1881.

Siblings

Mabel	b. 1881 Stow
Augustus	b. 1883 Stow
Harold John	b. 1885 Stow
Horace A	b. 1886 Stow
Claud Cyril	b. 1888 Stow
Lucian R	b. 1890 Stow
Septimus	b. 1894 Stow (stillborn)
Reginald O	b. 1895 Stow
Edward F) twins	b. 1899 Stow
Decimus)	b. 1899 Stow

Cemetery Gaza War Cemetery, Israel. Gaza is three kilometres inland from the Mediterranean coast, 65 kilometres south east of Tel Aviv. Some of the earliest burials were made by the troops that captured the city in November 1917. About two thirds were brought into the cemetery after the Armistice. The cemetery contains 2317 Commonwealth burials of the First World War.

Notes

Eustace was christened in St Edward's by the Rev R W Hippisley on 20 March 1892. His father's occupation was given as Bandmaster in the Baptism Register in 1899 when his twin brothers

The Military Medal

Gaza War Cemetery, Israel

were christened and in the 1901 census as Stonemason and Teacher of Phonography. His father built Hope Cottage himself for the family.

In the 1901 census Eustace's brothers Horace and Claud were listed as Errand boys. His brother Harold became the father-in-law of Frank Joslin – *see page 270*.

Eustace had been in the Territorial Army and enlisted in Biggleswade, joining 1/5th Battalion, Bedfordshire Regiment, when that Territorial unit was mobilised on 4 August 1914 at Gwyn Street, Bedford. The Battalion formed part of the East Midland Brigade, 54th (East Anglian) Division.

After nearly a year spent in training, the Battalion embarked at Devonport on 26 July 1915 in the *Braemar Castle* and sailed at 5.30 pm. On 3 August they called at Malta and three days later at Alexandria, before eventually landing at Suvla Bay on the Gallipoli peninsula on 11 August 1915. On 15 August they moved forward for an attack on Kidney Hill, which they captured with extraordinary dash and swept everything before them. They held on for 48 hours before being ordered to withdraw – they had advanced further than the regiments on either side and were pulled back to straighten the line. In this action, they were given the nickname of "the yellow devils" because of the sunlight glinting on their metal flashes. For the next four months there was stalemate until finally on 3 December 1915, 1/5th Battalion, Bedfordshire Regiment, was evacuated from the peninsula and sailed for Mudros on the island of Lemnos. From there the battalion went on to Egypt to be rebuilt between January and March 1916 after which a year-long posting to guard the Suez Canal followed. In 1916 the Sinai desert separated the British forces in Egypt from the Turks in Palestine. In January 1917 the British advanced across Sinai, constructing a supply railway and water pipeline in support and succeeded in driving the Turks back out of Sinai to Gaza and Beersheba. The railway was pushed forward to Deir el Belah and an aerodrome and camps were established there.

At 2.30 am. on 26 March 1917 the (British) Eastern Expeditionary Force attacked Gaza but was hindered by a thick fog. By 6 pm. the city was surrounded but the attack was broken off when Turkish reinforcements were reported to be approaching from the north. The Second Battle of Gaza, from 17 to 19 April 1917, again left the Turks in possession. Both battles had ended in costly failure.

After the failed attempts to capture Gaza in March and April 1917, the Allied army settled in front of the Turkish defences. In June 1917 General Sir Archibald Murray was replaced by General Edmund Allenby. He built the Allied position up slowly using subterfuge, deliberately misleading the Turks into believing the attack would fall on a different area than it eventually did. The 5th Bedfords were assigned to conduct a major raid on Turkish positions in front of Gaza. They held the line opposite Umbrella Hill which would be their target. The raids were so successful that all future raids were carried out in precisely the same way and the 54th Divisional symbol became an umbrella blown inside out because of the success of these operations.

Following the success of a first raid on 20th July, orders were received to repeat the raid on

STOW-ON-THE-WOLD WAR MEMORIAL

Two views of Gaza War Cemetery

the night of 27th/28th July using 5 officers and 111 Other Ranks. The moonlight was bright and zero hour was set for 9 pm. A hurricane barrage opened up on enemy positions as the raiders set off through gaps in the wire. The raiders were divided into four sections. The Turkish machine guns opened fire as the raiders fell upon the front trench but each objective fell after some hard bombing and bayonet duels. As the Turks started wavering, a whistle blew calling the raiders back to their assembly positions. The raiders were back to their own front line trenches by 9.35 pm. Their casualties were 9 killed, 7 missing and 23 wounded.

It is noted in the Battalion War Diary that on 2 August 1917 at 16.45 Military Medals were distributed by the General Officer Commanding 54th Division. Eustace was awarded his Military Medal for gallantry during the second raid on Umbrella Hill.

Skirmishing continued throughout the summer and autumn. On 5 October the Battalion Diary records that the day passed without incident. At 1800 hours two patrols went out with the objective of the first patrol drawing the Turks into the line of fire of the Lewis guns of the second patrol. Both patrols withdrew under heavy fire and had returned by 0400 hours when it was found that 2nd Lieutenant Dennis and Sergeant Clifford were missing. A letter dated 7 October 1917 from 2nd Lieutenant Dennis, now a prisoner of war, was dropped into British lines by enemy aircraft and gave the news that Sergeant Clifford had also been captured but died of wounds on 5 October 1917.

The Third Battle of Gaza began on 27 October 1917 and ended with the capture by the British of the ruined and deserted city on 7 November.

Eustace's award of the Military Medal was announced in the London Gazette of 18 October 1917, issue 30340. The Military Medal was instituted by Royal Warrant in 1916, born out of the need to recognise the almost daily acts of gallantry during the First World War. The reverse of the medal bears the words "For Bravery In The Field". He was also awarded the Victory Medal, the British War Medal and the 1914-15 Star.

Cap Badge of the Royal Garrison Artillery

Gunner Horace Clifford

Horace Clifford

Date of Birth	1881 – Stow
Service	110817 Gunner, 342nd Siege Battery, Royal Garrison Artillery
Date of Death	Killed in action on 29 November 1917 – age 36
Stow Address	Park Street (the cottage, now demolished, was on the site of Parkland Mews) - childhood home
	9 Evesham Road - married home

Parents

Henry Clifford	b. 1858 Stow
Hannah Clifford (nee Tidmarsh)	b. 1863 Little Compton

They were married in Stow in the spring of 1880.

Siblings

Ernest Lee	b. 1880 Lower Swell
Henry Lambert	b. 1883 Stow
Frank	b. 1885 Stow
Sydney	b. 1887 Stow
Mabel	b. 1889 Stow
Edith	b. 1892 Stow
Cecil Raymond	b. 1894 Stow – *see page 66*
Oswald Eric) twins	b. 1897 Stow
Myra Helen)	b. 1897 Stow
Nora Olwen	b. 1901 Stow
Gilbert Leslie	b. 1903 Stow

Wife

Elizabeth Clifford (nee Scarrott)	b. 1884 Stow

Horace and Lizzie were married on 12 October 1904 in St Edward's by the Rev J T Evans.

Children

Noreen Mary	b. 08 November 1907 Leamington
Leslie Horace	b. 27 August 1908 Stow
Reginald Boyce	b. 16 September 1914 Guiting Power

Cemetery Steenkerke Belgian Military Cemetery, Veurne, Belgium. The village of Steenkerke lies south of the town of Veurne (formerly Furnes), off the road which runs west from Ypres to Veurne. The Belgian Military Cemetery contains a plot of 30 Commonwealth burials of the First World War, 17 of them men of the Royal Garrison Artillery.

Horace's grave in Steenkerke Belgian Military Cemetery

Steenkerke Belgian Military Cemetery, Belgium

Notes

Horace and Ernest were baptised in St Edward's by the Rev R W Hippisley on 5 April 1895.

In 1901 Horace's father was working as a Slater, Horace himself as a Slater and Plasterer and his brothers Ernest as a Blacksmith, Henry as a Groom and Frank as a Page Domestic at Maugersbury Manor for Mr John Hewitt.

The Rev J T Evans christened two of Horace's children in St Edward's: Noreen on 31 January 1908 and Leslie on 19 November 1908. When Noreen and Leslie started at school in Stow in 1915, there was a note in their respective school registers stating that they had previously been at Stirchley School. Stirchley lies five miles south west of Birmingham.

Horace enlisted in the Army at the Recruiting Office in Suffolk Street, Birmingham on 5 June 1916. He was 35 years and 7 months old. His address was 24 Franklin Road, Bournville, Birmingham and his trade was given as Temp Chocolate Maker (Bricklayer and Plasterer). He had been in the Royal Engineers Volunteers for three years. He served at home until the spring of 1917 when he was sent to Belgium to join the British Expeditionary Force on 29th May.

From the Evesham Journal – Saturday December 15 1917
STOW-ON-THE-WOLD MAN KILLED
Mrs Horace Clifford has received a letter stating that her husband was killed on 29th November. He joined up 16 months ago and had been in France 6 months. Two years ago his brother Cecil Raymond Clifford died of wounds. There are still five brothers on active service. Mr and Mrs Henry Clifford, Park Street, Stow are his parents and there are also a widow and three young children. Much sympathy is extended to the relatives. The Chaplain writes as follows:- "If you have not already heard, I am afraid that I have very sad news for you tonight. It concerns your dear husband, Gunner H Clifford, 110817 RGA. Yesterday the enemy shelled near the battery and before your husband had taken suitable cover, he was killed instantly. I can assure you that there was no pain. It was all over in a brief second. Today we brought the body back to a quiet little village cemetery a few miles behind the front line and at 2.30 pm. I conducted the funeral service. The grave has been carefully marked and registered and in a few days a little cross with the name thereon will mark the sacred spot. In the course of a month or two the War Office will let you know the location of the cemetery. It is all so sad and I want to assure you of all our sympathy. Out here we mourn with you for your husband had proved himself a valuable soldier and a popular comrade. What can I say to comfort you? Your dear husband has given his life in an assuredly righteous cause and my prayer is that God will not forget his and your sacrifice. My prayer is that in this dark hour you may find hope and comfort in Jesus Christ, who taught us those blessed truths enshrined in our creed, "The resurrection of the body and the life everlasting."

Horace was awarded the Victory Medal and the British War Medal. Mrs Elizabeth Clifford, Horace's widow, received a pension of 29 shillings with effect from 24 June 1918.

Cap Badge of the South Staffordshire Regiment

Lance Corporal Tom Clifford

A Rhyme Of The South Staffordshires

South Staffs, you're the men for the work,
We know that you'll never shirk.
Where ever danger may lurk,
You are ready and steady.
True to your country,
True to your pal,
True to your honour,
True to your gal.
String up the Germans and don't waste a shot,
But use a strong South Staffordshire knot.

Tom Bernard Gregory Clifford

Date of Birth	28 March 1882 – Stow
Service	6799 Lance Corporal, 1st Battalion, South Staffordshire Regiment
Date of Death	1 March 1916 – age 33
Stow Address	High Street (1888), Fosse Road (1901), High Street (1913)
Parents	William Thomas Clifford b. 21 July 1847 Stow
	Mary Ann Clifford (nee Hill) b. 1846 Rugby
	They were married on 16 July 1870 in St Mary's, Lower Swell. Mary Ann had been employed at Quarwood. The witnesses were Edward John Clifford and Mary Elizabeth Clifford, brother and sister of William.
Siblings	Ernest b. 1870 Stow
	Victor b. 1878 Stow
	Edgar b. 1871 Stow
	Gertrude b. 1880 Stow
	Bertha b. 1873 Stow
	Margaret b. 1884 Stow
	George b. 1874 Stow
	Richard b. 1886 Stow
	Eva b. 1875 Stow
	Percival b. 1890 Stow
	Cathleen b. 1877 Stow
Wife	Maud Clifford (nee Spiller) b. 1891 Devonport
	Tom and Maud were married in Devonport in 1914.
Children	Bernard J b. 1914 Devonport
	Margaret Lilian Mary b. 21 July 1916 Devonport d. April 1917 Devonport
Cemetery	Weston Mill Cemetery, Devonport.

Notes

Tom was christened on 27 August 1882 in St Edward's by the Rev R W Hippisley. He was educated firstly at Stow Infants and Boys Schools. Tom, his brother Victor and sister Eva all left their Stow Board Schools on 21 March 1890, age 8, 11 and 13 respectively. The family was still

South Staffordshire Regimental Memorial in Walsall Town Hall

living in the High Street a year later at the time of the 1891 census when Tom's father's occupation was given as Mason/Bricklayer.

By 1901 the family was scattered. Tom's father had died, age 49, on 6 November 1896. Tom was working as a Plumber and living on his own, aged 19, in a cottage on the Fosseway (beside the traffic lights at the Evesham road junction). His brother Edgar had gone to Great Yarmouth in Norfolk as a Hairdresser, brother Victor was a Wheelwright in Reading and the youngest brother Richard, age 14, was a General Domestic Servant in the household of Frederick Smith, Baker, at the Bakery in Broadwell. His sister Bertha had married Joseph Howes in 1899 and gone to live in Marylebone, London and his sister Margaret was working as a Kitchenmaid in Kensington. By the time of the 1911 census Tom had joined the army and was listed in the census as "Overseas Military". He was serving in the 1st Battalion, South Staffordshire Regiment. In the 1913 Stow Electoral Roll Tom was listed as "Ownership Voter – freehold house in the High Street". However, the following year he was married in Devonport where his son Bernard was born later in 1914.

After the start of the war in August 1914, 1st Battalion, South Staffordshire Regiment, which formed part of 7th Division, was based at Lyndhurst between August and October 1914. The Battalion landed at Zeebrugge on 6 October 1914 with orders to proceed to Antwerp but the city surrendered to the Germans four days later and the Division halted at Ypres and dug in. They fought in the First Battle of Ypres later that month with all units suffering grievous losses.

Tom was severely wounded at Ypres on 27 October 1914. He was eventually transferred to a hospital in England in May 1915 and was discharged from the army on 6 November 1915.

He went to live at Admiralty Street, Keyham in Devonport and got a job there as a postman but died very soon afterwards of pleurisy on 1 March 1916. His funeral took place at Weston Mill Cemetery in Devonport on 6 March 1916. Four months after Tom had died, his daughter Margaret was born on 21 July 1916 at 9 Northbrook Street, Devonport. Sadly, she too died, aged only eight months, and was buried in the same grave as her father on 21 April 1917.

Tom's mother died in Stow almost exactly a year later on 20 April 1918.

Tom was awarded the 1914 Star, the Victory Medal and the British War Medal.

Cap Badge of the Royal Regiment of Artillery

Corporal William Cooke

The Royal Regiment Of Artillery

The Royal Regiment of Artillery was divided into two groups, mounted and unmounted. Royal Horse Artillery and Royal Field Artillery comprised the mounted group while Coastal Defence, Mountain, Heavy and Siege Batteries formed the unmounted Royal Garrison Artillery. In 1914 there was one four gun battery of 60 pounder guns per Division. During the war the heavy artillery was massively expanded, serving 6655 guns by 1918.

William Cooke

Date of Birth	29 November 1889 – Stow
Service	35462 Corporal, 195th Siege Battery, Royal Garrison Artillery
Date of Death	Killed in action on 24 April 1917 – age 27
Stow Address	Union Street (1888)
	Well Lane (1894)
Parents	George Bridgeman Cooke b. 1848 Upper Slaughter
	Rachel Cooke (nee Davis) b. 1854 Stow
	They were married in Stow in 1885.
Siblings	Bertha b. 1876 Stow
	Hannah b. 1881 Stow
	Jane b. 1885 Stow
	Ellen b. 1887 Stow
	Nora b. 1888 Stow
	Edith b. 1892 Stow
Cemetery	Bully-Grenay Communal Cemetery, British Extension, France. Bully and Grenay are two villages some 20 kilometres north of Arras. The British Extension was begun at the end of April 1916. From April 1917 to March 1918 it was very largely an artillery burial ground. After the Armistice graves were brought in from isolated positions and small burial grounds on the battlefield. There are now 803 Commonwealth burials and commemorations of the First World War in the British Extension which was designed by Sir Edwin Lutyens.

Notes

William was educated at Stow Infants and Boys Schools. He left in March 1902, aged 13, the register being marked "Left – gone to work." In 1901 William's father was employed as a Farm Labourer. The Rev J T Evans christened two of William's sisters in St Edward's: Ellen on 18 March 1903 and Edith Alice on 29 January 1913.

William was 19 years and 10 months old when he joined the Regular Army in 1909. He had previously been working as a Farm Labourer. He was 5 feet 6 inches tall, weighed 149 pounds with a fresh complexion, blue eyes and brown hair. He served in England until 1913 when he was sent to Singapore. William Cooke and Edward Castle (*see page 48*) were both regular soldiers in the Royal Garrison Artillery. They were serving together in Singapore in 1914 where they

Two views of Bully Grenay Communal Cemetery, British Extension

played in the same football team. By 01 November 1916 William was back in England for three weeks before leaving for France. He embarked at Southampton on 28 November and disembarked at Le Havre the following day. On 01 February 1917 William was promoted in the field to Corporal, backdated to 26 November 1916. Two months later he was killed on 24 April 1917.

From the Evesham Journal – Saturday May 19 1917
ANOTHER STOW MAN MISSING
Mr George Cooke of this town has been notified by the War Office that his son, Corporal W Cooke of the Siege Battery, Royal Garrison Artillery, has been killed in action on April 28 somewhere in France. Corporal Cooke has been in the army for nearly nine years.

After William's death, his father George B Cooke and the family completed forms on 16 August 1917 indicating that any possessions belonging to William should be forwarded to his father at Shepherds Row in Stow. More than two years later on 21 February 1920 the family instructed that any personal possessions or medals should be sent to William's sisters of the full blood – Mrs Jane Hickman (35) of Shepherds Way, Stow; Mrs Ellen Davis (30) of The Crescent, Maugersbury and Miss Edith Cooke (26). On 06 June 1923 Mrs Ellen Davis signed the receipt for William's medals.

STOW-ON-THE-WOLD WAR MEMORIAL

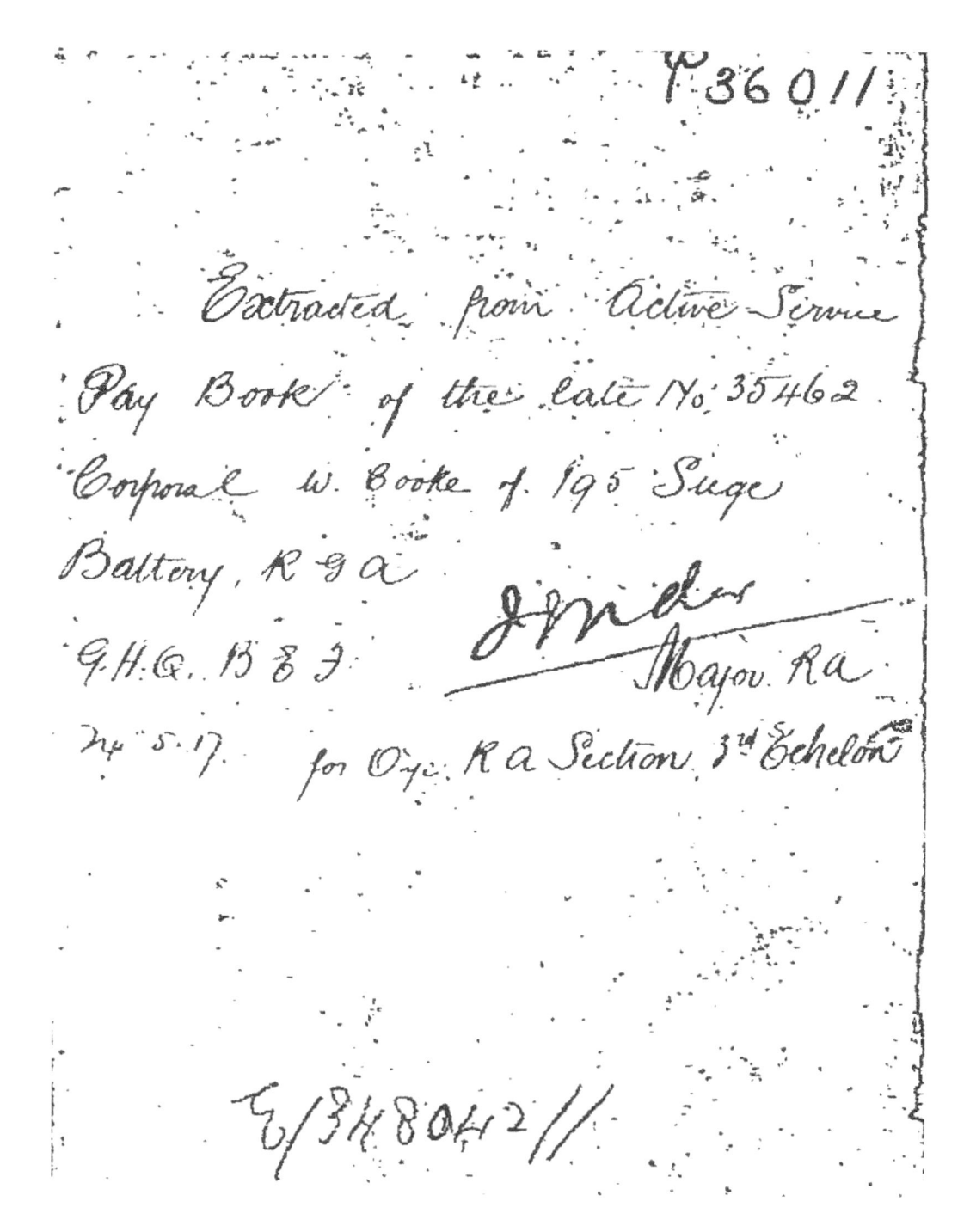

> Y 36011
>
> Extracted from Active Service Pay Book of the late No. 35462 Corporal W. Cooke of 195 Siege Battery, R.G.A.
>
> G.H.Q. B.E.F.
> 24.5.17.
>
> J. Miller
> Major R.A.
> for O/c. R.A. Section, 3rd Echelon
>
> E/348042//

Facing sheet of Corporal Cooke's will

WILL.

In the event of my death I give the whole of my property and effects to my Father,

George Bridgeman Cooke
Shepherds Row
Stow on the Wold
Glos

William Cooke
Cpl. No 35462
Royal Garr Arty
10th Dec 1916

The will of Corporal William Cooke

Cap Badge of the Army Service Corps

Private Charles Curtis

Charles Curtis

Date of Birth	21 April 1875 – Kempston, Bedfordshire
Service	M2/034055 Private, Mechanical Transport, Army Service Corps
Date of Death	6 February 1915 – age 39
Stow Address	Park Lodge, Park Street
Parents	Levi Curtis — b. 1837 Wootton, Bedfordshire
	Julia Curtis — b. 1842 Wootton, Bedfordshire
	Levi and Julia were married in 1860 and their marriage was registered in Bedford.
Siblings	Emily Amelia — b. 1869 Wootton
	Harriet Annie — b. 1871 Wootton
	Frederick — b. 1877 Kempston
Wife	Jane Curtis (nee Nye) — b. 1871
	Charles and Jane married on 13 August 1902 at Kempston.
Children	Ada May — b. 04 March 1904 Northill, Bedfordshire
	Arthur Stanley — b. 13 January 1907 Tamworth, Staffordshire
Cemetery	St Sever Cemetery, Rouen. St Sever Cemetery is about 3 kilometres south of Rouen and contains 3083 Commonwealth burials of the First World War. The Commonwealth section was designed by Sir Reginald Blomfield.

Notes

In 1881 Charles' parents were living at Green End, Kempston, Bedfordshire where his father worked as an Agricultural Labourer. Charles was employed as a Bricklayer's Labourer and then as a Motor Lorry Driver. At the outbreak of war he was working for Mr John Hewitt at Maugersbury Manor as his Chauffeur. A Medical History form was completed for Charles by Dr Edward Dening in Stow on 18 January 1915. His trade was given as Chauffeur, then crossed out and Motor Driver inserted. He was 5 feet 8 inches tall, weight 151 pounds. Charles enlisted in the army in London the next day. He was sent to Grove Park, Lee, SE and trained for eight days before joining the British Expeditionary Force at the Base Depot, Rouen in France on 27 January 1915. He died eleven days later, on 6 February, of pneumonia in No. 6 General Hospital at Rouen where Commonwealth camps and hospitals were stationed on the southern outskirts of the city.

Charles was awarded the 1914-15 Star, the British War Medal and the Victory Medal. His widow was awarded a pension of 15 shillings for herself and 3 shillings each for the children, a total of 21 shillings a week.

Park Lodge

St Sever Cemetery, Rouen, France

On 24 April 1919 in St Edward's, Jane Curtis, widow, age 48, married Edward Basil Wood, Farmer, age 42, of Stow. Charles' son Arthur was a pupil at Stow Boys School from September 1914 until March 1921. Charles' daughter May, who had attended Stow Girls School, worked in Stow Infant School as a Monitress from 8 October 1919 to 31 July 1923. On 15 December 1921 she was allowed to leave early, at 2.30 pm, to attend the War Memorial Dedication Service.

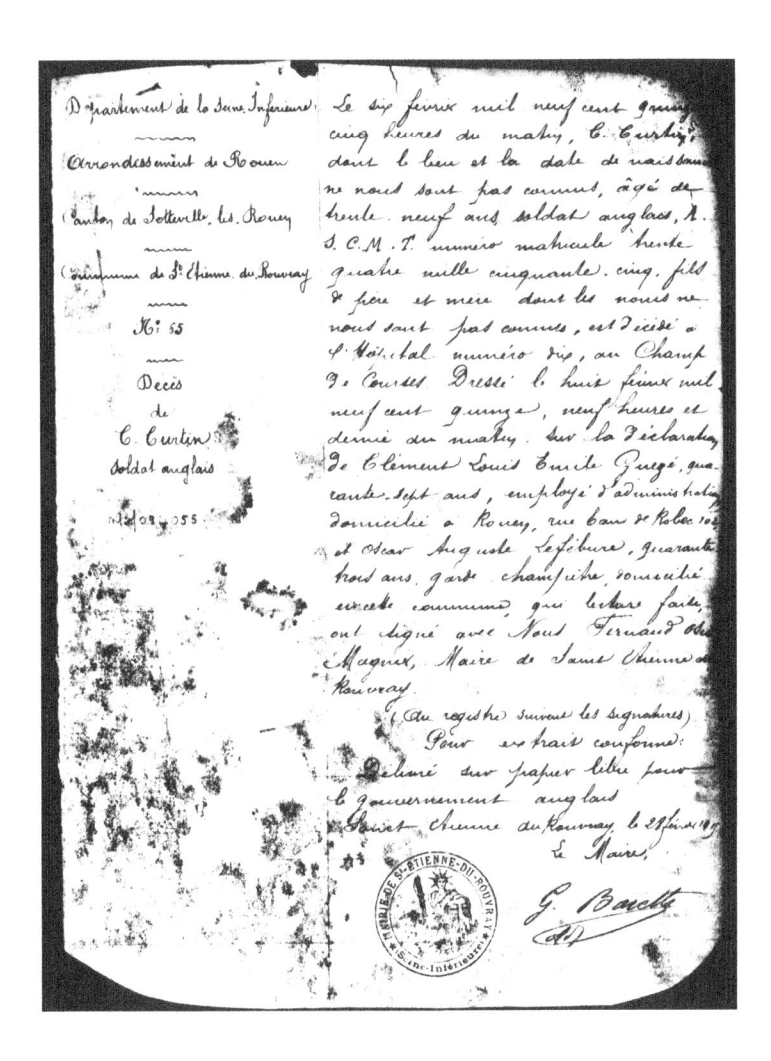

Extract from the French report of Charles' Death

Le six fevrier mil neuf cents quinze a cinq heures du matin, C Curtis, dont le lieu et la date de naissance ne nous sont pas connus, age de trente neuf ans, soldat anglais, ASC MT numero trente quatre mille cinquante cinq matricule, fils de pere et mere dont les noms ne nous sont pas connus, est decede a l'hopital numero six au Champs de Courses. Dresse le huit fevrier mil neuf cents quinze, neuf heures et demie du matin sur la declaration de Clement Emile Louis Gueze, quarante sept ans, employe d'administration domicilie a Rouen, rue Cau de Robec 102, et Oscar Auguste Lefebure, quarante trois ans, garde champetre, domicilie en cette commune, qui lecture faite, ont signe avec Nous Fernand Oscar de Maguex, Maire de St Etienne du Rouvray. (Au registre suivent les signatures) pour extrait conforme Delivre sur papier libre pour le gouvernement anglais.
St Etienne du Rouvray le 28 fevrier 1915. "Le Maire" G Barette dep.

Cap Badge of the Royal Regiment of Artillery

Cap Badge of the Labour Corps

The entry for Philip's birth in the Dance family bible

Philip Dance

Date of Birth	7 August 1891 – Marlcliff, Warwickshire	
Service	130236 Driver, Royal Field Artillery	
	transferred to 143146 Private, Labour Corps	
Date of Death	28 June 1918 – age 26	
Stow Address	Chapel Street – the home of his wife's parents	
Parents	William Dance	b. 1839 Salwarpe, Worcestershire
	Sarah Dance	b. 1845 Broadway, Worcestershire
Siblings	Florence	b. 1866 South Littleton, Worcs
	Arthur	b. 1869 Wormington, Glos
	Sarah Jane	b. 1872 Wick, Worcs
	John George	b. 1874 Wick, Worcs
	Thomas	b. 1878 Pensham, Worcs
	Charles	b. 1881 Aldington, Worcs
	William	b. 1882, died in infancy
	Edith	b. 1884 registered Alcester
	Walter	b. 1889 Marlcliff, Warwickshire
Wife	Annie Elizabeth Dance (nee Betteridge)	b. 1897 Stow
	Philip and Annie were married in the Baptist Chapel in Stow on 21 May 1914.	
Children	Philip	b. 1915, birth registered in Alcester
	William	b. 1916 Stow
Cemetery	Commonwealth War Grave, Stow-on-the-Wold Cemetery	
	Also commemorated on the War Memorial in Bidford-on-Avon	

Notes

Philip's wife Annie was christened on 19 October 1897 in St Edward's by the Rev R W Hippisley. Her father, Thomas Betteridge's occupation was given as Farrier in the Baptism Register and in a later entry as Shoeing-Smith. At that time the Betteridge family lived in Union Street.

In 1901 Philip's father was working as a General Labourer, his mother as a Dressmaker and his brother Charles as a Carter on a Farm.

Horse team pulling a gun

Philip's grave in Stow-On-The-Wold Cemetery

After leaving school, Philip worked for Messrs Bomford & Evershed as a Steamroller Driver's assistant. Later Philip moved to Stow to work as a Groom and lived in Camp Gardens.

After his marriage to Annie Betteridge in 1914, Philip lived with her family who had now moved to Chapel Street.

In March 1915 Philip enlisted in the army in Stratford on Avon. He became a driver in the Royal Field Artillery, which in those days meant working with horses. He was wounded in France and when he recovered, he was medically downgraded and transferred to the Labour Corps.

In 1916 the need was acknowledged for a force of unskilled labour which would leave all trained soldiers free to serve at the front. With the introduction of conscription in 1916 a category of men was introduced into the Army who were not suitable for service in the trenches – this included men already serving, such as Philip, but who had a reduced medical category because of injuries. The first labour units were created in February 1916 and on 21 February 1917 all such units were brought together to form the Labour Corps.

After his transfer to the Labour Corps, Philip was posted to 449th Agricultural Company, which had its headquarters at Taunton although this was mainly an administrative base. The men usually lived at home or on the farm where they worked. Philip was sent to Manor Farm, Chedzoy in Somerset where he worked with horses. His wife moved down from Stow to Manor Farm to be with him. One day Philip was kicked in the abdomen by a horse and suffered serious injuries. He was admitted to hospital in Bridgwater but died there of peritonitis on 28 June 1918. An inquest took place in Bridgwater on 1 July 1918.

A military funeral was held for Philip in Stow Cemetery on 3 July 1918 conducted by the Rev J T Evans.

Philip was awarded the Victory Medal and the British War Medal.

Cap Badge of the Australian Imperial Force

Private Arthur Eaton

Arthur Ernest Wilson Eaton

Date of Birth	1892 – Tiddington, Warwickshire
Service	1335 Private, 11th Battalion, Australian Infantry
Date of Death	Killed in action on 1 August 1915 – age 23
Stow Address	Chapel Street (1908) – sometimes referred to as The Pits
	Park Street (1910)
Parents	George Wilson Eaton — b. 1865 Stow
	Harriet Elizabeth Eaton (nee Arthurs) — b. 1866 Little Rissington
	They were married in Stow in 1888.
Siblings	Edward — b. 1889 Upper Oddington
	Beatrice — b. 1891 Upper Oddington
	George — b. 1894 Shipston-on-Stour
	Emily — b. 1897 Stow
	William — b. 1899 Stow
	Norah — b. 1900 Weston-on-Avon
	John — b. 1904 Drayton
Cemetery	Shell Green Cemetery, Gallipoli, Turkey. Shell Green was a sloping cotton field on the seaward side of Bolton's Ridge at the southern end of the Anzac area on the Gallipoli peninsula. The cemetery was used from May to December 1915 and contains 409 burials.
	Also commemorated on the Australian War Memorial, Canberra.

Notes

In the 1901 census Arthur and his family were living at Drayton Cottage in the civil parish of Old Stratford and Drayton. His father's occupation was given as a Gardener not Domestic. His mother was the sister of John Thomas Arthurs (*see page 22*). His grandfather, Frederick Eaton, age 73 and born in Stow, was living with them. When Arthur's brother William started at Stow Boys School and his sisters Emily and Norah at the Girls School in January 1908, it was noted in the school registers that they had previously been at school in Studley, Warwickshire.

After leaving school, Arthur worked as a farmhand and dairy assistant, then emigrated to

Shell Green Cemetery

Arthur's grave at Shell Green

Australia in 1913. He sailed from Liverpool in the *Zealandic*, a White Star/Shaw, Savill & Albion Joint Service ship, which was launched in Belfast in June 1911. Her maiden voyage had been from Liverpool to Wellington in New Zealand but she was chartered for a time in 1913 by the government of Western Australia as an immigrant carrier. The journey took about six weeks and the ship called at Cape Town. He disembarked in Fremantle on 8 November 1913.

Arthur enlisted in the Australian Imperial Force (AIF) at Perth, Western Australia and was sent to the military training camp at Blackboy Hill. Arthur's unit embarked on 22 February 1915 on *HMAT Ionus* and was diverted to Egypt from its original destination of western Europe. The AIF spent several months training there before being committed to its first campaign – against the Turks. The Allies landed at Gallipoli on 25/26 April 1915. Shell Green was captured by the 28th Australian Infantry Battalion on the morning of 25 April.

From the Evesham Journal – Saturday September 18 1915
STOW MAN KILLED IN GALLIPOLI
Mr and Mrs George Eaton of Stow-on-the-Wold have received the news of the death of their son, Arthur Ernest Wilson Eaton, who was killed in action in Gallipoli on August 1st. He emigrated to Australia three or four years ago and on the outbreak of war had joined an Australian battalion. His age was 23. Much sympathy is extended to his relatives.

Australian War Memorial, Canberra

The idea of a national museum to commemorate the sacrifice of Australians at Gallipoli was first mooted in 1915. The following year, after Australian divisions suffered 23,000 casualties in less than seven weeks of fighting at Pozieres in France, it was decided to create a place in Australia where families could grieve for those buried in places far away and difficult to visit. Work began in 1933 but the start of the Second World War delayed the official opening until Remembrance Day, 11 November 1941.

The Memorial is set among lawns and eucalypts at the head of a wide ceremonial avenue. Kangaroos occasionally stray there from the nearby hills. At the entrance to the Memorial are two medieval stone lions that previously stood at the gateway of the Menin road at Ypres and were damaged during the First World War. The lions were presented to the Memorial by the city of Ypres in 1936. In 1993 the remains of an unknown Australian soldier killed in France in the First World War were brought and interred in the tomb of the Unknown Soldier in the centre of the Hall of Memory. The walls and dome of the Hall are lined with one of the largest mosaics in the world. Over six million glass tesserae imported from Italy were used and the installation took three years to complete. In the Commemorative courtyard in front of the Hall of Memory is the Pool of Reflection crowned by the Eternal Flame. To left and right are stone cloisters with the bronze panels of the Roll of Honour.

Philip Summersbee *(see page 204)* is also commemorated on this Memorial.

STOW-ON-THE-WOLD WAR MEMORIAL

Looking out over the Aegean Sea from Arthur's Grave

Looking down on Shell Green Cemetery from the track leading up to Lone Pine Cemetery

Commemorative courtyard in the Australian war memorial in Canberra

Medieval stone lion presented by the city of Ypres to the Australian war memorial

STOW-ON-THE-WOLD WAR MEMORIAL

Stone cloisters in the commemorative courtyard in the Australian war memorial, Canberra

Arthur's name on panel 62 on the Australian war memorial in Canberra

Arthur's attestation document which he completed on joining the Australian Army on 30th October 1914

Front and back cap badges of the Gloucestershire Regiment

St Sever Cemetery Extension, Rouen, France

Alfred Frederick Ellens

Date of Birth	25 July 1885 – Stow
Service	201825 Lance Corporal, 8th Battalion, Gloucestershire Regiment
Date of Death	1 December 1918 – age 33
Stow Address	20 Well Lane
Parents	Charles James Ellens — b. 1846 Stow
	Matilda Ellens (nee Pearson) — b. 1849 Winchcombe
	They were married in Stow in 1868.
Siblings	Henry — b. 1870 Stow
	Anne — b. 1872 Stow
	Sam — b. 1875 Stow
	Kate — b. 1876 Stow
	Charles — b. 1879 Stow
	Percy — b. 1880 Stow
	Arthur — b. 1882 Stow
	Talbot — b. 1883 Stow
	Florence Jane — b. 1888 Stow
	Winifred — b. 1890 Stow
	Raymond — b. 1892 Stow
Cemetery	St Sever Cemetery Extension, Rouen
	Also commemorated on the family tombstone in Stow-on-the-Wold cemetery.
	For notes on St Sever Cemetery, Rouen, see page 93.

Notes

Alfred, Florence, Winifred and Raymond were all christened in St Edward's on 12 January 1897 by the Rev R W Hippisley. In 1901 Alfred's father was working as a Plasterer. Alfred was a Farm Labourer and he was also in the Territorial Army.

From the Evesham Journal – Saturday July 10 1915
STOW-ON-THE-WOLD PETTY SESSIONS
Thursday – Before Mr G F Moore (chairman), Mr W M Scott and Mr E W Kendall
In Search of Conies – Alfred Ellens, Stow, was summoned on a charge of trespassing on ground

Facing Bazentin-le-Petit across the fields today

The Ellens family grave in Stow Cemetery

in the occupation of Mrs Leigh at Broadwell on the 27th June, in search of conies. PS Parsloe said that in consequence of complaints received from Mr Timms, Mrs Leigh's gamekeeper, he watched the plantation and the calling on the Moreton road. He saw a dog chasing a rabbit. The rabbit got into the ground and the dog was barking at the hole. He kept quiet for some minutes and defendant came running down the plantation. Defendant was fined 5 shillings.

Alfred joined 8th Battalion, Gloucestershire Regiment some time after conscription was introduced in 1916. The Battalion was awarded twenty three battle honours between 1915 and 1918 and served on the Western Front from July 1915 as part of 57th Brigade, 19th Division.

In April 1916 the Battalion was in training in preparation for the big battle on the Somme. On 1 July they moved to positions north of Albert but pulled back to the town four days later having suffered 302 casualties. On 23 July they attacked Switch Line but were driven off and suffered a further 200 casualties. On 29 July they then moved to trenches facing Bazentin-le-Petit and launched an attack at 6.30 pm. the next evening but this failed and they suffered 169 more casualties, an appalling total of 671 casualties during the month. In an attack near Grandcourt on 18 November the Battalion obtained its objectives but at a cost of another 295 casualties.

By the beginning of May 1917 they were in the Ypres area and assisted in the repulse of a German attack on 9 May. At 3.10 am. on 7 June nineteen mines were exploded under German positions at Messines. 57th Brigade advanced at 8.10 am., consolidated captured positions and continued to attack. At dawn on 8 June they attacked again and the next day dug in and prepared defences. On 20 August 8th Gloucesters advanced over very boggy ground near Ravine Wood and suffered heavy casualties in taking their objectives. On 20 September at the Battle of the Menin Road, part of the Third Battle of Ypres, they obtained their objectives but were driven back. In December they were in the Ribecourt sector undergoing training and improving defences.

On 21 March 1918, 76 German Divisions launched a massive attack against 18 British Divisions with 11 in reserve. 19th Division was ordered to counterattack at Doignies at 7 pm. They reached Doignies church but with casualties mounting, the Battalion had to withdraw. At 4 am. next morning 8th Glosters again attacked Doignies but were driven off. The Germans then attacked their position three times but were repulsed each time. On 23 March the Battalion was withdrawn to Fremicourt but moved on to Bancourt next day where German attacks continued on 25 and 26 March. The Brigade was relieved at 1 pm. on 26 March.

In May they moved to a quieter sector on the Rheims/Verdun front but faced attacks on 27 May and again on 6 June. By August, however the Germans were in retreat and the Division advanced and fought minor actions over the next three months. By November they were at Montrecourt and Haussy and on 11 November 1918 the Battalion was in the Flamengrie area when the war ended.

The Battalion was at Candas clearing up on 1 December 1918. On that date Alfred died of influenza in hospital in Rouen. He was awarded the Victory Medal and the British War Medal.

STOW-ON-THE-WOLD WAR MEMORIAL

Cap Badge of the York and Lancaster Regiment

The silver alms dish presented to St Edward's by John's parents after his death

Richard John Francis

Date of Birth	9 May 1893 – Stow
Service	Lieutenant, 2nd Battalion, York & Lancaster Regiment
Date of Death	Died of wounds on 31 March 1915 – age 21
Stow Address	The Bryn (now the Youth Hostel), The Square (1901)
	Beechwood, Lower Swell
Parents	Edward Francis — b. 1859 Maugersbury
	Margaret Mary Francis (nee Lloyd-Williams) — b. 1865 Denbigh
	They were married in St Asaph, Denbighshire in 1892.
Siblings	Edward Lloyd — b. 1896 Stow – Lieutenant, 2nd Battalion, Wiltshire Regiment
Cemetery	Cite Bonjean Military Cemetery, Armentieres, France. Armentieres is close to the Belgian frontier, 14 kilometres north west of Lille. The cemetery was begun in October 1914 and during the winter of 1914-1915 it was used for civilian burials too as the town cemetery was greatly exposed. It contains 2132 Commonwealth burials of the First World War and was designed by Sir Herbert Baker.
	Also commemorated on the Lower Swell War Memorial.

Notes

John's father was a solicitor and sat on many committees in Stow: he was Clerk to the Board of Guardians at the Workhouse, Clerk to the Rural District Council and Clerk to the Board of Magistrates amongst other duties. He was also a Churchwarden at St Edward's.

John was baptised in St Edward's by the Rev R W Hippisley on 4 June 1893. He was educated at Fairfield, Great Malvern from 1902 to 1907 and then at Bradfield College near Reading from April 1907 (pupil number 2383). He left in December 1910 to go to the Royal Military College, Sandhurst, where he started on 1 February 1911 as a cadet in F Company. The cadet's fee paid by his parents was £150. He left the RMC on 21 December 1911, having won the Musketry prize and achieved 105th position in the order of merit (out of approximately 200). He was commissioned into 2nd Battalion, York and Lancaster Regiment, on 14 February 1912.

At the outbreak of war, 2nd Battalion, York & Lancaster Regiment, was stationed at Limerick, however, by September 1914 they had arrived in France as part of 16th Brigade, 6th Division. Armentieres was occupied by the Division on 17 October 1914. John was wounded on 29 March

John's grave in Armentieres, France

Cite Bonjean Military Cemetery, Armentieres, France

1915 and died two days later. He was awarded the Victory Medal, the British War Medal and the 1914 Star.

After John's death, his parents presented St Edward's with a massive and handsome silver alms dish which was dedicated on All Saints Day 1915. It bears the badges of Bradfield College and the York & Lancaster Regiment.

From the Evesham Journal – Saturday August 7 1915
MR EDWARD FRANCIS'S SON WOUNDED
News was received in Stow-on-the-Wold on Sunday morning by Mr and Mrs Edward Francis that their only surviving son, Lieut Lloyd Francis of the 2nd Wilts, had been seriously wounded in the head. Mr and Mrs Francis left the same day for France in the hope of seeing him. Their elder son, Lieut Richard John Francis of the 2nd York & Lancaster Regiment, was killed in action four months ago. The deepest sympathy is felt for Mr and Mrs Francis.

Lloyd Francis had joined the 2nd Battalion, Wiltshire Regiment at La Boutillerie in France on 25 November 1914. On 10 March 1915 he was wounded in the foot during an attack on German trenches. He rejoined the Battalion in July but only two weeks later he was again injured. The Battalion Diary records on 29 July:- "Peaceful day in the trenches. Work of thickening parapets continued during the night. Lieut E L Francis wounded whilst in front of trenches." Such work was usually carried out after dark. The head wound Lloyd sustained was a shattered jaw. He was mentioned in despatches for gallant and distinguished service in the field. He survived and after he left the army, he went on to study law and became a partner in his father's firm, which changed its name to Francis & Son.

Front and back cap badges of the Gloucestershire Regiment

The Menin Gate Memorial, Ypres, Belgium looking west towards the Square and the Cloth Hall

George Hathaway

Date of Birth	19 February 1897 – Stow
Service	10076 Private, 2nd Battalion, Gloucestershire Regiment
Date of Death	Killed in action on 9 May 1915 – age 18
Stow Address	Union Street (1900) – sometimes called Workhouse Lane
	Oddfellows Row (1908)

Parents

Frederick Hathaway	b. 1869 Stow – son of James Hathaway
Kate Hathaway (nee Hathaway)	b. 1872 Lower Swell – daughter of George Hathaway.

They were married in St Edward's on 26 November 1892.

Siblings

Annie	b. 1893 Stow
Eva	b. 1899 Stow, d. 1904
Norman	b. 1902 Stow
Winifred	b. 1905 Stow
Sydney	b. 1907, died aged 3 months
Phyllis	b. 1909 Stow
Victor	b. 1911 Stow

Memorial   Menin Gate Memorial, Ypres, Belgium – *see note on page 119.*

Notes

George was christened in St Edward's on 16 May 1897 by the Rev R W Hippisley. His name is given as "Frederick George" in the Baptism Register and his father's occupation as Labourer. George attended Stow Infants and Boys Schools, leaving on 16 February 1911.

After the Boxer Rebellion in 1900, the Chinese government was forced to agree to European powers maintaining military forces in China. Consequently when war broke out in Europe in August 1914, 2nd Battalion, Gloucestershire Regiment, was stationed at Tientsin on the north China coast, some 50 miles from Beijing. The Battalion immediately returned to England, landing at Southampton on 8 November 1914 and moved to a camp near Winchester.

George enlisted at Stow and was posted to B Company, 2nd Battalion, Gloucestershire Regiment. On 18 December 1914 the Battalion embarked at Southampton aboard the *City of Chester.* They were now part of 81st Brigade along with 1st Battalion, Royal Scots, 2nd Battalion,

Panel 22, Menin Gate Memorial

The Menin Gate Memorial, Ypres, Belgium, looking east

Cameron Highlanders, and 1st Battalion, Argyll & Sutherland Highlanders. They arrived at Le Havre and moved to Aire by train.

The 2nd Battalion was in the trenches near St Eloi from January to March 1915. George joined the Battalion in France on 25 March 1915. They moved east of Ypres in April where, from 18 to 21 April, their lines were shelled. On 24 April George was slightly wounded at Potijze Chateau, which was within British lines throughout almost all the war. The Chateau was used as an Advanced Dressing Station but was eventually destroyed by shellfire.

On 8 May they were heavily engaged by a German attack at Frezenberg. On 9 May after a heavy bombardment which hit the front line, the Germans advanced and broke into the Glosters' trenches. During this action the Glosters' Commanding Officer was killed. The Battalion was relieved the next day with 5 officers and 140 men's names on the casualty list of dead, wounded or missing. George was one of the missing, believed killed on 9 May.

He was awarded the 1914-15 Star, the Victory Medal and the British War Medal.

The Menin Gate Memorial, Ypres

The Menin Gate Memorial at Ypres is one of four memorials to the missing in the area known as the Ypres Salient. The site of the Memorial was chosen because of the thousands of men who passed through the gate on their way to the battlefields. It commemorates casualties who died before 16 August 1917. The Memorial bears the names of 54,332 officers and men who have no known grave. It was designed by Sir Reginald Blomfield with sculpture by Sir William Reid-Dick and was unveiled by Lord Plumer on Sunday 24 July 1927.

The Memorial is situated on the eastern side of the town and each night at 8 pm. the traffic is stopped at the Menin Gate while members of the local Fire Brigade sound the Last Post in the roadway under the Memorial's arches.

Note:
George Hathaway's age is given as 21 on the St Edward's War Memorial and by the Commonwealth War Graves Commission. However, there was no other George Hathaway in Stow of the right age so the son of Frederick and Kate Hathaway would appear to be the correct person.

Cap Badge of the Somerset Light Infantry

Cap Badge of the Oxfordshire & Buckinghamshire Light Infantry

Private George Hemmings

George Hemmings

Date of Birth	1873 – Stow
Service	11913 Private, 1st Battalion, Somerset Light Infantry
	transferred to 20227 Private, 1st Garrison Battalion, Oxfordshire & Buckinghamshire Light Infantry
Date of Death	2 May 1916 – age 42
Stow Address	Well Lane (1913)
	Chapel Street (1916)
Parents	Arthur Hemmings b. 1821 Stow
	Mary Hemmings (nee Cairns) b. 1831 Wyck Rissington
	They were married in Stow in 1870.
Wife	Ellen Hemmings (nee Jacques)
	George and Ellen were married in 1905 in Stow.
Children	William b. 08.06.1907 Stow
	Frederick b. 21.07.1908 Stow
	Harold b. 06.01.1910 Stow
	Charles b. 21.08.1913 Stow
	Ivy b. 05.06.1914 Stow
	Cynthia b. 08.1916 Stow
Cemetery	Trimulgherry Cantonment Cemetery and also commemorated on the Madras 1914-1918 War Memorial in Madras War Cemetery, Chennai, India, which bears the names of more than 1000 First World War servicemen who lie in many civil and cantonment cemeteries in various parts of India.

Notes

George was baptised by the Rev R W Hippisley in St Edward's on 1 June 1873. His father's occupation was given as Stonemason in the Baptism Register. George worked as a Bricklayer. He enlisted in Kitchener's New Army in Bristol and was in France with 1st Battalion, Somerset Light Infantry, by 3 December 1914. He was wounded almost immediately, on 19 December, and came home to convalesce.

    1st Garrison Battalion, Oxfordshire & Buckinghamshire Light Infantry, was formed at Portland in September 1915 and went to India in February 1916 where it became part of the Secunderabad Brigade, 9th (Indian) Division. In the 18th century the Nizam of Hyderabad and

Madras War Cemetery, India

the East India Company signed a deed for political and military co-operation. Secunderabad, in the state of Hyderabad, became one of the chief British military stations in India. Winston Churchill was stationed there as a subaltern in the 1890s.

Trimulgherry Fort, an artillery cantonment three miles north of Secunderabad and surrounded by a moat almost three miles in circumference, once had a barracks, arsenals, stables, a station hospital and a military prison. In 1914 the British military force in India comprised units of the British Army and the Indian Army, mixed together in the same command structure to provide a field force as well as forces for internal security duties.

From the Evesham Journal – Saturday May 13 1916
A STOW SOLDIER KILLED IN INDIA
News has been received by Mrs George Hemmings of this town of the death of her husband, Pte George Hemmings, which occurred on May 2 at Trimulgherry, India, where he had been for the past two months. The death was the result of an accident by which the deceased sustained a fracture of the skull. Pte Hemmings was in the Oxford & Bucks Light Infantry and had seen service in France, where he was wounded on December 19 1914. He was nursed back to health in a hospital at Norwich and was later stationed at Plymouth. He was home in the January of 1915 and again in November of that year, that being the last time his relatives saw him. Deceased was the son of the late Arthur Hemmings and was a native of Stow. He leaves a widow and four children. *(There were actually five children and a sixth, Cynthia, was born shortly after George's death).*

The following two letters were received by George's widow Ellen. The first letter was dated 6 May 1916.
"Very sorry to give you the sad news of your loving husband Pte G Hemmings who died on Tuesday morning about 4 o'clock. He was buried the same day about 6 pm. He passed away very peacefully in his sleep. All the men of the Drums wish me to convey to you their deepest sympathy in your irreparable loss of your dear husband. He was buried with full military honours and I am very pleased to state he was well respected by his comrades of his day and also the band and drums."

The second letter, dated 7 July 1916, was from CQMS A Hold, B Company, 1st Garrison Battalion, Ox & Bucks, Trimulgherry, Deccan, India.
"I am writing a few lines to you to tell you that today I have forwarded a money order. You will get notification from the post office at Stow-on-the-Wold when it arrives. You will no doubt ask whom the money is from, it was collected by me from the officers, warrant officers, NCOs and the men of your late husband's Company just to show the high esteem that he held amongst us all. I am only sorry dear Madam that it has took so long for us to show our appreciation – of course you will understand when I tell you that our men are at several places and hundreds of miles apart."

George was awarded the 1914-15 Star, the Victory Medal and the British War Medal.

Cap Badge of the Royal Air Force 1918

Longuenesse Souvenir Cemetery, St Omer, France

Tom Hiatt

Date of Birth	1 May 1888 – Stow
Service	268377 Aircraftsman 1st Class, 1st Aircraft Supply Depot, Royal Air Force
Date of Death	26 February 1919 – age 30
Stow Address	Digbeth Street (1881)
	The Square – the house on the south side of the King's Arms (1901)
Parents	Thomas Hiatt — b. 1842 Hook Norton
	Harriet Hiatt (nee Herbert) — b. 1850 Stow
	Their marriage in 1877 was registered at Headington, Oxfordshire.
Siblings	Joseph Bernard — b. 1880 Stow
	Clarice — b. 1883 Stow
	Mildred — b. 1884 Stow
	Olive — b. 1886 Stow
Wife	Hilda Mary Hiatt (nee Hiatt) b. 1893 Hook Norton
	Tom and Hilda married on 4 June 1918 at Erdington, Warwickshire.
Cemetery	Longuenesse Souvenir Cemetery, St Omer, France. St Omer is a large town 45 kilometres south east of Calais and Longuenesse is on the southern outskirts. The Commonwealth section of the cemetery contains 2874 Commonwealth burials of the First World War and was designed by Sir Herbert Baker.
	Also commemorated on the Hook Norton war memorial.

Notes

In the 1901 census Tom's father's occupation was given as Draper and his mother's as Boot and Fancy Goods Dealer. The family's draper's shop in Church Street, T & W Hiatt, which belonged to Tom's father and uncle William, is now Baggott's Antiques and the doorstep still reads "Frank Hiatt". Frank was Tom's cousin and the son of William Hiatt.

Before the war Tom worked as a Motor Mechanic and was a Volunteer in the Oxford Yeomanry. In the 1911 census he was working as a Chauffeur at Guiting Grange. He emigrated to Canada from Bristol in 1913 and then in 1915 returned to the UK from New York. He joined the Royal Air Force on 15 July 1918. He was posted to France in August 1918 to 1st Aircraft Supply Depot. On 20 February 1919 he reported sick with influenza and died six days later of broncho pneumonia. St Omer, where Tom died, was the General Headquarters of the British Expeditionary Force from October 1914 to March 1916. Field Marshal Lord Roberts died there

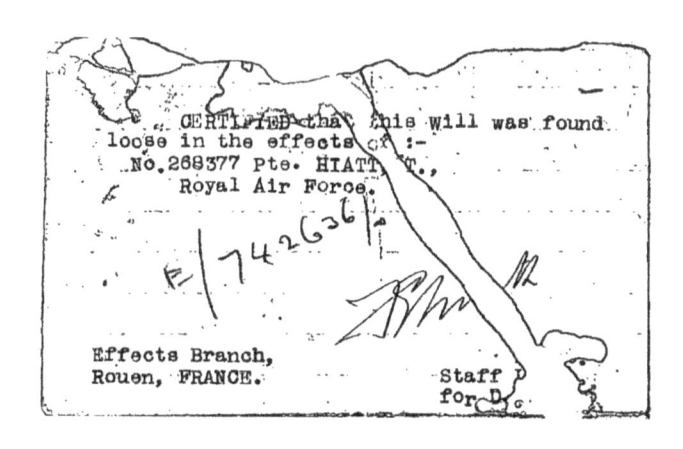

Facing pages of Tom Hiatt's will

in November 1914. Although in his eighties, he had come to visit the troops. He contracted a chill which became pneumonia and subsequently died.

Tom was awarded the RAF France Medal, the Victory Medal and the British War Medal.

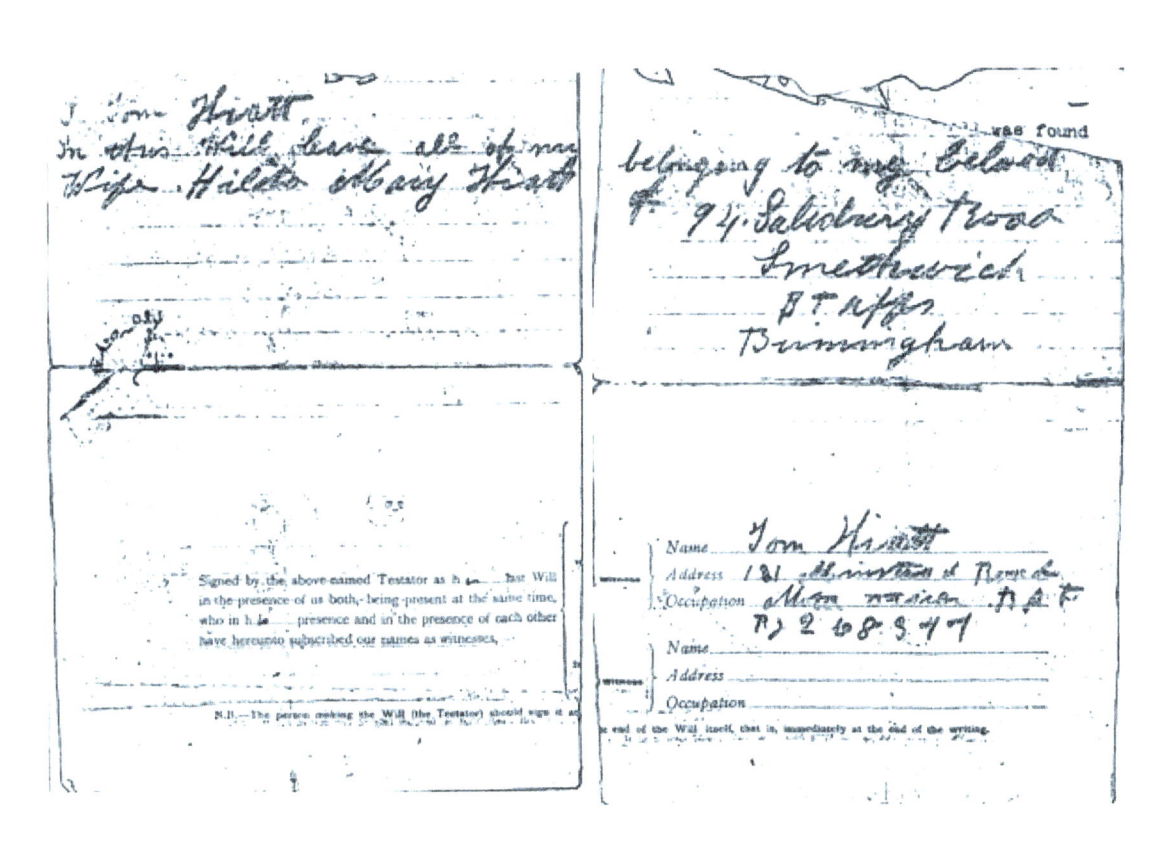

Tom Hiatt's will

Cap Badge of the Worcestershire Regiment

The badge is similar to that of the Coldstream Guards as it is believed to symbolise a link between the two regiments when the 29th Foot was raised in 1694 by Colonel Farrington, who was previously in the Coldstreams. Successive Colonels have also come from the Guards and the badge was adopted in the 18th century.

Rocquigny-Equancourt Road, British Cemetery, France

Francis Alfred John Hicks

Date of Birth	20 October 1878 – Stow
Service	20258 Private, 2nd Battalion, Worcestershire Regiment
Date of Death	Died of wounds on 25 October 1918 – age 40
Stow Address	Park Street (1888)
	Sheep Street (1891)
	Union Street (1901)
	Park Street (1913)
Parents	George Hicks — b. 1852 Great Rissington
	Jane Hicks (nee Hyde) — b. 1853 Stow
	They were married in St Edward's on 24 April 1872.
Siblings	Thomas — b. 1877 Stow
	Annie — b. 1882 Stow
	Bertram — b. 1884 Stow
	Walter — b. 1889 Stow
	Percy — b. 1896 Stow – *see page 134*
Cemetery	Rocquigny-Equancourt Road British Cemetery, Manancourt, France. Rocquigny and Equancourt are two villages in the Department of the Somme about 12 kilometres south east of Bapaume. The British Cemetery lies about halfway between the two villages at the crossing from Etricourt to Ytres. The cemetery was begun in 1917 and contains 1838 Commonwealth burials and commemorations of the First World War. It was designed by Sir Reginald Blomfield.

Notes

Frank was baptised in St Edward's by the Rev R W Hippisley on 19 January 1879. He was educated at Stow Infants and Boys Schools, leaving in March 1891.

In 1901 Frank's father was working as a Butcher, his brothers Thomas as a Cowman and Bertram as a Grocer's porter. Frank himself was a Labourer (chemist's).

Frank enlisted in Bourton-on-the-Water in 1914. He joined 2nd Battalion, Worcestershire Regiment, which had mobilised at Aldershot on the outbreak of war and formed part of 5th Brigade, 2nd Division. The Battalion, comprising 12 officers and 977 men, sailed from Southampton in two transports, *Lake Michigan* and *Herschel*, on 13 August to Boulogne to join the British Expeditionary Force.

The meeting of the Worcestershire Regiment and the South Wales Borderers in the grounds of Gheluvelt Chateau

Gheluvelt Chateau restored

On 16 August they went by train through Amiens and Arras to Wassigny, then marched to Lesquielles St Germain where they were received cordially by the inhabitants on whom they were billeted.

Before dawn on the morning of Sunday 23 August the Battalion crossed the Belgian frontier and marched through Malplaquet. The German artillery had already opened fire at Mons and by the time the Battalion came up, the British front line was hotly engaged. By the end of the day, withdrawal was ordered to a defensive line but thereafter retreat continued for the rest of the month and into September.

On 31 October 1914 the Battalion was in reserve at Polygon Wood, near Ypres, when the Germans broke through the British line. The situation was very serious and the Battalion was ordered to counter attack. The Battalion could not muster more than 500 men but unless the gap could be closed, the British army was facing disaster. They charged with fixed bayonets and surprised the enemy by the impetuous speed of the attack. The Germans, though far superior in numbers, gave way and Gheluvelt Chateau was held by the Allies against terrific odds. 2nd Battalion, Worcestershire Regiment, linked up with the remnants of the South Wales Borderers and the line was secured. General Sir John French said that if any one unit could be singled out for special praise that day, it was the Worcestershires. It is rare that the action of one unit can exert such a profound influence as this counter attack did.

Thereafter the actions in which the Battalion took part continued across the battlefields of France and Flanders. Frank landed in France on 19 July 1915. In December 1915 the Battalion was transferred to 100th Brigade, 33rd Division. During July 1916 at the Battle of the Somme whilst attacking a strong German position, the Battalion lost the majority of their officers and senior NCOs.

In the autumn of 1916 General Paul von Hindenburg, Chief of Staff of the German Army, ordered the construction of a system of defence fortifications behind the northern and central sectors of the Western Front – the Hindenburg Line.

The town of Etricourt in Alsace, near where Frank is buried, was lost to the Germans on 23 March 1918 at the start of their massive spring offensive when the British were pushed back 40 miles. By July, however, having failed to make the key breakthrough, the Germans retreated back to the Hindenburg Line. A massive Allied attack was launched against the Hindenburg Line in the region of the St Quentin Canal on 29 September 1918. The assault began at 5.30 am. The 2nd Worcesters were not involved in the main attack but in a diversionary one to the left of the line. By 10 am. their offensive had failed – every officer and man of the four platoons which led the attack had been mown down and killed while the ground behind them was covered by the dead and wounded of the following platoons. However, the main attack further south was successful, the canal was crossed and the Hindenburg Line broken. Allied forces advanced four to five miles into what had been German territory.

Frank died of his wounds on 25 October 1918. He was awarded the Victory Medal and the British War Medal.

STOW-ON-THE-WOLD WAR MEMORIAL

INFORMAL WILL.

W.O. No.: E/692525/1   DOMICILE. England

Record No. 483/797949 18/19

Name: Francis Alfred John Hicks

The enclosed document dated Nil and signed Hicks F.

Regtl. No. and Rank: No. 20258 Private

Regt. 2nd Bn. Worcestershire Regt.

Died at: France

Date of Death: 25/10/18.

appears to have been written or executed by the person named in the margin while he was "in actual military service" within the meaning of the Wills Act, 1837, and has been recognised by the War Department as constituting a valid will.

WAR OFFICE.

Date 7th March 1919.

U. W. A. Parkes,
for the Assistant Financial Secretary.

Facing page of Frank Hicks's will

132

Francis Alfred John Hicks

18
WILL.

In the Event of my Death I Bequeath the whole of my property & Effects to

Mrs Harrington
15 Tea The [...]
Plymouth
[...]

Signature *Hicks F*
Rank and Regt. *Pte*
Date _____

Frank Hicks' will

STOW-ON-THE-WOLD WAR MEMORIAL

Front and back cap badges of the Gloucestershire Regiment

Private Percy Hicks

Percy Hicks

Date of Birth	13 January 1896 – Stow
Service	29334 Private, 13th Battalion, Gloucestershire Regiment
Date of Death	Died of wounds on 6 April 1918 – age 22
Stow Address	Park Street (1888)
	Sheep Street (1891)
	Union Street (1901)
	Park Street (1913)
Parents	George Hicks — b. 1852 Great Rissington
	Jane Hicks (nee Hyde) — b. 1853 Stow
	They were married in St Edward's on 24 April 1872.
Siblings	Thomas — b. 1877 Stow
	Frank — b. 1878 Stow – *see page 128*
	Annie — b. 1882 Stow
	Bertram — b. 1884 Stow
	Walter — b. 1889 Stow
Wife	Elsie Winniferd Hicks (nee Hutt) — b. 1891 Finstock, Oxfordshire
	Percy (age 20) and Elsie (age 25) were married on 22 December 1915 in St Edward's by the Rev J T Evans.
Child	Marion Ruby — b. 2.11.1917 Stow
Cemetery	Abbeville Communal Cemetery Extension, France. The town of Abbeville is on the main road from Paris to Boulogne in the Department of the Somme. The Cemetery Extension was begun in September 1916 and contains 1754 First World War burials. The Commonwealth section of the Extension was designed by Sir Reginald Blomfield.

Notes

Percy was christened by the Rev R W Hippisley in St Edward's on 31 May 1896. His father's occupation was given as Butcher in the Baptism Register.

Percy was educated at Stow Infants and Boys Schools, leaving in April 1909. Before the war Percy worked as a Labourer.

Abbeville Communal Cemetery Extension, France

He enlisted in the Army at Stow in 1914 and was posted firstly to the Wiltshire Regiment (Private 23213) before transferring to 13th Battalion, Gloucestershire Regiment.

Formed in December 1914, 13th Battalion, Gloucestershire Regiment, (known as the Forest of Dean Service Battalion), left for France in March 1916, sailing in the *Marguerite* and the *Maidan* for Le Havre. In the ensuing two years they won nine battle honours, including Ypres and the Somme, and lost 10 officers and 292 men.

For much of the First World War, Abbeville was the headquarters of the Commonwealth lines of communication and three hospitals were stationed there at various times between October 1914 and January 1920. Percy was wounded and died in hospital in Abbeville on 6 April 1918.

From the Evesham Journal – Saturday May 4 1918
ANOTHER STOW MAN KILLED
Information has been received of the death in Abbeville Australian Hospital of Private Percy Hicks of the Gloucester Regt. Pte Hicks had received a gunshot wound in the chest and had been removed to the above-named hospital for treatment. Pneumonia supervened with fatal result on April 6 last. His bereaved wife and friends will be accorded a large share of sympathy.

He was awarded the Victory Medal and the British War Medal.

Percy's daughter Marion was christened on 6 December 1917 by the Rev J T Evans in St Edward's.

Cap Badge of the Bedfordshire Regiment
The 16th Regiment of Foot

Lance Corporal John Hillier

John Henry Hillier

Date of Birth	18 June 1876 – Camden Town, London
Service	33405 Lance Corporal, 8th Battalion, Bedfordshire Regiment
Date of Death	Killed in action on 4 October 1917 – age 41
Stow Address	Sheep Street
Parents	John Hillier — b. 1836 St Pancras, London, d. 1888 Stow
	Ann Maria Hillier (nee Hunt) — b. 1847 Stow
	They were married in Stow in 1875.
Siblings	Frank — b. 1878 Camden Town, London
	Frances Maria — b. 1880 Stow
Cemetery	Loos British Cemetery, Pas de Calais, France. Loos is a village to the north of the road from Lens to Bethune. The cemetery was begun in 1917 and enlarged after the Armistice by the concentration of graves from the battlefields and smaller cemeteries over a wide area to the north and east of the village. There are nearly 3000 First World War burials in this cemetery.

Notes

John's father was a widower when he married Ann Maria Hunt in St Edward's on 7 September 1875. His occupation was given as Post Office official. John was baptised in St Edward's on 30 July 1876 by the Rev R W Hippisley. He was educated at Stow Infants and Boys Schools, leaving in August 1889.

In 1891 George Lawrence, the Schoolmaster at Kingham, was a Boarder in the Hillier household.

John's father died in 1888 and his mother, Mrs Ann Maria Hillier, widow, married Frederick Arthurs, widower, in St Edward's on 11 March 1896. Frederick Arthurs was the father of John Thomas Arthurs – *see page 24*.

John enlisted in Warley, Essex at which time he was living at Chelmsford. He was posted to 8th (Service) Battalion, Bedfordshire Regiment, which was formed at Bedford in September 1914 as part of 71st Brigade, 24th Division.

From the Evesham Journal – Saturday October 20 1917
STOW MAN KILLED
Mrs J Arthurs of Stow-on-the-Wold has received an intimation of the death of her eldest son,

John's grave in Loos British Cemetery, France

Loos British Cemetery, France

Lance-Corporal J Hillier of the Bedfordshire Regiment, who resided in Stow from his infancy till his manhood. He was apprenticed to the late Mr T Blizard and became assistant to Messrs T & W Hiatt. He was killed on October 4.

His lieutenant writes as follows:- "Dear Madam, With deep regret I have to inform you that your son, Lance-Corporal Hillier, was killed in action on the night of October 4. He was killed instantaneously so suffered no pain. He was taken to the rear of the lines for proper burial and after the war, you can obtain from the Graves Registration Committee the name of the place of burial.

Your son was a most capable soldier and NCO and it is a great loss to his platoon and company, both as a soldier and comrade. All the company officers wish to join me in offering our sincere sympathy in your great loss. Yours faithfully, Thomas Dunn, 2nd Lieut." Lance-Corporal Hillier was 41 years of age.

John was awarded the Victory Medal and the British War Medal.

STOW-ON-THE-WOLD WAR MEMORIAL

Private Percy Hodgkins

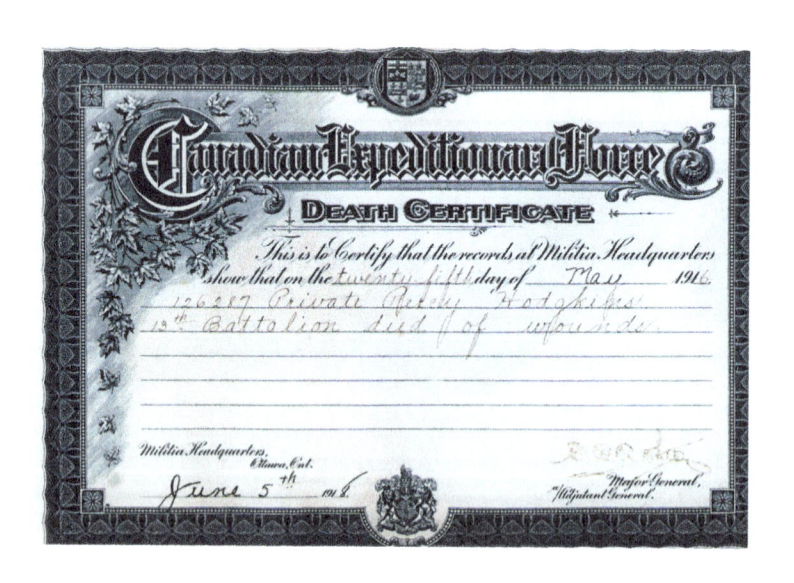

Canadian Expeditionary Force Death Certificate
"This is to certify that the records at Militia Headquarters show that on the twenty-fifth day of May 1916 126287 Private Percy Hodgkins 13th Battalion died of wounds."

Percy Hodgkins

Date of Birth	10 October 1895 – Stow
Service	126287 Private, 13th Battalion, Canadian Infantry (Quebec Regiment)
Date of Death	Died of wounds on 25 May 1916 – age 20
Stow Address	Church Street (1895)
	Parkers Cottages, Lower Oddington (1901)
Parents	William Hodgkins — b. 1848 Warwick, d. 1896 Stow
	Elizabeth Catherine Hodgkins (nee Keen) — b. 1862 Stow
	They were married in St Edward's on 20 November 1886.
Siblings	Herbert — b. 1887 Stow
	Frederick — b. 1889 Adlestrop
	Florence — b. 1890 Adlestrop
	Mabel — b. 1891 Stow
	Mary — b. 1893 Stow
Cemetery	Lijssenthoek Military Cemetery, West Flanders, Belgium. The cemetery is located 12 kilometres west of Ypres town centre. It began to be used by casualty clearing stations of the Commonwealth forces in June 1915 and contains 9901 Commonwealth burials of the First World War, which includes 1051 Canadians. It is the second largest Commonwealth cemetery in Belgium and was designed by Sir Reginald Blomfield.

Notes

In the censuses of 1881 and 1891 Percy's father was working as a Groom in the employ of Captain Stanley Arnold, Royal Lancashire Artillery, at the Mansion House, Adlestrop. The Hodgkins family lived in rooms over the stables.

Percy's father died in 1896 and his mother, Mrs Elizabeth Hodgkins, widow, married Walter Jennings, a Gardener, in Stow in the autumn of 1899. In 1901 they were living in Oddington. They ultimately had five children – Beatrice in 1900, Dora in 1903, Eva in 1906, Gladys in 1908 and Albert in 1910 – whose births were all registered in Stow.

Mr and Mrs Jennings and their children plus Fred and Percy Hodgkins emigrated to Canada. However, the Jennings family later returned to Stow but Fred and Percy chose to remain in Canada.

Percy's grave in Lijssenthoek Cemetery

Lijssenthoek Military Cemetery, Belgium

Percy's sister Mary married John James Murray in 1916 – *see page 164*.

On 7 September 1915 in Woodstock, Ontario, Percy enlisted in the Canadian army. His pre-war occupation was given as Knitter. 13th Battalion, Canadian Infantry, arrived in England on 1 December 1915.

In March 1916 Percy spent nineteen days in hospital at Shorncliffe in Kent suffering from German measles. Having recovered, he joined his unit in France in April 1916.

During the First World War, the village of Lijssenthoek was situated on the main communication line between the Allied military bases in the rear and the Ypres battlefields. Close to the front line but out of the extreme range of most of the German artillery, it became a natural place to establish casualty clearing stations. Percy was wounded on 25 May and died the same day at 4.15 pm. in No. 3 Casualty Clearing Station, Lijssenthoek.

From the Evesham Journal – Saturday June 24 1916
STOW SOLDIER'S DEATH
The sad news has been received by Mrs Walter Jennings (formerly Hodgkins) of the death of her son, Pte Percy Hodgkins, 13th Battalion, 3rd Canadian Regiment, which occurred on May 25 at No. 3 Casualty Clearing Station, of gunshot wounds in thigh, chest and right arm. Mrs Jennings has received a message of sympathy from His Majesty and the Queen and the chaplain who attended him at the last writes:- "Dear boy, he did his bit nobly." Pte Hodgkins was born in Church Street, Stow-on-the-Wold and was in his 21st year.

Cap Badge of the Queen's (Royal West Surrey) Regiment

Raised in September 1661 as part of the Tangier Garrison and styled the Tangier Regiment, from 1684 it was called The Queen's Regiment in honour of Charles II's wife, Queen Catherine of Braganza.

Cap Badge of the Labour Corps

Robert's name carved on the ringing chamber wall in St Edward's

The ringing chamber in the tower of St Edward's church

Robert Hookham

Date of Birth	15 June 1876 – Stow
Service	33934 Private, 3rd Battalion, The Queen's (Royal West Surrey) Regiment transferred to 66258 Private, 111th Company, Labour Corps
Date of Death	3 July 1918 – age 42
Stow Address	Sheep Street (1881)
	South Hill Cottage, Station Road
Parents	Henry Hookham b. 1823 Stow
	Elizabeth Hookham b. 1838 Stow
	Henry and Elizabeth married in Stow in 1866.
Siblings	Charles Frank b. 1868
	William Ernest b. 1872 Stow
	Margaret Annie b. 1874 Stow
	Edward b. 1878 Stow
Wife	Alice Hookham (nee Noble) b. 1876 Nether Swell
	Robert (aged 37) and Alice (aged 38) were married in St Edward's on 14 April 1914 by the Rev J T Evans.
Cemetery	Terlincthun British Cemetery, Wimille, France. The cemetery is on the northern outskirts of Boulogne and was begun in June 1918 when the space available for service burials in the civil cemeteries of Boulogne and Wimereux was exhausted. It suffered considerable damage during the Second World War during the withdrawal to Dunkirk. It now contains 4378 Commonwealth burials of the First World War and was designed by Sir Herbert Baker.
	Also commemorated on the Lower Swell war memorial.

Notes

In 1881 Robert's father was employed as a Slater & Plasterer but by 1891 Robert's mother was a widow and working as a Monthly Nurse.

On 3 April 1892 Robert (age 16) was christened with his brothers Ernest (age 20) and Edwin (age 14) in St Edward's by the Rev R W Hippisley. His deceased father's occupation was given as Slater. Robert worked as a Painter and Decorator. In his spare time he was a Volunteer in 1 Company, 2nd Gloucestershire Regiment, (Private 5972).

STOW-ON-THE-WOLD WAR MEMORIAL

Terlincthun British Cemetery, Wimille, France

Another view of Terlincthun British Cemetery, Wimille, France

This is the official letter which came with Robert's possessions that were returned to his widow, Alice. These were: "Silver watch and chain, Purse (with) Farthing, bar Soap, 2 Keys, Small Strop, match Box cover, 3 Wooden …?, Cap Badge, Leather Case."

Two thirds of World War One service records were lost due to bombing in the Second World War. Those records which survived were often charred at the edges, as is the one above.

Robert became a bell ringer in St Edward's and his name is carved on the wall in the ringing chamber in the tower. On 25 March 1914 he took part in ringing a peal of 5040 changes of Grandsire Triples, which was rung in three hours, the first such peal ever to be rung by an entirely local team.

Robert enlisted in Stow on 11 December 1915. The Magistrate who signed his Attestation was Colonel Henry Railston *(see page 184)*. Robert must have been rather overweight as his medical record states: "Too much adipose tissue." 3rd Battalion, The Queen's (Royal West Surrey) Regiment stayed in the United Kingdom and supplied drafts to the regular battalions overseas. Robert spent a week in hospital in Colchester in October 1916 suffering from pneumonia. He joined the British Expeditionary Force in France on 16 January 1917. On 9 May 1917 he transferred to the Labour Corps although from 15 April 1917 to 27 May 1917 he was attached to 41st Squadron Royal Flying Corps. He was on leave in England from 12 to 26 January 1918.

From the Evesham Journal – Saturday July 13 1918
DEATH OF A STOW SOLDIER FROM PNEUMONIA
News was received on Saturday of the death in a USA base hospital of Pte Robert Hookham of Queen's Own West Surreys (Labour Battalion). The deceased was a native of Stow and his age was 42. He had been in France for a year or more. Recently he suffered from an attack of influenza, which was followed by pneumonia and this proved unexpectedly fatal, death taking place on Wednesday July 3. He was buried in Wimereux. Mrs Hookham received an intimation of the above from a USA chaplain (E M Penbody) on Sunday morning. Muffled peals were rung on Sunday evening and very general sympathy is extended to her and other relatives.

From the Evesham Journal – Saturday July 20 1918
STOW MAN DIES OF ILLNESS
Mrs R Hookham of Stow-on-the-Wold has received official notice that her husband, Pte R Hookham of a Labour Company, died in hospital in Boulogne of broncho-pneumonia following an attack of influenza. Pte Hookham joined the 4th Glosters on June 16 1916 and was drafted into the West Surreys, and later into a Labour Battalion. Lieut Joblin writing to Mrs Hookham in reference to the death of her husband says:- "He was in my platoon for a long time and was a man I greatly admired for his diligence and devotion to duty. Knowing him as I did, I can all the more appreciate your loss and offer you my deepest and heartfelt sympathy. I trust you will find some little solace in this thought, that though he died in hospital and not from enemy action, he died a soldier and the knowledge that whatever the circumstances, and they have been trying at times, your husband never failed in his duty and always did his best."

Robert was awarded the Victory Medal and the British War Medal. His widow Alice was awarded a pension of 15 shillings a week with effect from 13 January 1919. Later she moved to Church Cottage, Broad Street, Banbury. At the time of Robert's death his Army Service Record listed his living relatives as his widow Alice and his brothers Ernest of Adlestrop and Edward of Stow.

INFORMAL WILL.

W.O. No. 1 E/619931/1 DOMICILE. English

Record No. 446/743323/18/19

Name Robert Hookham

The enclosed document dated 15·1·17 and signed Robert Hookham

Regtl. No. and Rank 66258 Private

Regt. 111 Labour Coy. Labour Corps.

Died at France

Date of Death 3·7·18

appears to have been written or executed by the person named in the margin while he was "in actual military service" within the meaning of the Wills Act, 1837, and has been recognised by the War Department as constituting a valid will.

WAR OFFICE.

Date 16/10/18

X. Waller
for the Assistant Financial Secretary.

CERTIFIED that this WILL was found loose in the A.B.64 of No. 1/66258, Pte HOOKHAM, R., No. 111 Labour Coy.

P/619931.

Captain,
Staff Captain.

Facing pages of Robert Hookham's will
AB64 is Army Book 64 – Soldiers Service & Pay Book

13

WILL.

In the event of my death I give the whole of my property & effects to my wife

Mrs Alice Hookham
South Hill Cottage
Stow on the Wold
Glos

Signature *Robert Hookham*
Rank and Regt. Pte No. ~~23984~~ 66258
3rd Infantry Labour Coy Lucan R.W.3
Date January 15 1917

The will of Robert Hookham

Front and back cap badges of the Gloucestershire Regiment

Private Leonard King

Leonard King

Date of Birth	3 November 1897 – Wyck Rissington
Service	2466 Private (Signaller), 8th Battalion, Gloucestershire Regiment
Date of Death	Missing believed killed in action on 18 November 1916 – age 19
Stow Address	Half Moon House, Maugersbury (1914)
Parents	Harry King — b. 1863 Maugersbury
	Fanny King (nee Smith) — b. 1867 Upper Swell
	They married in Stow in 1886.
Siblings	Harry — b. 1887 Lower Swell
	Louis — b. 1890 Upper Swell
	Eliza — b. 1892 Wyck Rissington
	Frederick — b. 1895 Wyck Rissington – *served in the Life Guards*
	Gertrude — b. 1900 Wyck Rissington
	Alfreda May (Primrose) — b. 1904 Stow
	Hiram John — b. 1907 Herefordshire
Memorial	Thiepval Memorial, France. The Memorial is off the main Bapaume to Albert road and is the Memorial to the missing of the Somme. It bears the names of some 72,000 officers and men of the United Kingdom who have no known grave, the majority of whom died between July and November 1916. The Memorial, designed by Sir Edwin Lutyens, was unveiled by the Prince of Wales in the presence of the President of France on 31 July 1932.

Notes

In 1891 Leonard's father was working as a Domestic Servant in Wyck Rissington and in 1901 he was working there as a Groom. When Leonard and Gertrude started as pupils at school in Stow in 1909, the register was marked "Previously at school in Lugwardine, Herefordshire." His home address was given as Half Moon House, Maugersbury. In later life his parents moved to The Forge in Maugersbury. Leonard left school in November 1911.

Leonard's brother Harry was the father of Frederick Harold King – *see page 274*.

Leonard enlisted at Bourton-on-the-Water in 1914 and was posted to 8th (Service) Battalion, Gloucestershire Regiment, which was formed at Bristol in September 1914 as part of 57th Brigade, 19th Division. In December 1914 the Battalion moved to billets in Weston and Clevedon. In

STOW-ON-THE-WOLD WAR MEMORIAL

Half Moon House, Maugersbury

Thiepval Memorial, France

March 1915 they were in training at Tidworth and finally embarked for France in July 1915. They moved up to the front line on 28 August 1915 and were in reserve during the Battle of Loos.

On 1 July 1916, the Battalion took up position north of Albert. Thirteen Divisions of Commonwealth forces launched an offensive that day in the Battle of the Somme but, despite a preliminary bombardment lasting seven days, the German defences were barely touched. Allied losses were catastrophic and the initial attack was a failure.

In the following weeks, huge resources of manpower and equipment were deployed. 8th Glosters were involved in a series of attacks but by 6 August had been sent to Bailleul where they awaited reinforcements and stayed there in training for two months. Attacks north and east continued throughout these months in increasingly difficult weather conditions. On 24 October they moved up to the front line east of Thiepval, returned to the reserves on 30 October and then up to the front line trenches again on 2 November. It was a similar pattern over the next fortnight. The Battle of the Somme finally ended on 18 November with the onset of winter. On that day the Battalion attacked near Grandcourt at 06.10 am. and took their objectives but at a cost of 295 casualties, one of whom was Leonard.

From the Evesham Journal – Saturday December 23 1916
MAUGERSBURY MAN MISSING
Mr and Mrs H King of this village have received official information that their son Leonard King, a Private in the Glosters, a signaller, has been missing since November 18. He was in France. Private King, who was 19 years of age, enlisted in August 1914. *(Leonard was only 16 years 9 months in August 1914).*

Three months after Leonard was posted missing, his parents were still seeking news of him, hoping against hope that he might have survived and been taken prisoner but it was not to be and he was eventually declared missing believed killed in action.

Leonard was awarded the Victory Medal and the British War Medal.

STOW-ON-THE-WOLD WAR MEMORIAL

Thiepval Memorial, France

Pier and face 5a from inside the Thiepval Memorial, France

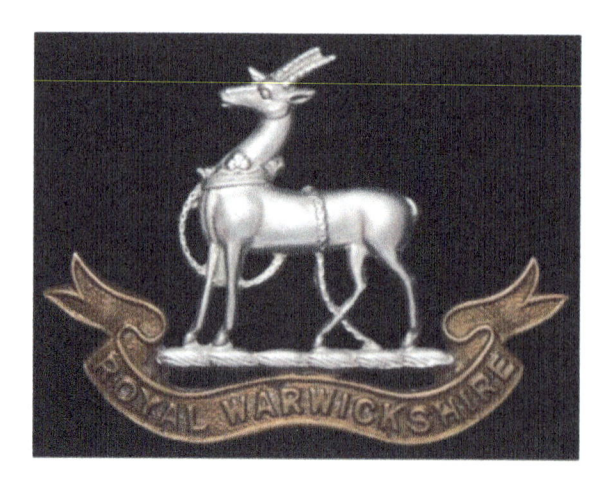

Cap Badge of the Royal Warwickshire Regiment (6th of foot)
The 'Royal' title was awarded by King William IV in recognition of loyal and faithful service.

British soldiers at Ypres in 1914

Richard Edward Minchin

Date of Birth	19 July 1896 – Stow	
Service	15866 Private, 2nd Battalion, Royal Warwickshire Regiment	
Date of Death	Died of wounds on 7 September 1916 – age 20	
Stow Address	Back Walls (1893)	
Parents	Richard W Minchin	b. 1852 Bampton, Oxfordshire
	Elizabeth Minchin	b. 1860 Longborough
	Their marriage was registered in Chipping Norton in 1884.	
Siblings	Thomas	b. 1885 Stow, d.1896
	Emma	b. 1887 Stow
	Louisa	b. 1890 Stow – *married Alfred Sansom, see page 194*
	Elsie	b. 1899 Stow
	Gertrude	b. 1902 Stow
	Alice	b. 1904 Stow
Cemetery	Peronne Road Cemetery, Maricourt, France. Maricourt is a village on the Albert-Peronne road in the Department of Somme. In 1916, Maricourt was the point of junction of the British and French forces and very close to the front line. The cemetery was begun in 1916 and there are 1348 First World War burials there.	

Notes

Richard was christened 'Richard Edwin' by the Rev R W Hippisley in St Edward's on 17 May 1897 and received as 'Richard Edward' by the Rev E Lyon Harrison, Curate in Charge, on 8 July 1898. His father's occupation was given as Labourer in the Baptism Register.

Richard attended Stow Infants and Boys Schools. According to the 1913 Electoral Roll, his family was living at Meadow Farm, Stow, but Richard had gone to work in Rugby where he enlisted in the Army in 1914 at the outbreak of war.

He was posted to 2nd Battalion, Royal Warwickshire Regiment, which had been in Malta in August 1914. The Battalion reached England on 19 September and formed part of 22nd Brigade, 7th Division at Lyndhurst. They sailed for Belgium and landed at Zeebrugge on 7 October. Later that month, the Battalion took part in the First Battle of Ypres in October and November 1914 and then in the Second Battle of Ypres which ended on 13 May 1915.

At Festubert from 16-18 May 1915 they were under continual artillery fire before advancing, capturing and holding German trenches. The months of June, July and August were relatively uneventful.

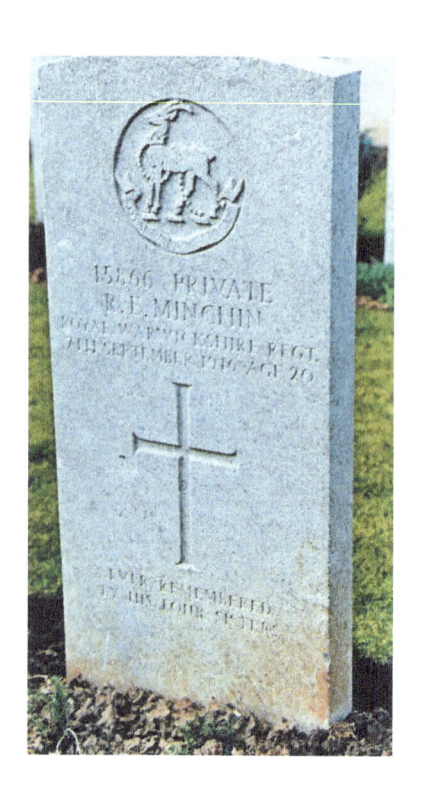

Richard's grave in Peronne Road Cemetery, France

Peronne Road Cemetery, France

The village of Loos gave its name to the battle which lasted from 25 September to 8 October 1915. The Battalion suffered severe losses. They went over the top at 0630 on 25 September 1915 in the face of terrific fire. Private Arthur Vickers won the Victoria Cross for cutting gaps in the German wire while under intense fire, thus enabling the Battalion to continue its advance. They were halted at St Elie but held on until dusk when they were forced to withdraw. At midnight when the Battalion mustered, there were no officers and only 140 men. By 8 October Loos had finally been captured from the Germans.

The following year was a build up to the Battle of the Somme which began on 1 July 1916 at which date 2nd Warwicks were entrenched before Mametz. As a result of offensives over the next five days, the attack on the southern end of the line was successful and the German line was captured over a front of six miles.

In August 1916 the Battalion was rested.

On 3 September in an attack along the whole front, the Battalion reached Ginchy but it was decided in the afternoon to withdraw them in view of the heavy casualties sustained, although this order was difficult to communicate to some of the men in advanced positions. One detachment held out for 36 hours and another for five days. Richard died of his wounds on 7 September 1916. His death was reported in the daily Casualty List published in the Birmingham Post on 6 October 1916.

Richard was awarded the Victory Medal and the British War Medal.

In the Commonwealth War Graves Commission records, Richard is listed as the brother of Mrs Elsie Lane of Boxbush, Great Rissington.

Badge of the Royal Warwickshire Regiment (6th of foot)
The 'Royal' title was awarded by King William IV in recognition of loyal and faithful service.

Locket with picture of John's daughter Kathleen

John James Murray

Date of Birth	1890 Cardiff, Monmouthshire
Service	610 Corporal, 1st Battalion, Royal Warwickshire Regiment
Date of Death	14 December 1919 – age 29
Stow Address	Enoch's Row
Parents	Timothy Murray b. 1851
	Cath Murray
	Timothy and Cath were married in Cardiff in 1878.
Wife	Mary Murray (nee Hodgkins) b. 1892 Stow
	John and Mary were married on 8 January 1916 in Newport, Isle of Wight
Child	Kathleen Mary b. 24 June 1917 Stow – d. 6 December 1919 Stow
Cemetery	Commonwealth War Grave, Stow-on-the-Wold

Notes

John's father was a Merchant Seaman. John's wife Mary was the sister of Percy Hodgkins (*see page 142*). At the time of their marriage, John was stationed at the Barracks, Parkhurst, Isle of Wight and Mary was working at 69 Crocker Street, Newport, Isle of Wight. Their daughter Kathleen was christened in St Edward's on 30 September 1917 by the Rev J T Evans.

On 3 November 1905 John had a medical examination at Stratford-upon-Avon. The record shows his age was 15 ½ years, height 4 feet 6 inches and weight 68 lbs and his occupation was given as "Musician". On 14 November he enlisted in the Royal Warwickshire Regiment and the next day he was sent to Portland in Dorset. From there he travelled on a troopship to Quetta in the north west of India, where he arrived on 28 February 1906 to join the 1st Battalion. After two years in Quetta the Battalion moved to Peshawar in 1908 and then to Bombay in 1910. After leaving the Royal Military Academy, Sandhurst in 1908, Field Marshal Viscount Montgomery joined the 1st Battalion, Royal Warwickshire Regiment, in India as a second lieutenant.

The 1st Battalion, Royal Warwickshire Regiment, sailed from Bombay aboard the troopship *Rewa* on 12 December 1912 and arrived at Southampton on 2 January 1913 having served overseas for seventeen years. John had been with the battalion for nearly seven years during which time he suffered from several bouts of malaria. The Warwicks were stationed at Shorncliffe from January 1913 until the outbreak of war. They then formed part of 10th Brigade, 4th Division, along with 2nd Battalion, Seaforth Highlanders, 1st Battalion, Royal Irish Fusiliers, and 2nd Battalion, Royal Dublin Fusiliers.

Silver War Badge

Around the rim of the badge was inscribed "For King and Empire – Services Rendered". For this reason it also became known as the "Services Rendered Badge". Each badge was engraved with a unique number on the reverse although this number was not related to the recipient's Service Number. The recipient would also receive a certificate with the badge. The badge was made of Sterling Silver and was intended to be worn on the right breast of civilian clothing. It could not be worn on military uniform.

The battalion mobilised on 4 August 1914 and moved to York, then to Strensall before proceeding to Southampton. On 22 August they sailed on the *Caledonia* to Boulogne. Three days later at Beaumont they were under heavy fire. Having received orders to retire, they moved off at 11 pm. It rained a good deal and no rations had arrived. They marched for twelve miles and bivouacked in a cornfield at 4.30 am. near Ancourt. A week later the Battalion was at Chantelupe only fifteen miles from Paris, then they moved north crossing the Rivers Marne and Aisne. By mid October they were on the Belgian border at Bailleul.

They endured heavy shelling for ten days after which the battle raged to the north but the Battalion was quiet although they faced constant sniping. On 18/19 December 1914, 10th Brigade assisted 11th Brigade in an attack at Ploegsteert Wood. The soldiers had their own names for the various types of German shell fired at them and on one day in this particular attack they recorded that seven White Hopes and twelve Little Willies had been dropped on them.

On Christmas Day at St Yves the Battalion Diary reads: "A local truce. British and Germans intermingle between the trenches. The dead in front of the trenches buried. No shot fired all day." An officer of the 1st Warwicks wrote home to his family: "The German trenches were only 80 yards away occupied by 134th Saxon Regiment. On Christmas Eve the Germans called out greetings and we replied in our best German, wishing them Frohliche Weinachten. On Christmas Day we were woken by the sergeants singing carols. At daybreak we met the Germans in No Mans Land and made arrangements there would be no shooting on either side during the day and Boxing Day. We had our photo taken in a group Germans, Tommies and officers."

In March 1915 the Battalion Diary records: "Lt Tillver reported that a boring machine had been heard in German lines – probably mining our trench – later discovered to be a Bull Frog heralding the spring!"

On 25 April at 4.30 am. the Brigade attacked outside Ypres – the battle lasted ten days. By July they were in the trenches at Mailly-Maillet on the Somme. On 25 October 10th Brigade was inspected in the grounds of Acheux Chateau by HM King George V accompanied by M. Poincare, President of the French Republic, and the Prince of Wales. The weather that day was awful – incessant rain with a strong north east wind.

By late 1915 John was attached to the 3rd Battalion, Royal Warwickshire Regiment, at Parkhurst Barracks on the Isle of Wight. It is likely that he had been wounded and was convalescing because the following year he was awarded the Silver War Badge. This badge was awarded from 12th September 1916 to officers and men who were discharged or temporarily retired from the military forces as a result of sickness or injury caused by their war service. It was on the Isle of Wight that he met Mary Hodgkins, a Stow girl who was working there as a nanny. They were married in Newport Register Office on 8th January 1916.

In late 1916 or early 1917 John returned to serve with the 1st Battalion in France. In 1917 the Allies attacked the remnant of the old German line located at Arras and Vimy Ridge. The attack

John's grave in Stow-On-The-Wold Cemetery

opened on 9 April. The German line fell. The Canadians took Vimy Ridge and the British 3rd Army swept through the marshy valley of the River Scarpe towards Fampoux.

After heavy fighting which lasted from 9 April to 12 May in trenches around the chateau, chemical works and the cemetery and having suffered many casualties, the British pushed back the German forces and took the town. During that period they had broken through and held four lines of German trenches. Their general, when later congratulating them and commending their conduct, called it the finest action of the war. For John Murray, however, it had spelt disaster. He was listed as missing in the daily Casualty List published in the Birmingham Post on 15 June 1917 and then on Thursday 19 July he was listed as "previously reported missing, now reported a Prisoner of War in German hands." It is most likely that he was captured on 3 May.

Whilst a prisoner of war, John contracted tuberculosis and was seriously ill by the time he was repatriated some twenty months later after the end of the war. His daughter Kathleen, aged 2, who caught the disease from him, died on 6 December 1919 and was buried in Stow Cemetery. Her funeral service was taken by the Rev J T Evans four days later. John himself died of tuberculosis on 14 December 1919 and was buried on 17 December in the same grave as his daughter, the service again being conducted by Mr Evans.

John was awarded the 1914 Star, the Victory Medal and the British War Medal.

Mrs Mary Murray, widow, married Joseph Long, Groundsman, in 1921.

Cap Badge of the Royal Regiment of Artillery

Battery gun at Passchendaele, 1918

Hubert Conroy Newcombe

Date of Birth	1885 – Withington, Gloucestershire
Service	322380 Gunner, 263rd Siege Battery, Royal Garrison Artillery
Date of Death	Died of wounds on 25 April 1918 – age 32
Stow Address	4 room cottage, Maugersbury (1911)
Parents	Charles Newcombe — b. 1851 Elkstone, Glos
	Elizabeth Newcombe — b. 1851 Elkstone, Glos
Siblings	Agnes — b. 1877 Elkstone
	William — b. 1879 Elkstone
	Charles — b. 1891 Withington
Wife	Ada Newcombe (nee Dando)
	Hubert and Ada were married in Lymington in the summer of 1908.
Children	Sidney Charles — b. 17.03.1909 Maugersbury
	Stanley Herbert — b. 15.08.1912 Maugersbury
	Doris Ellen Ada — b. 20.01.1916 Maugersbury
Cemetery	La Clytte Military Cemetery, Belgium. The cemetery is located eight kilometres west of Ypres. The first burial took place on 1 November 1914. The cemetery was enlarged after the Armistice when graves were brought in from isolated sites and small burial grounds in the surrounding area. There are now 1082 casualties of the First World War buried or commemorated in the cemetery, which was designed by Sir Edwin Lutyens. Fifty men of the Royal Garrison Artillery are buried in La Clytte Military Cemetery.

Notes

In 1881 Hubert's parents were living at Pinchley Bottom, Withington, Gloucestershire. In the 1901 census Hubert's occupation was given as Plasterer's Labourer at Withington and his father was working there as an Agricultural Labourer. Hubert's parents later moved to Pegglesworth, near Andoversford.

Hubert's children were all christened by the Rev J T Evans in St Edward's: Sidney on 30 May 1909, Stanley on 23 October 1912 and Doris on 10 May 1916. Hubert's occupation was given as Estate Mason in the pre-war entries in the Baptism Register.

In the 1913 Electoral Roll for Maugersbury, Hubert is entered as an "Ownership Voter – dwelling house in village".

Hubert's grave at La Clytte Cemetery

La Clytte Military Cemetery, Belgium

He enlisted in the army in Stow.

From the Evesham Journal – Saturday May 18 1918
MAUGERSBURY MAN KILLED
The relatives of Gunner Hubert Conroy Newcombe of the RGA have received news of his death. The following letter from Lieut Schlotel was received by his mother:-
"Dear Mrs Newcombe, I am writing to you to express the sympathy of all the battery officers and men in the matter of the death of your son. Nothing I can say will alleviate the great sorrow which has come to you. Your son was severely wounded during a terrific attack by the Germans. Every attention was paid to his wounds and he was carried to the hospital by his comrades, where he passed quietly away. We, as officers, had always noticed in Gunner Newcombe a man of great courage and the highest qualities and he was most popular among his comrades. I thought it my duty as senior officer left of the battery to write to express our sympathy for you in your irreparable loss. Believe me, Yours sincerely, L C Schlotel, Lt, RGA."
Gunner Newcombe had been two years in the Army and had been in France seven months. Just previous to going out he was at home on leave and was looking very fit. He was a man of sterling qualities. His age was 32. Besides his mother, he leaves a widow and three children.

Hubert was awarded the Victory Medal and the British War Medal.

In the Stow School register it is noted that the Newcombe family removed to Cheltenham in August 1918. They went to live at 15 Corpus Street, Cheltenham.

Cap Badge of the Oxfordshire & Buckinghamshire Light Infantry

At home in England, eggs were collected and despatched to hospitals near the front for the benefit of the wounded. Occasionally, people wrote their name and address on the eggshell and some received a letter of thanks from the recipient.

> *From the Evesham Journal – Saturday March 18 1916*
> AN EGG-CELLENT LETTER
> Miss Kathleen Collett, daughter of Mr W Collett of Stow-on-the-Wold, has received the following letter from a private in the Middlesex Regiment, somewhere in France: -"Just a line or two to tell you I had the pleasure through being in hospital for a few days of tasting one of your eggs, and I must say they are trae bon as they say here, that is very good or very nice in this case. I hope you don't think it impertinent of me writing but your name was so plain on the egg so I simply had to write. It is very funny weather out here: heavy falls of snow last week; now it is raining, which has made it warmer. It was terribly cold last week. I hear the Zepps have been your way. Did you see anything of them? Well, I think this is all now."

Abbeville Communal Cemetery, France

William Harold Phipps

Date of Birth	24 July 1892 – Stow
Service	18952 Lance Corporal, 3rd Battalion, Oxfordshire & Buckinghamshire Light Infantry
Date of Death	Died of wounds on 16 August 1916 – age 24
Stow Address	Sheep Street (1896)
	Park Street (1913)
Parents	Ralph Phipps — b. 1852 Hook Norton
	Mary Ann Phipps (nee Wilcox) — b. 1866 Northleach
	They were married in 1887 in Stow.
Sibling	Ralph — b. 1888 Stow
Cemetery	Abbeville Communal Cemetery, France
	For details of Abbeville Communal Cemetery, see page 135.

Notes

Harold was baptised in the Methodist Chapel in Stow on 18 September 1892. His father was a Tailor. Harold attended Stow Boys School from 1899 to 1904. In the 1911 census he was listed as working as a shop assistant in Warwickshire. 3rd (Reserve) Battalion, Oxfordshire & Buckinghamshire Light Infantry, remained in England and supplied drafts to the regular battalions overseas. Harold enlisted in Leamington Spa. He was later sent to France where he landed on 30 September 1915.

> *From the Evesham Journal – Saturday August 19 1916*
> STOW-ON-THE-WOLD MAN WOUNDED
> Lance Corporal Harold Phipps, of the Oxon & Bucks Light Infantry, was badly wounded on the 2nd inst. He was in an advanced trench which the enemy was shelling and was struck by a piece of shell on the thigh and chest. He is now lying in the South African General Hospital at Abbeville from whence he has written a letter to his parents, Mr and Mrs Ralph Phipps of this town. No details of the injuries are known here.
>
> *From the Evesham Journal – Saturday August 26 1916*
> STOW MAN DEAD
> Lance Corporal Harold Phipps, who we reported last week to have been wounded, succumbed to his wounds on Wednesday in last week. Much sympathy is evinced towards his parents, Mr and Mrs Ralph Phipps of this town.

Harold was awarded the 1914-15 Star, the Victory Medal and the British War Medal.

STOW-ON-THE-WOLD WAR MEMORIAL

Cap badge of the Grenadier Guards

Lance Corporal Frank Pratley

Boulogne Eastern Cemetery, France

Frank Pratley

Date of Birth	14 June 1895 – Kingham
Service	19595 Lance Corporal, 4th Battalion, Grenadier Guards
Date of Death	Died of wounds on 7 August 1916 – age 21
Stow Address	Park Street (1898), Camp Gardens (1899), Well Lane (1904), Union Street (1916)
Parents	Alfred Pratley — b. 1854 Kingham
	Sarah Ann Martha Pratley — b. 1853 Stow, d. 23.10.1916
	Their marriage was registered in Chipping Norton in 1877.
Siblings	Alban Alfred b. 1879 Kingham Rose b. 1891 Kingham
	Agnes b. 1881 Kingham Walter b. 1881 Kingham
	Florence b. 1887 Kingham Tom b. 1897 Kingham
	Albert b. 1888 Kingham Beatrice b. 1898 Stow
Cemetery	Boulogne Eastern Cemetery, Pas de Calais, France. The cemetery contains 5577 Commonwealth burials of the First Word War. The Commonwealth plots were designed by Charles Holden.

Notes

Frank's father was a Cowman. Frank attended Stow Boys School from 1902 to 1908. He enlisted in the Army in 1914 at Bourton-on-the-Water and in July 1915 transferred to 4th Battalion, Grenadier Guards, newly formed at Marlow. The Battalion proceeded to France on 14 July 1915 where on 15 August it became part of 3rd Guards Brigade, Guards Division, and assembled near St Omer. The Division's first action was at the Battle of Loos in September 1915, fighting at Hill 70 and the Hohenzollern Redoubt.

The Division was in the front line at the Battle of the Somme, which commenced on 1 July 1916, where they gained one of the battle honours now displayed on the Colours of the Regiment.

Frank was wounded in the head during the battle on 20 July and died of his wounds nearly three weeks later on 7 August 1916. He was awarded the 1914-15 Star, the Victory Medal and the British War Medal.

From the Evesham Journal – Saturday August 19 1916
REPORTED DEAD
Pte Frank Pratley, Stow-on-the-Wold, 3rd Co Grenadier Guards, is reported to have died of wounds on Monday August 7.

Cap Badge of the Army Veterinary Corps

The British Bantams
(Nickname of 14th Battalion, Gloucestershire Regiment)

There is a bonnie breed of Bantams
As yet unknown to fame
Who have joined the British roosters
To earn a glorious name.
They are sturdy, they are willing
And sure to stand the test,
What price the German eagle
When the Bantams leave the nest?

Benjamin William Thomas Pulham

Date of Birth	17 July 1895 – Stow
Service	24826 Private, 14th Battalion, Gloucester Regiment
	Re-enlisted – SE/34649 Private, Army Veterinary Corps
Date of Death	28 October 1918 – age 23
Stow Address	Park Street (1902) – the Pulham home was sometimes referred to as "by Banning's Alley".
	Back Walls (1909)
Parents	Thomas Pulham b. 1863 Stow
	Emily Pulham (nee Boulton) b. 1869 Stow
	They were married in Stow in 1894.
Siblings	Phoebe b. 1897 Stow
	Ethel Lilian b. 1899 Stow
	Mary Jane b. 1901 Stow
	Emily Elizabeth b. 1902 Stow
Wife	Eliza Pulham (nee Holmes) b. 1896 Bradford
	Benjamin and Eliza were married in Bradford in 1918.
Cemetery	Scholemoor Cemetery, Bradford, Yorkshire. There are 138 First World War burials in this cemetery.

Notes

Benjamin was christened with Phoebe on 1 July 1898 in St Edward's by the Rev E Lyon Harrison, Curate in Charge. His father's occupation was given as General Labourer in the Baptism Register.

Benjamin was educated at Stow Infants and Boys Schools, leaving in May 1909, shortly before his 14th birthday, and got a job as a Farm Labourer.

14th Battalion, Gloucestershire Regiment, was known as the West of England Bantams. Posters had been displayed on village greens and outside pubs advertising for recruits for a "Bantam Battalion – Height 5 feet 3 inches, chest expansion 34 inches." It was raised in Bristol from senior NCOs of the 12th Battalion with a few local recruits but the majority came from Birmingham. Benjamin enlisted at Chiseldon Barracks, Gloucester on 22 October 1915. His Attestation was signed by Colonel Henry Railston *(see page 184)* and Benjamin was posted to the

Benjamin's shared grave in Scholemoor Cemetery, Bradford

Gloucester Bantams. His height was 4 feet 8 and a half inches, weight 94 pounds and chest expansion 32 inches so he was small even for the Bantams.

The Battalion moved to Tidworth on 22 November 1915 and in January embarked for France where they landed on 30 January 1916. They moved to the front line at Festubert and Givenchy.

After a rest period, it was back to the front, this time at Lavantie and later at Neuve Chapelle. On 8 June 1916 the Battalion took part in a night raid, capturing an enemy machine gun. Another rest period followed involving training and preparation for the battle of the Somme in July when they went into the front line at Trones Wood.

Benjamin was in hospital in Birmingham from 14 July 1916 to 20 July with myalgia. He was then discharged from the Army on 30 August 1916. The Battalion records show that he had been ill overseas and that he was no longer fit for service.

At some point during the next two years he re-enlisted in the Army and was posted to the Army Veterinary Corps, which had been formed in 1903 to unite all Veterinary Officers under one badge and to provide a trained resource of soldiers to assist them.

In the summer of 1918 he was married in Bradford and then returned to his unit. Benjamin died in the Red Cross Hospital, 18 St Thomas Street, Winchester on 28 October 1918 of influenza followed by broncho pneumonia. His body was taken to Bradford for burial at Scholemoor Cemetery but his young widow did not have money to buy a plot in the churchyard so he was buried in a public grave. This grave is shared with Private G Partridge of the Royal Defence Corps.

He was awarded the Victory Medal and the British War Medal.

His widow lived at 107 Gracechurch Street, Lumb Lane, Bradford.

Cap Badge of the Royal Defence Corps

Front and back cap badges of the Gloucestershire Regiment

Frank's grave in Stow-on-the-Wold Cemetery

Frank Pulham

Date of Birth	15 April 1885 – Stow
Service	28990 Private, Gloucestershire Regiment, transferred to 71944 Private, 462nd Protection Company, Royal Defence Corps
Date of Death	1 December 1918 – age 33
Stow Address	Sheep Street (1889), Park Street (1894)
Parents	Thomas Pulham — b. 1838 Stow
	Mary Pulham — b. 1842 Little Barrow, Gloucestershire
Siblings	William b. 1867 Stow; Frances Ellen b. 1877 Stow
	Thomas b. 1872 Stow; Edwin b. 1879 Stow
	Emma b. 1874 Stow; Annie b. 1883 Stow
Wife	Lavinia Jane Pulham (nee Perkins) b. 1884 Aston, Warwickshire
	Frank and Lavinia were married in 1908 in Stow.
Children	William b. 1909 Stow; Mary b. 1910 Stow
	Eric b. 1913 Stow; Frank Harold b. 1917 Stow
Cemetery	Commonwealth War Grave, Stow-on-the-Wold Cemetery

Notes

Frank was christened Stephen Frank by the Rev R W Hippisley on 5 December 1886. He was educated at Stow Infants and Boys Schools. He and his father both worked as Farm Labourers although his father had earlier worked as a labourer at the brewery.

Frank's children Mary, William and Eric were all christened by the Rev J T Evans in St Edward's: Mary on 3 May 1911, William on 25 May 1911 and Eric on 15 April 1914. His son Frank was also christened there on 17 August 1921 by the Rev Sidney P Reade, Rector of Woodeaton, Oxon. Lavinia Pulham and the children later moved to 70 King George's Field, Stow.

The Royal Defence Corps was formed in 1916, made up of soldiers who were beyond the age for combatant service in the First World War. Their job was to guard railways, roads and ports thus relieving other troops for frontline service. Following Frank's death from influenza after six days in the Military Hospital at Buttevant in County Cork, Ireland, his body was brought back to England. He was buried in Stow Cemetery, the funeral service being taken by the Rev J T Evans on 6 December 1918. Frank was awarded the Victory Medal and the British War Medal.

Cap Badge of 18th King George's Own Lancers

Cap Badge of the 4th Royal Irish Dragoon Guards

Lieutenant Julian Railston

Spencer Julian Wilfred Railston

Date of Birth	1889 – Hamilton, Lanarkshire, Scotland	
Service	Lieutenant, 18th King George's Own Lancers (Indian Army) seconded to 4th (Royal Irish) Dragoon Guards	
Date of Death	Killed in action on 30 October 1914 – age 25	
Stow Address	Ivy Cottage, Camp Gardens	
Parents	Colonel Henry E Railston	b. 1851 Newcastle
	Magdalen Railston (nee Oakley)	b. 1860 Wickwar, Gloucestershire
	They were married in Marylebone, London in 1884.	
Sibling	Henry George Moreton	b. 1886 Hamilton, Lanarkshire – Captain, 1st Battalion, Rifle Brigade. He was awarded a DSO, announced in the London Gazette of 3 July 1915, for "Great gallantry at Hannebeck".
Memorial	Menin Gate Memorial, Ypres, Belgium.	
	For details of the Menin Gate Memorial, see page 119.	

Notes

Colonel Railston, Julian's father, served in The Cameronians (Scottish Rifles). At the time of the 1901 census the family was on holiday at Carisbrooke on the Isle of Wight and Colonel Railston's occupation was given as Lieutenant Colonel, 2nd Royal Rifle Reserve Regiment, and JP for Hertfordshire. Julian's parents owned a house at 23 Queen's Gate, London SW7 and later also acquired Ivy Cottage in Stow.

Julian commenced his studies in D Company at the Royal Military College, Sandhurst on 12 September 1906. On entrance he was 131st in the order of merit out of about 200 cadets. After the Junior Term he had risen to 20th place and after the Senior Term he finished in 10th position. The twelve subjects covered included military law and administration, engineering, tactics, topography, drill and musketry. He was commissioned into the Indian Army on 17 August 1907 but was initially attached to the Scottish Rifles. In November 1908 Julian joined 18th King George's Own Lancers in Delhi. The Regiment had been raised in Gwalior in 1858 and was composed of three squadrons of Punjabi Musulmans and one of Sikhs. The Regiment moved to Meerut in October 1909. In 1911 King George V and Queen Mary travelled to Delhi to attend the spectacular Delhi Durbar.

Aerial view of Ypres with the Menin Gate in the background

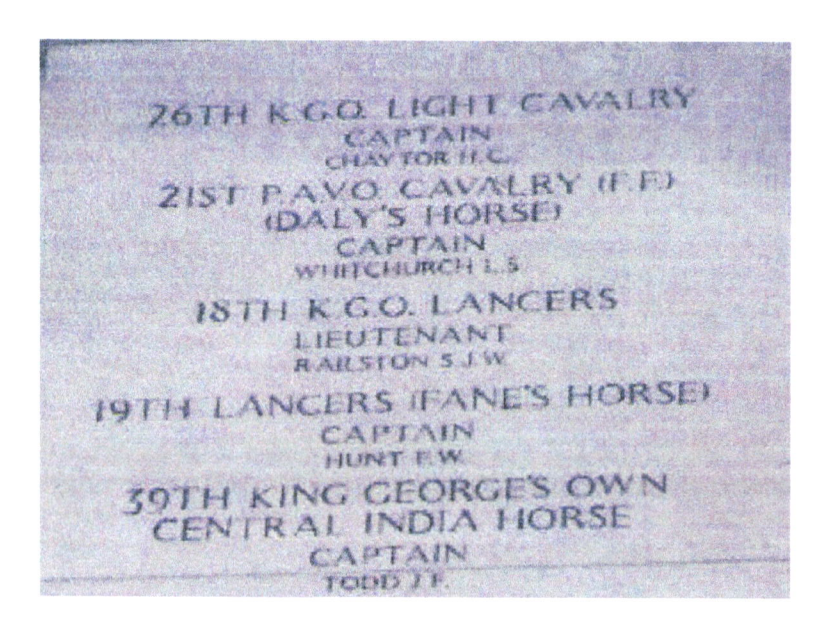

Panel 1, Menin Gate Memorial

Following the outbreak of war Lord Kitchener, Secretary of State for War, advocated forming a volunteer army. The new regiments required officers and the government called up all reserve list officers and any British Indian Army officer who happened to be on leave in the United Kingdom. Having been granted six months home leave from India dating from 24 May 1914, Julian was in England and was seconded to 4th (Royal Irish) Dragoon Guards, who were at Tidworth as part of 2nd Cavalry Brigade.

The Brigade left for France on 15 August 1914. The crossing took 18 hours and it was a relief to all on board when their ship steamed into harbour at Boulogne on the morning of Sunday 16 August. On the evening of 21 August a squadron of 120 cavalrymen of 4th Dragoon Guards were sent forward to reconnoitre ahead of the British Expeditionary Force, no contact having yet been made with the Germans who were reported to be advancing south from Brussels. The squadron spent a tense night halted in a cornfield close to Casteau on the Mons-Brussels road. They moved off at 6 am. the next morning and within half an hour had been sighted by a small German patrol who immediately turned their horses round and headed back the way they had come. However, the Dragoons gave chase and Corporal Thomas, a Drummer of C Squadron, fired first – the first shot of World War One. The whole action lasted no more than a few minutes. The British captured three wounded Germans but there were no British casualties except among the horses. One mare had been shot in the stomach and although she managed to bring her man out, she had to be pole-axed in a village nearby and was handed over to a Belgian butcher.

Ironically the final shots of World War One were fired only yards away from the site of this opening engagement. A plaque dedicated to 116th Canadian Infantry Regiment, which ended up at Casteau after the capture of Mons on 11 November 1918, is on a wall only fifty yards away from a stone memorial marking the location of the Dragoons' exploits of 22 August 1914.

With the failure of the German offensive at the Battle of the Marne in September 1914, a race to the North Sea began as both armies moved north and west, constructing trench lines that came to characterise the war on the Western Front until 1918. By early October 1914 the Allies were at Nieuwpoort in Belgium but by 6 October the Germans had forced the Belgian Army out of Antwerp from where they advanced and captured Ypres. The British Expeditionary Force recaptured the town but a German counter attack took place on 15 October. The BEF held their position over the next few days in spite of suffering heavy losses. On 23 October there were furious attacks near Langemarck and the next day the Germans occupied Polygon Wood but failed in their attempt to break through Allied lines. Heavy fighting continued for the rest of the week. Julian was killed in desperate fighting at Messines Ridge near Ypres on Friday 30 October 1914. After his death, Julian's estate was administered by the Indian Army.

In February 1918 Colonel Henry Railston applied for the 1914 Star to be awarded posthumously to his son.

St Leonard's Church, Tortworth

From the Evesham Journal – Saturday November 20 1914
HOW LIEUT RAILSTON FELL
Lieut S J W Railston, 18th King George's Own Lancers, attached to the 4th Dragoon Guards, son of Colonel and Mrs Railston of Ivy Cottage, Stow-on-the-Wold, whose name was in Wednesday's casualty list, appears from letters received from brother officers to have lost his life in a gallant attempt to bring in a wounded peasant woman who, in very heavy village fighting, had got between the British and German lines. Lieut Railston left his cover to do this and was immediately killed by many bullets from a Maxim battery.

Julian's maternal grandmother, Lady Georgina Oakley, was the sister of Henry, 3rd Earl of Ducie, whose home was at Tortworth Court, near Wotton-under-Edge in Gloucestershire. On the south wall inside St Leonard's Church at Tortworth is a fine marble and alabaster memorial to Julian. It is edged with a beautiful border of vine leaves against an azure blue background and the text in the centre gives details of his military service.

Cap Badge of the King's Royal Rifle Corps

In 1755 it was decided to recruit in America a unique regiment of four battalions, the 62nd (Royal American) Regiment, to defend the frontiers of the 13 American colonies against attack from the French and their Red Indian allies. Soon afterwards the Regiment was renumbered the 60th Royal Americans, later becoming the King's Royal Rifle Corps. They carry no colours, battle honours being inscribed on their cap badge.

Arras 1917
Soldiers leaving the trenches at the start of the attack

George Robbins

Date of Birth	5 July 1892 – Stow
Service	R/34054 Rifleman, 16th Battalion, King's Royal Rifle Corps
Date of Death	Missing believed killed in action on 20 May 1917 – age 24
Stow Address	Burford Road (1899)
	Cemetery Walk (1901) – also called Wraggs Row
	Station Road (1917)
Grandparents	Richard Robbins b. 1849 Barton-on-the-Heath, Warwickshire
	Sarah Jane Robbins (nee Lane) b. 1848 Little Rissington
	Their marriage in 1870 was registered in Chipping Norton.
Mother	Harriet Alice Robbins b. 1875 Barton-on-the-Heath, Warwickshire
Memorial	Arras Memorial, France. The Memorial is in the Faubourg d'Amiens Cemetery in Arras. The Commonwealth section of the cemetery was begun in March 1916. The Memorial commemorates almost 35,000 servicemen from the United Kingdom, South Africa and New Zealand who died in the Arras sector between the spring of 1916 and 7 August 1918 and have no known grave. Both cemetery and memorial were designed by Sir Edwin Lutyens with sculpture by Sir William Reid-Dick.
	Also commemorated on the Lower Swell War Memorial.

Notes

In 1881 George's mother Harriet Robbins and her parents, sisters Hannah and Bertha and brothers Herbert and John were living in James's Cottages, Lower Swell. Sister Beatrice and brothers Charles and Alfred were later additions to the family.

George was christened privately in St Mary's, Lower Swell on 24 August 1894 by the Rev R W Hippisley. His mother Harriet was an unmarried Domestic Servant and he was brought up by his grandparents.

He was educated at Stow Infants and Boys Schools. In the 1901 census George was noted as a schoolboy living with his grandparents. He enlisted in Stow in 1914 and was posted to 16th (Service) Battalion, King's Royal Rifle Corps, which was formed in September 1914 by Field Marshal Lord Grenfell, Commandant of the Church Lads Brigade, from current and previous members of that organisation. The Battalion became part of 100th Brigade, 33rd Division and was in France by 1 December 1915.

STOW-ON-THE-WOLD WAR MEMORIAL

Two views of the Arras Memorial, France

The Battalion Diary for the two weeks commencing 6 July 1916 gives a picture of what life was like for troops in France at that time. On that date the Battalion received orders to be ready to move off at half an hour's notice and eventually departed at 11.30 pm.

They marched all night, arriving at new billets at 5.30 am. They rested for the next two days, then set off by train at 01.15 am. on 9 July. After a journey lasting seven hours, they then marched seventeen miles to billets in an old silk mill by the canal, west of Amiens.

For the next four days they alternately marched and rested until on 14 July they moved to an assembly point where picks, shovels and extra ammunition were issued, plus two sandbags per man. On the next day, 15 July 1916, they went into attack at High Wood, advancing through the wood and suffering many casualties. They held this position until they were relieved the next morning and marched back to the rear. They improved the trenches in the morning and rested when possible. A new draft of 79 men and three second lieutenants joined the Battalion. The weather was very hot and they had a quiet day with no shelling near their lines. At 9.30 pm. orders were received to stand to at 4 am. and be ready to move at short notice. At 4 am. orders came through from Brigade Headquarters to occupy a forward trench and cover the withdrawal from High Wood. This was a typical fortnight.

The French handed over Arras to Commonwealth forces in the spring of 1916 and the system of tunnels upon which the town is built were then used and developed in preparation for the major offensive planned for April 1917. The Battle of Arras began in a snowstorm on Easter Monday, 9 April 1917, when Canadian Divisions fought at Vimy Ridge six miles to the north of the British at Arras, who attacked a heavily fortified line held by the Germans. After a massive artillery bombardment the British managed to advance up to four and a half miles in some places as far as the third line of German trenches. It was one of the largest advances since the start of trench warfare. A simultaneous French attack further south was a total failure resulting in mutiny among the French divisions. On 23 April the Battalion supported 1st Queen's Regiment in an unsuccessful attack near Croisilles. Two tanks allotted in support failed to appear. Casualties for the day (killed and wounded) were 270. The battle continued on through May. The daily casualty rate was even worse than at the Somme in 1916 with 155,000 men killed in 39 days. George was listed as missing believed killed in action on 20 May 1917.

From the Evesham Journal – Saturday June 23 1917
STOW MAN MISSING
Mr and Mrs Robbins, Station Road, Stow-on-the-Wold, have received an intimation from the War Office that their grandson, Pte George Robbins, of the King's Royal Rifles, has been missing since May 20 last.

George was awarded the 1914-15 Star, the Victory Medal and the British War Medal.

Badge of the Worcestershire Regiment

The badge is similar to that of the Coldstream Guards as it is believed to symbolise a link between the two regiments when the 29th Foot was raised in 1694 by Colonel Farrington, who was previously in the Coldstreams. Successive Colonels have also come from the Guards and the badge was adopted in the 18th century.

British troops in gas masks 1918

Alfred Charles Sansom

Date of Birth	1882 – Sutton, Surrey
Service	18703 Private, 14th Battalion, Worcestershire Regiment (Severn Valley Pioneers)
Date of Death	Died of injuries on 7 November 1918 – age 36
Stow Address	Union Street
Parents	John Sansom — b. 1858 Lower Norwood, Surrey
	Clara Sansom — b. 1860 Waltham St Lawrence, Berkshire
Wife	Louisa Sansom (nee Minchin) b. 1890 Stow
	They were married at Plympton St Mary, Devon in 1910.
Children	Clara Louise — b. 25.08.1910 Stow
	Dorothy Lilian) twins — b. 16.04.1918 Stow
	Elizabeth May) — b. 16.04.1918 Stow
Cemetery	Querenaing Communal Cemetery, France. Querenaing is a small village in the Department of Nord, 5 kilometres south of Valenciennes. There are now 21 First World War casualties commemorated in this cemetery, the majority of whom were buried by their comrades in late October and early November 1918.

Notes

At the time of Alfred's birth, his father was working as a Coachman for William Appleton, a Tea Merchant, who lived at The Arches, Angel Hill, Sutton in Surrey. In the 1901 census Alfred's occupation was given as Footman. He was at Merrist Wood, Worplesdon in Surrey in the household of a widow, Mrs Emily Shrubb, and her two sons, Charles and Henry. There were four other servants besides Alfred, – a Housekeeper, two Housemaids and a Kitchenmaid.

Alfred's wife Louisa was the sister of Richard Minchin *(see page 160)*. In 1917 Alfred's daughter Clara was admitted to Stow Girls School. She had previously been a pupil at Sloane Square School, London. She stayed until 1921 when the register was marked "Left Stow". The twins were christened by the Rev J T Evans in St Edward's on 16 April 1919, their first birthday, and five months after their father's death.

Alfred enlisted in Bourton-on-the-Water on 19 July 1915 and was sent to join the 14th (Pioneer) Battalion, Worcestershire Regiment, which was formed in September 1915 by Lt Col H Webb, MP, as a combatant battalion to supplement the field work of the Engineers and taken over by the War Office in March 1916. On 20 June 1916 the Battalion sailed for France at 6.30 pm. where, on arrival at Le Havre, they formed part of 63rd (Royal Naval) Division.

STOW-ON-THE-WOLD WAR MEMORIAL

Passchendaele – crossing the duckboards

Map showing the location of the village of Querenaing where Alfred is buried.

They remained in the Vimy Ridge area for the next three months. In October 1916 they were moved to the Somme front in preparation for an attack on 13 November in the valley of the River Ancre. For most of 1917 the Pioneer Battalion was employed in the Arras area, moving to the Ypres Salient at the end of September. They took part in the battle of Poelcapelle in October 1917 and in fighting on the Passchendaele Ridge, where the ground on which the troops had to fight became increasingly muddy due to heavy rain and the artillery's destruction of the ancient drainage systems that helped keep the land dry. The shell holes filled with water and men and horses drowned in the mud. The advancing British soldiers also had to endure mustard gas attacks. After a long hard struggle, the village of Passchendaele was finally captured on 6 November 1917 by British and Canadian infantry. The whole offensive cost the British Expeditionary Force nearly 310,000 casualties.

In January 1918 the weather was very cold with much snow. After 15 January it changed to rain and bitter sleet with a driving wind which brought an extreme of misery and much sickness among the troops. On the Cambrai front where 14th Battalion were now positioned, a German attack forced back the British front line and the Pioneers had much hard work to do in the entrenchment of new positions. They were shelled constantly and casualties were numerous. On 23 January they moved back into reserve until mid February when they returned to the front line with their Battalion Headquarters situated on the old Hindenburg Line.

At 10 pm. on 11 March the Germans opened an intense bombardment of gas shells over the whole area. For three days gas lay thick in the valley. Although the Pioneers obeyed strictly the order that no man was to leave the dugout without his mask, most of the casualties occurred when they got back to the dugouts and took off their masks. Their clothes were saturated with gas and they literally gassed each other.

The German bombardment on 21 March marked the start of their successful spring offensive and the British withdrawal back across the Somme front for which they had battled so hard in the summer of 1916. At dawn on 21 August 1918 the British attacked on a wide front forcing the Germans back and by September they had regained most of the ground lost in March with the advancing Divisions almost reaching the Hindenburg Line. The role of the Pioneers in the battle was to follow close behind the attacking troops and repair as fast as possible the shattered roadways.

Just after 5 am. on 27 September the British attacked on the line of the Canal du Nord, stormed the German defences and advanced towards Cambrai. The Pioneers worked furiously during the five days of the battle to build bridges and causeways over the canal for guns and limbers to cross. After a few days rest in reserve, they were ordered forward again to take part in the final battle of Cambrai between 7 and 9 October. The Battalion moved to the rear for the rest of the month but was again at the front on 1 November when they transferred to the area around Valenciennes. They laboured valiantly in bitter cold and drizzling rain to enable the guns to move forward to the battle line. Alfred died of injuries on 7 November 1918. He was awarded the 1914-15 Star, the Victory Medal and the British War Medal.

Alfred's grave in Querenaing Communal Cemetery, France

The Commonwealth War graves section at Querenaing Communal Cemetery, France

A general view of the cemetery

Front and back cap badges of the Gloucestershire Regiment

Private Fred Stephens and his Brother, Private George Stephens

Fred Albert Stephens

Date of Birth	18 March 1894 – Stow
Service	11259 Private, 7th Battalion, Gloucestershire Regiment
Date of Death	Missing believed killed in action on 8 August 1915 – age 21
Stow Address	Cemetery Walk (1901) – also called Wraggs Row (1913)
Parents	George Stephens — b. 1845 Stow
	Rizpah Stephens (nee Holtom) — b. 1853 Condicote
	They were married in St Edward's on 1 March 1873.
Siblings	Emily — b. 1874 Stow
	William — b. 1876 Stow
	George — b. 1880 Stow
	Thomas — b. 1885 Stow
	Frank — b. 1888 Stow
	Minnie — b. 1889 Stow
	Rose — b. 1891 Stow
Memorial	Helles Memorial, Gallipoli, Turkey. The Memorial stands on the tip of the Gallipoli peninsula. It is an obelisk over 30 metres high that can be seen by ships passing through the Dardanelles and bears nearly 21,000 names of servicemen who died in operations throughout the peninsula and have no known grave.7

Notes

Fred, Minnie and Rose were all christened on 4 February 1898 in St Edward's by the Rev E Lyon Harrison, Assistant Curate. Their father's occupation was given as Mason in the Baptism Register. Fred's mother's unusual name comes from the Old Testament, 2 Samuel chapter 3: "Now Saul had a concubine called Rizpah."

Fred enlisted in Birmingham in 1914 and was posted to 7th Battalion, Gloucestershire Regiment, which was formed at Bristol in August 1914, forming part of 39th Brigade, 13th Division. They moved to Tidworth for training and eventually sailed from Avonmouth in June 1915 bound for Gallipoli.

The eight month campaign in Gallipoli was fought by Commonwealth and French forces in an attempt to force Turkey out of the war, to relieve the deadlock of the Western Front in France

The view from Chunuk Bair Ridge

Helles Memorial, Gallipoli

and Belgium and to open a supply route to Russia through the Dardanelles and the Black Sea.

The Battalion landed on the peninsula in July 1915. From early morning on 7 August British, Australian, New Zealand, Indian and Gurkha soldiers fought to take and hold the peaks of Chunuk Bair. Resisting them were Turkish soldiers led by Colonel Mustafa Kemal. At 4.15 am. on 8 August 1915 the Battalion advanced on Chunuk Bair ridge. The New Zealand Wellington Brigade, with the Glosters in support, captured the summit and were able to look down on the objective of the whole campaign – the straits of the Dardanelles at the Narrows. The Glosters suffered appalling losses but still fought on unflinchingly. By evening only 181 unwounded men remained out of the 1000 who had gone into action that morning.

Fred was killed on that day, 8 August 1915. He was awarded the 1914-15 Star, the Victory Medal and the British War Medal.

From the Evesham Journal – Saturday September 25 1915
STOW MAN MISSING
News has been received by the parents of Pte F Stephens that their son, who was in 7th Glosters and was in the trenches at Gallipoli, is missing.

Fred's parents advertised in the Gloucester Graphic in October 1915: "Mr and Mrs Stephens, Cemetery Walk, Stow-on-the-Wold would be grateful for any information of their son Fred, missing since going into action in the Dardanelles on August 8."

Lance Corporal George Stephens of the Worcestershire Regiment, Fred's elder brother, who was reported missing on 22 July 1916, wrote home in September 1916 saying he was a Prisoner of War at Dulmen in Westphalia.. He requested a food parcel, which was promptly despatched.

STOW-ON-THE-WOLD WAR MEMORIAL

*Cap Badge of the Australian
Imperial Force*

*The grave of an unknown
Australian soldier*

*Janet, Doris and Sophie Summersbee with their mother Clara and their brother Philip
outside the family shop in Park Street around 1907.*

My thanks to Bob Sharp for the use of this photograph.

Austin Philip Summersbee

Date of Birth	28 March 1893 – Stow
Service	968 Private, 12th Battalion, Australian Infantry
Date of Death	Missing believed killed in action on 25 April 1915 – age 22
Stow Address	Park Street – next door to the Campin family (1901)
	Sheep Street (1913)

Parents

John Thomas Summersbee	b. 1851 Stow
Clara Summersbee (nee Palmer)	b. 1864 St Pancras, London

They were married in Stow in 1880.

Siblings

Henry Fred	b. 1886 Stow
Stephen John	b. 1888 Stow
Arthur Vivian	b. 1890 Stow – *served in HMS Amphitrite*
Janet	b. 1895 Stow
Doris	b. 1897 Stow
Sophie Elizabeth	b. 1903 Stow

Memorial Lone Pine Memorial, Gallipoli, Turkey. The Memorial stands over the centre of the Turkish trenches and tunnels which were the scene of the fiercest fighting during the August offensive. It commemorates more than 4900 Australian and New Zealand servicemen who died in the Anzac area and have no known grave.

Also commemorated on:

(1) the Australian War Memorial, Canberra – *for details of the Australian War Memorial, see page 103.*

(2) the Summersbee family grave in Stow-on-the-Wold Cemetery.

Notes

Philip was baptised in the Methodist Chapel in Stow on 4 June 1893. In the 1901 census his father's occupation was given as Builder and he also worked as a Joiner.

The photograph on the opposite page of Mrs Clara Summersbee and her three daughters and one son with his bicycle outside the family shop has been used as a post card. It is addressed to Miss E Dowler, 11 William Street, Weymouth and postmarked "Stow-on-the-Wold 5.10 pm. July ? 07". The text reads: "Dear E, I hope you are not very tired with the journey. I am sorry I

Bugler Philip Summersbee

could not come to wish you goodbye. Please remember me to Mrs B. and I hope you will all benefit from the sea. C.S." Miss Dowler was the sister of the stationmaster at Stow and aunt of Arthur John Dowler – *see page 59*.

Philip worked as a Builder's assistant, then in 1913 aged 20, he emigrated to Australia. He sailed from Liverpool on the SS *Medic*, a White Star liner, built in 1898 by Harland & Wolff. The ship called at Cape Town and the journey would have taken six weeks. Philip disembarked at Albany on 29 May 1913. He took with him three testimonials which he had been given on board ship to help him in his search for a job.

The first read:-

"SS *Medic* at Albany 29 May 1913

The bearer Philip Summersbee of his own free will worked with my staff on the passage from England, he proved a good worker. I can recommend him to anyone requiring an Assistant Steward or similar capacity.

Peter Gronit, Chief Steward"

The second read:-

"SS *Medic* At Albany 29/5/1913

To whom it may concern

The bearer Philip Summersbee worked aboard the above ship as a voluntary steward from L'pool to Australian Ports. I can recommend him with confidence to anyone wishing to employ an Asst Steward as he is a capable and willing man.

J W Dodd, 2nd Steward"

The third read:-

"SS *Medic* At Albany WA May 29/1913

Philip Summersbee has been a very popular Passenger on the above ship since leaving Liverpool. As Chairman of the various committees on the voyage I have noticed with pleasure the many ways in which he has placed himself at the convenience of the Passengers. This culminated in his gratuitously offering his service as a Steward, which proved acceptable to both passengers and crew. His readiness to please, combined with his pleasure in honest work, make it a very fortunate circumstance for anyone who would wish for a capable servant and I have genuine pleasure in giving him this unsolicited testimonial.

Signed Gilbert Hough

Schoolmaster, Salford Education Committee"

On the outbreak of war Philip enlisted as a Bugler in the Australian Imperial Force (AIF) at Perth, Western Australia. The response to enlistment exceeded all expectations and on 1 November

STOW-ON-THE-WOLD WAR MEMORIAL

Lone Pine Memorial, Gallipoli, Turkey

The name Lone Pine originates from a single tree which grew on the site of the battle. Before it was destroyed by artillery fire, the soldiers called it the Lonesome Pine after a popular song of the era by Laurel and Hardy entitled "Trail of the Lonesome Pine". Seeds from the original tree were collected and taken back to Australia to germinate. When mature enough, a tree was returned to the site of the Lone Pine battle where it now stands as a major feature of the Memorial.

1914 the first contingent sailed for Europe from Albany. Diverted to Egypt from its original destination, the AIF spent several months in Egypt before being committed to its first campaign – in Gallipoli against the Turks.

The Australian and New Zealand Corps landed on 25 April north of Gaba Tepe on the west coast, an area which soon became known as Anzac Bay. Good Friday, 25 April 1915, the day on which Philip died and the first day of the landings at Gallipoli, is nowadays commemorated as Anzac Day.

From the Evesham Journal – Saturday October 16 1915
STOW MAN MISSING
Bugler Philip Summersbee, of the Tasmanian Contingent, is officially reported missing since the end of April last. He was in the Dardanelles. His parents, Mr and Mrs J Summersbee, are old inhabitants of this town of which their son was a native.

John Frederick Summersbee, nephew of Philip, was lost in HM Submarine Thistle in April 1940, age 28.

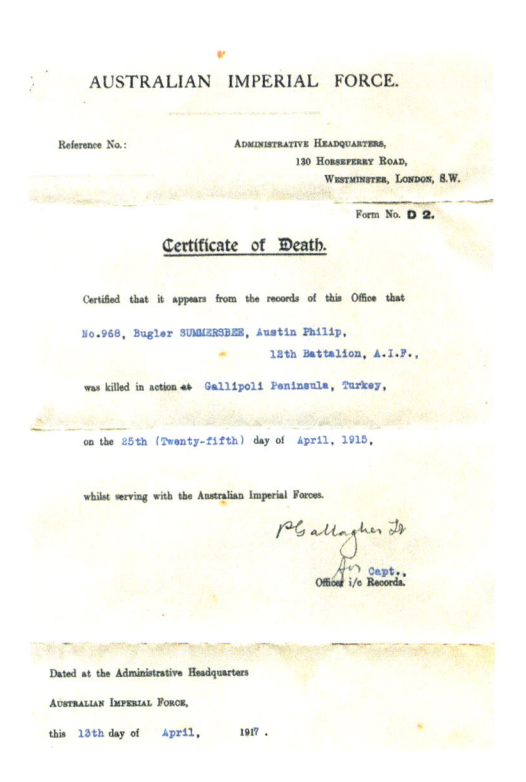

The death certificate sent to Philip's family

Panel 35 on the Lone Pine Memorial

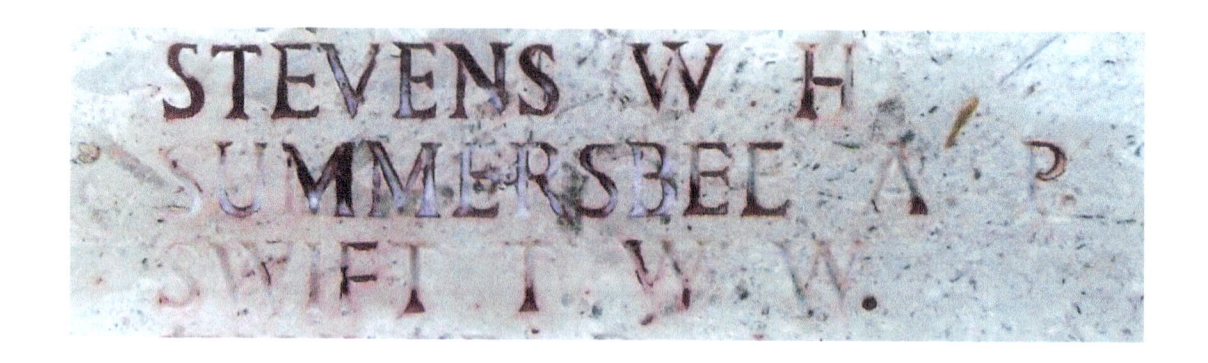

Philip's name on Panel 35

Looking down to Lone Pine Cemetery from the Turkish war memorial

Front and back cap badges of the Gloucestershire Regiment

British troops in the trenches at Ypres 1917

William George Taylor

Date of Birth	22 December 1887 – Stow	
Service	22482 Private, 8th Battalion, Gloucestershire Regiment	
Date of Death	24 May 1919 – age 31	
Stow Address	Enoch's Row	
Parents	George Taylor	b. 1851 Stow
	Sarah Taylor (nee Clifford)	b. 1865 Stow
	They were married in 1887 in Stow.	
Siblings	Maud Winifred	b. 1889 Stow
	Dorothy	b. 1890 Stow
	Florence Maria	b. 1891 Stow
	Rhoda Violet	b. 1894 Stow, d. 1896
	Daisy Hannah	b. 1896 Stow
	Reginald Percival	b. 1898 Stow
	Norman Victor	b. 1901 Stow
	Lucy May Ellen	b. 1903 Stow
Cemetery	Commonwealth War Grave, Stow-on-the-Wold Cemetery	

Notes

William was educated at Stow Infants and Boys Schools. In the 1901 census William's father's occupation was given as a Foundry Labourer. Hannah Clifford, William's maternal grandmother, was staying with the family at the time the 1901 census was completed.

William's sister Lucy was christened in St Edward's on 2 August 1903 by the Rev Walter P Chamberlayne, half-brother of Rupert Ingles-Chamberlayne – *see page 55*.

William enlisted in 1914 and was posted to 8th Battalion, Gloucestershire Regiment, which was formed at Bristol in September, part of 57th Brigade, 19th Division. It was formed on Salisbury Plain and in December moved into billets in Weston and Clevedon.

In June 1915 King George V inspected the Division. The Battalion landed in France on 18 July 1915. On 28 August they were in the front line but were in reserve during the Battle of Loos in the autumn of that year.

On 1 July 1916 they moved to positions north of Albert at the start of the Battle of the Somme.

On 3 July 1916 at La Boiselle the commanding officers of the other three battalions in the

William's grave in Stow-on-the-Wold Cemetery

Division were all wounded and Lt Colonel Carton de Wiart, Commanding Officer of 8th Glosters, took command of all four battalions. Firstly he led the attack, then a strong German counter attack was repulsed and the position was held. He was awarded the Victoria Cross for his bravery on that day.

In October the Battalion was in the front line east of Thiepval. They attacked at Grandcourt on 18 November and took their objectives but at a cost of 295 casualties. In May 1917 they were in the Ypres area and in June attacked German positions at Messines. They again suffered heavy casualties in August when they attacked at 05.30 over very boggy ground at Ravine Wood on the Ypres Salient.

In 1918 with the collapse of Russia in the east, many German Divisions were transferred to the western front for a spring offensive which began on 21 March. The Germans massed artillery all along the line. The Battalion was commended for their gallantry in covering the withdrawal of the guns as the British retreated in face of the onslaught. In April the Germans again launched a heavy bombardment and 8th Glosters assisted in holding the line. They were again under heavy attack in May but by August the situation had improved and patrols were being sent out to keep in touch with the now retreating Germans. The Battalion advanced over the next weeks and fought minor actions. On 20 October the Brigade crossed the River Selle near Haussy in heavy rain and launched an attack at 2 am. By 5.30 am. all objectives had been taken. On 11 November the Battalion was in the Flamengrie area when the war ended.

In January 1919 full demobilisation of the Division started.

William died on 24 May 1919 in 2/1st Southern General Hospital, Birmingham.. He was buried on 29 May in Stow cemetery, the service being taken by the Rev E G Keed.

In May 1915 the old Poor Law Infirmary on Dudley Road, Birmingham was taken over as a hospital to treat the flood of casualties from the front. By 1916 it had been expanded to 1560 beds. In May 1917 it was established as a hospital in its own right, adopting the title 2/1st Southern General Hospital. The convoys of wounded and sick were unloaded at Soho & Winson Green GWR goods station where a special platform was erected for the purpose.

William was awarded the 1914-15 Star, the Victory Medal and the British War Medal.

Facing page of William Taylor's will

WILL.

April 14th 1918

In the event of my death - I give the whole of my money also insurances money to my mother, Mrs Geo. Taylor, Enochs Terrace, Stow-on-the-Wold, Gloucestershire

Signature *William G. Taylor*

Rank and Regiment *Private 22482. 8th Glosters Regiment*

Date *April 14th 1918*

William Taylor's will

STOW-ON-THE-WOLD WAR MEMORIAL

Cap badge of the Grenadier Guards

Private John Timms

John William Timms

Date of Birth	6 June 1898 – Stow
Service	29066 Private, 2nd Battalion, Grenadier Guards
Date of Death	Killed in action on 28 March 1918 – age 19
Stow Address	Sheep Street (1897), Park Street (1901)
Parents	John Timms — b. 1868 Woodstock
	Sarah Timms (nee Fisher) — b. 1864 Stow
	They were married in St Edward's on 8 June 1886.
Siblings	Ellen b. 1883 Campden Kate b. 1892 Stow
	Horace b. 1888 Stow Harry b. 1894 Stow
	Ethel b. 1890 Stow Frank b. 1896 Stow
	Cecil Edward, twin brother of John, b. 1898 Stow
Memorial	Arras Memorial, France. Also commemorated on the family grave in Stow Cemetery. *For details of the Arras Memorial, see page 191.*

Notes

John and Cecil were christened on 23 September 1898 in St Edward's by the Rev E Lyon Harrison, Curate in Charge. John's father's occupation was given as Grocer's Porter in the Baptism Register. In the 1901 census he was working as a Railway Carrier's Labourer and John's mother was working as a Laundress. John was educated at Stow Infants and Boys Schools. He left in June 1911 (age 13) with an Exemption Certificate, which meant he had a job to go to. His twin brother Cecil stayed on until June 1912.

2nd Battalion, Grenadier Guards, was formed at Chelsea in London in August 1914 and later that month became part of 1st Guards Brigade in France. Arras, 28 March 1918, (the date of John Timms' death), was awarded as a Battle Honour to the Grenadier Guards and the name is displayed on their Regimental Colours.

From the Evesham Journal – Saturday April 27 1918
STOW MAN KILLED
Mrs John Timms has received official information that her son Jack has been killed in action on March 28 on the Western Front. The deceased was a Private in the Grenadier Guards. He was a bright, active boy. His mother has received very general sympathy. There are three other sons in the army.

On the Commonwealth War Graves Commission record for John, he is listed as son of Mrs Sarah Jane Timms of 31 Boyworth, Abingdon, Bucks. John was awarded the Victory Medal and the British War Medal.

Badge of the Sherwood Foresters

The Regimental War Memorial of the Sherwood Foresters at Crich in Derbyshire

Frank Webb

Date of Birth	1893 – Stow
Service	3152 Private, 1/6th Battalion, Sherwood Foresters (Nottinghamshire & Derbyshire) Regiment
Date of Death	Died of wounds on 26 July 1916 – age 23
Stow Address	Park Street (1898), Church Street (1901)
Parents	John Webb b. 1859 Stow
	Elizabeth Webb (nee Watkins) b. 1864 Stroud
	They were married in Stow in the summer of 1886.
Siblings	Harold John b. 1887 Stow William b. 1895 Stow – *see page 222*
	Thomas b. 1889 Stow Harry b. 1898 Stow
Memorial	Arras Memorial, France. *For details of the Memorial, see page 191.*

Notes

In 1881 Frank's grandfather was the Innkeeper at the Crown & Anchor pub in The Square, Stow. Frank's father was a Hairdresser with his own premises in Church Street. He was also a Churchwarden at St Edward's for several years. Frank's parents later moved to Corona, Cirencester Road, Charlton Kings.

Frank enlisted in Chesterfield, Derbyshire on 22 October 1914. He gave his address as 12A Newbold Road, Chesterfield and his trade as Hairdresser. He was 5 feet 8 inches tall with blue eyes and dark brown hair. The Territorial Battalions of the Sherwood Foresters mobilised on the outbreak of war and formed 139 (Forester) Infantry Brigade which, in February 1915, had the distinction of being part of the first Territorial Division to land in France. Frank embarked from Southampton and landed in France on 11 June 1916. The Battalion gained special recognition for its valour on the opening day of the Battle of the Somme – 1 July 1916.

From the Evesham Journal – Saturday August 5 1916
STOW MAN MISSING
Mr J Webb of Stow-on-the-Wold has received news from the front somewhere in France that his son, Private Frank Webb of the Sherwood Foresters, is missing. He was sent out with three others on the night of July 24 on patrol work and he has not been heard of. It is probable that he has fallen into German hands as a prisoner.
(*On the night of 24 July 1916, Frank volunteered for patrol duty. He and his Commanding Officer were captured by the Germans and Frank died of wounds two days later*).
He was awarded the Victory Medal and the British War Medal.

STOW-ON-THE-WOLD WAR MEMORIAL

Cap Badge of the London Regiment

Private William Webb

John Webb, William's father, standing in the door of his shop in Church Street

William Webb

Date of Birth	1895 – Stow
Service	6155 Private, 21st Battalion, London Regiment
	7759 Private, 12th Battalion, London Regiment
	473980 Rifleman, 12th Battalion, London Regiment (The Rangers)
Date of Death	Killed in action on 22 September 1917 – age 22
Stow Address	Park Street (1898)
	Church Street (1901)
Parents	John Webb — b. 1859 Stow
	Elizabeth Webb (nee Watkins) — b. 1864 Stroud
	They were married in Stow in the summer of 1886.
Siblings	Harold John — b. 1887 Stow
	Thomas — b. 1889 Stow
	Frank — b. 1893 Stow – *see page 220*
	Harry — b. 1898 Stow
Cemetery	Morchies Military Cemetery, France. Morchies is a village eight kilometres north east of Bapaume in the Pas de Calais. The cemetery was begun in April 1917 and used until January 1918. There are now over 150 First World War casualties commemorated at this site.

Notes

In 1881 William's grandfather was the Innkeeper at the Crown & Anchor pub in The Square, Stow. William's father was a Hairdresser with his own premises in Church Street. He was also a Churchwarden at St Edward's for several years. William's parents later moved to Corona, Cirencester Road, Charlton Kings

William enlisted in Stow and was posted initially to the 21st Battalion, London Regiment, later transferring to 12th Battalion. The London Regiment raised over 80 battalions and formed four entire Divisions from Greater London and Middlesex. They were affiliated to regular regiments but without change of battalion titles. In August 1914 12th Battalion from Holborn formed part of 3rd London Brigade, 1st London Division. In December 1914 the Battalion moved to France and joined Lines of Communication on Christmas Day 1914. On 20 May 1915 they were transferred to GHQ Troops and formed a composite Battalion with 5th and 13th Battalions.

William's grave at Morchies Cemetery, France

Morchies Military Cemetery, France

From the Evesham Journal – Saturday October 6 1917
RIFLEMAN W WEBB KILLED
Very general and sincere sympathy is felt for Mr and Mrs John Webb of Stow-on-the-Wold in their sad bereavement.

From the Evesham Journal – Saturday October 6 1917 (continued)
Their fourth son, William, who was serving with the forces at the front, was killed instantaneously by a trench mortar shell on the 22nd ult. He belonged to the Scout Section, London Regiment. This is the second son lost by Mr and Mrs Webb; their son Frank was killed fourteen months ago.

The following letter was received by the parents from his lieutenant:-

"Dear Mr Webb, What I have to write to you about touches me deeply. Your son, as God wills it, died like a hero last night. Whilst carrying out his duties in the front line as an observer, a heavy trench mortar shell dropped near him and killed him instantaneously. His death is a source of great sorrow to me and his comrades; my heart is too full for words to express my grief. Your son was my best man in most things. Nobly and well has he performed his duties in the past. It is a comfort for us to know he was killed outright. We brought him out of the trenches and buried him with due ceremony near a French cemetery, a peaceful spot, where others of his comrades are laid. The padre was with me this afternoon and we held the service by his side. My sympathy for you in your bereavement is great. We all miss your boy as if he was our brother. May God in his mercy comfort you. Yours very sincerely, W E Wood, Lieut. – Batt, The Rangers, 12th London Regt, BEF." Mr Webb has also received a letter from the Chaplain who officiated at his son's funeral, expressive of deep sympathy and of high esteem for the boy who has gone home.

William was awarded the Victory Medal and the British War Medal.

STOW-ON-THE-WOLD WAR MEMORIAL

Cap Badge of the Wiltshire Regiment 99

Cap Badge of the Labour Corps

Private John Webley's Medal Record Card

These medals were returned by John's family for amendment as the surname was incorrectly shown as "Webling". The correct medals were re-issued on 27 June 1922.

226

John Robert Webley

Date of Birth	1888 Deptford, Kent
Service	9939 Private, Wiltshire Regiment (Duke of Edinburgh's) transferred to 599442 Private, Labour Corps
Date of Death	14 November 1918 – age 30
Stow Address	Little Rissington
Parents	Robert Webley — b. 1862 Little Rissington
	Elizabeth Webley — b. 1862 Ockenden, Essex
Siblings	Daniel — b. 1884 Grays, Essex
	William — b. 1890 Lewisham, Kent
	Arthur John — b. 1898 Battersea, London
Cemetery	Grangegorman Military Cemetery, County Dublin, Republic of Ireland. The cemetery was opened in 1876 and was used for the burial of British service personnel and their near relatives. There are 613 Commonwealth burials of the First World War in this cemetery.

Notes

John's father Robert was born in Little Rissington and was the brother of William Webley. John and Robert Webley *(see page 230)* were first cousins. In the 1891 census Robert and Elizabeth, John's parents, and their sons Daniel, John and William are listed at 38 Parkham Street, Battersea with Robert's job given as Excavator. In the 1901 census Robert and Elizabeth and their 2 year old son Arthur are listed in Battersea but there is no mention of their other three sons. Robert's occupation is given as "Ganges Navy". The second HMS Ganges, the last sailing ship to be a sea-going flagship, was built at the Bombay Dockyard and fitted out at Portsmouth in 1822. It was paid off in 1861 and converted to a boys' training ship, based first at Falmouth and from 1899 at Harwich.

John enlisted into 3rd (Militia) Battalion of the Wiltshire Regiment in Devizes on 31 August 1914. The 3rd Battalion was a reserve battalion responsible for the recruitment and part training of soldiers of the Regiment prior to them being posted on active service. 2nd Battalion, Wiltshire Regiment arrived back in England from Gibraltar on 4 September 1914 and became part of 21st Infantry Brigade at Lyndhurst in Hampshire. The Battalion landed at Zeebrugge on 7 October 1914. The Battalion Diary for Christmas Day 1914 records:- "No firing. An unofficial armistice took place and troops of both sides met and buried the dead. The Battalion fixed up a board with

Grangegorman Military Cemetery, Ireland

Regimental badges on the hillside at Fovant

"A Merry Xmas" written on it in German midway between the trenches and was evidently much appreciated by the enemy." John was serving in France with this Battalion by 20 January 1915.

The first major engagement in which the Battalion was involved was at Neuve Chapelle in March 1915 when they were commended for stubborn fighting in difficult trench country. On 1 June 1915 at 4 pm. the Battalion lined the roads in which their billets were situated at Rebecq for a casual inspection by Mr Asquith, the Prime Minister, accompanied by General Haig. Apart from artillery duels and occasional sniper action the 2nd Wiltshires saw no major action again until the Somme in July 1916 when they attacked at Trones Wood near Maricourt. By October they were in trenches near Pommiers in the valley of the River Aisne. At 3.40 am. on 18 October 21st Brigade attacked, 2nd Wiltshires on the left, 18th King's Liverpools in the centre and 2nd Yorkshires on the right. They reached their objectives but failed to take them. The Wiltshires incurred casualties of 14 officers and 350 other ranks.

On 21 March 1918 the Battalion was in trenches near Rouvral. An intense enemy bombardment continued throughout the day and the Battalion was surrounded in spite of strong resistance. A message was received by pigeon carrier from the colonel that he was holding out with 50 men but no further news was received. The German advance continued over the next ten days and it was not until 2 April that casualty figures for the recent action could finally be established. Of the officers, 1 was killed, 17 were missing and 4 wounded. In the other ranks, 4 were killed, 9 wounded and 597 were missing. Those who survived were formed into a composite battalion with 2nd Bedfordshires.

Most likely after recovering from being wounded, John was transferred to the Labour Corps during the summer of 1918, possibly to 653 Company based at Dublin, whose role was to support military establishments there. On 14 November 1918 he died in King George V Hospital, North Dublin, of pneumonia following influenza.

John was awarded the 1914-15 Star, the Victory Medal and the British War Medal.

On his Death Certificate, John's address was given as 28 Parkside Street, Battersea Park Road, London. This was the home of John's parents, Robert and Elizabeth Webley. They are listed there in the Electoral Register for Battersea North in June 1918. His brother, Arthur Webley, is listed as an Absent Voter at that address in spring 1919. He was serving as a Rifleman in 3rd Battalion, King's Royal Rifle Corps.

At the outbreak of war in 1914 there was an urgent need for the provision of training and transit camps for the Army. One of these was established at Fovant in Wiltshire on the chalk downs between Salisbury and Shaftesbury. Many of the regiments stationed there carved replicas of their cap badges into the hillside. Only eight of these badges now remain and these are scheduled as Ancient Monuments. 6th Battalion City of London Regiment, the Australian Imperial Force, the London Rifle Brigade, the Post Office Rifles and the Devonshire Regiment were all cut in 1916. The Wiltshire Regiment and the Royal Wiltshire Yeomanry were cut in 1950/51 and the Royal Corps of Signals in 1970. All other badges have been allowed to grass over.

Front and back cap badges of the Gloucestershire Regiment

Private Robert Webley (left) and his brother, Private John Webley (right)

Robert Webley

Date of Birth	15 May 1883 – Stow
Service	23706 Private, 7th Battalion, Gloucestershire Regiment
Date of Death	Died of sunstroke on 10 August 1916 – age 33
Stow Address	Park Street (1888)
	Union Street (1893)
	Chapel Street (1904)
Parents	William Webley — b. 1852 Little Rissington
	Fanny Webley — b. 1857 Ford
Siblings	Albert — b. 12.05.1877 Stow
	Frank — b. 20.08.1878 Stow
	Walter — b. 20.09.1885 Stow
	Alfred — b. 06.07.1892 Stow
	Eva — b. 29.06.1894 Stow
	May — b. 01.05.1896 Stow
	John — b. 28.02.1898 Stow
Cemetery	Basra War Cemetery, Iraq. Basra is a town on the west bank of the Shatt-al-Arab waterway, 90 kilometres from its mouth in the Persian Gulf. The cemetery contains 2551 burials of the First World War.
	It came under sustained shell fire during the Iran/Iraq war of the 1980s with the gravestones being scattered and smashed and the panels with the names of the dead stripped from the screen wall. The Commonwealth War Graves Commission is hopeful that as events stabilize in Iraq, restoration may be undertaken.

Notes

Robert had two more siblings: sister Ada (b. 1880) and brother Edward (b. 1882), both of whom died in infancy. John Robert Webley (*see page 226*) was Robert's cousin.

In the 1901 census Robert's father's occupation was noted as Sawyer; brother Albert was a Police Constable in Kingswood, Gloucestershire; Frank had gone to Islington in London to work on the railway and Walter and Robert himself were Builder's Labourers in Stow.

Robert's sisters Eva and May were both christened in St Edward's by the Rev J T Evans: Eva on 8 February 1911 and May on 12 February 1913.

Robert enlisted in Stow and was posted to 7th Battalion, Gloucestershire Regiment, which formed part of 39th Brigade, 13th Division.

British troops march through Kut-el-Amara after they recaptured the city on 25 February 1917.

The Battalion sailed from Avonmouth in June 1915 bound for Gallipoli in Turkey. The Turkish Ottoman Empire had entered the war on the German side in 1914. After the failure of the Gallipoli campaign, the peninsula was evacuated in December 1915.

7th Battalion, Gloucestershire Regiment, as part of 13th Division, plus four other Divisions, all under the command of General Fenton Aylmer, moved to Egypt. In January 1916 a British expedition, the Tigris Corps, sailed to Mesopotamia in an attempt to relieve Kut-el-Amara, a small town on the east bank of the River Tigris, which had been occupied by the British under General Sir Charles Townshend since September 1915. Townshend's advance to Baghdad had been halted by the Turks and after the British failed to capture Ctesiphon, they fell back to Kut in December 1915 where they were besieged by Turkish forces. The Tigris Corps under General Aylmer made their base at Ali Gharbi, about fifty miles downstream from Kut.

After three costly and unsuccessful clashes in January and a further failure in March, Aylmer was replaced by General George Gorringe. However, weakened by disease and having suffered heavy losses of around 23,000 killed or wounded, the relieving British troops withdrew at the beginning of April. Kut could not be saved and, forced by hunger, the British garrison of 8,000 men surrendered to the Turks on 29 April 1916 and were made prisoners. The captured soldiers were impressed into slave labour until the fall of the Ottoman Empire in 1918.

7th Battalion was in Orah on 10 August 1916 in searing heat when Robert died there of sunstroke.

Kut was captured in February 1917 and the Allied forces went on to take Baghdad in March.

Robert's youngest brother John joined the Gloucestershire Regiment while still under age. In the Gloucester Graphic of 31 August 1918, under John's picture it states:- "Private J Webley, DCM, MM, West Riding Regiment, wounded for the fifth time and now in hospital abroad. He was awarded the MM for showing great gallantry in the field although twice wounded and the DCM for bringing wounded in under heavy shell fire. Son of Mr and Mrs W Webley of Chapel Street, Stow-on-the-Wold."

Front and back cap badges of the Gloucestershire Regiment

Private Ernest Young

Ernest Albert Young

Date of Birth	1878 – Castle Combe, Wiltshire	
Service	15298 Private, 10th Battalion, Gloucestershire Regiment	
Date of Death	Died of wounds on 1 October 1915 – age 37	
Stow Address	Park Street	
Parents	Albert Young	b. 1845 Nettleton, Wiltshire
	Elizabeth Young	b. 1845 Littleton Drew, Wiltshire
Siblings	Charles	b. 1869 Castle Combe
	William	b. 1874 Castle Combe
	George	b. 1876 Castle Combe
	James	b. 1880 Castle Combe
Wife	Annie Maria Young (nee Haynes)	
	Ernest and Annie were married in Castle Combe in 1902.	
Children	Gertrude Ellen (Nell)	b. 05.02.1903 Castle Combe
	Elizabeth Rose	b. 27.03.1906 Stow
	George Frederick	b. 29.07.1909 Birmingham
Cemetery	Etaples Military Cemetery, Pas de Calais, France. Etaples is a town 27 kilometres south of Boulogne. The cemetery contains 10,769 Commonwealth burials of the First World War, the earliest dating from 1915. The cemetery, the largest Commonwealth War Graves cemetery in France, was designed by Sir Edwin Lutyens. Also commemorated on the Castle Combe War Memorial.	

Notes

In the 1881 census the Young family was living at 5 Water Street, Castle Combe. By the 1901 census Ernest's mother had died and his father was living at 22 Oakfield Grove, Castle Combe and employed as a Jobbing Gardener.

In 1901 Ernest was working as a Groom and was a Boarder in the household of Robert and Mary Bowes at 19 King Street, Melton Mowbray. The Bowes had six children ranging in age from Robert junior at 16, down to baby Lily, who was nine months old at the time of the census. Robert Bowes was 44, a Yorkshireman and also a Groom.

Ernest's children Elizabeth and George were both christened by the Rev J T Evans in St Edward's: Elizabeth on 6 June 1906 and George on 20 October 1909. Ernest's occupation was given as Gardener in the Baptism Register.

Ernest's grave in Etaples Military Cemetery

Etaples Military Cemetery, France

After enlistment in Stow, Ernest initially served as Private 19886 in the Grenadier Guards but then transferred to 10th (Service) Battalion, Gloucestershire Regiment, which was formed at Bristol in September 1914. It was recruited mainly from the Gloucester and Cheltenham area with its Headquarters at Lansdown Crescent, Cheltenham. Training took place on Cleeve Hill. On 6 May 1915 the Battalion left Cheltenham by train for Salisbury Plain, later crossing from Southampton to France where they landed at Le Havre on 9 August. They formed 1st Brigade, 1st Division with 8th Royal Berkshires, 1st Black Watch, 1st Cameron Highlanders and 1/14th London Scottish.

On 17 August the Battalion arrived at Bethune, near the front line. The Glosters and the Berkshires were appointed to lead the big attack at Loos when six British Divisions would advance along a six mile front. The artillery barrage started on 21 September and shells were poured onto the German lines for the next four days. On 22 September they left rest camp to move up to the front line although 95 men with mumps had to be left behind. 10th Battalion, Gloucestershire Regiment, was in the centre of the British line when at 6.30 am. on 25 September, the whistle was blown and the battle opened. Gas was being used by the British for the first time but this was a doubtful asset as the wind changed and the British troops suffered from the effects of their own gas. By 3.30 pm. the German line was taken but at huge cost. 150 Glosters had died in No Man's Land, 14 out of 21 officers were lost and only 60 of the men in 10th Battalion had not become casualties. The Battalion was commended for their gallantry on that day.

Ernest had been wounded and died of his injuries a week later on 1 October in St John's Hospital, Etaples.

From the Evesham Journal – Saturday October 9 1915
DEATH OF ANOTHER STOW MAN
News has been received of the death of Pte Ernest Albert Young, 10th Glosters, at St John's Hospital, Etaples. The deceased was reported at the end of last week to be dangerously wounded in the thigh and on Sunday his wife received a telegram announcing his death in the above hospital. Deceased was a native of Castle Combe, Wiltshire. He had lived in Stow for some years. He leaves a widow and three little children, who will receive the very sincere sympathy of the townspeople.

WORLD WAR TWO

Declaration of War – 3 September 1939

Victory In Europe Day – 8 May 1945

Victory In Japan Day – 15 August 1945

The Memorial – The Second World War Men

		Date of Death	Age
1.	BAILEY, Anthony	24.07.1941	31
2.	BAILEY, Christopher Sidney	15.09.1942	27
3.	BANNING, Frederick Anthony	26.01.1945	19
4.	COLDICOTT, Keith John	25.08.1944	21
5.	FOSTER, Richard Norman	31.01.1944	21
6.	JONES, Maurice Edwin	05.06.1942	23
7.	JOSLIN, Frank	08.07.1942	30
8.	KING, Frederick Harold	12.08.1944	28
9.	LOFF, Victor Charles	17.06.1940	40
10.	MILLER, Frederick	16.02.1942	26
11.	MILLER, George	24.01.1942	28
12.	ROSE, Joseph	Not known	?
13.	SMITH, Henry Toomer	11.10.1941	21
14.	SUMPTION, John Barnett	30.04.1944	21

STOW-ON-THE-WOLD WAR MEMORIAL

The railings round the cross in The Square were taken away during World War Two to aid the war effort

My thanks to Bob Sharp for use of this photograph.

Second World War
Their Home Addresses In Stow & District

Back Walls	-	Joseph Rose
Church Street	-	Maurice Jones
Evesham Road	-	Frederick Miller
	-	George Miller
King George's Field	- no. 1	Frederick Banning
Park Street	- Rath Cottage	Frederick King
	-	Victor Loff
Sheep Street	- Rutland House	Henry Toomer Smith
Spring Gardens	- no. 16	Frank Joslin
The Square	- Lloyds Bank House	Keith Coldicott
	- Little Elms	John Barnett Sumption
Maugersbury	- Dower House	Anthony Bailey
	- Rock House	Christopher Bailey
Upper Swell	- Greenfields	Richard Foster

HMS Prince of Wales in 1941
Frederick Miller served on this ship

Second World War
Their Service In The Royal Navy, Army And Royal Air Force

ROYAL NAVY

HMS Manners   Able Seaman Frederick Banning
HMS Prince of Wales   Able Seaman Frederick Miller

ARMY

Royal Armoured Corps
    4th Queen's Own Hussars   Captain Christopher Bailey
    Royal Tank Regiment   Lance Corporal Frank Joslin - 5th Battalion
Royal Engineers   Sgt George Miller
Gloucestershire Regiment   Pte Maurice Jones - 1st Battalion
                                          Pte Frederick King - 2nd Battalion

Parachute Regiment   Pte Keith Coldicott
Pioneer Corps   Pte Victor Loff – 46th Coy, Aux Mil

RAF VOLUNTEER RESERVE

57 Squadron   Sgt (Observer) Henry Toomer Smith
183 Squadron   Flying Officer Richard Foster

Air Transport Auxiliary   Anthony Bailey

Not known: Joseph Rose

Anthony Bailey's grave in Broadwell Churchyard

Second World War
Their Memorials Or The Cemeteries Where They Are Buried

Alamein Memorial	Christopher Bailey
Alamein War Cemetery	Frank Joslin
Bayeux War Cemetery	Frederick King
Broadwell, St Paul's Churchyard	Anthony Bailey
Dunkirk Memorial	Victor Loff
Guidel Communal Cemetery	Richard Foster
Pietermaritzburg, Fort Napier Cemetery	George Miller
Portsmouth Naval Memorial	Frederick Banning
Prestbury, St Mary's Churchyard	John Barnett Sumption
Plymouth Naval Memorial	Frederick Miller
Rangoon Memorial	Maurice Jones
Ranville War Cemetery	Keith Coldicott
Rheinberg War Cemetery	Henry Toomer Smith

Not known: Joseph Rose

When I Come Home From The East

"When I come home from the East"
Said the soldier,
"They say I'll feel the cold
But I shan't care
If Stow's still there –
If Stow's still there on the Wold."

"When I come home from the East"
Said the soldier,
"The North wind may be harsh
But I shan't mind
If I can find
Moreton still in the Marsh."

"When I come home from the East"
Said the soldier,
"It'll like as not be snowing
But that's naught to me
If I can see
The River Windrush flowing."

A.W.B.

Published in "Punch" 29th November 1944

Second World War Dates Of Death Chronologically And Cause Of Death

1940

17 June	Victor Loff	Killed in Action

1941

24 July	Anthony Bailey	Accident
11 October	Harry Toomer Smith	Killed in Action

1942

24 January	George Miller	Illness
16 February	Frederick Miller	Killed in Action
05 June	Maurice Jones	Killed in Action
08 July	Frank Joslin	Killed in Action
15 September	Christopher Bailey	Died of wounds

1944

31 January	Richard Foster	Killed in Action
30 April	John Barnett Sumption	Illness
12 August	Frederick King	Killed in Action
25 August	Keith Coldicott	Killed in Action

1945

26 January	Frederick Banning	Killed in Action

Not known: Joseph Rose

STOW-ON-THE-WOLD WAR MEMORIAL

Badge of the Air Transport Auxiliary

Anthony Bailey

Anthony Bailey

Date of Birth	13 July 1910 – London
Service	Pilot, Air Transport Auxiliary
Date of Death	Killed in a flying accident on 24 July 1941 – age 31
Stow Address	Fosseway House (1921-25), Rock House, Maugersbury – childhood homes
	Dower House, Maugersbury – home of the Dickinson family
Parents	Colonel Percy James Bailey, DSO, OBE – late 12th Lancers
	Dorothy Jessica Bailey (nee Bowles) b. 1886 Kensington, London
	They were married in London in 1907.
Siblings	Richard (1908 – 69)
	Christopher (1915-42) – *see page 251*
	Timothy (1918-86) – *see page 251*
Wife	Desiree Dorothy Bailey (nee Dickinson) b. 1914 London – known as Rab
	Anthony and Rab were married on 16 March 1940 in St Edward's by the Rev Christian Hare.
Cemetery	St Paul's Churchyard, Broadwell *(see page 244)*

Notes

Anthony's widow, Mrs Rab Bailey, served on the PCC and also as a sidesman at St Edward's.

Anthony was educated at the Royal Naval College, Dartmouth from January 1924 and left in August 1927. He was duly commissioned into the Royal Navy at 18. He resigned in 1936 and trained as a civilian pilot with North Eastern Airways. On the outbreak of war he was considered too old to become an RAF pilot but was recruited into the Air Transport Auxiliary. He was killed in a crash at Speke Airport, Liverpool, caused by a fighter plane cutting in as he landed his bomber.

In 1939 Britain needed pilots to ferry new aircraft from factories to service airfields and military bases across the country. Rather than tie up RAF pilots, civilians who held a pilot's A licence and had logged at least 250 flying hours were recruited. Gerald D'Erlanger, director of BOAC, became administrator of the new organisation, the Air Transport Auxiliary. Wartime strength of the ATA was 1752 pilots of whom about 600 were women. They lost 174 personnel during the war, one of whom was Amy Johnson, who lost her bearings in thick fog, ran out of fuel, ditched in the Thames Estuary and was drowned.

Badge of the 4th King's Own Hussars

Captain Christopher Bailey

Christopher Sidney Bailey

Date of Birth	12 February 1915 – London
Service	141129 Captain, 4th Queen's Own Hussars, Royal Armoured Corps
Date of Death	Died of wounds on 15 September 1942 – age 27
Stow Address	Fosseway House (1921-25)
	Rock House, Maugersbury
Parents	Colonel Percy Bailey, DSO, OBE – late 12th Lancers
	Dorothy Jessica Bailey (nee Bowles) b. 1886 Kensington, London
	They were married in London in 1907.
Siblings	Richard (1908-69)
	Anthony (1910-41) – *see page 248*
	Timothy (1918-86) – *served in 12th Lancers, was taken prisoner in 1940 and was a POW for 5 years.*
Memorial	El Alamein Memorial, Egypt. Alamein is a village approximately 130 kilometres west of Alexandria on the road to Mersa Matruh. The Memorial forms the entrance to the Alamein War Cemetery. The Land Forces panels commemorate more than 8500 soldiers of the Commonwealth who died in the campaigns in Egypt and Libya and in the operations of the Eighth Army in Tunisia up to 19 February 1943 and who have no known grave.

Notes

Colonel Percy Bailey was a member of the PCC at St Edward's and he and Mrs Dorothy Bailey were both sidesmen. Mrs Bailey was the sister of Lady Redesdale and consequently aunt to the six Mitford sisters and their brother Tom, who was killed in Burma in 1945. As a boy Christopher was close to his cousin Unity Mitford, later notorious for her friendship with Adolf Hitler. Unity's sister, Deborah, Dowager Duchess of Devonshire, recalls a furious row when her father Lord Redesdale found Christopher and Unity stealing peaches in the glasshouses at Swinbrook.

In summer at the home of the four Bailey boys, the annual "Bailey Week" was held, which included cricket, tennis, walks, riding, picnics and dancing. It was like a mini-season and their Mitford cousins and James Lees-Milne, the diarist, were among the guests who enjoyed the fun. Christopher was educated at Marlborough College from January 1928 to December 1931. He played hockey, cricket and rugby for his house.

Christopher was a temperance worker in 1933 and later in the 1930s he went to live in Cyprus

STOW-ON-THE-WOLD WAR MEMORIAL

Stow-on-the-Wold Cub Scouts 1933
The Cub Leader is Mrs Percy Bailey
The house in the background, The Forge, was the home of Harry and Fanny King
(see page 154) and later belonged to Colonel and Mrs Percy Bailey

Inscription at the El Alamein Memorial

where he ran an inn which was known for its good food. On the outbreak of war he joined the Cyprus Mule Company, then returned to England and was commissioned into the 4th Queen's Own Hussars.

In 1941 4th Queen's Own Hussars had taken part in the defence of Greece during which they fought a series of rearguard actions, two of which were at Proasteion and the Corinth Canal. They covered the withdrawal from the Yugoslav border to the southern beaches. By the end of April 1941 the Germans had occupied Athens and the evacuation, where possible, of British troops from Greece to Egypt was completed although most of the senior officers and 400 men of 4th Hussars were amongst the 10,000 taken prisoner.

In January 1942 Christopher was posted to 8th Army Headquarters in Cairo. After reforming in Cairo, 4th Hussars were ready by April 1942 to take part in the fighting in North Africa. The campaign in the Western Desert was fought between Commonwealth forces based in Egypt and the Axis forces based in Libya. The battlefield across which the fighting surged back and forth between 1940 and 1942 was the thousand kilometres of desert between Alexandria in Egypt and Benghazi in Libya.

In July 1942 Christopher was approached by Major David Stirling and invited to join a new organisation which Major Stirling had set up the previous year to carry out sabotage operations behind enemy lines. It was the start of the Special Air Service. In the first sortie in which Christopher was involved, in an attack on the aerodrome at Fuka, west of El Alamein, sixteen aircraft, thirty new aircraft engines, three workshop hangars and several ammunition dumps were all destroyed.

The next action planned for September 1942 was to be a much larger raid on Benghazi. The raiding party made their way in small groups across the desert to the rendezvous point where they met on 14th September. On the night of 14th/15th September they moved up closer to Benghazi. Before dawn on the morning of 15th September Christopher led off the attack. Taking three men with him, their task was to attack and destroy an Italian fort and radio station on top of an escarpment to the south of the town. Unfortunately as they entered the building Christopher was shot through the lungs and two of the others were also wounded. However, the remaining member of Christopher's party made it back to the main force and brought reinforcements of three officers and ten men who captured the fort and the radio link was destroyed. The three wounded men were taken back to the rendezvous point in the hills to the east.

After all elements of the attack had been carried out and everyone was accounted for, the party moved in small groups to the original rendezvous twenty five miles further south. The next afternoon enemy aircraft circled over the desert trying to spot the raiding party. There were never less than fifteen aircraft in the skies above them.

The group in which Christopher was travelling was located and attacked. Several trucks were destroyed and Christopher was wounded again in the strafing. Some of them, Christopher included, were too badly wounded to move.

STOW-ON-THE-WOLD WAR MEMORIAL

El Alamein Memorial, Egypt

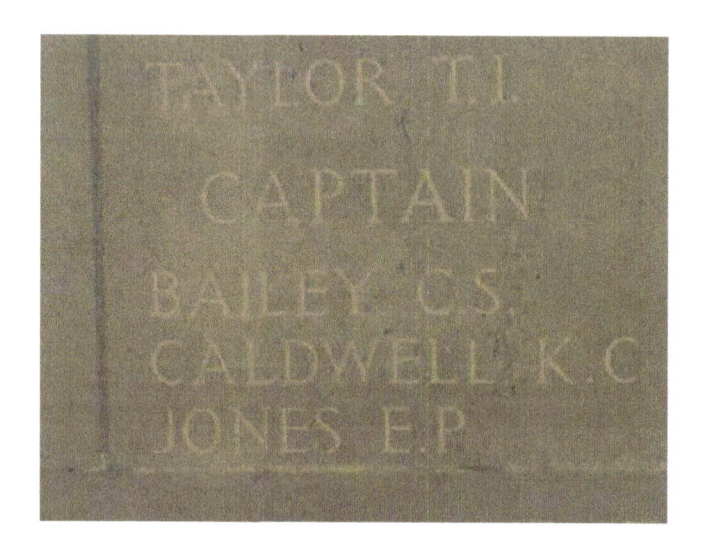

Christopher's name on the memorial

One of the medical orderlies volunteered to drive back to Benghazi in a Bantam with a flag of truce to seek medical aid and lead out an ambulance in spite of the fact that this meant he would certainly spend the rest of the war as a prisoner. Having made the injured as comfortable as possible, the remainder of the group headed for Jalo. Sadly Christopher died of his wounds before any medical help reached him.

Winston Churchill was appointed Colonel of the 4th Queen's Own Hussars on 22 October 1941 and remained so until his death. In 1896 as a young subaltern, he had served with the regiment in India. His son Randolph also served in the regiment during the Second World War.

El Alamein War Cemetery and Memorial

STOW-ON-THE-WOLD WAR MEMORIAL

Insignia of the Royal Navy

Able Seaman Frederick Banning

Frederick Anthony Banning

Date of Birth	7 February 1926 – Stow
Service	P/JX 624910 Able Seaman, HMS Manners, Royal Navy
Date of Death	Lost at sea on 26 January 1945 – age 18
Stow Address	Well Lane (1926)
	1 King George's Field
Parents	Frederick John Banning b. 1893 Stow
	Annie Banning (nee Brennan)
	Their marriage was registered at Winchcombe in 1919.
Siblings	Margaret Minnie b. 1919 Stow
	Anne Patricia b. 1920 Stow
	Veronica Marion b. 1922 Stow
	Agnes Lavinia b. 1923 Stow
	John b. 1928 Stow, d. 1933
	Sheila Teresa b. 1930 Stow
	Edward George b. 1933 Stow
	Norah b. 1935 Stow
	Terence b. 1937 Stow
Cemetery	Portsmouth Naval Memorial. The Memorial commemorates almost 10,000 sailors of the First World War and almost 15,000 from the Second World War who have no known grave.

Notes

Frederick's father was a Farm Labourer and his grandfather was listed in the 1901 census as a Cattle Dealer. Frederick's sister Margaret was christened in St Edward's on 25 January 1920 by the Rev J T Evans. Frederick and his other siblings were all christened in Stow's new Catholic Church of Our Lady and St Kenelm.

    HMS Manners (K568), a frigate of the Captain class, was built in Boston, Massachusetts and launched on 24 September 1943. It was torpedoed by the German submarine U-1051 on 26 January 1945 in the Irish Sea, 19 miles off Holyhead. The ship broke in half and the stern sheered off and sank with the loss of four officers and 39 ratings, one of whom was Frederick. 15 others were injured. The forward section was towed into Barrow-in-Furness. The submarine U-1051 which destroyed HMS Manners was itself sunk with all hands within a few hours by HMS

STOW-ON-THE-WOLD WAR MEMORIAL

Portsmouth Naval Memorial

Manners' sister ships, HMS Aylmer, Calder and Bentinck. German naval records show that the submarine did not return from that patrol. The wreck of HMS Manners was sold in 1946 and scrapped in Piraeus in Greece the following year.

From the Evesham Journal – Saturday February 17 1945
STOW SAILOR'S DEATH
News has been received from official sources by Mr and Mrs Frederick J Banning of 1 King George's Field, Stow-on-the-Wold, that their eldest son, Able Seaman Frederick Anthony Banning, has been lost at sea and must be presumed dead. Able Seaman Banning, who had been in the Royal Navy for two years, for which he volunteered, was home on leave about three weeks ago. Nineteen years of age, he was a torpedo gunner. He was educated at Stow-on-the-Wold School and, before joining the Navy, was a messenger in the Stow Fire Service. He was employed by Mr Wheeler, builder, of Slaughter. Able Seaman Banning's grandfather, Mr John Banning, is a well-known cattle dealer in the Cotswolds.

Lieutenant Commander James Cole, RN, was a Petty Officer Telegraphist on board HMS Manners at the time the ship was torpedoed. He wrote an account of the end of HMS Manners, an extract from which follows.

"On Christmas morning 1944, we heard the healthy throb of the Manners' diesels for the first time. We get a cheer from the American dockyard workers as the ship slowly eases itself from the dockyard walls.

On 26th January there is a huge explosion at the stern of the ship. We immediately lose way and steering. The Officer of the Watch yells down the voice pipe: "Signal Most Immediate: Have been mined or torpedoed, am uncertain which, in position Holyhead 102-15 miles." The signalman also sent the signal by light to the two ships ahead. The Asdic operator had called out seconds before the explosion: "Torpedo screws, starboard quarter." We are stationary in the water and the ship's company are racing to action stations. Then a second torpedo struck the ship abaft the funnel, level with the main engine room. The ship shuddered violently and split in two. At the time the second torpedo struck, more than half of the ship's company had been on the quarterdeck or down below in the stern half of the ship. All lights went off but after a few seconds the low power emergency lighting came on. I rushed from the office and, looking aft, saw the stern of the ship upside down and settling slowly. We could see heads bobbing in the water around the rapidly disappearing stern. To our amazement the bow portion of the ship lurched to starboard, righted itself and levelled off still high in the water. We released three Carley floats into the water. Although there was water coming into the motor room, it was not critical but with no power the pumps could not be started. Then there were more violent explosions as the depth charges on the sinking stern of the ship reached their depth settings. We were lifted up on the mushroom of the explosion astern and tons of water cascaded onto the ship. Many of the survivors in the water were killed but a few managed to swim away, climb into the Carley floats and were rescued. Later that evening, while we were being towed to Barrow, I had to send the dreaded signal to the Admiralty reporting the names of all the dead."

Badge of the Parachute Regiment

Keith as a schoolboy

Ranville War Cemetery, France

Keith John Coldicott

Date of Birth	1923 – Evesham	
Service	5192890 Private, 8th Battalion, Parachute Regiment	
Date of Death	Killed in action on 25 August 1944 – age 21	
Stow Address	Lloyd's Bank House, The Square	
Parents	John Garfield Coldicott	b. 1895 Mickleton Wood Farm, Glos.
	Catherine May Coldicott (nee Lissaman)	b. 1895 Mickleton
Siblings	Aisla	b. 1926 Evesham
	Pauline	b. 1927 Evesham
Cemetery	Ranville War Cemetery, Calvados, France. Ranville lies north east of Caen and was the first village to be liberated in 1944.	
	Private E Corteil of 9th Battalion, Parachute Regiment, is also buried at Ranville. He died on 6 June 1944 and his dog Glenn, the regimental mascot, is buried in the same grave.	

Notes

Keith was educated at Pate's Grammar School in Cheltenham and joined the Army straight from school.

His father was Manager of Lloyd's Bank in Stow and was a member of the PCC at St Edward's. Two of his father's brothers, Keith's uncles Charles and Harry Coldicott, died during the First World War. Charles was a sergeant in the Warwickshire Yeomanry and died of enteric fever in Alexandria in 1915 and Harry died of wounds while fighting with the Australian Light Horse Regiment in Belgium in June 1917.

On D Day, 6 June 1944, 8th Battalion, Parachute Regiment, part of 6th Airborne Division, comprised a force of about 760 men commanded by Lt Colonel Alastair Pearson, MC, DSO and two bars. Their task was to capture and destroy three bridges over the River Dives in Normandy and then to hold that position on the eastern flank of Sword beach against German attack. Gold, Juno and Sword were the code names for the three Normandy beaches where British troops landed on D Day.

All the objectives were achieved although, because of adverse weather conditions, the troops, who landed by glider or parachute, had been widely scattered. Heavy fighting continued for some weeks in Normandy against German counter attacks until on 17 August, 6th Airborne Division started the advance eastwards, reaching the River Seine on 26 August. Keith was killed in this advance on 25 August 1944.

STOW-ON-THE-WOLD WAR MEMORIAL

Cap Badge of the Royal Air Force

Pilot Officer Dick Foster

Richard Norman Foster

Date of Birth	22 November 1922 – Upper Swell
Service	149358 Flying Officer (Pilot), 183 Squadron, Royal Air Force Volunteer Reserve
Date of Death	Killed in action on 31 January 1944 – age 21
Stow Address	The Manor House, Upper Swell
	Greenfields, Upper Swell (1927)
Parents	William W Foster
	Marion Foster (nee Thick)
Siblings	William — b. 1906 Upper Swell
	Marjorie — b. 1908 Upper Swell
	Edwin — b. 1909 Upper Swell
	Robert — b. Upper Swell – *World Motor Cycle Champion 1950*
	Noel — b. Upper Swell
	Mary — b. 1916 Upper Swell
Cemetery	Guidel Communal Cemetery, Morbihan, France. Guidel is a village 60 kilometres north west of Vannes. There are now over 100 war casualties commemorated at this site.

Notes

Dick's father was Manager of the Abbotswood estate at Lower Swell for Mr Mark Fenwick, a steel magnate. When Mr Fenwick sold the estate in 1927, the Foster family moved to Greenfields.

Dr Edward Dening was the family doctor in Stow for many years. When the first six Foster children were born, Dr Dening charged £1 on each occasion for the confinement fee. By the time Dick was born, six years after Mary, Dr Leonard King had taken over the practice and prices had gone up – the cost for Dick's delivery was seven guineas, more than all the others put together!

From 1932 to 1968 Stow Rugby Club played on a field at the Foster farm on the Broadway road.

Dick joined the Royal Air Force Volunteer Reserve in April 1941 and after initial training was posted to 183 Squadron, which was formed in May 1942 as a Typhoon squadron. It did not become operational until April 1943 when it started carrying out cross Channel sweeps with fighter bombers. The Squadron moved to Cornwall in September 1943 from where attacks were made on enemy shipping and airfields. In November they began to use rockets rather than bombs.

Guidel Communal Cemetery, France

On the night of 30/31 January 1944, Dick's plane took off from an airfield in Cornwall and was shot down by anti-aircraft fire whilst attacking an airfield in France.
Dick and the other members of the crew were all killed.

Dick's brother Edwin (Ned) was a Lieutenant in the Royal Artillery and was awarded a Military Cross for gallantry in action in Italy in 1944.

In July 1948 Ned visited France in an attempt to find out where Dick had been buried as at that time he had no known grave. Ned managed to establish with the help of local French people the exact whereabouts of Dick's original grave. He then liaised with the Commonwealth War Graves Commission and had the identification accepted and the headstone in Guidel Cemetery was amended from "Known to God" to give Dick's personal details.

From the Evesham Journal – Saturday February 5 1944
STOW AIRMAN MISSING
Flying Officer Richard Norman Foster, the youngest son of Mr and Mrs W W Foster, of Greenfields, Stow-on-the-Wold, has been reported missing believed killed after air operations over the Channel.

Dick Foster, who had his 21st birthday in November, was educated at Campden Grammar School and after leaving there, he worked for a time as a fitter at an aerodrome. He joined the RAF in April 1941 and was sent to America for training as a pilot. He came back home in May 1942, having won his "Wings" and was posted to a Typhoon squadron. He obtained his commission in May 1943 and was gazetted Flying Officer in October.

He was of a very genial nature and was always ready with a helping hand and his many friends will miss his smile and treasure his acquaintance. Sincere sympathy is felt by a host of friends with his parents and their family in their anxiety.

Front and back cap badges of the Gloucestershire Regiment

Maurice in Rangoon – July 1939

Maurice Edwin Jones

Date of Birth	11 November 1918 – Stow (Armistice Day)
Service	5184139 Private, 1st Battalion, Gloucestershire Regiment
Date of Death	Missing believed killed on 5 June 1942 – age 23
Stow Address	Church Street (now the offices of Harrison & Hardie, Estate Agents)
Parents	Edwin Jones — b. 1883 Donnington
	Rose Margaret Jones (nee Summerell) — b. Paddington, London
	They were married in Stow in 1912.
Siblings	Margaret (Mollie) — b. 1914 Stow
	Beryl — b. 1923 Stow
Memorial	Rangoon Memorial, Burma. The Memorial is situated in Taukkyan War Cemetery and bears the names of almost 27,000 men of the Commonwealth land forces who died during the campaigns in Burma and who have no known grave. Taukkyan is the largest of three war cemeteries in Burma.

Notes

In 1901 Maurice's father was working as a Carter on a farm. Later he worked at Donnington Brewery.

After he left school, Maurice had various jobs as a Labourer and then in October 1937 he joined the Army – 1st Battalion, Gloucestershire Regiment. He was already in Burma at the outbreak of war in 1939.

1st Battalion, Gloucestershire Regiment, had moved to Burma from India in November 1938 and was stationed at Mingaladon, a few miles north of Rangoon, with 'A' Company in Rangoon. After the Japanese entered the war on 7th December 1941, the Battalion was mobilised on 17th December. The Regimental Colours were sent by air to Lloyd's Bank in Delhi and the regimental silver was initially sent by road to Maymyo. When Maymyo was evacuated in May 1942, the cases containing the regimental silver were buried in the jungle, unfortunately never to be seen again – it was purloined by persons unknown. The one case that was kept with the Battalion was carried throughout the long retreat and ultimately reached India safely.

There were Japanese air raids on Mingaladon and Rangoon on 23rd December and Christmas Day 1941. In the Christmas Day raid, all ranks were ordered to take cover in the trenches but the cooks remained in the cookhouse and directly the raid ended, turkey and Christmas pudding were served to the men by the officers and NCOs in the traditional manner.

STOW-ON-THE-WOLD WAR MEMORIAL

The Rangoon Memorial, Burma

By March 1942 the Japanese had penetrated across the eastern frontier from Siam and a general retreat from Burma was ordered with 1st Gloucesters acting as rearguard. At Taukkyan, twenty one miles north of Rangoon, they encountered a road block held by about 500 Japanese, which had to be cleared before the long column could continue northward. Throughout the withdrawal, the battalion, commanded by Lt Colonel Charles Bagot, was almost continuously in contact with the enemy and managed at Letpadan to inflict defeat on the Japanese Advanced Guard Battalion, the first defeat the Japanese had suffered.

There were also fierce actions at Paungde on 27th March and Shwedaung a few days later to delay the Japanese advance. The Battalion arrived at Yenangyuang on 13th April, by now reduced to two companies with most of the officers killed or wounded. They were ordered to cover the demolition of the oil installations there before continuing on towards Mandalay. The army next withdrew from Mandalay to Kalewa on the River Chindwin. It was a race with the Japanese to see who would get to Kalewa first. If the Japanese had arrived first, the whole army would have been trapped in Burma. By 9th May the Battalion had crossed the River Chindwin with the enemy only a few hours behind. They climbed the jungle-clad mountains between Burma and Assam marching in the cool of the night to avoid the great heat of May, then moved on to cross the Tamu Pass (6500 feet above sea level), carrying their wounded with them. They reached Imphal and arrived at Kohima by 1st June. Maurice died on 5th June 1942. The Battalion had covered 600 miles and lost eight officers killed and eleven wounded. 156 Other Ranks were either killed or died of wounds. Only four of the officers who had been with the battalion in Rangoon remained.

The Rangoon Memorial

The Rangoon Memorial was begun in 1951 for the reception of graves from four battlefield cemeteries at Akyab, Mandalay, Meiktila and Sahmaw which were difficult to access and could not be maintained. The graves have been grouped together at Taukkyan to preserve the individuality of these battlefield cemeteries. Burials were also transferred from civil and cantonment cemeteries and from a number of isolated jungle and roadside sites. The total number of identified casualties is 26,866.

Cap Badge of the Royal Tank Regiment

Frank's grave in El Alamein War Cemetery

Frank Joslin

Date of Birth	25 July 1911 – Bristol
Service	7883701 Lance Corporal, 5th Royal Tank Regiment, Royal Armoured Corps
Date of Death	8 July 1942 – age 30
Stow Address	16 Spring Gardens – the home of his wife's parents
Parents	Edmund Brailey Joslin b. 1875 Bedminster, Bristol
	Lily Mary Joslin (nee Hill)
	They were married in Bristol in 1901.
Wife	Ethel May Joslin (nee Clifford) b. 11.12.1914 Stow
	Frank and Ethel were married in St Edward's on 25 November 1939.
Child	Philip Wilfred b. 16 March 1941 Stow
Cemetery	Alamein War Cemetery, Egypt. The cemetery contains the graves of men who died at all stages in the Western Desert campaigns. It now contains 7239 Commonwealth burials of the Second World War.

Notes

Frank was born at home, 36 Victoria Place, Spring Street, Bristol. His father was a Tannery worker. Frank's wife Ethel was the niece of Eustace Clifford *(see page 73)*. At the time of their marriage, Frank was in the Royal Tank Corps at Harpenden, Hertfordshire and Ethel was working as a Clerk. Their son Philip was christened on 11 May 1941 by the Rev F M Christian Hare in St Edward's.

When war was declared on 3rd September 1939 5th Royal Tank Regiment was stationed at Perham Down in Wiltshire as part of 1st Heavy Armoured Brigade, 1st Armoured Division. It fought as part of the British Expeditionary force in France in May 1940 and became caught up in the withdrawal to Dunkirk. Frank was one of the many thousands of servicemen rescued from the beaches at Dunkirk in June 1940.

The Regiment was re-equipped and then sent to North Africa where, having survived losses in Cyrenaica in Libya in April 1941, it fell back on Tobruk. There it formed part of the Tobruk garrison until 14th April when the regiment embarked for Egypt and joined 4th Armoured Brigade in Cairo. The siege of Tobruk had commenced on 10th April. On 15 June 1941 in Operation Battleaxe the British launched a large counterattack in an unsuccessful attempt to relieve Tobruk. In September the Regiment returned to the desert and continued training before the start of Operation Crusader in November when the newly created British 8th Army pushed Rommel back to his starting point at Mersa el Braga.

STOW-ON-THE-WOLD WAR MEMORIAL

Entrance to El Alamein War Cemetery

View across the cemetery at El Alamein

A fierce tank battle ensued against Rommel's Panzer Divisions, in particular around the Sidi Rezegh airfield until, after nearly three weeks, the Germans began to withdraw to the north west. This successful Allied offensive relieved Tobruk and pushed on to El Agheila. Tobruk was finally relieved after a siege of 242 days on 7th December. The Italians lost half of their army and the Germans a quarter of theirs.

In January 1942 Rommel counterattacked driving the British back and Benghazi fell to the Germans. In late May 1942 in the battle of Gazala reinforced Axis forces advanced across the desert and attacked the Allied line west of Tobruk. The Allies were heavily defeated and forced to withdraw to Mersa Matruh. Tobruk fell on 21st June with the loss of 35,000 prisoners. Rommel was promoted to Field Marshal.

The Germans advanced towards Alexandria and Cairo and on 1st July attacked the British line at El Alamein, an insignificant railway station on the coast, but the British line held. On 2nd July 4th Armoured Brigade drove back repeated attacks by Axis armour who withdrew before dusk. The next day the Germans resumed the attack but by this time the strength of the Afrika Corps was greatly reduced and they were suffering from the extended length of their supply lines. The Axis advance was halted and they were forced onto the defensive. General Auchinleck launched a new attack in great force on 8 July. Frank was killed on that day.

Another view across El Alamein Cemetery

STOW-ON-THE-WOLD WAR MEMORIAL

Front and back cap badges of the Gloucestershire Regiment

Private Frederick King

Frederick Harold King

Date of Birth	16 June 1916 – Stow	
Service	5188140 Private, 2nd Battalion, Gloucestershire Regiment	
Date of Death	Killed in action on 12 August 1944 – age 28	
Stow Address	Park Street – Rath Cottage	
Parents	Harry King	b. 1887 Lower Swell
	Alice Jane King (nee Shelton)	b. 1888 Stow
Siblings	Percival Shelton	b. 16.06 1907 Stow – *Royal Artillery*
	Cyril Leonard	b. 08.08.1920 Stow – *Tank tester and fitter*
	Lionel Bert	b. 28.10.1922 Stow – *In the Home Guard*
Wife	Mary King (nee Illes)	b. 1919 Lower Swell
	Fred and Mary were married on 30 September 1940 in St Mary's, Lower Swell.	
Child	Norma Mary	b. 25 December 1942 Lower Swell
Cemetery	Bayeux War Cemetery, Normandy, France. The town of Bayeux lies 24 kilometres north west of Caen. The cemetery is the largest Commonwealth cemetery of the Second World War in France and contains 4144 Commonwealth burials.	

Notes

In 1901 Fred's father was working as a Stable Boy in Cheltenham. He was the brother of Leonard King *(see page 155)*.

Fred was christened in St Edward's on 9 August 1916 by the Rev Sydney E Martin and his father's occupation was given as Grocer's Porter in the Baptism Register. In later life he worked as a Chauffeur and also in a garage in Stow. Before the war Fred worked as a Painter and Decorator.

Both Fred and his brother Cyril sang in the choir at St Edward's.

In 1807 a mineral spring was discovered in Lower Swell. It is covered by a spa house, now a terrace of four cottages. The family of Fred's wife Mary lived in The Spa House and after their marriage Fred stayed there too whenever he was on leave.

2nd Battalion, Gloucestershire Regiment, came successfully through the D Day landings at about 11 am. on 6 June 1944 although the crossing was rough and many troops were seasick.

By 7 June 1944 the Battalion was outside Bayeux and proceeded to advance cautiously across Normandy. They were engaged in the assault on Tilly on 11 June and met great difficulties as German snipers had been left at every vantage point. During these operations a Platoon

Fred and Mary outside Spa Cottage on their wedding day

Bayeux War Cemetery

Commander had a curious experience. He captured a German despatch rider and, anxious to bring him in without loss of time, rode pillion behind him and directed his prisoner to Battalion Headquarters where he then handed him over.

On 1 August the Battalion moved forward to occupy Anctonville and Fossard. On 8 August they travelled by bus on a three hour journey to an area west of the River Orne and advanced on 9 August to establish a bridgehead near Courmeron. At 6.50 am. on 12 August a patrol of ten men penetrated the outskirts of Thury-Harcourt coming under heavy fire in which Fred was killed by a sniper.

After the war, Fred's widow and daughter moved to Southfields, London.

Fred King's grave

Cap Badge of the Pioneer Corps

The Lancastria in the River Thames before the war

Victor Charles Loff

Date of Birth	1900 – St James's, London
Service	13002604 Private, 46 Company Auxiliary Military Pioneer Corps
Date of Death	Died of wounds on 17 June 1940 – age 40
Stow Address	Park Street (1942) – c/o Mrs Scarrott
	Sheep Street (1946) – beside the Post Office
Parents	Rudolph Charles Loffhagen — b. 1872 St James's, London
	Emily Elizabeth Loffhagen (nee Elmore) — b. 1878 St James's, London
	They married in Westminster in 1895.
Siblings	Emily — b. 1896 St James, London
	Adelaide — b. 1898 St James, London
Wife	Winifred Loff (nee Warren) — b. 1912 Stow
	Victor and Winifred married in Paddington, London in 1936.
Children	Victor — b. 1937 Paddington, London
	Pamela — b. 1938 Paddington, London
Memorial	Dunkirk Memorial, France. The Memorial stands at the entrance to the British War Graves Section of Dunkirk Town Cemetery and commemorates more than 4,500 casualties of the British Expeditionary Force who died in the 1939-40 campaign and who have no known grave. The Memorial was designed by Philip Hepworth and the engraved glass panel depicting the evacuation was by John Hutton.

Notes

Victor's grandfather, also Victor Charles Loffhagen, was born in St Petersburg in 1833. He came to the UK in 1860, became naturalised British and married Harriet Brackenridge, a Scotswoman. He was a master tailor who worked with his sons in Carnaby Street, London and made waistcoats for a firm in Savile Row. In the 1901 census, Victor's parents were living at 24 Great Windmill Street, St James's, London. Their occupations were given as Tailor and Tailoress. Victor's age was given as sixteen months.

Victor's wife was christened Lydia Winifred on 22 January 1913 in St Edward's by the Rev J T Evans. Before the war Victor worked as a Costermonger in London.

The Auxiliary Military Pioneer Corps was raised in 1939 changing its name in 1940 to Pioneer Corps. Victor was serving in France in June 1940.

STOW-ON-THE-WOLD WAR MEMORIAL

The Dunkirk Memorial, France

An Extraordinary Occurrence

One Stow resident, John Brown, future newsagent, member of the PCC and sidesman at St Edward's, was more fortunate than Victor Loff. He served in a Motorised Transport unit and as the German army forced the BEF back to Dunkirk, his unit received the order "Each for yourself". He and a companion made their way to Dunkirk and arrived to find a hectic scene with troops standing in lines all along the beach, waiting to be rescued by a flotilla of small boats. Exhausted, they lay down in the sand dunes to rest and fell asleep. When they awoke, all was quiet – the boats had gone, the troops had gone and they were on their own. Somehow they obtained a canoe and, using their rifles as paddles, set off for England. Half way across the Channel, to their alarm and amazement, a submarine surfaced beside them and an English voice said: "Want a lift?"

The 16,000 ton SS *Lancastria* (originally called the *Tyrrhenia*) was built in Glasgow and launched in 1922. The *Lancastria* spent many years as a Cunard cruise liner and in September 1939 was in the Bahamas. She was converted in New York for her war time role of cargo and transport duties.

At 6.00 am. on 17 June 1940 the *Lancastria*, now His Majesty's Troopship, was guided into the sea lanes off the Loire estuary and anchored a few miles off St Nazaire at Charpentier Roads. Almost immediately the evacuation began of soldiers of the British Expeditionary Force along with some RAF personnel and a few civilians. There were so many to evacuate that ferrying to and fro continued into the afternoon. The number on board is not known but almost certainly exceeded 6000. At about 1300 hours the red alert sounded and a German bomber attacked the *Oronsay* which lay some miles off. German Dornier aircraft spotted the cruise liner, anchored and undefended. She was hit by four bombs, one of which was a bull's eye, dropping straight down the funnel and exploding in the engine room. The *Lancastria* sank at 16.15. There were survivors – two lifeboats had been launched but the rescue operation was very difficult due to enemy aircraft action and fuel oil which had leaked from the ruptured tanks of the liner. However, 2447 people were saved. Victor went down with the ship. The site of the wreck is now an official war grave.

Owing to the scale of the tragedy (it is Britain's worst ever maritime disaster), Winston Churchill forbade publication of the news in the interests of public morale. Survivors were forbidden under King's Regulations to mention the disaster and people killed were listed as "missing in action". The official report is still sealed until the year 2040.

After Victor's death, his widow and their two children returned to live in Stow. Several years later, Winifred and her daughter Pamela emigrated to Australia.

Insignia of the Royal Navy

Fred Miller and Fred King in the Stow-on-the-Wold Schoolboys football team 1929/30

Able Seaman Frederick Miller

Frederick Miller

Date of Birth	29 January 1916 – Little Compton
Service	D/JX213495 Able Seaman, HMS *Prince of Wales*, Royal Navy
Date of Death	Missing believed killed on 16 February 1942 – age 26
Stow Address	Sheep Street (1922)
	5 Evesham Road (1925)
Parents	Edward Miller
	Catherine Miller (nee Forgie)
	They were married in Brentford in 1910.
Siblings	Nora — b. 08.10.1911 Little Compton
	George — b. 17.07.1913 Little Compton – *see page 288*.
	Alexander — b. 20.11.1917 Little Compton – *was a Prisoner of War*
	Donald — b. 23.09.1919 Little Compton
Wife	Dinah Miller (nee Sparrow) of Wellesbourne, Warwickshire
	Frederick and Dinah were married in Moreton-in-Marsh in 1941.
Child	James b. 26.12.1941 Moreton-in-Marsh
Memorial	Plymouth Naval Memorial. The Memorial is on The Hoe and commemorates more than 7000 sailors of the First World War and almost 16,000 from the Second World War with no known grave.

Notes

Frederick was christened in St Denis's Church, Little Compton on 27 February 1916. His father's occupation was given as Motor Driver in the Baptism Register. The Miller family moved to Stow in 1922. After leaving school Frederick worked as a telegraph boy for the Post Office. Following the outbreak of war, he joined the Navy and in 1941 he was posted to the new battleship HMS *Prince of Wales*, which was built in the Cammell Laird shipyard at Birkenhead and had been launched on 3rd May 1939. During commissioning in Liverpool in January 1941 a German bomb landed very close to *Prince of Wales* and as a precaution the ship was moved to the Rosyth dockyard where commissioning work was completed by 31 March 1941. The ship then sailed to Scapa Flow to carry out sea and gunnery trials.

On 19 May 1941 the new German battleship *Bismarck* accompanied by the heavy cruiser *Prinz Eugen* left the port of Gotenhafen (now Gdynia) and headed out into the Baltic. A friendly

*Divine Service on board HMS Prince Of Wales Sunday 10 August 1941
Placentia Bay, Newfoundland*

President Roosevelt and Mr Churchill are seated facing the left hand gun

Swedish diplomat passed on the information that the ships were bound for Bergen in Norway. This was confirmed by an RAF Spitfire reconnaissance flight showing the German ships at anchor near Bergen.

Prince of Wales and *Hood* were ordered to sea to intercept the German ships and although there were still over a hundred civilian technicians on board *Prince of Wales,* she sailed within two hours of receiving the order. On 23 May the two German ships were detected by the heavy cruisers *Norfolk* and *Suffolk* in the Denmark Strait between Greenland and Iceland. Fire was exchanged but the outgunned British cruisers withdrew.

The next day, Saturday 24th May, *Prince of Wales* and *Hood* caught up with the German ships. At 05.52 *Hood* opened fire at a range of about 12.5 miles. Soon after 6 am. *Hood* was hit amidships, split in half and sank within three minutes. There were only three survivors. Over 1400 men died. *Prince of Wales* had to turn to avoid the wreckage. Her gunfire had caused damage to *Bismarck* but she had received seven hits and as all but one of her main guns were out of action, the captain decided to disengage under cover of a smokescreen. Having rendezvoused with *Norfolk* and *Suffolk*, *Prince of Wales* headed for Iceland to carry out temporary repairs and then returned to the dockyard at Rosyth. Two days later *Bismarck* was again attacked by British ships and the Fleet Air Arm and finally sunk. Whilst undergoing repairs in Rosyth an unexploded torpedo was found on board *Prince of Wales*, which caused some consternation until it had been successfully dealt with.

In August 1941 HMS *Prince of Wales* carried Winston Churchill to Ship Harbor, Placentia Bay, Newfoundland. There from 9th to 12th August he joined US President Franklin D Roosevelt on the USS *Augusta* for the Atlantic Conference. On Sunday 10 August the President and his entourage joined the ship's company on board *Prince of Wales* for divine service. The President gave a gift bag containing fruit, chocolate and cigarettes to every man on board. On 14 August 1941 the two leaders issued the Atlantic Charter, which formed the basis of the United Nations Charter. It was to be a blue print for the post-war period.

In September *Prince of Wales* was assigned to escort duty for the first major Malta convoy of the war, code name Operation Halberd. Nine transports ran from Gibraltar to Malta escorted by *Ark Royal, Nelson, Rodney* and *Prince of Wales*. The Italians sailed to intercept but aborted and returned home. *Nelson* was damaged by a torpedo south of Sardinia and the British capital ships returned to Gibraltar. The transport *Imperial Star* was sunk by an aerial torpedo but all her crew were rescued and the convoy reached Malta safely.

Ordered to the Far East to counter the developing Japanese threat, *Prince of Wales* left Greenock on 25 October 1941. In order to avoid submarines in the Mediterranean, the ship sailed down the west coast of Africa and called at Freetown, Cape Town and then across the Indian Ocean to Colombo before finally arriving in Singapore on 2 December. On 7 December the Japanese attacked the American fleet in Pearl Harbor and Britain and the United States immediately declared war on Japan. The next day Japanese troop landings in the north of Malaya

STOW-ON-THE-WOLD WAR MEMORIAL

Plymouth Naval Memorial

were reported. *Prince of Wales*, HMS *Repulse* and four escort destroyers (collectively known as Force Z) were sent to investigate.

Finding no signs of an invasion, the British ships turned and were heading back to Singapore when on the morning of 10 December they were located by enemy aircraft fifty miles off the Malaysian coast near Kuantan. A torpedo attack by 86 Japanese warplanes commenced at 11.18 am. The British ships had no air cover to help protect them and a high level bombing attack developed. One bomb penetrated the hull of *Prince of Wales* causing extensive casualties. She soon started to go down and the order to abandon ship was given. *Repulse* was sunk at 12.35 pm. followed by *Prince of Wales* fifty minutes later with a total loss of 840 men. Some survivors were picked up and Frederick was amongst them. The survivors were taken into Singapore and those who were fit enough were assigned to shore duties.

The Japanese advanced so rapidly down the Malayan peninsula that the British were taken by surprise. It was the first time they had faced a Japanese attack and they had expected it to come from the sea, not overland through the jungle. Kuala Lumpur was captured on 11 January 1942. The British forces were driven back onto Singapore Island where after two weeks of fierce fighting, the island's defences were overcome and the GOC, General Arthur Percival, formally surrendered shortly after 5.15pm with hostilities to cease at 8.30pm on 15 February 1942.

Frederick was one of fifteen sailors from *Prince of Wales* posted as missing believed killed the next day, 16 February 1942.

STOW-ON-THE-WOLD WAR MEMORIAL

Cap Badge of the Corps Of Royal Engineers

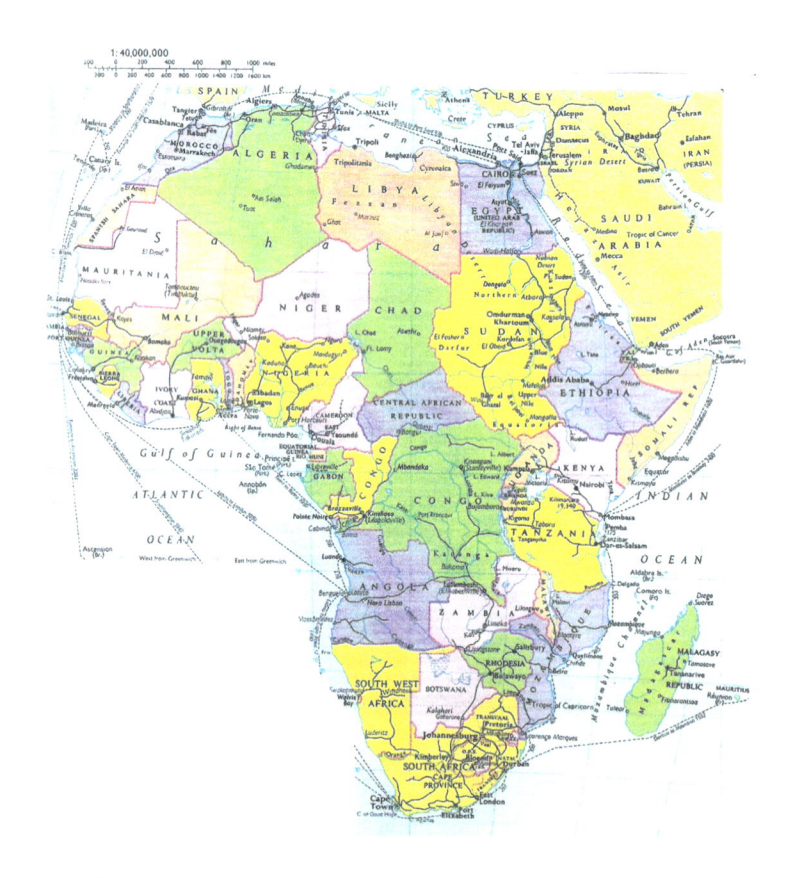

Pietermaritzburg is about 80 miles inland from Durban in South Africa

George Edward Miller

Date of Birth	17 July 1913 – Little Compton
Service	1866811 Sergeant, 22 Field Company, Royal Engineers
Date of Death	24 January 1942 – age 28
Stow Address	Sheep Street (1922)
	5 Evesham Road (1925)
Parents	Edward Miller
	Catherine Miller (nee Forgie)
	They were married in Brentford in 1910.
Siblings	Nora — b. 08.10.1911 Little Compton
	Frederick — b. 29.01.1916 Little Compton – *see page 282*
	Alexander — b. 20.11.1917 Little Compton – *was a Prisoner of War*
	Donald — b. 23.09.1919 Little Compton
Cemetery	Pietermaritzburg, Fort Napier Cemetery, Kwazulu Natal, South Africa. The cemetery contains 112 Commonwealth burials of the Second World War.

Notes

George was christened in St Denis's Church, Little Compton on 31 August 1917. His father's occupation was given as Soldier in the Baptism Register. When George was admitted to Stow Boys School in 1922, it was noted in the School Register that he had previously been at school in Little Compton. He left school in 1927 and joined the Army as a boy soldier.

During the Second World War a large transit and disposal camp was established in the Oribi area close to Pietermaritzburg. This camp was served by the Oribi Military Hospital, a convalescent depot which operated in the area in the hills overlooking the city.

Hospital ships brought sick and wounded troops from the western desert south to the hospital at Oribi. This solved the difficulty of moving casualties from North Africa to the United Kingdom because of dangers at sea and a lack of hospital capacity at home.

George died in hospital at Oribi on 24 January 1942 of pulmonary tuberculosis.

One summer Sunday morning at Maugersbury Manor c. 1938
Back Row: Ken Halford and Cyril King
Front Row: Joseph Rose and Tom Webley

Joseph Rose

Date of Birth	17 January 1921
Service	
Date of Death	
Stow Address	Back Walls – the cottage is now used by the staff of The Grapevine Hotel
Parents	Joseph Rose b. 1887 Westcote
	Mary Ann Rose (nee King)
Siblings	Iris Mary b. 1923 Stow
	John b. 1928 Stow
	Leslie George b. 1931 Stow
Cemetery	

Notes

Joseph's father (age 14) was working as a Farm Labourer at the time of the census in 1901 and living in Cemetery Walk, Stow, where he lodged with Linda Clifford, a widow (age 77), who was a small shopkeeper.

Joseph and his siblings were all christened in the Church of Our Lady and St Kenelm, Stow.

Joseph was a pupil at Stow Boys School and left in 1935.

Note:

I very much regret that I have been unable to trace what Joseph Rose did during World War Two that warranted his inclusion amongst the names of the men who are commemorated on the war memorial. There is no Commonwealth War Graves Commission record for him. It has been suggested that he served in the Merchant Navy but again I can find no record either on the Tower Hill Memorial (which records the names of 24,000 British merchant seamen from World War Two who have no known grave) or in the Seamen's Pouches, which are held in the National Archives at Kew and give details of individual seamen and the vessels they served on but 95,000 of these pouches were destroyed in the mid 20th century. I have not even been able to trace a Death Certificate for Joseph.

STOW-ON-THE-WOLD WAR MEMORIAL

Badge of 57 Squadron, Royal Air Force

Sergeant Observer Harry Toomer Smith

Henry Toomer Smith

Date of Birth	21 December 1919 – Stow
Service	926528 Sergeant (Observer), 57 Squadron, Royal Air Force Volunteer Force
Date of Death	Killed in action on 11 October 1941 – age 21
Stow Address	Church Street
	Sheep Street – Rutland House
Parents	Reginald Toomer Smith
	Emma Mary Smith (nee Castle) b. 1890 Moreton-in-Marsh
	They married in St Edward's on 6 August 1913.
Siblings	Rohilla Creama Toomer b. 12.03.1916 Stow
	Stella Letitia Toomer b. 29.04.1922 Stow
Cemetery	Rheinberg War Cemetery, Germany. Rheinberg is 24 kilometres north of Krefeld. There are over 3300 servicemen buried in this cemetery, most of them airmen who died in bombing raids over Germany. Some were first buried in isolated graves where their plane had crashed and were brought in to Rheinberg after the war. The cemetery was designed by Philip Hepworth and opened in 1946.
	Also commemorated on the family grave in Stow-on-the-Wold Cemetery.

Notes

Rutland House, Sheep Street, was originally the Swan Inn from 1446 to 1700. It is now called Peppercorns House.

Harry's father worked as a Horse Breaker and Trainer. In the 1930s he advertised in a tourist brochure for the North Cotswolds as "Reg T Smith's Riding School". He had stables in Well Lane. He was a widower (age 43) when he married Harry's mother (age 25) in 1913. She was the sister of Edward William Castle *(see page 48)*.

Harry was christened by the Rev J T Evans in St Edward's on 29 February 1920.

In July 1940 Harry volunteered to join the Royal Air Force and having trained as a navigator, joined 57 Squadron.

57 Squadron was at Lossiemouth from June 1940 where it took part in anti-shipping patrols. At the turn of the year they moved to Wyton in Huntingdonshire, flying Wellington night time bombers as part of Bomber Command Main Force.

At midnight on 10/11 October 1941 Harry's plane took off from Feltwell in Norfolk. It was

Rheinberg War Cemetery, Germany

a Wellington, number 9756, setting out to attack targets in Cologne. The plane was shot down near the city of Cologne and Harry and all the other crew members were killed.

From the Evesham Journal – Saturday October 18 1941
STOW SERGEANT OBSERVER MISSING
News has been received by Mr and Mrs R T Smith of Rutland House, Stow-on-the-Wold, that one of their sons, Sergeant-Observer Henry Toomer Smith of the RAF, is missing as the result of air operations.

Sergeant Smith, popularly known as "Harry", is aged 21 years. He was educated at Westwood Grammar School, Northleach and served his apprenticeship on leaving school with Mr G A French, Stow-on-the-Wold, as a grocer. He was an ardent sportsman and goalkeeper to the Stow AFC eleven in pre-war days. He entered the RAF in July 1940.

John Sumption

St Mary's Churchyard, Prestbury

John Barnett Sumption

Date of Birth   1922 – Prestbury
Service
Date of Death   30 April 1944 – age 21
Stow Address   Little Elms, The Square
Parents   Thomas Sebastian Sumption   b. 1884 Prestbury, Gloucestershire
                      Elsie May Sumption (nee Robinson)
Siblings   Josephine Mary   b. 1920, d. 1921 Prestbury
                      Constance
Cemetery   St Mary's Churchyard, Prestbury

Notes

At the time of the census in 1901, John's father, age 17, was working as a Grocer's assistant. The Sumption family owned the grocer's shop and post office in Prestbury and the Robinson family owned the bakery next door. The Sumptions have been sub-postmasters at Prestbury for several generations.

John's uncle, Major John F Sumption of the Canadian forces, died of wounds on 22 October 1916 and is commemorated on the Prestbury war memorial. He was a partner in the Montreal firm of Sumption & Hughes.

When John's sister Josephine was christened in St Mary's Church, Prestbury in 1920, the family's address was given as Greenmount, Oaklands. After his father's death in 1927 at the early age of 43, John's mother took a job as companion housekeeper to Mrs Howman at Little Elms, The Square, Stow.

John died at Highnam Isolation Hospital, Gloucestershire of pulmonary tuberculosis. His death was registered by his aunt, Miss A F Robinson, and on his Death Certificate he was described as Plumber's apprentice of The Elms, Stow-on-the-Wold. He was buried in the churchyard at Prestbury in the same grave as his father and baby sister Josephine. John's Sumption and Robinson grandparents are all buried close by.

Note:

I very much regret that I have been unable to trace what John Sumption did during World War Two that warranted his inclusion amongst the names of the men who are commemorated on the war memorial. There is no Commonwealth War Graves Commission record for him and although John is wearing uniform in his photograph, neither the Army Personnel Centre Historical Disclosures Department nor the Royal Air Force Personnel Management Agency have any record for him in their archives.

STOW-ON-THE-WOLD WAR MEMORIAL

The Cross Of Wood

God be with you and us who go our way
And leave you dead upon the ground you won;
For you at last the long fatigue is done,
The hard march ended, you have rest today.

You were our friends, with you we watched the dawn
Gleam through the rain of the long winter night,
With you we labored till the morning light
Broke on the village, shell-destroyed and torn.

Not now for you the glorious return
To steep Strand valleys, to the Severn leas
By Tewkesbury and Gloucester, or the trees
Of Cheltenham under high Cotswold stern.

For you no medals such as others wear –
A cross of bronze for those approved brave –
To you is given, above a shallow grave,
The wooden Cross that marks you resting there.

Rest you content, more honourable far
Than all the Orders is the Cross of Wood
The Symbol of self-sacrifice that stood
Bearing the God whose brethren you are.

This poem was written by Lieutenant Cyril Winterbotham of 1/5th Battalion Gloucestershire Regiment a month before his death. He was killed attacking a German trench near Ovillers on the Somme on 27th August 1916.

COOK ONCE
EAT TWICE

NADIYA HUSSAIN

MICHAEL JOSEPH

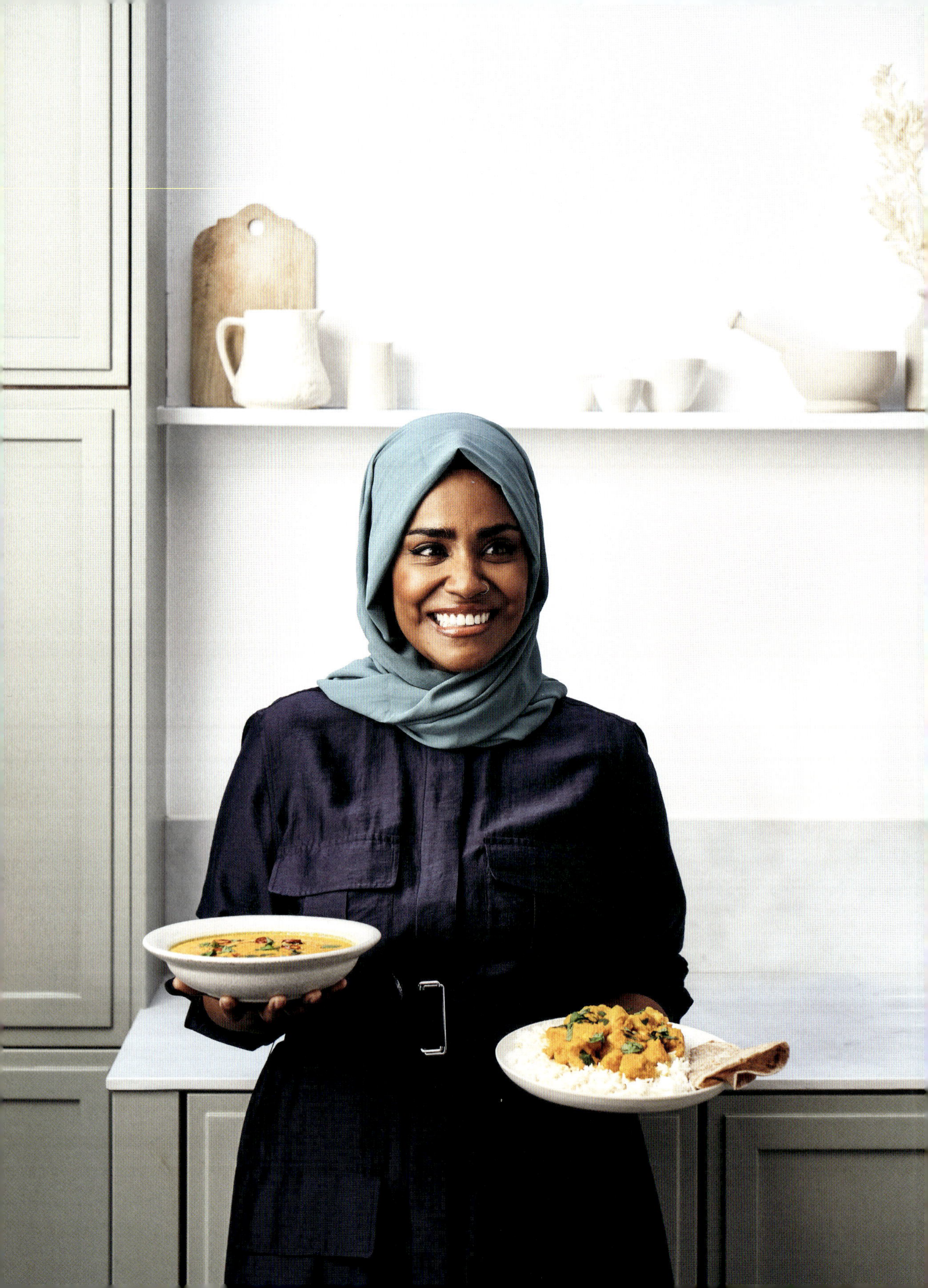

COOK ONCE
EAT TWICE

NADIYA HUSSAIN

Photography by Chris Terry

Based on the programme from BBC

THIS IS FOR ABDAL, THE MAN THAT TRULY APPRECIATES THE 'EAT TWICE' ELEMENT OF THIS BOOK.

CONTENTS

INTRODUCTION 6–7

HOW THIS BOOK WORKS 8–10

SAVVY SHOPPING ON A BUDGET 12–13

NADIYA'S ESSENTIAL KITCHEN KIT 14–15

DEFROSTING INSTRUCTIONS 16–17

BACK TO BASICS 18–57
LOVIN' YOUR LEFTOVERS 58–95
READY MEALS 96–131
TWO DISHES 132–165
NEVER WASTED AGAIN 166–197
EASY BAKES 198–225
WASTE NOT WANT NOT 226–245

INDEX 246–252

THANKS 254–55

INTRODUCTION

As a mother raising three children, how I cook and what I cook is ever-changing. Every year, we face new challenges with a growing family, and with those challenges come changes in the way we live, and these changes almost always affect how we eat and what we eat. This means I've had lots of practice at finding new ways of stretching ingredients to feed the whole family as well as to make life easier. I've always got a few clever uses for leftovers, delicious ideas for the ingredients we waste the most, recipes for cooking two meals out of one set of ingredients, and dishes and bakes that keep the longest in the fridge and freezer. These are the ways of cooking that make my everyday easy and tasty, and I want to share them all with you.

As the kids get older, their curiosities towards the basic day-to-day home-cooked meals increases. I've been asked, how do I poach an egg properly? How can I make a simple lasagne? What do I do with the leftovers? These are just a few questions of many that I have answered in this book. It has been the relentless questioning from them that has spurred me on to put everything in one place.

As they teeter on the brink of adulthood and full independence, I wanted to write a cookbook that is stripped back and has all the essentials anyone would need. Not just for children becoming adults, but also for adults who don't cook much or at all; for people who want to get more confident in the kitchen; for those who need inspiration for their everyday staples; or for anyone who simply wants a taste of some of the food we love to make and eat at home.

So, I have worked to include everything I know you will need to make this the most useful book on your shelf. Leaving you feeling inspired, accomplished and with a full belly.

Nadiya x

INTRODUCTION / 7

HOW THIS BOOK WORKS

This book is made up of seven chapters, each one serving its own great purpose. First, you have '**BACK TO BASICS**', with all the recipes that make a great foundation for a good meal, including Ultimate Mashed Potatoes, an easy recipe for bread, a simple staple tomato sauce, and a straightforward best roast chicken. In my opinion these are some of the most important recipes to learn and love, because they are the ones that you will make time and time again.

Now, if like me you don't like waste, but you do like the satisfaction of making the most of your ingredients and you are looking for ways to up your game when it comes to using leftovers, the chapter for you is '**LOVIN' YOUR LEFTOVERS**'. There are delicious recipes like a simple Courgette Spaghetti, that you can turn into a quick frittata using the leftovers. Or a mouthwatering Mongolian beef that can be enjoyed again as Seaweed Rice Wraps. Nothing in your kitchen need be wasted and this chapter can really change how you cook and how you think in the kitchen too.

Even though I am someone who has never bought a supermarket ready meal, I do appreciate the ease of knowing there is something in the freezer for a speedy mealtime when I need one. Something that can be taken out, heated up and eaten in the time it takes for you to shower and get into your PJs. So you will love my '**READY MEALS**' chapter. There are great crowd-pleasing meals, like Beef Stew and Dumplings, Meatball Marinara, Teriyaki Salmon and many more. All of these are make-ahead recipes that are prepared on a day where you have a little bit more time, cooled and frozen, ready to enjoy at a later date, when you need that ready meal, ready!

'**TWO DISHES**' is a magical chapter that allows you to make a dish that is halved before one of the two batches gets transformed into something entirely different by introducing a handful of new ingredients. Like transforming a Carrot Soup into a Carrot and Cod Curry or making a Stroganoff and then turning one half into a Hand-held Pie. What's not to love about cooking once but ending up with two completely different and delicious meals?

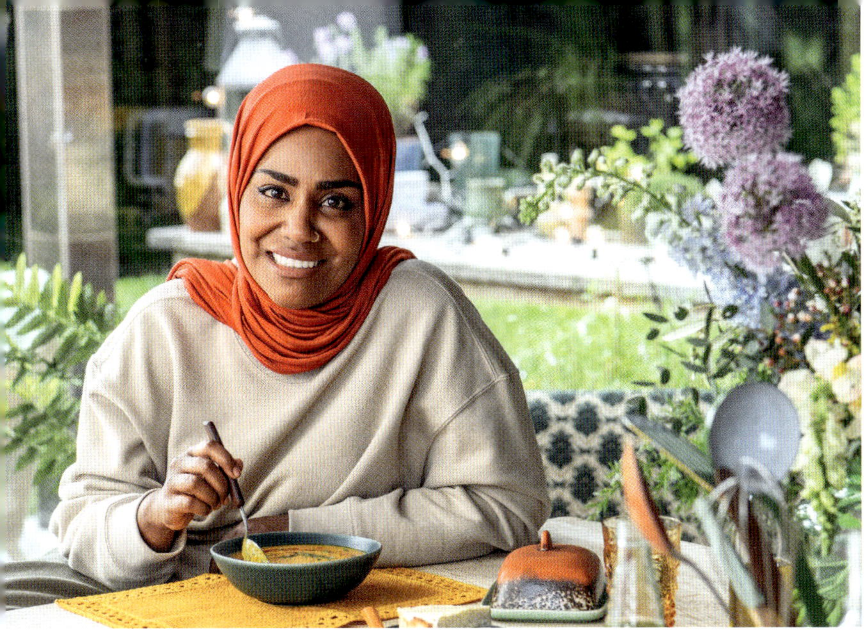
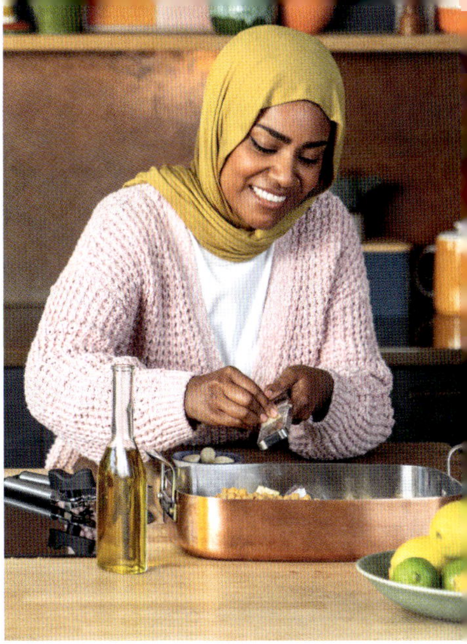
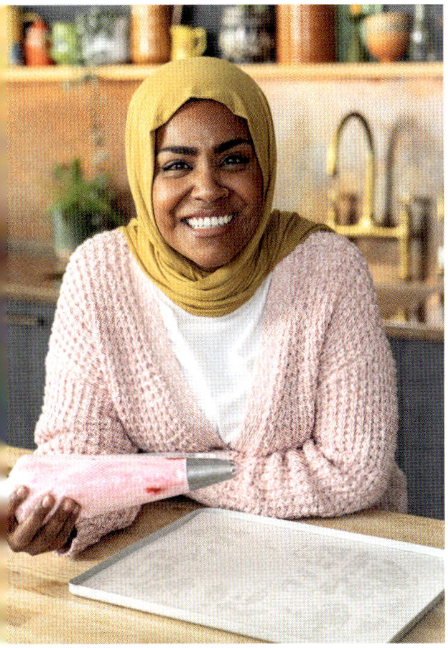
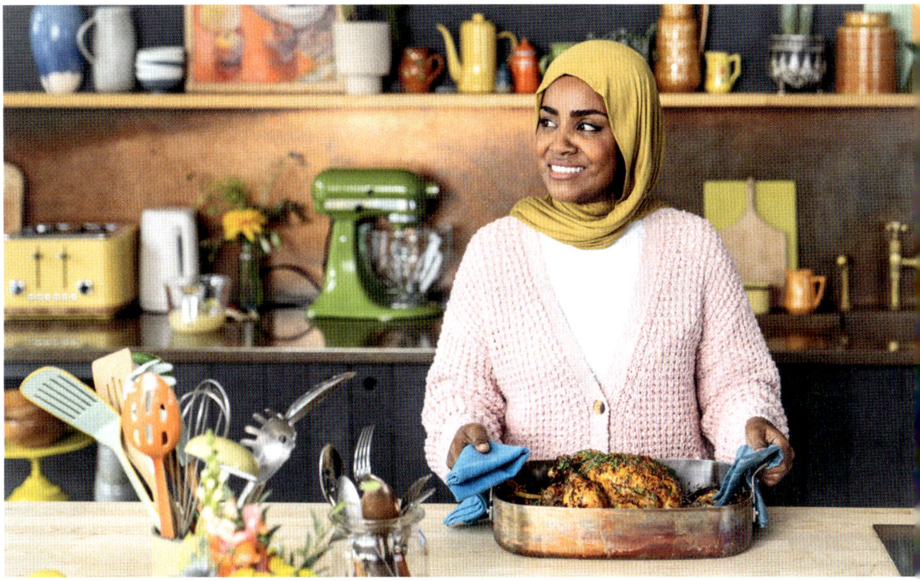
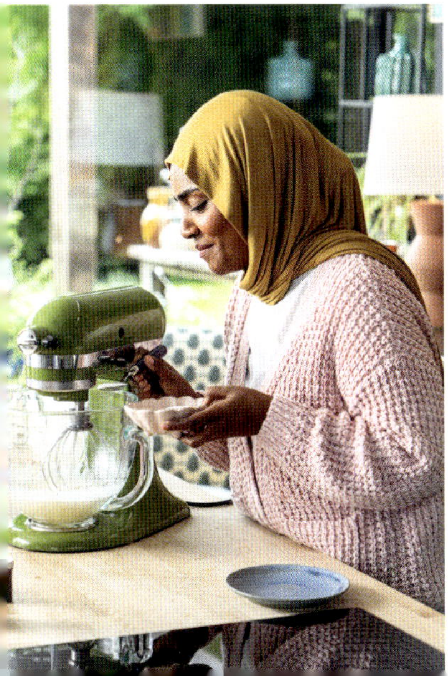
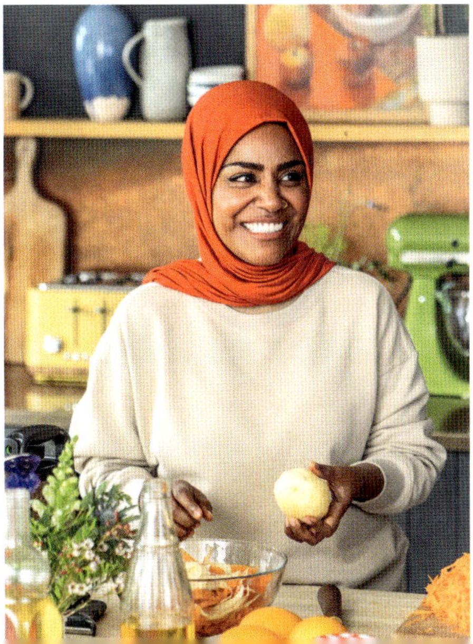
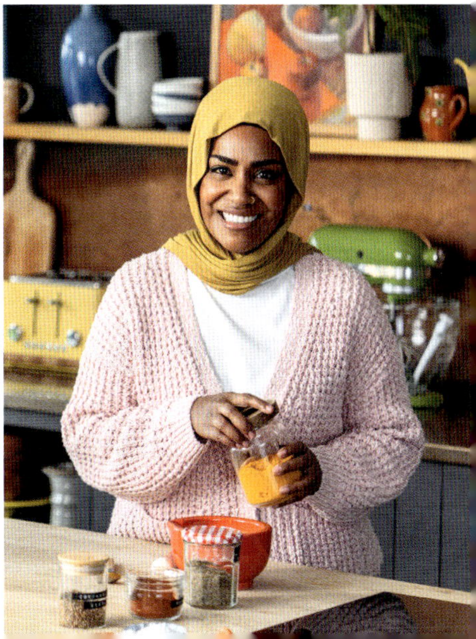

'**NEVER WASTED AGAIN**' is one of my favourite chapters. This chapter takes the key ingredients that are the most thrown away in the UK, such as milk, bread, cheese, potatoes, bagged salad, bananas and more, and gives you a whole section of mouth-watering recipes so that you never have to throw these ingredients out ever again. Try the Bagged Salad Green Chutney, Buttermilk Pancakes, Banana and Brown Sugar Drop Doughnuts and so many more.

'**EASY BAKES**' guides you through the world of baking with simple sweet recipes that won't leave you flustered. These treats have a long storage life, so they make the most of the time you spend baking and you'll always have something delicious tucked away in the fridge or a cake tin. You could make the Espresso Chocolate Cake, or perhaps the Raspberry Pudding Pots. Or how about the Peach and Pecan Crumble?

Finally, think about all the things we throw into the food waste bins. Well, imagine taking apple peels and making an apple jam. Or prawn shells destined to be thrown away but instead made into a fragrant oil, or perhaps date pips that get discarded without a second thought, imagine making a date coffee that is completely caffeine free. '**WASTE NOT WANT NOT**' is the chapter that shows you how to truly make the most of every last part of your ingredients. It'll save you money and get you thinking differently about what you can cook with.

Cook Once, Eat Twice has everything you need to get started in the kitchen in a way that will simplify your week and make life more convenient. Equipping yourself with the basics is essential to cooking delicious recipes that will be everything but basic. Having quick, home-made 'ready' meals stashed away in your freezer will save time when you need dinner on the table, and fast. Making two recipes out of one dish will help your food and your money go further. Clever ideas for using up your leftovers and ingredients that would otherwise be thrown out will build your confidence when you are confronted with just a few things left in the cupboard. And delicious, speedy treats that keep well, will make you more inclined to bake them so you'll always have something sweet and ready-to-go.

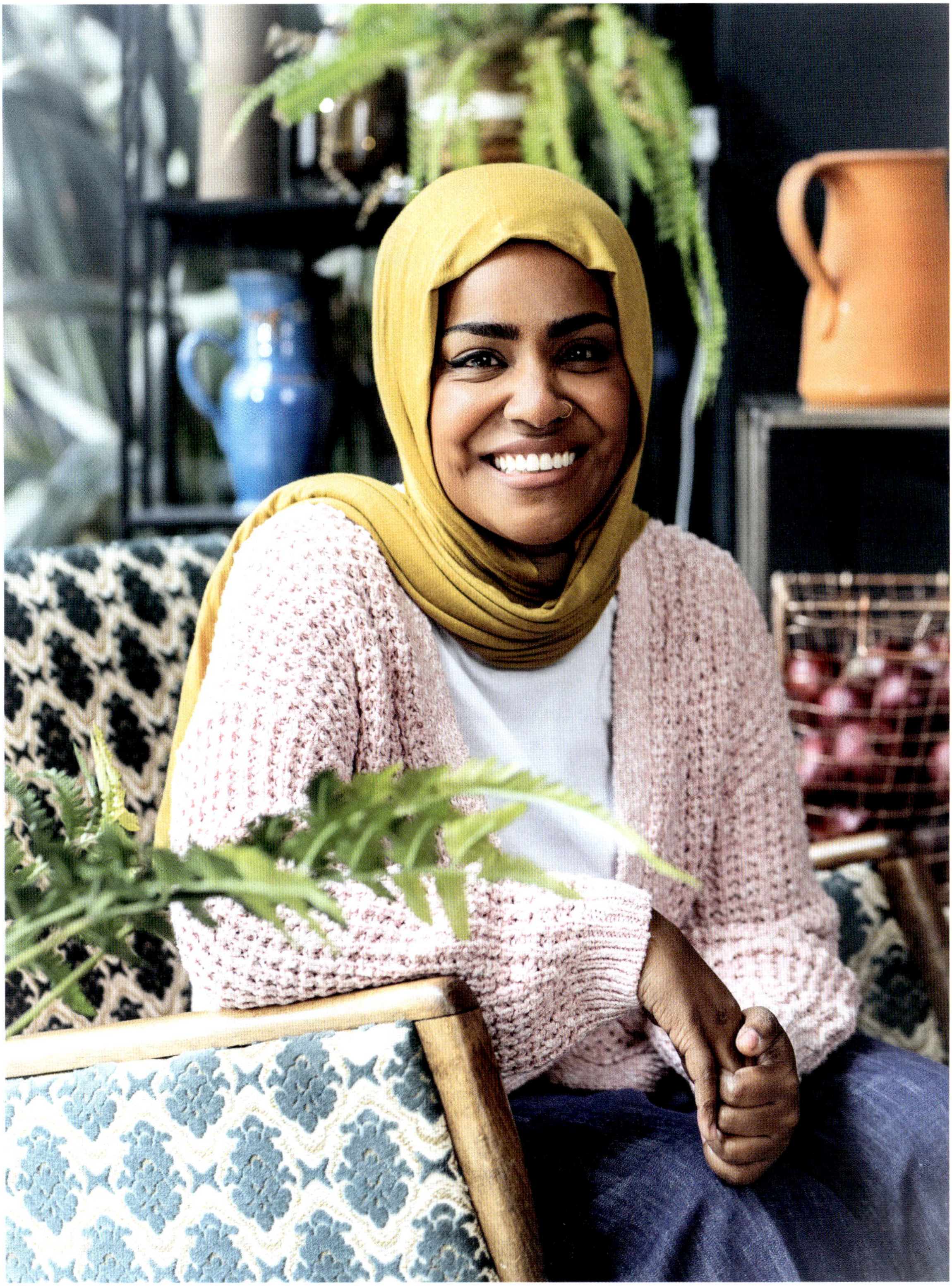

SAVVY SHOPPING ON A BUDGET

Fridge organization is so important when it comes to savvy supermarket shopping. If you arrange and label all your essentials in the fridge, freezer and cupboards, you will know when things are running low by sight, before you avoid buying things you don't need. That way you contribute to wasting less before you have even started.

Have a shopping list attached to your fridge or saved on your phone. As soon as something needs purchasing, put it straight onto the list ready for the next time you go to the shops.

Once you know what you need to restock you can start planning your meals for the week ahead. It doesn't need to be set in stone but having an idea of which nights are the busy ones and knowing which members of your family will be in on which day means that you can have a clearer idea of options for meals and identify the moments where you can cook ahead. Plus having a rough plan will help you stay focused in the supermarket so you don't waste money on ingredients you don't need.

Another thing to remember is that own and value branded items are, for the most part, often just as good as more expensive brands. A lot of the time you are paying for pretty packaging but what is inside isn't necessarily better.

Every recipe in this book I've written with accessible ingredients in mind. This is the food that we are most likely to buy, the ingredients that we are most likely to waste and that you can find in supermarkets everywhere, which means that whoever and wherever you are, this book will be an incredibly helpful one.

SAVVY SHOPPING ON A BUDGET / 13

NADIYA'S ESSENTIAL KITCHEN KIT

Before you get started, here are some pointers. Make sure you have a few very good staple kitchen essentials; these tools will help you to get the best out of your time in the kitchen.

- **A GOOD KITCHEN KNIFE**
  For easy chopping and prep

- **KNIFE SHARPENER**
  So you can easily slice ingredients precisely. Be very careful when your knife is sharpened.

- **A REALLY GOOD POTATO PEELER OF YOUR CHOICE**
  For all of your peeling needs. Remember to keep your potato or fruit skins!

- **LARGE SERVING SPOON OR LADLE**
  For dividing meals up into containers

- **WEIGHING SCALES**
  For baking

- **ROLLING PIN**
  For pastry

- **HAND BLENDER**
  For soups, curries and sauces

- **TWO HEAVY-BASED FRYING PANS OR CASSEROLE DISHES**
  For making two meals at once

- **SMALL BAKING DISHES**
  For cooking individual portions that can go straight in the fridge or freezer

- **MEAL PREP DISHES & RESEALABLE FREEZER BAGS**
  For easy food storage

- **LABEL MAKER**
  Not essential, but great to have to put labels on your containers of leftovers and ready meals

- **MASKING TAPE**
  If you haven't got a label maker, I find masking tape a great way to label and organize your meals

- **MARKER PEN OR PENCIL**
  For marking up labels

- **MASON JARS AND JAM JARS**
  For food storage

- **TIN FOIL**
  For covering meals that are being kept in the fridge or freezer

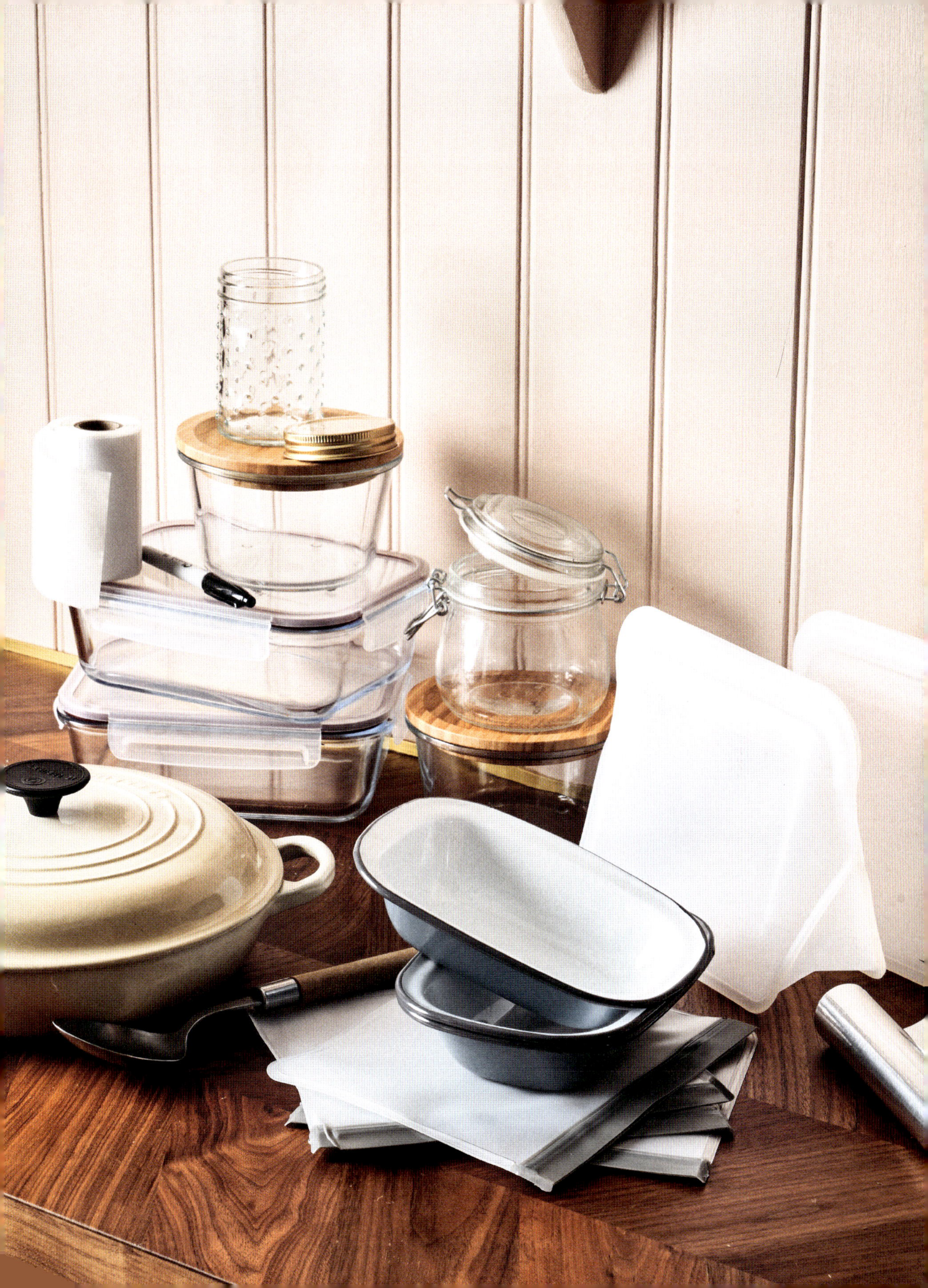

DEFROSTING INSTRUCTIONS

Lots of the recipes in this book can be cooked straight from the freezer, but if you plan on defrosting meals before heating them up, then I always advise to defrost in the fridge. <u>Note</u>: always lay a cloth or piece of kitchen paper underneath it to mop up any condensation.

❄ Once any meal is defrosted, heat until piping hot and eat within 24 hours.

❄ Leftovers can be stored in the fridge and should be eaten within 2–3 days. **<u>Do not refreeze or refrigerate again after warming</u>**.

❄ If you are keeping rice, cool thoroughly, place in the fridge and eat within 1 day. Again, if reheating make sure it's piping hot.

❄ Make sure that any leftovers or meals for the fridge or freezer are properly cooled before putting them inside, otherwise you may increase the temperature and create somewhere that bacteria can multiply.

Now let's get on and do some cooking!

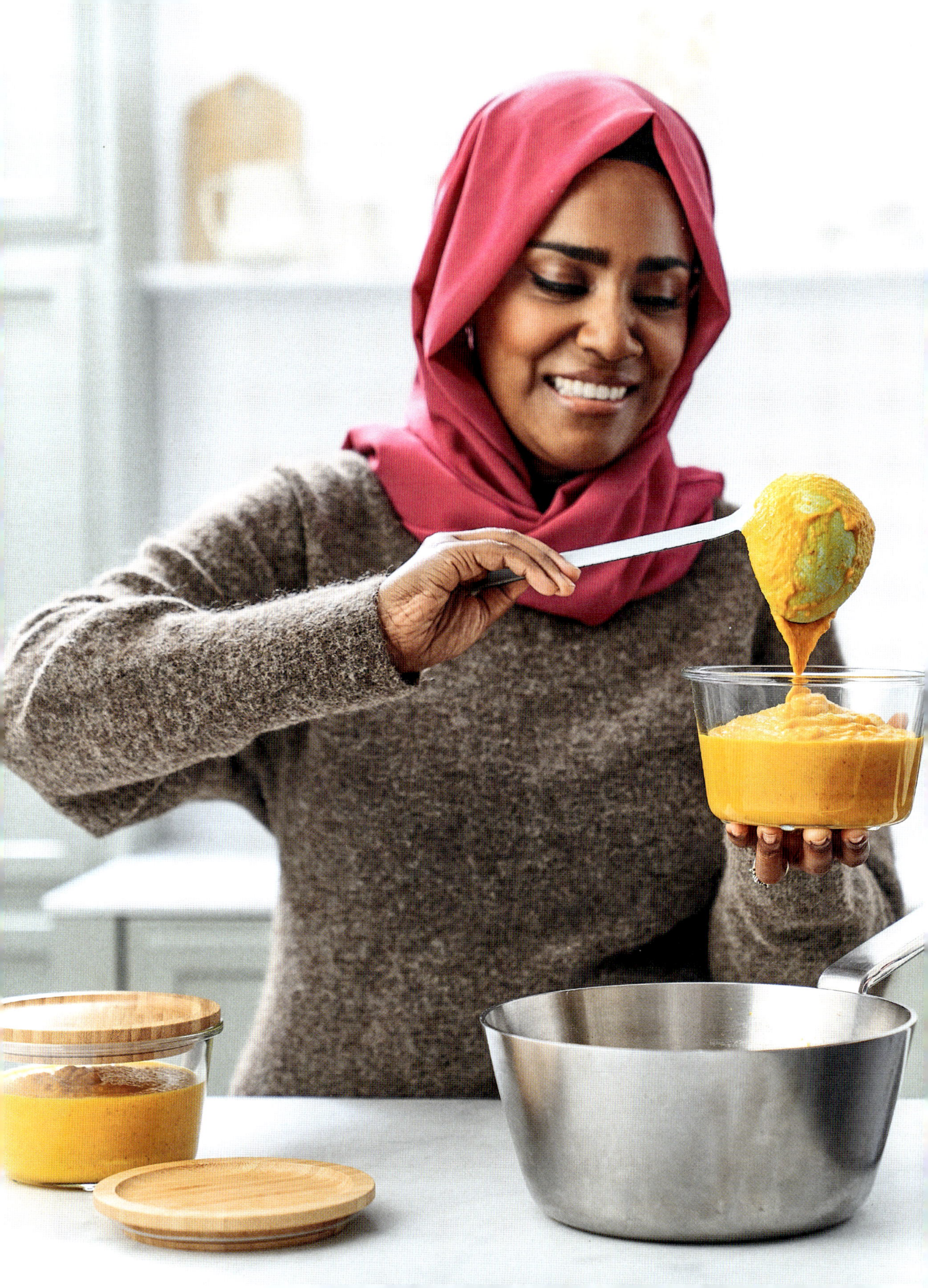

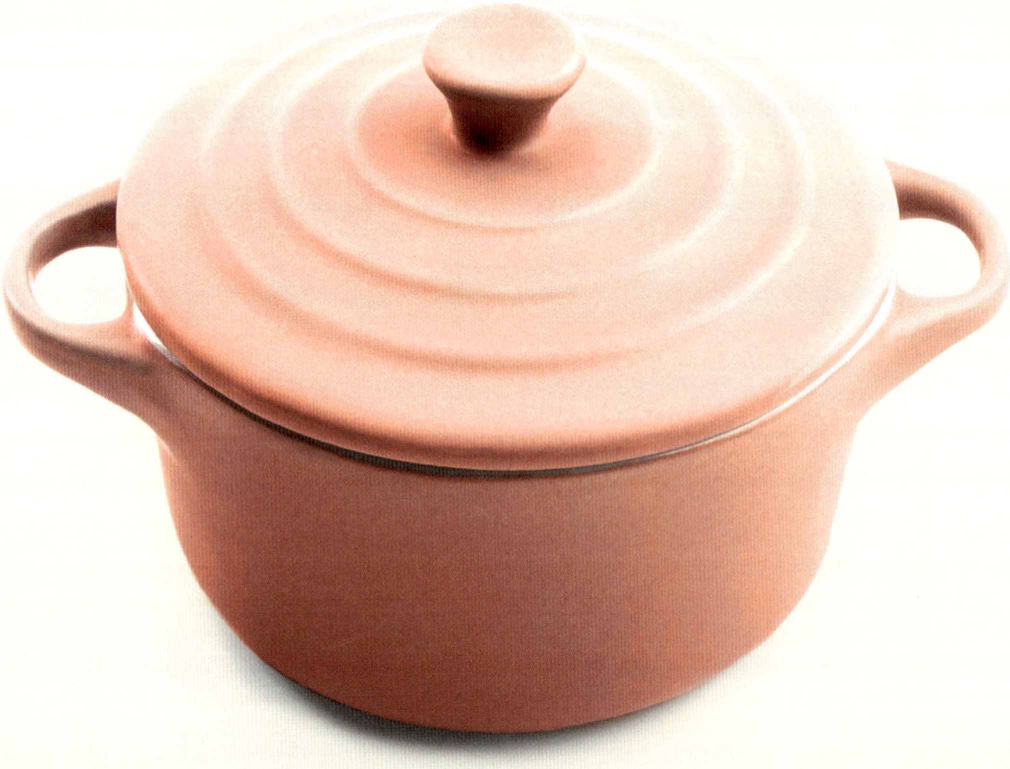

BACK TO

↓
BASICS

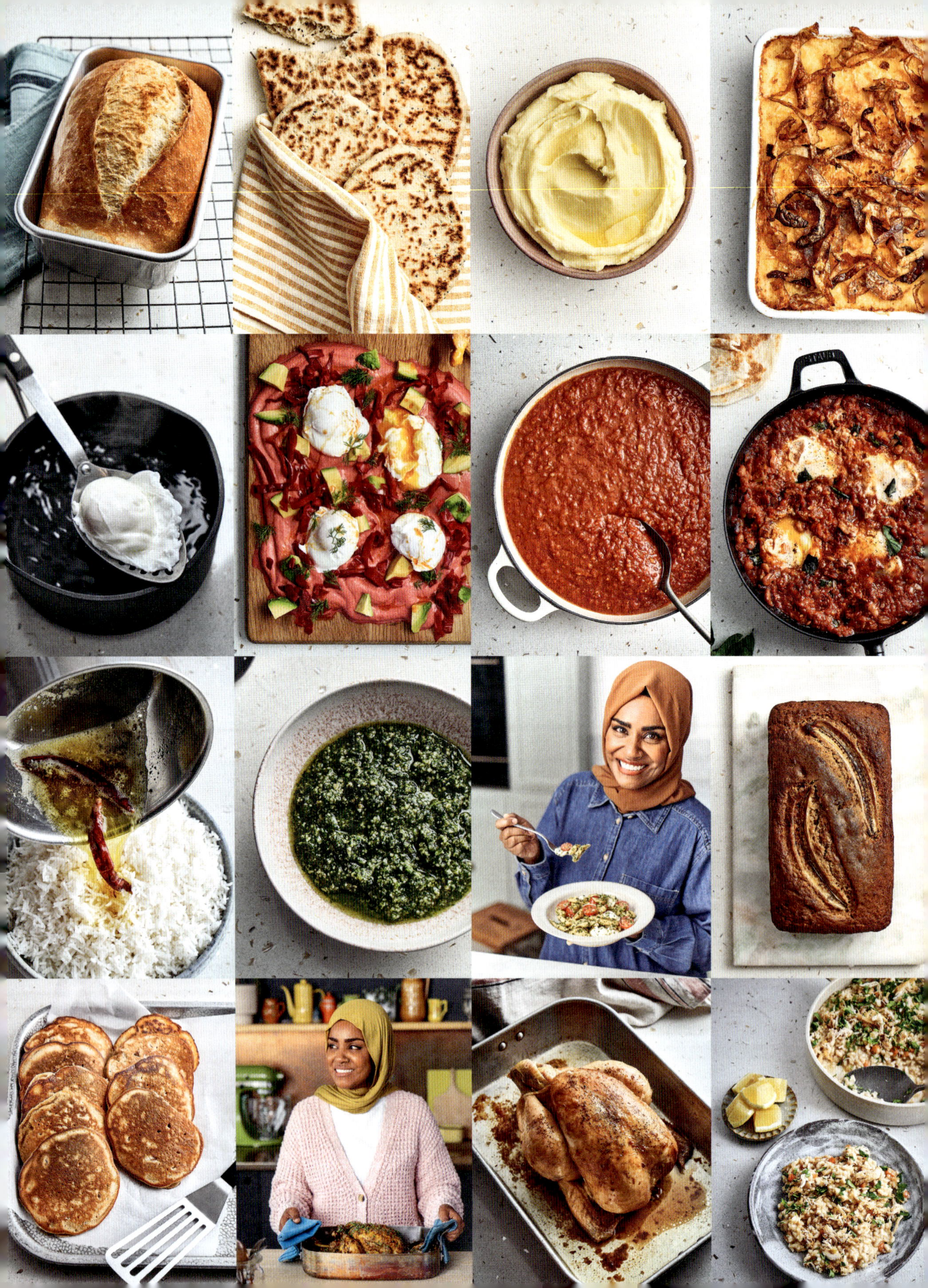

BACK TO BASICS

A chapter of easy essential staples that are simply great to have in your repertoire rather than buying convenience versions. Each is accompanied by a second recipe which can be made using that same meal so that you can get the most from your basics and use every inch.

LOAF OF BREAD
↓
NO-NONSENSE NAAN

ULTIMATE MASHED POTATO
↓
CHEESE FEST POTATO BAKE

POACHED EGGS MADE SIMPLE
↓
POACHED EGG BREAKFAST BOARD

EVERYTHING TOMATO SAUCE
↓
TOMATO BEAN SHAKSHUKA

SIMPLE RICE
↓
CHEAT'S PILAU

PERFECT HERBY PESTO
↓
SCISSOR CUT PESTO PASTA

BASIC BANANA BREAD
↓
BANANA BREAD PANCAKES

JUST ROAST CHICKEN
↓
CARCASS RISOTTO

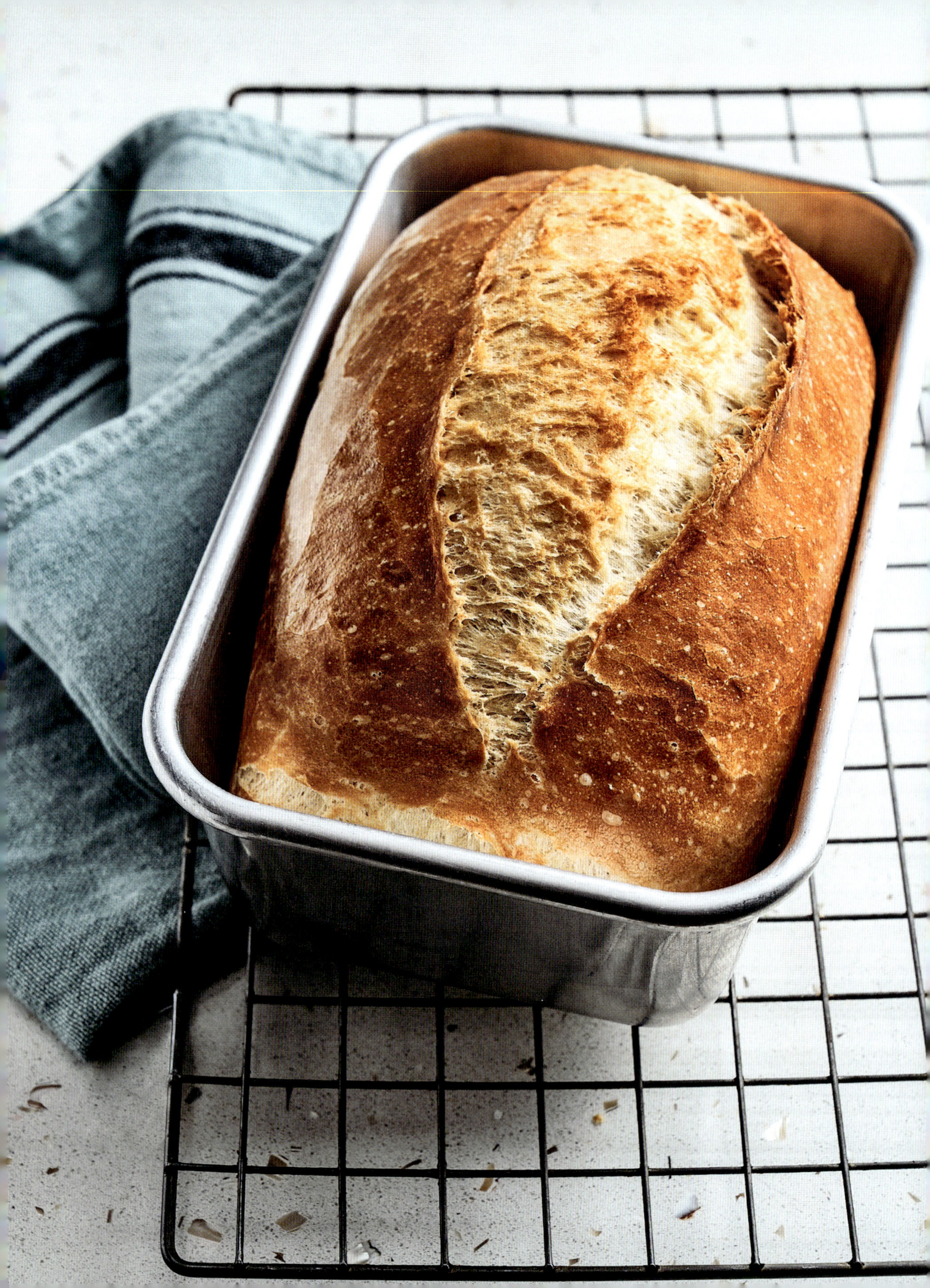

LOAF OF BREAD

I know it's easy to buy a loaf of bread, but it's so worth knowing how to make your own loaf from scratch. And one thing I can guarantee is that it will always taste better than a loaf of bread bought from the shops.

ALSO MAKES: NO-NONSENSE NAAN (PAGE 24)

PREP: 25 MINS **PROVE:** 1–2 HOURS
BAKE: 45 MINS
MAKES: 1 LOAF

500g strong bread flour, plus extra for dusting

7g fast-action yeast

1 teaspoon salt

3 teaspoons caster sugar

350ml lukewarm water

Start by making the dough. Put the strong bread flour in a large mixing bowl along with the fast-action yeast, salt and caster sugar. Give it all a good mix so everything is well combined. Make a well in the centre and pour in the lukewarm water. Mix and bring the dough together till you have no more floury bits left in the bowl.

If you are using a stand mixer, attach a dough hook and knead the mixture on a high speed till the dough is stretchy and smooth. If you are kneading by hand, lightly flour the worktop and knead for 10 minutes until you have a dough that is smooth and stretchy.

Cover and leave in a greased bowl in a warm place till the dough has doubled in size. This can take longer than an hour or less depending on how warm it is. Once doubled, knock the dough back to remove all the air bubbles.

Place the dough onto a floured surface and have a 900g non-stick loaf tin at the ready.

Roll out the dough and tuck the ends in. Drop into the tin, seam-side down. Cover and leave to prove for about 30 minutes till the dough has filled the tin and risen.

Preheat the oven to 170°C with a baking tray in the base.

Uncover the dough, slash down the middle (lengthways) using a sharp knife and pop into the middle of the oven. Add some hot water to the tray in the base – creating steam in the oven makes for a loaf with a delicious crust. Bake for 45 minutes.

Once baked, remove from the tin and cool on a wire rack.

As soon as it is cool enough, you will be ready to devour your bread. I promise you, once you have baked your first loaf you will keep on coming back for more.

TIP *Bread can be sliced and frozen, then toasted from frozen in a toaster and you will never have to see mouldy bread again!*

NO-NONSENSE NAAN

We grew up on naan, not because it was traditional, but because Dad would make an extra few naan, whack them in a foil packet and bring them home to us. They were at their best warm and straight out of the bag. This recipe is a great starter one for making very simple naan using a bread dough recipe, as on the previous page.

PREP: 30 MINS
PROVE: 1–2 HOURS
COOK: 15 MINS
MAKES: 6 NAAN

- 500g strong bread flour, plus extra for dusting
- 2 tablespoons onion seeds
- 7g fast-action yeast
- 1 teaspoon salt
- 3 teaspoons caster sugar
- 350ml lukewarm water

For the butter

- 150g salted butter, melted
- Pinch of salt
- 1 clove of garlic, minced

Start by making the dough. Put the strong bread flour in a large mixing bowl along with the onion seeds, fast-action yeast, salt and caster sugar. Give it all a good mix so everything is well combined.

Make a well in the centre and pour in the lukewarm water. Mix and bring the dough together till you have no more floury bits left in the bowl.

If you are using a stand mixer, attach a dough hook and knead the mixture on a high speed till the dough is stretchy and smooth. If you are kneading by hand, lightly flour the worktop and knead for 10 minutes until you have a dough that is smooth and stretchy.

Cover and leave in a greased bowl in a warm place till the dough has doubled in size. This can take longer than an hour or less depending on where you place the bowl and how hot it is in that spot. Once doubled, knock the dough back to remove all the air bubbles.

Divide the mixture into six equal mounds on a baking tray. Cover with some greased clingfilm and leave to double in size in the fridge. This process will take longer for them to double, but it will make it easier for them to be rolled out and much easier to handle.

Make the flavoured butter by mixing the melted butter, salt and garlic together.

Once the naan have risen, take each ball and, on a lightly floured surface, roll the dough out to about 3mm thin.

Heat a non-stick pan over a medium to high heat – this is the best way to achieve the scorch marks that you would traditionally get in a tandoor. Put a naan in the pan and cook for 3 minutes on each side.

Brush the naan with the flavoured butter and then do the same with the rest of the dough till you have cooked them all. Enjoy your fluffy, buttery naan!

TIP *You can do so much to flavour these naan, so go to town and make naan your way. Try adding cumin seeds, caraway seeds, ajwain, chilli flakes or sesame seeds.*

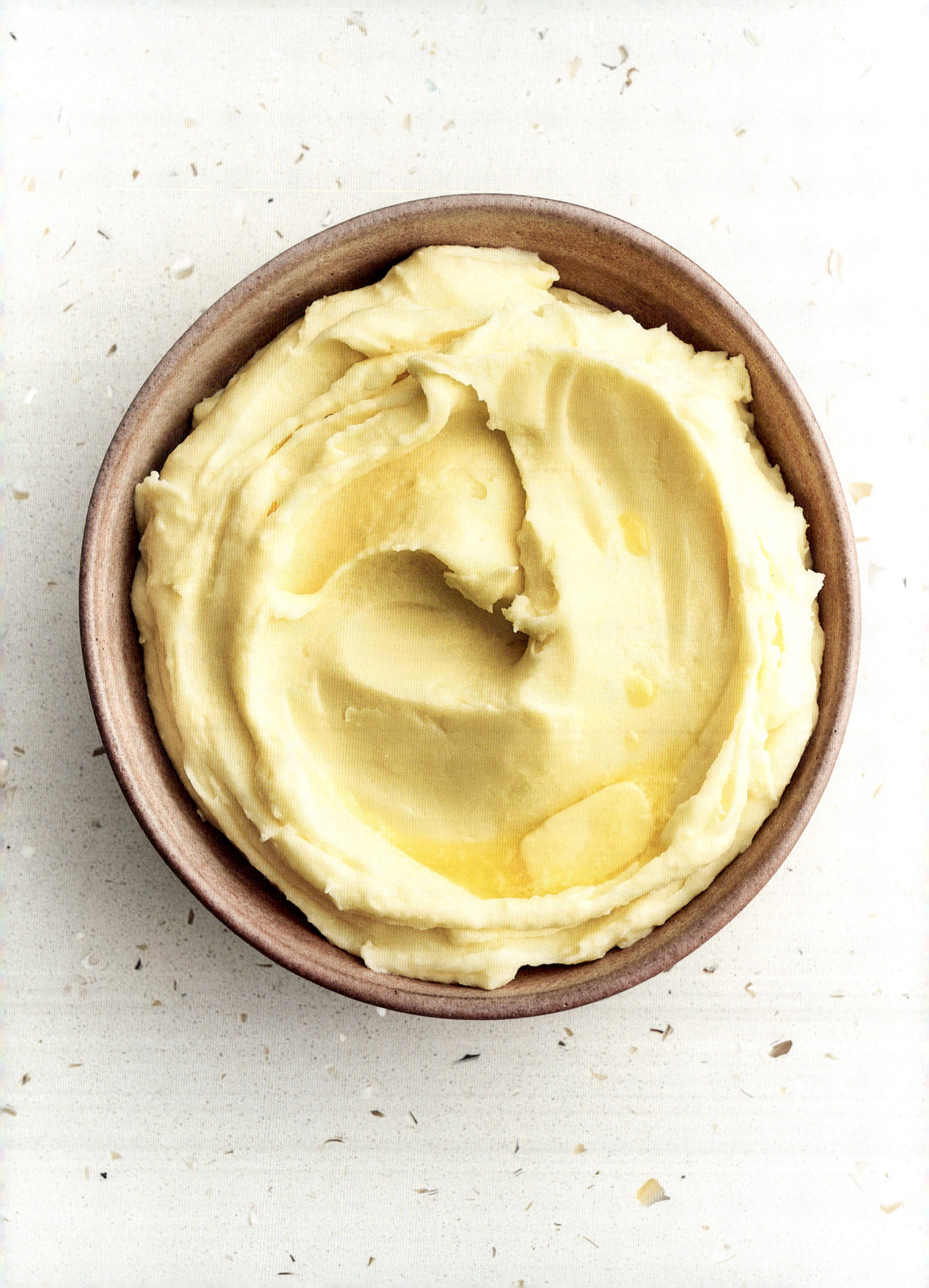

ULTIMATE MASHED POTATO

My niece Aleesha categorically says that I make the best mash in the world and she might not be wrong. If I make mash, I cannot eat it without her and I often send her a small Tupperware with her name on so she can enjoy it in all its buttery goodness. I can't gatekeep something this good!

ALSO MAKES: CHEESE FEST POTATO BAKE (PAGE 28–29)

PREP: 10 MINS **COOK:** 20–25 MINS

SERVES: 6

1.5kg Maris Piper potatoes

250ml cream

150g salted butter

2 teaspoons salt, plus an extra pinch

5 tablespoons full-fat mayonnaise

TIP *If you have saved the potato water and it has cooled, use it for your house plants. Potato water has a natural fungicide in it so it's great to keep away any fungi, nasties and bugs. So, water your house plants with this cooled water whenever you can.*

When making mashed potato, it is so important to get the right potato – something that is fluffy and breaks down well. So, Maris Piper potatoes work best for mash.

A little care needs to be taken in prepping them too. Peel the potatoes and cube them so that the potatoes are roughly the same size and will cook evenly. What you don't want is some potatoes that are cooked right down to mush and others that are still rock solid.

Now we've done some admin, let's make some mash! Put the potatoes in a large, roomy pan, so the potatoes have room to move as they boil and bounce. Pour in cold water till they are completely submerged, then add a generous pinch of salt and boil over a high heat for 20–25 minutes.

You will know the potatoes are cooked by inserting a skewer or knife into a potato. If it slides off, the potatoes are cooked and if it stays on there, they need some more time. Drain the potatoes into a colander but be sure to pop a bowl underneath and reserve that water (for anyone who has plants, this is for you, see tip below).

Leave the water to cool and the potatoes to air-dry for 10 minutes. Pop the cooked potatoes back into the same pan.

One by one, squeeze each potato through a ricer till you have done them all. You can absolutely use a masher, but I much prefer a ricer as this guarantees no lumps. Don't use a stick blender as this just creates mash that has the texture of wallpaper glue!

Once the potatoes have gone through the ricer, add the cream, butter, salt and mayo and mix till the butter has melted and you have a smooth, creamy mashed potato. It should be velvety, buttery-smooth and seasoned to perfection. If this is the only reason my niece visits, I don't care! Great mash, happy family!

CHEESE FEST POTATO BAKE

As if my kids don't already like mashed potatoes enough, this is up there as a firm top five in my family. It's great for when you want something stodgy, filling, yummy and simple. Perfect for serving your mash up in a different way.

PREP: 10 MINS **COOK:** 35–45 MINS

SERVES: 6

1.5kg Maris Piper potatoes

250ml cream

150g salted butter

2 teaspoons salt, plus an extra pinch

5 tablespoons full-fat mayonnaise

For the potato skins

3 tablespoons olive oil

3 teaspoons paprika

½ teaspoon salt

For the cheesy breadcrumbs

350g mature Cheddar cheese, grated

175g white breadcrumbs

Peel the potatoes, reserving the peels, then cube the potatoes so that they are roughly the same size and will cook evenly. Put the potatoes in a large, roomy pan, so the potatoes have room to move as they boil and bounce. Pour in cold water till they are completely submerged, then add a generous pinch of salt and boil over a high heat for 20–25 minutes.

While they are cooking, start on the potato peels. Put the potato peels in a bowl, drizzle over the olive oil and, using your hands, make sure the skins are coated. Now add the paprika and salt, making sure they are evenly distributed.

You can now crisp these up in an air fryer at 200°C for 15–18 minutes. If you don't have an air fryer, this can also be done in an oven at 200°C for the same time or until they are crispy. Once they are done, set aside.

Now, back to the mash. You will know the potatoes are cooked by inserting a skewer or knife into a potato. If it slides off, the potatoes are cooked and if it stays on there, they need some more time. Drain the potatoes into a colander but be sure to pop a bowl underneath and reserve that water (for anyone who has plants, this is for you, see tip on page 27).

Leave the water to cool and the potatoes to air-dry for 10 minutes. Pop the cooked potatoes back into the same pan.

One by one, squeeze each potato through a ricer till you have done them all. You can absolutely use a masher, but I much prefer a ricer as this guarantees no lumps. Don't use a stick blender as this just creates mash that has the texture of wallpaper glue!

Once the potatoes have gone through the ricer, add the cream, butter, salt and mayo and mix till the butter has melted and you have a smooth, creamy mashed potato.

Preheat the oven to 200°C if not already on. Have a 25cm roasting dish at the ready.

Mix the cheese and breadcrumbs in a bowl together and set aside. Take half the mash mixture, spoon into the roasting dish and create an even layer. Add half the cheese/breadcrumb mixture right on top in an even layer, then add the rest of the potato on top. Finally, sprinkle over the rest of the cheese breadcrumb mixture.

Sprinkle over the spiced-up potato peels and bake in the oven for 25 minutes till the cheese is bubbling and you have an appetite!

TIP *Mayo in mash makes it really rich and creamy, but why not try other condiments to make your mash extra special. Sriracha, Kewpie, mustard… I love a bit of salad cream for tang!*

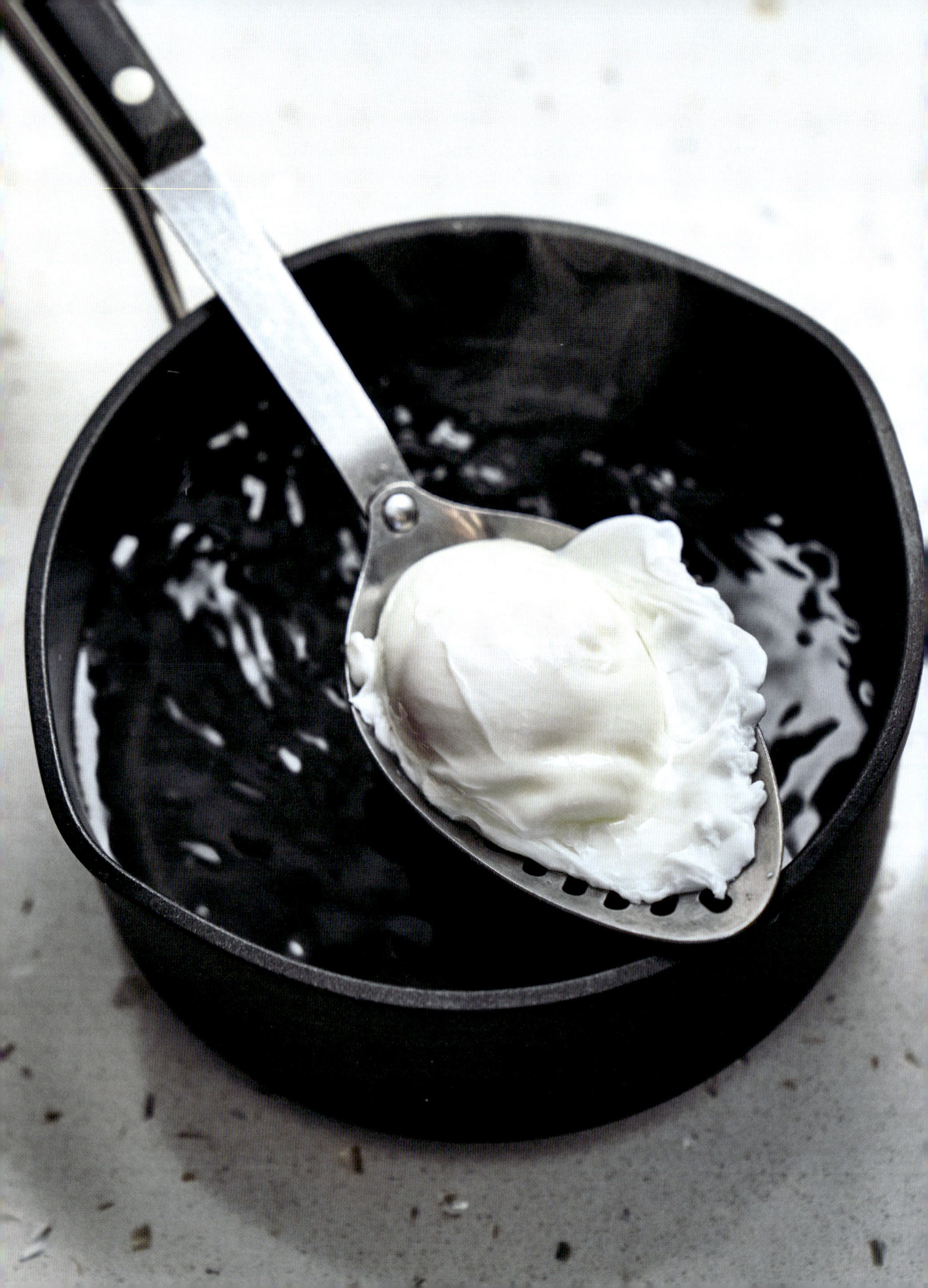

POACHED EGGS MADE SIMPLE

I never used to make poached eggs because everyone made such a fuss: right way, wrong way, vinegar, no vinegar, to swirl or not to swirl? Honestly, guys, this is how I do it and I hope it makes life easy enough for you to want to poach an egg every single day for the rest of your lives!

ALSO MAKES: POACHED EGG BREAKFAST BOARD (PAGE 32)

PREP: 5 MINS **COOK:** 12 MINS

MAKES: 4 EGGS

4 fresh eggs

Start with fresh eggs. The fresher the egg, the tighter the end result. The less fresh they are, the more likely you are to have the wispy bits you can get when poaching an egg. Crack each egg into a small bowl and set aside.

Get a pan large enough to be able to comfortably hold four eggs and deep enough for a lot of water. Pour water into the pan and bring to a boil. As soon as the water boils, turn the heat right down.

Have a bowl of cold water large enough for the four eggs set to the side. Add a few cubes of ice if you have ice, if not, don't worry about it (and you can skip this step entirely if you are eating your eggs straight away).

Stir the water to remove any air bubbles and leave the water to become still. As soon as the water is still, take a bowl with an egg and gently lower it right down to the surface of the water, allowing the egg to just drop in. Do the same with the other three eggs in quick succession so they cook for roughly around the same time.

Leave to sit for 3 minutes, then remove the eggs one by one with a slotted spoon and eat immediately or drop carefully into the cold water to stop them from cooking any further.

There you have it, poached eggs to eat however you like to eat your poached eggs. But if you want a fun new way to eat them, head over the page to find a recipe for a delicious poached egg breakfast board. See you there!

TIP *When making poached eggs, try not to crowd the pan. Remember you need enough space to allow a spoon in to pick the eggs up, so always have that in mind. Also, don't forget to have fun – making poached eggs is fun!*

POACHED EGG BREAKFAST BOARD

This is the kind of thing I like to make when I want a delicious breakfast to serve in the middle of the table. It's a fun way of enjoying poached eggs. In fact, it's my new favourite way, with creamy beetroot, avocado, runny eggs and lots of crisp toast to swish it up with.

PREP: 5 MINS **COOK:** 18 MINS

SERVES: 4

4 fresh eggs

Toast, to serve

For the creamy beetroot

250g cooked beetroot

200ml crème fraîche

1 clove of garlic, peeled

Pinch of salt

For the toppings

1 avocado, cut into cubes and sprinkled with some lemon

Pickled red cabbage

Crispy chilli oil

Finely sliced fresh dill

Runny honey

Crack each egg into a small bowl and set aside.

Get a pan large enough to be able to comfortably hold four eggs and deep enough for a lot of water. Pour water into the pan and bring to a boil. As soon as the water boils, turn the heat right down.

Have a bowl of cold water large enough for the four eggs set to the side. Add a few cubes of ice if you have ice, if not, don't worry about it (and you can skip this step entirely if you are eating your eggs straight away).

Stir the water to remove any air bubbles and leave the water to become still. As soon as the water is still, take a bowl with an egg and gently lower it right down to the surface of the water, allowing the egg to just drop in. Do the same with the other three eggs in quick succession so they cook for roughly around the same time.

Leave to sit for 3 minutes, then remove the eggs one by one with a slotted spoon and eat immediately or drop carefully into the cold water to stop them from cooking any further.

For the beetroot, put the cooked beetroot in a blender with the crème fraîche, garlic and salt. Blitz till you have a smooth, thick paste. Spread all over a wooden board or flat platter.

Sprinkle over the diced avocado and the pickled red cabbage, then drizzle over the crispy chilli oil. Add the eggs on top. Sprinkle over the dill and then do another sprinkling of crispy chilli oil and honey.

Serve with buttered crisp toast and dig right in.

TIP *If you are struggling to find crispy chilli oil, you can make your own by combining chilli flakes, oil and crispy fried onions. Give it a mix and you are good to go. The best thing about making it yourself is that you can control the chilli: add more (if you are like my husband) or less (if you are like me).*

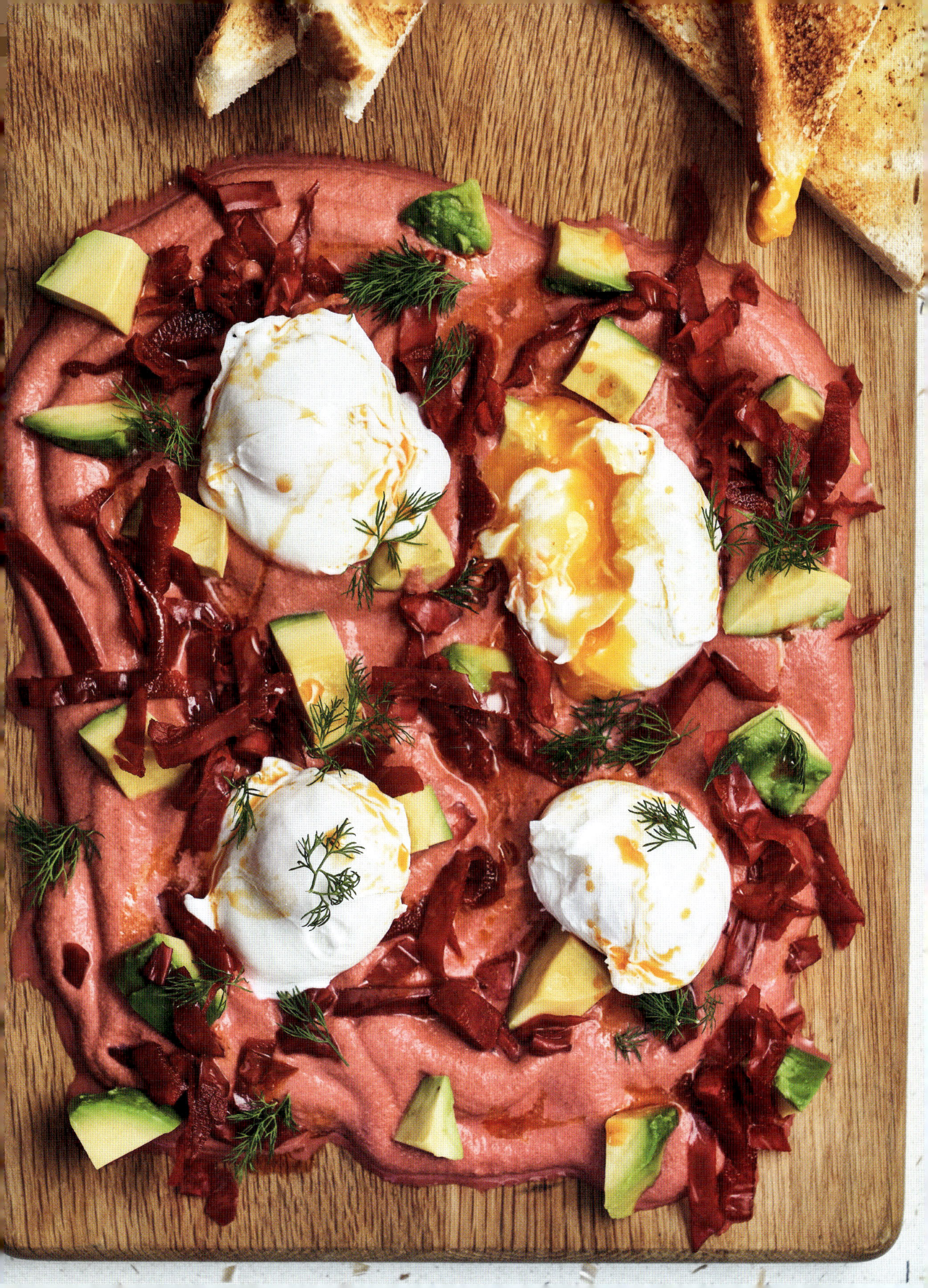

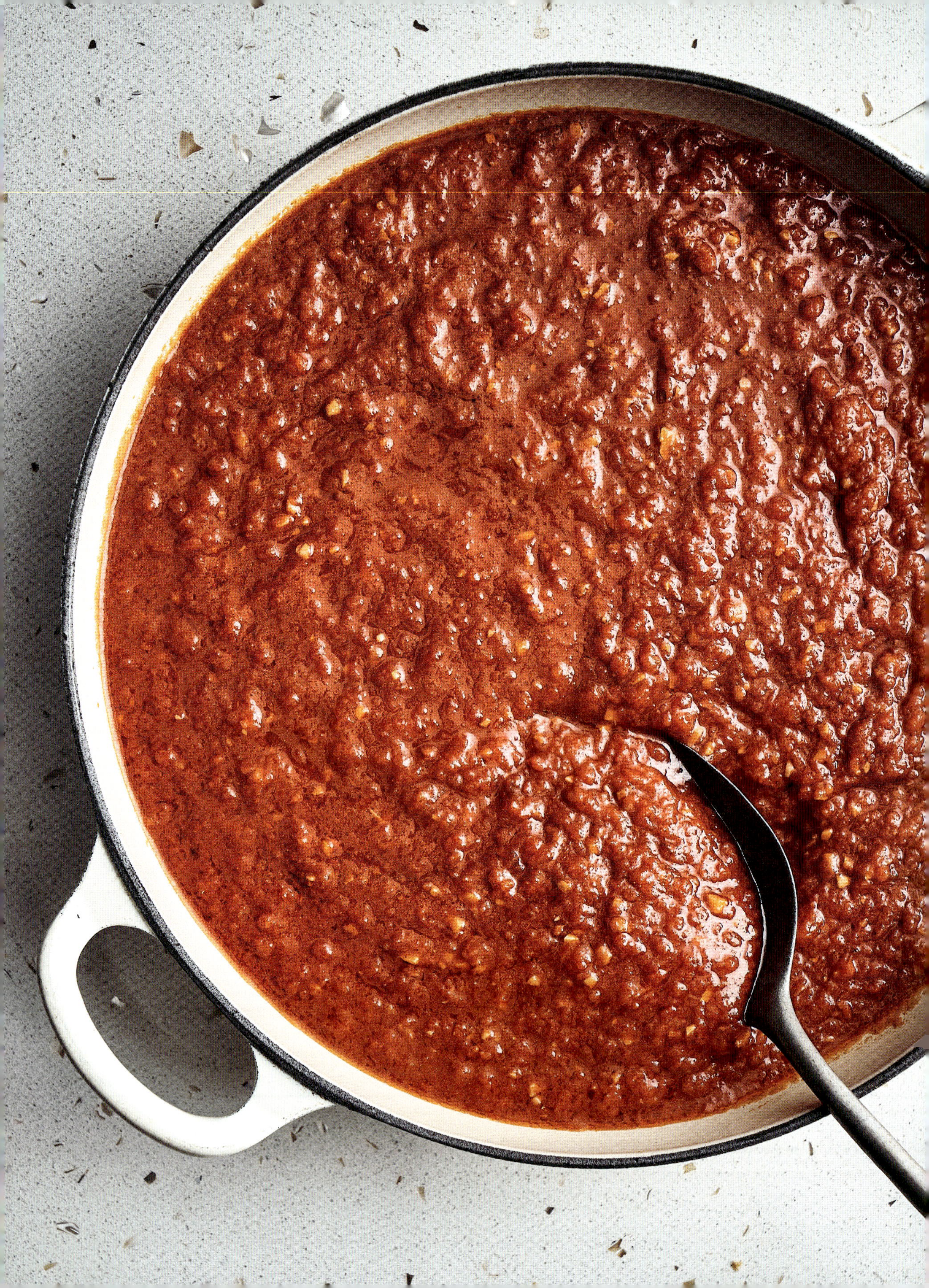

EVERYTHING TOMATO SAUCE

This sauce is a staple and that is why I had to share it. It's made simply with tinned tomatoes, so we are already ahead, but we are amping up the flavour. Once this sauce is made, you can use it in so many ways. You can add mince and make Bolognese; you can mix in veg for a ratatouille; it can be a simple pasta sauce or is the perfect base for a pizza. Make a load of this and pop it into your freezer. And if you are looking for a hearty way to eat this sauce, I've got a recipe just for you over the page.

ALSO MAKES: TOMATO BEAN SHAKSHUKA (PAGE 36)

PREP: 5 MINS **COOK:** 45 MINS

MAKES: 1 LARGE BATCH

100ml olive oil

1 large bulb of garlic, cloves peeled and minced

2 teaspoons salt

3 tablespoons balsamic vinegar

4 tablespoons tomato purée

3 x 400g tins of chopped tomatoes

100ml whole milk

2 teaspoons caster sugar

Start with a large pan that has a lid that fits. Get the pan onto a high heat and pour in the oil.

As soon as the oil is hot, add the garlic and cook till it is a dark brown. Lower the heat and add the salt, balsamic and tomato purée, mix and cook through for a few minutes. Add the tins of tomatoes and milk and mix through.

Leave the lid on and cook over a medium heat for 30 minutes till the whole mixture has thickened.

After 30 minutes, stir in the sugar and the sauce is ready to use immediately or to divide up and pop into the freezer.

TIP *If you are going to use this sauce for pizza, I would recommend reducing it till it's a little thicker and tearing in some basil at the end for an extra oomph!*

BACK TO BASICS / 35

TOMATO BEAN SHAKSHUKA

I love shakshuka but I prefer it with some substance and not just tomato sauce, so I like to make mine using my simple tomato sauce recipe and then really fill it up with tinned beans, which are soft and delicious, making my delicious tomato sauce stretch a little further.

PREP: 5 MINS
COOK: 1 HOUR 8 MINS
SERVES: 4

For the tomato sauce
- 100ml olive oil
- 1 large bulb of garlic, cloves peeled and minced
- 2 teaspoons salt
- 3 tablespoons balsamic vinegar
- 4 tablespoons tomato purée
- 3 x 400g tins of chopped tomatoes
- 100ml whole milk
- 2 teaspoons caster sugar

For the shakshuka
- 2 tablespoons olive oil
- 2 onions, thinly sliced
- ½ teaspoon salt
- 1 teaspoon chilli powder (optional)
- 2 teaspoons cumin (I use seeds)
- 2 x 400g tins of mixed beans (or cooked beans of your choice), drained
- 4 medium eggs
- Small handful of fresh basil
- Grated Parmesan cheese

Start with a large pan that has a lid that fits. Get the pan onto a high heat and pour in the oil.

As soon as the oil is hot, add the garlic and cook till it is a dark brown. Lower the heat and add the salt, balsamic and tomato purée, mix and cook through for a few minutes. Add the tins of tomatoes and milk and mix through.

Leave the lid on and cook over a medium heat for 30 minutes till the whole mixture has thickened.

After 30 minutes, stir in the sugar and the sauce is ready to use. For this recipe, I am going to take half, cool and freeze for another time, then use the other half to make some yummy shakshuka.

For the shakshuka, pour the olive oil into a large non-stick pan. When the oil is hot, add the onion and salt and cook till the onion is soft.

Add the chilli powder and cumin along with the drained mixed beans and the half batch of tomato sauce. Cook over a high heat till the mixture is quite thick.

Make four dents in the mixture where you can crack in the eggs. Crack the eggs in, tear up the basil and add on top along with the cheese. Pop the lid on, allowing the eggs enough time to steam until the whites are cooked but the yolks are still runny.

I love eating this hot with cooked rice, right in front of the telly box!

TIP *When adding herbs like basil, try tearing rather than cutting. When you cut too much, the herbs release oils and most of that good flavour ends up on your board and not in your dish.*

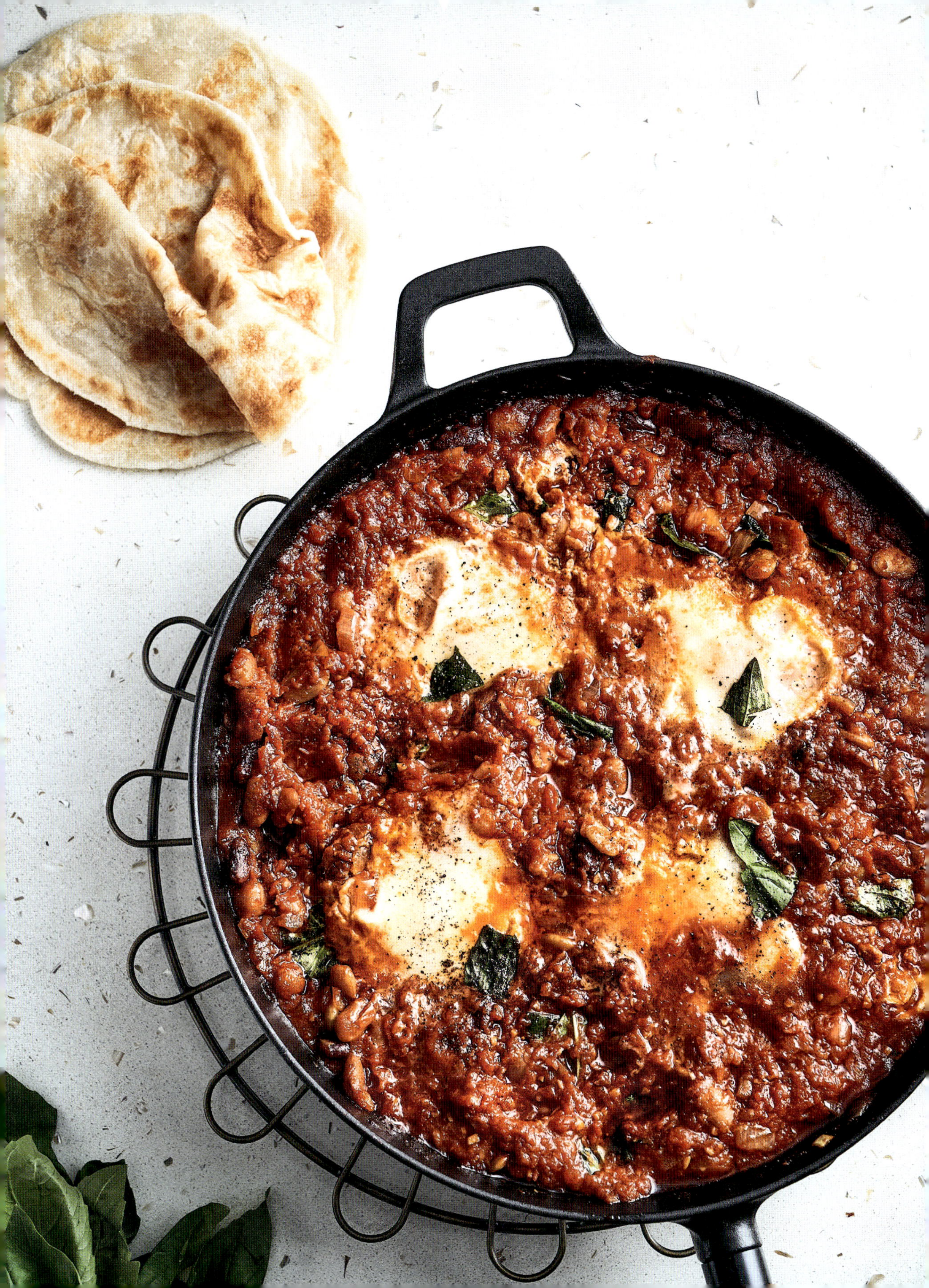

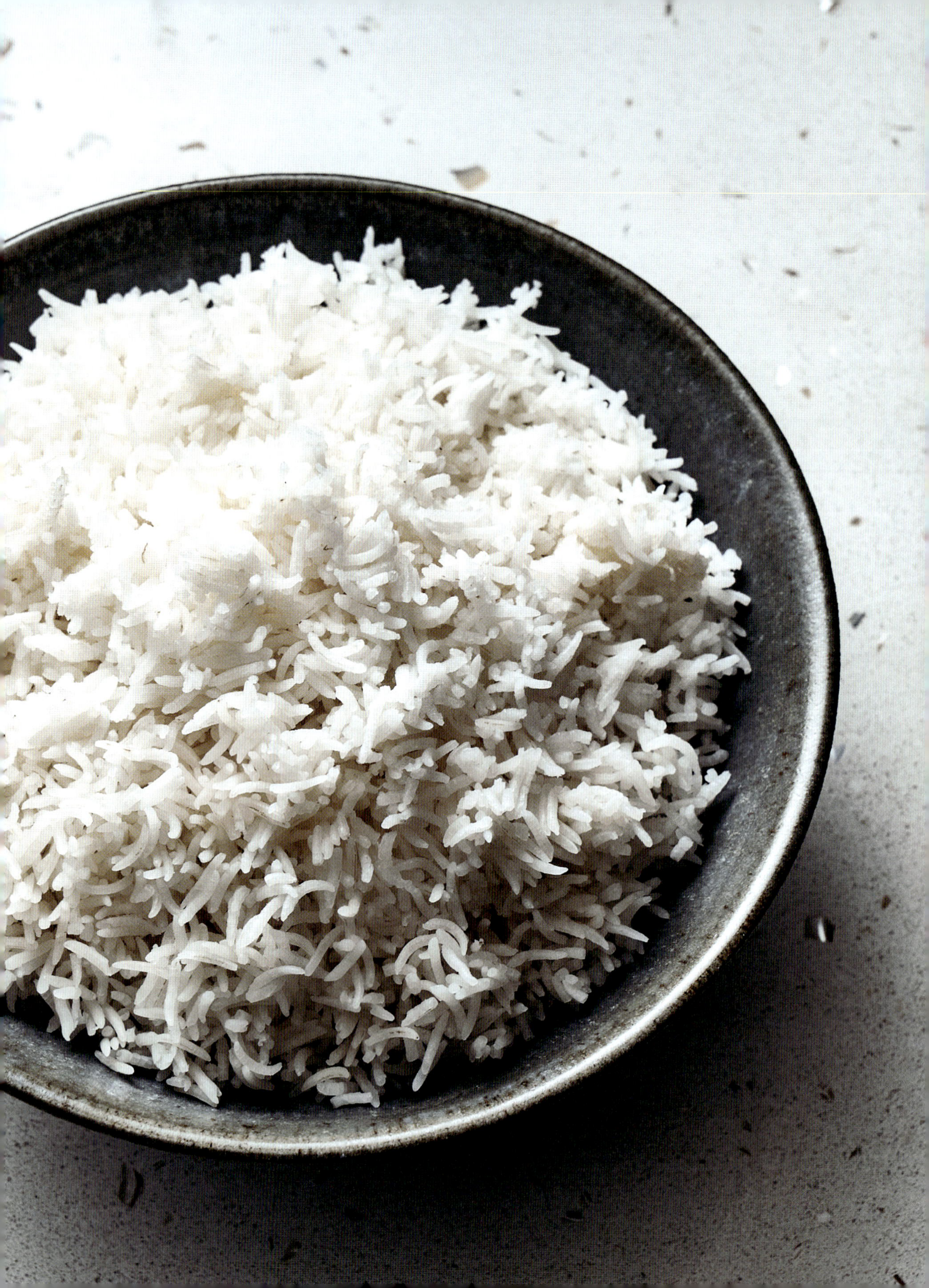

SIMPLE RICE

I think people fret over rice a lot. I have met people who are amazing cooks and bakers, but they still don't want to cook rice. But rice does not have to be tricky at all. Take it from the granddaughter of a rice farmer (that's me, by the way!), I learnt to cook rice while still very young and I promise you with these simple-to-follow tips and tricks you will become an expert rice cooker too!

ALSO MAKES: CHEAT'S PILAU (PAGE 40)

PREP: 5 MINS **COOK:** 28 MINS

SERVES: 4

280g basmati rice
1 teaspoon salt

So, I go with a standard measurement of 280g for four people. That is the standard size of a mug, so if you don't have weighing scales, just use one of those. We eat a lot of rice in our house, so make sure to scale up like me if rice is your family's go-to.

Place the rice in a bowl or a large sieve and wash the rice, mixing it and removing the starch. You will start off with water that is very cloudy and the longer you wash, the clearer the water will become. When that water runs clear, you are ready to start cooking your rice.

Pop your rice into a pan, making sure it's a good-sized pan. The rice will grow up to three times its original size, so it will need room as it steams. If the rice is too compacted and tight, it will become stodgy. Now add enough cold water so the water is 2cm above the rice level.

Pop the pan onto a high heat. It's important to mix the rice. If you leave it to boil and don't move it, the rice will stay still on the base and burn, so every minute or so, move that rice so it's swirling about in the pan.

Once the rice starts to boil, you will see that the water is starting to thicken, really slowing the grains of rice down. As soon as the liquid has completely thickened and evaporated and you can see all the grains and no water, lower the heat, put the lid on and leave to steam for 10 minutes.

Take the lid off, fluff the rice up with a fork and your rice, that you cooked, is ready to eat! Well done, it was all you!

TIP *There are so many great tips here to get your rice right every time. Remember that this works with any amount of rice. Just be sure to follow the tips and increase the size of the pan depending on how much rice you are cooking.*

CHEAT'S PILAU

Well, once you have mastered plain rice, I want you to be able to take the next step and feel confident adding lots of flavour. There are more complicated ways to make this, but I wanted you to have this cheat's version before we get into anything too tricky.

PREP: 3 MINS **COOK:** 33 MINS

SERVES: 4

For the rice
280g basmati rice
1 teaspoon salt

For the flavoured ghee
75g ghee or butter
2 dried red chillies
2 teaspoons black mustard seeds
Large pinch of saffron
½ teaspoon salt

Place the rice in a bowl or a large sieve and wash the rice, mixing it and removing the starch. You will start off with water that is very cloudy and the longer you wash, the clearer the water will become. When that water runs clear, you are ready to start cooking your rice.

Pop your rice into a pan, making sure it's a good-sized pan. Now add enough cold water so the water is 2cm above the rice level.

Pop the pan onto a high heat. It's important to mix the rice. If you leave it to boil and don't move it, the rice will stay still on the base and burn, so every minute or so, move that rice so it's swirling about in the pan.

As soon as the rice starts to boil, you will see that the water is starting to thicken, really slowing the grains of rice down. As soon as the liquid has completely thickened and evaporated and you can see all the grains and no water, lower the heat, put the lid on and leave to steam for 10 minutes.

Meanwhile, make the flavoured ghee by melting the ghee in a small pan. As soon as the ghee is hot, add the dried red chillies and black mustard seeds. As soon as the seeds start to pop, remove the pan from the heat, add the saffron and salt and mix through well.

Take the lid off the rice, fluff up with a fork, pour in the flavoured ghee and mix through till every grain is covered. This is such a great way to add flavour to simple rice. Before too long, you will be a rice expert!

TIP *Ghee has a higher smoking point than other oils, so if you see it smoking, don't be alarmed – it can go as high as 250°C. Ghee is great in cooking – it has a delicious flavour and nutty aroma. If you've never given it a try, why not now?*

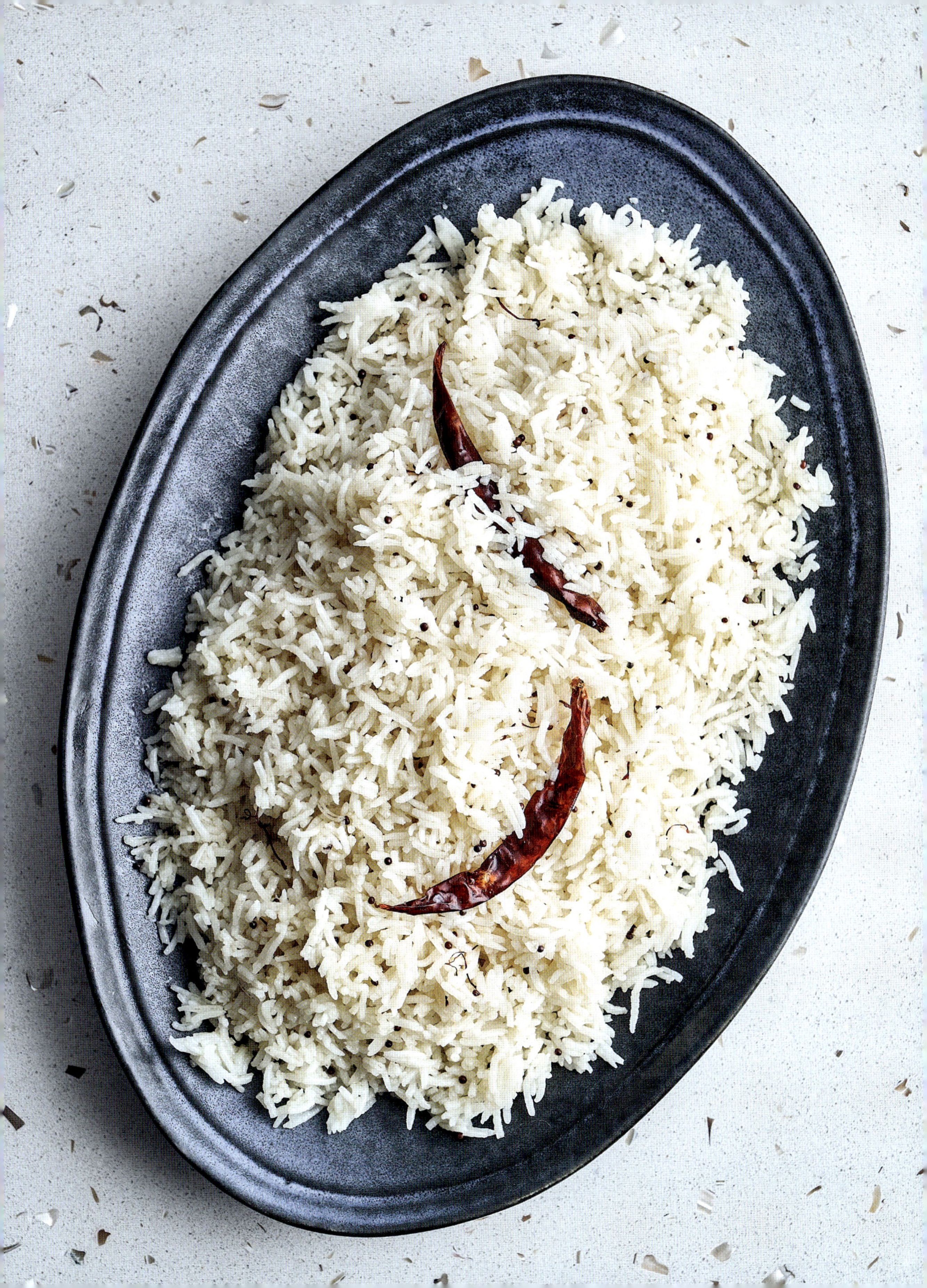

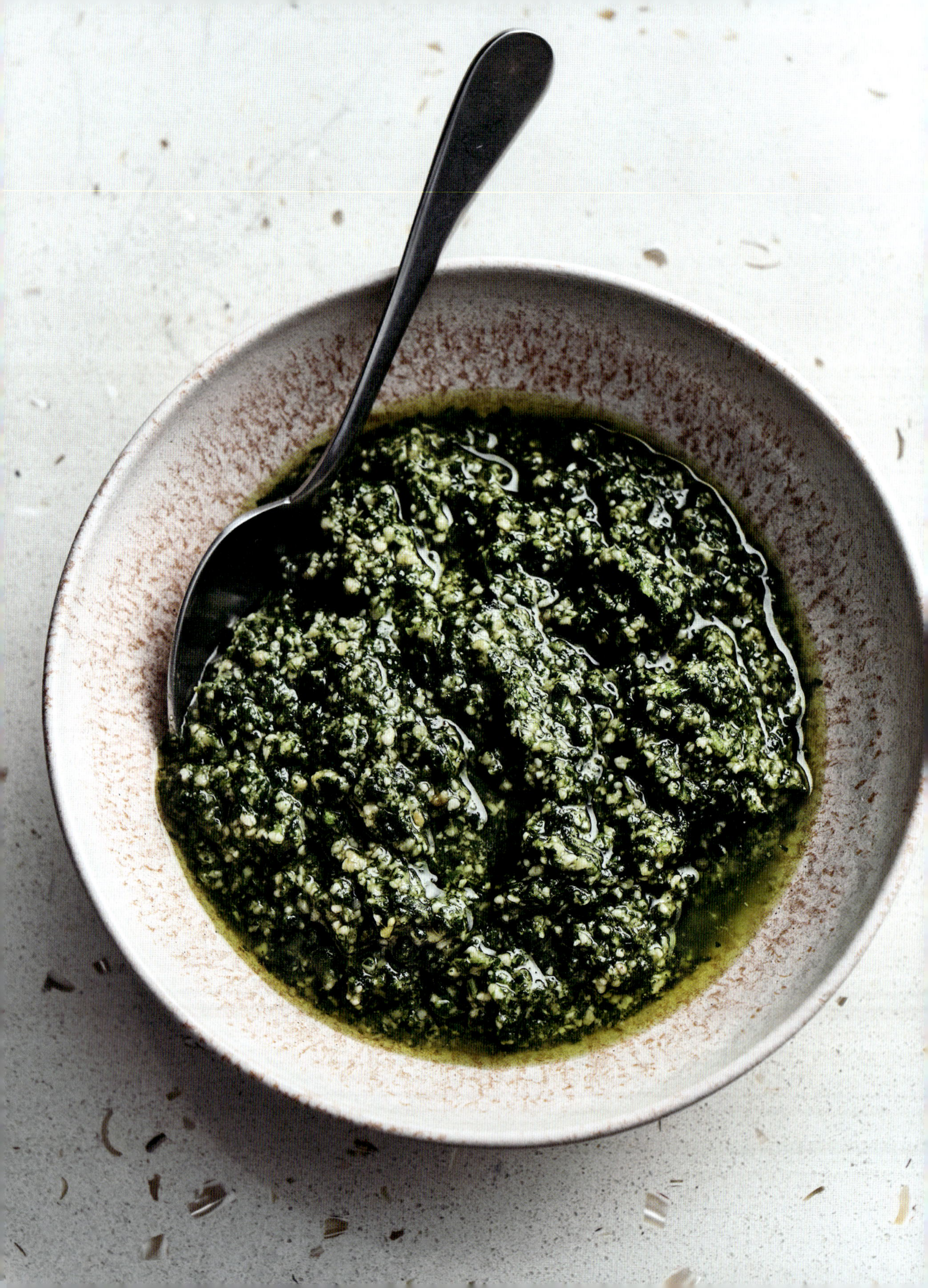

PERFECT HERBY PESTO

Pesto is such a go-to for me now and was even more so when my children were small. Once it's made it is so versatile to add to sauces, mix with pasta, use as a marinade and so on. It is quite literally a lifesaver. You guys are going to love this delicious herby pesto.

ALSO MAKES: SCISSOR CUT PESTO PASTA (PAGE 44)

PREP: 12 MINS **COOK:** 5 MINS

MAKES: 2 MEDIUM JARS

50g pine nuts

100g fresh basil leaves

25 fresh chives, chopped

4 cloves of garlic

50g Parmesan cheese, grated

½ lemon, juice only

150ml olive oil, plus extra for the top

½ teaspoon salt

2 teaspoons ground black pepper

Start by toasting the pine nuts in a pan till they are golden brown and really toasted. This will enhance that nutty flavour. Cool the nuts down and pop into the jug of a blender.

Add the basil, chives, garlic, Parmesan, lemon juice, olive oil, salt and ground black pepper. Blend till you have a smooth, beautiful green pesto.

Pop into the jars and pour a little oil on top to help preserve it.

Store in the fridge for up to 2 weeks till you are ready to use.

TIP *Nuts can go off very quickly, especially pine nuts. The best way to store them is in the freezer. Just defrost and use as you would normally.*

BACK TO BASICS / 43

SCISSOR CUT PESTO PASTA

Pasta is so easy to make and once you've made it, you won't want to buy dried pasta again. I mean, that's a lie – you will always buy dried pasta because it's super convenient! But when you make this, you will feel accomplished and really pleased with yourself, enough to make you want to do it over and over again. What's even better is that you don't have to shape the dough. We are just going to cut the pasta straight into the hot salty water.

PREP: 22 MINS **COOK:** 12 MINS

SERVES: 4

For the pasta

200g strong bread flour, sifted

2 large eggs

Salt, for the water

For the pesto

100g pine nuts

100g fresh basil leaves

25 fresh chives, chopped

4 cloves of garlic

50g Parmesan cheese, grated

150ml olive oil

2 teaspoons ground black pepper

To finish

100g cherry tomatoes halves

170g mozzarella pearls

Start by making the pasta (I do this first to allow it some time to rest). Pour the flour onto the work surface and make a well in the centre. Crack the 2 eggs into the centre and, working your way from the centre and in circular motions, bring the flour together till you have a dough.

As soon as you have no more flour left, bring the dough together and knead till you have a smooth dough that is lovely and shiny. Cover the dough on the work surface with a tea towel and leave to rest while you make the pesto.

To make the pesto, start by toasting the pine nuts in a pan till they are golden brown and really toasted. This will enhance that nutty flavour. Cool the nuts down and pop into the jug of a blender.

Add the basil, chives, garlic, Parmesan, olive oil and ground black pepper. Blend till you have a smooth, beautiful green pesto.

You only need 3 tablespoons for this recipe, so pop the rest into a jar and add a little oil on top to help preserve it. Store in the fridge till you are ready to use. It will last in the fridge for up to 2 weeks.

Bring a large pan filled with water to a boil, add plenty of salt and take the dough into your hands. Take a pair of sharp scissors, grease and cut the dough straight into the water. Cook the pasta for a few minutes till it begins to come to the surface – fresh pasta cooks faster than dried. You can also cut onto a floured tray if you are not cooking straight away.

Drain the pasta and add straight back to the pan. Add your pesto, along with the tomatoes and mozzarella, and mix through. It is now ready to demolish!

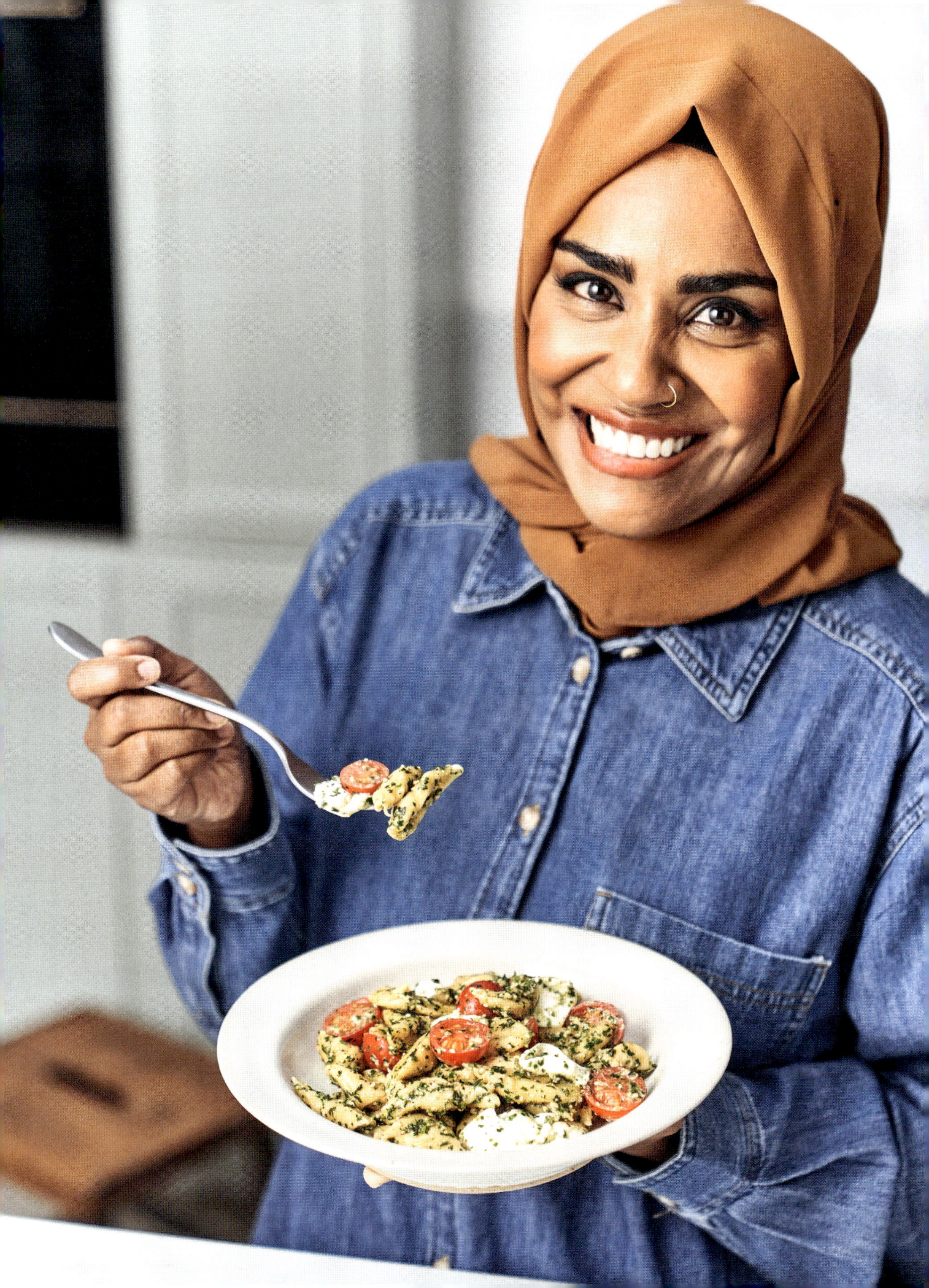

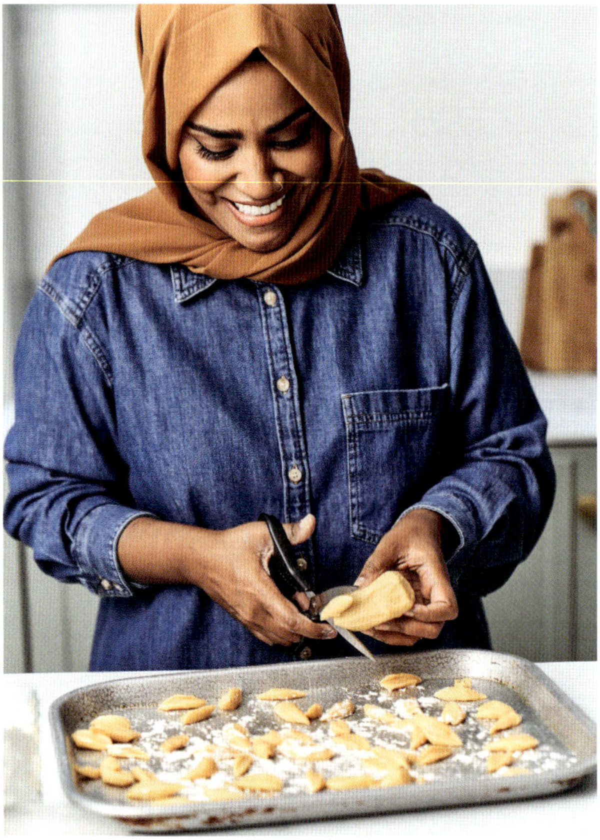
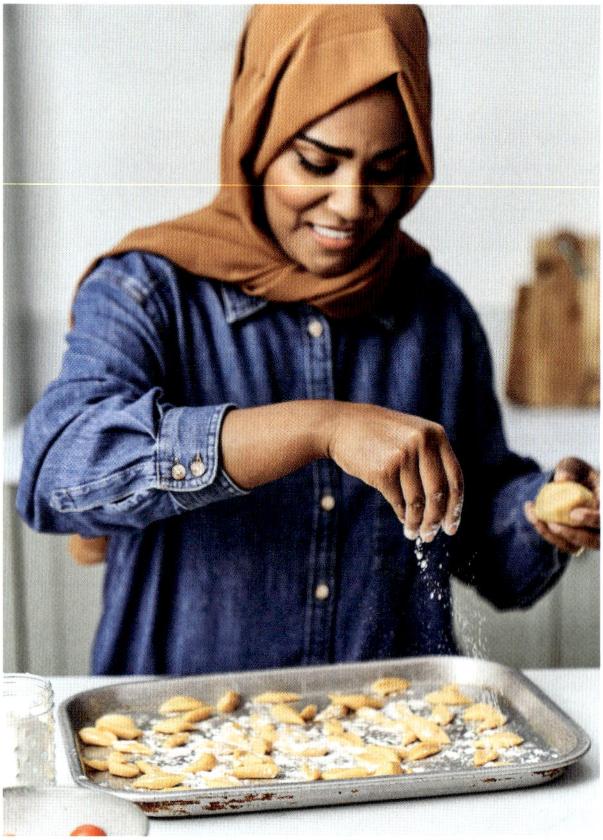
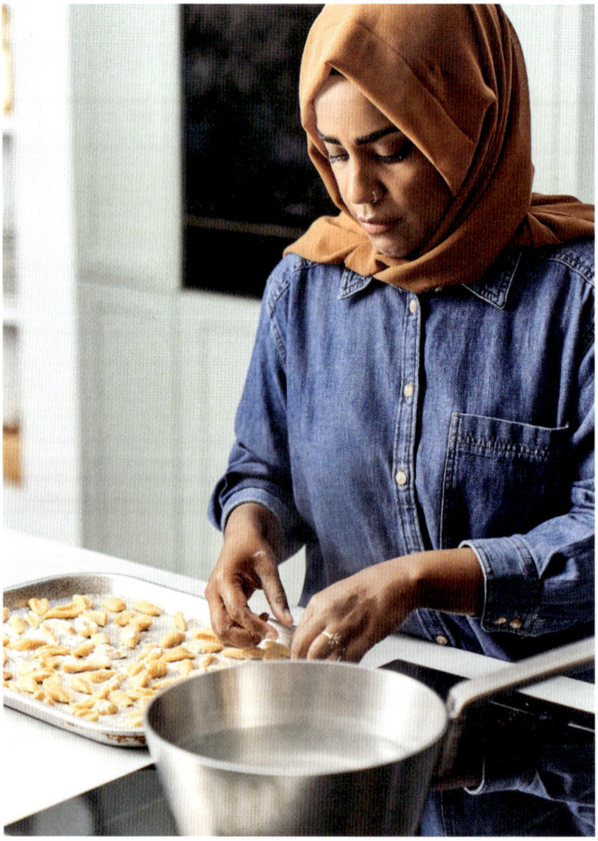
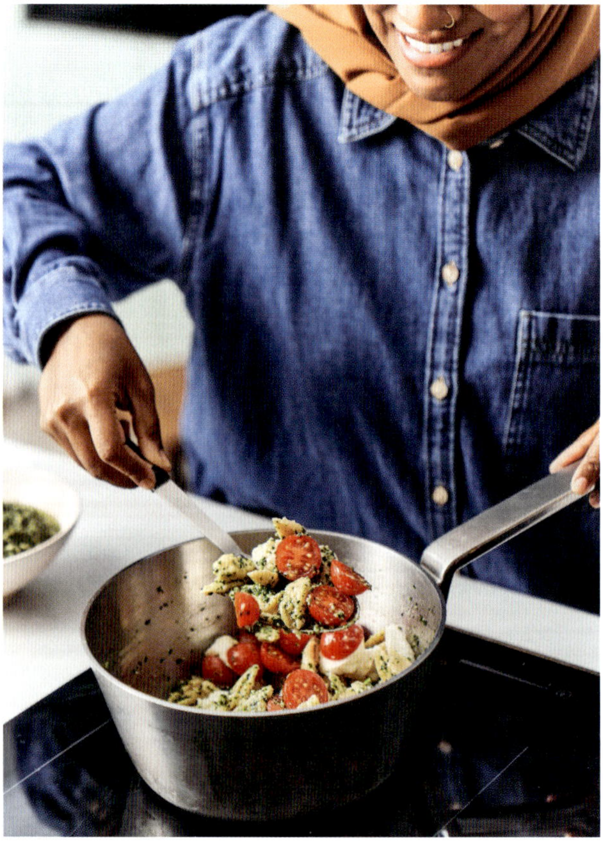

TIP *Fresh pasta once shaped can be frozen, but you can also make an extra dough ball and pop it into the freezer. Just defrost and cut straight into water! Fresh pasta every single time.*

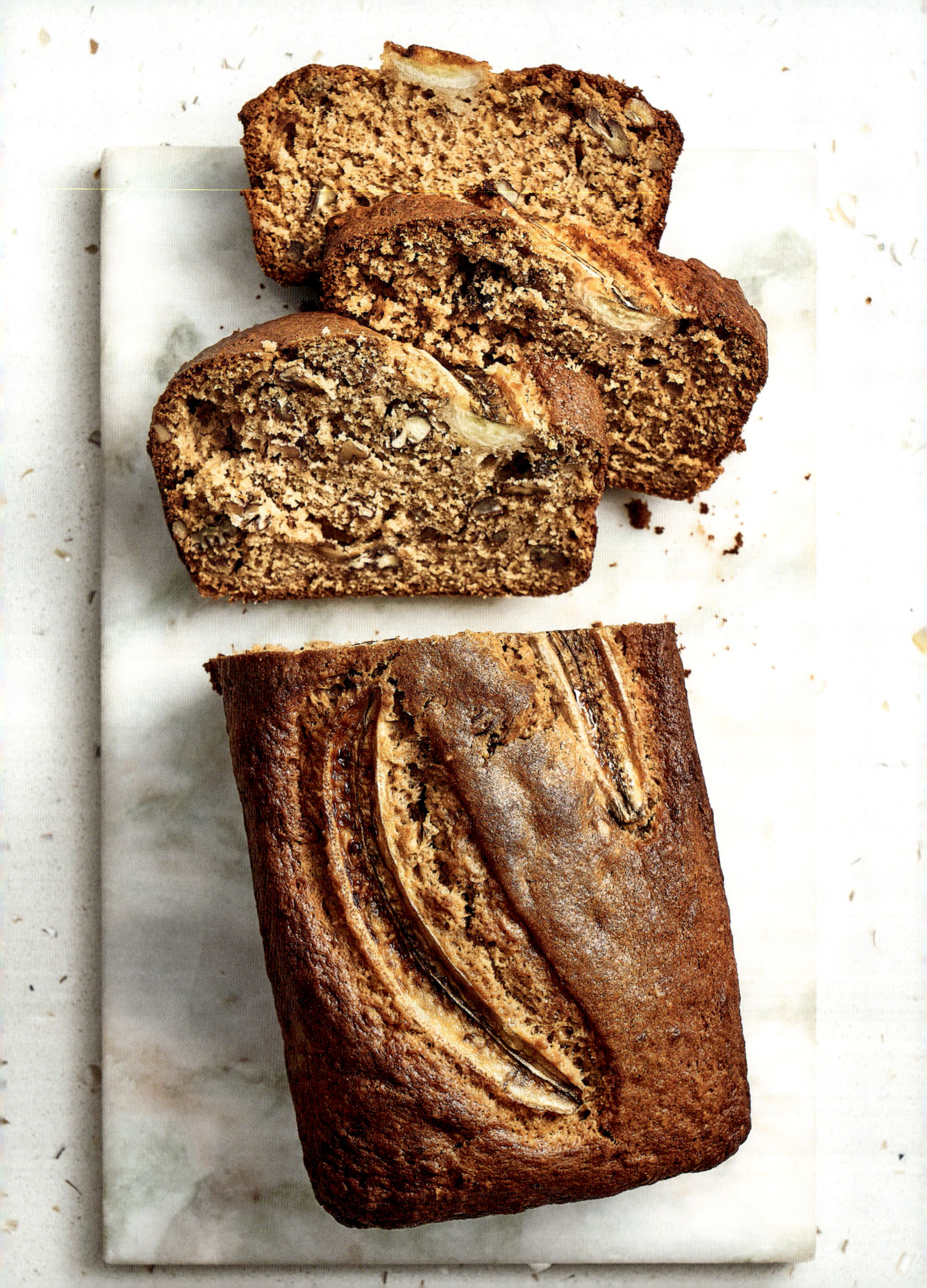

BASIC BANANA BREAD

Banana bread is, and always will be, a staple in our house. It's something I think I could make with my eyes shut and hands tied behind my back and no doubt that is the same for many people. This recipe is simple enough for you to eat with whatever you will.

ALSO MAKES: BANANA BREAD PANCAKES (PAGE 50)

PREP: 12 MINS **COOK:** 45 MINS–1 HOUR

REST: 30 MINS

SERVES: 10

100g salted butter, softened

175g soft brown sugar

2 medium eggs

1 teaspoon vanilla extract

1 teaspoon almond extract

2 ripe bananas, mashed, plus 1 whole banana for the top

225g self-raising flour, sifted

1 teaspoon baking powder

2 teaspoons ground cinnamon

100g pecans, roughly chopped

Preheat the oven to 170°C. Grease and base line a 900g loaf tin.

Put the butter and soft brown sugar in a large mixing bowl and whisk till you have a mixture that is creamy and almost white. Now add the eggs, vanilla, almond extract and mashed banana.

Add the flour, baking powder, cinnamon and pecans and mix everything till you have a smooth, even batter.

Spoon the mixture into a prepared tin, then take the tin and tap sharply on the worktop to level off the top of the batter. Take the whole banana and slice horizontally so you have two long halves. Lay the halves on top.

Now bake the cake on the middle shelf for 45 minutes–1 hour, till a skewer inserted comes out clean. Leave in the tin for 10 minutes and then cool on a wire rack.

TIP *If the bananas are microwaved before adding to the batter, this makes the solids separate from the liquid and reduces the liquid to give the bread a more caramel-like flavour.*

BANANA BREAD PANCAKES

These are exactly what they sound like: banana bread batter but cooked like pancakes. So, all the loveliness of banana bread with the instant deliciousness of pancakes. Cinnamon sweet, nutty and full of bananas.

PREP: 6 MINS **COOK:** 16 MINS

SERVES: 4–6

For the pancakes

100g salted butter, melted

150g soft brown sugar

2 medium eggs

2 ripe bananas

1 teaspoon vanilla extract

1 teaspoon almond extract

225g self-raising flour, sifted

1 teaspoon baking powder

2 teaspoons ground cinnamon

120ml whole milk

100g pecans, roughly chopped

Butter, for frying

To serve

Whipped cream

Golden syrup

Fresh fruit

For the pancake batter, put the melted butter, soft brown sugar, eggs, bananas, vanilla extract, almond extract, self-raising flour, baking powder, cinnamon and milk into a blender jug and blitz till you have thick batter.

Transfer the batter to a bowl with a ladle, add the chopped pecans to the batter and mix through.

Take a non-stick pan and set it over a low to medium heat. Brush the pan with a little butter and ladle in small spoonfuls of the batter to create small pancakes or larger ladlesful for bigger pancakes.

Cook over a medium heat till the surface of the pancakes has bubbles and looks dry, then turn and fry on the other side.

Keep cooking till you have made them all. We love to serve these with whipped cream, golden syrup and tons of fresh fruit!

TIP *When making pancakes, I always have a few leftovers. I pop them in the freezer and simply toast them from frozen. Perfect for when you want to make a quick dash out of the door but still want to eat delicious pancakes.*

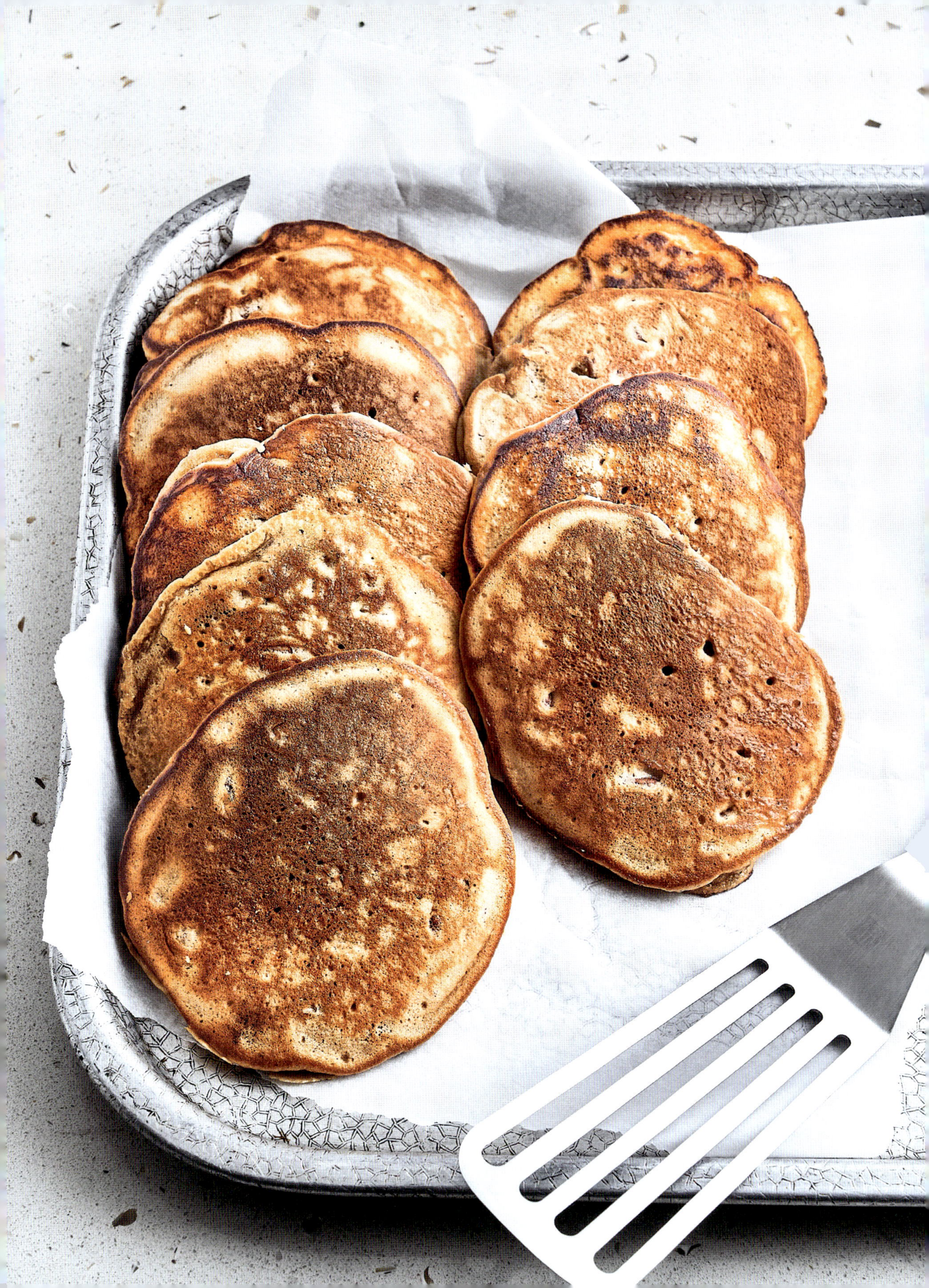

JUST ROAST CHICKEN

I love a roast chicken – none of the frills, just a roast chicken. And not just for a roast dinner, but for the sake of having a chicken that you can do anything with. For me, it's ripping bits of cold chicken out of the fridge that makes me happy. It's great for sandwiches and to add protein to your lunch through the week. So, let me show you how to make a delicious, moist roast chicken – perfectly!

ALSO MAKES: CARCASS RISOTTO (PAGE 57)

BRINE: 4 HOURS **PREP:** 5 MINS
COOK: 1 HOUR 20 MINS
REST: 15 MINS
SERVES: 4

3 litres water
300g fine salt
1.6kg whole chicken
Salt and ground black pepper

Start by getting a large pan or bowl and make a brine by pouring the water into the pan/bowl along with the salt and mixing till the salt has dissolved.

Add the chicken and submerge completely, using a plate to weigh it down if you need to. The size of your pan/bowl will affect how much water you need to completely cover the chicken, so always remember that salt to water should be a 10% ratio, e.g. 300g salt to 3 litres water, 400g salt to 4 litres water, and so on. Ideally I would do this overnight. If you can do that and you are prone to pre-planning, then do that. If you can't, 4 hours will suffice. This will give you ultimate moistness, which is what we want!

Preheat the oven to 170°C.

Remove the chicken from the water, drain and pat dry. Put in a roasting dish and sprinkle with salt and pepper all over – be generous. Lay the chicken breast-side up. Cover with foil and pop into the oven for 1 hour.

After 1 hour, remove the foil and bake for another 20 minutes. This gives your chicken a beautiful golden colour and finishes off the cooking at the same time. Take out and leave to rest before serving.

There are many ways to know when a chicken is ready. Here are a few ways of being sure:

When a chicken is cooked, it changes colour to an opaque white.

Insert a skewer into the thickest part of the chicken – the breast near the bone – and if the liquid runs clear, it is cooked. If there is a pink tinge, then it needs more time.

But if you want to be absolutely sure, invest in a meat thermometer. Insert the thermometer into the thickest part of the chicken, making sure not to touch the bone. If the temperate is 70°C, then the chicken is cooked.

Now to eat! There are so many ways to serve a roast chicken – be adventurous and show me on Insta! Whatever you do, make sure you don't throw away the carcass. I have a great use for it on page 57.

> **TIP** *Never wash your chicken. By washing you can, without realizing, spread salmonella. And if you are handling chicken, make sure to be aware of where you may be spreading chicken juices/liquid.*

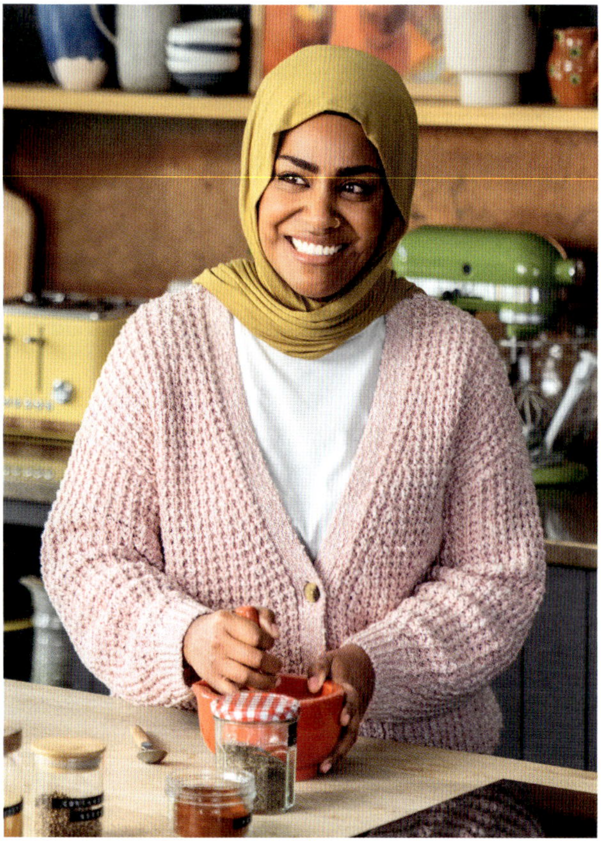
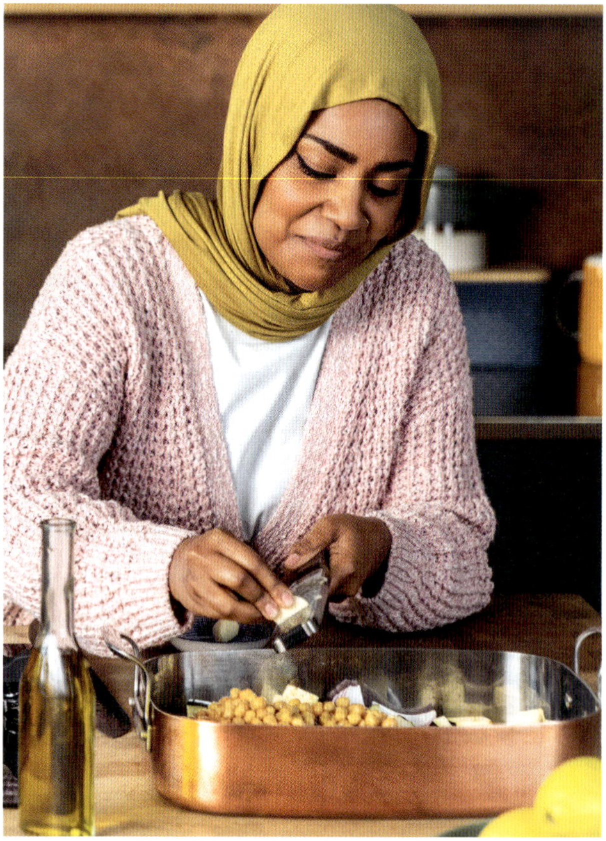
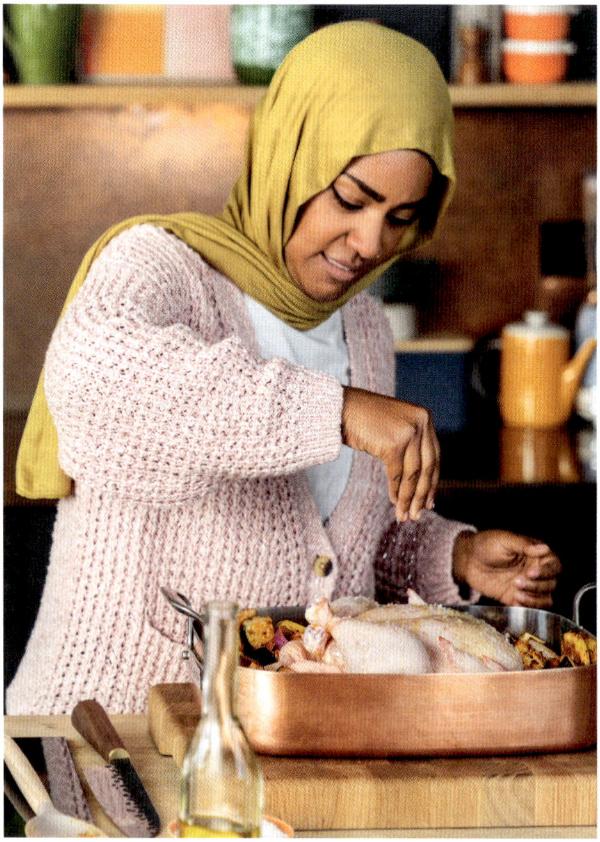
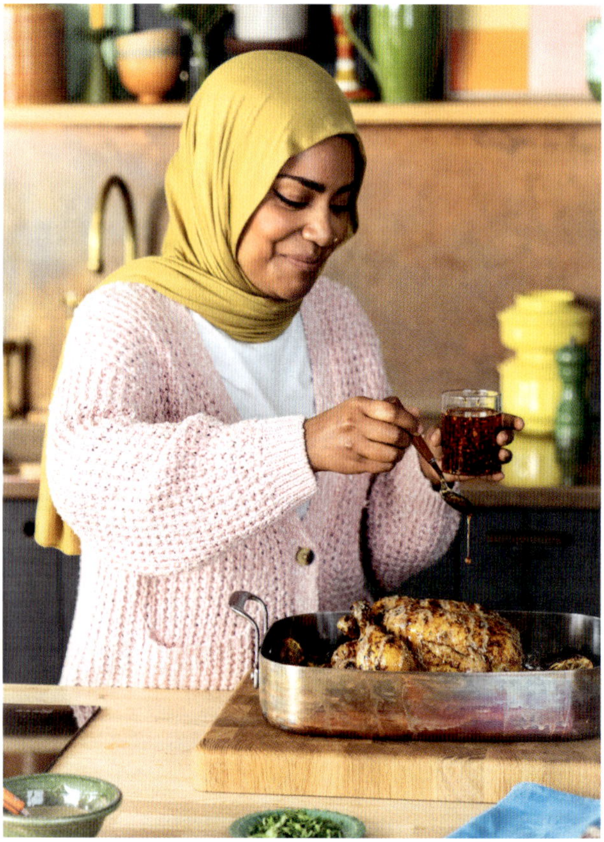

TIP *Why not spice-up your roast chicken by turning to page 81 and following the recipe for the Chickpea and Chicken Traybake, swapping the drumsticks for your whole roast chicken and using the chicken roasting time and temperature from page 52. Serve with loads of tahini, chilli oil and fresh coriander leaves.*

TIP *If you have any wilted herbs, don't throw them out. Pop them in the microwave and zap for 5 seconds at a time till the herbs are dry. Scrunch into a jar and save.*

CARCASS RISOTTO

I love risotto so much. It's literally one of my fave things to eat, especially when it makes use of something that would otherwise have been dumped. Making your own stock after cooking a roast is the perfect way to get at any leftover chicken and use up all those juices from the bones of the bird. This risotto is creamy and packed with flavour.

PREP: 5 MINS
COOK: 45 MINS
SERVES: 4

For the stock

1.5 litres cold water

2 tablespoons chicken stock powder

Carcass of a whole chicken (see page 52)

For the risotto

Oil, for frying

2 tablespoons butter

4 cloves of garlic, minced

2 celery sticks, diced

1 onion, diced

1 carrot, diced

400g risotto rice

100g Parmesan cheese, grated

25g fresh flat-leaf parsley, chopped

Salt

Start by making the stock. Pour the cold water into a large pan and add the stock powder and the chicken carcass.

Pop onto a high heat and bring to the boil, then leave to fast simmer till any flesh from the bones has cooked off completely and the bones are clean.

Drain through a sieve or small-holed colander, making sure you place a bowl underneath so you catch the stock. I have made that very mistake and watched my beautiful stock gush down the drain at lightning speed.

Set the stock aside. Remove the bones from the colander and place the shreds of chicken in another bowl, making sure to remove any excess moisture from the chicken.

Take a large non-stick pan with high sides, add a dash of oil and get the oil nice and hot. Add the chicken shreds and fry over a high heat till the chicken is crispy. Take out of the pan, sprinkle with salt and set aside.

Now for the risotto. Add some oil and the butter to the same pan and as soon as the butter has melted, add the garlic, celery, onion and carrot and cook till the onion is browned and the carrot is softened.

Add the rice and cook for 5 minutes over a high heat till the rice starts to stick a little. Pour the stock into another pan and heat until warmed through.

Add the hot stock, one ladle at a time, till it starts to evaporate, then keep adding till you have used up all the liquid. If your rice still needs a little more cooking and you've used up all your stock, just add hot water until the rice is done.

When the mixture is thick and the liquid has evaporated, turn the heat off. Pop on the lid for about 2 minutes. Add the grated Parmesan to the risotto and mix through, then check the seasoning and adjust if necessary.

Sprinkle over the crispy chicken and parsley. Serve with wedges of lemon and enjoy this delicious risotto that started off life as a carcass – not bad, right?!

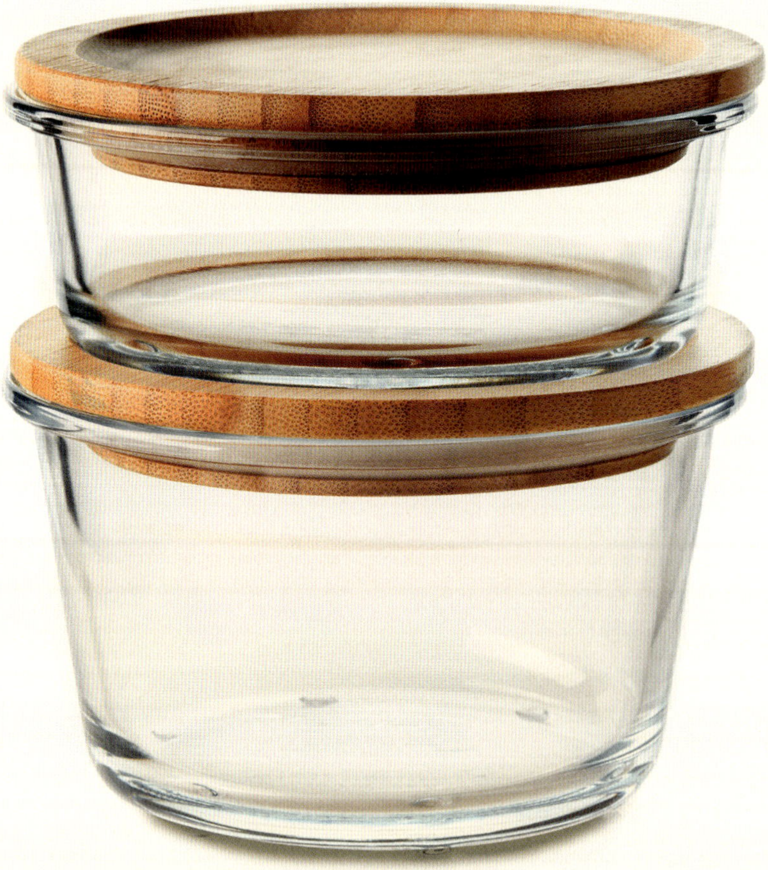

LOVIN' YOUR ⬇ LEFT OVERS

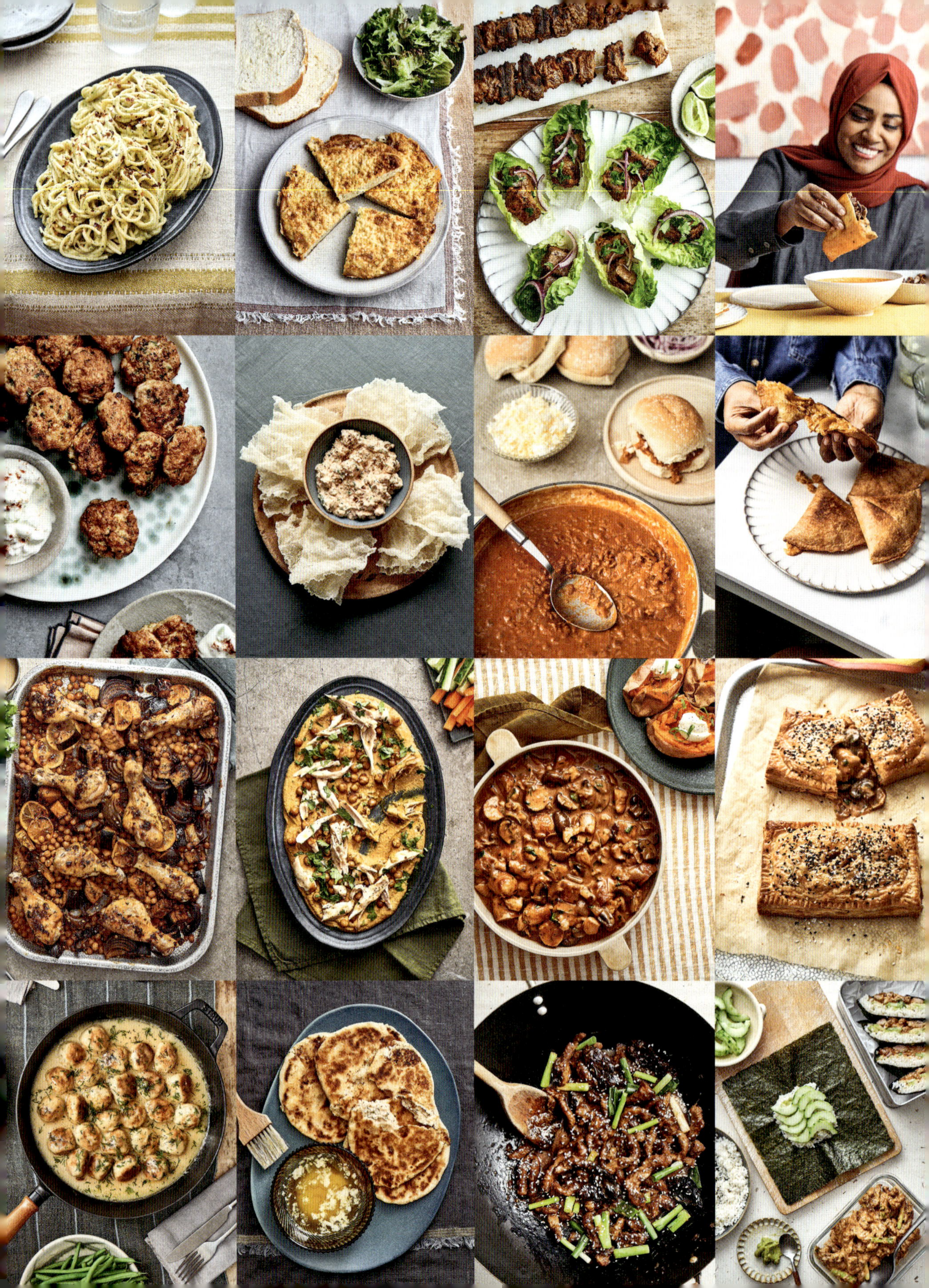

LOVIN' YOUR LEFTOVERS

A collection of family-friendly meals, each followed by a second recipe to level up the leftovers. This chapter is filled with leftovers you'll look forward to.

COURGETTE SPAGHETTI
↓
COURGETTE SPAGHETTI FRITTATA

BEEF SUYA KEBABS
↓
CHEAT'S BIRRIA

CHICKEN AND PRAWN KOFTAS
↓
RICE PAPER CHIPS AND DIPS

SLOPPY JOES
↓
CHEESE AND LAMB SAMOSAS

CHICKPEA AND CHICKEN TRAYBAKE
↓
SPICED CHICKEN-TOPPED HUMMUS

CHICKEN SAUSAGE MUSHROOM CASSEROLE
↓
CREAMY SAUSAGE HANDHELD PIES

SWEDISH-STYLE MEATBALLS
↓
MEATBALL PARATHAS

MONGOLIAN BEEF WITH STICKY RICE
↓
MONGOLIAN BEEF SEAWEED RICE WRAPS

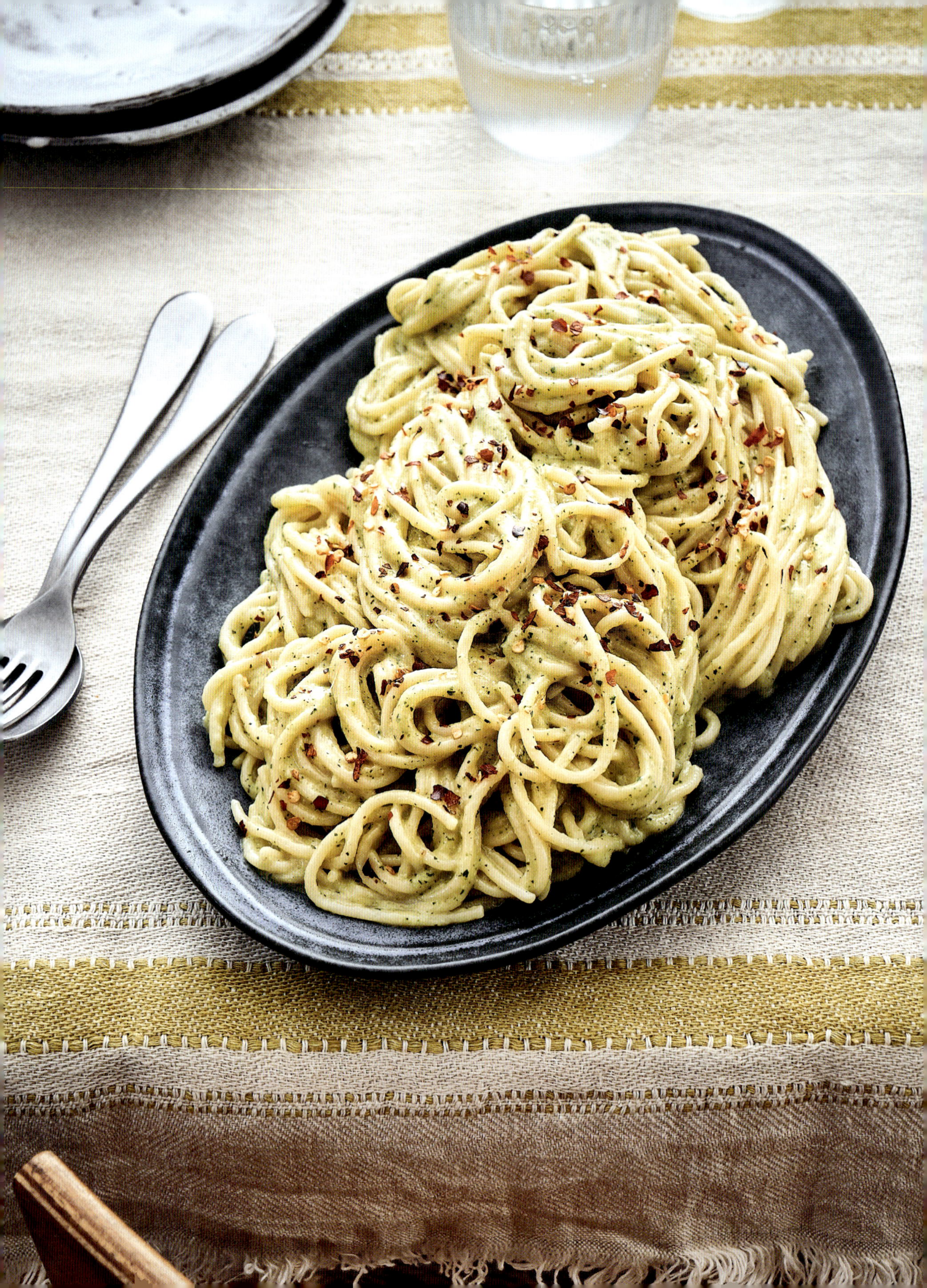

COURGETTE SPAGHETTI

I love this simple dish – it's literally a few ingredients thrown together to make a sublime spaghetti. I make this a lot when my parents have grown way too many courgettes and have a glut that they don't know what to do with. So, I do this. Simply cooked courgettes, garlic, nice olive oil and cheese!

ALSO MAKES: COURGETTE SPAGHETTI FRITTATA (PAGE 64)

PREP: 5 MINS **COOK:** 30 MINS

SERVES: 4

Oil, for deep-frying

500g courgettes, halved and thinly sliced into half-moons

6 cloves of garlic, peeled and sliced

400g dried spaghetti

200ml olive oil

1 teaspoon salt

100g Gruyère cheese, grated

Chilli flakes (optional)

So, let's start by deep-frying those courgettes. Take a large pan and pour in the oil about two-thirds of the way up.

Bring the oil up to a high heat, drop one courgette slice in and if it starts to sizzle, add some more slices to the pan. Deep-fry them in batches – adding too much at the same time will lower the temperature and you'll be frying forever, so be sure not to overcrowd that pan.

Keep frying till you have done all the courgettes – they should be crispy and golden. Have a plate ready with some kitchen paper lining the base to drain any excess oil.

Now add the sliced garlic and deep-fry till the garlic is a deep golden brown. Take it as far as you can without burning for the best flavour. Drain with the courgette and set aside.

Meanwhile, cook your pasta as per the cooking instructions.

Make the sauce by pouring the olive oil into a blender, adding the salt, fried courgettes and the garlic and blitzing to a smooth paste.

Drain the pasta, being sure to save a cupful of the starchy water. Add the pasta back into the pan with the sauce from the blender and the saved pasta water and mix till you have a sauce that beautifully sticks to the spaghetti.

Add the cheese and stir through, then serve with a sprinkling of chilli flakes, if you fancy it, and enjoy your big bowl of simple spaghetti.

TIP *If you are ever deep-frying courgettes to make them crispy for eating as is (unlike this recipe), always salt beforehand. This removes any excess moisture, making sure you get really crispy courgettes. This also works well with other vegetables that have lots of moisture.*

COURGETTE SPAGHETTI FRITTATA

I love a frittata. They are traditionally made with potatoes, but I think they are delicious with anything that is carby and that's why spaghetti works well. My eyes are bigger than my stomach and I always make more than I can eat, so I make a lot of frittatas. This one I think you will really like.

PREP: 5 MINS **COOK:** 25 MINS

SERVES: 2

150g leftover courgette spaghetti, cooled (see page 63)

3 medium eggs

2 teaspoons ground cumin

Pinch of salt

100g Gruyère cheese, grated

Hot sauce (optional)

Start by roughly chopping the cooled spaghetti (this just makes it easier to mix with the eggs).

Put the eggs, ground cumin and salt in a medium-sized bowl and whisk. Add the cold spaghetti and mix through.

Pop a non-stick pan over a medium heat and as soon as it is hot, add half the cheese and allow it to melt a little and start to get some colour.

Pour in the spaghetti egg mix and make sure it is in an even layer. Pop a lid on and let it steam for 10 minutes. Take the lid off, add the remaining cheese and the hot sauce on top and grill till bubbly and melted.

Wait 15 minutes before serving, so you can get a nice cut. This is perfect served with a fresh green salad or even better in between two slices of buttered bread. Carb on carb heaven!

TIP *If you want to know if your eggs are fresh, pop into a bowl of cold water. If an egg sinks, it's good to use, if it floats, throw it out or, better still, dig a hole near where you are planting veg in a garden, break in the egg, including the shell, and cover it up. This will give your plants much-needed nutrients!*

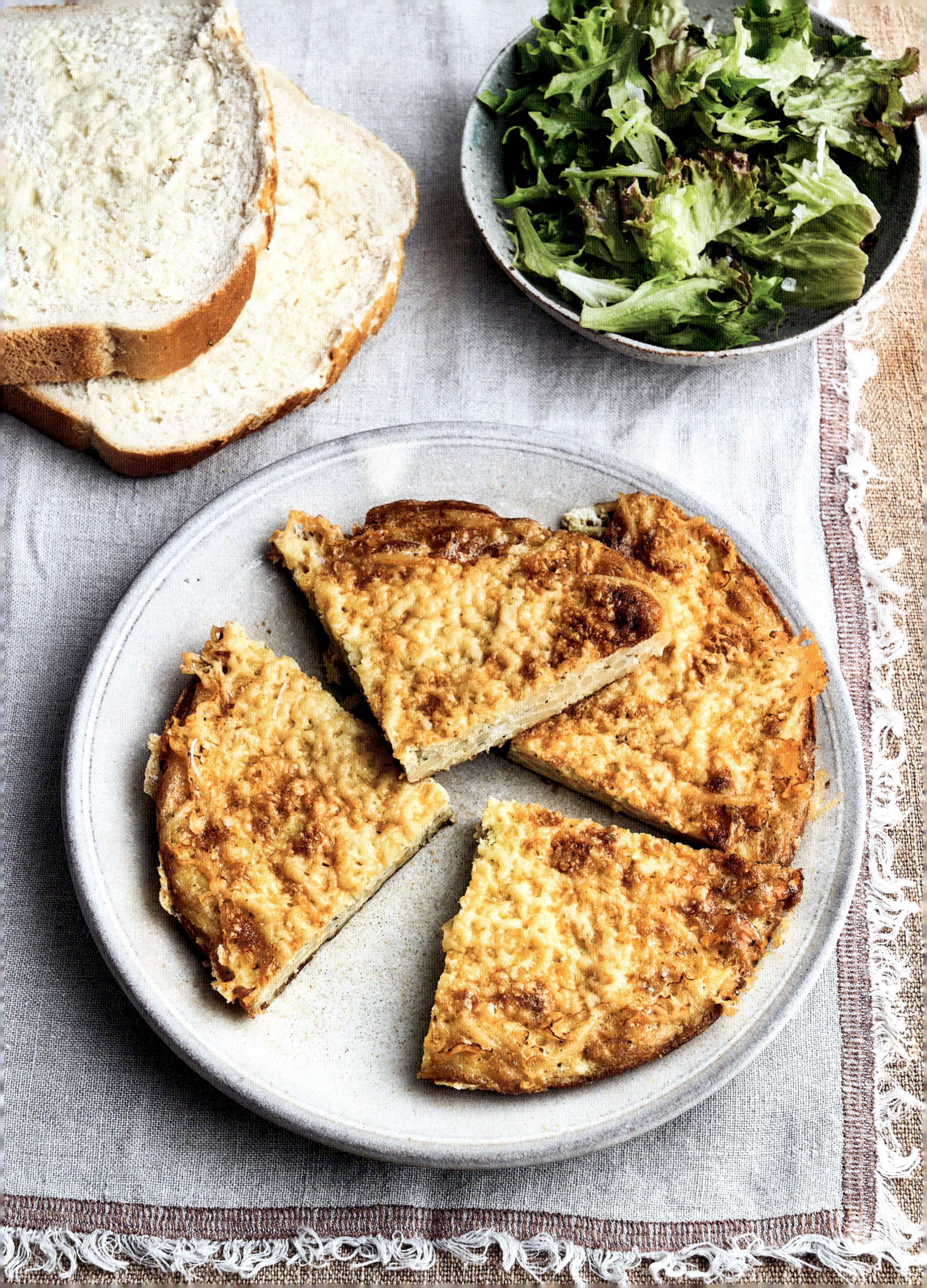

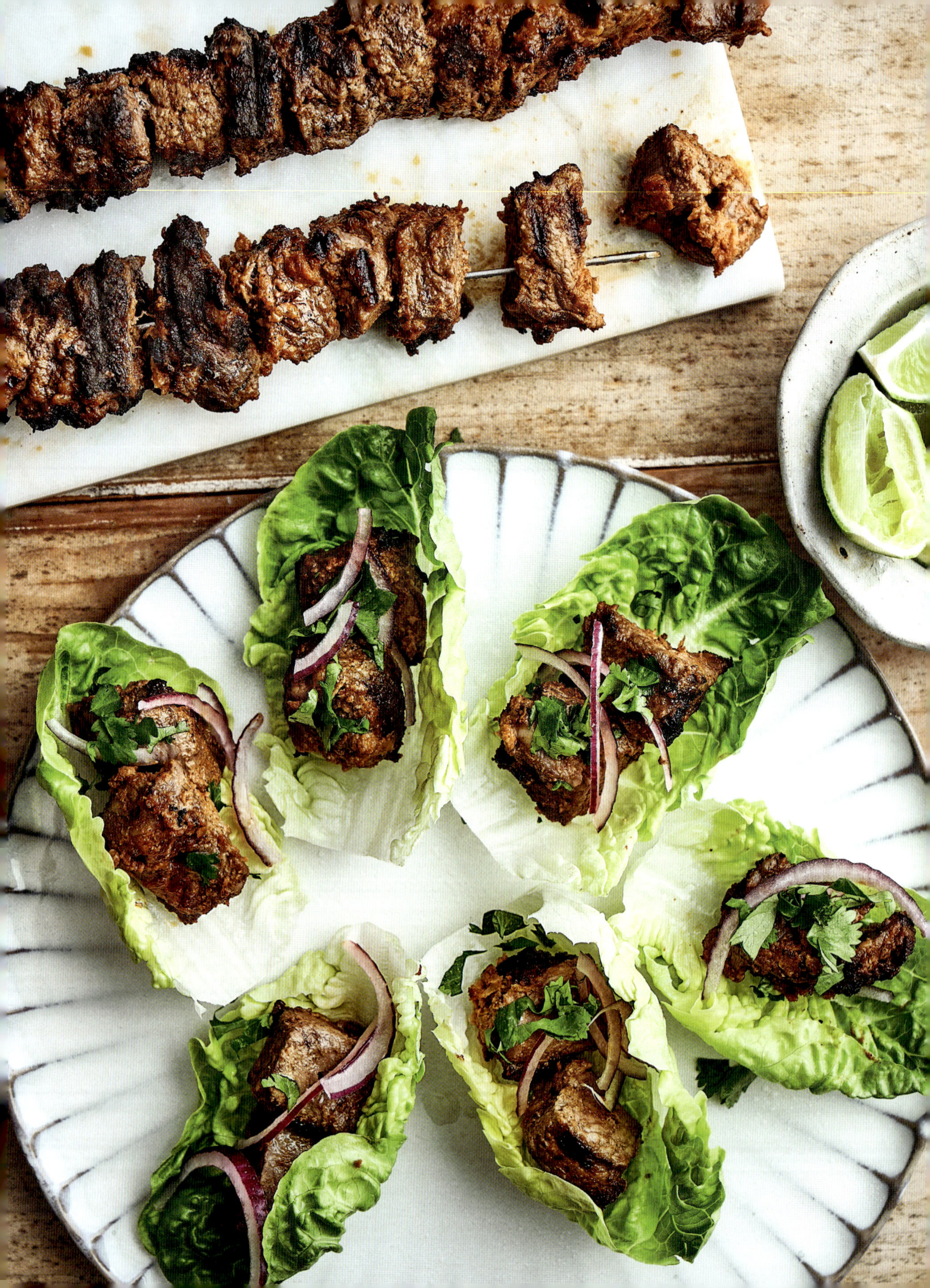

BEEF SUYA KEBABS

I absolutely love these skewered kebabs. This is my take on Nigerian suya kebabs, which are aromatic and creamy and that I make using things I have at home.

ALSO MAKES: CHEAT'S BIRRIA (PAGE 68)

PREP: 10–15 MINS (+ MARINATING) **COOK:** 28 MINS

MAKES: 12 KEBABS

For the beef

- 100g smooth peanut butter
- 50ml vegetable oil
- 1 onion, grated
- 2 tablespoons ginger paste
- 2 tablespoons garlic paste
- 1 tablespoon smoked paprika
- 1 tablespoon cayenne
- 1 tablespoon salt
- ½ teaspoon ground cloves
- 1 lemon, juice only
- 1.5kg beef, cubed

To serve

- Large lettuce leaves
- Sliced red onion
- Chopped fresh coriander
- Lime wedges
- 12 wooden or metal skewers

Start by making the marinade. Put the peanut butter, vegetable oil, grated onion, ginger paste and garlic paste in a large bowl. Now in with your spices – add the smoked paprika, cayenne, salt, ground cloves and the lemon juice. Mix everything so you have a smooth, even paste.

Add the beef and mix to make sure each piece is covered in the delicious marinade. Leave in the fridge for 4 hours or overnight if you can.

Prepare the skewers by fully submerging them in water to soak for 15 minutes or use metal skewers.

Skewer the meat onto the skewers and pop on a tray till you are ready to grill these.

Put a griddle pan over a high heat and brush with oil. Place the skewers on a few at a time, cooking them for 4 minutes on each side. These are also great on the barbecue when the weather is nice. This is my favourite way to cook them, so you get that smoky flavour, but that doesn't mean that this can't be a great midweek meal too.

I love serving these with large lettuce leaves to wrap the beef in, garnished with sliced red onion, coriander and lime wedges.

TIP *When making things like kebabs, try and make sure the meat is the same size. This way it will all cook evenly and at the same time.*

CHEAT'S BIRRIA

This is great if you have any beef left over from the suya kebabs. This simple, spicy broth means you can really jazz up the beef by just sitting it in a taco and dipping it!

PREP: 5 MINS **COOK:** 32 MINS

SERVES: 4

For the birria sauce
2 tablespoons vegetable oil
1 bay leaf
3 cloves of garlic, minced
4 dried chillies
2 tablespoons tomato purée
1 onion, chopped
3 tomatoes, grated
1 teaspoon salt
1 teaspoon dried oregano
1 teaspoon ground cumin
1 teaspoon ground cinnamon
1 teaspoon ground ginger
500ml beef stock
1 teaspoon apple cider vinegar

For the tacos
Chilli oil, for frying
4 tortilla wraps, quartered
400g leftover beef suya kebabs, shredded or chopped (see page 67)

Start by making the rich birria sauce. Put a deep pan over a medium heat and pour in the oil. As soon as the oil gets hot, add the bay leaf, minced garlic and the dried chillies. As soon as everything is sizzling, add the tomato purée, onion and tomatoes with the salt and cook for 10 minutes.

Now add the oregano, ground cumin, cinnamon and ginger and cook for 5 minutes.

Pour in the beef stock and apple cider vinegar. As soon as it comes to the boil, leave to simmer for 10 minutes. Remove the bay leaf and, using a stick blender, blend so you have a smooth sauce. Take off the heat.

To prepare the tortillas, pour some chilli oil into a frying pan and, one by one, quickly fry so they are just warmed through and gently stained by the spicy oil.

To eat this is a beautiful thing. Take a chilli oil-stained tortilla and fill with beef. Then dip the entire thing into the warm birria sauce and enjoy, letting it drip down your chin. Stick the birria in the middle of your table and enjoy the sweet silence of deliciousness!

TIP *This sauce can be frozen, so if you have any left over, be sure to freeze so you can enjoy birria another time.*

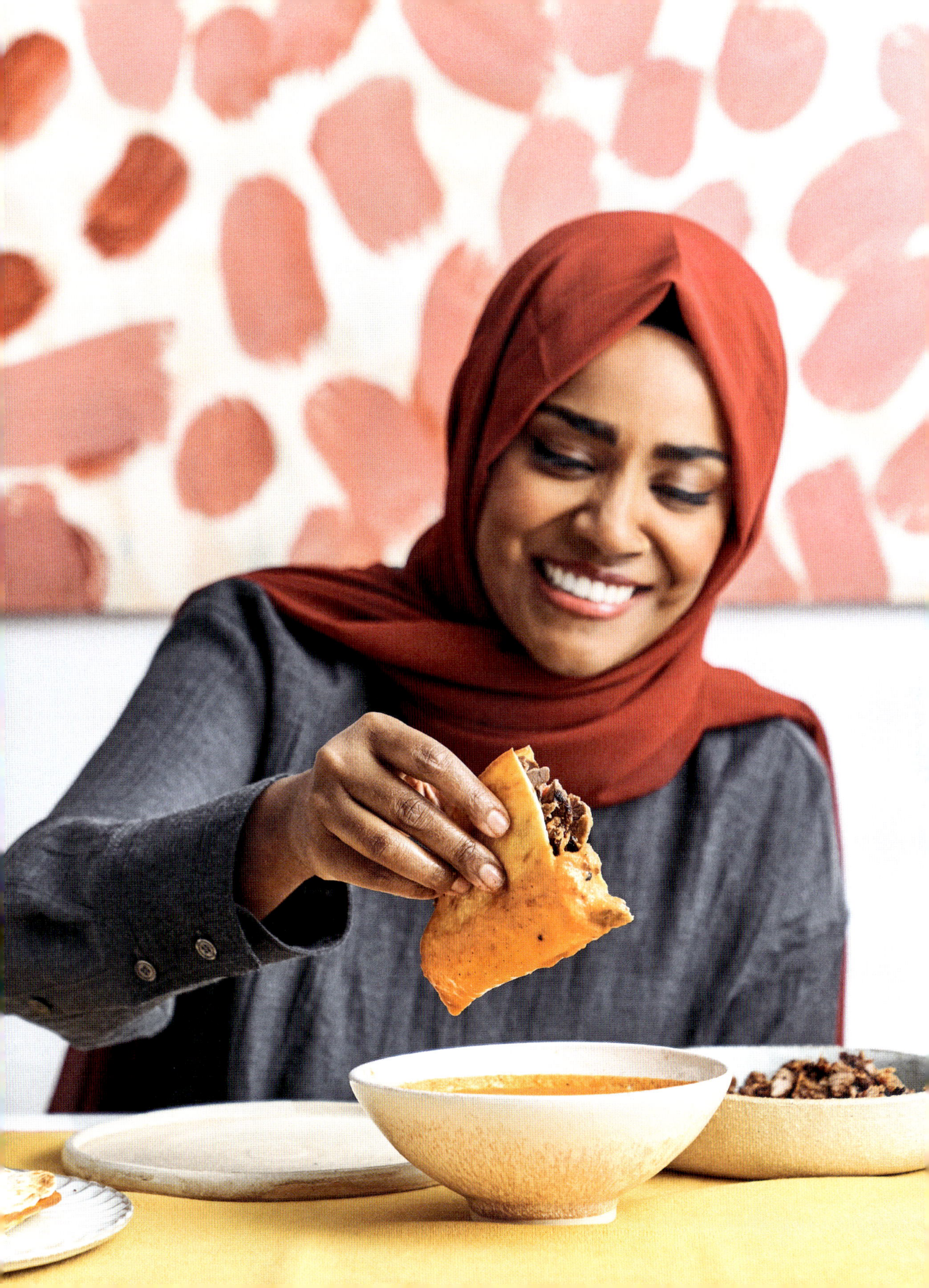

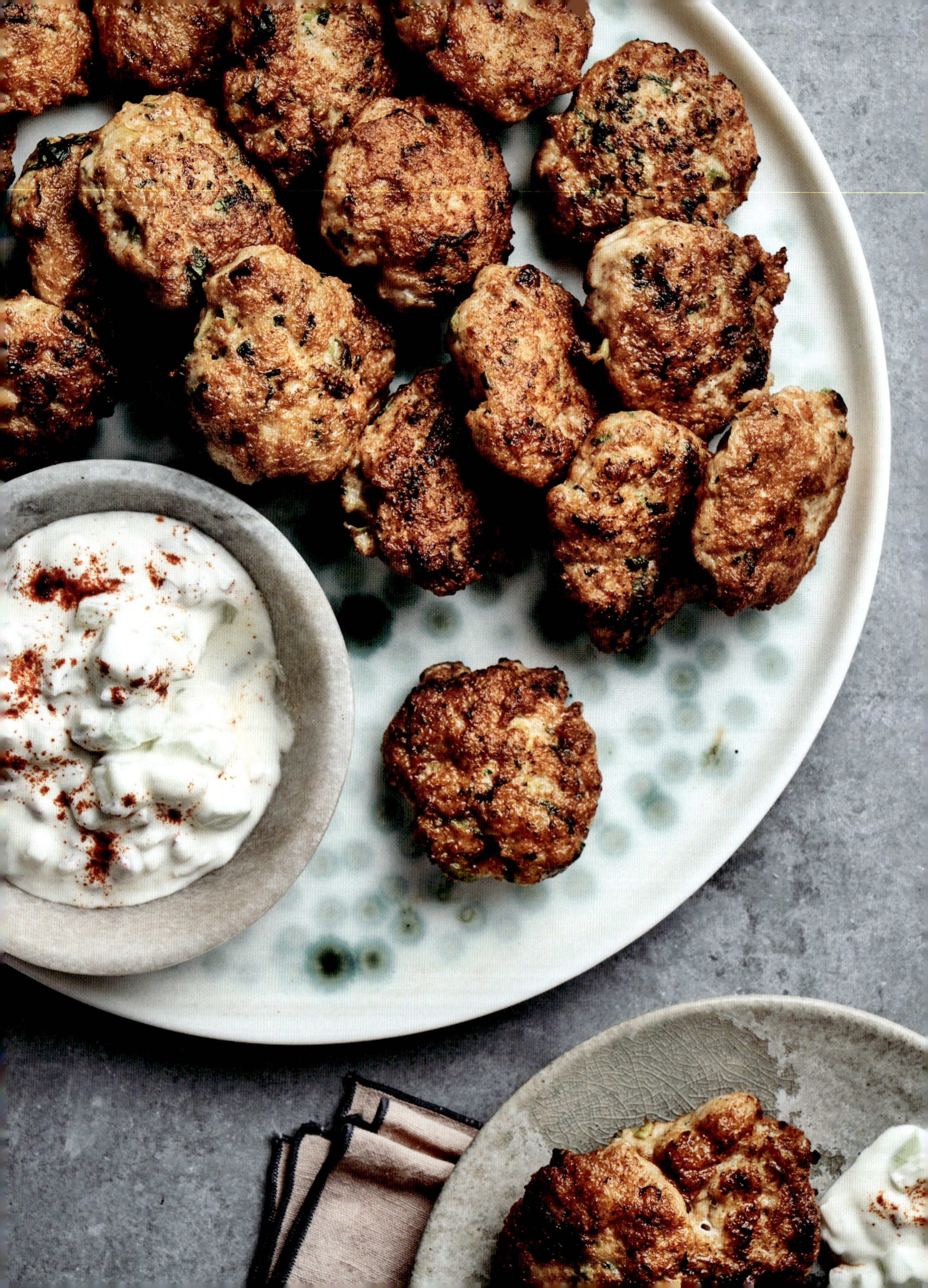

CHICKEN AND PRAWN KOFTAS

A mixture of prawns and chicken makes for a really lovely texture, and these are delicious and easy to make for something a little different. Serve with a cooling soured cream dip.

ALSO MAKES: RICE PAPER CHIPS AND DIPS (PAGE 72)

PREP: 5 MINS **COOK:** 30 MINS

SERVES: 4

For the koftas

- 250g boneless chicken thighs, diced
- 400g raw prawns, shells and tails removed
- 1 teaspoon salt
- 2 tablespoons ginger paste
- 1 tablespoon garlic paste
- 1 tablespoon garam masala
- 4 spring onions, thinly sliced
- Small handful of fresh coriander, finely chopped
- Oil, for frying

For the dip

- ½ cucumber, peeled, seeds removed and diced
- ½ red onion, finely diced
- Pinch of salt
- 1 teaspoon honey
- 1 lime, juice only
- 300ml soured cream
- Splash of milk
- Paprika, for sprinkling

Start by making the koftas. Put the chicken thighs into a food processor along with the raw prawns and salt and blend till you have a smooth paste.

Now add the ginger paste, garlic paste and garam masala and blend till you have a mixture that looks even. Tip out into a bowl, add the spring onion and coriander and mix well.

Pop a non-stick frying pan over a medium heat and pour in some oil so we can lightly fry these koftas.

Grease your hands to stop the mixture from sticking. Take a walnut-sized amount, create a flat patty and pop into the hot oil. Do this till you have a few in the pan but be sure not to overcrowd. Fry for about 4 minutes on each side and keep going till you have cooked them all.

Make the dip by putting the cubed cucumber in a bowl with the red onion and a pinch of salt. Add the honey and lime juice and mix through, then mix in the soured cream. Pour in a splash of milk just to make it a little runnier.

Sprinkle paprika on top of the dip, and the koftas and dip are ready to serve.

TIP *The moistest part of a chicken is the thighs, so when you are making something like this it's best to use the thigh as it will mean you have really juicy koftas. However, if you wanted to you could also use breast.*

RICE PAPER CHIPS AND DIPS

I am going to show you guys how to make a really hearty dip using leftover koftas. This recipe just stretches what you already have into something new and fresh. The 'chips' are crisps made with rice paper, so they are crisp and light and work beautifully with our dip.

PREP: 5 MINS **COOK:** 20 MINS

SERVES: 4

For the dip

3 tablespoons oil

2 teaspoons coriander seeds, crushed

½ teaspoon salt

1½ teaspoons chilli powder (optional)

1 clove of garlic, minced

1 celery stick, diced into small cubes

3 tablespoons crispy fried onions

Small handful of fresh coriander, finely chopped

300g Greek yoghurt

100g leftover chicken and prawn koftas, cooled and diced (see page 71)

For the rice paper chips

Oil, for frying

4 sheets of rice paper

For the dip, start by heating the oil in a small pan over a medium heat. As soon as the oil is hot, add the crushed coriander seeds and allow them to sizzle a little. As soon as they sizzle, pour the mixture into a bowl.

To the bowl, add the salt, chilli powder, garlic, celery, crispy onions and coriander and mix them all together.

Add the yoghurt and koftas and mix together, then set aside and get ready to fry the rice paper.

This bit is a lot of fun. Find a frying pan that is big enough to fit the rice paper, with space to fry and room around the edges for the tongs to be able to pick up the rice paper. Have a plate ready, lined with some kitchen paper.

You will need about 2–3cm of oil in the pan. Get the oil hot over a medium heat. Gently lower a sheet of rice paper into the oil and let go. It should puff up instantly and become all knobbly and crispy – this will take seconds. Take out and leave to drain, then do this to all the rice paper.

Once they are fried and cooled, break into shards and serve them alongside your yummy kofta dip!

TIP *Why not try crispy rice paper as a delicious crunchy topping for your salads!*

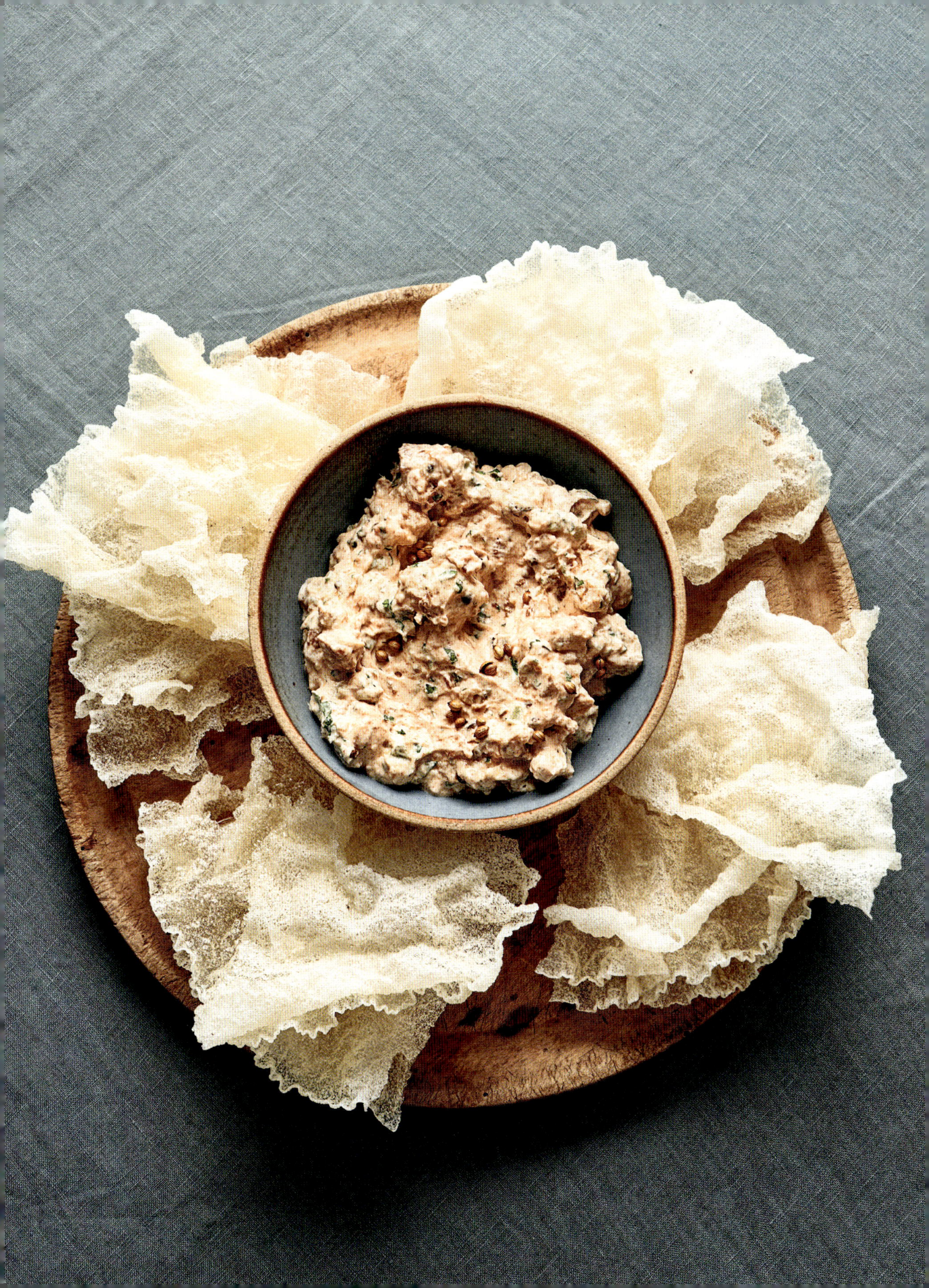

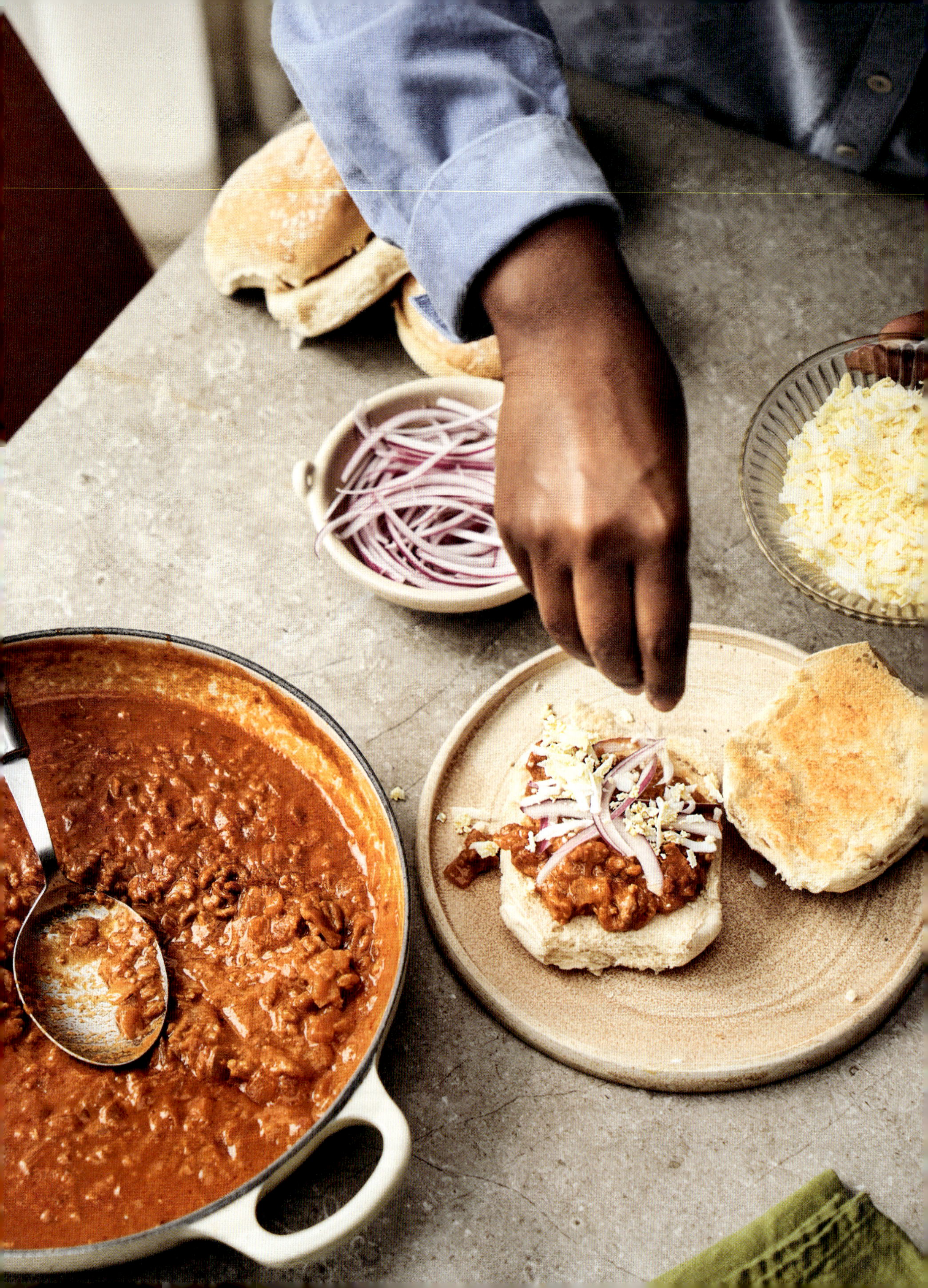

SLOPPY JOES

These are the burgers that you see all over teen American movies, served up by grumpy kitchen staff to even grumpier teenagers. Don't believe everything you see in teen movies – they are absolutely delicious. The mince is cooked till rich and thick and it's served with tangy pickled eggs and onions, all in a floured bap!

ALSO MAKES: CHEESE AND LAMB SAMOSAS (PAGE 78)

PREP: 5 MINS **COOK:** 1 HOUR

MAKES: 8 BURGERS

For the mince

- 3 tablespoons vegetable oil
- 6 cloves of garlic, minced
- 2 onions, finely diced
- 1 teaspoon salt
- 4 tablespoons tomato purée
- 2 x 400g tins of cream of tomato soup
- 4 tablespoons Worcestershire sauce
- 2 teaspoons yeast extract
- 3 tablespoons ground cumin
- 2 tablespoons chilli flakes (optional)
- 1kg lamb mince
- 100ml whole milk
- 2 tablespoons gravy granules

To serve

- 8 large floury baps
- 4 pickled eggs, grated
- 1 red onion, thinly sliced

Let's start by making the sloppy part of the sloppy Joe (who is Joe anyway?). Pour the olive oil into a deep pan and place over a medium heat. As soon as the oil is hot, add the garlic and cook till golden brown.

Now add the onion and salt and cook till the onion is translucent, golden brown and soft. Add the tomato purée and cook into the onion for a few minutes.

Pour in the cream of tomato soup and add the Worcestershire sauce, yeast extract, ground cumin and chilli flakes, mix through and leave to simmer till the yeast extract has melted away.

Crumble in the lamb mince and stir, breaking up the meat while it cooks in the sauce to prevent any huge clumps of mince.

Pour in the milk and simmer for about 30 minutes till the sauce has thickened and really coated the meat. Add the gravy granules, stir and let the granules dissolve. Leave on the lowest heat, covered with a lid, for 10 minutes and then take off the heat.

To serve, cut open the baps and toast them on both sides under the grill or in a toaster. To each one add a generous helping of the mince, sprinkle on the pickled egg and red onion, top with a bap and get it in your mouth!

TIP *Gravy granules are not just great for instant gravy, they are amazing as a thickener for curries, casseroles, stews and sauces.*

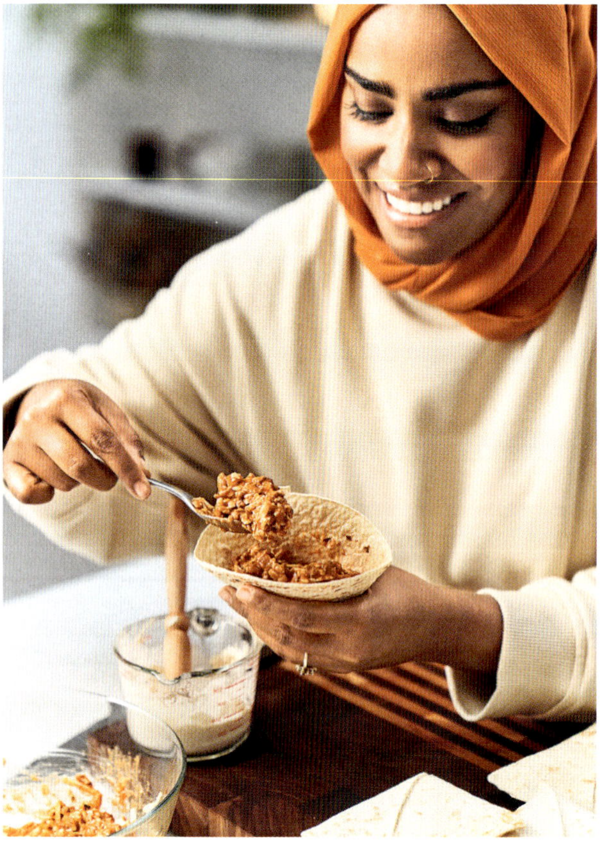
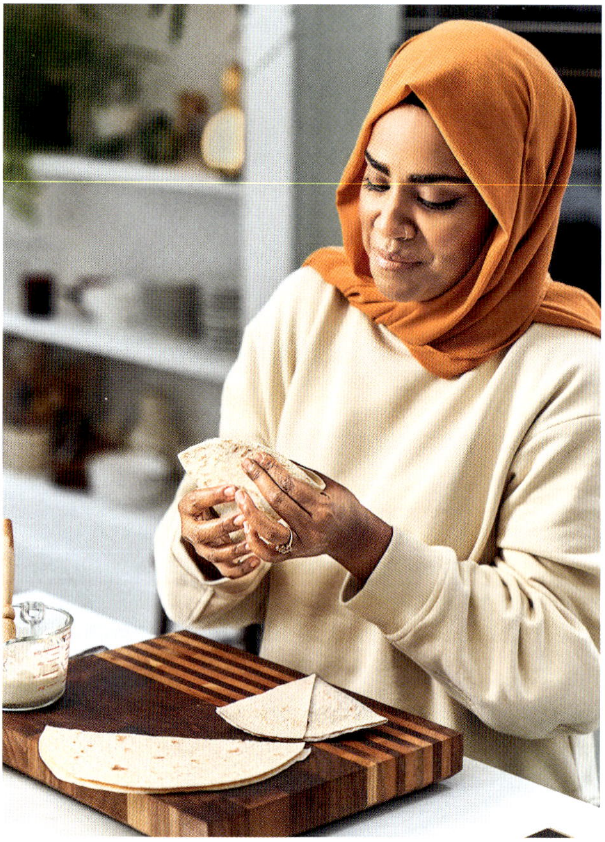
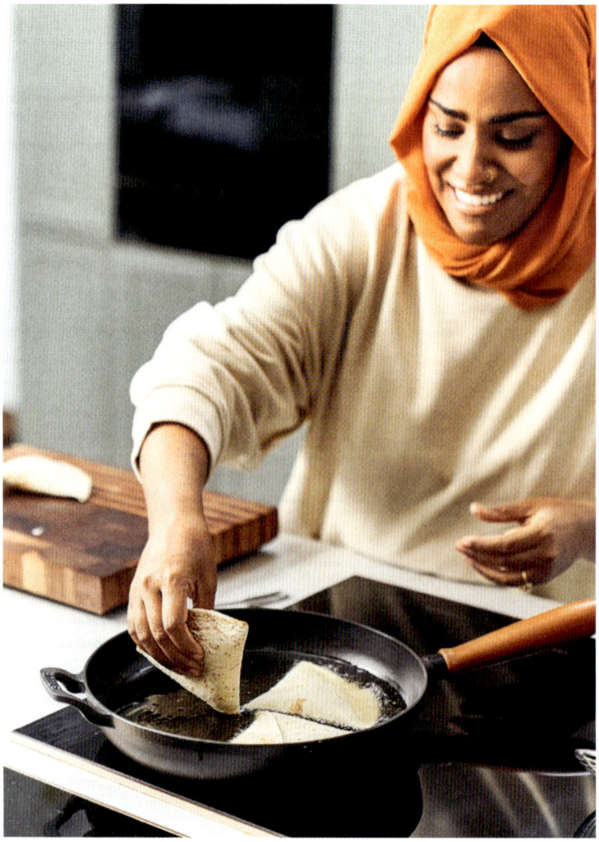
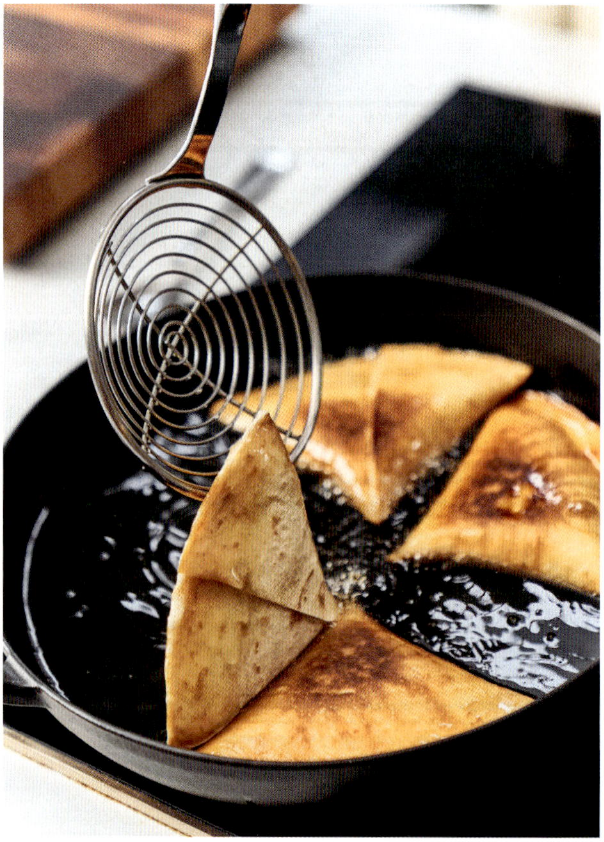

LOVIN' YOUR LEFTOVERS / 77

CHEESE AND LAMB SAMOSAS

I love samosas and the best samosas are made using leftovers. This kind of filling is perfect for that. These samosas are great with cheese and are made so simply using tortilla wraps.

PREP: 12 MINS **COOK:** 16 MINS

MAKES: 4 SAMOSAS

For the glue
50g plain flour
Water

For the samosas
250g leftover Sloppy Joes mince (see page 75), chilled
100g Cheddar cheese, grated
2 tortilla wraps, halved
Oil, for deep-frying

Start by making the glue. This is so simple – just put the flour in a bowl with enough water to make a thick paste, like the consistency of pancake batter. Set that aside.

Preheat the oven to 180°C.

To a large bowl, add the mince filling and the cheese and mix through well so the cheese is evenly incorporated.

Now take a tortilla half and create a cone shape by bringing the two straight edges together, making sure to overlap by about 3cm. Brush on your glue and fix the two edges together, being sure to press hard to make them adhere.

Fill the inside of the cone with the mince, but not too full, just enough to be able to close it comfortably. Glue the rounded edge and press firmly. Do this to all the samosas.

Put a large frying pan over a medium heat, add oil about 2cm deep and pop the samosas in a couple at a time as these are huge. I know! I love a massive samosa! These will only take a few minutes on each side till the tortilla is golden and the filling warmed up.

Leave to drain on a plate lined with kitchen paper before eating.

TIP *Samosas make a great snack. When these have cooled, if you have any left over, freeze and then cook from frozen in the air fryer or oven.*

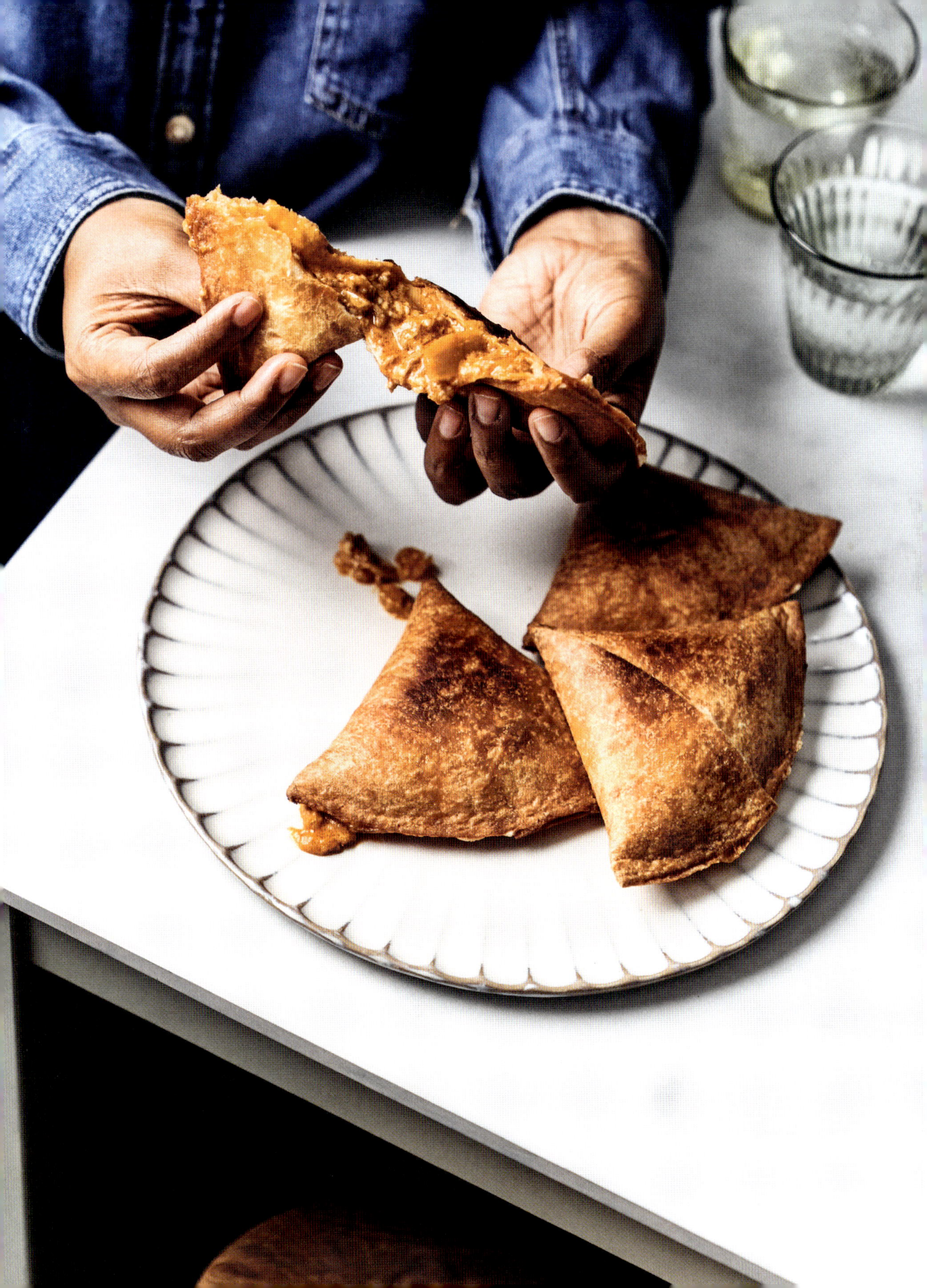

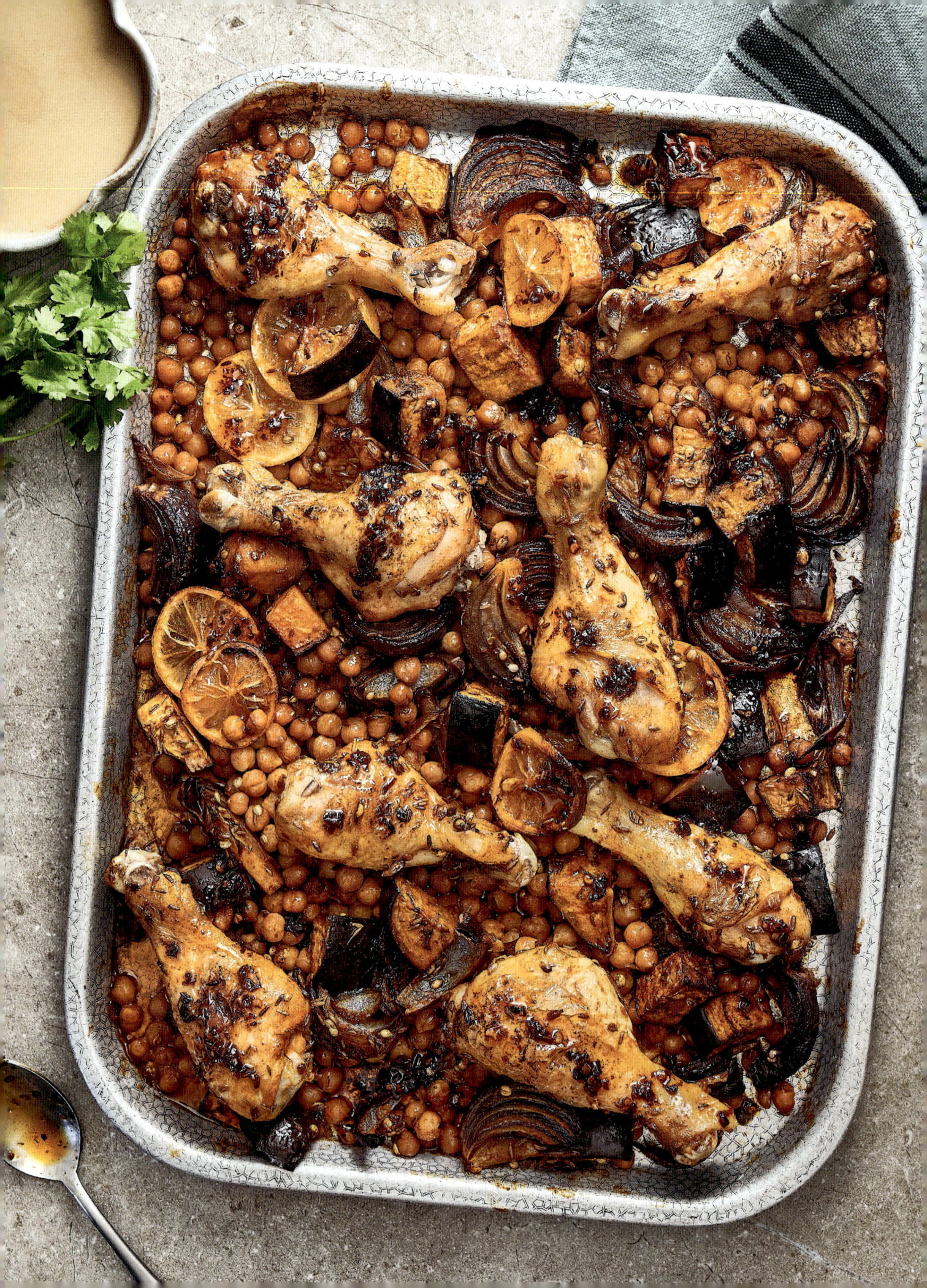

CHICKPEA AND CHICKEN TRAYBAKE

I love a traybake and this one is no less loved than all the others that I make! Packed full of veg and flavour, this is the kind of thing I make on repeat for an easy life and a delicious dinner each and every single time.

ALSO MAKES: SPICED CHICKEN-TOPPED HUMMUS (PAGE 82)

PREP: 8 MINS **COOK:** 45 MINS

SERVES: 4

For the traybake

Oil, for frying

4 cloves of garlic, minced

2 red onions, cut into chunks

1 medium aubergine, cut into chunks

2 x 400g tins of chickpeas, drained

1 lemon, topped and tailed and thinly sliced

2 teaspoons coriander seeds

2 teaspoons cumin seeds

1½ teaspoons salt

2 teaspoons paprika

½ teaspoon ground turmeric

8 chicken drumsticks

To serve

Chopped fresh coriander

Tahini

Chilli oil

Preheat the oven to 180°C and have a large roasting dish ready to put this beautiful thing together.

Pour a generous drizzle of oil into the base of the dish and now it's time to get it all in. Add the garlic, red onion, aubergine, chickpeas and lemon slices.

Using a pestle and mortar, lightly crush the coriander and cumin seeds. Add with the salt, paprika, turmeric and the chicken drumsticks. Get your hands in and give everything a really good mix around so it's all coated.

Pop into the oven for 45 minutes till the chicken is cooked and the vegetables are tender.

To serve, sprinkle over the chopped coriander and drizzle over the tahini and chilli oil. It is now ready to take to the middle of the table.

TIP *Never throw away the liquid from chickpea water – you can make great vegan meringues with it!*

SPICED CHICKEN-TOPPED HUMMUS

I love making and eating hummus and if you have never made it, give it a go. Hummus is so easy and so easy to flavour! I think you will absolutely love it.

PREP: 10–15 MINS

SERVES: 4–6

200g leftover chickpea and chicken traybake, cooled (see page 81)

2 tablespoons tahini

50ml olive oil, plus extra for drizzling

1 lemon, juice only

3 ice cubes

Good pinch of salt

Fresh coriander, for sprinkling

To serve

Warm pittas

Vegetable sticks

Take your leftover vegetables and chickpeas, minus the chicken, and put into a blender. Shred the chicken and set aside.

Add your tahini, olive oil and lemon juice and blend the whole thing till you have a broken-down mixture. Now add your ice cubes and blend till you have a smooth, creamy mixture.

Pour into a flat serving dish and spread out. Sprinkle with coriander, a few extra chickpeas and the shredded chicken and drizzle over some olive oil. I love to serve this with warm pittas and vegetable sticks.

TIP *Adding ice to the hummus while making it creates the most deliciously smooth dip – totally worth a try!*

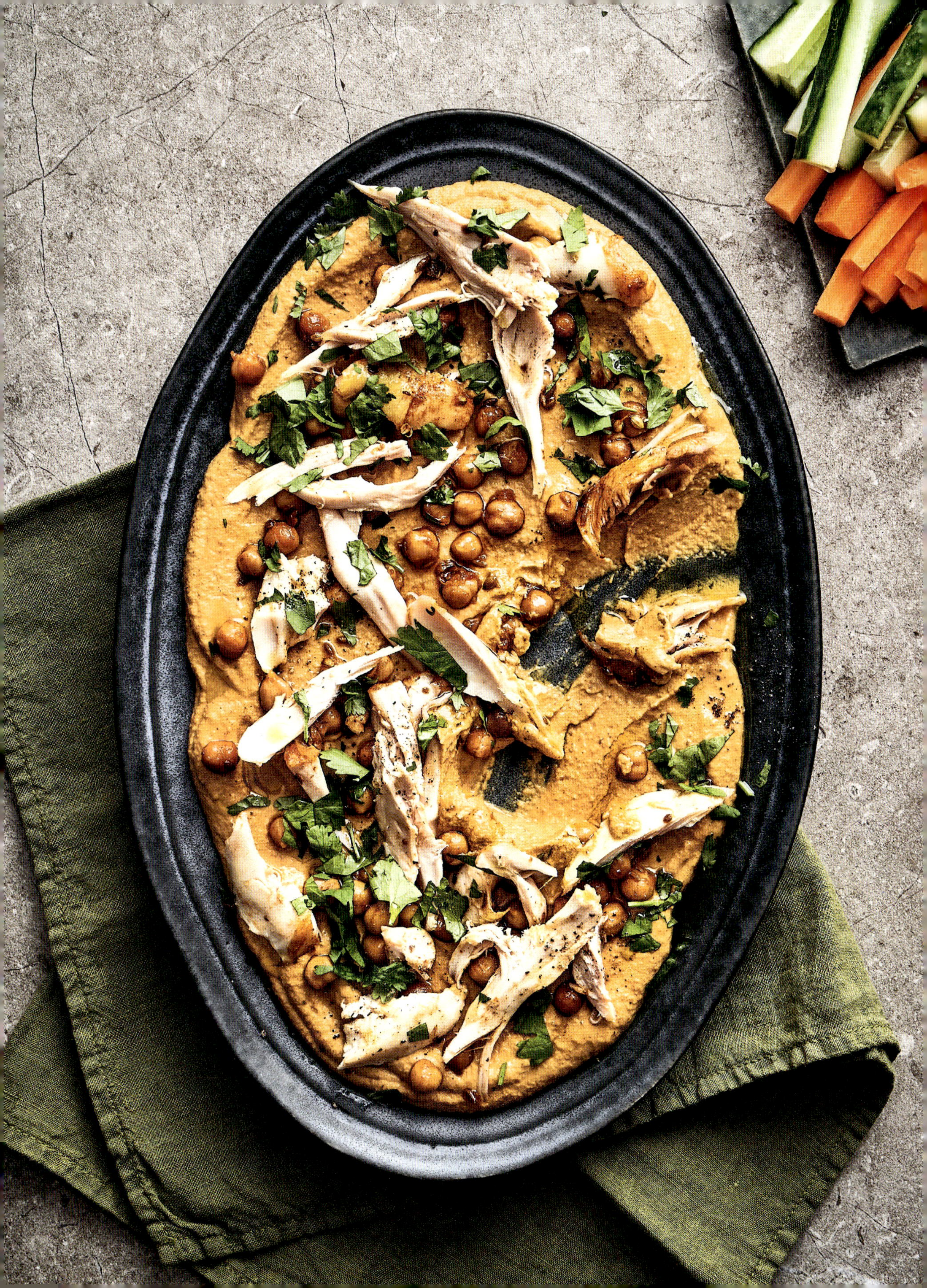

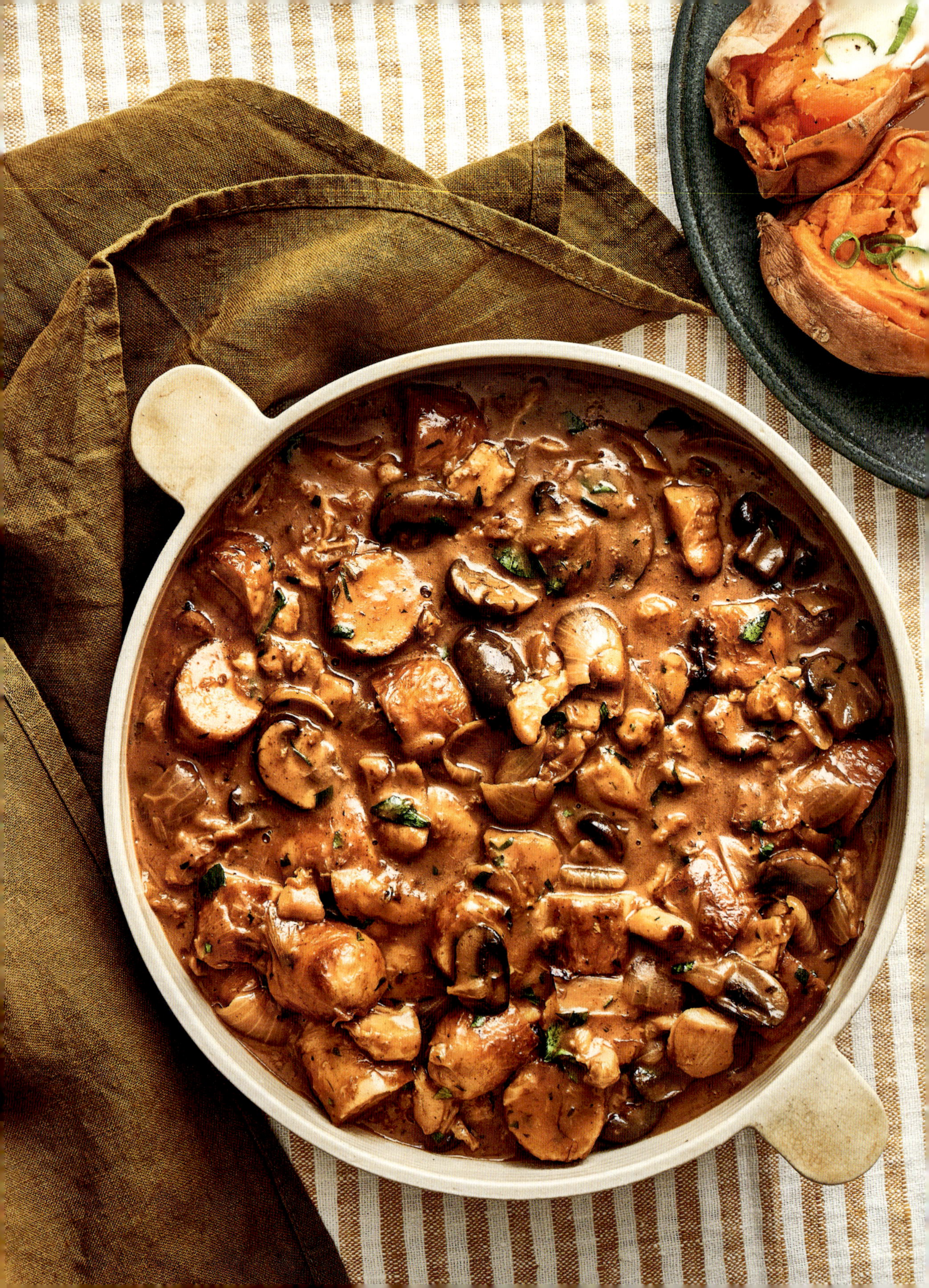

CHICKEN SAUSAGE MUSHROOM CASSEROLE

I love making casseroles, mostly because you can make, put a lid on and leave. This combination of chicken, sausage and mushroom is a winner dinner in our house. Earthy, herby and scrummy.

ALSO MAKES: CREAMY SAUSAGE HANDHELD PIES (PAGE 86)

PREP: 5 MINS **COOK:** 1 HOUR 40 MINS

SERVES: 4–6

For the casserole

Oil, for frying

1 bay leaf

500g boneless chicken thighs, diced

6 sausages, quartered

2 onions, chopped into big chunks

50ml vegetable oil

50g plain flour

3 cloves of garlic, minced

Large sprig of fresh lemon thyme

1 teaspoon salt

1 tablespoon yeast extract

3 tablespoons Worcestershire sauce

2 tablespoons ground black pepper

1 teaspoon smoked sweet paprika

200g mushrooms

400ml chicken stock

100ml crème fraîche

To serve

Chopped fresh parsley

Pour oil into a large casserole dish and set over a high heat. Add the bay leaf and as soon as the bay sizzles, add the chicken, in batches, and cook till golden brown on the outside. Put the chicken in a bowl and continue cooking until all the chicken is browned. Set the chicken aside.

In the same dish, fry the sausages till golden and place with the cooked chicken. Do the same with the onion, cook till golden brown and place with the chicken and sausage.

Add the vegetable oil to the now-empty casserole dish and set over a medium heat. Stir in the plain flour and cook till golden and the flour starts to smell nutty.

It's time to get everything in. Add the garlic, sprig of lemon thyme, salt, yeast extract, Worcestershire sauce, black pepper and smoked sweet paprika, then tip the bowl of chicken, sausage and onion back in.

Add the mushrooms and chicken stock and mix everything through. Bring the whole thing to a boil, reduce to a medium heat, cover and leave to simmer for 45 minutes.

After 45 minutes, add the crème fraîche and mix through. Leave to simmer for another 15 minutes, till the mixture is thicker.

Take off the heat and sprinkle over the parsley. I love to serve this with a baked sweet potato.

TIP *It's so easy to bake a sweet potato in the microwave. Pierce the potato and place directly onto the microwave plate, cook for 8–10 minutes and it should be fully cooked and super sweet.*

CREAMY SAUSAGE HANDHELD PIES

I make these handheld pies all the time and they are especially great with leftovers that have cooked long and slow. With all the hard work done, all we need to do is envelop them in ready-rolled puff pastry – easy as handheld pie, some might say!

PREP: 12 MINS **COOK:** 25 MINS

MAKES: 4 PIES

- 2 x 320g packs of ready-rolled puff pastry, defrosted if frozen
- 1 egg, beaten
- 400–450g leftover chicken sausage mushroom casserole, chilled (see page 85)
- Sesame seeds
- Rock salt

Preheat the oven to 200°C.

Start by laying out one sheet of puff pastry on a large baking sheet. Leave the paper it is already on, on. Place the long edge closest to you. Brush the outer edges of the pastry with egg and then brush a cross right onto the pastry. You should have four visible rectangles.

Now divide up your cooled casserole mixture among the rectangles.

Take your second sheet of pastry and roll it out a little more so it's big enough to sit on top. Using the sheet of paper attached to your pastry as a guide, place the pastry right on top of the casserole mixture, using the side of your hand to section off the four pies. Make sure it all touches the egg glue you brushed on the bottom sheet.

Now all you need to do is cut the pastry so you have four individual pies. Press and seal the edges and poke steam holes into the top of each one. Brush generously with the egg and sprinkle with the sesame seeds and rock salt.

Bake for 25 minutes. Take the pies out and if you can wait, wait for 10 minutes before eating. They will be piping hot . . . and delicious!

TIP *You can also make this recipe using shortcrust pastry if that's all you have or you fancy something different. This will give you a more biscuity texture rather than flaky.*

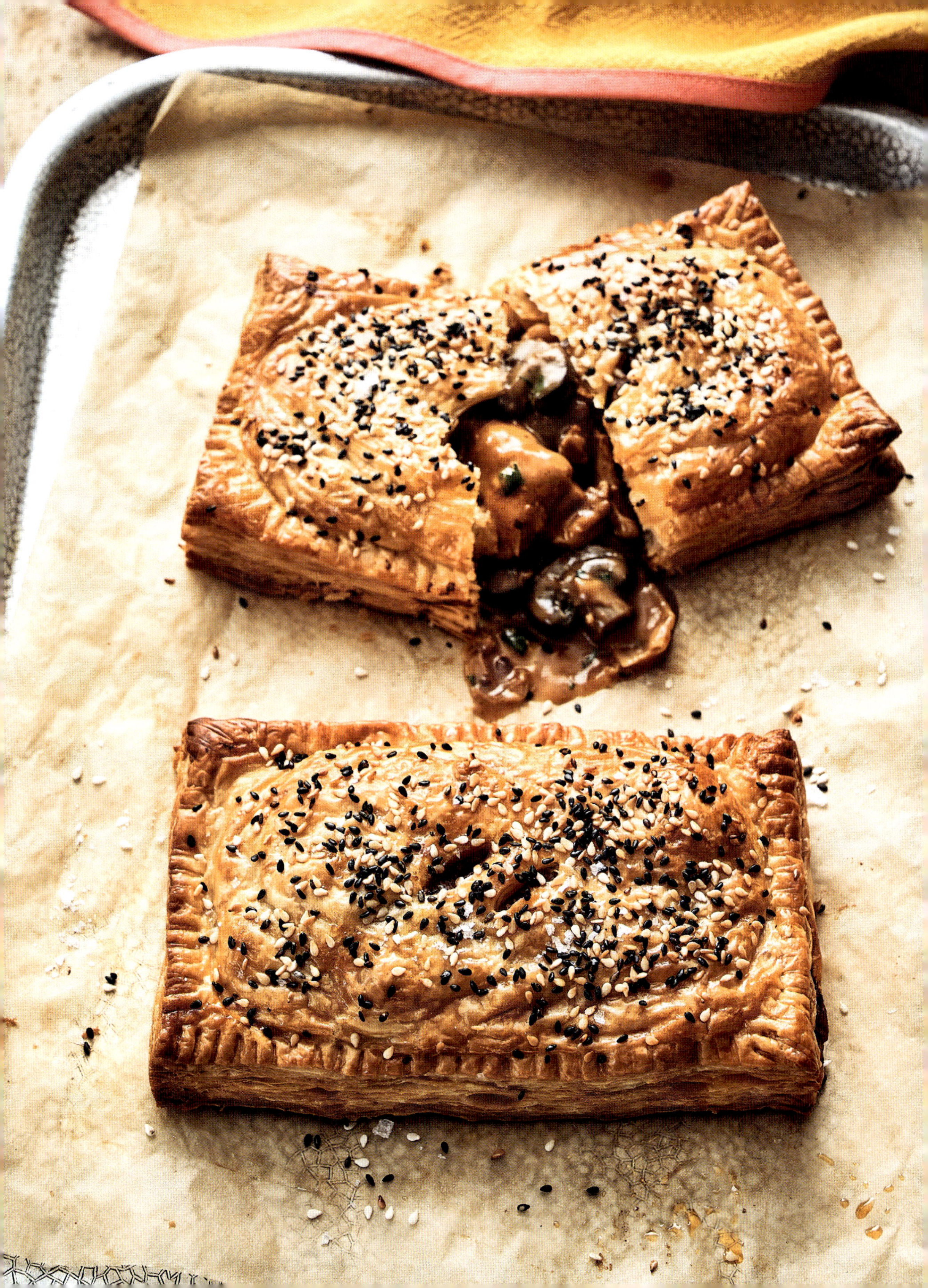

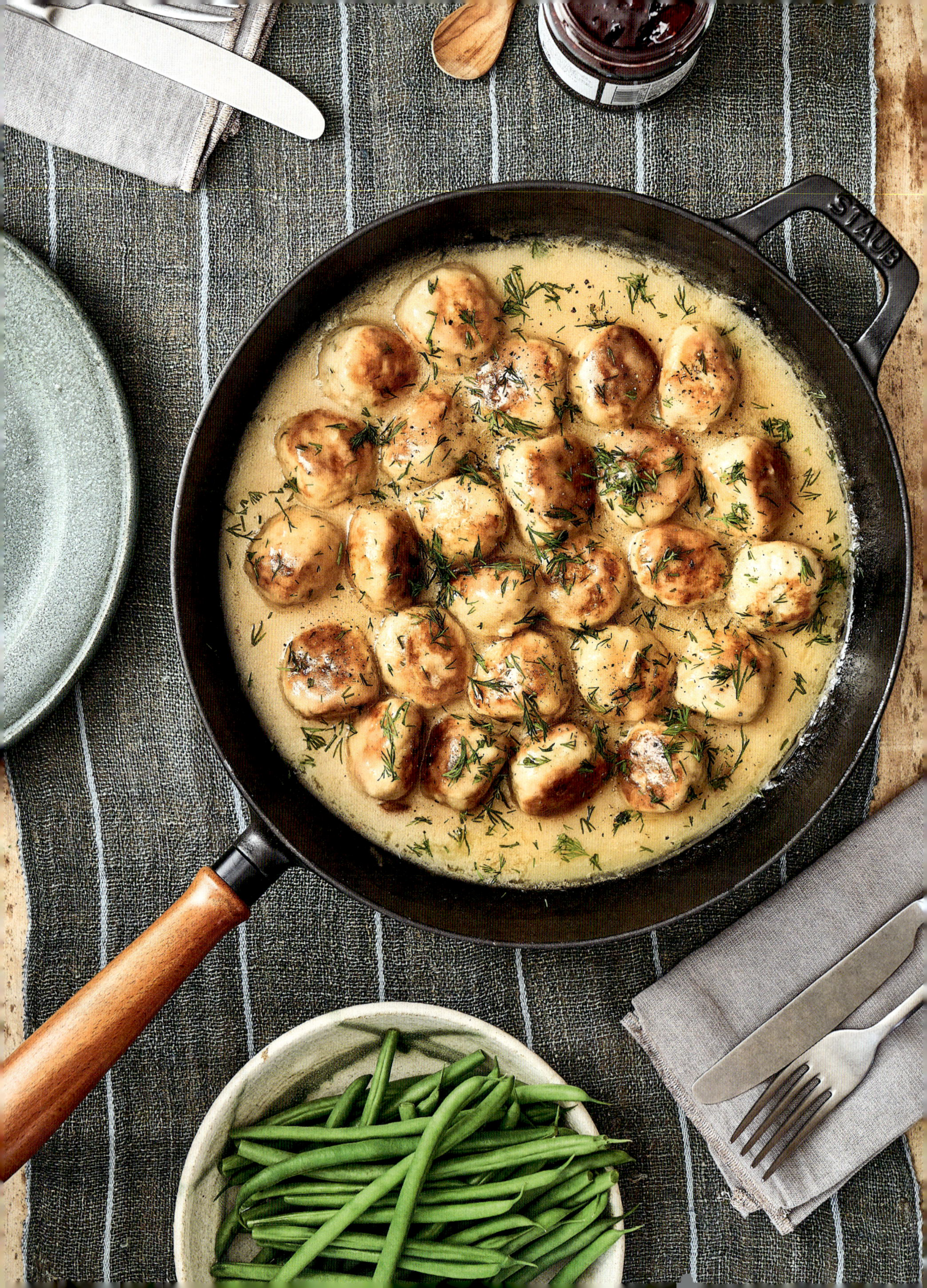
STAUB

SWEDISH-STYLE MEATBALLS

I know these are traditionally made with pork. I don't eat pork, but I don't think anyone should miss out, so I am making mine with chicken mince, simply flavoured with dill and garlic, all in a chicken stock sauce.

ALSO MAKES: MEATBALL PARATHAS (PAGE 90)

PREP: 10–12 MINS **COOK:** 18 MINS

SERVES: 4

For the meatballs
- 400g chicken or turkey mince
- 1 onion, very finely diced
- 2 cloves of garlic, minced
- ½ teaspoon salt
- 1 medium egg
- 85g breadcrumbs
- Small handful of fresh dill, finely chopped
- Oil, for frying

For the sauce
- 2 tablespoons oil
- 3 tablespoons plain four
- 500ml chicken stock
- 3 teaspoons miso paste

To serve
- Ultimate mashed potato (see page 27)
- Steamed green beans

Start by making the meatballs. Put the chicken mince in a large bowl along with the onion, garlic, salt and egg. Mix it all through so the egg is incorporated. Sprinkle in the breadcrumbs and dill, get your hands in and mix till you have an even mixture.

Wet your hands, take a pinch of the mixture that is the size of a whole walnut and mould tightly into a ball. Do this to all of the mixture and set the balls to one side to fry.

Pour some oil into a medium-sized non-stick pan, pop over a medium heat and start frying the balls, in batches, till they are golden brown and you have fried them all. They should take about 4 minutes to cook all the way through.

Now for the sauce. Add the oil and plain flour to the same pan and just gently cook the flour for a few minutes. Pour in the chicken stock and miso paste and whisk till you have a smooth, rich sauce that is packed with umami flavour.

Add your fried balls back into the pan with the sauce and toss them around till they are coated and warmed all the way through.

The balls are now ready, and you have the yummiest, simplest Swedish-style meatballs that everyone will, for sure, enjoy. I love to serve these with creamy mashed potato and steamed green beans. I don't love having it with the sweet jelly on the side, but you totally should if that is your thing!

TIP *You can make the meatballs ahead of time, shape them, fry, cool and freeze. When you are ready to eat, you just cook from frozen in the air fryer or oven.*

MEATBALL PARATHAS

Parathas are my love language. I am always cooking them, whether that is from the freezer, fresh that day or defrosted from the night before. The best parathas are the ones that use up leftovers because then you get to enjoy the same delicious flavour but in a whole other way!

PREP: 20 MINS **PROVE:** 15 MINS
COOK: 24 MINS
MAKES: 4 PARATHAS

150g leftover Swedish-style meatballs, cooled (see page 89)

For the dough

140g plain flour, plus extra for dusting

1 teaspoon salt

4 tablespoons oil

80–90ml hot water from the tap

Melted butter, for brushing

Make sure you have the leftover filling cooled. Pop into the blender and blend till you have a thick paste. Put into a bowl and set aside while you make the dough.

Put the flour in a bowl with the salt and oil. Get your hands in and rub the oil into the flour. Now add the water and, with your hands, mix till you have a dough. Be sure to not knead too much. Cover and leave for 15 minutes.

Uncover the dough and divide into four equal pieces. Roll one piece of the dough to about 10cm.

Take a quarter of the filling and add to the centre of the dough, then bring the dough to the centre and encase the filling. Pat down and flatten. On a floured surface, roll out to about 3mm thin.

Put a non-stick pan over a medium heat and, as soon as the pan is hot, put the paratha in the hot pan and fry for 3 minutes on each side. Take off the heat and brush with butter, then do the same with the other three. Enjoy hot!

TIP *To give another dimension to the flavour, you could add spices to your butter. Why not try paprika, garlic granules or za'atar – the list could go on and on.*

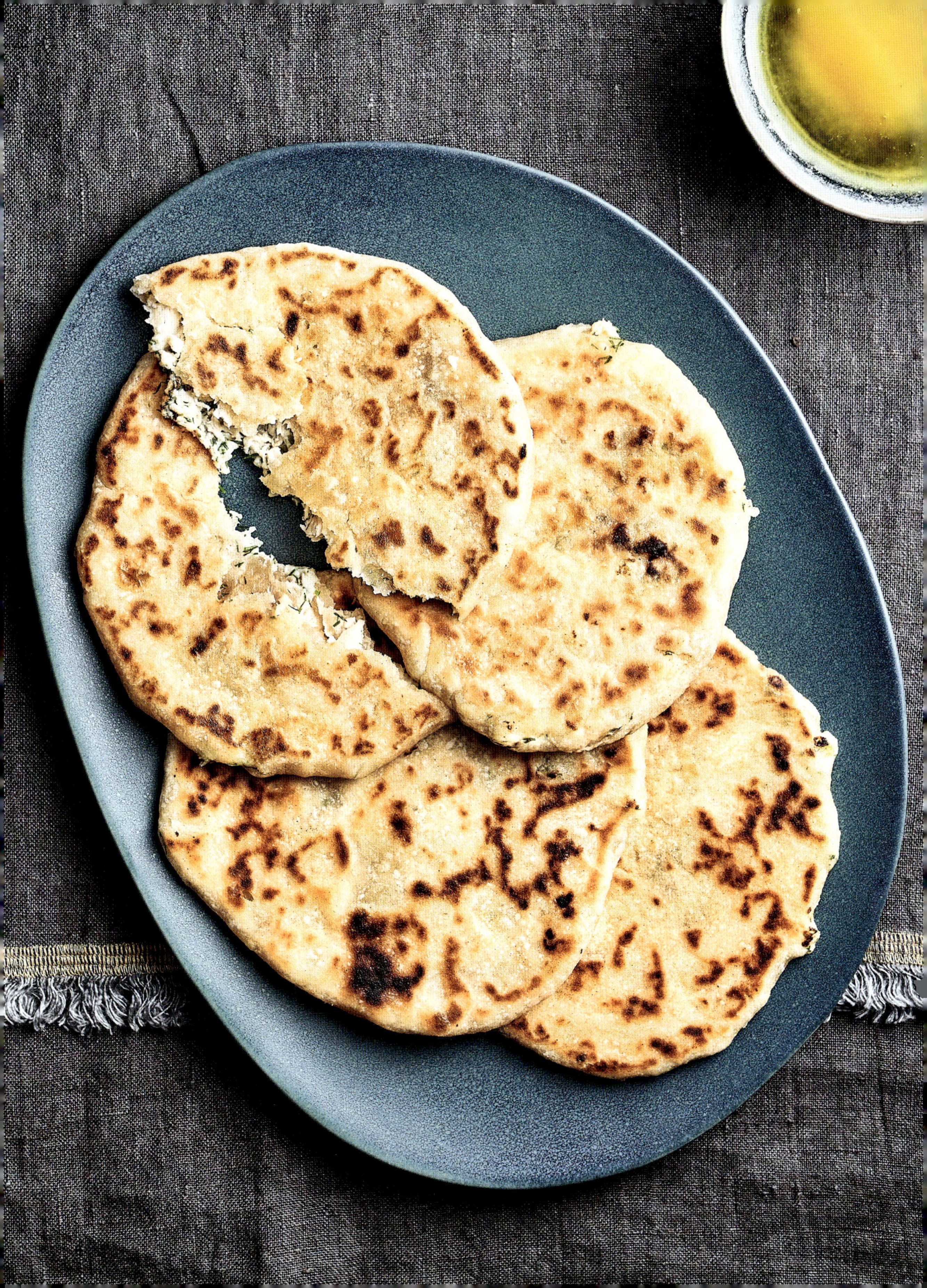

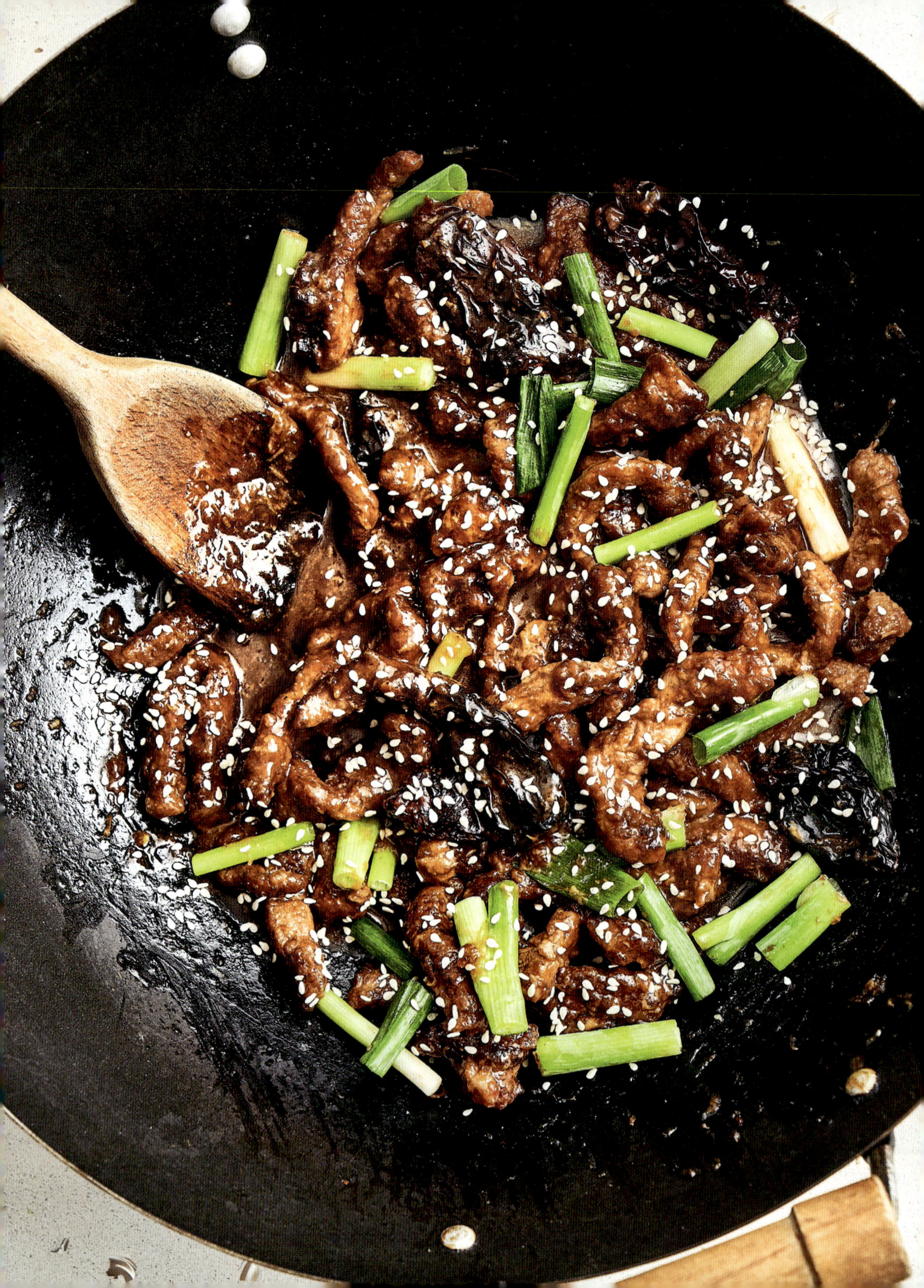

MONGOLIAN BEEF WITH STICKY RICE

I love dishes like this, that have maximum flavour and minimum work, using ingredients that we all most likely have at home. The beef is tender, sticky and sweet – you will love it.

ALSO MAKES: MONGOLIAN BEEF SEAWEED RICE WRAPS (PAGE 94)

PREP: 5 MINS **COOK:** 30 MINS

SERVES: 4

For the beef
- 500g beef steak, thinly sliced
- 1 teaspoon oil
- 2 teaspoons dark soy sauce
- 4 tablespoons cornflour

For the sauce
- Oil, for frying
- 7 cloves of garlic, minced
- 8 large dried red chillies
- 100ml water, plus 1 tablespoon for the slurry
- 2 tablespoons brown sugar
- 50ml dark soy sauce
- 1 teaspoon cornflour

To finish
- 3 spring onions, cut into 5cm pieces
- White sesame seeds

To serve
- 2 x 250g sticky rice packets

Start by taking the beef and putting it in a large bowl. Pour in the oil and soy, then add the cornflour and mix through till the beef is nicely coated.

To make the sauce, drizzle a dash of oil into a frying pan and get the oil hot. Add the garlic and chillies and cook until the garlic is a deep golden brown and the chillies almost blackened in places. Put the garlic and chillies aside in a bowl for later.

Then in the same pan over a high heat, cook the beef in batches till the beef is seared and dark brown. Remove the beef and set aside on a plate.

Mix the water, brown sugar and soy sauce together in a jug. Still using the same pan and adding a little oil if you need to (if there is some already in there, that is fine to use), pour the mixture into the pan and cook through for a few minutes over a medium heat.

Mix the cornflour with 1 tablespoon of water to make a slurry and add that to the pan. This should thicken the sauce instantly. Add the beef straight back in and stir through so the beef is glistening and covered in that shiny sauce. Throw the spring onions in and toss through.

Serve in a dish with the sesame seeds sprinkled over. I love to eat this with sticky rice straight out of a microwaved packet.

TIP *To cut any type of meat very thinly, I have a great trick: freeze for 4 hours in manageable chunks for cutting. Then take a sharp knife and cut as thin as you can. Freezing it for a few hours helps to stabilize the shape, making it easier to cut and hold the meat in place.*

MONGOLIAN BEEF SEAWEED RICE WRAPS

Seaweed is possibly the best way to eat leftover sticky rice. Add the Mongolian beef and you are on to a winner. These leftovers are simply wrapped and then sliced, ready to eat on the go.

PREP: 24 MINS
MAKES: 4 WRAPS

400g leftover Mongolian beef with sticky rice, chilled (see page 93)

4 tablespoons mayonnaise

2 tablespoons Sriracha

1 teaspoon black sesame seeds

4 seaweed wraps

Wasabi paste

½ cucumber, peeled, seeds removed and thinly sliced

Start by putting the leftover beef in a bowl with the mayonnaise, Sriracha and sesame seeds. Mix through well and set aside.

Take a sheet of seaweed and place down on the worktop, then spoon a quarter of the beef mixture into the centre. Top with a quarter of the rice so you have a roughly 7cm square.

Squeeze some wasabi on top and spread into a thin layer, then place some cucumber slices on top of that. Now encase the filling with the edges of the seaweed. You should have a neat square. Use a little water on the end of your fingers to stick the sides down. Wrap in clingfilm and make the other three.

These are best eaten the next day for lunch, giving the seaweed some time to soften.

TIP *If you can't get hold of wasabi or you don't like it but still want that kick of heat, you can use English mustard instead. Or how about trying horseradish?*

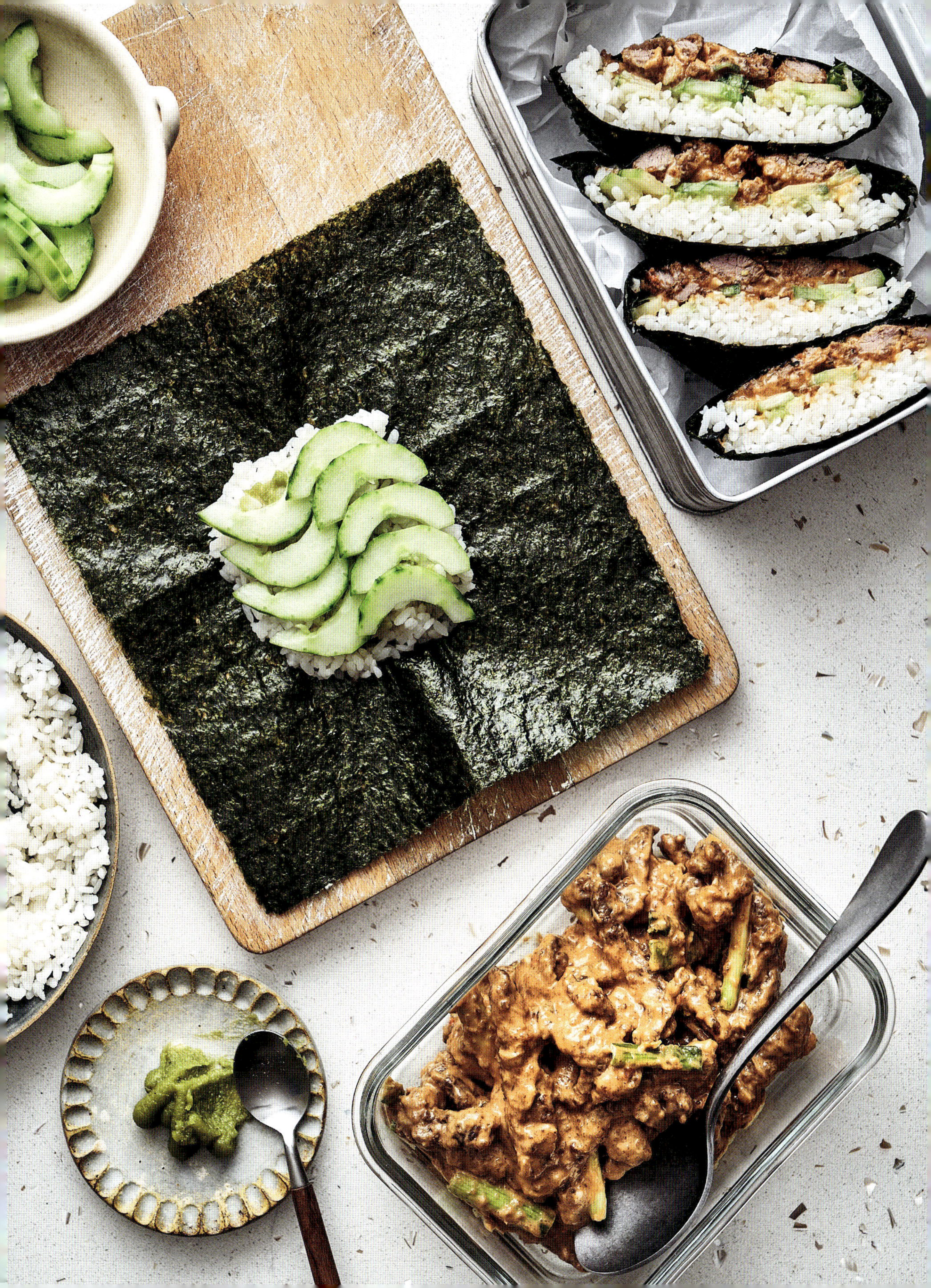

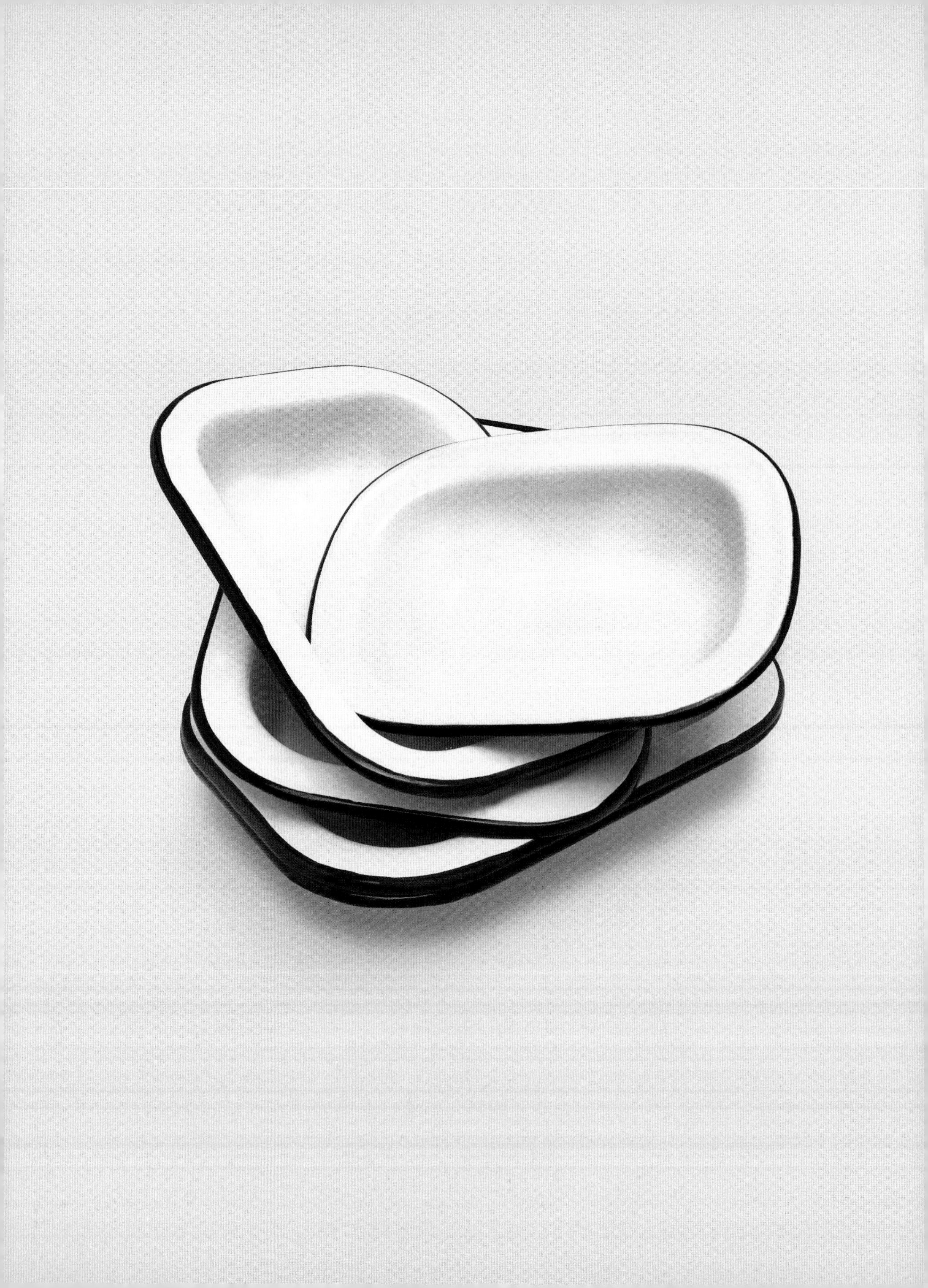

READY
↓
MEALS

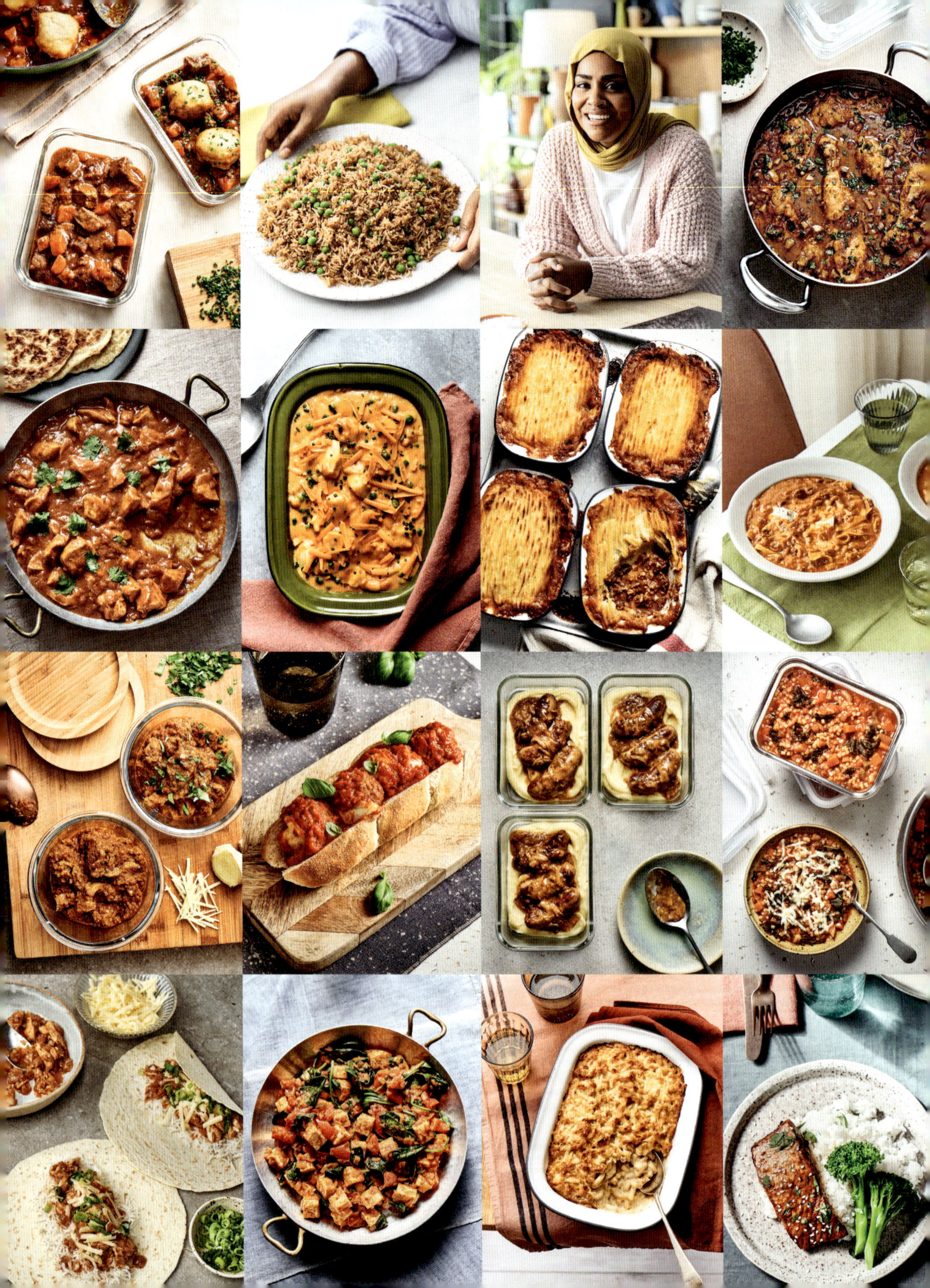

READY MEALS

Cook-ahead recipes that are perfect portions for the freezer, ready to be microwaved or baked from frozen at a later date.

BEEF STEW AND DUMPLINGS

BROWN RICE AND PEAS

CHICKEN CACCIATORE

CHICKEN TIKKA MASALA AND RICE

COD MORNAY

COTTAGE PIE

LASAGNE SOUP

LIME PICKLE LAMB

MEATBALL MARINARA

SAUSAGE, MASH AND MUSTARD GRAVY

MINESTRONE

SMOKY CHICKEN BURRITOS

PANEER KARAHI

MACARONI CHEESE

TERIYAKI SALMON AND STICKY RICE

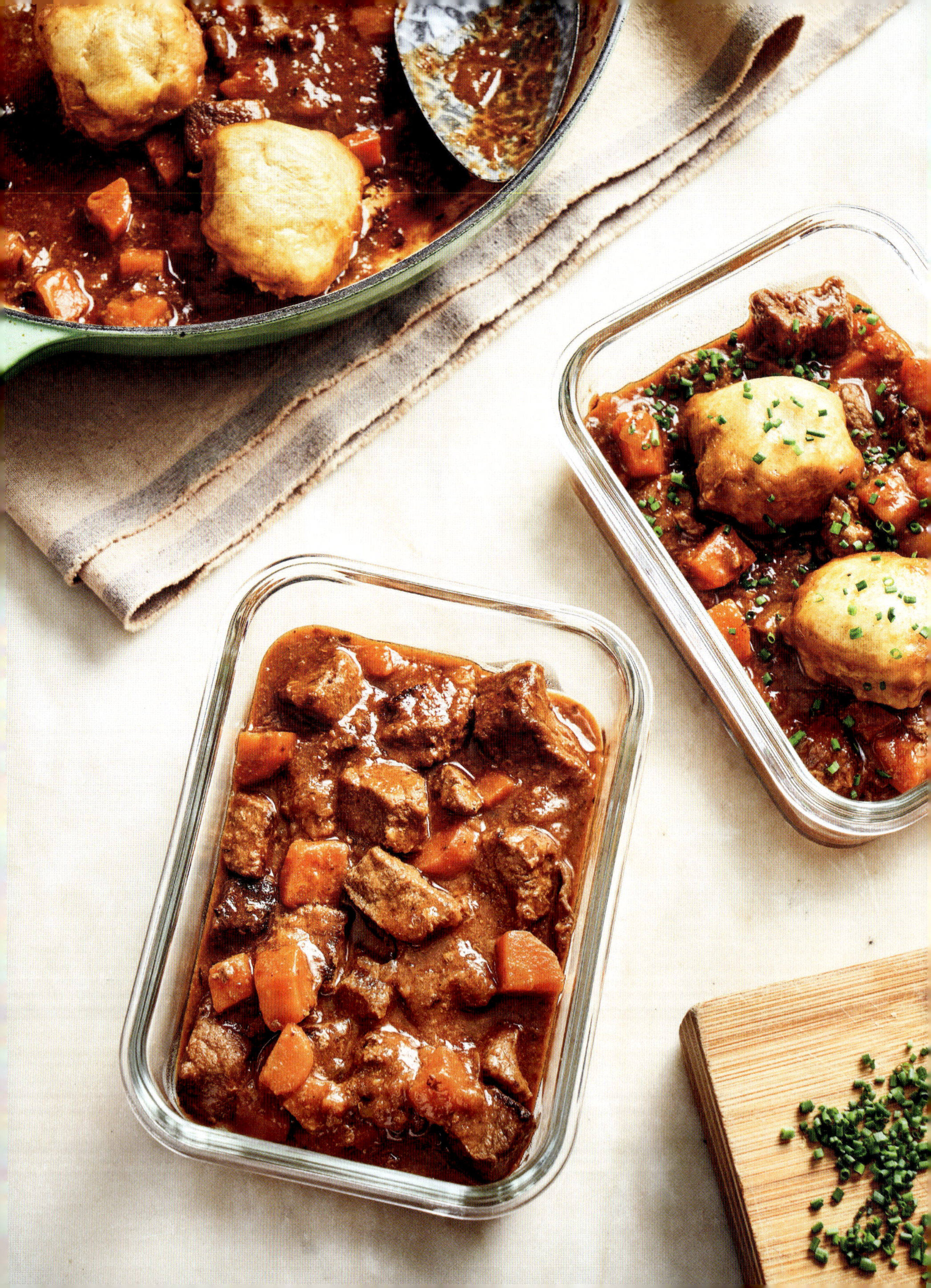

BEEF STEW AND DUMPLINGS

Beef stew is one of my sons' absolute favourites. There is something about a beef stew that fills a hole in your tummy that nothing else does. It's heart-filling and warming. I love making these with dumplings, so it's a meal in one, with no other fuss.

PREP: 6–8 MINS
COOK: 1 HOUR 30 MINS
MAKES: 4 MEALS

For the stew

- 3 tablespoons vegetable oil
- Large sprig of fresh lemon thyme
- 2 onions, cut into small chunks
- 2 teaspoons celery salt or fine salt
- 1 tablespoon garlic paste
- 3 carrots, peeled and cut into 1cm coins
- 500g beef chunks
- 2 tablespoons ground black pepper
- 2 tablespoons paprika
- 500ml water
- 4 tablespoons beef gravy granules

For the dumplings

- 200g self-raising flour
- 115g salted butter, cut into small chunks
- Pinch of salt
- 3 tablespoons water (you may need more)
- 1 egg, beaten
- Chopped fresh chives, to garnish

Start by making the stew. Pour the oil into a large non-stick pan (that has a lid that fits). As soon as the oil is hot, add the lemon thyme, onion and salt and cook till golden brown. If the onions get stuck to the base, don't worry, this will add flavour – just add a splash of water to unstick.

Get the garlic paste in, along with the carrot and beef chunks, and cook till the meat has browned. Add the black pepper and paprika, mix through and cook for a few minutes.

Pour in the water, mix and leave to cook over a low heat with the lid on for 45 minutes.

Make the dumplings by putting the flour in a bowl with the butter and salt. Rub the butter in till there are no lumps of butter left. Pour in the water and bring the dough together. Divide the mixture into eight equal balls and brush the top of each one with the egg.

Remove the lid of the stew, stir in the gravy granules and lower the heat. Add the dumplings straight on top, put the lid back on and steam on the lowest heat for 25 minutes.

Once cooked, remove from the heat, take out the thyme stalk and divide the mixture among four ovenproof freezer dishes/containers, popping two dumplings on top of each of the dishes. Sprinkle over the chives. Leave to cool and freeze.

You can cook this from frozen at 180°C for 45 minutes, with the lid off and the dish covered with some foil.

> **TIP** *Adding water to the onions while cooking enhances their sweetness, so when you are sweating them down, don't be afraid to add some not only to stop them from sticking, but also to make them sweeter.*

BROWN RICE AND PEAS

Ever need just a well-flavoured bowl of rice, but you can't be bothered? Well, let's make it once and eat it four times. This is so worth it for those delicious aromas and perfectly cooked rice.

PREP: 5 MINS **COOK:** 35 MINS

MAKES: 4 MEALS

150ml vegetable oil

2 onions, finely diced

2 teaspoons salt

2 teaspoons chilli flakes

3 teaspoons cumin seeds

4 tablespoons garam masala

400g basmati rice, washed and drained

800ml boiling water

300g frozen peas, defrosted

Start with a large non-stick pan, so the rice has plenty of room to expand and cook. Pour the oil into the pan and get it really hot. Add the onion and cook till it's really dark brown, but not burnt. Lower the heat and stir in the salt, chilli flakes, cumin seeds and garam masala.

Mix the basmati rice into the onion mixture and cook over a medium heat for about 3 minutes. Pour in the boiling water and boil over a high heat till most of the liquid has evaporated and the liquid becomes thick.

Mix in the peas, lower the heat, cover and steam for 10–12 minutes. Fluff up the rice and leave to cool completely. Divide into freezer dishes/containers and freeze.

To cook, pop into the microwave from frozen for 5–7 minutes, till hot all the way through. To serve, I would eat with a crispy fried or poached egg – it has to be an egg, any way you like.

TIP *Colouring onions until they are nearly black but not burnt adds a really intense flavour and colour.*

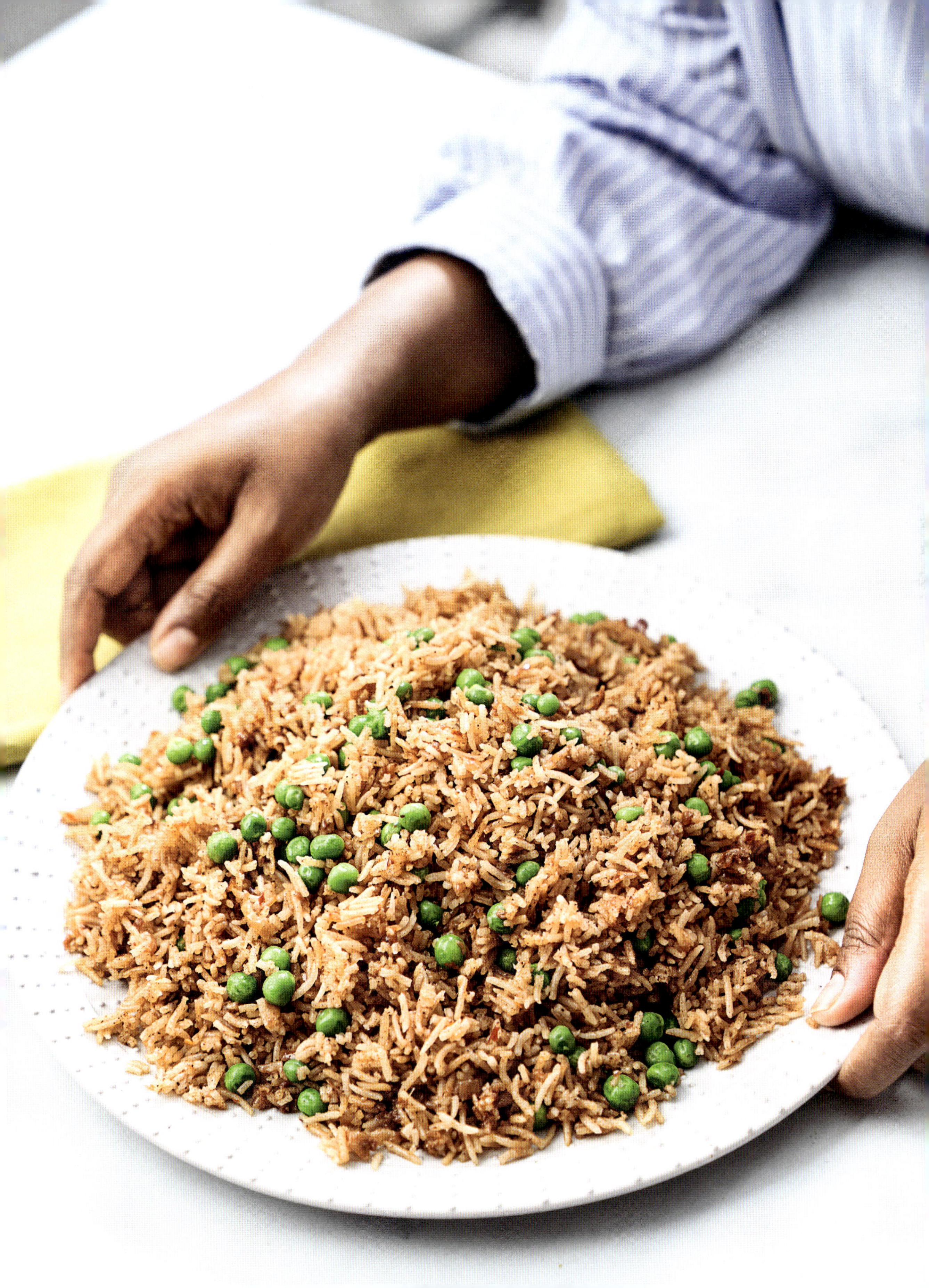

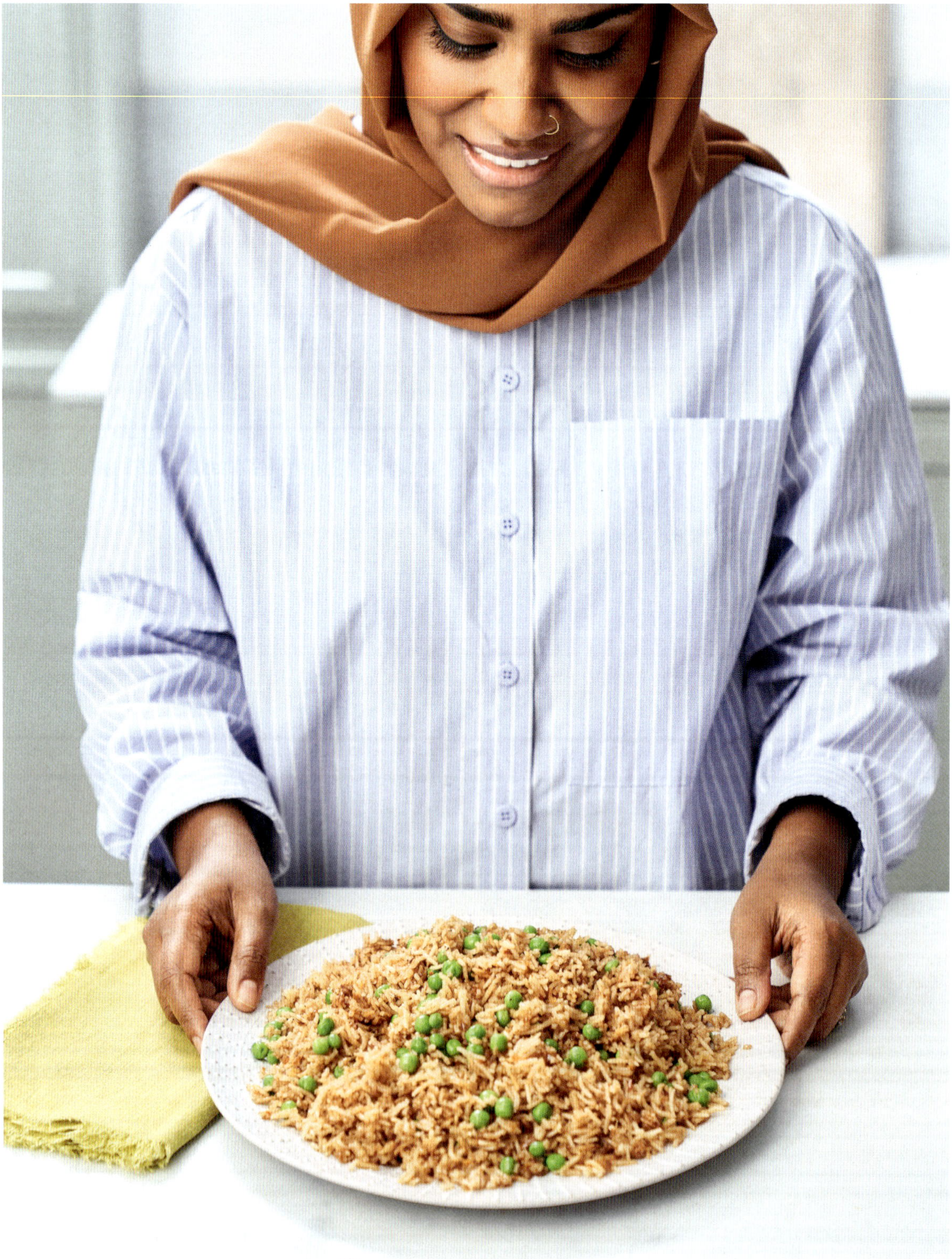

Brown rice & Peas

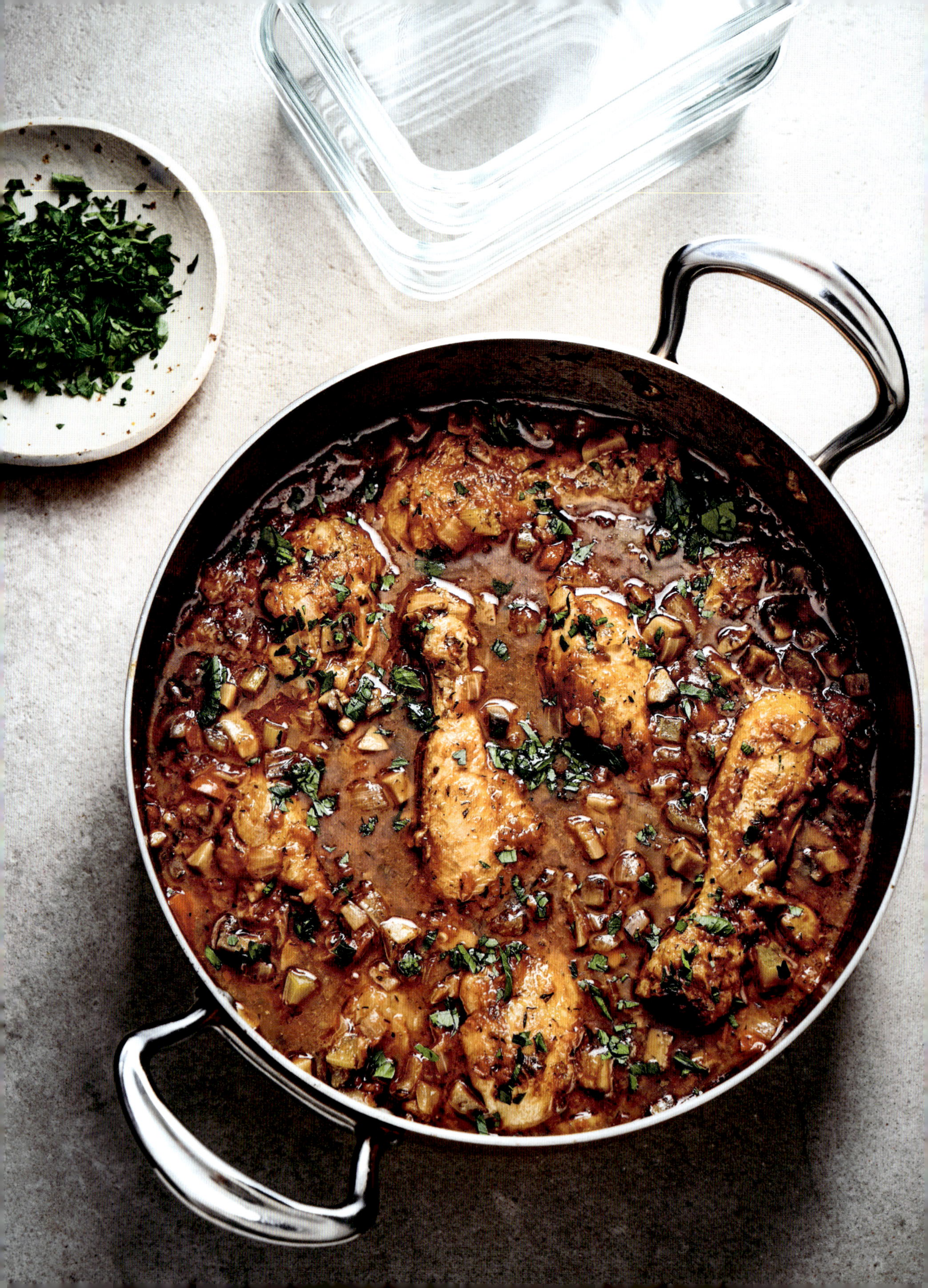

CHICKEN CACCIATORE

This is something that I used to make all the time without realizing it had a name, and what a great name at that too! This is a wholesome chicken dinner, full of veg – what's not to love?

PREP: 5 MINS **COOK:** 55 MINS

MAKES: 4

Oil, for frying

8 chicken drumsticks, skin on

4 cloves of garlic, minced

1 onion, diced

3 celery sticks, diced

1 red pepper, diced

300g mushrooms, diced

2 teaspoons salt

2 tablespoons ground black pepper

1 tablespoon dried oregano

1 tablespoon dried thyme

1 teaspoon dried parsley

400g tin of chopped tomatoes

400ml chicken stock

1 tablespoon cornflour

1 tablespoon water

Chopped fresh parsley, to garnish

Start with some oil in a pan over a medium heat. As soon as the oil is hot, add the chicken drumsticks, a few at a time, and brown – we're not cooking it through yet though. Set aside.

Pour a little more oil into the same pan, if you need to, and get the garlic in with the onion, celery, red pepper, mushrooms and salt. Cook until everything starts to soften.

Go ahead and add the black pepper, dried oregano, thyme, parsley, tomatoes and chicken stock, cooking until the liquid has started to evaporate. Add the chicken back in, cover and cook for 25 minutes.

Mix together the cornflour and water in a small bowl and add to the chicken to help the liquids thicken some more. Take off the heat and divide among your freezer dishes/containers, with two drumsticks in each dish. Leave to cool, sprinkle over the parsley and freeze.

Thaw out the night before and when you are ready to eat, microwave for 5–7 minutes.

TIP *Cooking chicken or meat with the bone still in makes the entire dish more flavourful.*

CHICKEN TIKKA MASALA AND RICE

The best thing to come out of an Indian restaurant is probably a chicken tikka masala, and if it is done right, it can be wonderful; done badly – I guess you're never going back! That's why I think you should make your own. It's delicious, easy, you can have it whenever you fancy and you don't even have to leave the house.

PREP: 5 MINS **COOK:** 35 MINS

MAKES: 4 MEALS

Oil, for frying

2 onions, chopped

1½ teaspoons salt

2 tablespoons garlic paste

2 tablespoons ginger paste

2 tablespoons tomato purée

1 tablespoon garam masala

2 tablespoons curry powder

750g skinless chicken thighs or breasts, diced

400g tin of cream of tomato soup

100ml water

Chopped fresh coriander, to garnish

Start by putting a medium-sized pan on a high heat with some oil. As soon as the oil is hot, add the onion and salt. Cook the onions till they are golden brown.

Now add the garlic paste, ginger paste and tomato purée and cook for a few minutes. Tip in the garam masala and curry powder and cook for a few minutes more. Add the chicken and cook till every piece is cooked through.

Pour in the tomato soup and water, mix and leave to simmer away. As soon as the sauce is thick and not watery, take off the heat and leave to cool. Portion out into freezer dishes/containers, sprinkle over the coriander and freeze.

To reheat, thaw out in the fridge and microwave for 5–7 minutes. I love to eat this with rice, always!

TIP *Curries are naturally gluten free, so the way to thicken the sauce is to start with lots of onions.*

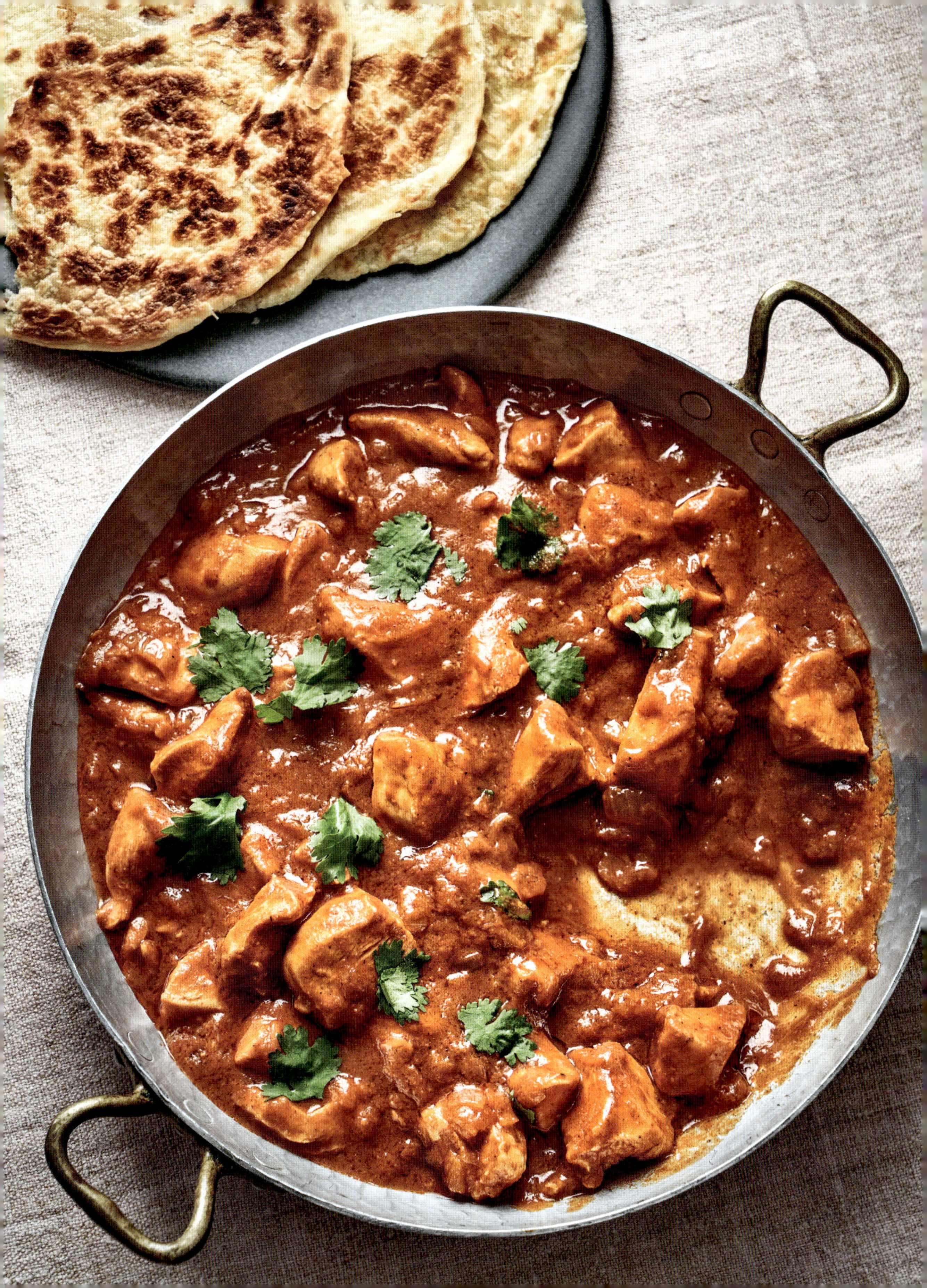

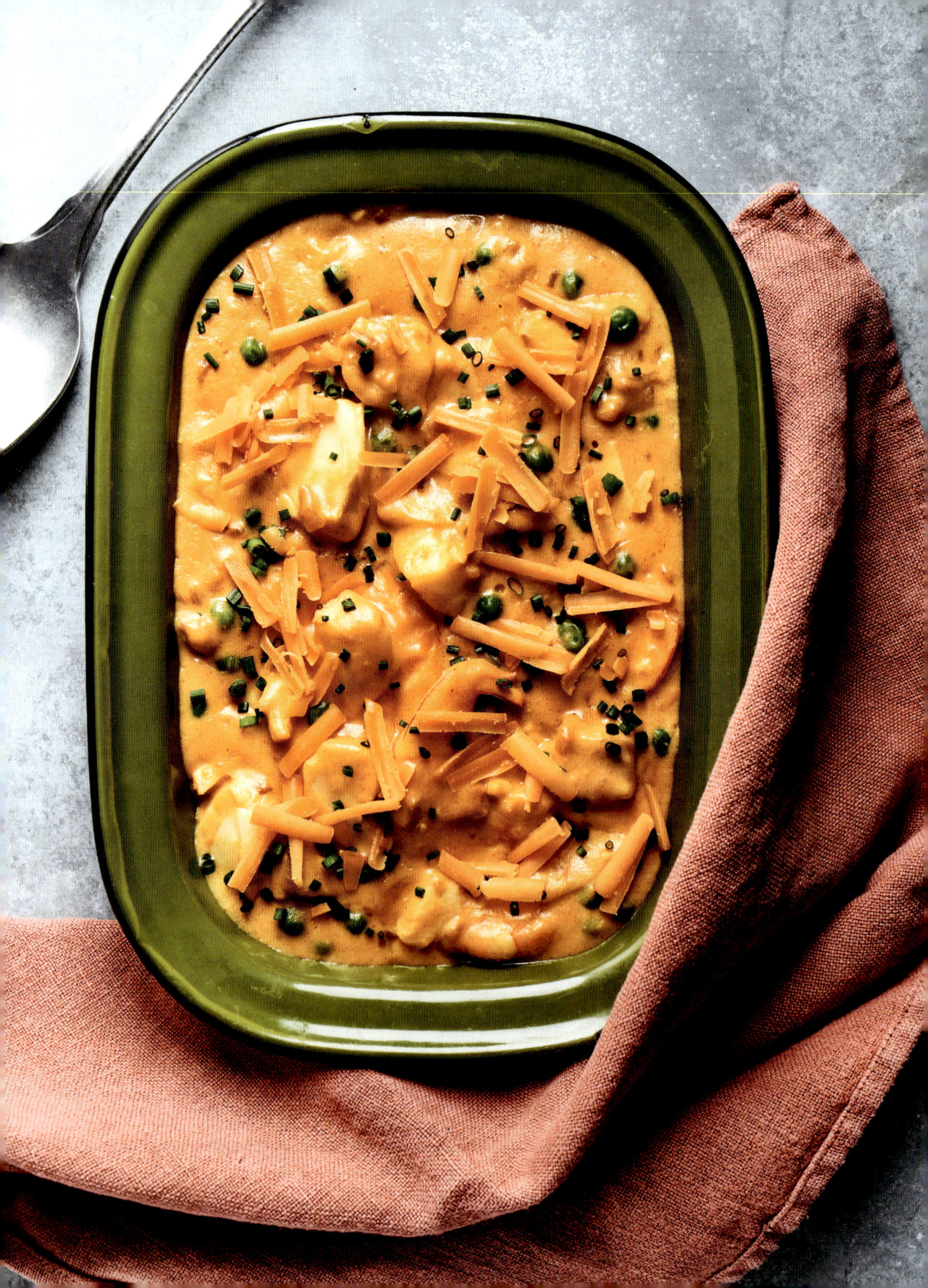

COD MORNAY

This is much like a fish pie but without the potatoes. You can absolutely eat this with mash, but I love the delicious, creamy fish with just some simple steamed veg.

PREP: 5 MINS **COOK:** 25 MINS

MAKES: 4 MEALS

40g salted butter

40g plain flour

¼ teaspoon ground turmeric

1 teaspoon paprika

500ml whole milk

1 teaspoon salt

200g Red Leicester cheese, grated

4 cloves of garlic, minced

50g crispy fried onions

285g cod fillets, cut into small chunks

165g raw prawns

200g frozen peas

50g Red Leicester or Cheddar cheese, grated

Chopped fresh chives, to garnish

Start by putting a pan on the hob over a medium heat. Put the butter in the pan and melt till golden brown.

Toss in the flour, turmeric and paprika and mix till you have a thick paste. Pour in half the milk and whisk whilst still on the heat, making sure there are no lumps. Add the rest of the milk and keep whisking till you have a thick sauce. Sprinkle in the salt, Red Leicester, garlic and crispy fried onions and mix through.

Get the cod fillet chunks and prawns in along with the peas and mix together. Put the lid on and let the fish cook for 15 minutes.

Take off the heat, divide into ovenproof freezer dishes/containers and, once cooled, sprinkle with more Red Leicester or Cheddar cheese and chives and get into the freezer.

To cook, thaw out and bake for 20 minutes at 180°C. Make sure it is cooked all the way through.

TIP *To preserve cheese for longer, rub butter all over the block to create a barrier to stop mould growing.*

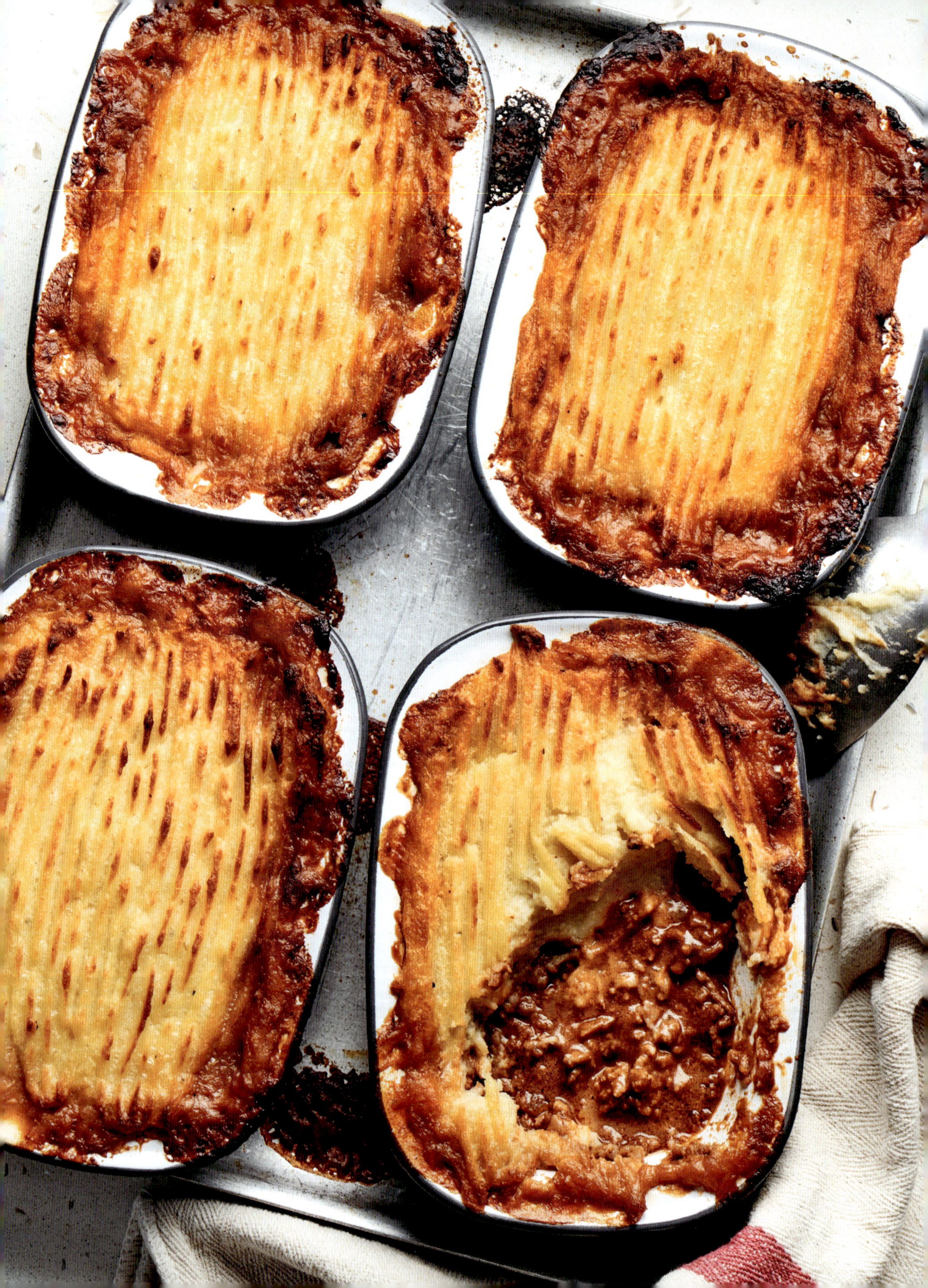

COTTAGE PIE

Cottage pie is one of the faves of the pies. I love a mashy top and a sauce that doesn't have tomatoes. So, this just ticks all the boxes. It makes for a great ready meal on a day when you want a quick dinner that is delicious too.

PREP: 5–8 MINS **COOK:** 1 HOUR 5 MINS

MAKES: 4 MEALS

For the mash

900g Maris Piper potatoes
250g salted butter
250ml milk
Salt

For the mince

4 tablespoons vegetable oil
1 onion, finely diced
2 cloves of garlic, minced
1 teaspoon salt
2 tablespoons ground black pepper
1 tablespoon dried thyme
2 tablespoons ground cumin
500g beef mince
3 tablespoons plain flour
500ml hot water
1 tablespoon yeast extract
4 tablespoons Worcestershire sauce
3 tablespoons brown sauce
1 tablespoon miso paste

Start by making the mash. Add the potatoes to a pan with cold water, heavily salt the water and boil the potatoes till tender and perfect for mashing. Drain and transfer back to the pan, then push the cooked potatoes through a ricer or use a masher.

Add the salted butter and milk along with a sprinkling of salt and mix till you have a smooth, creamy mash. Leave to one side and get onto making the mince base.

For the mince, get a medium pan on the heat, add the oil, onion, garlic and salt. Cook the onions till they are soft. Add the black pepper, thyme, cumin and beef mince and mix through till the mince has cooked. Now add the plain flour and stir through until the mince is coated.

To a jug add the hot water, yeast extract, Worcestershire sauce, brown sauce and miso paste. Stir well and pour into the mince mixture. Cook over a high heat and leave to simmer till the liquid is thick and the mince is coated. This should take about 30 minutes.

Divide the mixture into four ovenproof freezer dishes/containers. Top with the mash and leave to cool completely before freezing.

Bake from frozen for 35–40 minutes at 180°C.

TIP *Cumin really enhances that lamb flavour.*

LASAGNE SOUP

This is exactly like lasagne but without the layers, without the fuss and with all the flavour. Rich, tomatoey mince with sheets of lasagne and cheese, topped with a cream cheese and Parmesan drizzle.

PREP: 5 MINS **COOK:** 40–45 MINS

MAKES: 4 MEALS

Oil, for frying

2 onions, diced

2 teaspoons salt

6 cloves of garlic, minced

2 carrots, peeled and grated

500g lamb or beef mince

2 tablespoons yeast extract

2 teaspoons vinegar

2 tablespoons tomato purée

1 tablespoon ground cumin

1 tablespoon chilli flakes (optional)

2 x 400ml tins of cream of tomato soup

600ml water

250g lasagne sheets, smashed up

250g grated cheese

To serve

Cream cheese

Grated Parmesan cheese

Start by putting a large pan on the hob over a medium heat. Pour in the oil and when the oil is hot, get the onions in with the salt and cook and sweat down until golden and soft.

Get the garlic and carrots in and mix through. Now add in your mince along with the yeast extract, vinegar, tomato purée, ground cumin and chilli flakes. Cook over a high heat, then stir in the tomato soup and water and bring to the boil.

As soon as the soup boils, add your smashed lasagne sheets and mix in. Once it has boiled again, lower the heat and simmer for 25–30 minutes, then take off the heat and leave to cool completely.

Sprinkle in the grated cheese, mix through, portion out into freezer containers and freeze.

To reheat, defrost and then heat in a pan until piping hot. To serve, I like to add dollops of cream cheese and some grated Parmesan, if you fancy it.

TIP *If you want to make the soup extra creamy, you can add 100ml cream with the tomato soup and then reduce it down.*

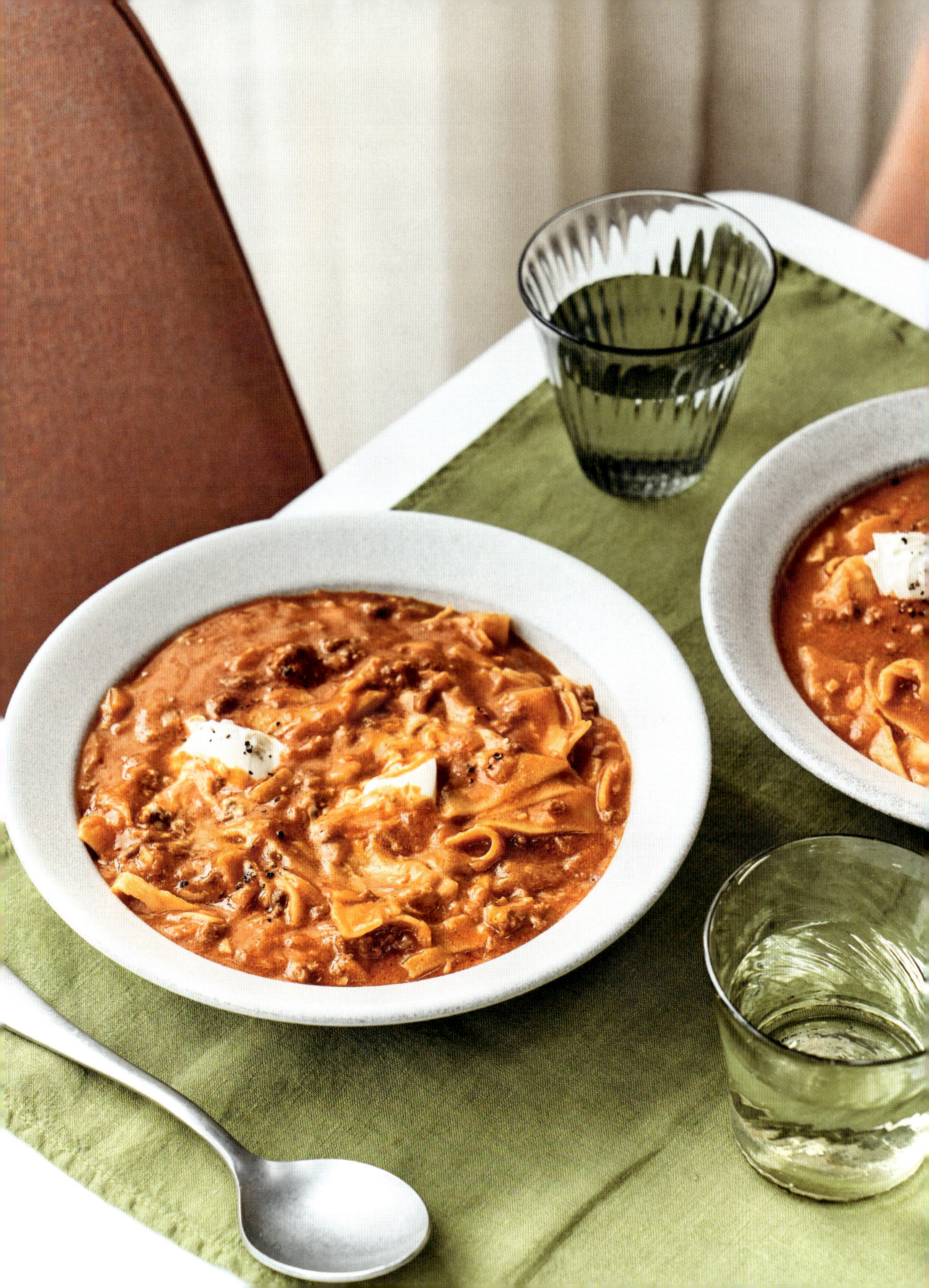

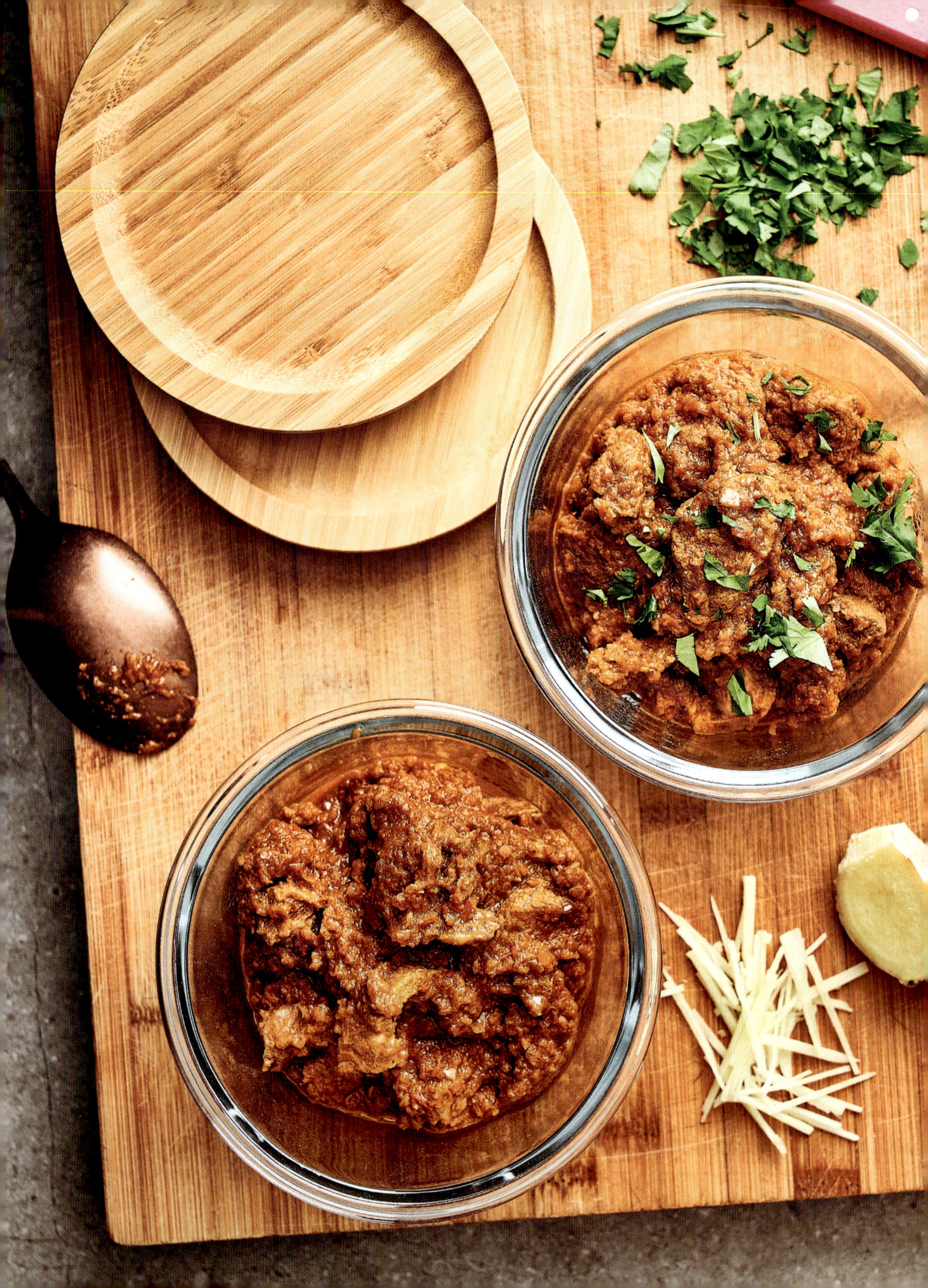

LIME PICKLE LAMB

Achari lamb is lamb cooked with Indian pickles. The pickles give the curry a unique tangy, spicy flavour that is perfectly balanced. A good pickle that has developed its flavour over months makes a great addition to an already delicious curry.

PREP: 6 MINS **COOK:** 48 MINS

MAKES: 4 MEALS

3 tablespoons garlic paste

3 tablespoons ginger paste

2 onions, roughly chopped

2 tomatoes, roughly diced

1 teaspoon salt

1½ tablespoons lime or mango pickle

2 tablespoons curry powder

2 tablespoons ground cumin

2 teaspoons chilli powder (optional)

200ml water

4 tablespoons oil

500g lamb, thinly sliced

To serve

Chopped fresh coriander

Thinly sliced peeled ginger

Start by making the easy paste. Put the garlic paste, ginger paste, onion and tomato in a blender. Blend the mixture till everything has really broken down and you don't have any huge lumps.

Now add the salt, lime or mango pickle, curry powder, ground cumin, chilli powder, if using, and water and blend till completely smooth.

To a medium pan add the oil. As soon as the oil is hot, add the paste from the blender and cook over a medium heat till the mixture is dry and coming away from the sides.

Add the lamb, mix through the sauce and cook over a high heat for 5 minutes. Reduce the heat, pop the lid on and leave to simmer for 30 minutes.

Take the lid off and cook for another 5 minutes over a high heat to reduce any watery liquid. Take off the heat and cool completely. Divide among four freezer dishes/containers, sprinkle with the coriander and ginger, put the lids on and freeze.

To reheat, remove from the freezer the night before and defrost. These can be heated in the microwave for 4 minutes. I like to serve this with rice, cooked fresh or straight out of a packet!

TIP *If you prefer a milder pickle flavour, go for a sweet mango pickle. It will still impart a ton of delicious flavour.*

MEATBALL MARINARA

Meatballs are one of our go-to meals. They're a great way to eat mince and a really good home-made ready meal. These are tomatoey and cheesy and can be eaten sandwiched into a toasted sub or with pasta.

PREP: 12–15 MINS **COOK:** 52 MINS

MAKES: 4 MEALS

For the meatballs
500g lamb mince
2 tablespoons dried breadcrumbs
2 teaspoons garlic granules
3 teaspoons onion granules
1 teaspoon ground black pepper
Salt

For the sauce
3 tablespoons oil
6 garlic cloves
2 x 400g tins of chopped tomatoes
1 red pepper
1 teaspoon salt
3 tablespoons tomato purée
1 teaspoon chilli flakes
1 tablespoon dried oregano

For the topping
2 x 150g mozzarella balls, drained
Fresh basil
Subs, fresh or frozen and defrosted

Begin by making the meatballs. Put the lamb mince and breadcrumbs into a bowl with the garlic granules, onion granules, ground black pepper and salt. Mix the whole lot by hand, then take walnut-sized pieces and squeeze tightly. Set aside the meatballs on a plate and get on to making the sauce.

For the sauce, get a wide, high-sided frying pan big enough for all the meatballs to sit in one even layer when they are being cooked. What you don't want is for them to be stacked on top of one another, as this will just risk them breaking apart.

Mince the garlic. Put the pan over a medium heat with the oil in it. Add the garlic and cook till just slightly golden brown.

Pour the tinned tomatoes into a blender, add the red pepper, salt and tomato purée and blend to a smooth paste. Gently pour into the pan and cook over a medium heat till the sauce is darker in colour and thicker in consistency. This should only take 10–15 minutes.

Sprinkle in the chilli flakes and dried oregano and mix through. One by one, add the meatballs in an even layer. Lower the heat, put the lid on and let them steam. This will help the meatballs keep that rounded shape.

Cook for 15 minutes, take off the lid, turn the balls and stir so they are completely coated. Tear in your mozzarella, dropping it in and around the meatballs, and leave to steam with the lid on for another 15 minutes. Take off the heat and tear in the basil. Divide into four ovenproof freezer dishes/containers and leave to cool completely. Cover and freeze.

These can be cooked from frozen for 35 minutes at 180°C with the lid off or microwaved for 10 minutes.

TIP *Adding breadcrumbs to the meatballs helps them to hold their shape and bind them and, as the meatballs cook, they also help thicken the sauce.*

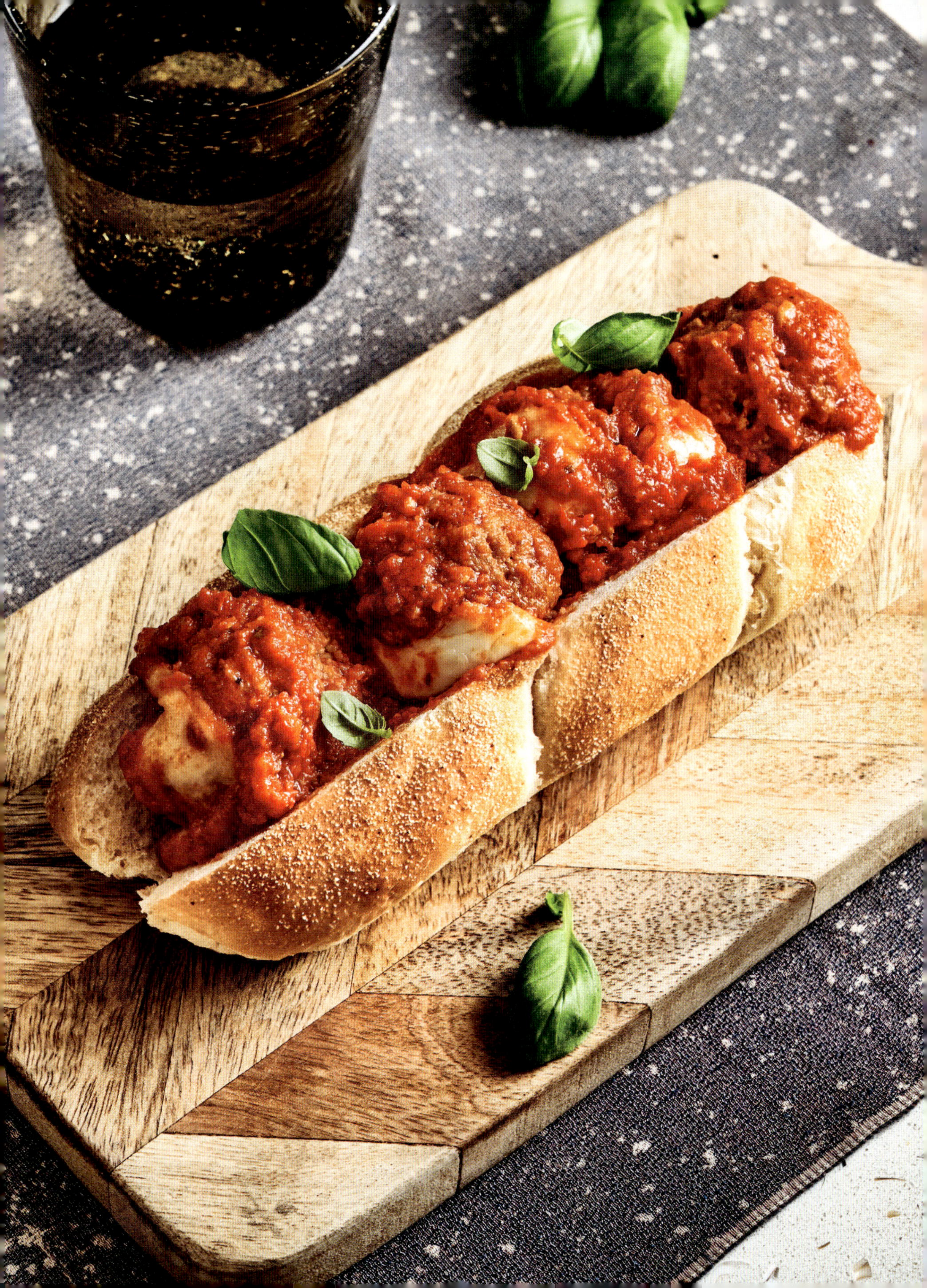

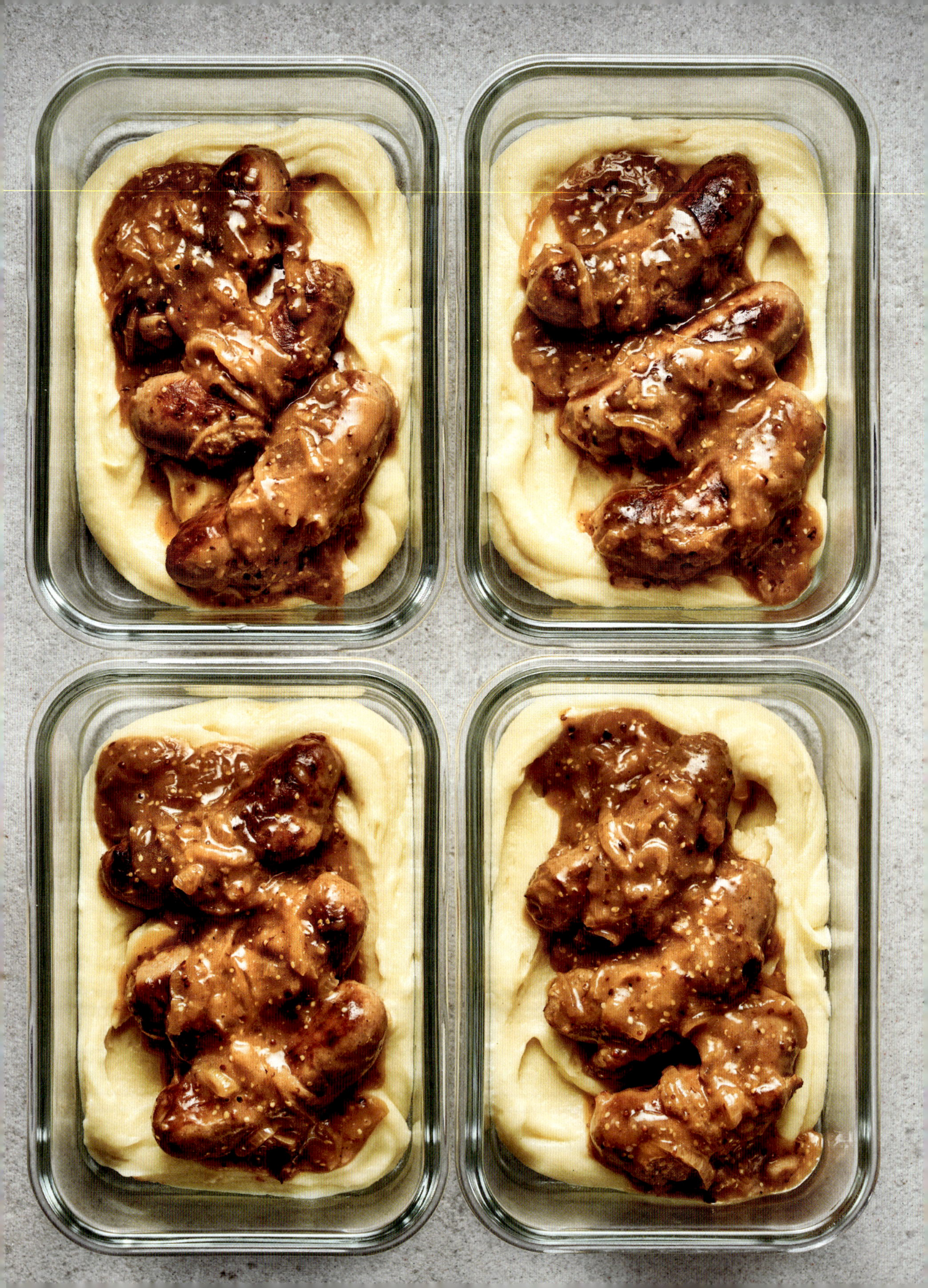

SAUSAGE, MASH AND MUSTARD GRAVY

I like making this meal because sausages are a firm favourite at my house and with a sauce and mash, you can make them go a really long way. The sauce is mustard and peppery and I think you guys will love it.

PREP: 10 MINS **COOK:** 1 HOUR

MAKES: 4 MEALS

Ultimate mashed potato (see page 27)

Oil, for frying

12 chicken sausages, slashed without going all the way through

50g butter

3 onions, thinly sliced

1 teaspoon salt

3 tablespoons wholegrain mustard

50g plain flour

500ml beef stock or water

I would start by making the mash before starting on the sausages.

Now, let's cook these sausages and make this sauce.

Pour some oil into a non-stick pan and add the slashed sausages. Cook the sausages all the way through, then remove them from the pan onto a separate plate.

To the same pan add the butter and cook till brown. Add the onion and salt and cook till really very brown and caramel coloured. Spoon in the mustard and mix through. Sprinkle in the flour and incorporate as best you can into the onion.

Pour in the beef stock or water and cook over a high heat till the gravy has thickened. As soon as it has, add the sausages back in and mix through.

To portion out, put a layer of the mash into the base of each ovenproof freezer dish/container, add three sausages each straight onto the mash and spoon in the gravy. Cool and freeze.

You can cook from frozen, covered, in the oven at 180°C for 35 minutes or cook for 10 minutes in the microwave.

TIP *Slit the sausages but not all the way through, so the flavour of the sauce can penetrate them.*

MINESTRONE

I love making soups. They are a great way of using up leftovers, but also are brilliant if you just want tons of good stuff in one bowl. That is what minestrone is all about.

PREP: 5 MINS **COOK:** 52 MINS

MAKES: 4 MEALS

Oil, for frying

5 cloves of garlic, minced

1 onion, diced

2 teaspoons salt

2 teaspoons smoked paprika

3 celery sticks, diced

3 carrots, peeled and diced

1 lemon, zest and juice

3 tablespoons tomato purée

400g tin of chopped tomatoes

400g tin of beans, drained

400ml hot water

Large handful of kale, roughly chopped

150g small pasta shapes

Grated cheese, to serve

Begin by pouring some oil into a large pan. When the oil is hot, add the garlic, onion and salt. Cook the onions till just brown.

Now add in the smoked paprika, celery, carrot, lemon zest and juice and tomato purée. Mix and cook for a few minutes. Pour in the tinned chopped tomatoes and half the beans, reserving the other half.

Take the other half of the beans and smash with the back of a fork. Add to the pan, which will help to naturally thicken the sauce without needing to add any flour.

Pour in the hot water, add the kale and pasta and bring everything to a boil, then boil for 5 minutes. Now reduce the heat and simmer for 30 minutes with the lid on.

Once cooked and thickened, transfer to your freezer dishes/containers. Leave to cool, then sprinkle over the grated cheese and freeze.

To reheat, I like to have a lid on, slightly ajar and cook in the microwave for 5–8 minutes.

TIP *Crush pasta or spaghetti if you can't find miniature pasta shapes – it all works the same way.*

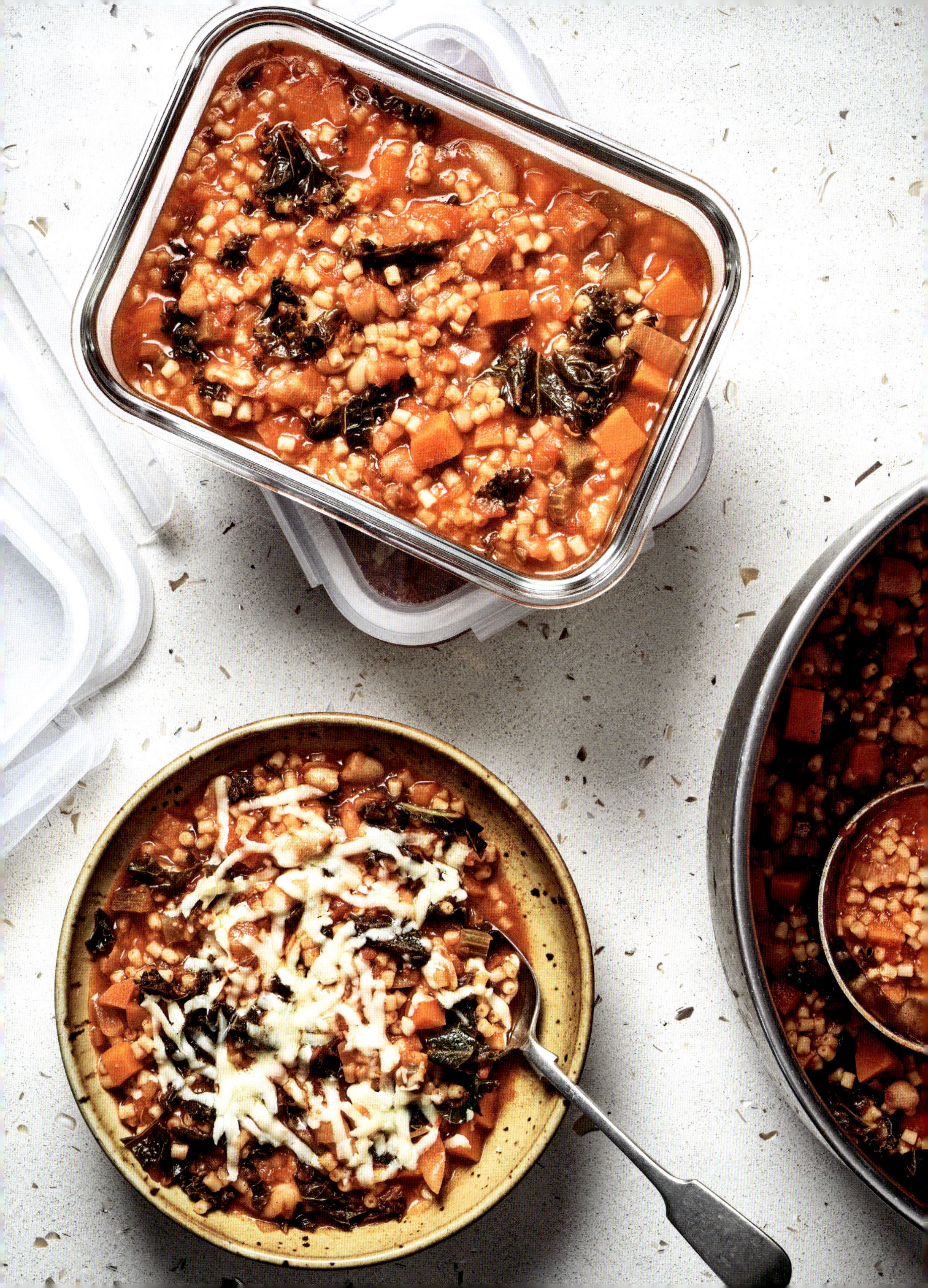

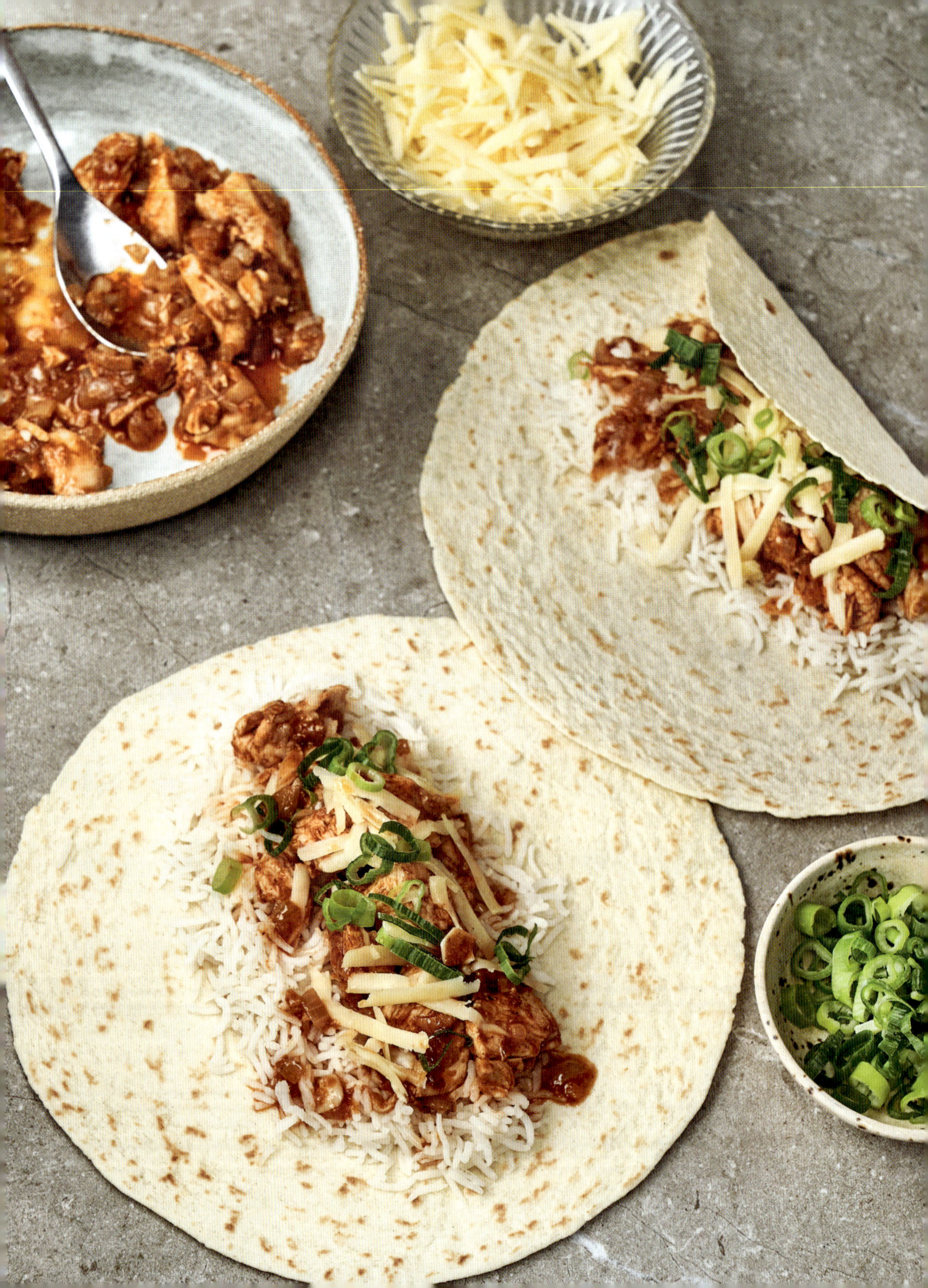

SMOKY CHICKEN BURRITOS

My family loves burritos and these can be made in advance and frozen. Filled with rice, onion and lots of cheese, they are the best for on-the-go meals if you know you don't have tons of time.

PREP: 5 MINS **COOL:** 5 MINS
COOK: 24 MINS
MAKES: 4 MEALS

Oil, for frying

1 clove of garlic, minced

1 onion, diced

1 teaspoon salt

2 chicken breasts, diced

1 lime, juice only

2 tablespoons chilli sauce

2 teaspoons smoked paprika

2 teaspoons ground cumin

2 spring onions, thinly sliced

100g Cheddar cheese, grated

250g microwave rice, cooked and cooled

4 large tortilla wraps

Pour your oil into a large frying pan and, as soon as the oil is hot, add the garlic and onion with the salt and cook till soft.

Now get the diced chicken breast in and cook with the lime juice and chilli sauce till there is no liquid left and the chicken is cooked.

Sprinkle in the smoked paprika and ground cumin and mix to cook through for just a few minutes. Transfer all of that to a bowl and leave to cool completely.

Once cooled, add the spring onions, cheese and cooked microwave rice. Mix well and divide among four tortilla wraps. Roll each tortilla up tight and wrap in foil before freezing.

Cook from frozen, in the foil, for 25–30 minutes on 180°C.

TIP *Smoked paprika enhances the smoked flavour and also adds a faux barbecue flavour.*

PANEER KARAHI

Essentially, a karahi is just the dish in which this curry is cooked. It is a rounded, deep pan with two handles. If you don't have one, this curry can also be done in a wok. This is a deep, rich curry, which is deliciously balanced with the creamy paneer. I love to eat this with naan!

PREP: 5 MINS **COOK:** 40 MINS

MAKES: 4 MEALS

Oil, for frying

500g paneer, cut into cubes

2 onions, diced

1 teaspoon salt

2 tablespoons garlic paste

4 tomatoes, diced

2 tablespoons tomato purée

½ teaspoon ground turmeric

2 tablespoons curry powder

1 teaspoon chilli powder (optional)

Large handful of spinach

Cream, for drizzling

Put a medium non-stick frying pan on the hob over a medium heat. Splash in a good drizzle of oil.

Get the paneer cubes in and leave them to cook, tossing and moving the paneer around occasionally. You want to keep frying till the paneer cubes all have a brown, crinkly texture.

Take the paneer out of the pan and set aside, then place the same pan back on a medium heat. Pour in a drizzle more oil. As soon as the oil is hot, add the onion along with the salt and cook till soft and golden.

Get the garlic paste in with the tomatoes, tomato purée, turmeric, curry powder and chilli powder and cook till the tomatoes have broken down and you have a rich sauce. Add a splash of water to prevent it catching on the bottom of the pan.

As it cooks, add the spinach in and mix through till wilted. Add the paneer back in, cover and cook for 15 minutes.

Once the curry has finished cooking, take it off the heat and transfer into your freezer containers. Leave to cool, then drizzle over some cream, cover and freeze.

To reheat, thaw out and heat in a pan or in the microwave until hot all the way through.

TIP *Pre-frying the paneer over a high heat creates an uneven texture that works really well to allow the sauce to cling to the cheese cubes.*

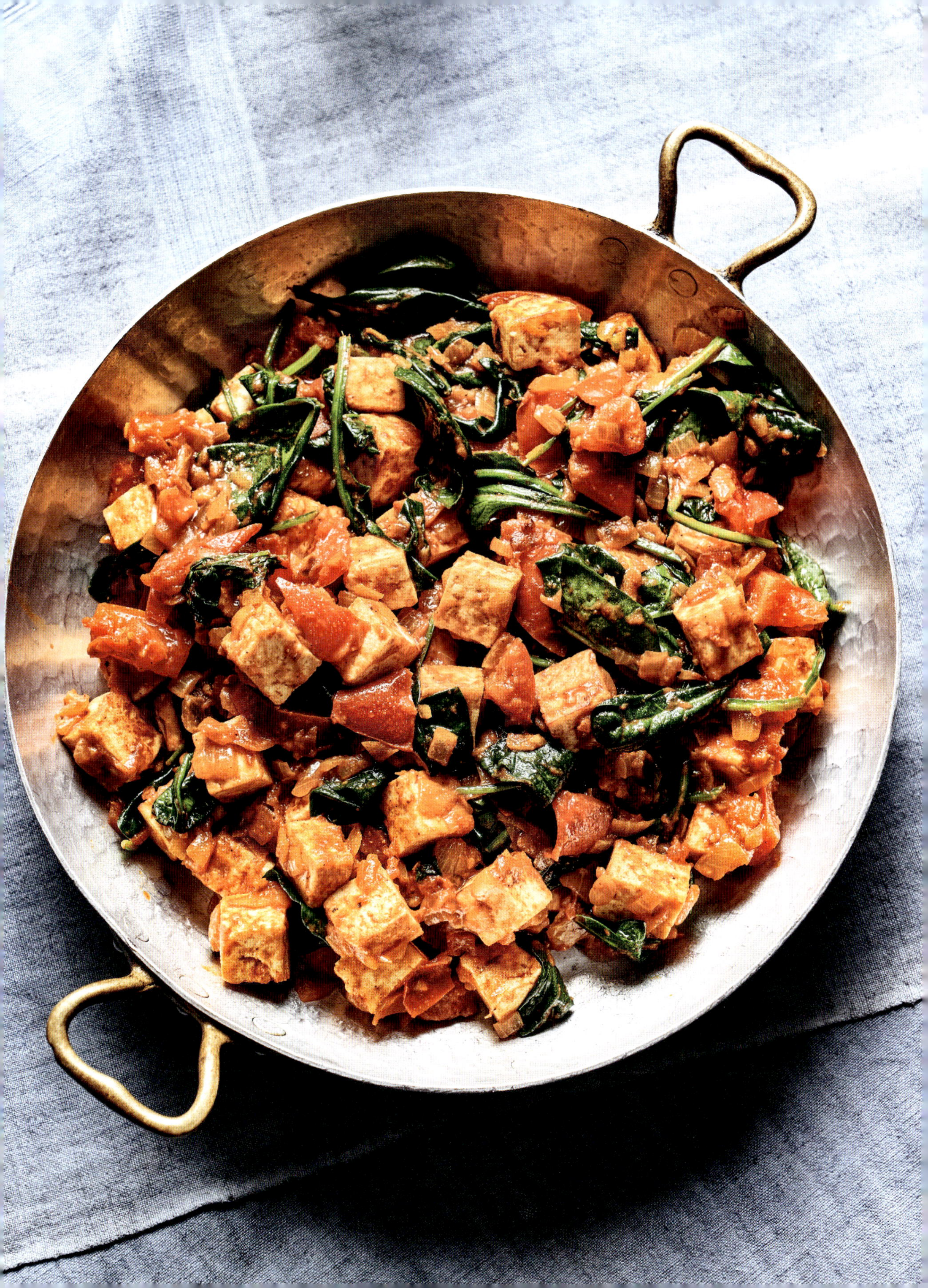

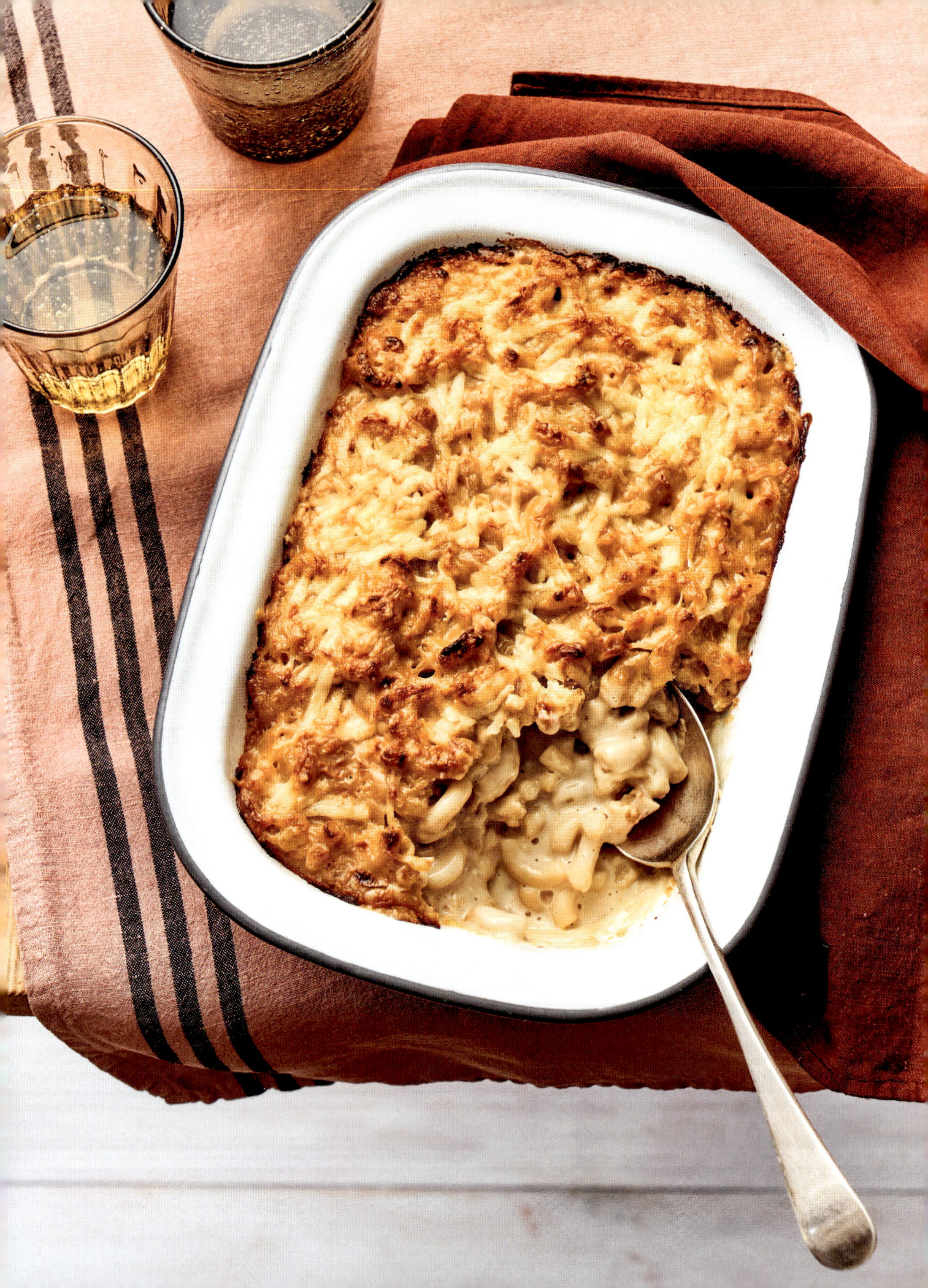

MACARONI CHEESE

The best one-pot dinner, this will be in my Top 10 for ever. There are so many ways of making macaroni cheese, all delicious, but I am going to show you the simplest and, best of all, it's also the cheesiest!

PREP: 5 MINS **COOK:** 40 MINS

MAKES: 4 MEALS

400g macaroni pasta
100g salted butter
100g plain flour
1 litre whole milk
1 tablespoon yeast extract
2 tablespoons Worcestershire sauce
2 teaspoons English mustard powder
1 teaspoon salt
300g Cheddar cheese, grated, plus an extra 100g for the top

Start by making the macaroni. Cook as per the instructions, drain, then run under cold water to prevent sticking and set aside.

Add the salted butter to a large non-stick pan or flat casserole dish. As soon as the butter has melted, keep heating till the butter gets brown. Now tip in the plain flour and whisk till combined.

Slowly add the milk, 100ml at a time, making sure to whisk all the time. Keep adding the milk until it has all been finished. Over a low heat, cook the sauce for about 5 minutes.

Now add the yeast extract, Worcestershire sauce, mustard powder and salt. Whisk till the yeast extract has disappeared and melted. Take off the heat and leave for 10 minutes before adding the cheese and mixing through.

Now add the cooked macaroni in and mix evenly through. Divide the mixture among four ovenproof freezer dishes/containers, sprinkle over the cheese and, once cooled, freeze.

Thaw out in the fridge the night before eating and bake in the oven, uncovered, at 180°C for 25 minutes.

TIP *The mustard naturally enhances the flavour of the cheese.*

TERIYAKI SALMON AND STICKY RICE

This is a really delicious teriyaki sauce using bits and bobs you might already have at home. It is dark and sticky and flavourful.

PREP: 4 MINS (+ MARINATING) **COOK:** 25 MINS

SERVES: 4

100ml dark soy sauce

2 tablespoons sesame oil

1 tablespoon ketchup

1 tablespoon brown sauce

1 tablespoon garlic paste

1 tablespoon ginger paste

1 tablespoon chilli sauce

2 tablespoons brown sugar

2 tablespoons lemon juice

1 teaspoon ground coriander

4 salmon fillets

Oil, for frying

To serve

Sticky rice

Sesame seeds

Fresh coriander

Get the dark soy sauce, sesame oil, ketchup, brown sauce, garlic paste, ginger paste, chilli sauce, brown sugar, lemon juice and ground coriander into a dish that will fit all four pieces of the fish comfortably and mix really well, making sure that the sugar has stirred in properly and started to dissolve.

Add the salmon fillets and cover in the marinade. Ideally leave this overnight or for at least 4 hours.

Put a non-stick pan on a high heat and pour in a splash of oil. When the oil is hot, add the fillets in and fry on both sides for about 4 minutes.

Take the fish out, add the marinade to the same pan and cook until the sauce has thickened. Take off the heat.

I like to eat this with sticky rice, so I take sticky rice out of a packet and place in my freezer dishes/containers. Now add your salmon on top of each one and drizzle over the sauce. Sprinkle with sesame seeds and fresh coriander. Cool and freeze.

To eat, thaw out and heat in a microwave for 5–7 minutes.

TIP *Cooking sauces and marinades mean you can use it again – make sure to refrigerate once cooled.*

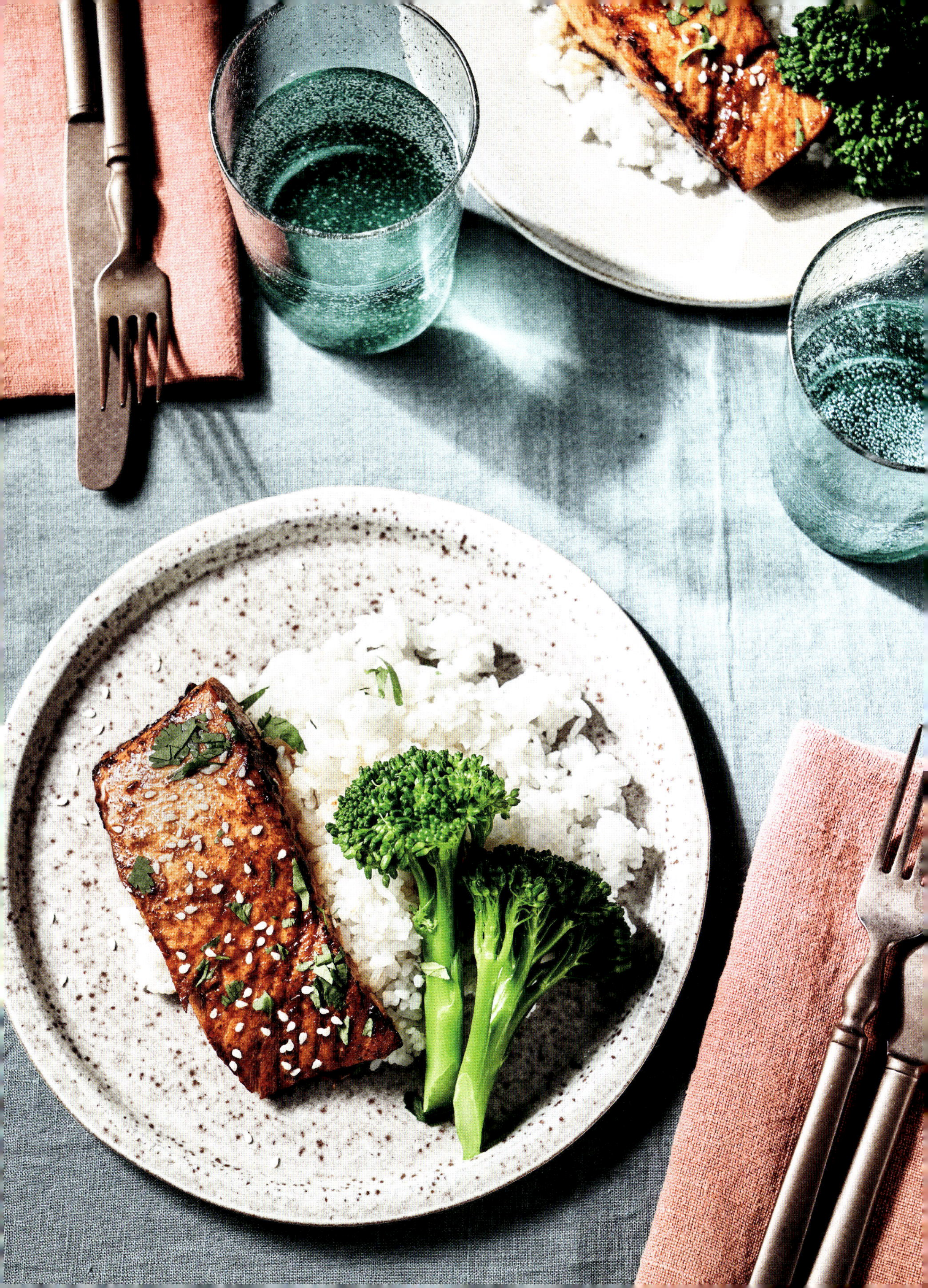

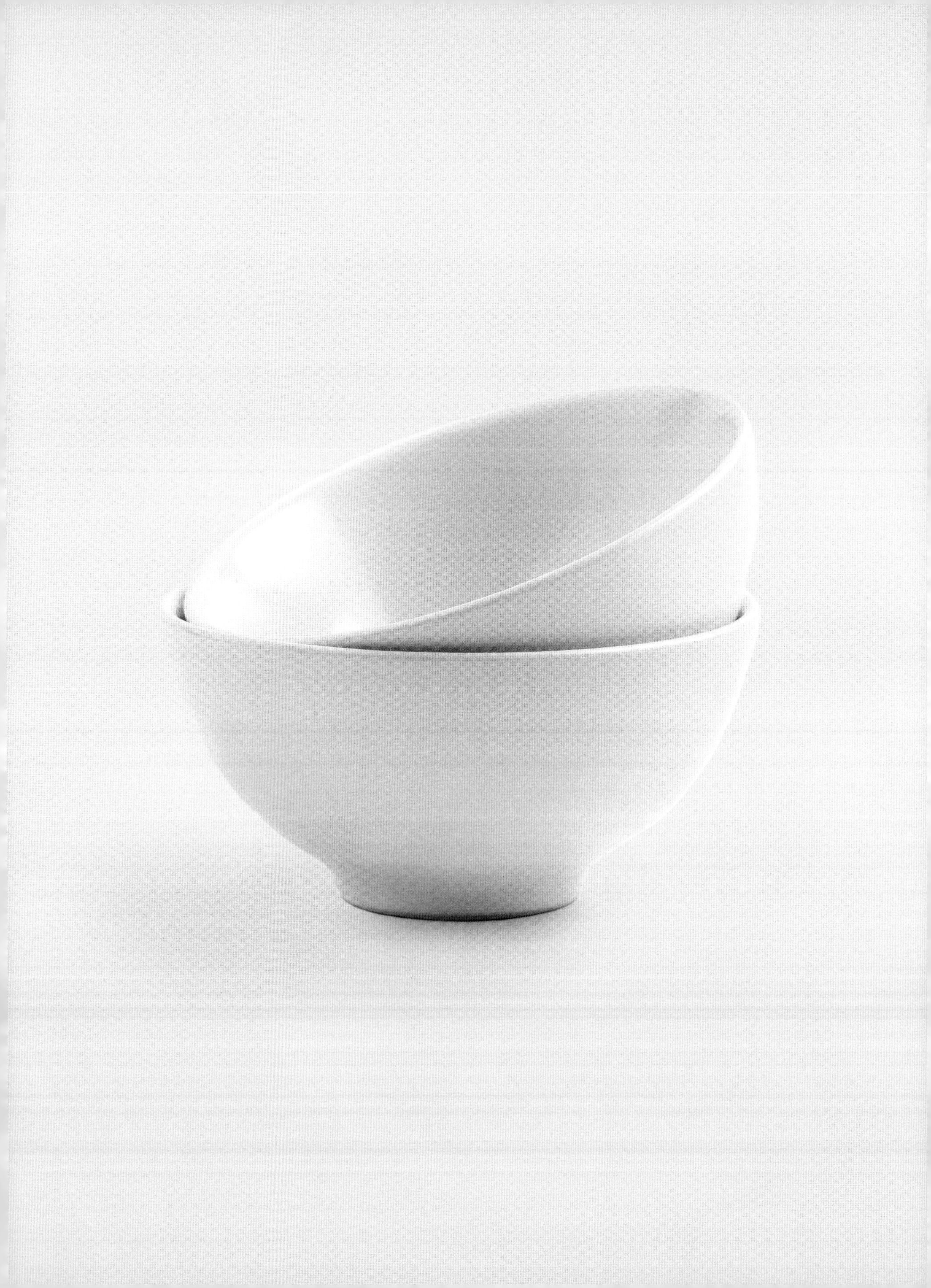

TWO
↓
DISHES

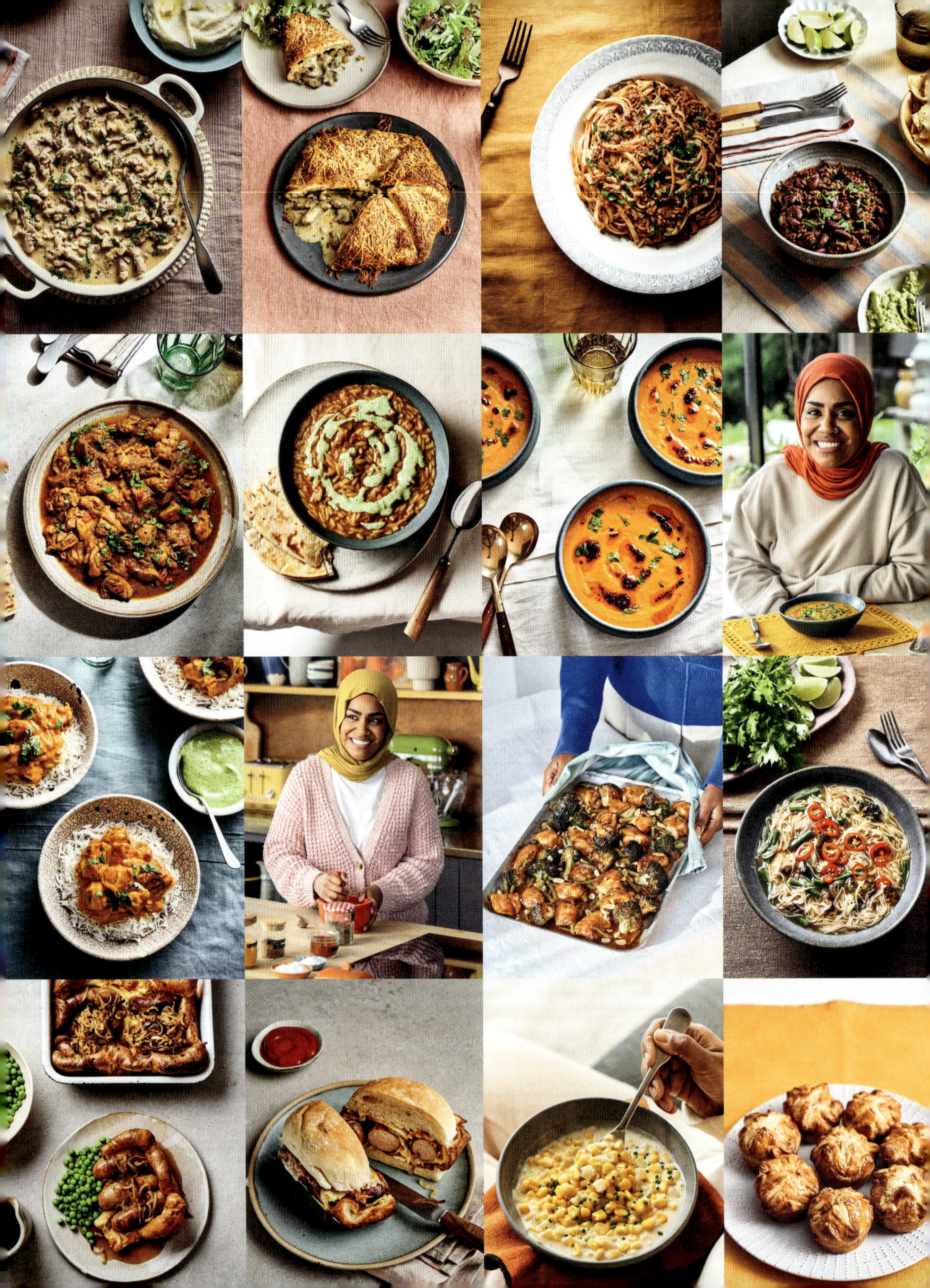

TWO DISHES

Double-duty recipes where one meal gets turned into two, e.g. making a Bolognese and adding kidney beans and spices to half of it for a second dish of chilli con carne. What's not to love about cooking from one set of ingredients for two completely different meals?!

BEEF STROGANOFF
↓
STROGANOFF FREE-FORM PIE

BOLOGNESE
↓
CHILLI

CHICKEN CURRY
↓
CHICKEN AND ORZO

CARROT SOUP
↓
CARROT AND COD CURRY

PEANUT CHICKEN TRAYBAKE
↓
NOODLE SOUP

HONEY MUSTARD TOAD-IN-THE-HOLE
↓
TOAD BURGERS

CORN CHOWDER
↓
CORN CHOWDER INDIVIDUAL PIES

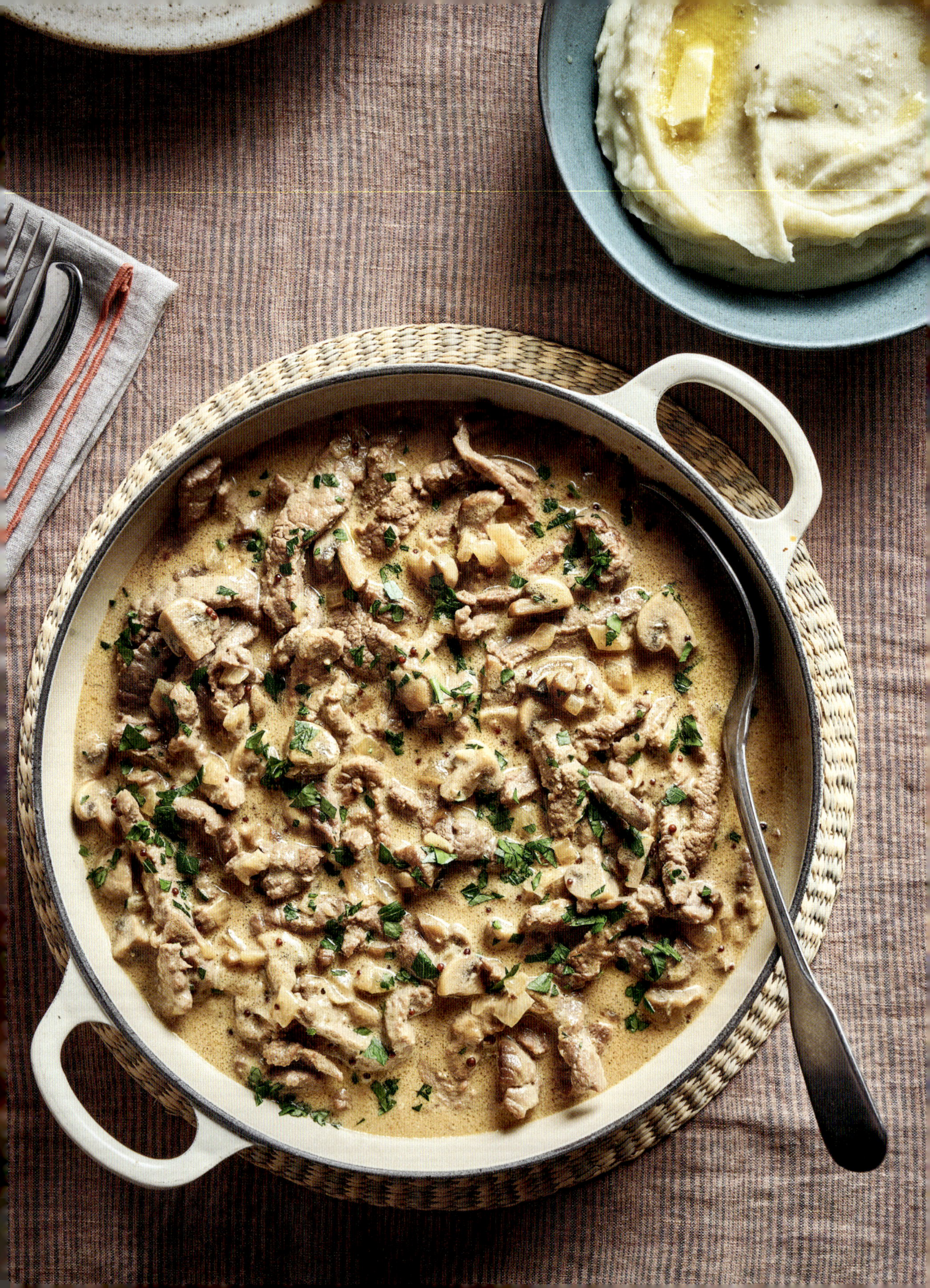

BEEF STROGANOFF

A stroganoff is the kind of thing that is wholesome and delicious and is a one-pot dish that can be really versatile. I love eating this with buttery mash or cooked tagliatelle.

ALSO MAKES: STROGANOFF FREE-FORM PIE (PAGE 138)

PREP: 5 MINS **COOK:** 1 HOUR 6 MINS

SERVES: 4

150g butter

2 tablespoons brown mustard seeds

4 cloves of garlic, minced

2 onions, diced

1 tablespoon salt

2 tablespoons English mustard

350g mushrooms, quartered

1kg beef, thinly sliced

400ml beef stock

100ml cream

3 tablespoons beef gravy granules

Fresh parsley, to serve

Put the butter in a pan and when the butter has melted, add the mustard seeds. As soon as the mustard seeds start popping, add the minced garlic and onion with the salt. Cook the onions till soft.

Spoon in the English mustard and mix through. Get the mushrooms and beef in and cook till the sliced beef is brown.

Pour in the beef stock and cream and boil on a high heat and leave to simmer with the lid off for 40 minutes.

Add the gravy granules, stir through, and then cook for a few minutes before taking off the heat and sprinkling over some parsley.

TIP *You don't have to make this with beef, you can use chicken instead.*

STROGANOFF FREE-FORM PIE

We are taking the filling and making a really cool free-form pie – so no tin, just pastry and yummy stroganoff filling.

PREP: 11 MINS **COOK:** 40 MINS **COOL:** 20 MINS

SERVES: 4

500g pack of shortcrust pastry

½ the beef stroganoff, cooled (see page 137)

1 egg, lightly beaten

50g Parmesan cheese, grated

Preheat the oven to 180°C and place a baking tray on the middle shelf of the oven. Have another baking tray ready with some baking paper.

Take the block of shortcrust pastry and roll out to a rough round, big enough to lay out the cooled stroganoff on and then to cover over the top.

Add the cooled stroganoff to the centre, making sure you have an even layer. Fold over the outer edge of the pastry into the middle, covering the filling, then pinch in the middle to bring it all together.

Place onto the baking tray with baking paper. Brush all over with egg, then sprinkle over the cheese. Use a sharp knife to create some steam holes.

Bake on top of the hot tray in the oven for 40 minutes. Take out and leave to cool for 20 minutes before serving with a simple salad.

TIP *Why not try this with puff pastry for a flakier pie.*

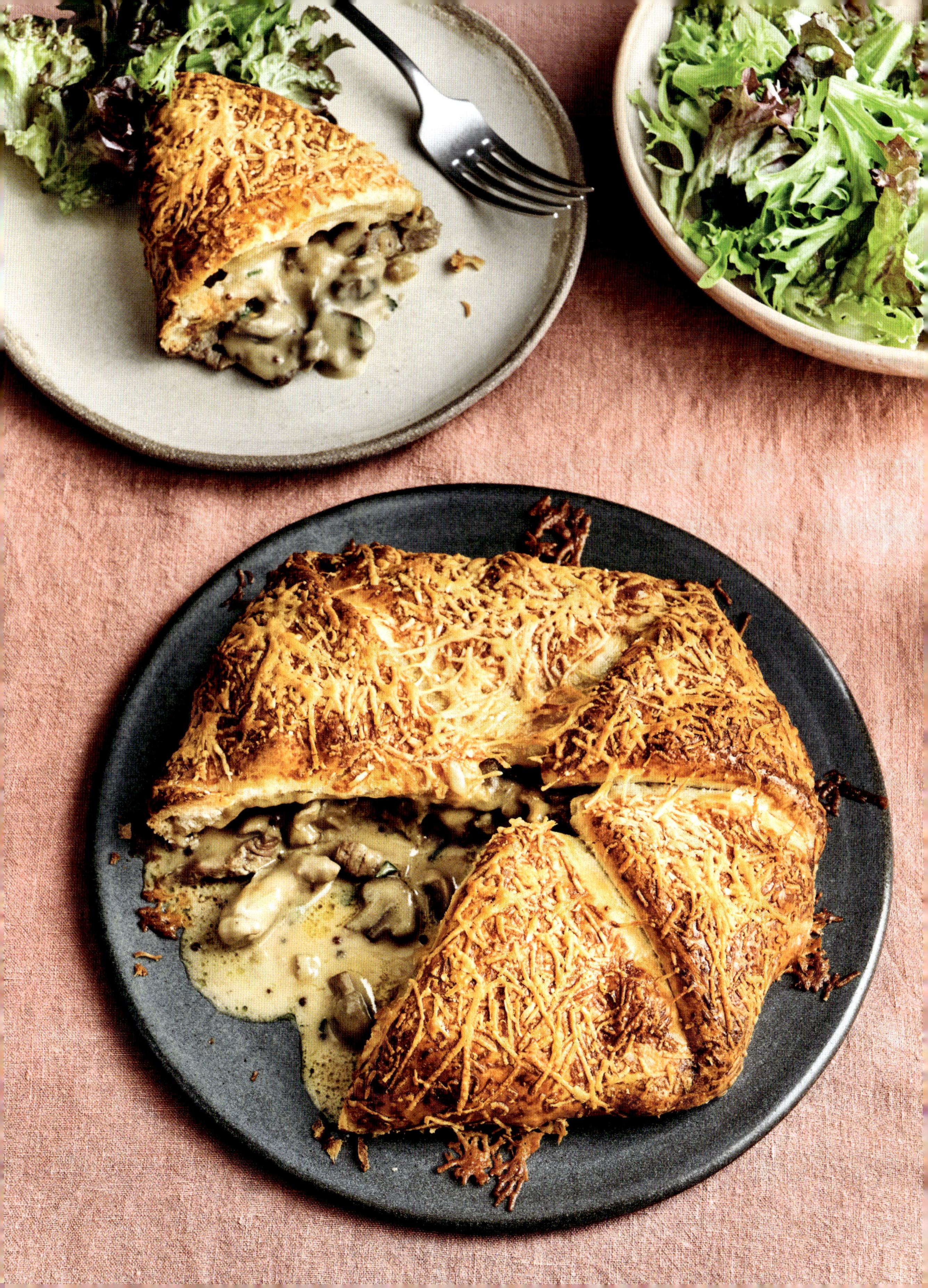

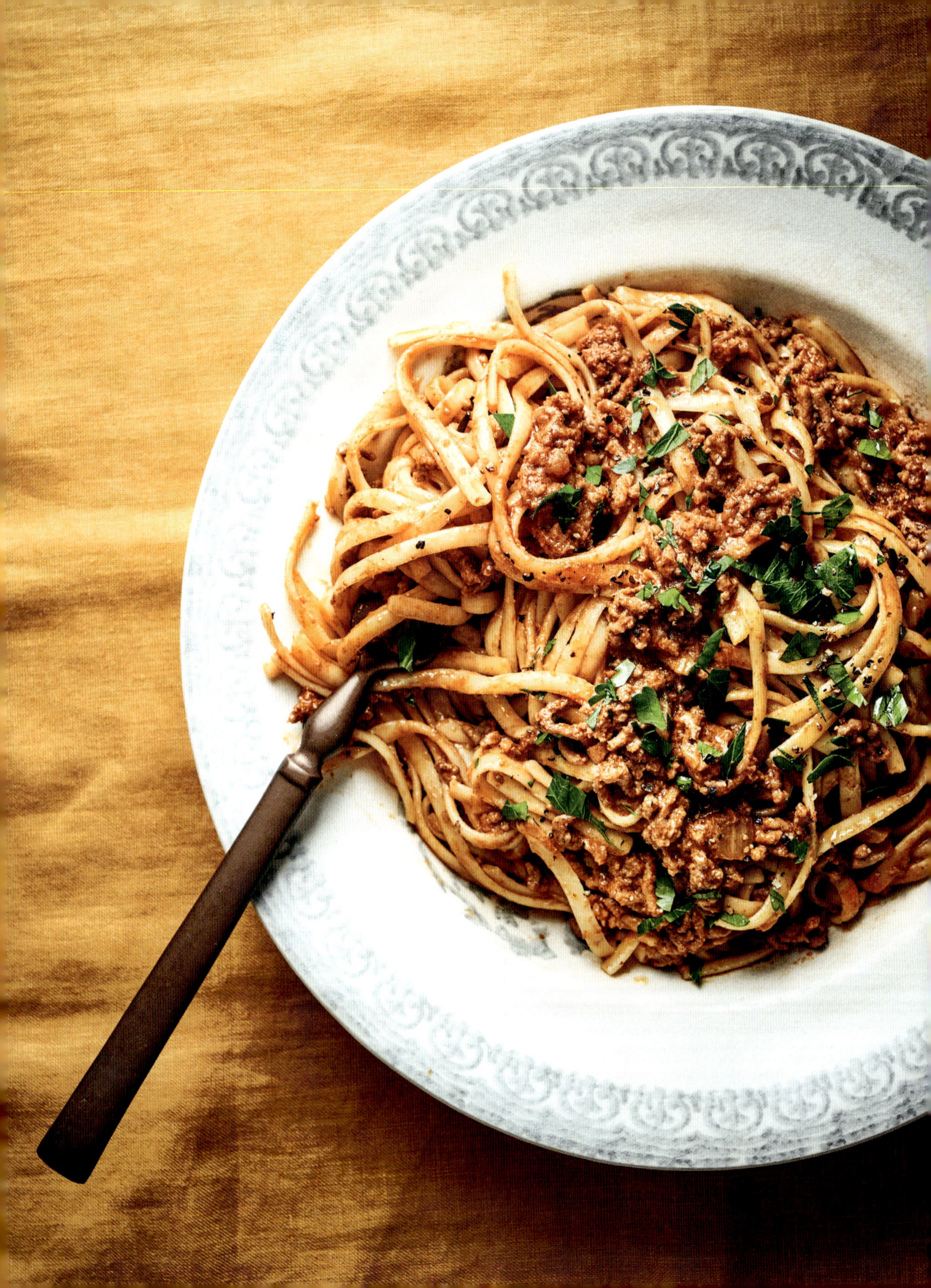

BOLOGNESE

Bolognese is a staple. It's a must-have go-to in most of our homes and rightfully so, as it's simple and easy to make. I will show you how to make it all in one pan and then, using the same base, change it up to make a simple chilli for another day.

ALSO MAKES: CHILLI (PAGE 142)

PREP: 5 MINS **COOK:** 50 MINS

SERVES: 4

- 100ml oil
- 1 large bulb of garlic, cloves peeled and minced
- 2 onions, diced
- 1 tablespoon salt
- 2kg mince, lamb/beef
- 2 tablespoons yeast extract
- 2 tablespoons chilli powder
- 3 tablespoons ground cumin
- 2 tablespoons tomato purée
- 2 tins of cream of tomato soup
- 400ml water

Start with a large pan and pour in the oil. As soon as the oil is hot, add the garlic. Add the onion and salt to the pan and cook till the onions are soft and just golden.

Get the mince in along with the yeast extract and cook till the mince is completely cooked through and browned. Spoon in the chilli powder, ground cumin and tomato purée and mix through.

Pour in the cream of tomato soup and water, mix through and leave to sit and bubble away for 30 minutes with the lid on. Serve with spaghetti or your pasta of choice.

TIP *You can substitute the soup with any tomato-based soup or tinned chopped tomatoes/passata.*

CHILLI

We are using this basic Bolognese recipe to create a chilli, so you have half the work and twice the dishes. Chilli is another classic favourite in our house because we love beans and this makes the mince go a long way.

PREP: 5 MINS **COOK:** 36 MINS

SERVES: 4

½ the Bolognese (see page 141)

2 x 400g tins of kidney beans, drained

1 tablespoon cocoa powder

200ml hot water

To serve

Fresh coriander

Avocado slices

Lime wedges

Nachos

Rice

Begin with half the Bolognese mixture heating in a pan. Add in the drained kidney beans.

Spoon the cocoa powder into a jug with the hot water and mix together. Pour into the pan and cook with the lid on for 30 minutes.

When it is cooked and ready to eat, serve the chilli sprinkled with coriander and with avocado, lime wedges, nachos and rice to make it a fuller meal.

TIP *If you don't have cocoa, add a few cubes of very dark chocolate and allow it to melt and cook through.*

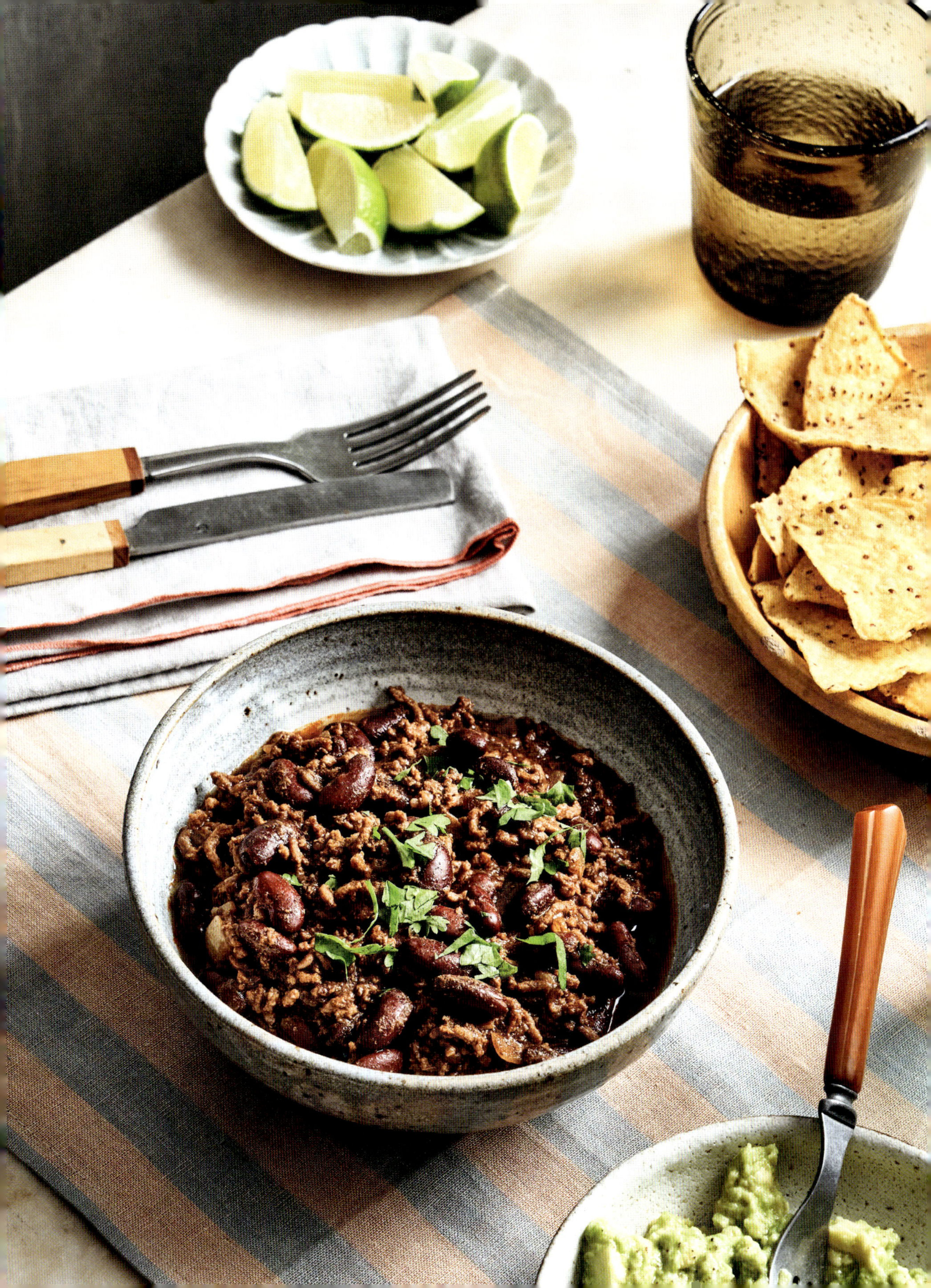

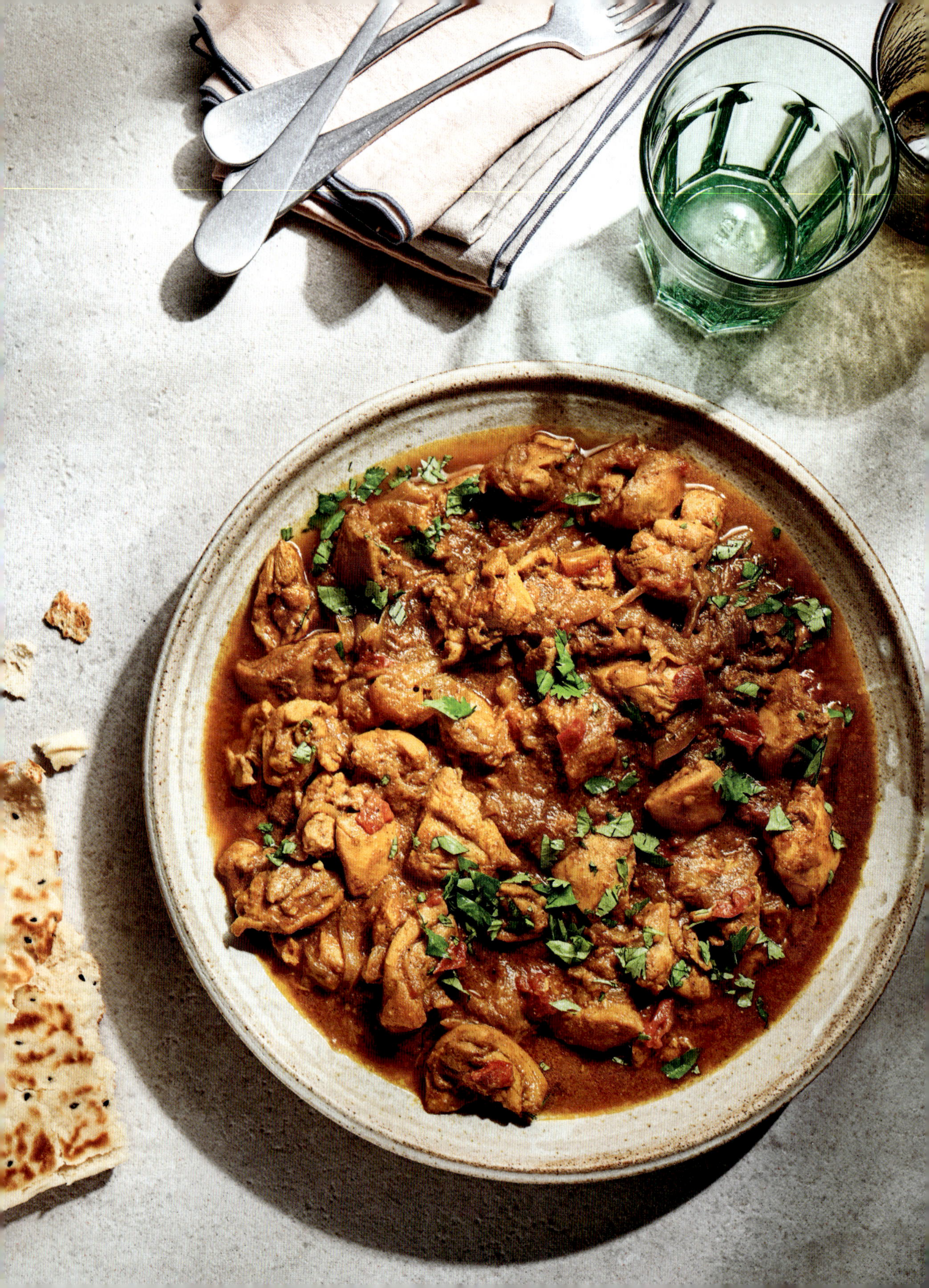

CHICKEN CURRY

This is the simplest curry you will ever make and even better because we are going to take half the curry and make another all-in-one dish. The only thing better than eating a curry once, is eating a curry twice.

ALSO MAKES: CHICKEN AND ORZO (PAGE 146)

PREP: 5 MINS **COOK:** 55 MINS

SERVES: 4

100ml oil

3 tablespoons garlic paste

2 tablespoons ginger paste

3 onions, sliced

2 tablespoons salt

3 tomatoes, diced

4 tablespoons garam masala

½ teaspoon ground turmeric

1 tablespoon chilli powder (optional)

2kg boneless chicken thighs, diced

Fresh coriander, to garnish

Begin by pouring the oil into a large pan over a high heat. As soon as the oil is hot, add the garlic and ginger paste and cook through for a few minutes.

Get the onions in with the salt and cook till golden brown and lovely and soft. If the onions start to catch, add a splash of water.

Now get the chopped tomatoes in and cook till the tomatoes have really broken down. Spoon in the garam masala, turmeric and chilli powder and cook the spices in the pan for a few minutes.

Put the boneless chicken thighs into the pan and cook over a high heat for 5 minutes, then reduce the heat, add a splash of water, cover with a lid and leave to cook for 30 minutes. Once the curry is ready, sprinkle with coriander and I would eat it with rice or naan or both.

TIP *If you want a curry with spice but less heat, add paprika instead of chilli powder as it is much milder.*

CHICKEN AND ORZO

This is an all-in-one dish that is made using half the curry. This is great for a meal that requires no faff, just warmed and straight into a bowl.

PREP: 5 MINS **COOK:** 25 MINS

SERVES: 4

½ the chicken curry (see page 145)
250g orzo
500ml boiling water

To serve

4 tablespoons natural yoghurt
Splash of oil
1 clove of garlic
1 lemon, juice only
Small handful of fresh coriander
Splash of milk

Begin by putting half the curry in a pan, adding the orzo and cooking over a high heat till the orzo is combined and starts to change in colour.

Pour in the boiling water, bring the whole thing to a boil and then reduce. Keep the lid off and cook till the orzo is tender and no longer has a crunchy centre. Take off the heat.

To serve, I like to add the yoghurt, oil, garlic, lemon juice and coriander to a blender and make a quick and flavourful drizzle. Add a splash of milk to loosen and drizzle all over your hot orzo.

TIP *You can use soured cream or mascarpone if you don't have yoghurt.*

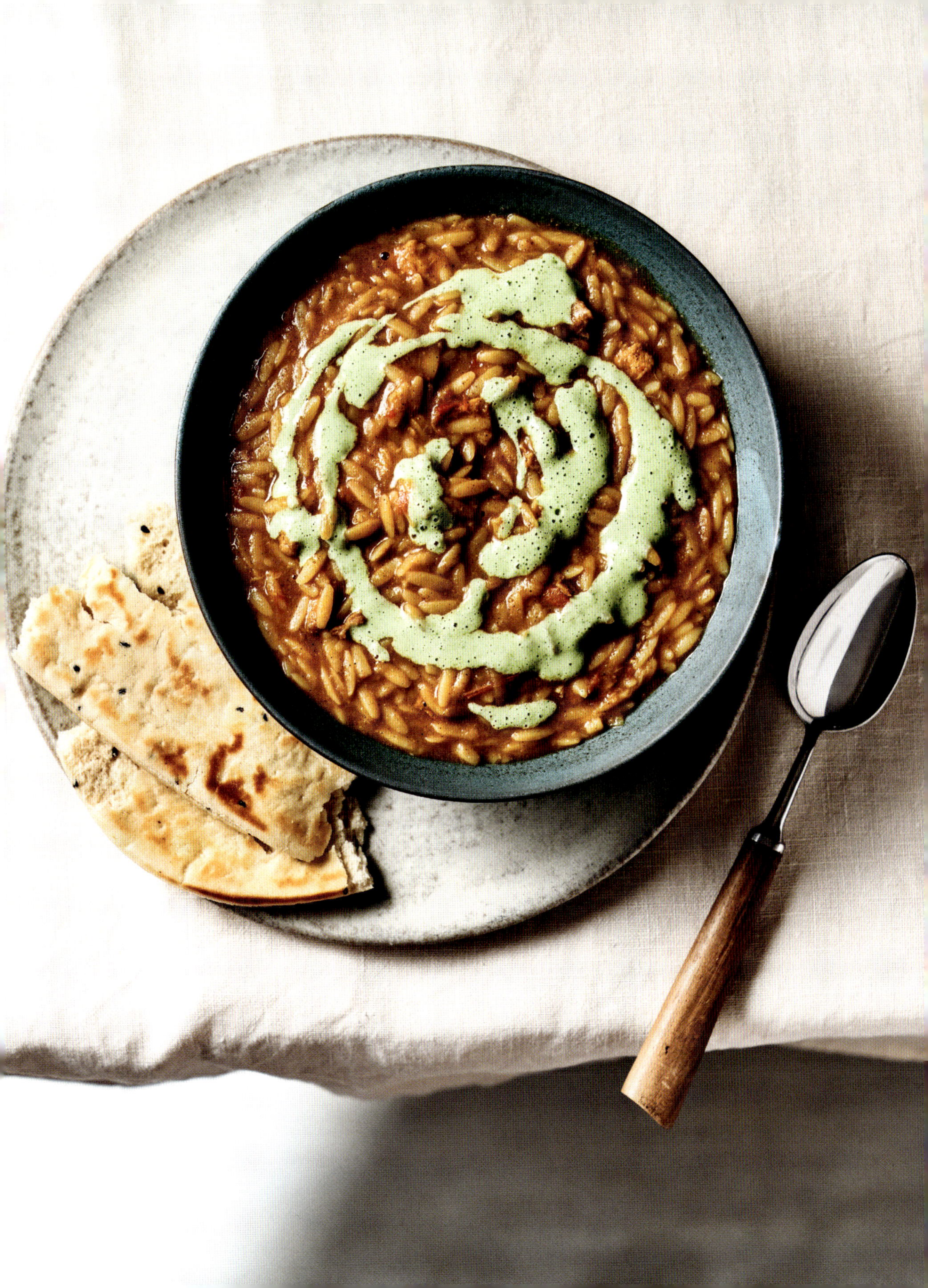

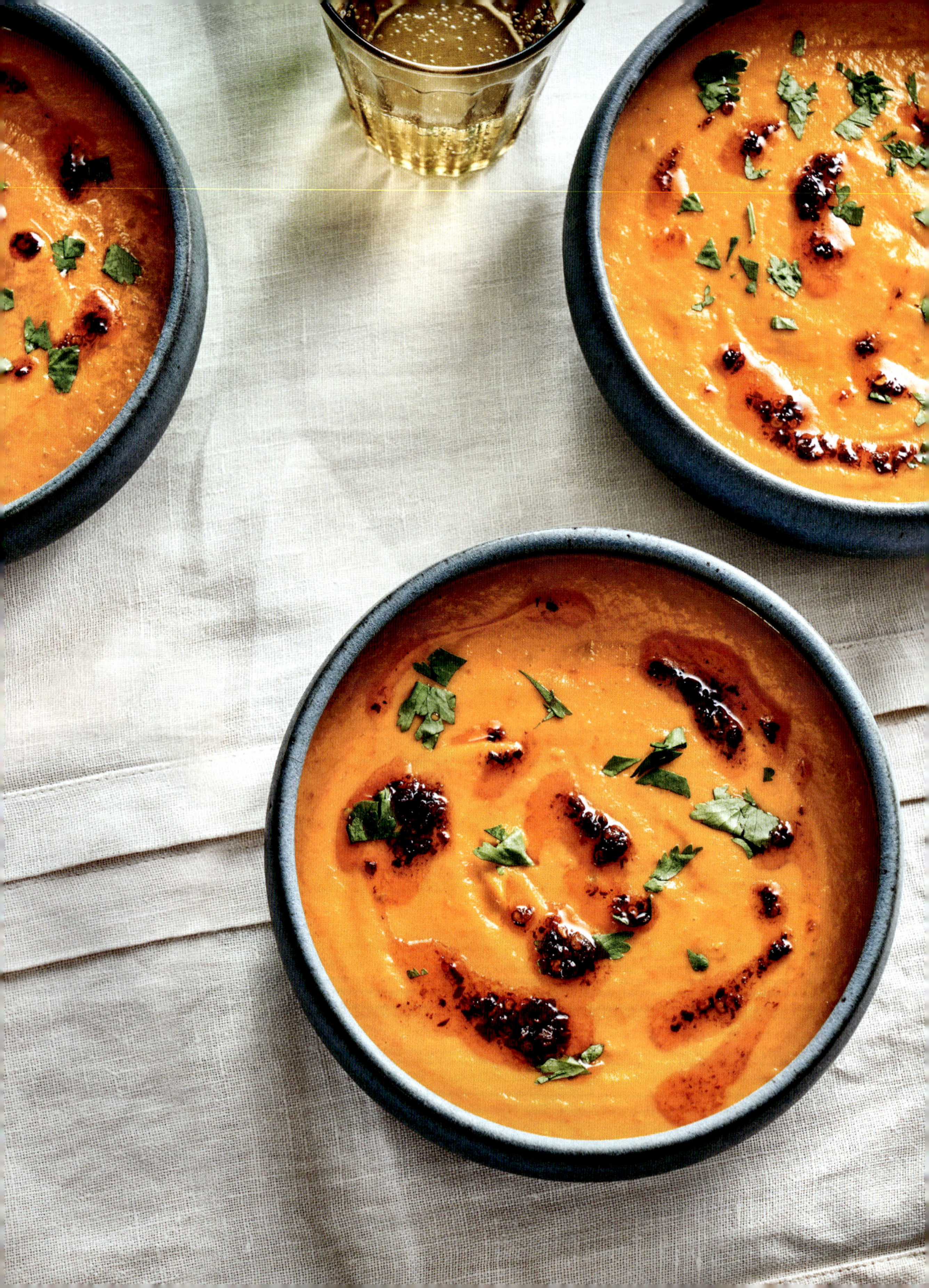

CARROT SOUP

I love a really hearty carrot soup. It's such a great way to use up carrots or just a great soup to make if you love carrots.

ALSO MAKES: CARROT AND COD CURRY (PAGE 152)

PREP: 5 MINS **COOK:** 1 HOUR

SERVES: 4

200g butter

2 tablespoons coriander seeds

2 tablespoons cumin seeds

1 teaspoon chilli flakes

½ teaspoon ground turmeric

6 cloves of garlic, minced

1 onion, diced

2 tablespoons salt

1kg carrots, peeled and grated

1 medium/large potato, peeled and grated

2 oranges, zest and juice

1 litre water or vegetable stock

To serve

Chilli oil

Fresh coriander

Put the butter in a large stockpot or pan, place over a medium heat and, as soon as the butter has melted, add the coriander seeds, cumin seeds, chilli flakes and turmeric and heat through for a few minutes.

Add the garlic, onion and salt and cook through till the onions are soft.

Get all the grated carrot in along with the grated potato and cook over a high heat, mixing to combine everything.

Add the orange juice and zest. Pour in the water or stock and boil rapidly for about 10 minutes, then turn the heat down and leave to simmer with the lid on for 30 minutes. As soon as the carrots are tender, purée with a blender to a smooth, creamy paste.

To serve, drizzle over some chilli oil and sprinkle on the coriander.

TIP *You can also use parsnips instead of carrots, or a mixture of both.*

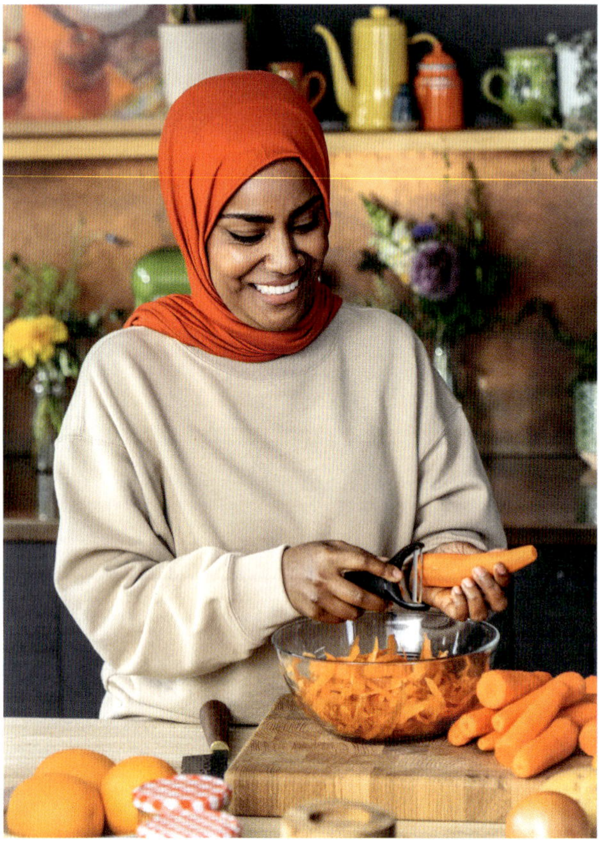
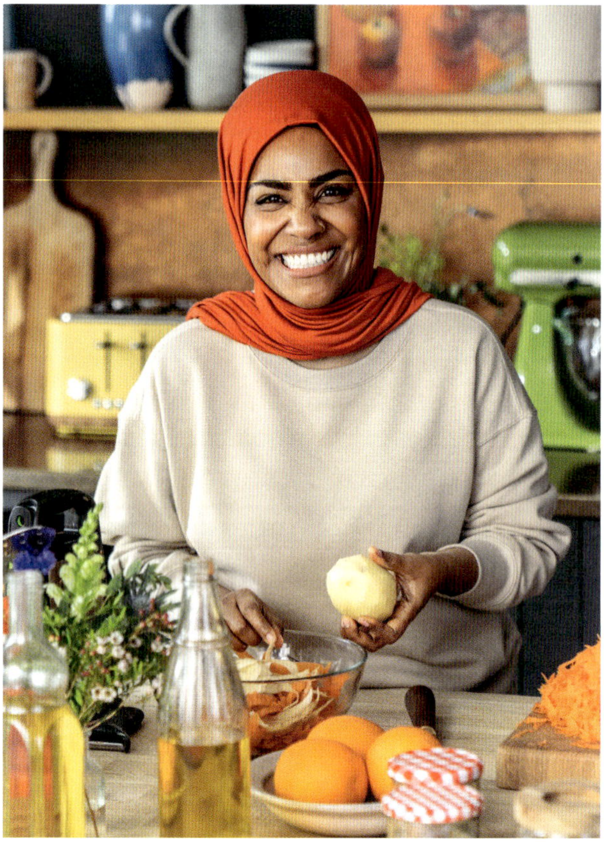
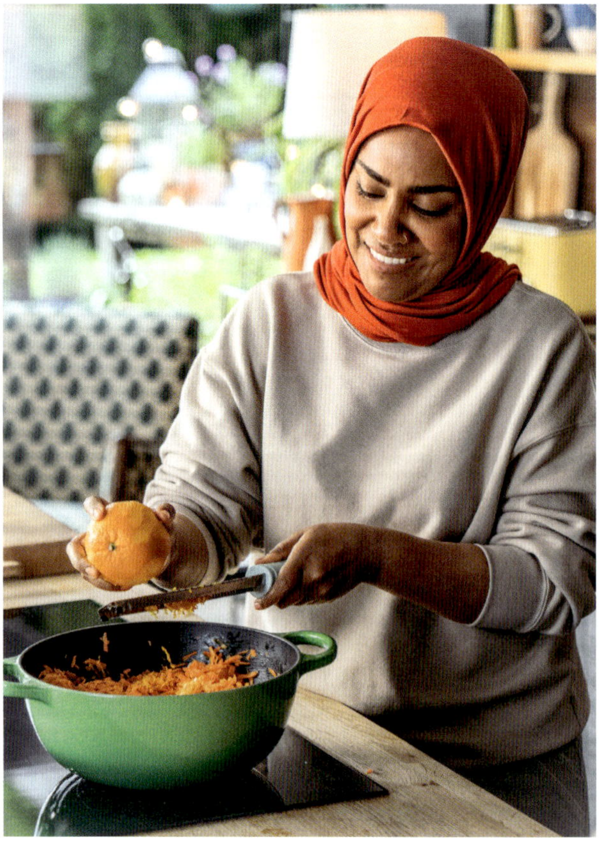
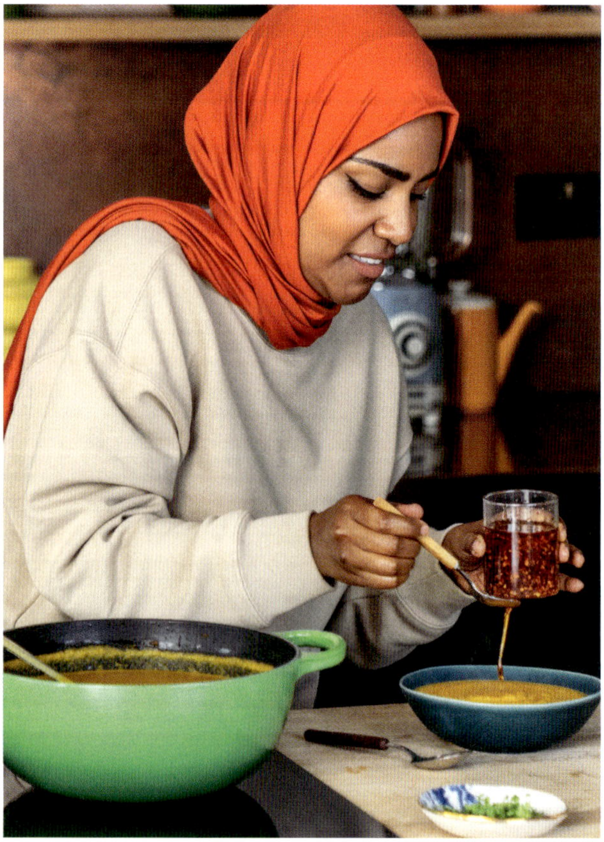

TWO DISHES / 151

CARROT AND COD CURRY

Carrot soup makes for a great base for a fish curry, so let me show you how delicious and easy it really is to make.

PREP: 5 MINS **COOK:** 54 MINS

SERVES: 4

- ½ the carrot soup (see page 149)
- 2 x 285g cod fillets, cut into chunks
- 2 teaspoons oil
- sprinkle of salt
- ½ teaspoon chilli powder
- Oil, for frying
- 4 spring onions, sliced into thin strips
- Fresh coriander, to serve

Put half the carrot soup in a pan over a medium heat and leave to bubble away and reduce.

Put the cod chunks into a bowl, drizzle over the oil, salt and chilli powder and mix till the fish is coated.

Take a non-stick frying pan and place over a medium heat. Pour some oil into the pan and, as soon as the oil is hot, add the chunks of fish so they get cooked and golden on each side. Do this in batches, so you don't overcrowd the pan. Set aside till you have done them all.

Now fry the spring onions and set aside with the fish.

Add the fish and spring onion to the reduced carrot soup, carefully mix through, cover and leave to cook for 20 minutes. As the curry cooks, the cod will flake and fall apart, but that is perfect – all that delicious flavour will get into every inch of the cod pieces.

Sprinkle over the coriander to serve. I love eating this with rice!

TIP *This can also be made with haddock and prawns or even crab sticks.*

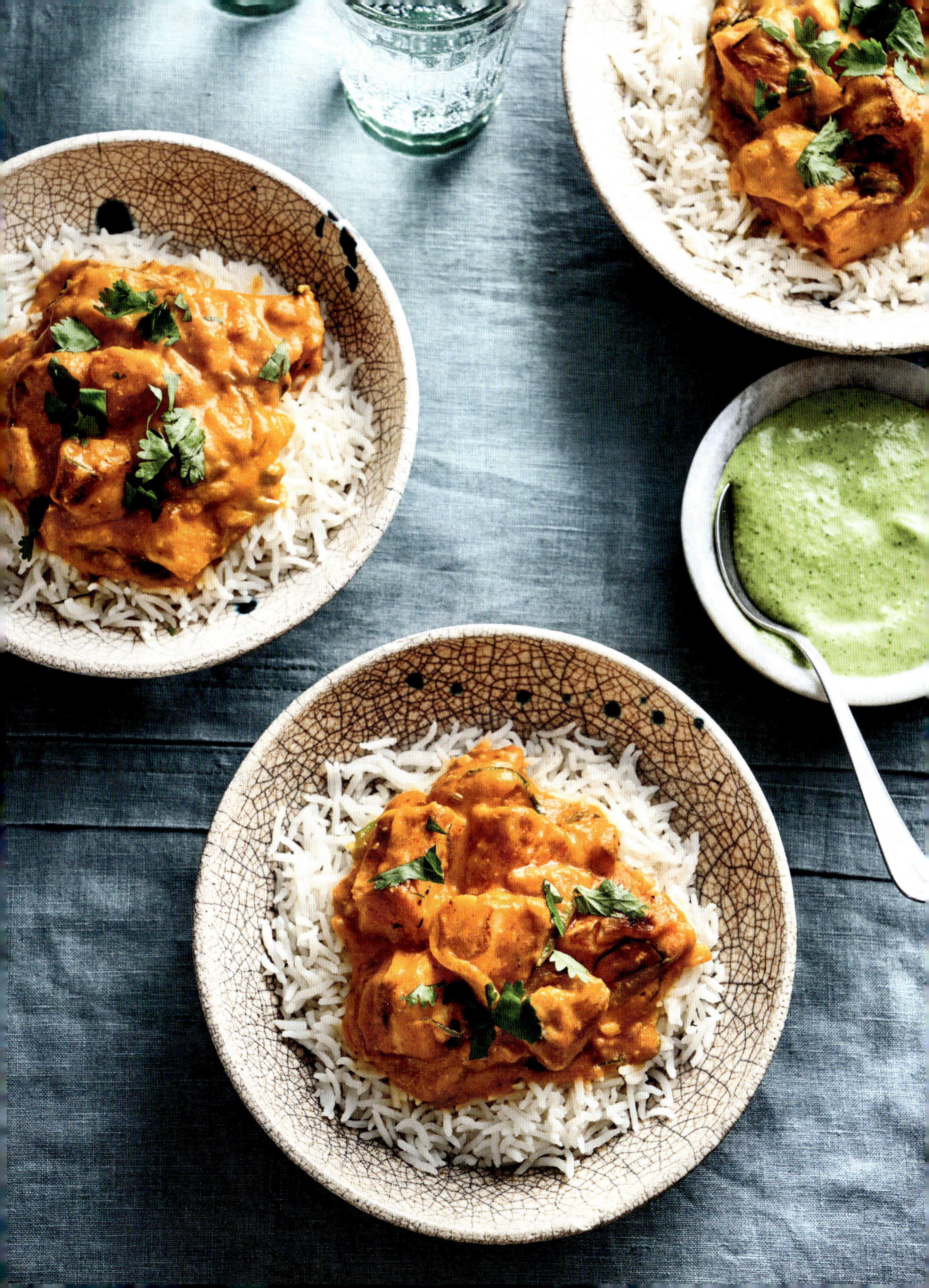

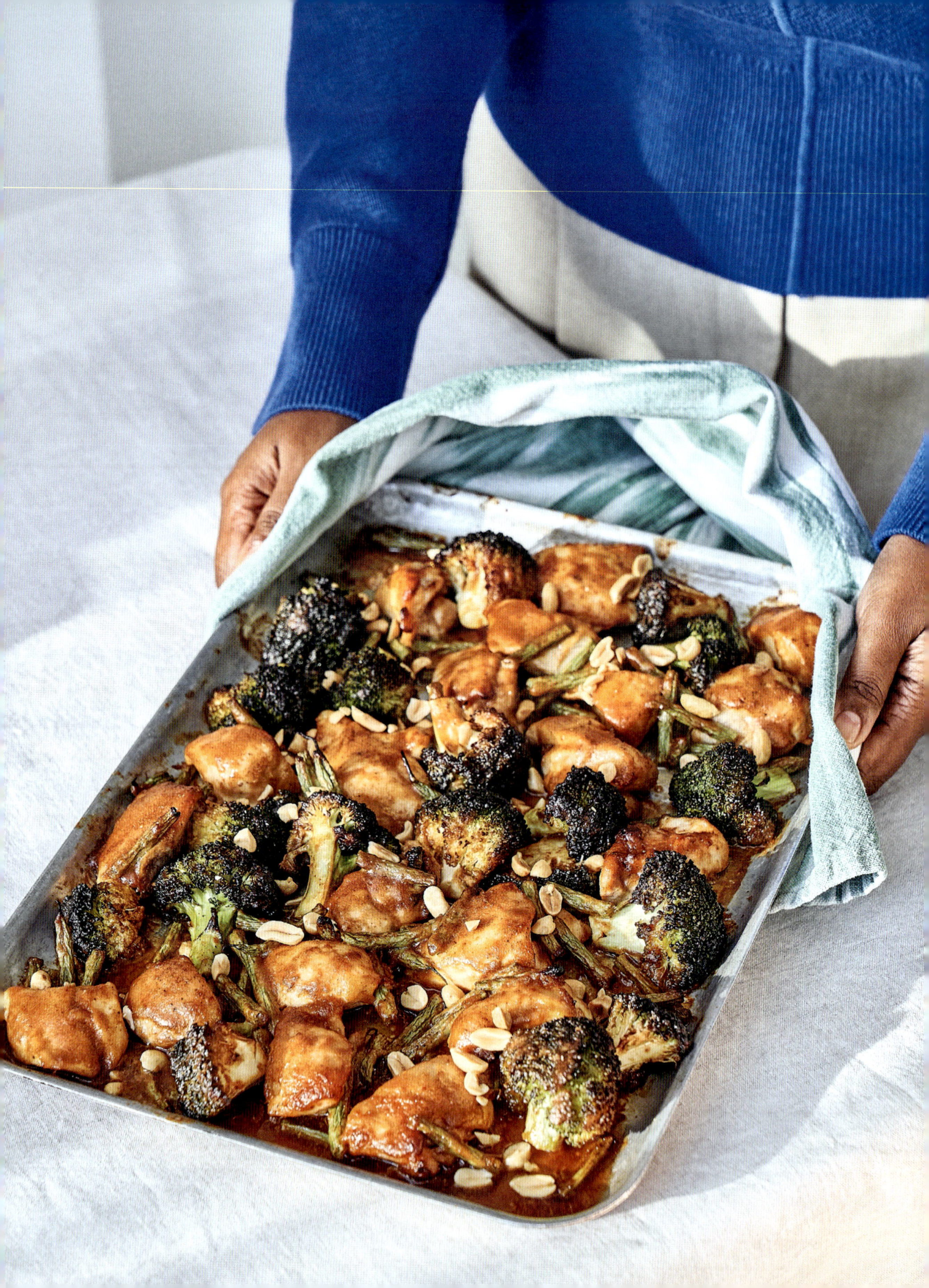

PEANUT CHICKEN TRAYBAKE

This one-pan chicken dish is packed with flavour and has everything you need for a mid-week meal.

ALSO MAKES: NOODLE SOUP (PAGE 156)
PREP: 5 MINS **COOK:** 45 MINS
SERVES: 4

- 150g smooth peanut butter
- 150ml oil
- 2 tablespoons garlic paste
- 2 tablespoons ginger paste
- 3 tablespoons chilli paste
- 3 tablespoons apple cider vinegar
- 2 tablespoons runny honey
- 100ml soy sauce
- 1kg chicken thighs, diced
- 400g broccoli florets
- 200g green beans, cut into 2–3cm slices
- 1 large cucumber, cut into semicircles
- 100g peanuts, roughly chopped

Start by putting the smooth peanut butter, oil, garlic paste, ginger paste, chilli paste, apple cider vinegar, runny honey and soy sauce in a large bowl. Mix really well and add the chicken in, making sure the chicken is totally covered.

Preheat the oven to 180°C and have a large roasting dish at the ready.

Add the broccoli and green beans to the dish, put the chicken on top and mix through with your hands. Sprinkle over the peanuts and bake for 45 minutes.

Take out and this one-tray dish is ready to devour.

TIP *This works really well with paneer or halloumi as a meat alternative.*

NOODLE SOUP

The traybake is the perfect base for a delicious noodle soup, so take half the traybake and make something totally different.

PREP: 5 MINS **COOK:** 38–40 MINS

SERVES: 4

- ½ the peanut chicken traybake (see page 155)
- 1–1.5 litres chicken stock
- 200g noodle nests
- 2 tablespoons cornflour
- 3 tablespoons water

To serve

Chopped fresh coriander

Lime wedges

Chopped chillies

Take half the traybake and pop into a deep saucepan along with the chicken stock. Bring the mixture to the boil.

Crush the noodles in your hand and add to the liquid. Simmer away for 30 minutes.

Make the cornflour slurry by mixing the water with the cornflour. Add to the noodle soup to thicken just slightly.

Take off the heat and serve with coriander, lime wedges and chopped chillies.

TIP *If you don't have any noodles, you can always crush up spaghetti and get that in there – it will taste just as good.*

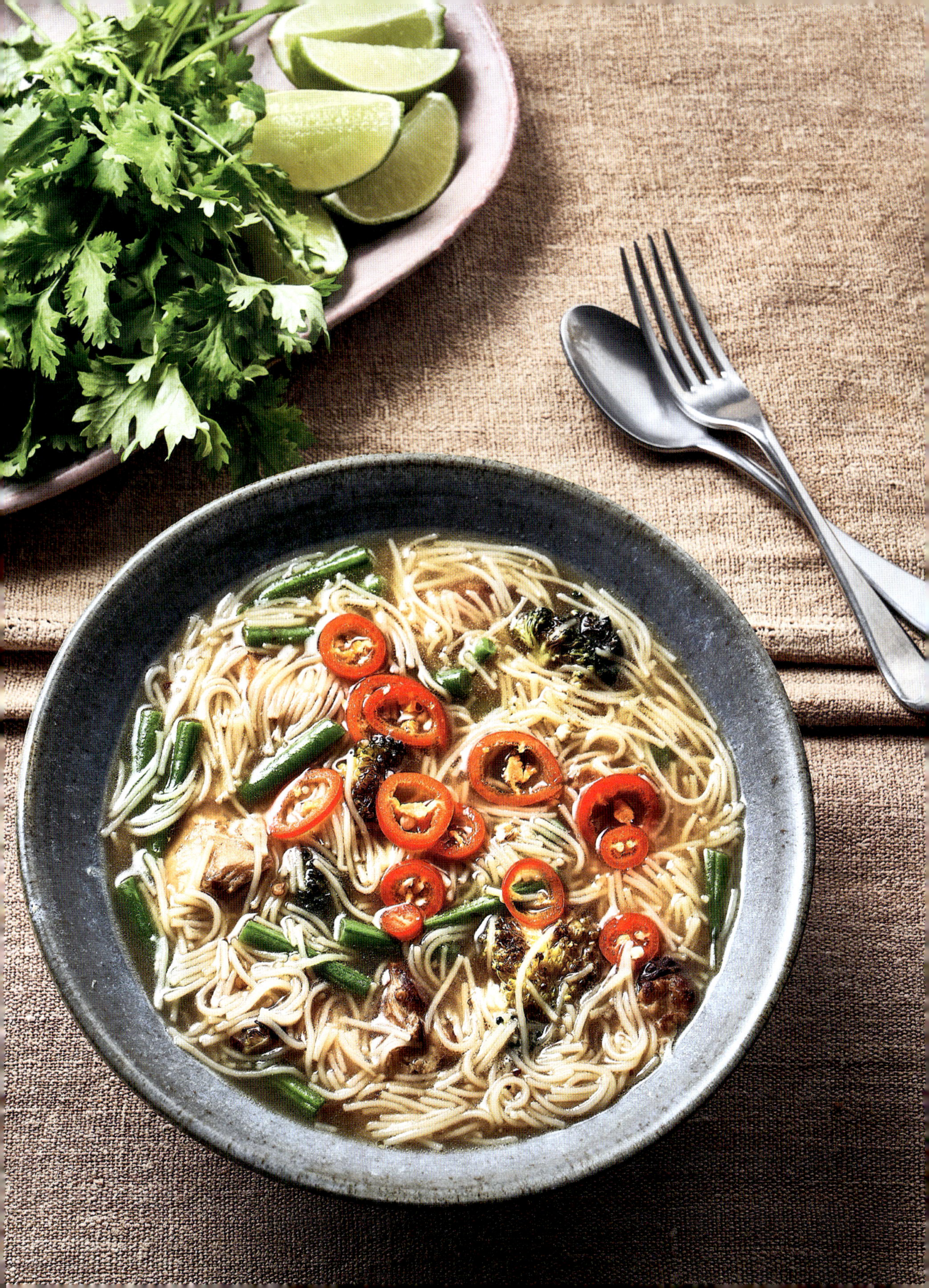

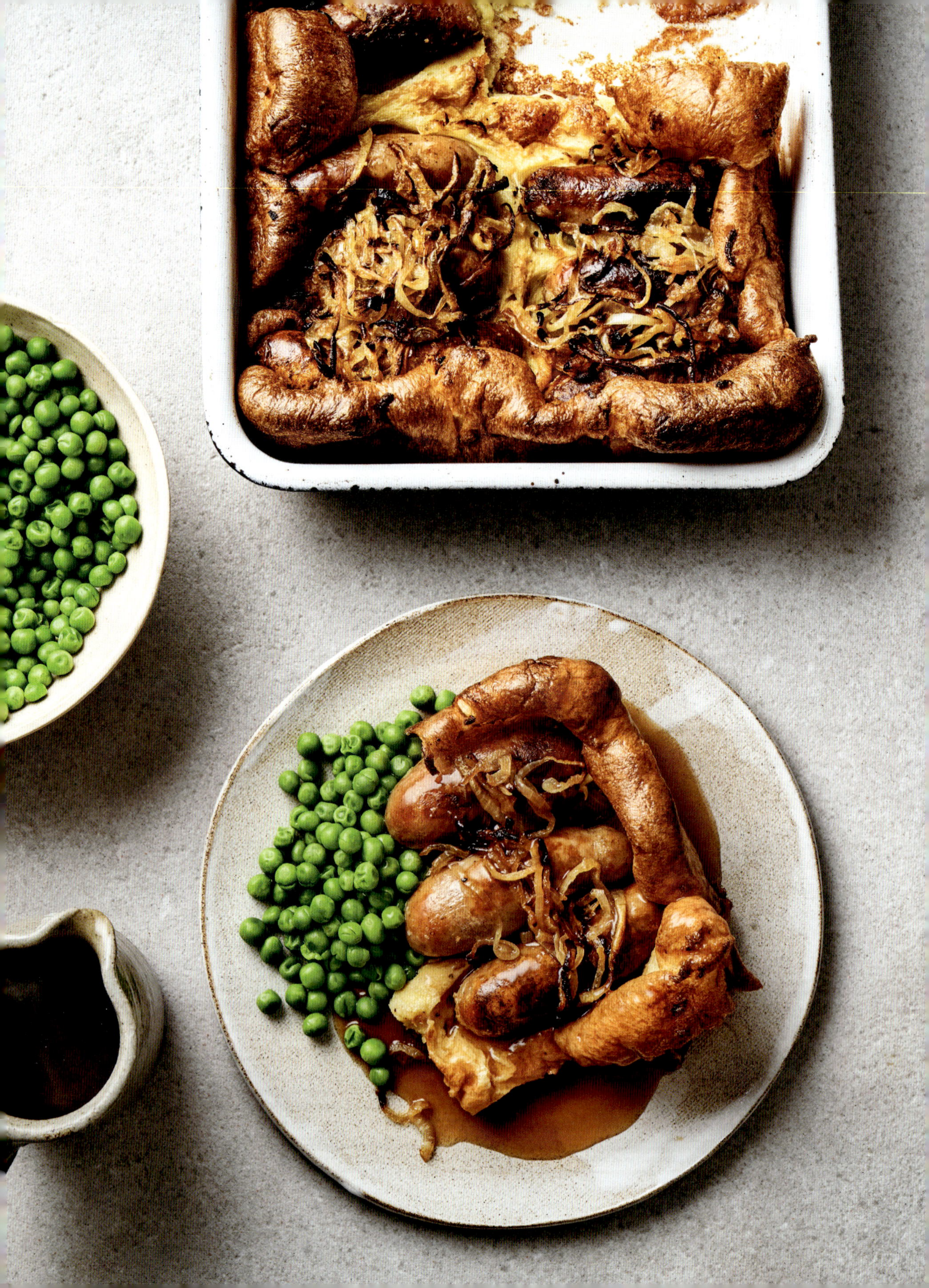

HONEY MUSTARD TOAD-IN-THE-HOLE

Toad-in-the-hole is Yorkshire pudding and sausage – literally the best combination. So simple you will wonder why you have never made it before.

ALSO MAKES: TOAD BURGERS (PAGE 160)

PREP: 6 MINS **COOK:** 1 HOUR 25 MINS

SERVES: 2

For the batter

115g plain flour
½ teaspoon salt
1 teaspoon ground black pepper
4 medium eggs
300ml whole milk
100ml oil

For the sausages

3 tablespoons oil
12 chicken sausages
3 onions, thinly sliced
1 teaspoon salt
1 teaspoon sugar
2 tablespoons wholegrain mustard

Start by making the batter. Put the plain flour in a bowl with the salt and black pepper. Whisk to combine. Add the eggs and whole milk and whisk to a smooth batter. Set aside in the fridge.

For the sausages, pour the oil into a frying pan and as soon as the oil is hot, add the sausages and cook till golden brown. Take out and set aside on a plate.

Pour another splash of oil into the pan and when the oil is hot, add the onion and salt and cook till golden brown and caramelized.

Now add the sugar and wholegrain mustard and warm through till the sugar has dissolved.

Preheat the oven to 200°C.

Get a large roasting dish and pour the remaining 100ml of oil into the dish. Add the sausages on top of the oil, making sure they are in threes so there are three per person in every portion. Now add the onions on top of the sausages.

Pop into the oven for 10 minutes. Take out and pour the batter in and around the sausages. Bake for 35–40 minutes.

Take out and this is ready to eat with gravy and peas – my personal fave way of eating it.

TIP *Don't be afraid to try this with vegetarian sausages – they are just as good!*

TWO DISHES / 159

TOAD BURGERS

No toads were harmed in the making of these burgers. They are pretty yummy though.

PREP: 2 MINS **COOK:** 15 MINS
SERVES: 2

2 large floured baps

Butter and yeast extract, for spreading

2 portions of the toad-in-the-hole (see page 159)

2 slices of strong Cheddar cheese

Worcestershire sauce

Mayo

Pop the grill on high.

Put the baps on a baking tray and grill till toasted. Butter, spread with yeast extract and set aside.

Put the toad-in-the-hole portions on the baking tray and place the cheese on top. Sprinkle generously with the Worcestershire sauce. Grill till the cheese has melted.

Place the toads onto the base of the baps, squeeze on the mayo, place the tops on and enjoy!

TIP *If you don't like yeast extract, spread a little beef extract on instead for the same sort of flavour.*

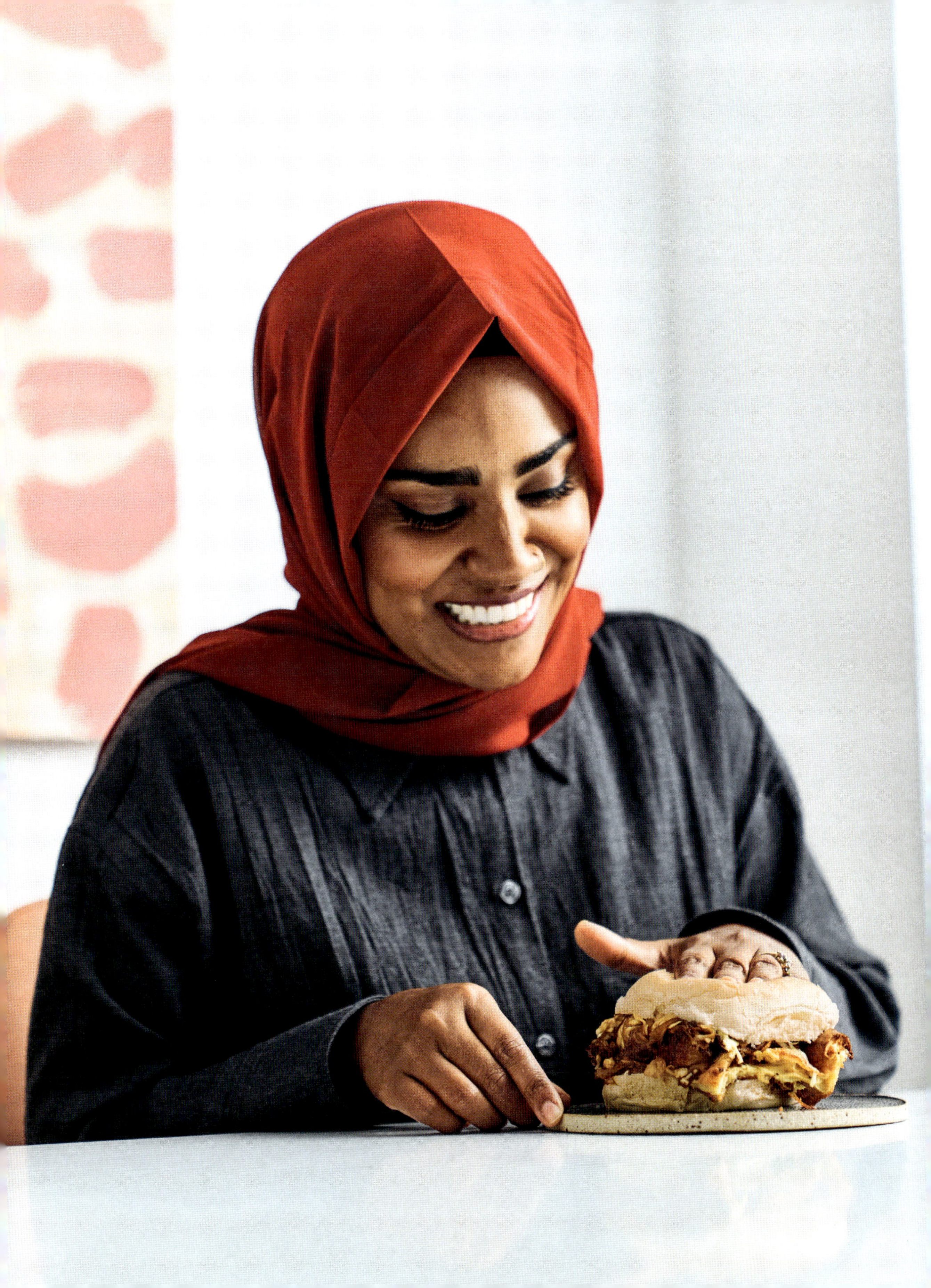

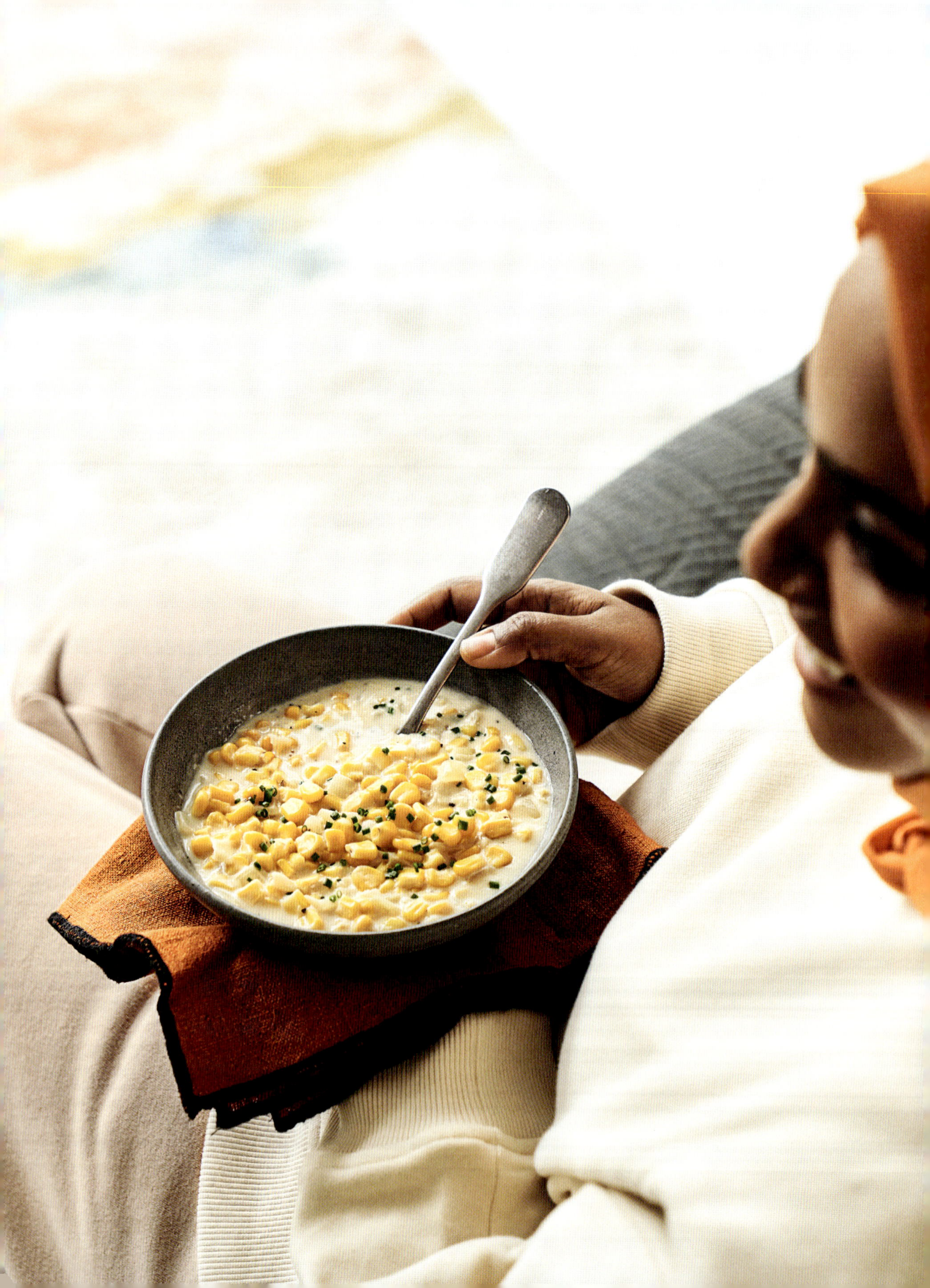

CORN CHOWDER

My daughter's absolute favourite dish to eat. She loves it so much I now make it for her two ways.

ALSO MAKES: CORN CHOWDER INDIVIDUAL PIES (PAGE 164)
PREP: 5 MINS **COOK:** 26–30 MINS
SERVES: 4

- 100g butter
- 3 onions, diced
- 3 cloves of garlic, minced
- 2 tablespoons ground black pepper
- 1 tablespoon salt
- 1kg frozen sweetcorn
- 4 tablespoons plain flour
- 750ml whole milk
- Chopped fresh chives, to garnish

Put the butter in a pan and heat till the butter has melted. Add the onion and cook till lovely and soft.

Now add the garlic, black pepper and salt and cook through for a few minutes. Stir in the frozen sweetcorn and cook for a few minutes till the corn has started to thaw out.

Get the flour in and mix through. Pour in the milk and cook over a high heat for a few minutes and then simmer till the whole mixture is lovely and thick.

Serve with a sprinkling of chopped chives.

TIP *Why not try this with peas – so different but still really good.*

CORN CHOWDER INDIVIDUAL PIES

These pies are buttery and delicious and perfect for a picnic or gathering.

PREP: 8–10 MINS **FREEZE:** 45 MINS **COOK:** 35–40 MINS
MAKES: 12 PIES

- ½ the corn chowder, cooled in the fridge (see page 163)
- 100g Cheddar cheese, grated
- 2 teaspoons chilli flakes
- 2 x 320g packs of ready-rolled puff pastry
- 1 egg, lightly beaten
- Sprinkle of salt

Take the chilled corn chowder and add the grated Cheddar and chilli flakes, mixing really well till everything is combined.

Have a deep 12-hole muffin tin ready.

Divide one pastry sheet into 12 equal squares. Put the squares into the cups of the muffin tray and tease into all the edges, manipulating the pastry to make sure it has covered the base and sides of each cup. Pop the tin into the freezer for 15 minutes.

Cut the other sheet into 12 equal pieces and pop the squares into the fridge.

Take the tin out and fill to the top with the corn mixture, then brush the edges with egg. Pop the squares of pastry on top of the filling. Seal the edges simply by pressing the edges, bringing any overhang into the centre. Pierce the tops for steam to escape. Pop into the freezer for 30 minutes.

Preheat the oven to 200°C.

Take the tin out, brush the tops with egg, sprinkle with salt and bake for 35–40 minutes.

TIP *To get the best shape, always freeze your pastry for 30 minutes before you bake. This really helps to keep that shape when baking in a hot oven.*

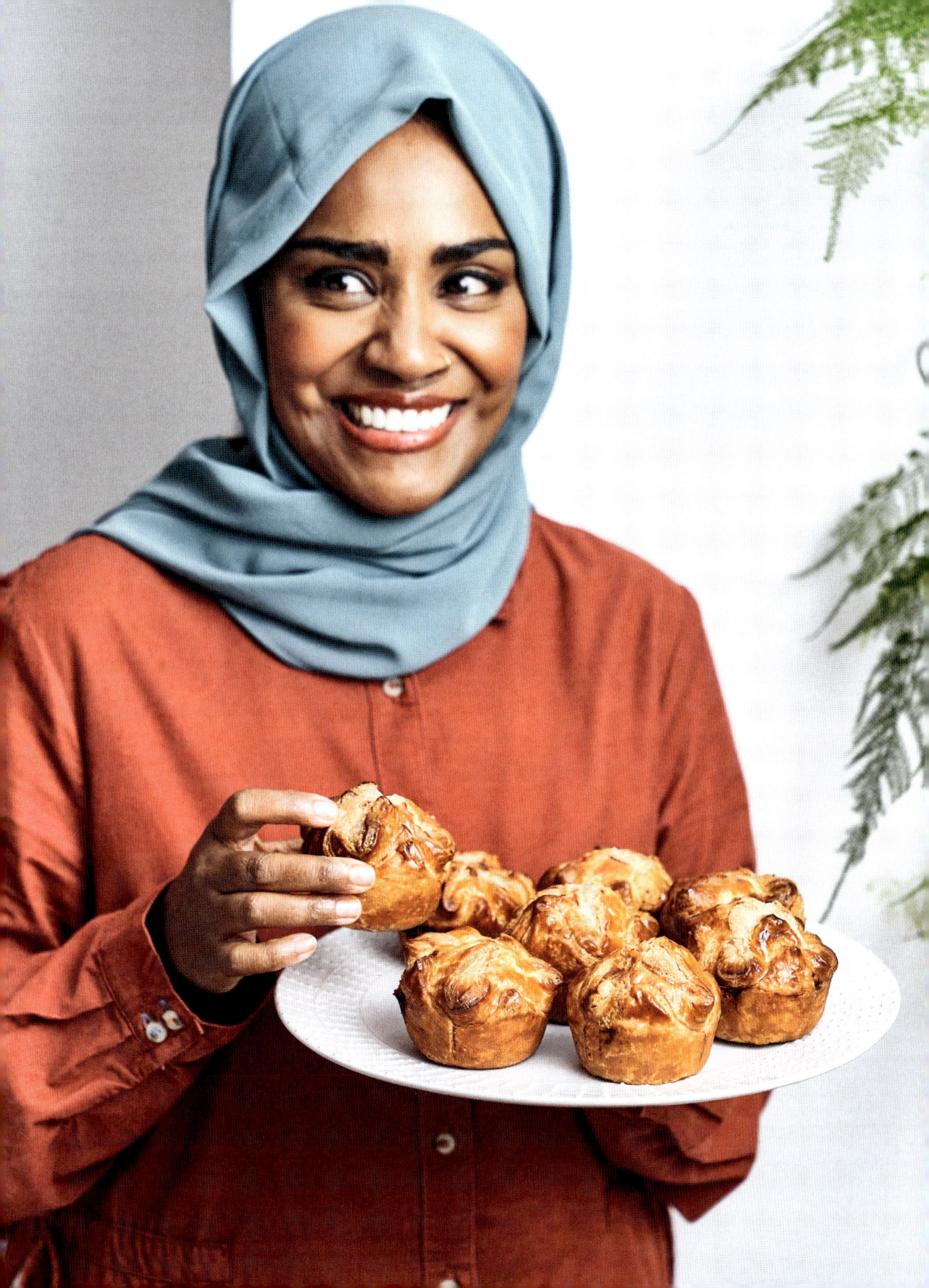

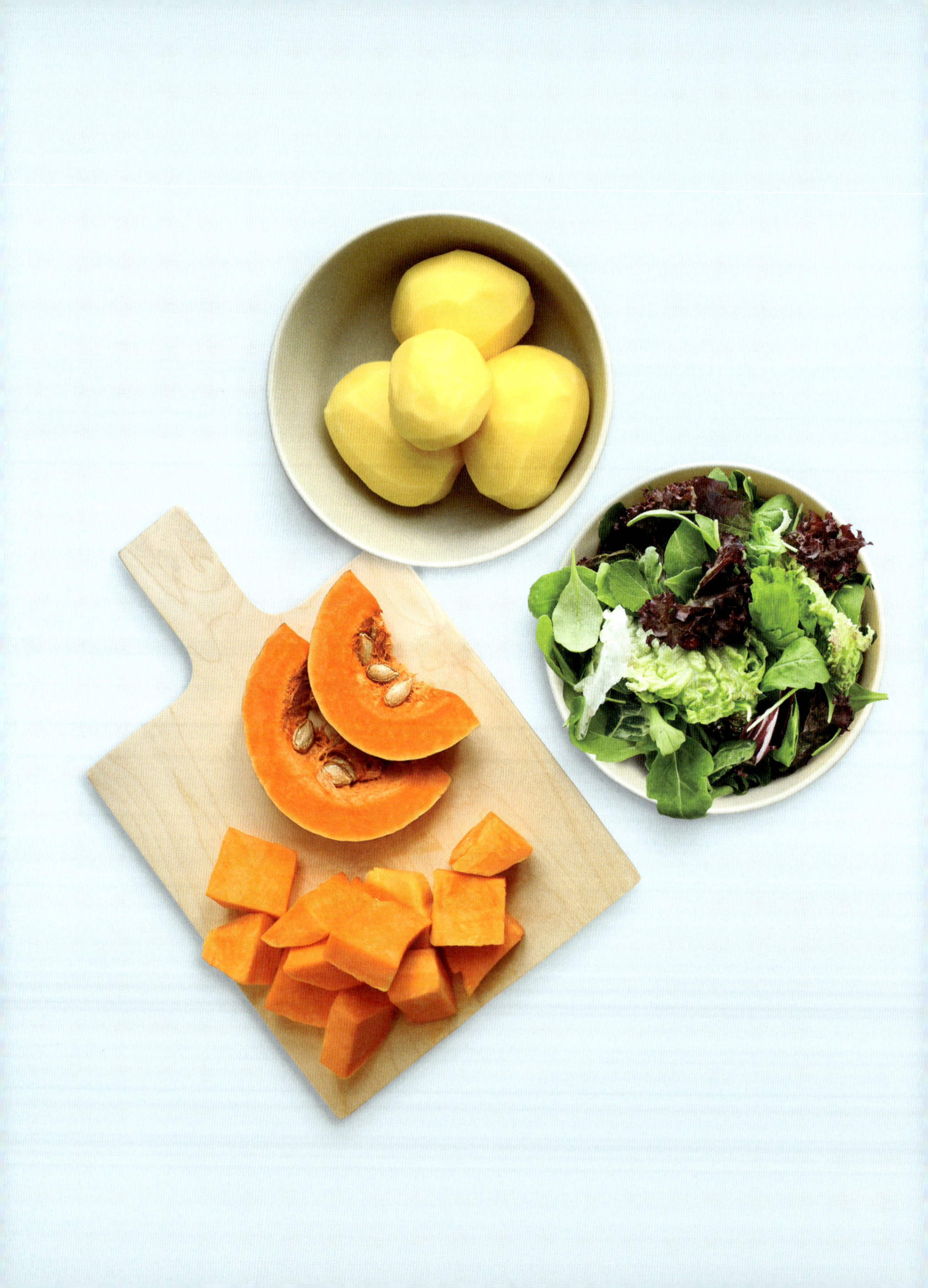

NEVER WASTED
↓
AGAIN

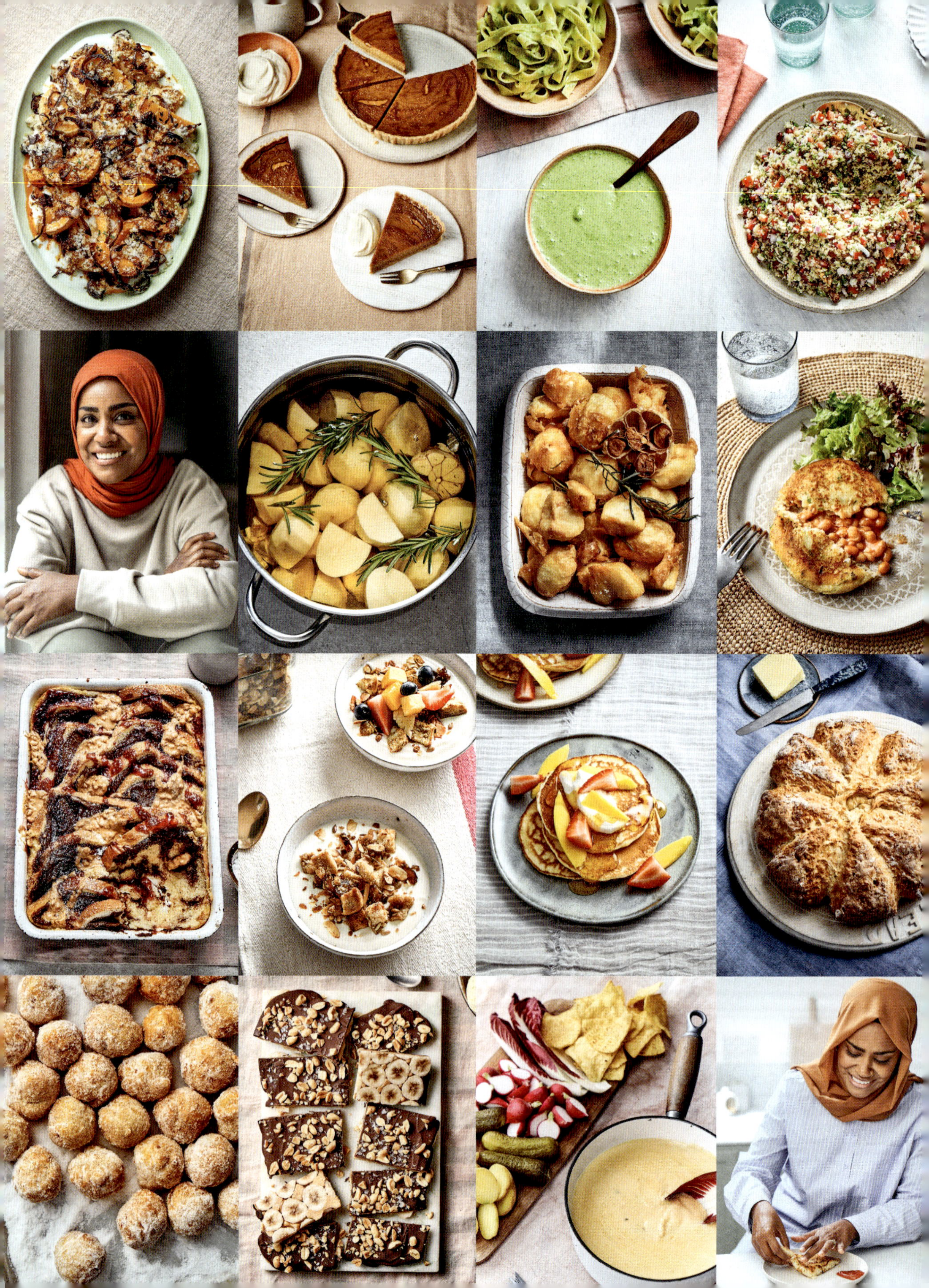

NEVER WASTED AGAIN

Focusing on the most commonly wasted ingredients, which rarely get finished in one go, this chapter gives a double dose of inspiration for cooking them in two different ways.

ROAST BUTTERNUT SQUASH
↓
BUTTERNUT SQUASH TART

BAG OF SALAD CHUTNEY
↓
TABBOULEH

CRISPY FRIED ROASTIES
↓
POTATO FARLS

BREAD AND BUTTER PUDDING
↓
CINNAMON BREAD GRANOLA

BUTTERMILK PANCAKES
↓
SODA BREAD

BANANA AND SUGAR DROP DOUGHNUTS
↓
BANANA PEANUT BARK

CHEESE FONDUE
↓
CHEESE AND ONION PANCAKE

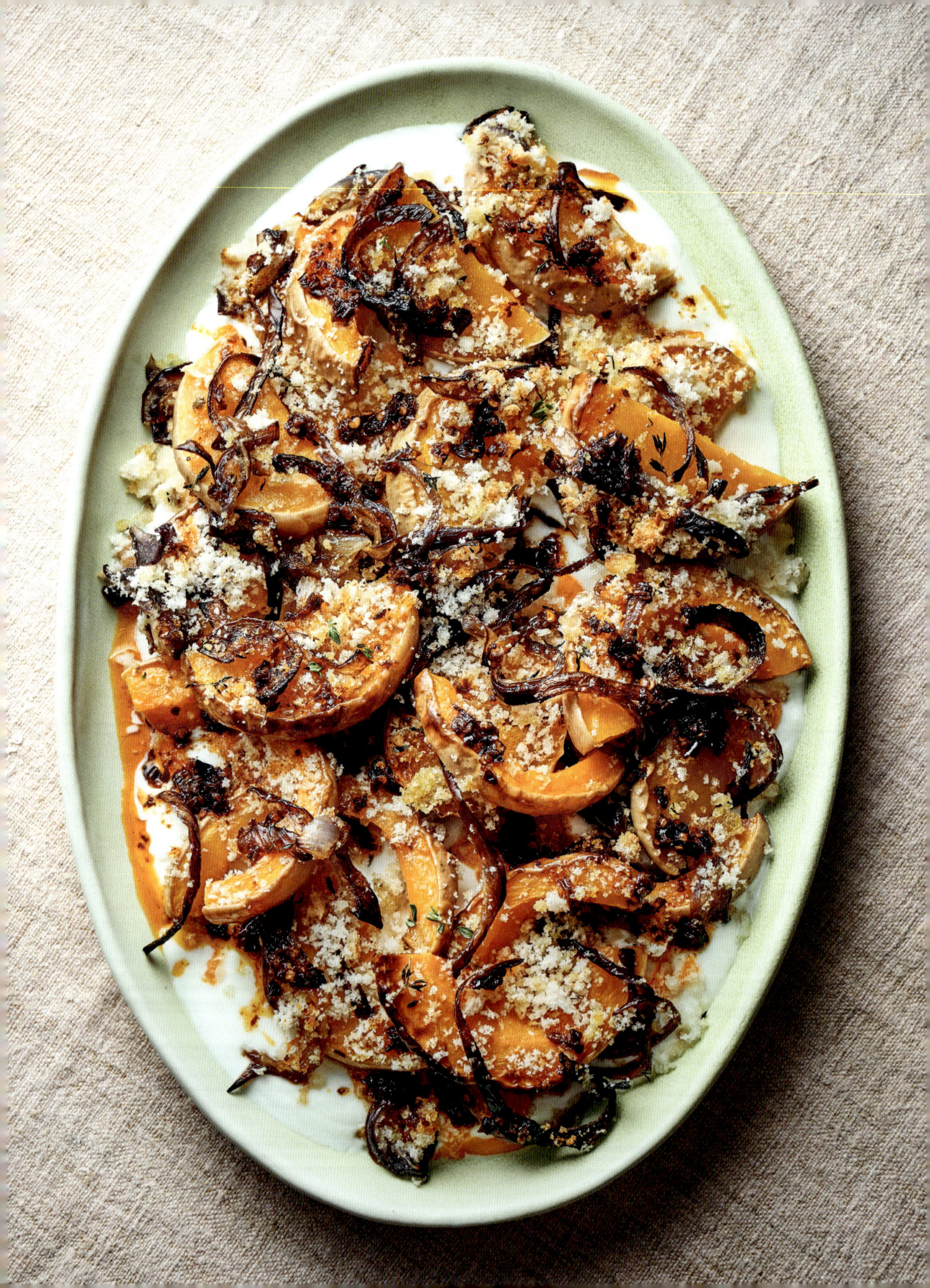

ROAST BUTTERNUT SQUASH

A whole butternut squash can be daunting but it need not be, so I am going to show you how to make this delicious roast squash. It takes very little effort and you will love it!

LEFTOVER SQUASH ALSO MAKES:
BUTTERNUT SQUASH TART (PAGE 172)

PREP: 16 MINS **COOK:** 55 MINS

SERVES: 4–6

1 large butternut squash

Oil, for drizzling

2 red onions, thinly sliced

Salt

For the crumb

200g dried or fresh white breadcrumbs

6 anchovies

3 cloves of garlic

Lemon thyme, leaves removed

To serve

Yoghurt

Chilli oil

Lemon juice

Preheat the oven to 180°C and have a large non-stick roasting dish ready.

Prepare the butternut squash by taking off the top and tail. Now cut lengthways so you have two lobe pieces with the inside hollow bit exposed. Lay one piece flat and cut into 1cm slices. Do the same to the other piece.

Drizzle the roasting dish with the oil. Pick up a half in one go and lay flat, fanning the slices out to fit the tray. Do the same with the other one and lay beside the first half.

Sprinkle with salt all over. Sprinkle over the red onion and then sprinkle with some more salt. Bake in the oven for 40 minutes.

For the crumb, put half the breadcrumbs in a food processor along with the anchovies, garlic and thyme and blend till you have an even crumb that is a bit clumpy. Add the rest of the crumbs and mix through.

Take the butternut squash out of the oven, sprinkle over the crumb and then bake for another 15 minutes.

Take the squash out and, to serve, get a serving plate and smother all over with some yoghurt. Place the squash on top. Drizzle over the chilli oil and squeeze some lemon juice on top, then you are ready to serve this wonderful squash.

TIP *You can do this with any type of pumpkin, keep the skin on and if it's too thick it can always just be removed as you eat it, there is no value in peeling a pumpkin, it's just life wasted!*

BUTTERNUT SQUASH TART

This is like an American pumpkin pie, but using a sweet butternut squash that is readily available here in the UK. We should never miss out on pudding or making something delicious because we think we can't find an ingredient – where there is a will, there is a way!

PREP: 25 MINS
COOK: 1 HOUR 50 MINS
SERVES: 8

600g butternut squash

Icing sugar, for dusting

350g shortcrust pasty

140g soft brown sugar

25g unsalted butter, melted

125ml whole milk

2 medium eggs

50g ground almonds, toasted

1 teaspoon ground cinnamon

1 teaspoon mixed spice

1 teaspoon ground ginger

Pinch of salt

75g caramelized biscuit spread, warmed

Mascarpone, to serve

Start by preparing the butternut squash. Peel and chop up the squash to roughly the same size.

Pop into a pan and bring to the boil. Boil the squash till tender, remove from the heat, drain and leave to cool completely.

Put the squash into a blender and blend to make a smooth paste. Set aside in a bowl.

Preheat the oven to 170°C and pop a baking tray on the shelf. Have a 22cm loose-bottom tart tin at the ready.

Dust the work surface with some icing sugar and roll the pastry out so it is large enough to line the base and sides of the tart tin, making sure there is some extra pastry for overhang.

Line the tart tin with the pastry, poking holes with a fork all over the base. Line the inside with some baking paper and fill with baking beans or dry lentils. Place onto the hot baking tray and bake for 15 minutes.

After 15 minutes, remove the paper and the beans and bake for another 10 minutes.

Set the tart to one side to cool and return the baking tray to the oven while you finish making the filling. Drop the oven temperature to 160°C.

To make the filling, put the soft brown sugar, melted butter, milk, eggs, ground almonds, cinnamon, mixed spice, ground ginger and salt in a bowl and whisk till you have a smooth paste. Pour into the tart shell. Take the warm caramelized biscuit spread and drizzle all over.

Bake the tart on top of the hot baking tray for 55 minutes–1 hour.

When the tart is ready, remove from the oven and leave to cool for 10 minutes, then cut off the overhang of pastry. Leave to cool completely before removing from the tart case.

Ideally chill in the fridge before cutting and serving. I love to serve this simply with a dollop of mascarpone cream.

TIP *This tart freezes really well, so if you make it and there are a few slices left, wrap in clingfilm and pop into the freezer. Thaw out and eat as you normally would.*

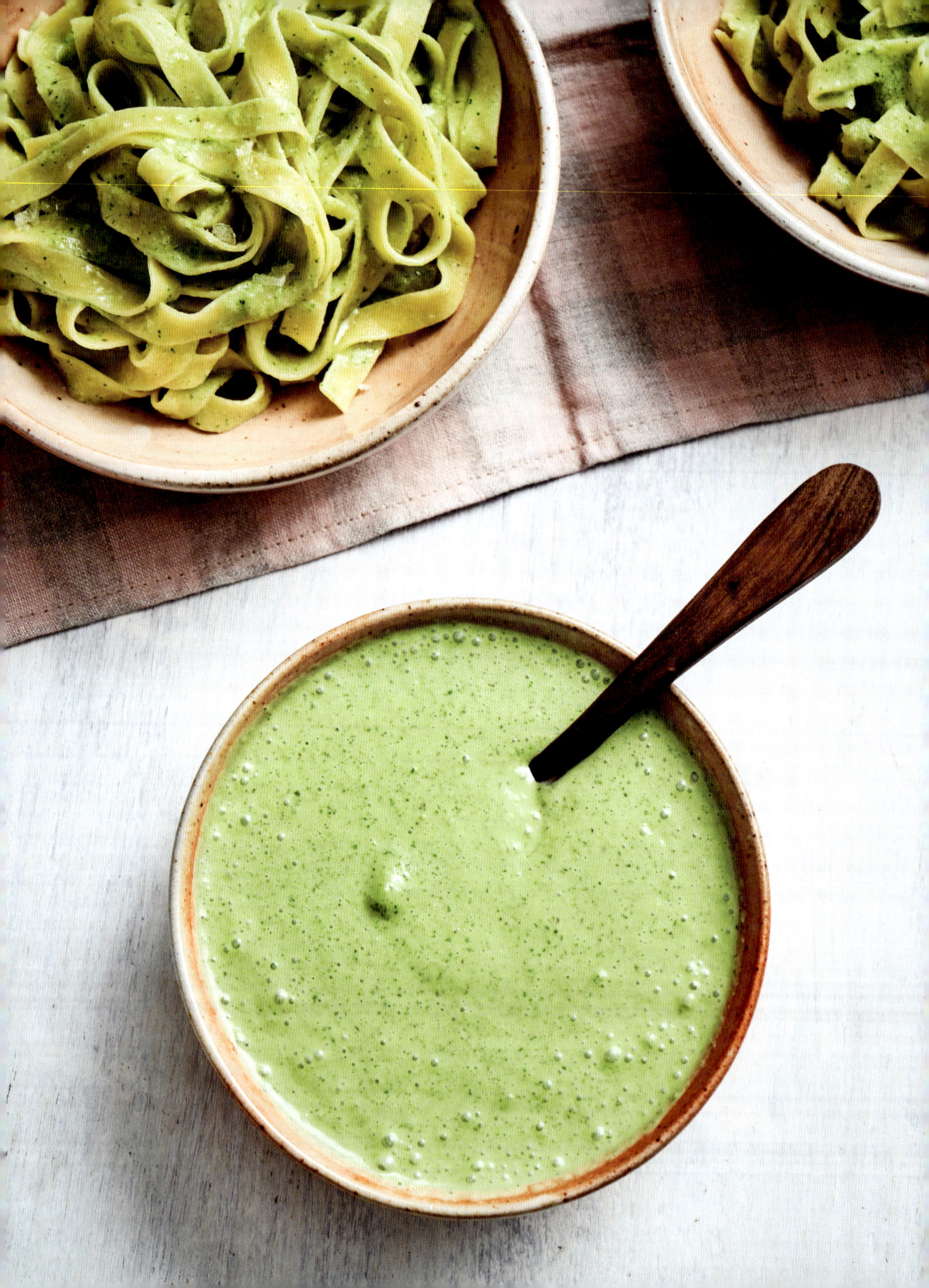

BAG OF SALAD CHUTNEY

This chutney is perfect for samosas, great as a dip for pakoras or as a sauce for tortillas or chips. You can even use it as a dressing for a potato or pasta salad. So simply made with any greens, you will love this.

LEFTOVER BAG OF SALAD ALSO MAKES:
TABBOULEH (PAGE 176)

PREP: 20–24 MINS

MAKES: 1 JAR

50g dried apricots
100g mixed salad bag
2 cloves of garlic
2 green chillies
Large handful of fresh coriander
150g Greek yoghurt
Salt

Start by soaking the dried apricots. Put the apricots in a bowl, submerge in hot water and leave for 15 minutes.

Add your mixed salad bag to a blender along with the garlic, green chillies, coriander and salt.

Take the hydrated apricots out of the water and add to the blender with a tiny bit of the water from the apricot bowl, then blend to a smooth paste.

Tip out the yoghurt into a bowl and mix to make smooth. Add the green mixture and mix till you have smooth, green, vibrant chutney. Taste and adjust the seasoning as you like.

You will find so many interesting ways of serving this, but when you are not, keep refrigerated.

TABBOULEH

A chopped salad has to be the most convenient and effective way of making and eating a salad, so here you have it, the best way to jazz up that sad bag of salad that could have been destined for the waste. Not today!

PREP: 30–36 MINS

SERVES: 2–4

150g couscous

1 vegetable stock cube

80g salad bag

25g fresh mint

4 medium tomatoes, deseeded

1 red onion, diced

1 pickled egg, grated

Walnuts, toasted and chopped

200g pomegranate

50ml olive oil

1 lemon, zest and juice

Salt

Start by making and cooling the couscous. Put the couscous in a bowl, crumble in the stock cube and pour in hot water till the water is just 1cm above the surface of the couscous. Cover and leave to steam for 20 minutes.

As soon as the couscous is cooked, uncover and use a fork to fluff it up. Transfer it to a large bowl.

Take the bag of salad, chop it up into small pieces along with the mint and add to the couscous. Dice the deseeded tomato into small cubes and add to the bowl.

Now add in the red onion, pickled egg, walnuts and pomegranate. Mix it all through.

Mix the olive oil, lemon zest and juice with some salt. Drizzle into the bowl and mix through really well – the salad is now ready to enjoy.

TIP *If you have a pulse function on your blender/food processor, this can be made in seconds.*

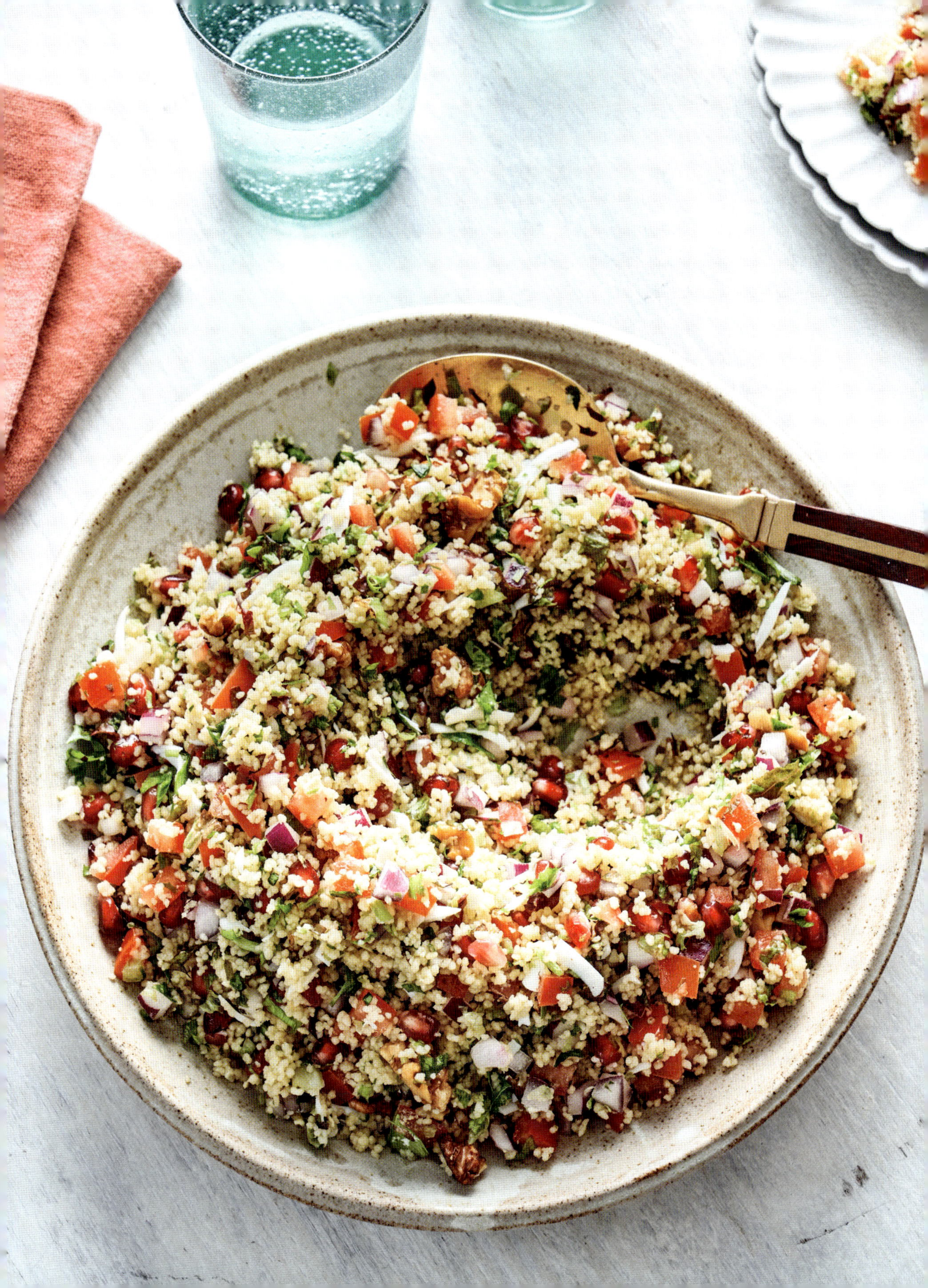

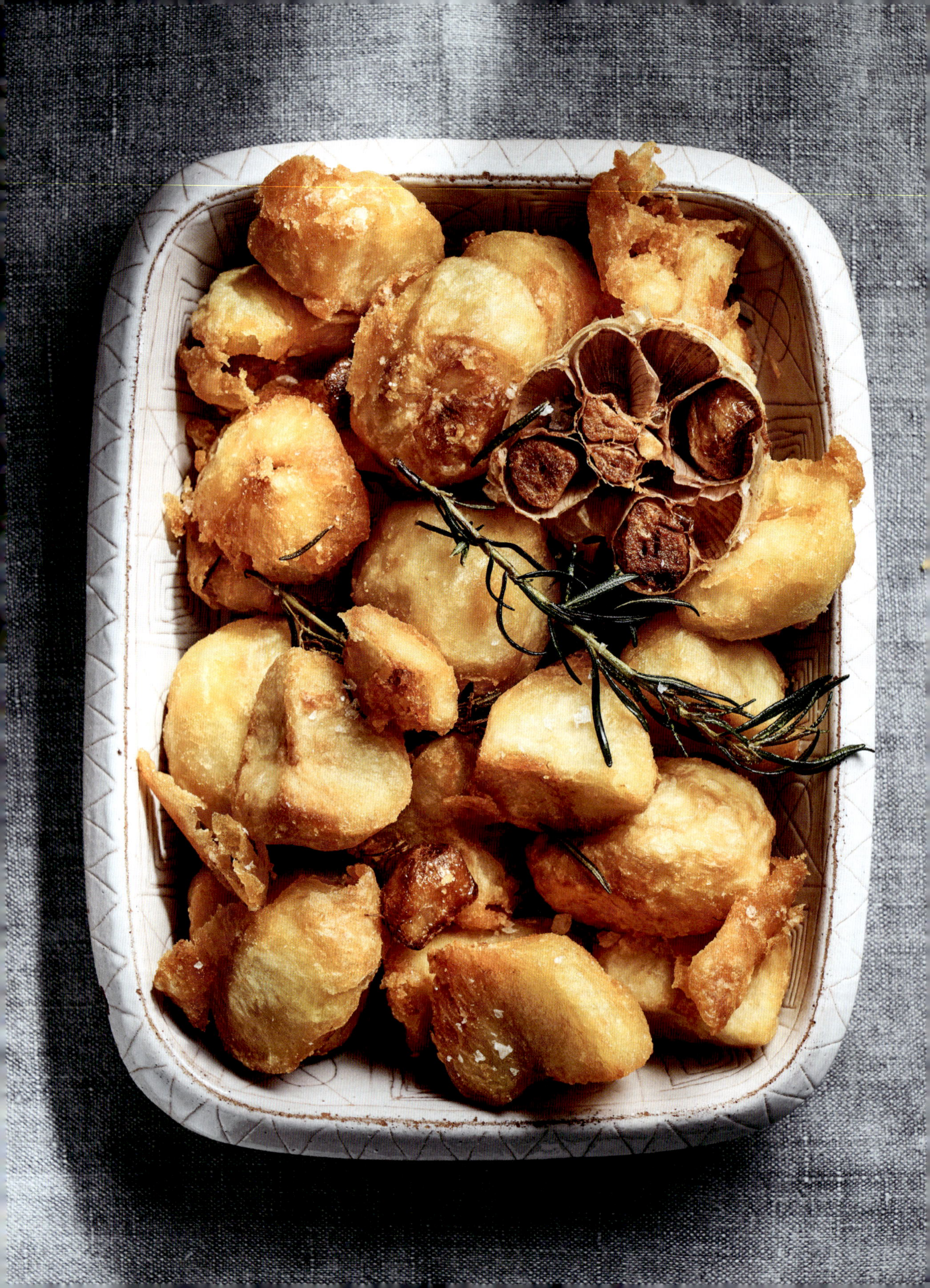

CRISPY FRIED ROASTIES

These roasties are like roasties but deep-fried. This gives you texture like nothing else really will. So, give these a go. No pre-boiling, just straight into oil and let the oil do all the work.

LEFTOVER POTATOES ALSO MAKES:
POTATO FARLS (PAGE 180)

PREP: 8–10 MINS **COOK:** 40–50 MINS

SERVES: 4

1kg potatoes

Oil, for deep-frying

2 tablespoons salt, plus extra

Large sprigs of fresh rosemary

1 bulb of garlic, cut in half

Start by preparing your potatoes. Peel the potatoes and cut so they are all as even in size as possible.

Pop into a large saucepan that fits all the potatoes so they are in roughly an even layer (it doesn't matter if they are crowded in a few places).

Add enough oil to fill the pan and cover the potatoes completely – the oil should go above the potatoes by about 2cm. Now sprinkle in all the salt and add the rosemary and bulb of garlic.

Put the pan over a high heat and as soon as the oil gets really hot, reduce the heat just slightly to medium and let the potatoes cook till they start to float.

When they are all floating, they are cooked and ready to eat. Drain on some kitchen paper and sprinkle with more salt.

TIP *This oil is heavily flavoured and perfectly seasoned, so use it to make a fresh mayo, in dressings or to cook other dishes.*

NEVER WASTED AGAIN / 179

POTATO FARLS

These are so yummy, like mashed potatoes slash jacket potatoes. A delicious hybrid that I know you need in your life.

PREP: 28 MINS **COOK:** 47 MINS **CHILL:** 30 MINS

MAKES: 4 FARLS

For the potato

400g potatoes

½ teaspoon salt

½ teaspoon ground black pepper

75g plain flour

1 teaspoon baking powder

3 spring onions, thinly sliced

For the filling

200g tin of baked beans, drained (reserving the sauce)

50g Cheddar cheese, grated

Sprinkle of chilli flakes

For the sauce

1 tablespoon chilli sauce

1 tablespoon ketchup

1 tablespoon mayonnaise

Start by preparing your potatoes. Peel the potatoes and cut so they are all as even in size as possible.

Boil the potatoes in a pan of salted water till tender. Drain and pass through a ricer for a smooth potato mixture.

Once completely cooled, add the salt, pepper, plain flour, baking powder and spring onions. Mix well, divide into four equal balls and set aside.

For the filling, take the drained baked beans and mix with the Cheddar and chilli flakes.

Now take each mound and flatten in the palm of your hands. If the mix is sticking, dunk your hand in cold water.

Add a quarter of the mixture to a potato mound and envelop the bean mix in the potato, so it is completely encased. Flatten in the palm of your hands. Do the same to the other three. Pop into the fridge for 30 minutes.

To cook these, add butter to a pan with the farls and gently cook for 7–8 minutes on each side, till golden and delicious and warm all the way through.

For the sauce, mix the bean juice with the chilli sauce, ketchup and mayonnaise and serve as a dip on the side.

TIP *These freeze really well so if you have any left over, freeze for a quick lunch or brunch emergency.*

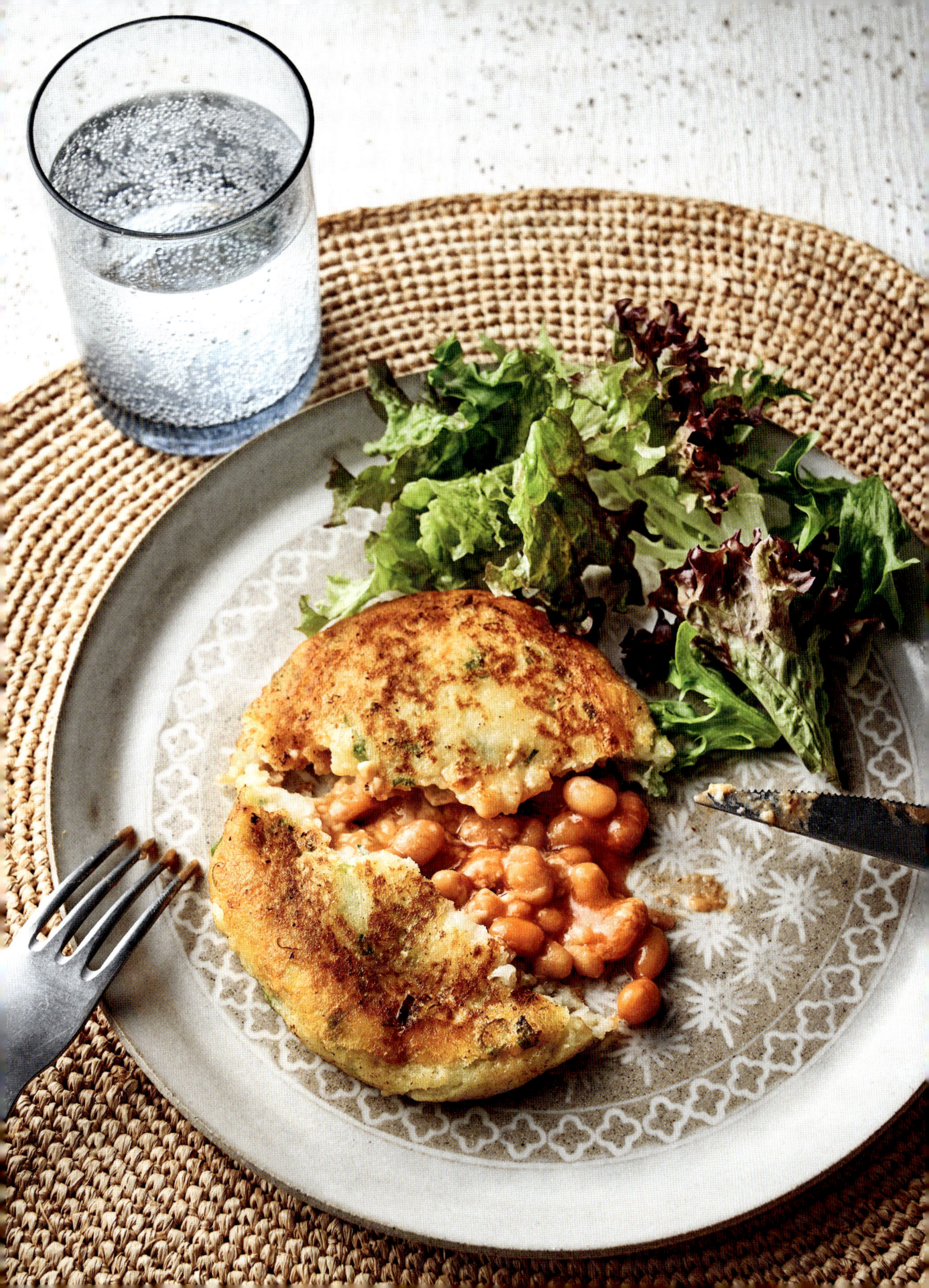

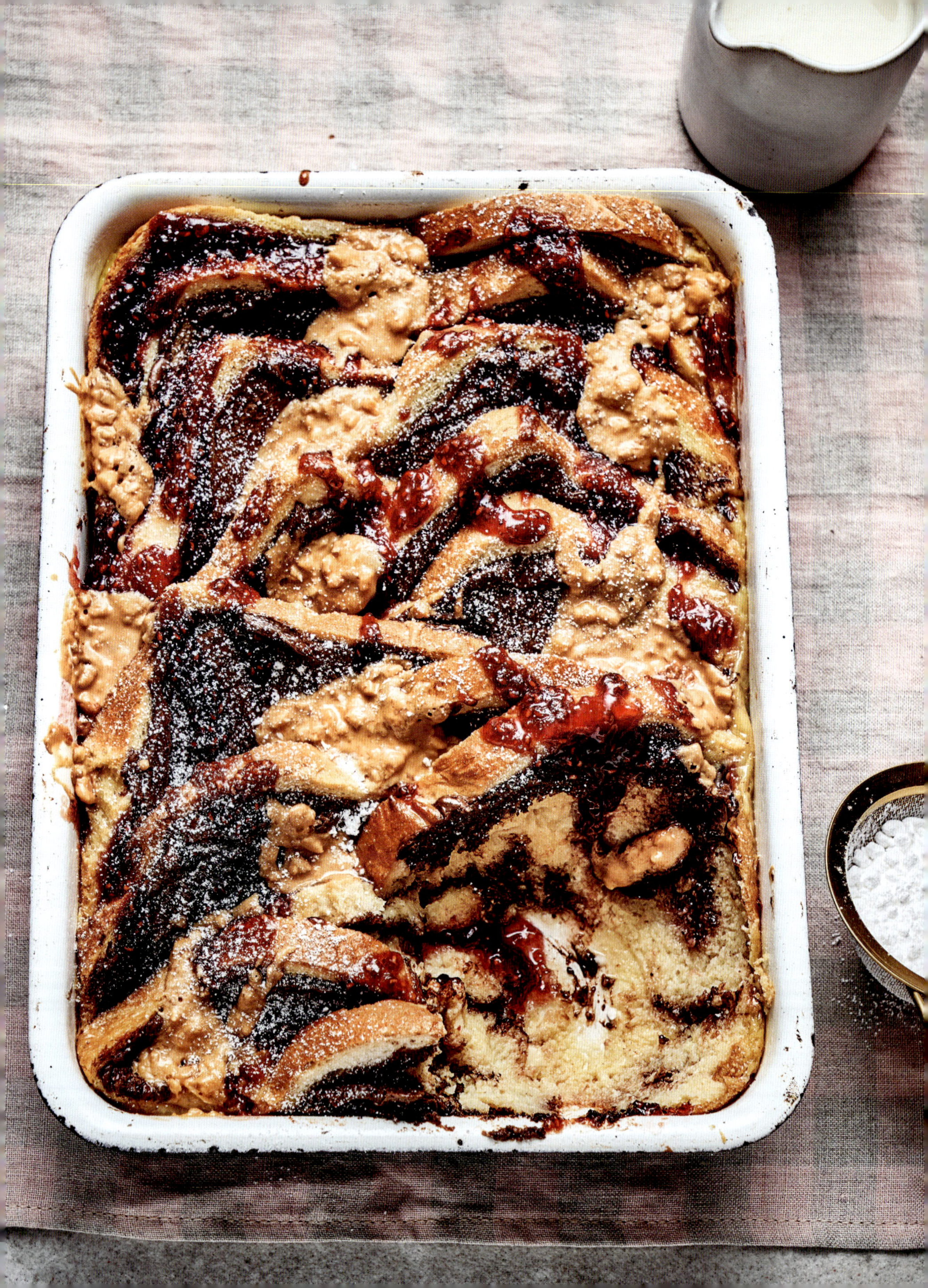

BREAD AND BUTTER PUDDING

This is a total classic and a great way to use up bread that is getting stale. In fact, for the best bread and butter pudding the staler the bread the better, as dry bread really soaks up that yummy custard. This is my peanut butter and jam easy bread and butter pudding.

LEFTOVER BREAD ALSO MAKES:
CINNAMON BREAD GRANOLA (PAGE 184)

PREP: 15 MINS
COOK: 42 MINS **REST:** 50 MINS
SERVES: 6

Butter, for greasing

300g stale bread slices

100g chocolate spread

3 medium eggs

150g caster sugar

450ml whole milk

100g raspberry jam

100g crunchy peanut butter, warmed through

Icing sugar, for dusting

Double cream, for serving

Grease the inside of a 28cm x 16cm roasting dish. Set aside.

Cut each of the stale bread slices into four triangles and spread each piece with the chocolate spread. Lay the pieces of bread side by side and angled until the dish is filled.

Make the custard by putting the three eggs into a bowl with the caster sugar and whisking till combined.

Pour the milk into a pan and heat till it just comes up to the boil, then remove from the heat. Carefully pour the hot milk into the egg mixture, making sure to whisk all the while. Once you have added all the milk, pour over the bread and leave the whole thing to sit for a minimum of 30 minutes.

Preheat the oven to 170°C.

Drizzle over the jam and peanut butter, then bake for 30 minutes.

Once the pudding is out, leave to sit for another 20 minutes before eating. Dust with icing sugar and serve with double cream.

TIP *If you have people in the family who don't like crusts, save them and place those slices in the freezer, then make this recipe when you have just enough bread!*

CINNAMON BREAD GRANOLA

Leftover bread can be made into a crisp, wholesome granola that you will adore. This is granola with a crunchy, cinnamon-bready twist.

PREP: 10 MINS **COOK:** 30–35 MINS

SERVES: 4

300g bread slices
200g sliced almonds
50g sunflower seeds
50g oats
25g desiccated coconut
200ml coconut oil, melted
200ml maple syrup
2 teaspoons vanilla extract
1 teaspoon almond extract
3 teaspoons ground cinnamon
1 orange, zest only
200g dates, chopped

To serve
Yoghurt
Fresh fruit and berries

Preheat the oven to 170°C. Get a large baking tray ready.

Take your bread slices, dice into 1cm cubes and pop them onto the large tray. Now add your sliced almonds, sunflower seeds, oats and desiccated coconut. Mix it all through.

To a small bowl or jug add the coconut oil, maple syrup, vanilla extract and almond extract, mix together and drizzle all over the bits in the tray. Get your hands in and make sure everything is coated.

Sprinkle over the cinnamon, grate over the zest of the orange and mix again with a spoon.

Bake for 30–35 minutes, stirring halfway to make sure everything is evenly golden. Once everything is crisp and golden, add the chopped dates and mix through.

Once cooled, store the granola in an airtight container. I love to generously sprinkle this on top of yoghurt and eat with fresh fruit and berries.

TIP *Slice the oranges when the zest is removed and freeze. They make instant flavoured ice for your drinks.*

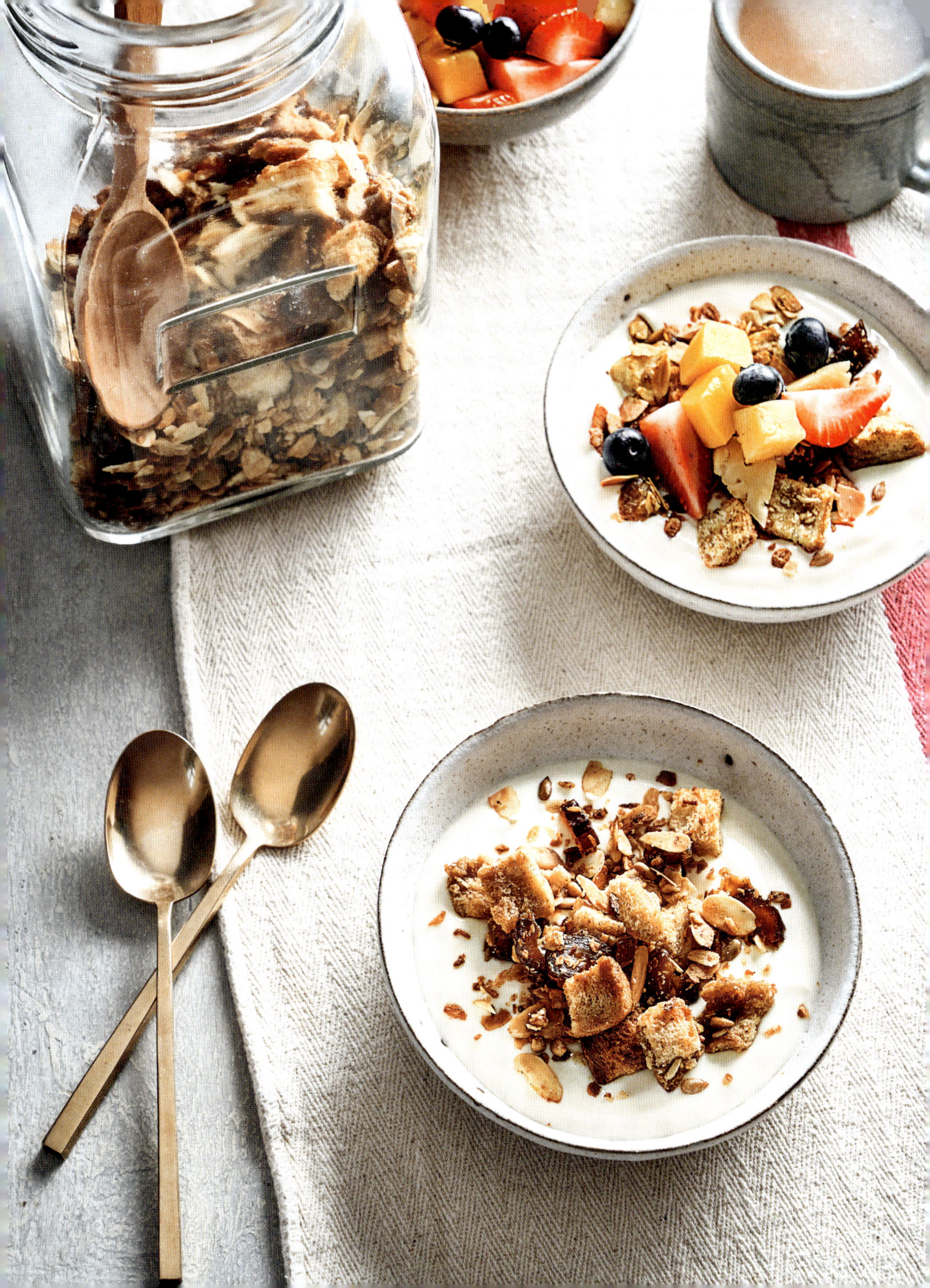

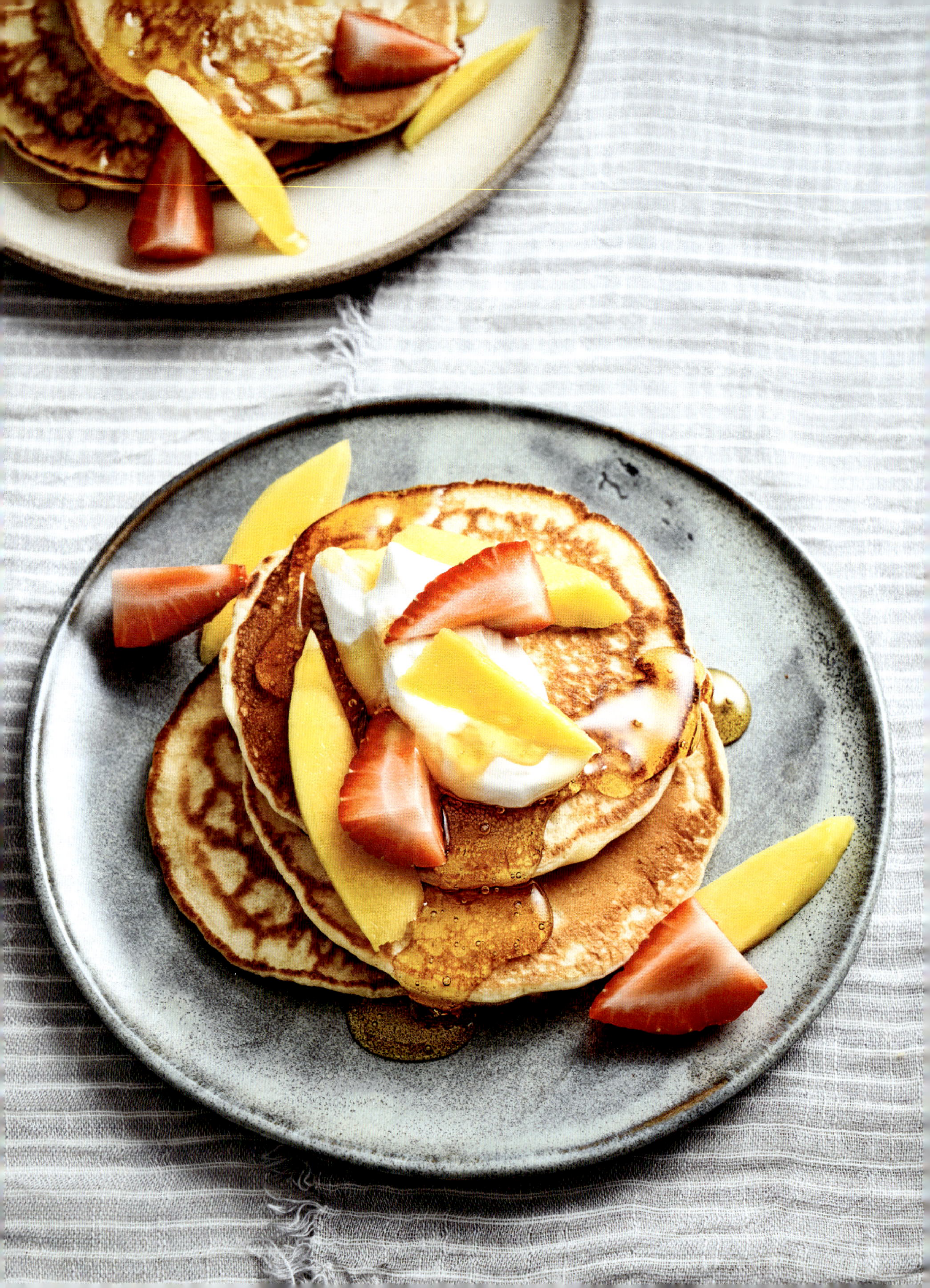

BUTTERMILK PANCAKES

Buttermilk pancakes are tender and moreish and are a great way of using up milk that is on its way out. I am going to show you how to use buttermilk in two ways to make delicious things.

LEFTOVER INGREDIENTS ALSO MAKES:
SODA BREAD (PAGE 188)

PREP: 10 MINS **COOK:** 24 MINS

SERVES: 4

300ml whole milk

3 tablespoons lemon juice

175g plain flour

½ teaspoon baking powder

½ teaspoon bicarbonate of soda

1 tablespoon caster sugar

Pinch of salt

2 medium eggs

3 tablespoons oil

Oil, for frying

To serve

Yoghurt

Fruit

Maple syrup

Start by making the buttermilk. Pour the whole milk into a jug with the lemon juice, stir well, set aside and leave to thicken.

Put the plain flour in a large bowl with the baking powder, bicarbonate of soda, caster sugar and salt. Whisk to combine.

Now pour in the buttermilk mixture along with the eggs and oil, then whisk till you have thick batter.

Brush some oil onto a hot non-stick pancake pan and spoon in the mixture. Cook till the surface of the pancake is bubbly and dry-looking, flip over and cook on the other side. Do this till you have made all your pancakes.

Serve hot, with yoghurt, fruit and maple syrup.

TIP *If you don't have lemon juice to make the buttermilk, you can use lime juice or vinegar.*

SODA BREAD

Of all the breads, soda bread is the easiest and fastest to make. If you have milk on the turn, it's the best for bread like this.

PREP: 26 MINS **COOK:** 30 MINS

MAKES: 1 LOAF

400ml whole milk

4 tablespoons lemon juice

500g plain flour

1 teaspoon salt

2 tablespoons caster sugar

1 teaspoon bicarbonate of soda

50g butter, softened

Start by making the buttermilk. Pour the whole milk into a jug with the lemon juice, stir well, set aside and leave to thicken.

Preheat the oven to 200°C. Line a baking tray with some baking paper.

Put the plain flour in a large bowl with the salt, caster sugar and bicarbonate of soda.

Add the butter to the bowl and rub the butter in till there are no large clumps.

Make a well in the centre and add the buttermilk, using a dinner knife to bring the dough together without kneading. Do this till you have little or no flour left.

Tip the dough out onto a worktop and bring together without kneading. Place on the lined baking tray and flatten to about 5cm thick. Use a sharp knife to cut all the way through into eight equal wedges.

Pop into the oven and bake for 30 minutes.

Take it out and leave to cool on a rack. While still warm, take a wedge, open and butter generously and enjoy!

TIP *This is such a great dough to flavour. You can use spices, dried fruit, nuts, zests, chocolate – there are so many creative possibilities.*

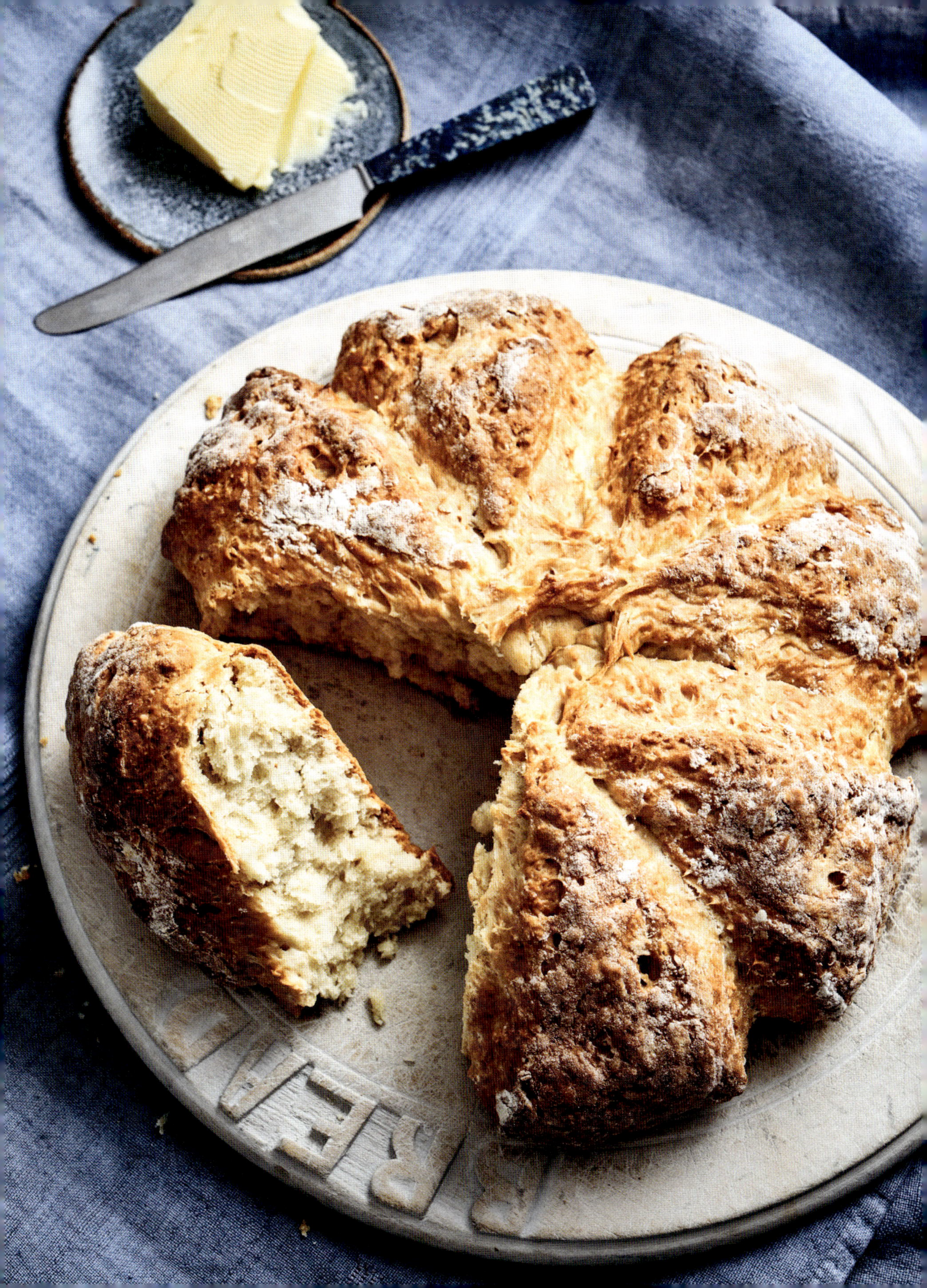

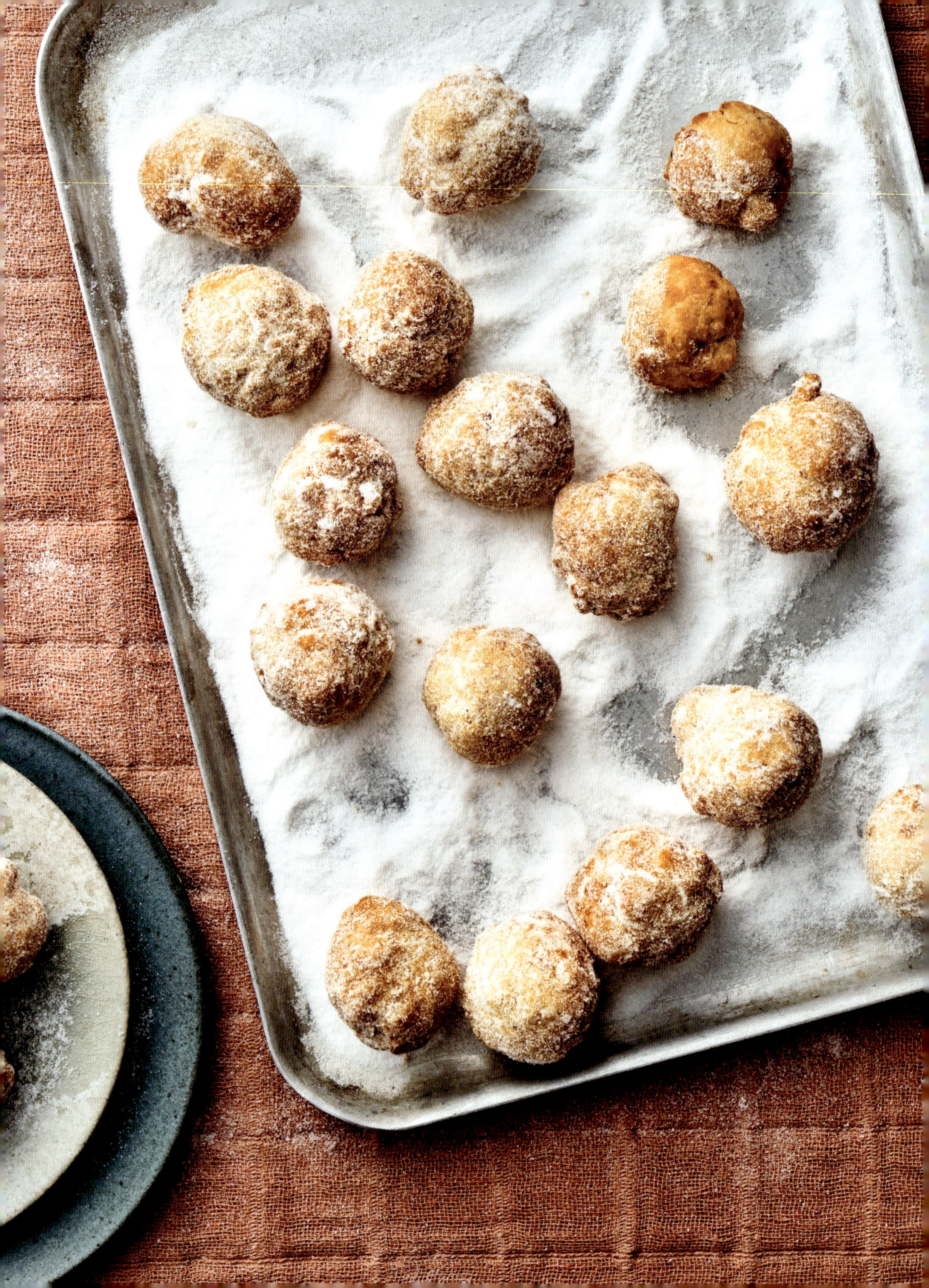

BANANA AND SUGAR DROP DOUGHNUTS

These doughnuts are the easy cheat's version of a doughnut – a batter made and dropped into oil, fried and coated in sugar. They are extra special because they use up leftover bananas, which make the doughnuts even more yummy.

LEFTOVER BANANA ALSO MAKES:
BANANA PEANUT BARK (PAGE 192)

PREP: 10 MINS **COOK:** 15 MINS

SERVES: 2–4

350g plain flour

3 teaspoons baking powder

Large pinch of salt

1 tablespoon caster sugar, plus extra for coating

1 banana

1 medium egg

2 teaspoons vanilla extract

3 tablespoons oil

175ml whole milk

Oil, for frying

Start by putting the plain flour in a bowl with the baking powder, salt and caster sugar and whisking through.

Put the banana in another bowl and mash to a smooth paste. Now add the egg, vanilla and oil.

Add all of this to the dry mix with the milk and whisk till you have a really thick, spoonable batter.

Set aside and start heating the oil in a medium pan. You need enough oil to be able to deep-fry these little balls. As soon as the oil gets to 150°C, drop the batter in 1 teaspoon at a time, using another teaspoon to tease the batter off the spoon.

Add enough so that you can still comfortably fry the balls and they can move around in the oil. They should only take 4–5 minutes to cook.

Drain onto some kitchen paper and roll in caster sugar. Do this to all of the batter and enjoy the doughnuts while they are still warm.

TIP *You can dust with icing sugar instead of caster sugar if you are after a powdered doughnut rather than a sugared doughnut.*

BANANA PEANUT BARK

One of the best ways to eat bananas is frozen, so I want to show you how to make this frozen bark that can be enjoyed without very much work. A layer of frozen banana slices, peanut butter and melted chocolate – perfect to eat as it is or as a topping for ice cream.

PREP: 22 MINS **COOK:** 5 HOURS

MAKES: 1 SHEET

3 bananas

250g smooth peanut butter, warmed

300g milk or dark chocolate

150g salted peanuts, roughly chopped

Good pinch of rock salt

Line and grease a medium baking tray.

Take your bananas, peel and slice into coins. Lay all over the prepared sheet in an even layer, making sure they are tightly packed. Pop into the freezer and leave for a few hours.

Take out and spread over the smooth peanut butter. Melt the chocolate and spread all over the layer of peanut butter. Sprinkle over the salted peanuts, then the salt.

Pop into the freezer and leave there for a couple of hours before eating.

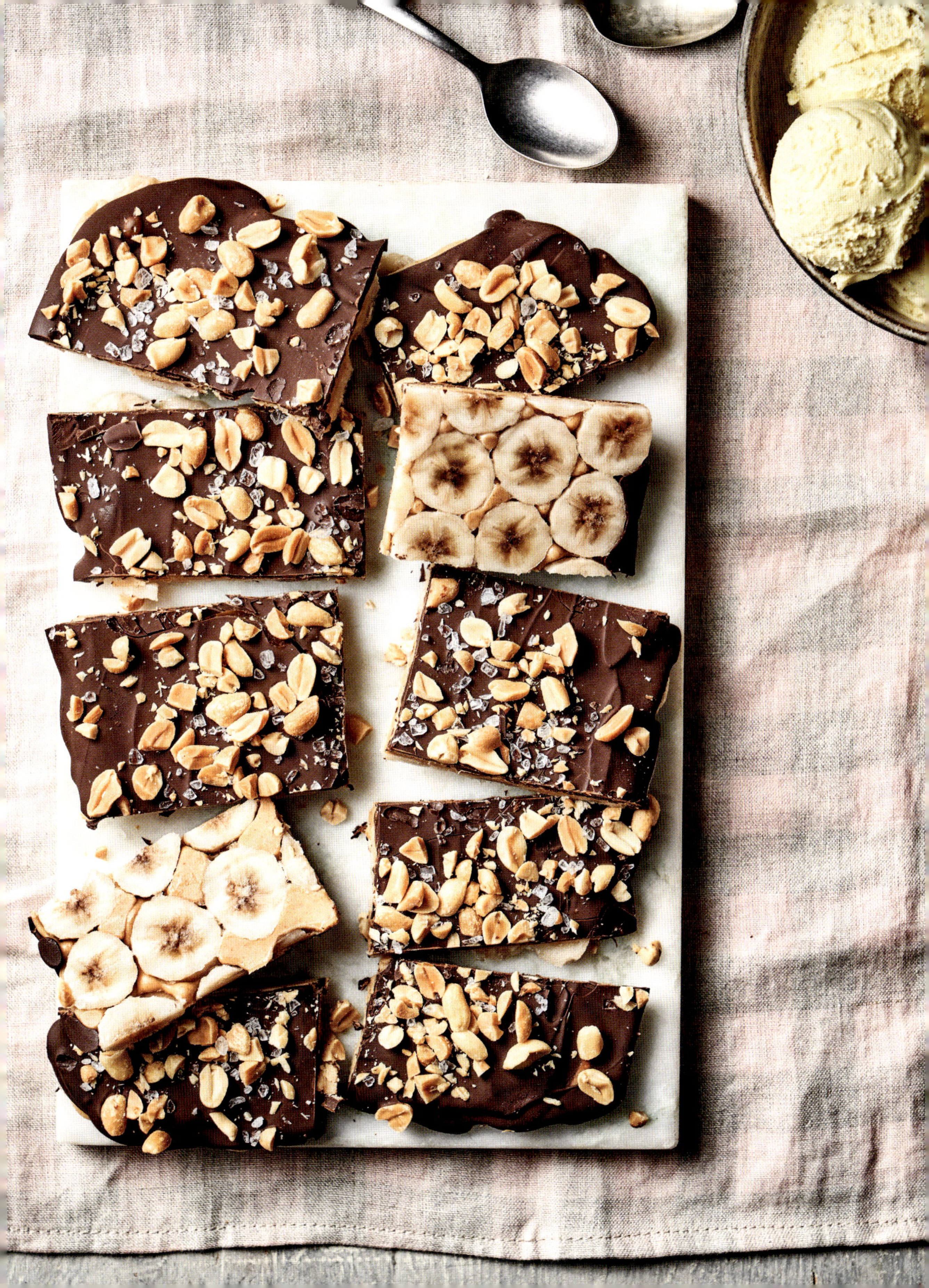

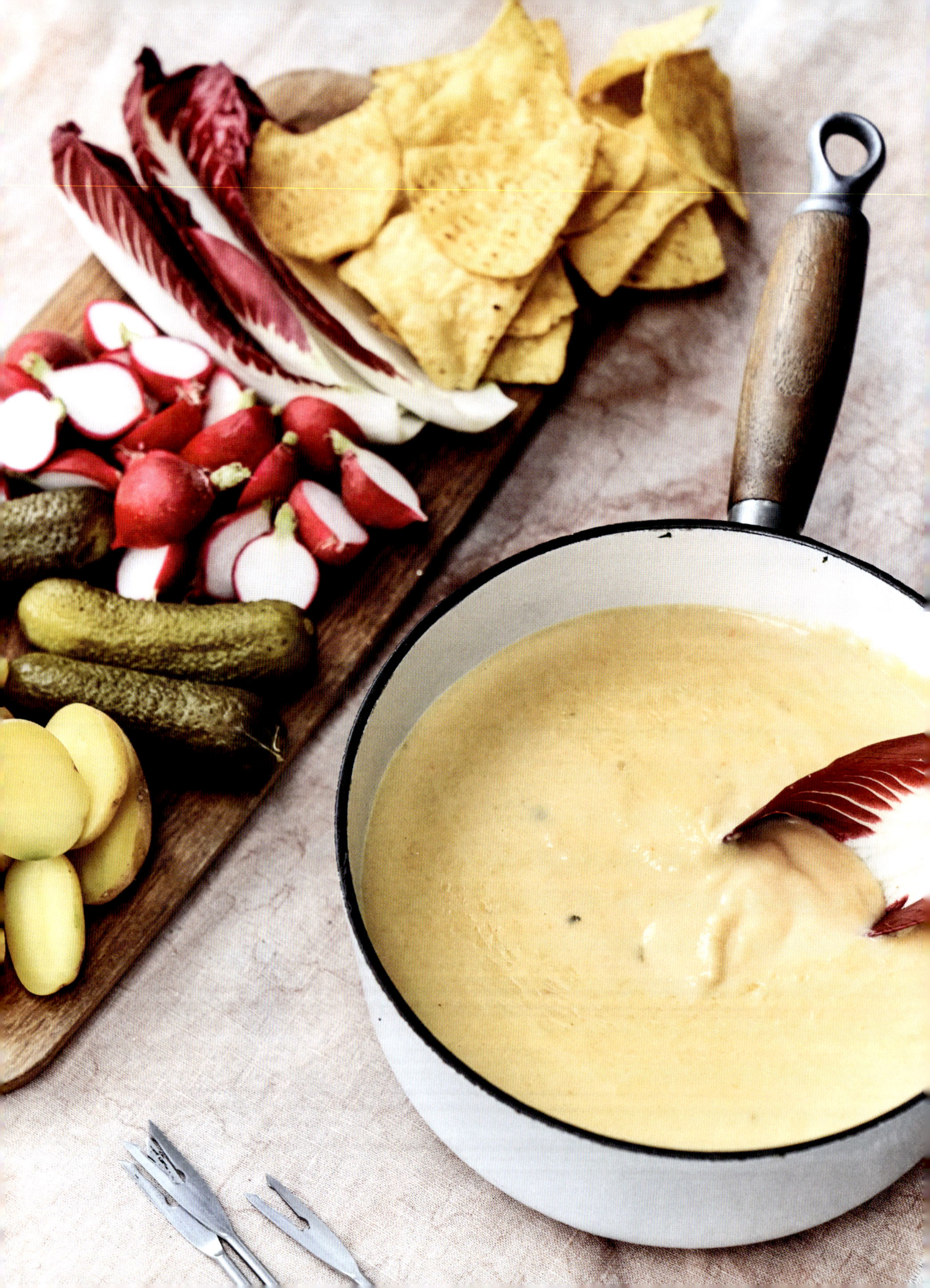

CHEESE FONDUE

Melted cheese with lots of bits to dip in it is my idea of heaven! So let me share with you my fondue recipe.

LEFTOVER CHEESE ALSO MAKES:
CHEESE AND ONION PANCAKE (PAGE 196)
PREP: 8 MINS **COOK:** 30 MINS **SERVES:** 4-6

- 200ml vegetable stock
- 1 teaspoon yeast extract
- 1 tablespoon miso paste
- 2 cloves of garlic, minced
- 1 tablespoon lemon juice
- 400g Cheddar cheese, grated
- 2 tablespoons cornflour
- 2 tablespoons water

To serve

Gherkins, pickled onions, boiled potatoes, bread, celery, crackers, radicchio, radishes, tortillas, jalapeños, pitta bread, etc.

The best thing to do to get ahead is to prep the bits to dip with in advance.

Make the fondue by putting the vegetable stock in a saucepan with the yeast extract, miso paste and minced garlic, then bring to the boil and simmer. Add the lemon juice and completely lower the heat. Take off the heat and leave for about 10 minutes.

Now start adding the cheese a little at a time, making sure to whisk with each addition. Keep adding till you have used up all the cheese.

Mix the cornflour with the water and add to the cheese. Simmer away on the lowest heat till thick.

Serve warm with all your picky bits and you are in for a fun night.

TIP *If you don't have a fancy warming thing for the fondue but you do have an instant pot, slow cooker or even a rice cooker, you can serve it in one of those on the keep warm setting.*

CHEESE AND ONION PANCAKE

You are going to be so glad you made this. What is not to love – cheese, potato, onion! Best combi in the world!

PREP: 6 MINS **COOK:** 30 MINS

SERVES: 4

Oil, for frying

2 cloves of garlic, minced

1 onion, thinly sliced

Large pinch of salt

2 medium potatoes, grated

200g Cheddar cheese, grated

Get a non-stick pan on the hob and pour some oil into it.

When the oil is hot, add the garlic and cook for a few seconds. Add the onion and salt and fry till the onions are a golden brown.

Take your grated potatoes and be sure to squeeze out any excess liquid. Now add to the onion mix and cook till everything is dry.

Add the grated cheese and mix through. When the cheese is starting to melt and has mixed with the potatoes, flatten and turn the heat up to create a really crisp base.

Turn out onto a plate, slide back into the pan and fry to crisp up the other side.

Cut into quarters, leave for 10 minutes to cool, and then enjoy.

TIP *Cheese can be preserved for longer if you smother it in a layer of butter, creating a protective barrier to stop any bacteria or mould growing on it.*

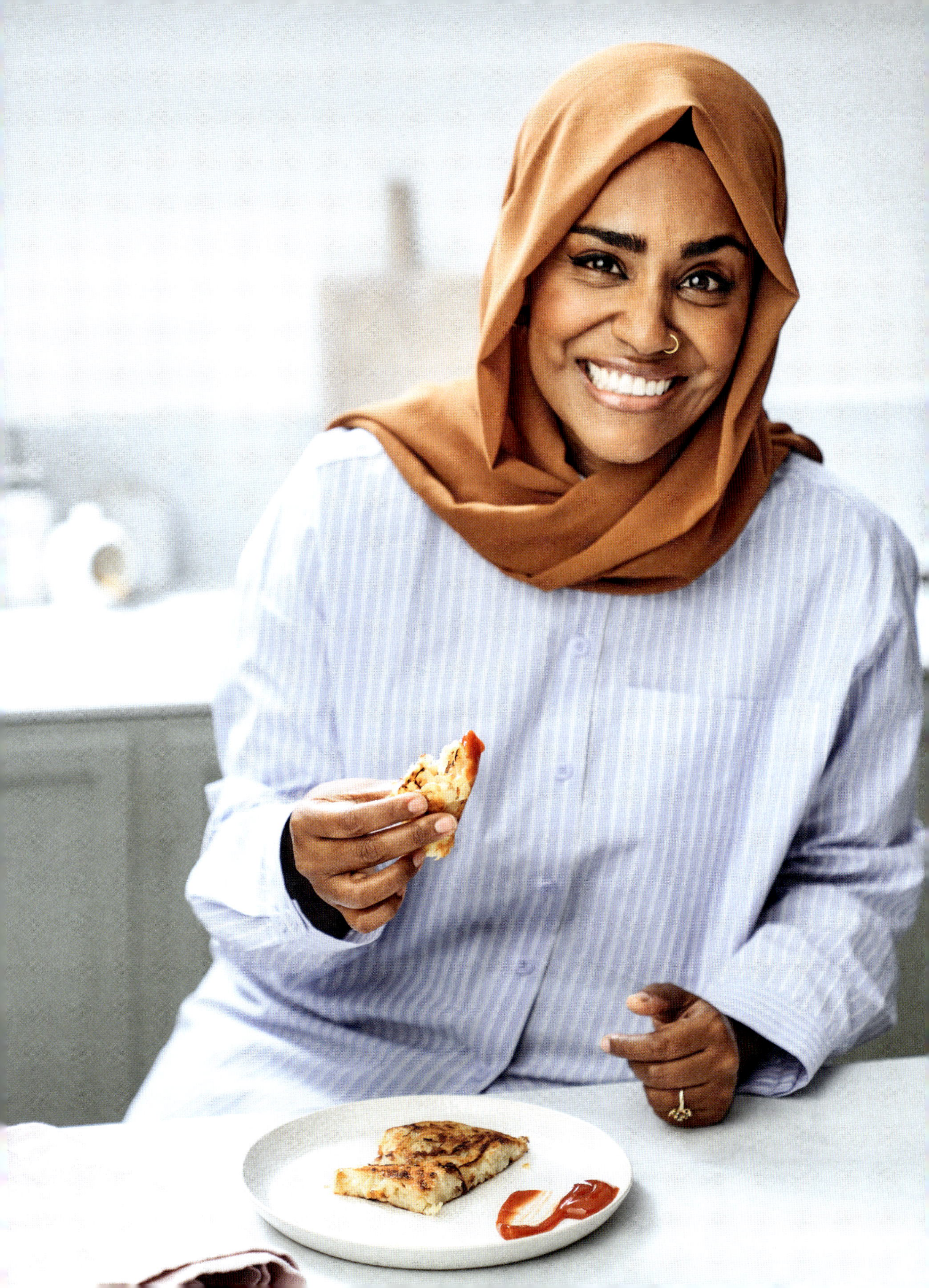

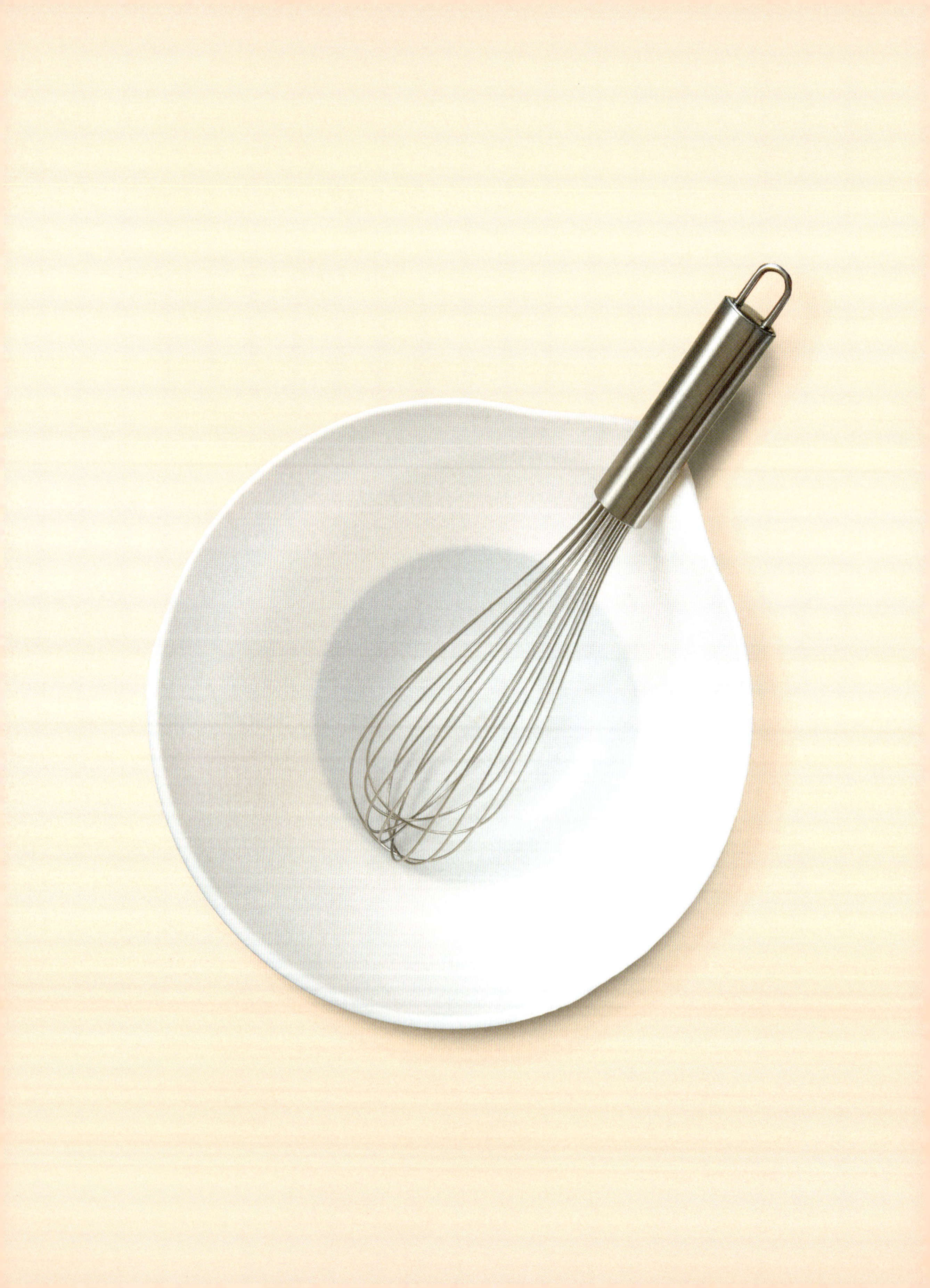

EASY
↓
BAKES

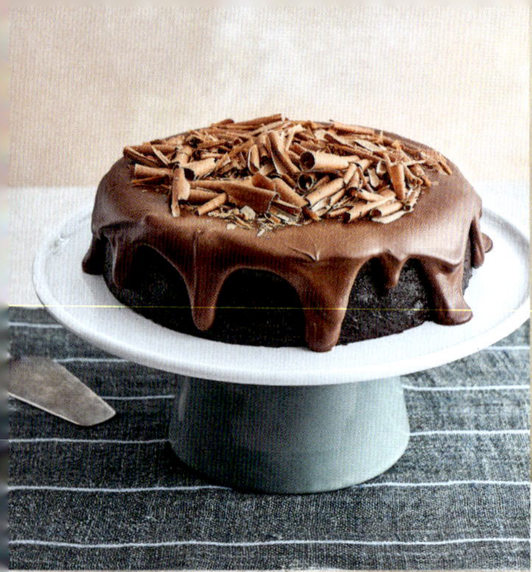
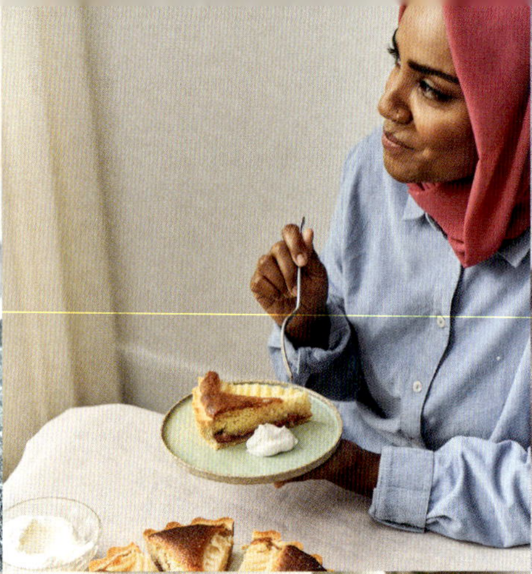
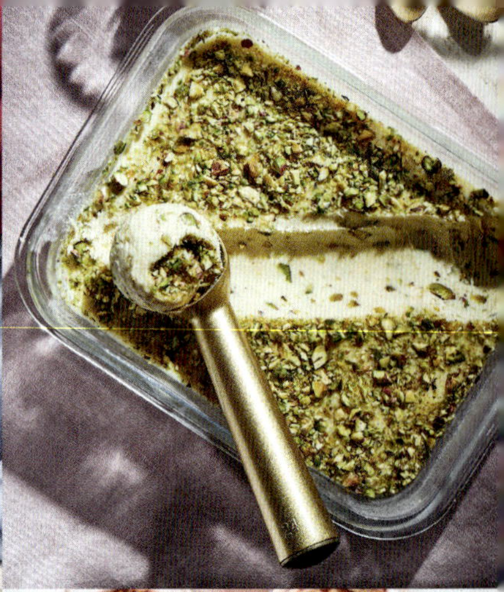
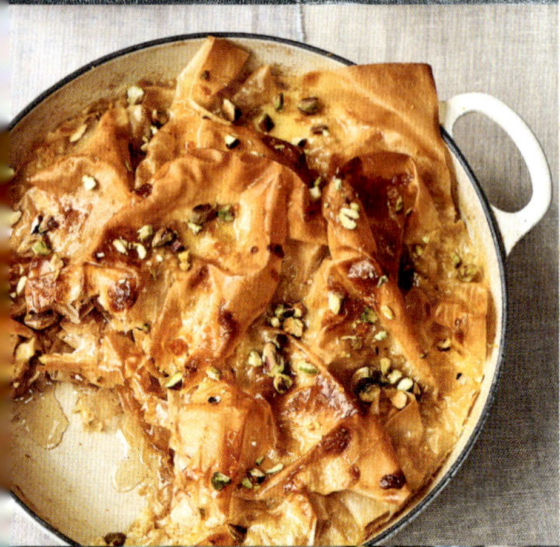
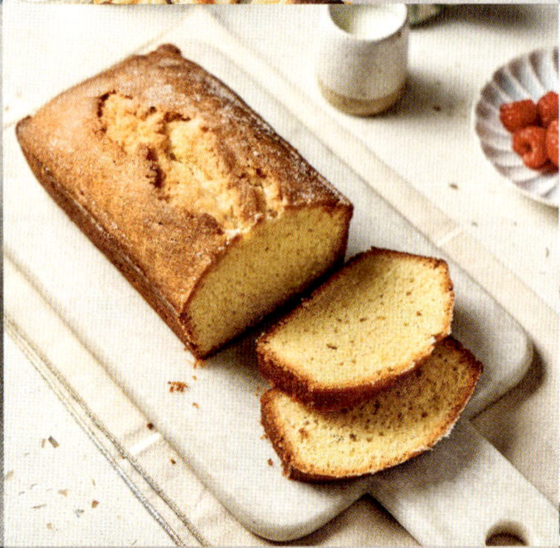
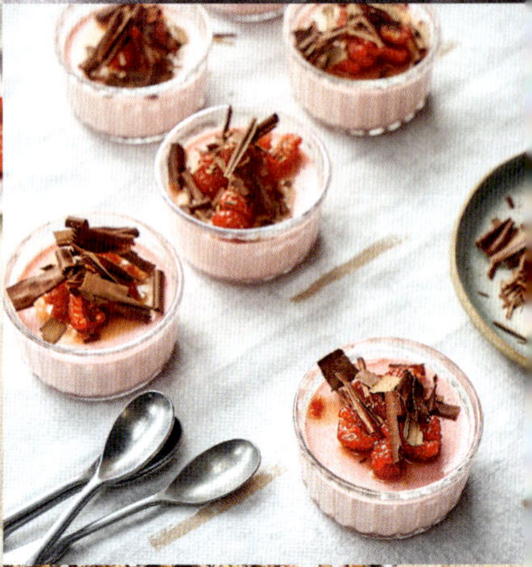
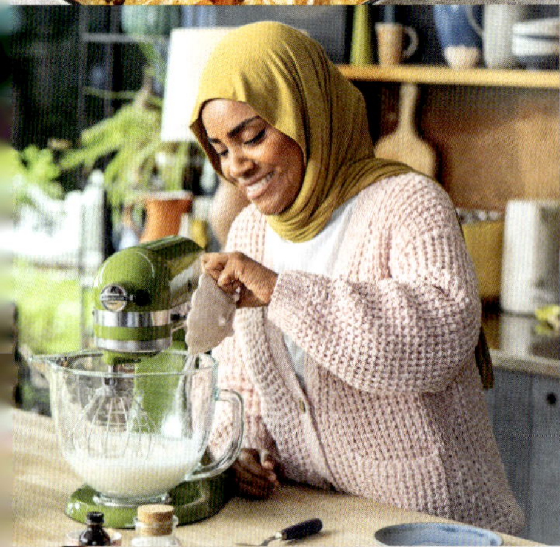
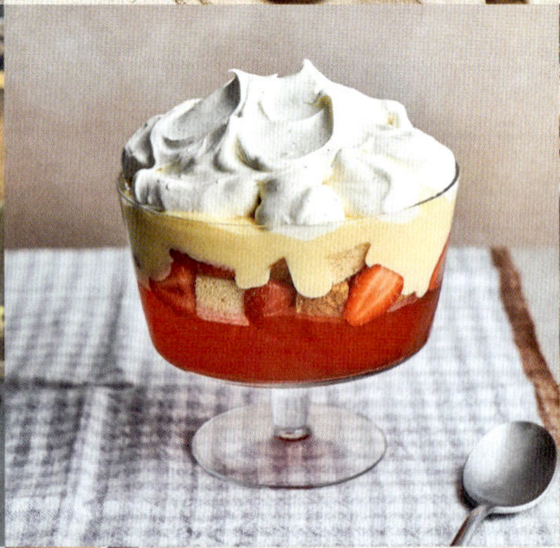
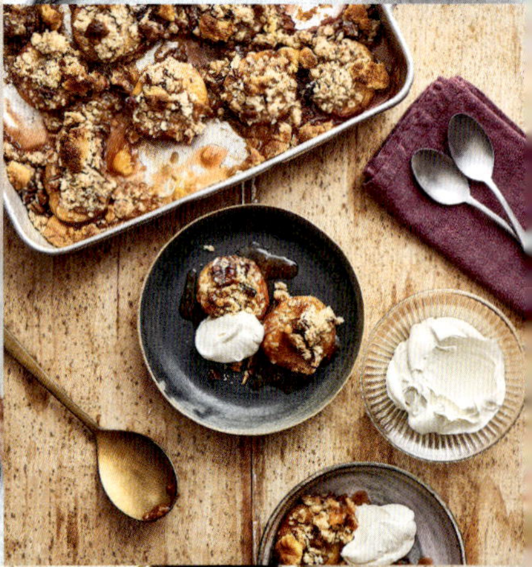
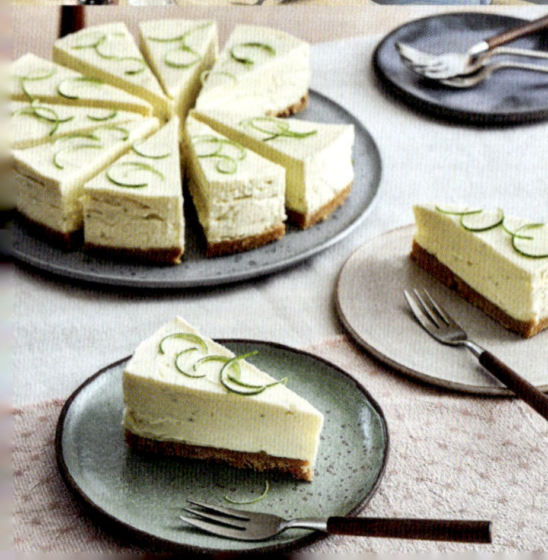
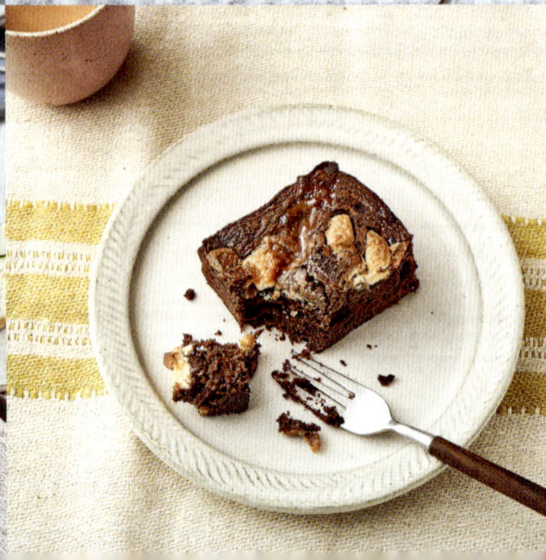
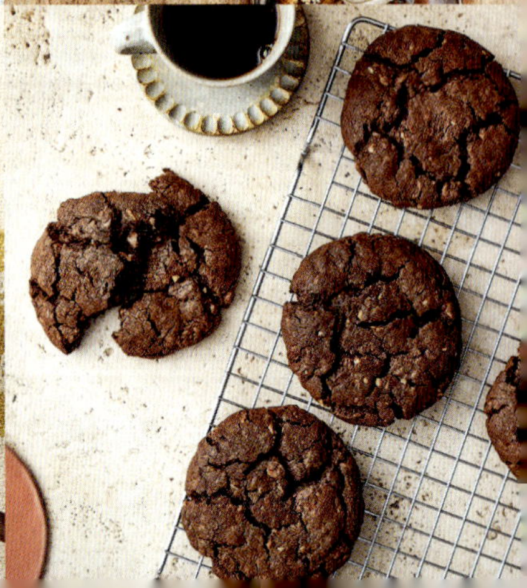

EASY BAKES

Simple, achievable bakes that can be stored, frozen, refrigerated or eaten later. It means you'll always have something sweet ready-to-go.

ESPRESSO CHOCOLATE CAKE

PEAR AND ROSE TART

KULFI ICE CREAM

FILO CRINKLE CAKE

SHERBET LEMON LOAF

EASY RASPBERRY PUDDING POTS

STRAWBERRY LEMONADE TRIFLE

PEACH PECAN CRUMBLE

LIME CHEESECAKE

WHITE CHOCOLATE AND CARAMEL BROWNIES

HAZELNUT CHOCOLATE COOKIES

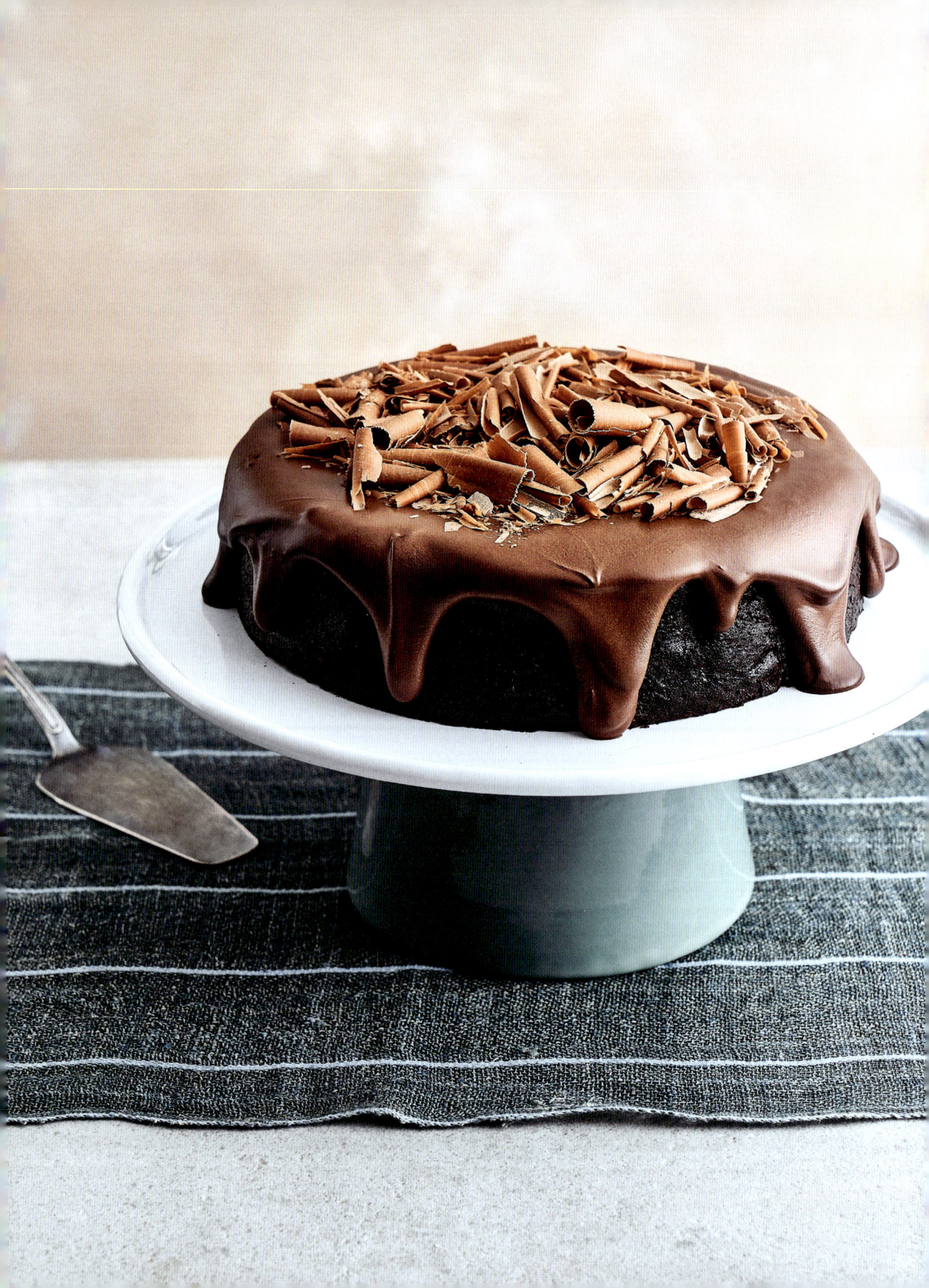

ESPRESSO CHOCOLATE CAKE

This is the simplest of cakes. Made with oil and hot water, it's also the moistest chocolate cake ever – it literally never dries out, even when left out! The intense coffee flavour makes it super special.

PREP: 35 MINS
BAKE: 55 MINS–1 HOUR
COOL: 10–15 MINS
MAKES: 12 SLICES

For the cake

- Oil, for greasing
- 225g plain flour, sifted
- 350g caster sugar
- 85g cocoa powder
- 1½ teaspoons baking powder
- 1½ teaspoons bicarbonate of soda
- 250ml whole milk
- 2 medium eggs, lightly beaten
- 125ml olive oil
- 250ml boiling water
- 3 tablespoons coffee granules

For the ganache

- 250g dark chocolate (70%), chopped
- 200ml boiling water
- 1 tablespoon coffee granules
- 100g milk chocolate, shaved, to serve

Start by preheating the oven to 170°C and lining and greasing a 20cm round cake tin. Set aside and get on to making the cake batter, which is really quick.

Place the flour in a large bowl along with the caster sugar, cocoa powder, baking powder and bicarbonate of soda. Whisk everything together till all the dry ingredients are mixed through.

Make a well in the centre and pour in the milk, then crack in the eggs, pour in the olive oil and whisk till you have a thick batter. Pour in the boiling water, along with the coffee, and mix it all through – you will have a very runny cake batter.

Pour into the prepared tin and bake on the middle shelf for 55 minutes–1 hour till a skewer inserted comes out clean and the cake is coming away from the edges. Take out of the oven and leave to cool in the tin completely.

Make the ganache by putting the dark chocolate in a bowl. Pour in the boiling water and sprinkle over the coffee granules. Mix till the chocolate has melted and you have a smooth ganache. To make it more quickly and for an ultra-smooth result, you can mix it using a stick blender. Pour the ganache all over the cake and spread it out evenly.

Sprinkle over the shaved milk chocolate, then pop into the fridge and leave to chill completely so the ganache can set. Take out of the tin, place onto a serving dish and cut into wedges to enjoy.

TIP *Adding coffee to chocolate enhances the cocoa flavour. But if you want to make this for kids, you can remove the coffee altogether and make as pure chocolate or experiment with extracts, such as vanilla, peppermint, orange and so on.*

PEAR AND ROSE TART

This is the kind of bake that appears really special because it has lots of layers, but it is not difficult to make. The recipe is full of shortcuts, but you still get all the flavours of the rose and pear and it is very much a special dessert.

PREP: 32 MINS **BAKE:** 1 HOUR

SERVES: 6–8

For the pastry
Icing sugar, for dusting
320g pack of ready-rolled shortcrust pastry

For the jam
100g seedless raspberry jam
1 organic rose head, petals only
1 teaspoon rose extract

For the filling
100g unsalted butter, softened
100g caster sugar
100g ground almonds, toasted and cooled
2 medium eggs
3 cardamom pods, seeds removed and crushed

For the pears and syrup
415g tin of pears in juice
Caster sugar

Start by preheating the oven to 180°C. Pop a baking tray on a shelf and have a 20cm loose-bottom fluted tart tin at the ready. Dust the work surface with icing sugar.

Take the defrosted shortcrust pastry out of the box, roll it out and cut to create enough surface area to cover the base and sides of the tart tin, making sure that there is some overhang.

Push the pastry into the edges and fluted parts of the tin. Prick the base of the tart all over to create a path for the steam to leave. Line with some baking paper and fill with baking beads or uncooked lentils to weigh it down.

Bake for 15 minutes. Remove the tart shell from the oven, take out the paper and the beads/dried lentils and pop back in for another 10 minutes. Take out of the oven and leave for just enough time for it to be cool enough for you to trim the edges of the pastry.

Now for the jam. Put the raspberry jam in a bowl, then thinly slice the rose and add to the bowl along with the rose extract. Mix well and spread all over the base of the pastry shell.

Make the filling by putting the butter in a bowl with the sugar and mixing to an even paste. Add the ground almonds along with the eggs and cardamom seeds, mix to a smooth paste and then spread it all over the jam layer.

For the pears, drain the pears of their juice, reserving the liquid. You will need five halves. Slice the halves into thin slices, keeping the halved pears together.

Place each pear half on top of the almond base, fanning out a little before placing them down.

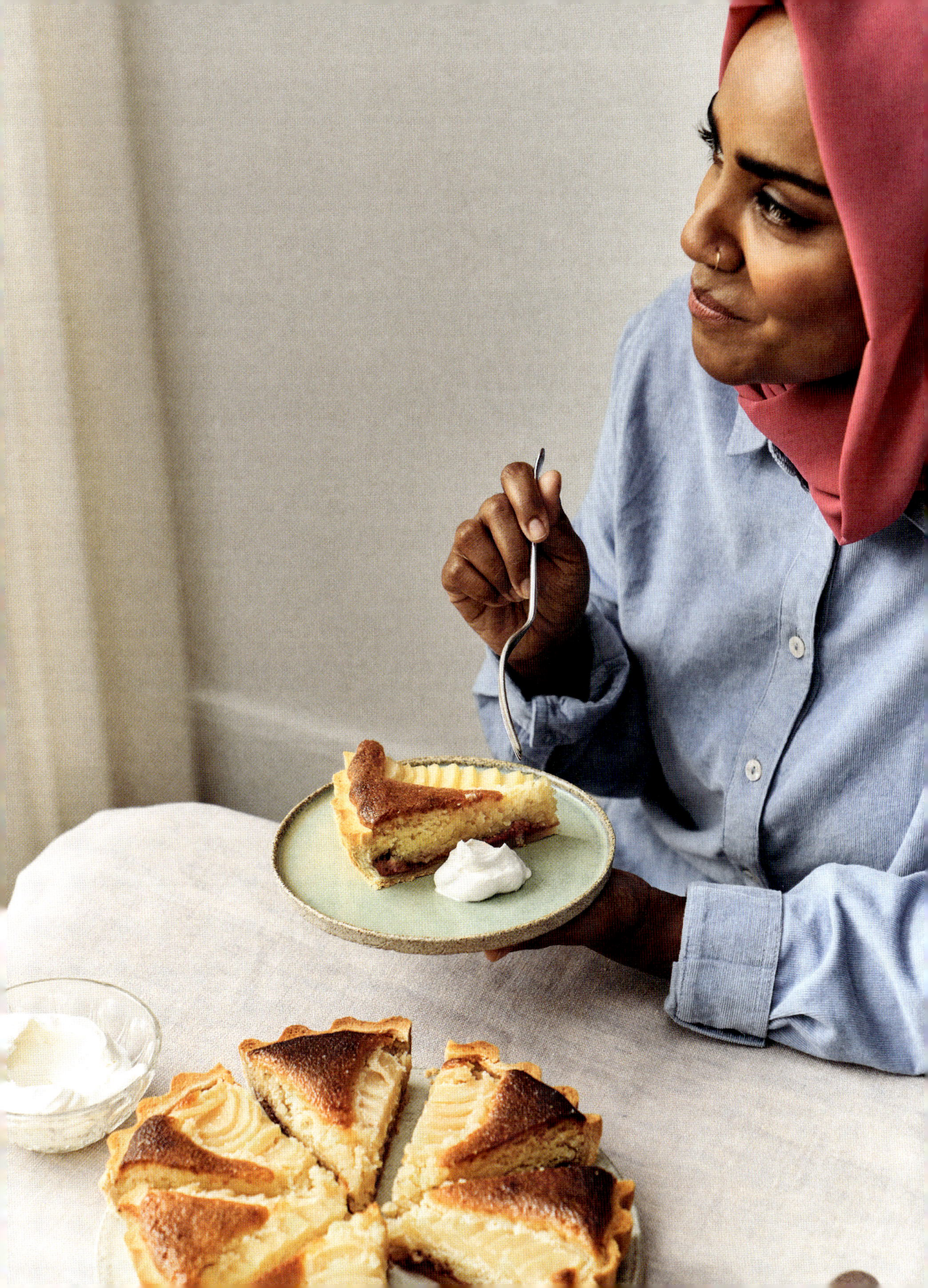

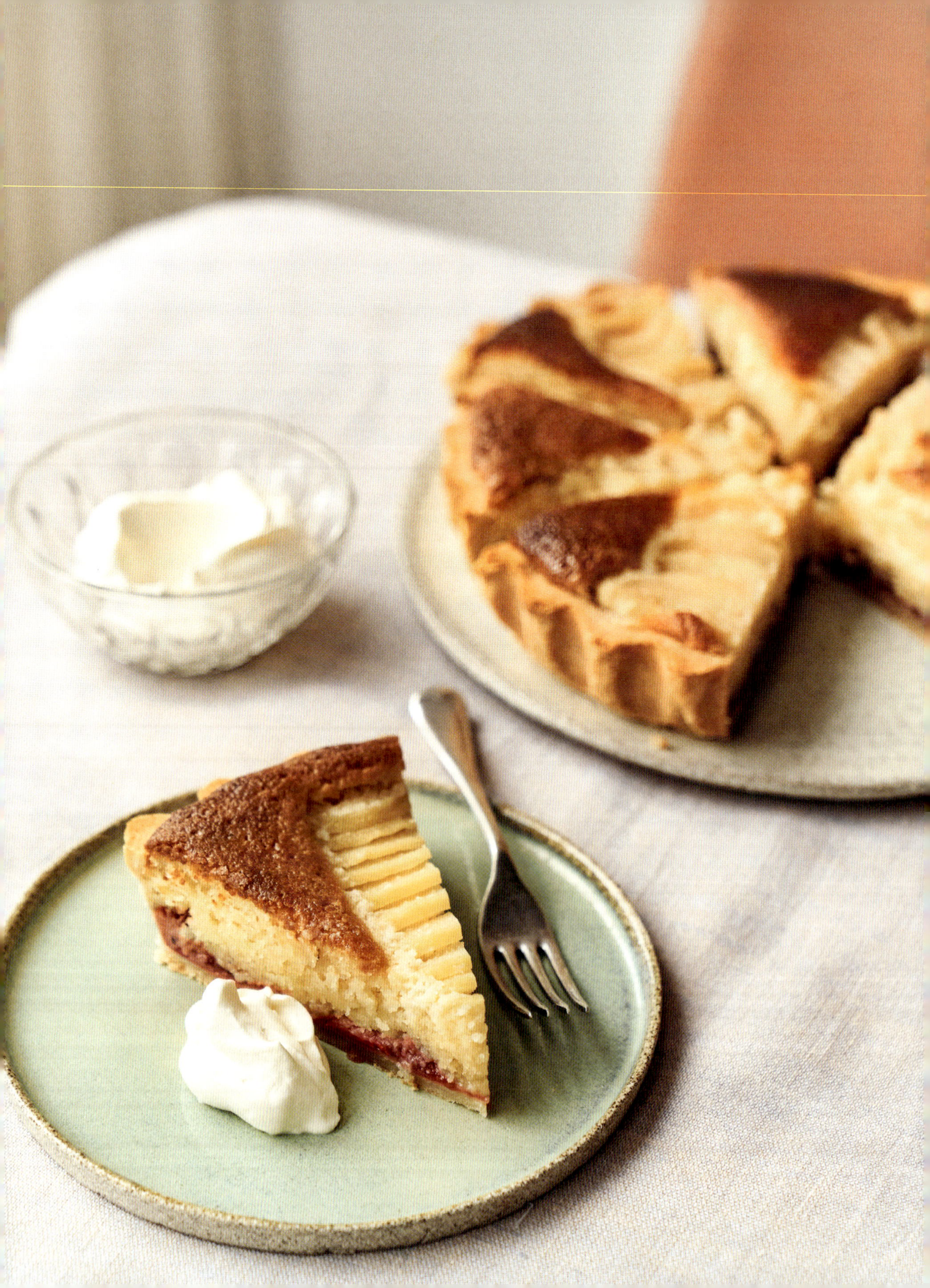

Bake in the oven for 25–30 minutes. Take out and leave to cool completely in the tin.

Make a syrup by putting the pear liquid in a bowl and measuring the juice. Add the same amount of caster sugar. Pour into a pan and boil and cook down till you have a thick, sticky syrup.

Brush the tart all over with the syrup and the tart is ready to eat, served with a dollop of thick double cream.

TIP *You can use any tinned or jarred fruit for this. The fruit is tender and doesn't require extra cooking, making it the simplest way to add fruit to a dessert without any extra work.*

KULFI ICE CREAM

This is traditional for me because this is all my dad served in his restaurant. If I had known then how easy this is to make, I would have convinced him to never buy it. You guys will love the creaminess of this ice cream and you don't even need an ice-cream machine.

PREP: 5 MINS **COOK:** 15 MINS
FREEZE: OVERNIGHT

SERVES: 2–4

397g tin of condensed milk

900ml double cream

10 cardamom pods, seeds removed and crushed

2 white bread slices, blitzed to a crumb

100g pistachios, toasted, cooled and roughly chopped

Start by pouring the condensed milk into a medium non-stick pan and begin cooking over a medium heat. Cook till the mixture is thick, coming away from the sides and light brown.

Pour in the cream and cook and simmer till the fudge has mixed in with the cream. Now add the cardamom pods and the white breadcrumbs and mix through. Simmer for 2 minutes over a low heat.

Take off the heat and strain through a sieve, being sure to push through any of those lumps. Stir in two-thirds of the pistachios.

Pour the whole thing into a freezer-safe tub, sprinkle over the remaining pistachios and freeze overnight. Before serving, thaw out for 5 minutes and then scoop.

TIP *For extra security, place the tub into a zip sealed bag for an extra layer. This stops the ice cream freezing solid and is a great thing to do whether you are making your own ice cream or the ice cream is shop-bought.*

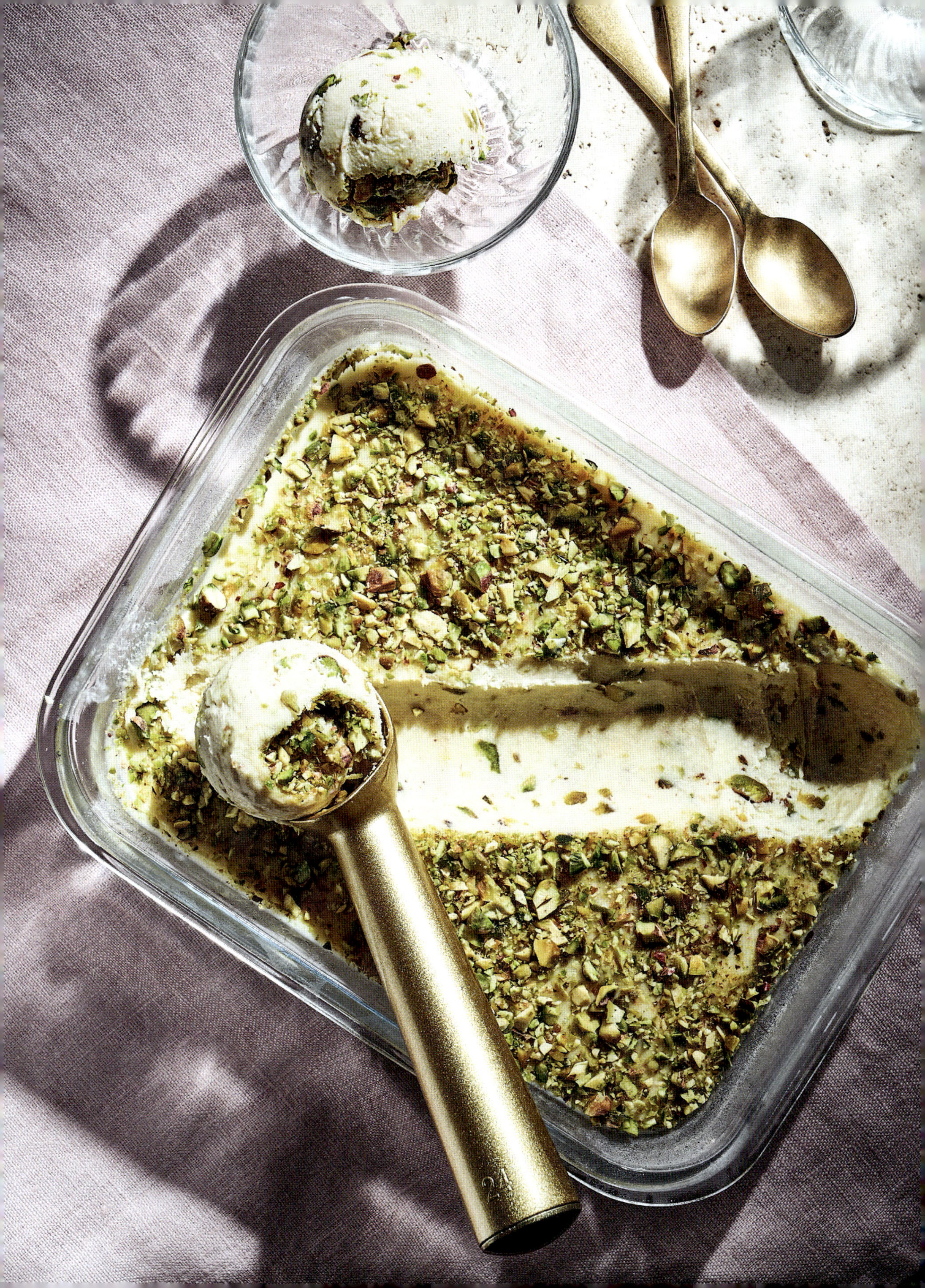

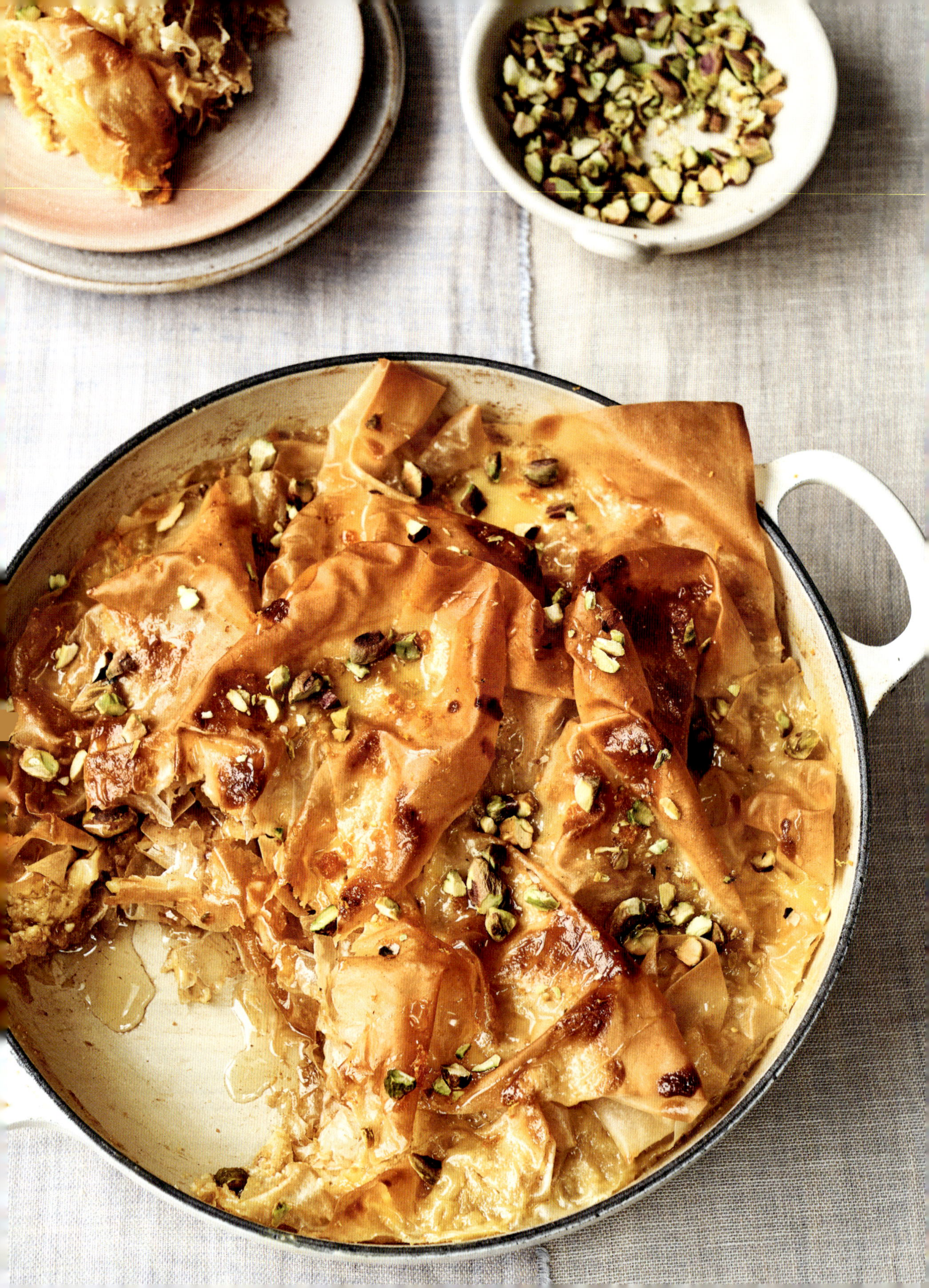

FILO CRINKLE CAKE

This is a delicious way to use filo pastry and the best thing about it is that there are no finicky folding methods. It's all a bit random and I am kind of in love with that. It's sweet, soft, crispy delicious and perfect for gatherings.

PREP: 15 MINS **BAKE:** 1 HOUR 20 MINS
CHILL: 1 HOUR
SERVES: 6–8

For the pastry
- 2 x 270g packs of filo pastry, defrosted
- 100g salted butter, melted, plus extra for greasing
- 1 teaspoon ground cinnamon

For the filling
- 3 egg yolks
- 1 tablespoon custard powder
- 100g caster sugar
- 400ml whole milk
- 3 teaspoons vanilla extract
- 100g pistachios, roasted and roughly chopped

To serve
- 1 orange
- Runny honey

Start by preheating the oven to 180°C and having a 23cm round skillet greased and at the ready (make sure it has a secure base – a loose bottom would not work in this case).

For the pastry, take the filo out of its box and packet and set aside. Mix the melted butter with the ground cinnamon.

Take a filo sheet and brush with the melted butter, then literally crinkle the filo and place inside the skillet, crumpled. Do this to each sheet and keep going, one crumpled sheet at a time, until you have filled the whole skillet.

Pop into the oven and bake for about 15–20 minutes till really golden and crispy. Take out and set aside.

Make the custard by putting the egg yolks in a bowl with the custard powder and caster sugar. Whisk till combined.

Heat the milk till it just comes up to the boil and then take off the heat. Add the vanilla extract. Slowly pour the milk into the egg yolk mixture, whisking all the time, till you have added all the milk.

Pour the mixture all over the baked filo and leave for 10 minutes for the custard to get into the layers.

Sprinkle over the pistachios and bake for 20–25 minutes. Take out and leave to cool in the tin.

To serve, grate the zest of the orange on top. Squeeze the juice of the orange all over and then drizzle over the honey generously. Leave to chill for 1 hour before slicing and enjoying.

TIP *This is the perfect recipe for filo that has dried up and crumbled in your freezer – you never have to throw away your filo ever again.*

SHERBET LEMON LOAF

This is a take on my favourite boiled sweet – sherbet lemons! The cake is lemony, buttery and a little bit tangy.

PREP: 12 MINS **BAKE:** 1 HOUR 5 MINS

SERVES: 8–10

For the cake

175g unsalted butter, softened

175g caster sugar

3 medium eggs, lightly beaten

3 lemons, zest only (see below)

1 teaspoon vanilla bean paste

1 teaspoon almond extract

1 teaspoon lemon extract

225g self-raising flour

2 tablespoons cornflour

For the lemon topping

3 lemons, juice only (see above)

Caster sugar

1 teaspoon citric acid (optional)

Start by preheating the oven to 160°C and lining and greasing a 900g loaf tin.

For the cake, put the unsalted butter in a bowl with the caster sugar and mix in a freestanding mixer till you have a mixture that is light, fluffy and almost white. Add the eggs in a steady stream while the mixer is still going till you have combined them all.

Go ahead and add the lemon zest, vanilla bean paste, almond extract, lemon extract, self-raising flour and cornflour. Fold together till you have a mixture that is shiny and smooth.

Spoon into the prepared loaf tin, level off and bake for 55 minutes–1 hour. Once baked, remove from the oven and leave to cool in the tin for a few minutes.

For the lemon topping, put the juice of the 3 lemons in a bowl and measure the juice. Add the same amount of caster sugar. I can't give you exacts because all lemons are different sizes, so each time the amount is unique. Add the citric acid (if you have it), mix in and pour the topping all over the hot cake, spreading the sugar so you have an even, crusty sherbet lemon layer. Allow the hot cake to absorb the lemon mix for a few minutes before removing it from the tin.

Leave to cool completely and for the sugar to harden. Cut into slices and enjoy.

TIP *Leftover cake need never be thrown away. Did you know that you have other options than just freezing? You can also bake slices of cake till they turn into biscuits – give it a go next time you have a few slices left.*

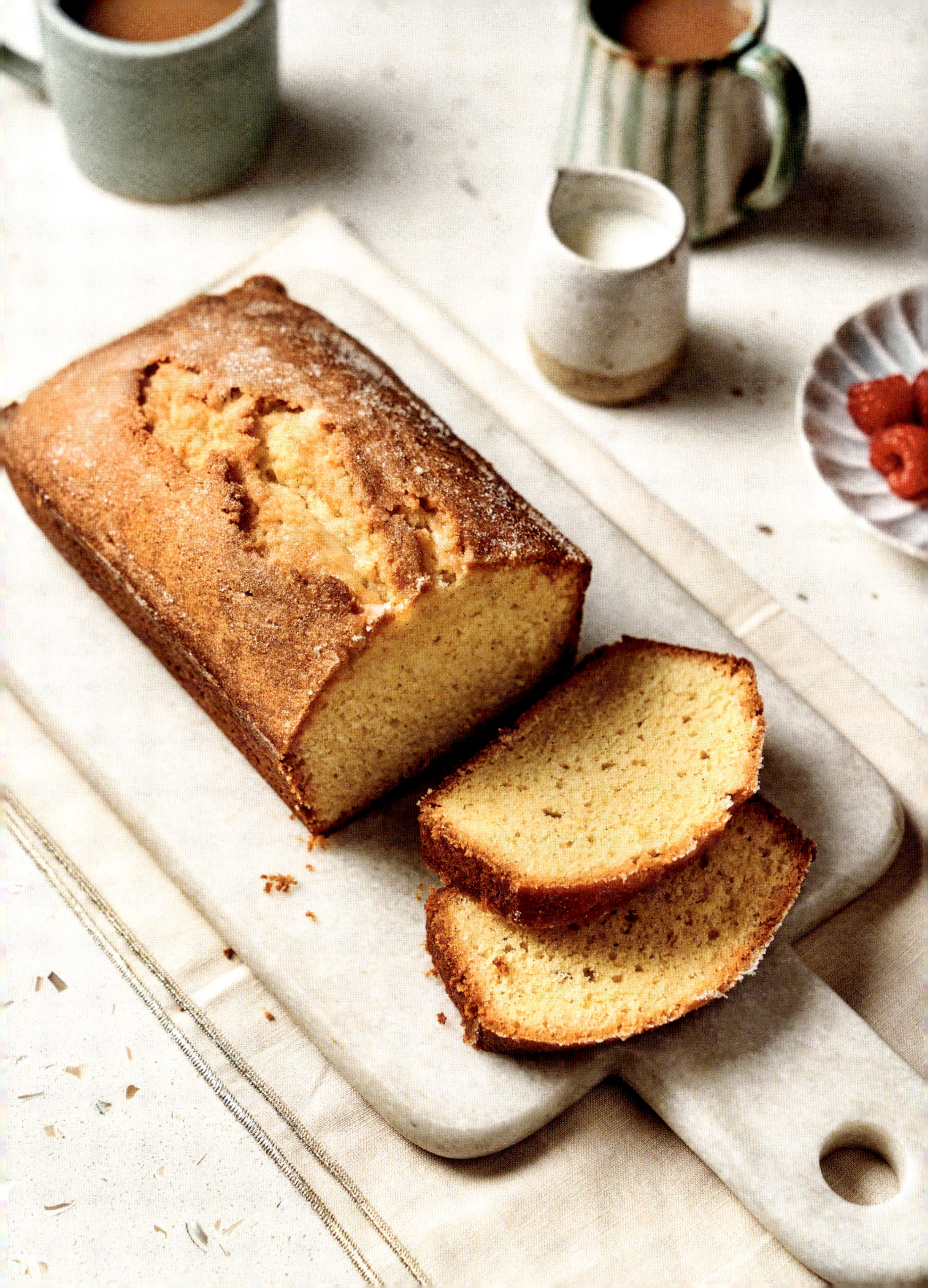

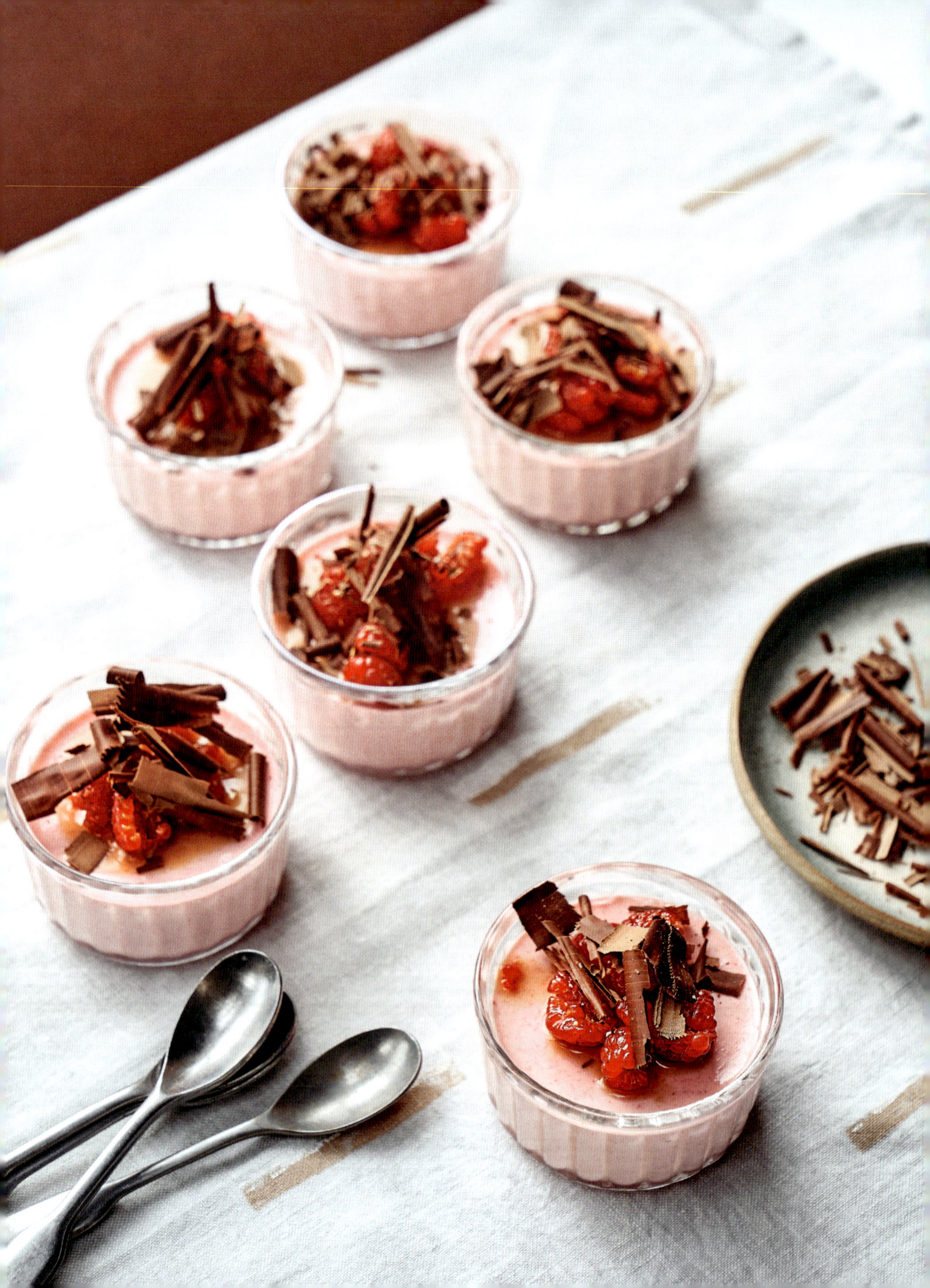

EASY RASPBERRY PUDDING POTS

This pudding is a delicious fruity and dense one. I am not a huge fan of airy mousses – I prefer the ones with a bit more richness and more like a set custard – so here we have a raspberry version that I think you will adore.

PREP: 8 MINS **COOK:** 16 MINS
CHILL: 4 HOURS–OVERNIGHT
MAKES: 6 POTS

For the mousse
300g raspberries
600ml double cream
150g caster sugar
1 lemon, zest and juice

To serve
150g raspberries
Zest of 1 lemon
3 tablespoons maple syrup
75g dark chocolate (70%), shaved

Start by getting your ramekins or pots ready, washed, dried and ready to fill. Set them aside.

Take half the raspberries, setting the other half aside. Blend the mixture, passing it through a sieve so you have a smooth purée. Set aside also.

Pour the double cream into a small pan along with the caster sugar and mix to combine. Put the pan over a medium heat and warm till the sugar has dissolved completely. Take off the heat and leave to one side to cool for 5 minutes.

Now add the lemon juice, along with the raspberry purée. Mix really well, strain through a sieve and pour equally into the waiting ramekins or pots. Place in the fridge for at least 4 hours or overnight if you can.

To serve, take the other raspberries, halve them, then add the lemon zest and mix in the maple syrup. Top each pot with the raspberries and sprinkle over the shaved chocolate.

TIP *You can totally use frozen berries for this if that is what you have available to you.*

STRAWBERRY LEMONADE TRIFLE

The best pudding for grown-ups and kids alike. My dad's ultimate favourite dessert, this is inspired by a raspberry lemonade.

PREP: 20 MINS **COOK:** 8 MINS (+ CHILLING)

MAKES: 1

For the jelly
2 x 23g sachets of strawberry jelly crystals

800ml lemonade, plus extra for brushing

For the cake
280g Madeira cake

For the fruit layer
300g strawberries

1 lemon, zest and juice

For the custard
500g readymade custard

For the cream
600ml double cream

4 tablespoons icing sugar

1 teaspoon vanilla bean paste

Start with the dish you are using. Ideally use a trifle dish as they are perfect for serving the trifle, but equally you can use a clear roasting dish that is deep enough to build up the layers.

Open the jelly sachets and put the crystals in a large jug or bowl with a spout. Take half the lemonade (400ml) and bring to the boil in a pan, then remove from the heat and pour straight into the jug. Make sure to whisk quickly so everything dissolves fast.

Now add the remaining 400ml lemonade and pour the whole lot into the trifle dish. Leave to cool and then set in the fridge.

When you're ready to assemble the trifle, slice up the Madeira cake, brushing some lemonade on top to moisten it.

Chop up the strawberries, mix with the lemon juice and zest and place along with the Madeira cake onto the jelly in an even layer. Pour in the custard in an even layer.

Whip up the double cream with the icing sugar and vanilla bean paste. Spoon right on top in peaks. Chill for a few hours before serving to get the best of this dessert.

TIP *This trifle can be frozen, so if you have any leftovers, divide into individual portions and pop into freezer containers.*

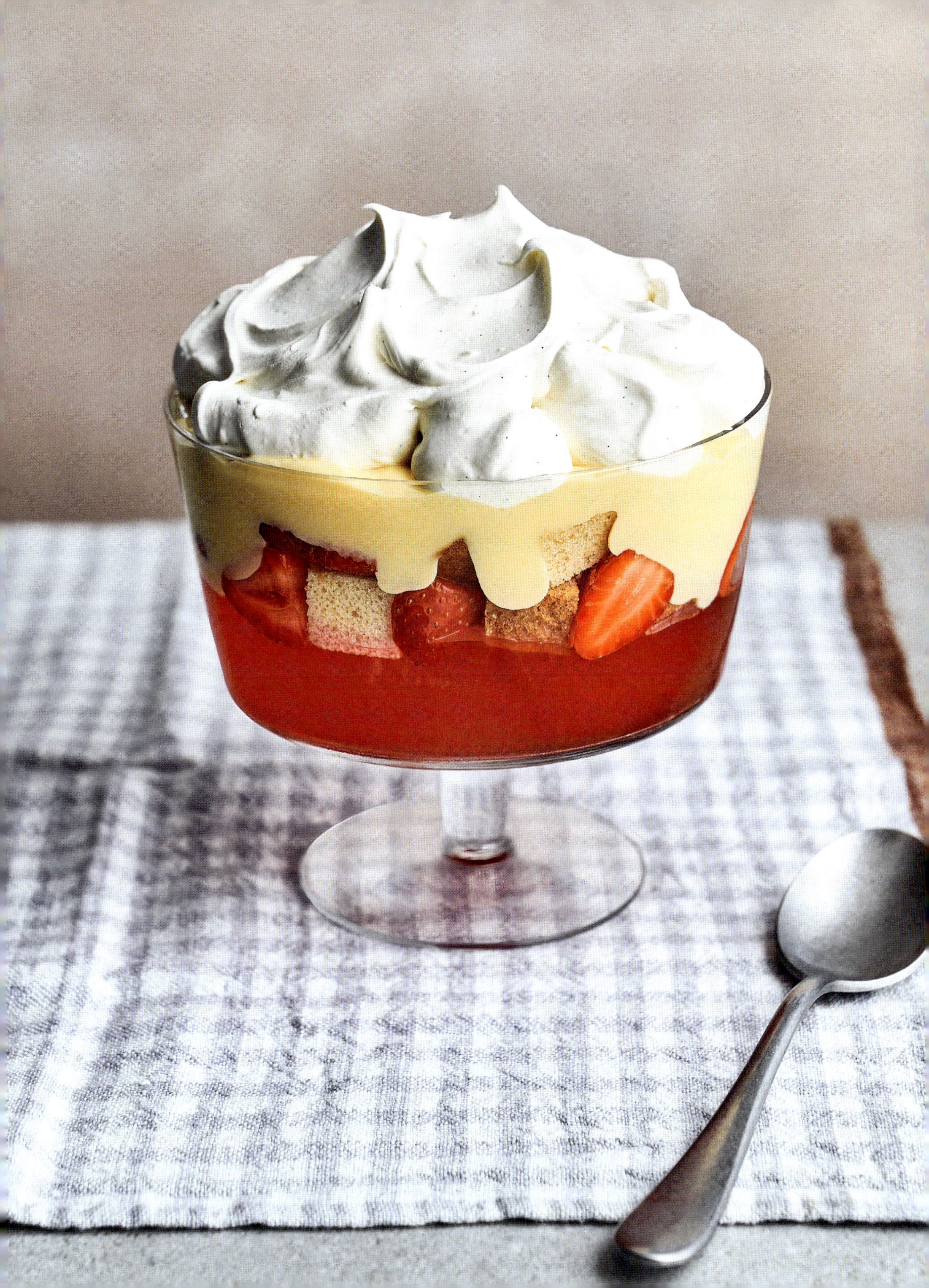

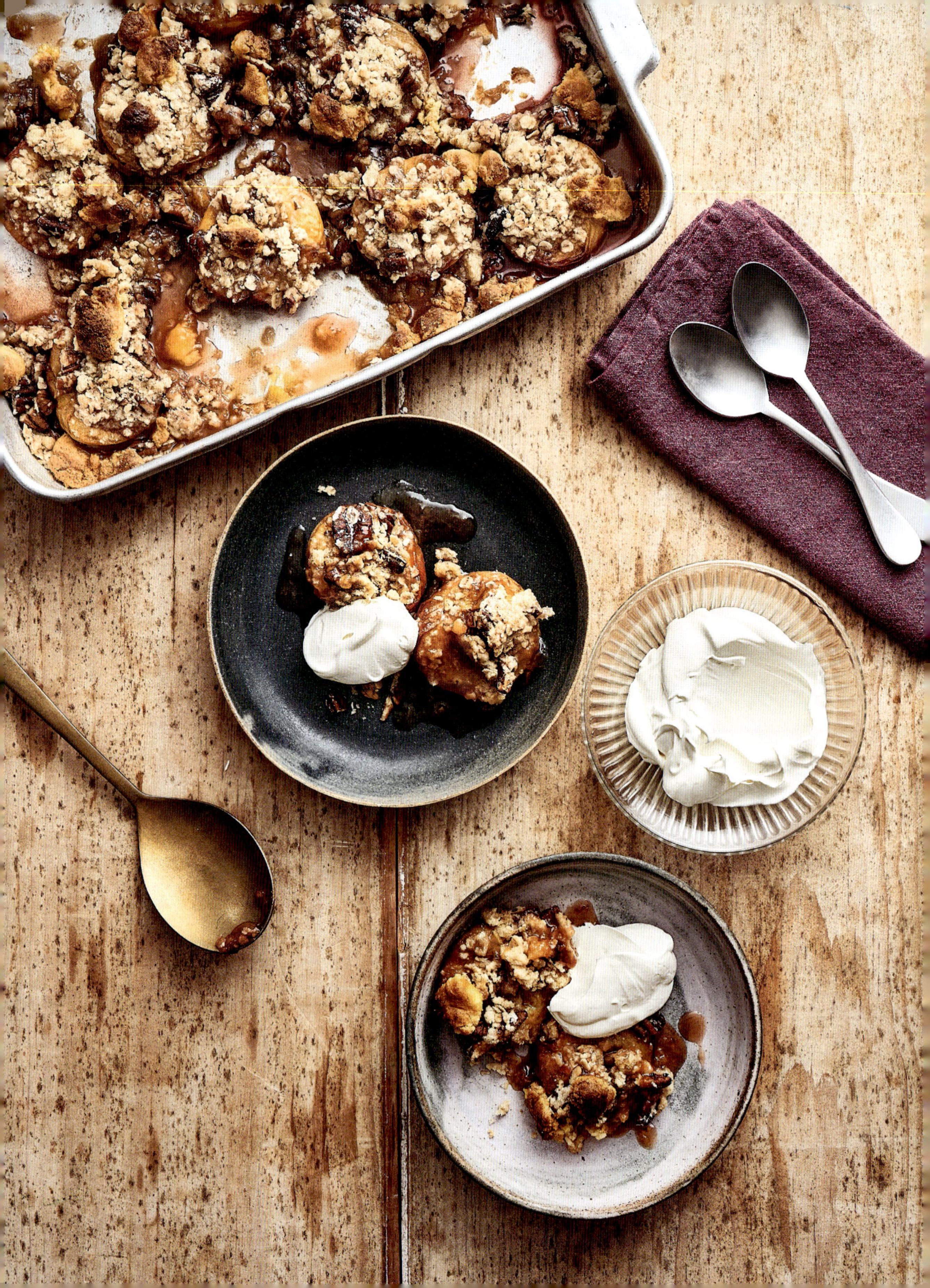

PEACH PECAN CRUMBLE

Crumbles can be so much more than what we were served for our school dinners. They were delicious, stodgy and sweet, but we can make our own version – peachy, nutty and sweet. Like a hug in a crumble.

PREP: 15 MINS **BAKE:** 1 HOUR 10 MINS

SERVES: 6

For the peaches

8 peaches, halved but stones still in

50g salted butter, melted

1 teaspoon ground cinnamon

50g caster sugar

For the crumble

100g pecans

100g plain flour

50g porridge oats

75g salted butter, cubed

60g demerara sugar

Pinch of salt

100g golden marzipan

Preheat the oven to 180°C. Grease the inside of a roasting dish that will happily sit the peaches in an even layer.

Put the peaches in the dish, keeping their stones in as roasting with these will enhance that peach taste. Peaches are naturally subtle, so this really helps to maximize the flavour.

Pour in the melted butter, cinnamon and caster sugar and mix through till well combined.

Pop into the oven to roast for 20 minutes. Take out and remove the seeds (see tip below).

For the crumble, toast the pecans in a dry pan till they are golden. Remove and set aside. As soon as they are cool, roughly chop.

Toast the plain flour and porridge oats till golden and then pop into a bowl and leave to cool completely.

Add the butter and rub in till you have no big lumps. Mix in the demerara sugar, chopped toasted pecans and a good pinch of salt.

Mix through and top the baked peaches. Take pinches of the golden marzipan and place all over.

Bake in the oven for 30–40 minutes. Serve hot with lashings of whipped cream, custard, ice cream or all of the above.

TIP *If you want you can save the peach seeds. Clean and dry the stones, then smash with a hammer to reveal the inside seed. These can be grated into creams and custards, revealing an almond vanilla flavour!*

LIME CHEESECAKE

This is the base for a simple cheesecake that doesn't need baking, but why not go a little extra and make it that bit more special. Top the buttery biscuit base and limey filling with a meringue straight out of a jar!

PREP: 22 MINS **FREEZE:** OVERNIGHT

SERVES: 6–8

For the base
- 200g digestive or oaty biscuits
- ½ teaspoon ground nutmeg
- 100g butter, melted
- Good pinch of salt

For the filling
- 600g full-fat cream cheese
- 2 teaspoons vanilla extract
- 200g white chocolate, melted
- 2 limes, zest only
- 400ml double cream
- 150g lime marmalade

To serve
- Lime zest

Line and grease the base and sides of a 20cm springform tin and set to one side.

Make the base by adding the digestive or oaty biscuits to a food processor and blitzing to a crumb. Sprinkle in the nutmeg, add the butter and salt and whizz till combined.

Drop into the tin and, using the back of a spoon, make a compacted, even layer of biscuit. Place in the freezer to set.

Make the filling by putting the full-fat cream cheese in a bowl and mixing till it is smooth. Add in the vanilla extract, melted white chocolate and lime zest. Whisk to combine.

Pour in the double cream and mix till you have a smooth cheesecake mixture. Spoon in the lime marmalade, gently fold in and pour on top of the biscuit base. Leave to chill in the fridge, ideally overnight.

Take out, serve and enjoy.

TIP *Don't throw away your limes. To remove any hardened limescale that may have built up on your taps, attach them to the ends of your taps and leave overnight.*

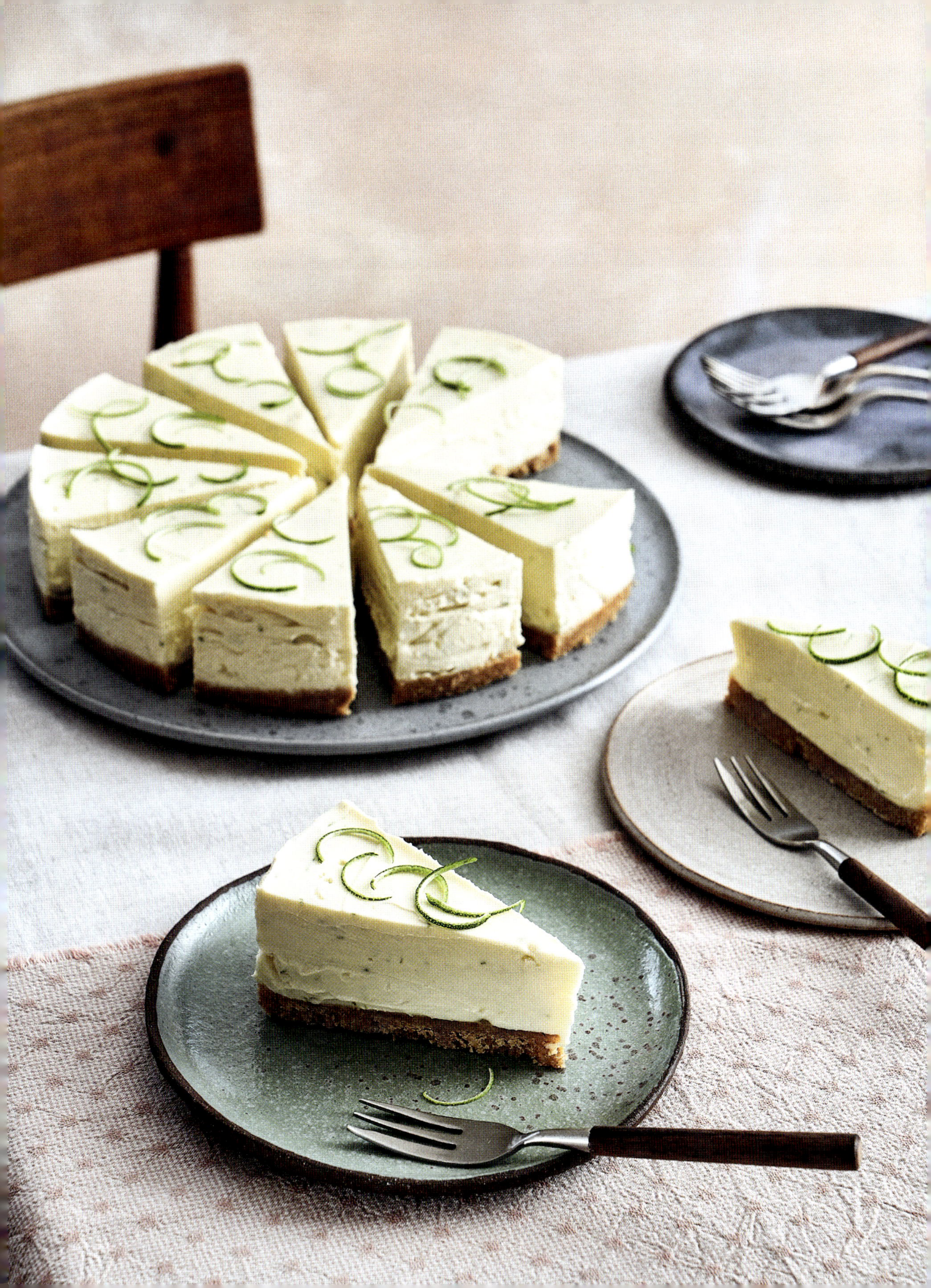

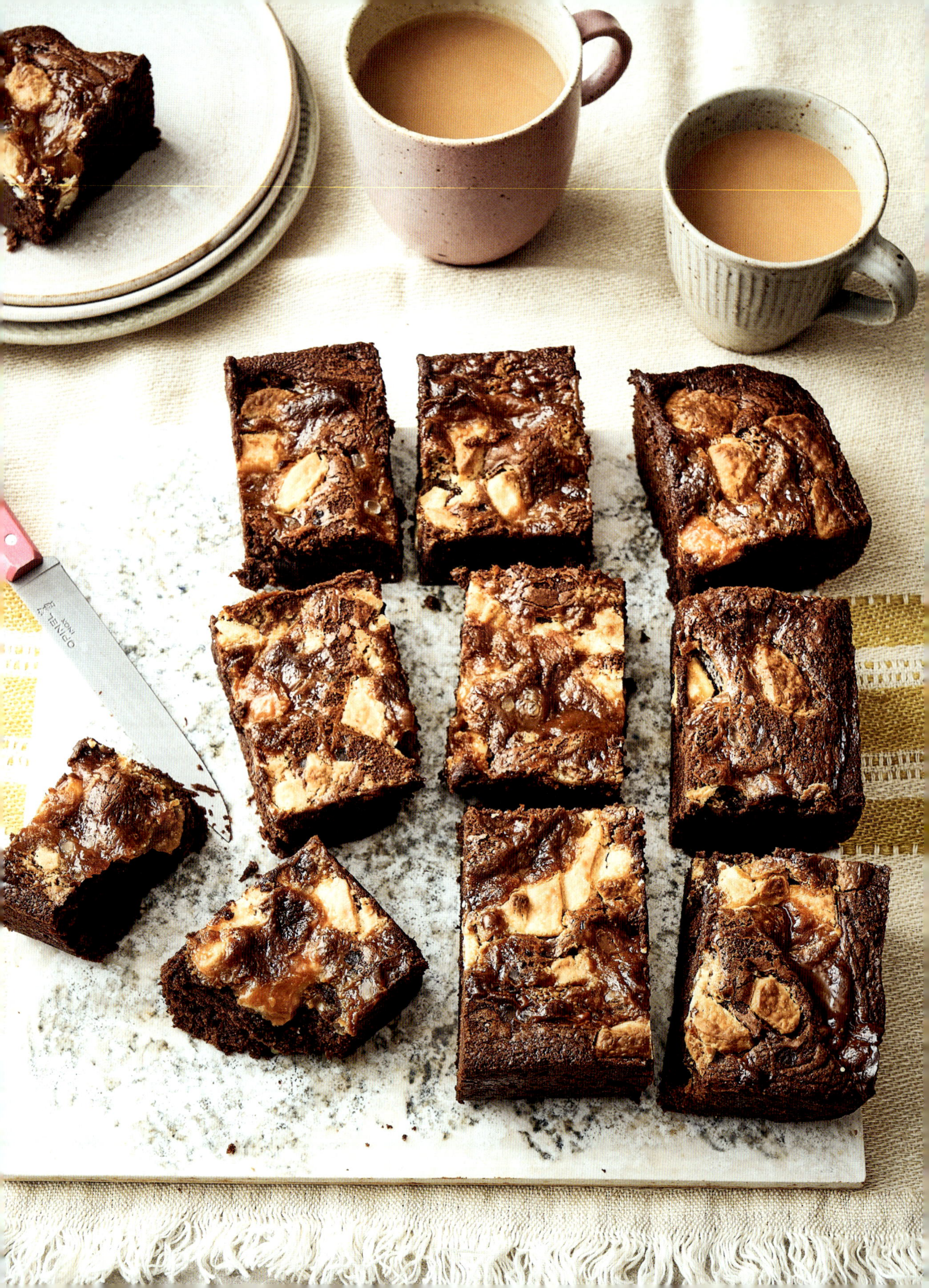

WHITE CHOCOLATE AND CARAMEL BROWNIES

Everyone needs a great brownie in their bag of tricks, nothing fancy, just a simple brownie base that can be expanded on through time, or just left as it is. A good dense, fudgy brownie is all the joy we need in life.

PREP: 25 MINS **BAKE:** 30 MINS
CHILL: 1 HOUR + OVERNIGHT
MAKES: 12 BROWNIES

- 250g salted butter, plus extra for greasing
- 250g dark chocolate (70%), broken up or roughly chopped
- 4 medium eggs
- 280g caster sugar
- 130g plain flour
- 20g cocoa powder

For the top
- 100g caramel
- 100g white chocolate, chopped
- Rock salt

Start by lining a 23cm square tin and greasing it lightly.

Melt the butter and dark chocolate in a pan till liquid, then take off the heat and leave to cool completely.

Once cool, put the eggs in a large mixing bowl along with the caster sugar and whisk till the mixture is really light in colour and very fluffy.

Sift in the plain flour and cocoa powder and mix through till you have a thick batter. Pour into the prepared tin and level off. Leave in the fridge for 1 hour.

Preheat the oven to 180°C.

Drizzle over caramel in random blobs and then sprinkle over the chocolate and salt. Bake for 30 minutes.

Take out and leave to cool in the tin completely. Chill in the fridge overnight. Chop into squares and revel in your efforts.

TIP *These freeze so well. Wrap them individually and pop into the freezer, then thaw out and enjoy as you would normally.*

HAZELNUT CHOCOLATE COOKIES

Everyone needs a great cookie recipe in their repertoire. So here is one that I think you will love and enjoy time and time again.

PREP: 20 MINS **COOK:** 12–14 MINS (+ CHILLING)

MAKES: 12 COOKIES

200g unsalted butter, plus extra for greasing

300g soft brown sugar

2 teaspoons vanilla extract

1 teaspoon almond extract

2 medium eggs

300g self-raising flour, sifted

80g cocoa

1 teaspoon baking powder

Large pinch of salt

200g milk chocolate chips

100g roasted chopped hazelnuts

Put the butter in a bowl with the soft brown sugar, vanilla extract and almond extract. Whisk till you have a mixture that is light and fluffy.

Add the eggs and mix until really well combined. Throw in the self-raising flour, the cocoa, baking powder, salt, milk chocolate chips and chopped hazelnuts and mix till you have a stiff dough.

Divide the mixture into twelve equal balls, flatten out with the palm of your hand and leave to sit in the fridge for as long as possible or overnight.

Preheat the oven to 170°C. Line three baking trays with baking paper and grease lightly.

Place four cookies on each tray with space for the cookies to spread. Bake for 12–14 minutes, till they are baked on the outside and just chewy in the middle.

Take out and leave on the tray till totally cooled. They are now ready to eat!

TIP *When you have measured the balls, they can be frozen and then baked from frozen at the same temperature for 18–20 minutes.*

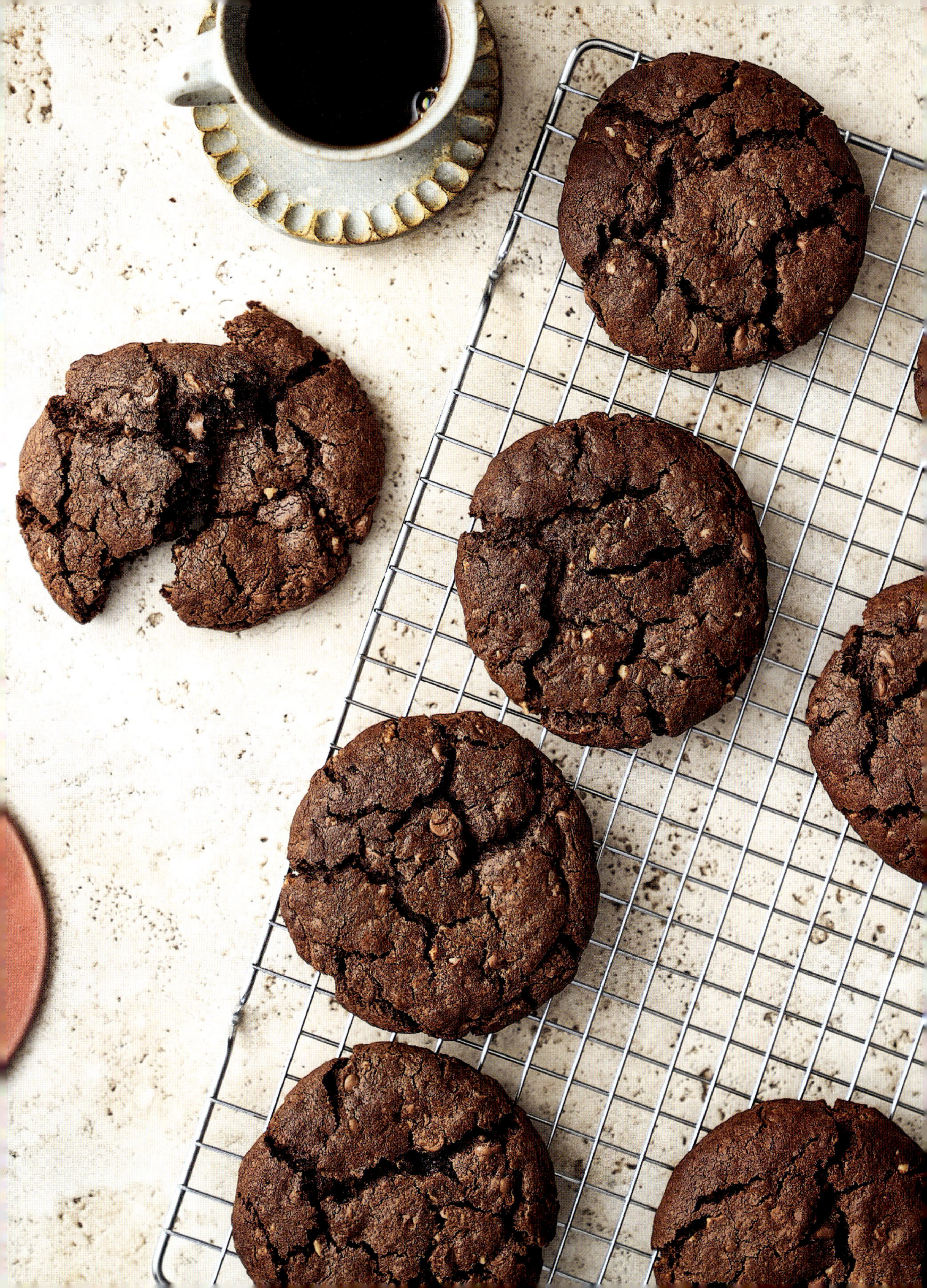

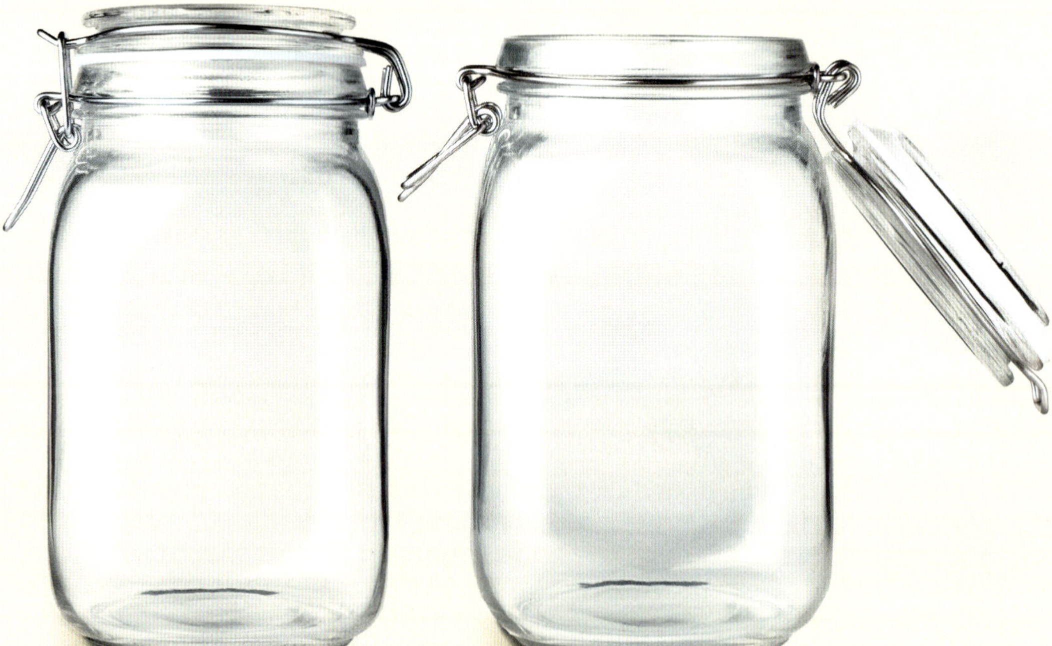

WASTE NOT
↓
WANT NOT

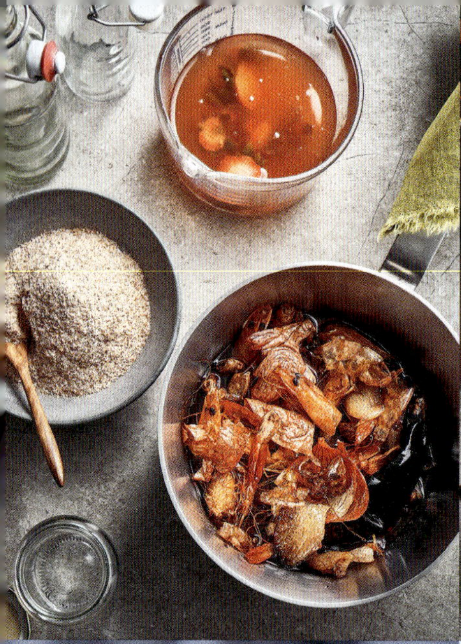
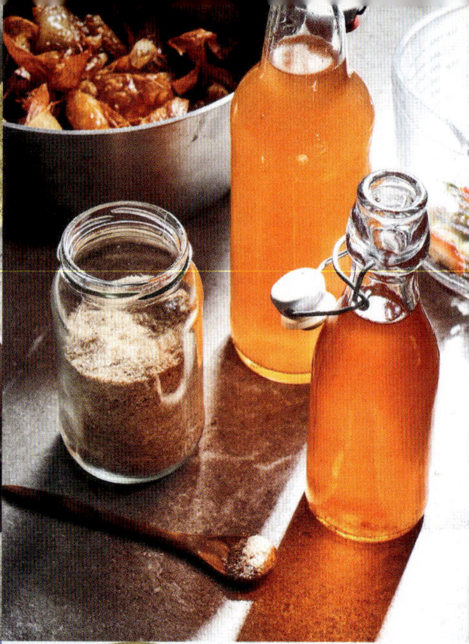
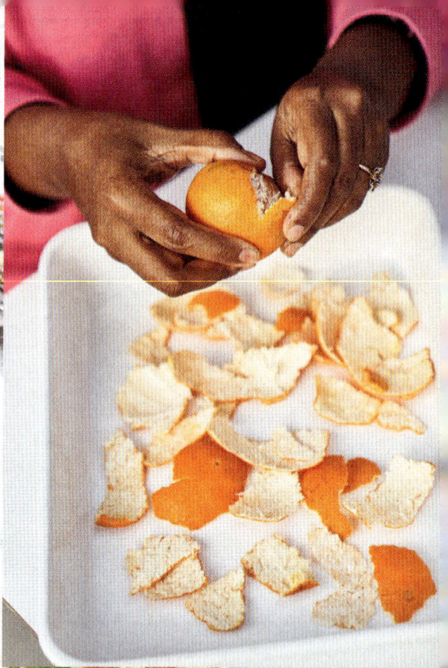
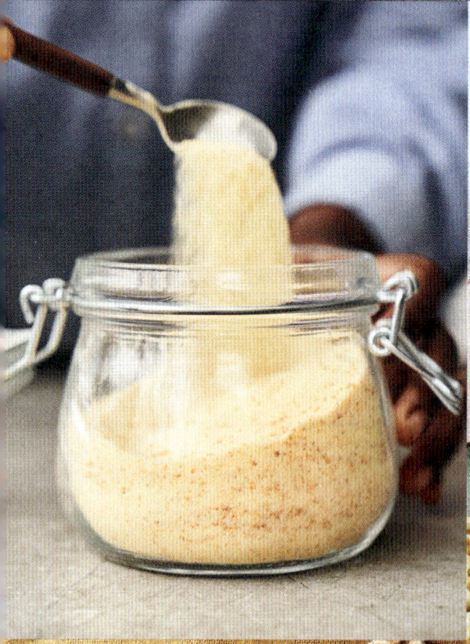
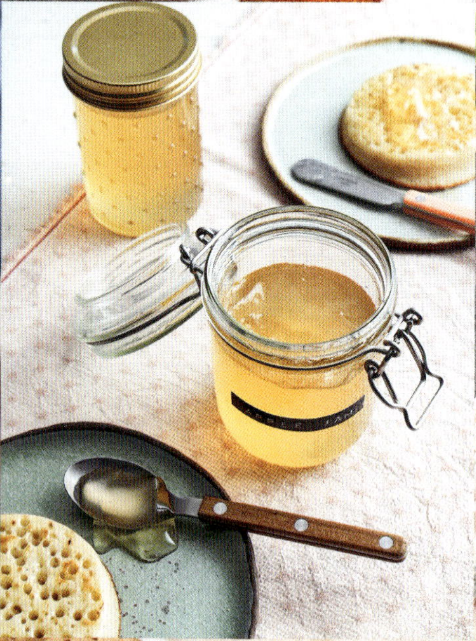
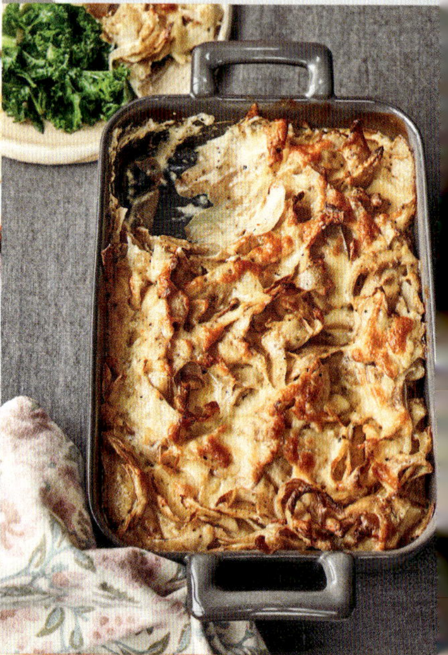
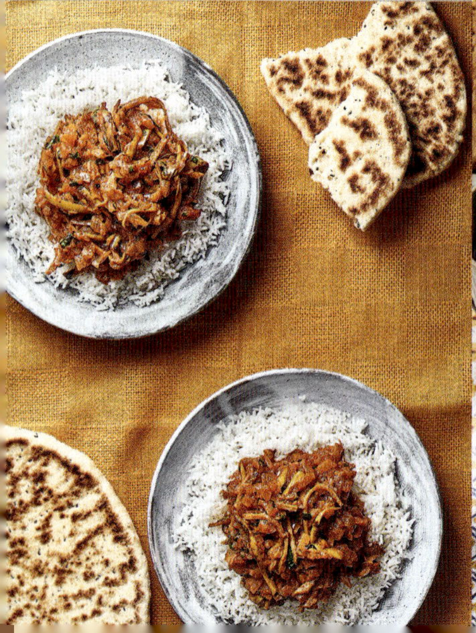
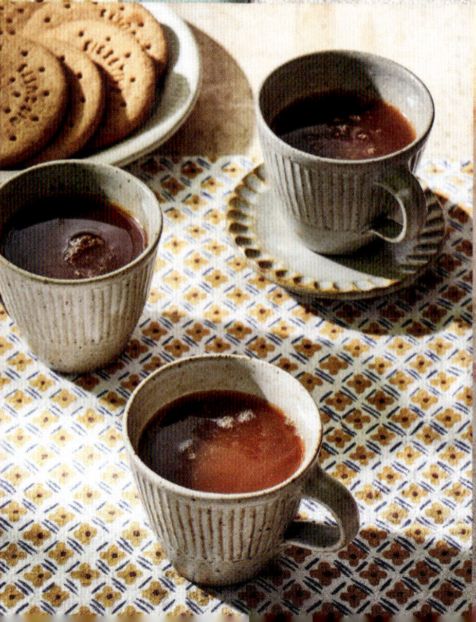
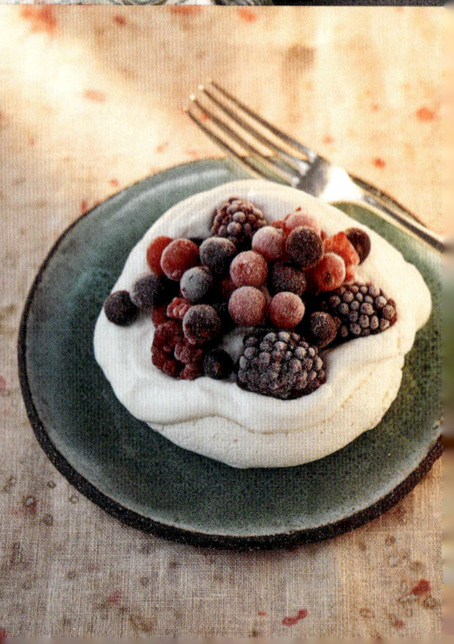

WASTE NOT WANT NOT

Brilliant bonus recipes to use up your scraps and peelings so that you can make the most of your ingredients.

PRAWN SHELL OIL

GARLIC POWDER SALT

STRAWBERRY VINEGAR

CLEMENTINE SUGAR

APPLE JAM

POTATO SKIN GRATIN

BANANA PEEL CURRY

DATE COFFEE

CHICKPEA WATER MERINGUES

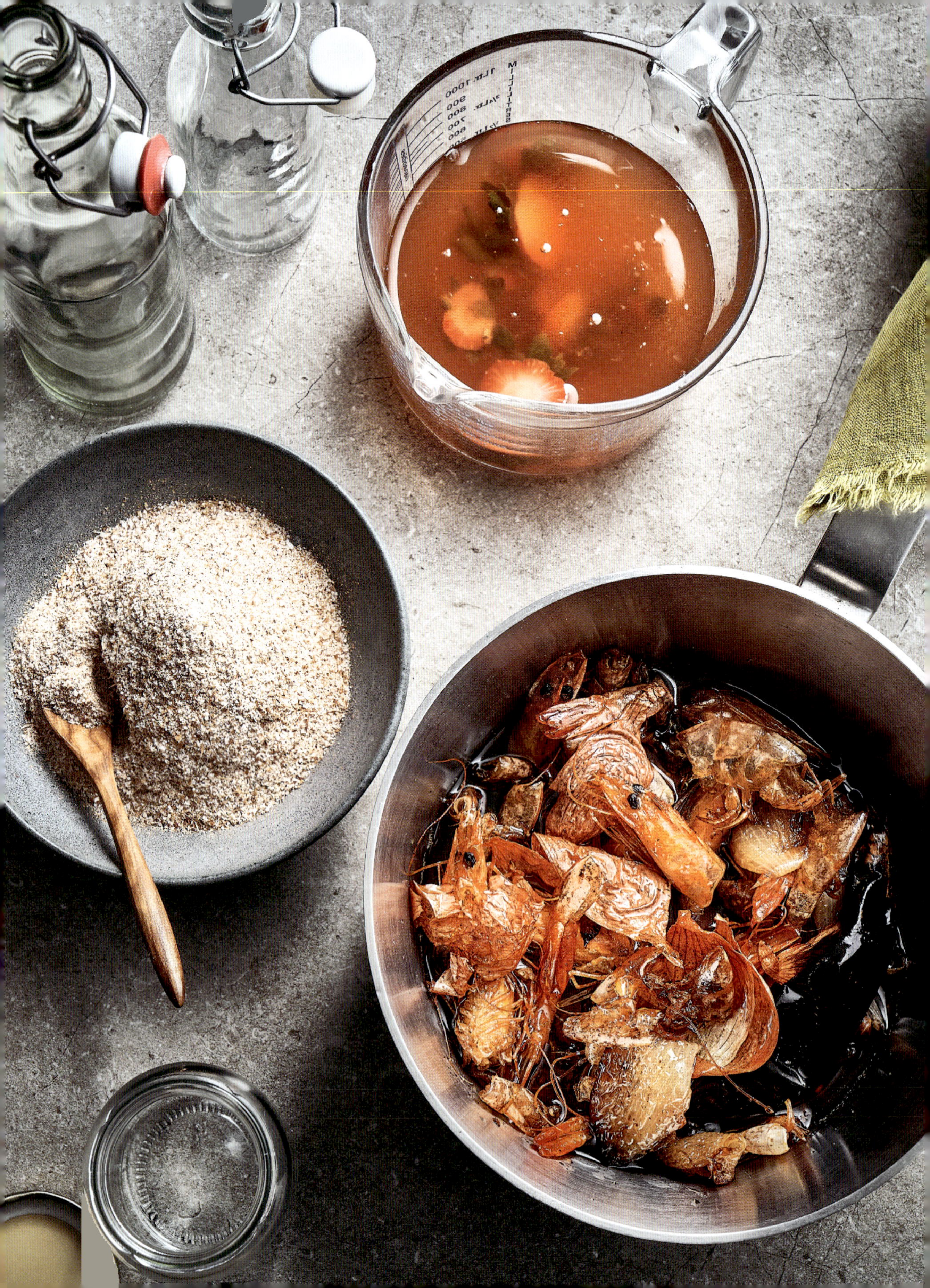

PRAWN SHELL OIL

I love cooking with prawns that have the shells, tails and heads still on as that is where you get the absolute best flavour. And I cannot bear for the shells and such like to go to waste. So for those moments where I don't have whole prawns, let me show you how to make simple, delicious prawn shell oil.

PREP: 1 HOUR 42 MINS
COOL: OVERNIGHT
MAKES: 500ML OIL

500ml olive oil

6 whole dried red chillies

3 whole cloves of garlic, peeled and lightly crushed

1 onion, quartered (with the root and peel still on)

150–200g prawn shells, tails and heads

Start by adding the flavour to this oil. Pour 100ml of the oil into a medium-sized pan.

Put the pan over a high heat and add the red chillies. As soon as the chillies just start to blacken, lower the heat. Get the garlic and onion in and cook till the garlic and onion are browned.

Now add your prawn shells, tails and heads and cook these till they turn golden brown. To really extract that prawn flavour, I would use a potato masher and break down the heads. Cook for about 5 minutes on a medium heat, stirring occasionally.

Pour in the remaining oil and heat the oil till everything is deep-frying. Deep-fry for 5 minutes and then lower the heat and leave to cook for 1 hour on the lowest setting.

Set aside and leave the oil to cool overnight. When the oil is completely cold, strain through a sieve and transfer to a bottle.

I love to use this oil in noodles or to finish off fish dishes with that delicious intense seafood flavour.

TIP *You can experiment with this oil and use all sorts of different herbs to flavour it along with the shells. My personal favourite is tarragon.*

GARLIC POWDER SALT

I use so much garlic that I cannot bring myself to throw away the skins. There is so much flavour in them, so I have found a way of using them and I save my garlic peels over time till I have enough to make this. Garlic salt is so versatile, perfect for cooking, for sprinkling – frankly great to have in your handbag to add flavour on the go. Yes, I have done that!

PREP: 3 MINS
COOK: 10–15 MINS
MAKES: 1 JAR

Peels of 10 bulbs of garlic
1 teaspoon cornflour
200g fine salt

Preheat the oven to 180°C.

Lay the garlic peels on a tray in one flat, even layer. Bake the peels till a deep golden brown. Remove the peels and leave to cool completely.

Crush the garlic peels in a spice grinder or blender with the cornflour and grind to a fine powder. Add the powder to a bowl with the salt and mix.

Transfer to jars or sprinklers and you are ready to enjoy your garlic salt, in and on everything.

TIP *A great way to peel garlic fast is to add the bulb to a jar, making sure it has room to bounce around. Remove the outermost husk before adding to the jar, then put the lid on and just shake to peel the cloves.*

WASTE NOT WANT NOT

STRAWBERRY VINEGAR

How often do we throw away the tops of our strawberries without even a thought? Not any more. Using the tops, you can make beautifully pink, strawberry-hinted vinegar.

COOK: 7–10 MINS
STEEP: OVERNIGHT
SERVES: 4

Tops of 300g punnet of strawberries

500ml apple cider vinegar

Start by putting the strawberries in a small pan and pouring in the vinegar, retaining the bottle.

Heat over a high heat and bring the liquid to a boil. As soon as it does, remove from the heat and set aside to cool completely and leave to steep overnight. This will really help with the colour and the flavour.

Strain through a colander and then transfer the strawberry vinegar back into the bottle.

CLEMENTINE SUGAR

I have kids, so I have easy peelers in the bowl all the time and I never throw away the peels. They sit on my windowsill and dry out so I can make this zesty sugar! You guys will love this one.

PREP: 6–8 MINS

MAKES: 1 LARGE JAR

Peels of 6 clementines, dried
1 teaspoon cornflour
300g caster sugar

Start by making sure the peels are dry. They should be really noisy when you drop them on a plate from a small height. You can dry them on the windowsill or you can also do this in a dehydrator.

When they are all dry, pop into a coffee grinder, spice grinder or smoothie maker with a milling blade. Add the cornflour and blend till you have a clementine powder.

Put the powder in a large jar with the sugar and pop the lid on. Shake till the mixture is even.

I love using this sprinkled on top of cakes, pancakes and porridge. It really brings a delicious zestiness that I know you will love.

TIP *You can use all citrus fruits to make this sugar – limes, lemons, grapefruits! Have fun!*

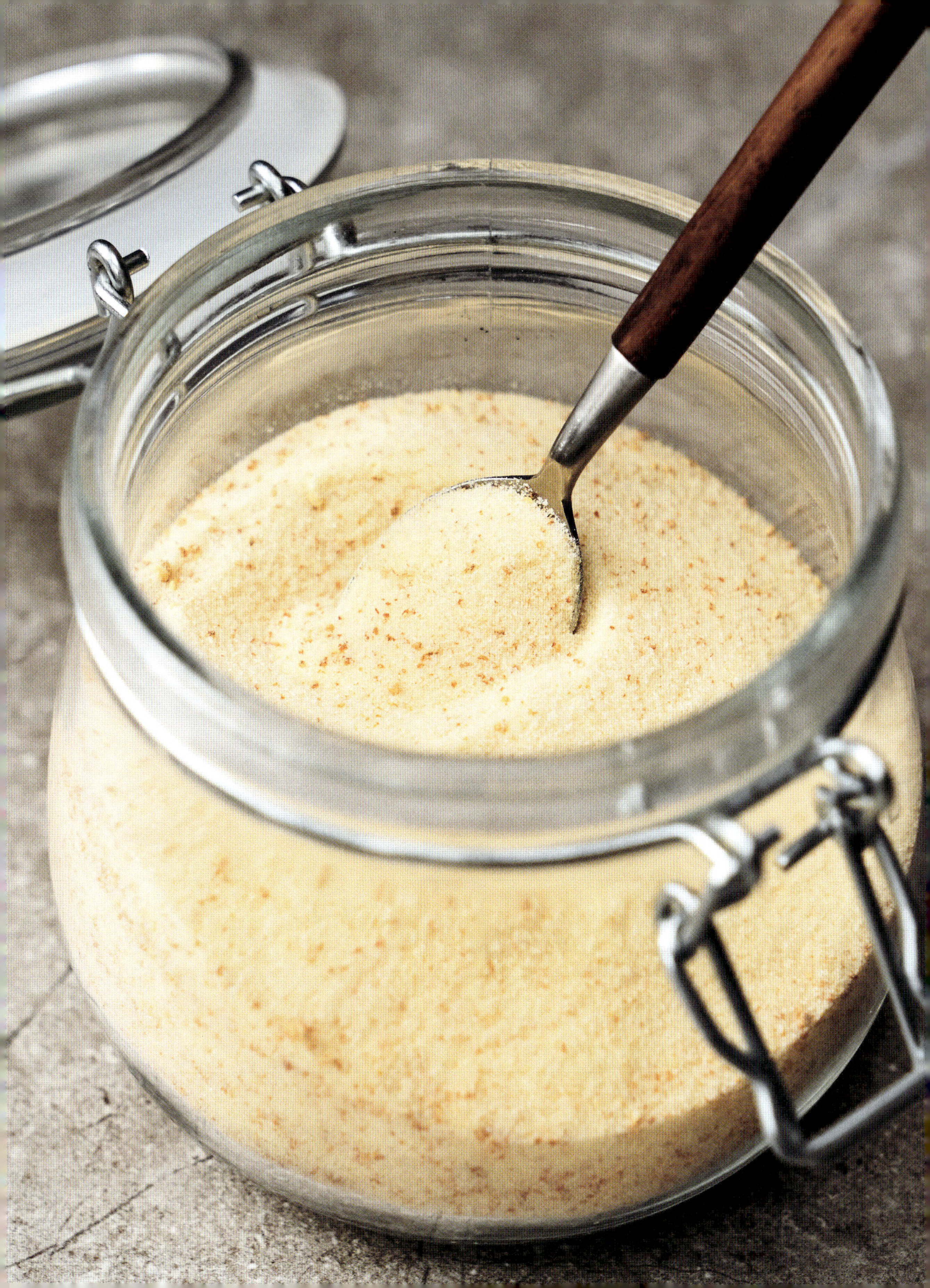

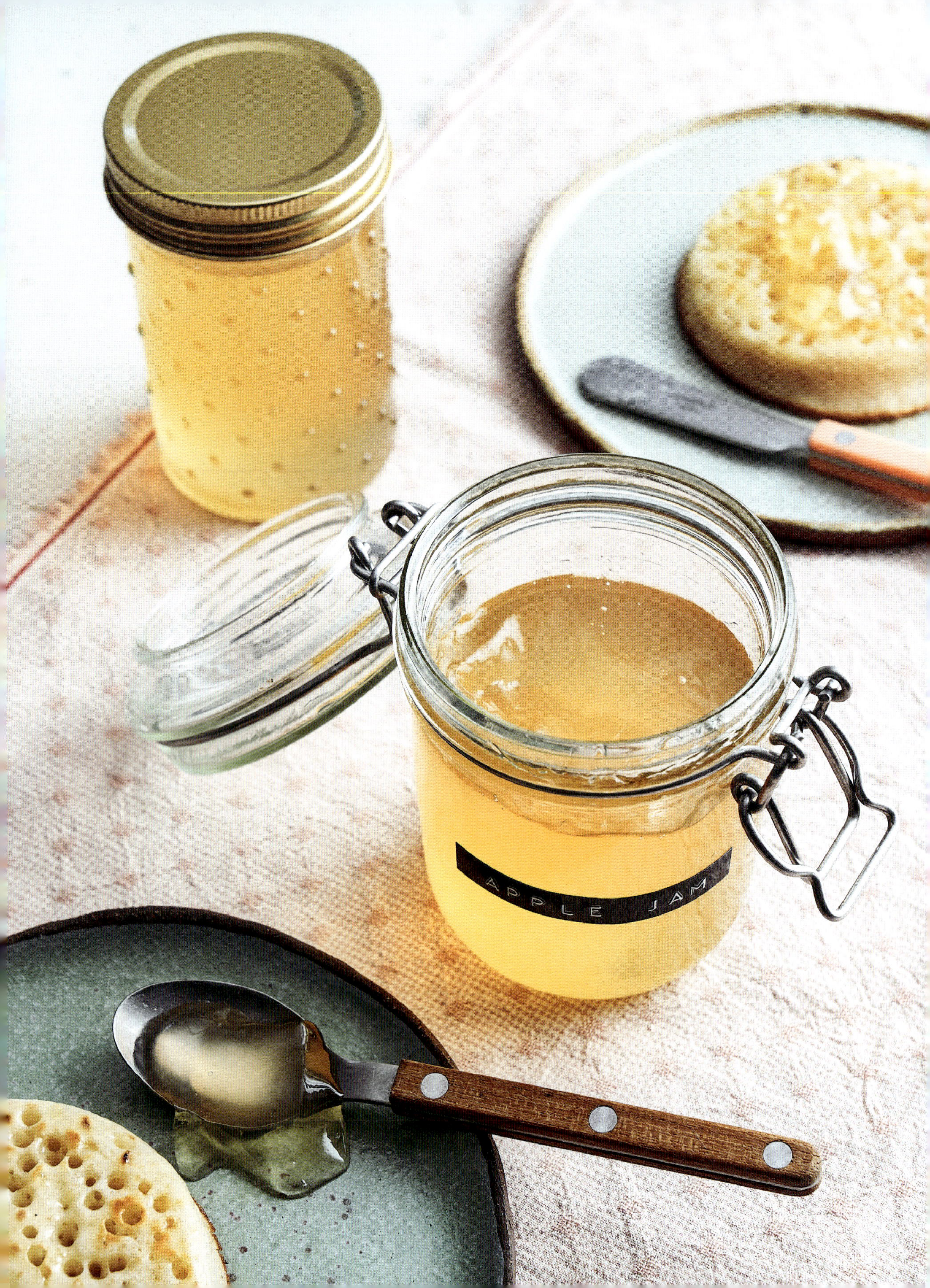
APPLE JAM

APPLE JAM

I love making this jam because I think it's super cool to be able to use the cores and peels of apples to make something so yummy. I make apple pie all the time, so if I'm making apple pie you best believe that an apple jam will follow.

PREP: 15 MINS **COOK:** 1 HOUR 15 MINS

MAKES: 250ML

Peels and cores of 6 green apples

750ml water

500g jam sugar (dependent on liquid after boiling)

2 tablespoons lemon juice/1 tablespoon citric acid

1 tablespoon coconut oil or butter

Start by putting the peels and cores in a large pan with the water. Bring the mixture to the boil and keep cooking till you have evaporated about a third of the liquid and the cores and peels are very soft.

Remove from the heat and strain the liquid into a large jug. Don't be tempted to push the mixture through – we don't want the flesh, we just want that golden clear liquid. As soon as the liquid has stopped dripping, remove the colander. You should have about 500ml of liquid.

Pour into a pan and add the jam sugar – whatever amount of liquid you have, make sure you add the exact same amount of sugar. Now add the lemon juice/citric acid.

Pop a small plate into the freezer for testing the jam.

Bring the mixture to the boil and leave to boil away. This can take up to 15 minutes. The mixture needs to come to 105°C if you are using a sugar thermometer, but another way to test it is to take out the plate from the freezer and pop a little of the mixture onto the cold plate. Leave it for 1 minute and use your finger to push the mixture. If it crinkles without breaking apart, it is ready. Take off the heat, add the coconut oil or butter, mix and set aside.

Sterilize your jars and lids by dipping into boiling water and then leaving to drain dry, which shouldn't take long.

Ladle the mixture into the jars and pop the lids on while still hot. These will keep for months and be enjoyed for just as long!

TIP *You can also freeze your apple peels and pop them into your smoothies for extra fibre in your morning drink.*

POTATO SKIN GRATIN

I save all my potato peelings for moments like this. As I cook through the week, I put the peels in the freezer so I can make dishes that essentially start their lives off as leftovers that would otherwise be thrown out or composted. This recipe makes a gratin like you would make with potato slices, but I like it better this way because with the skin on you have more texture, plus you still get that delicious creamy goodness of a good old gratin.

PREP: 15 MINS **COOK:** 1 HOUR
REST: 30 MINS
SERVES: 6

Butter, for greasing

1kg potato skins (defrosted if they are from the freezer)

300ml whole milk

3 cloves of garlic, minced

4 tablespoons onion powder

2 tablespoons black pepper

300ml double cream

100g Parmesan cheese, grated

Salt

Preheat the oven to 160°C. Get a rectangular, deep roasting dish ready, grease the inside with butter and set aside.

Start with your potato skins. Lay them out on a tea towel and make sure that they are dry by patting them down with kitchen paper.

Pour the milk into a saucepan and add the garlic, onion powder and black pepper. Bring the mixture to the boil and then take off the heat.

Add the peelings, then the cream, season well and stir together. Leave to sit for 10 minutes for the liquid to settle. Sprinkle over the cheese and bake for 40–45 minutes.

Take out and leave for at least 30 minutes before eating. This will give enough time for the cream to absorb into the potato skins and for everything to thicken up.

This is perfect as a side for a roast dinner or with a slab of grilled salmon.

TIP *If you have carrot, parsnip or beetroot peelings, you can use all of these things in the gratin. You don't have to be limited to just potato skins.*

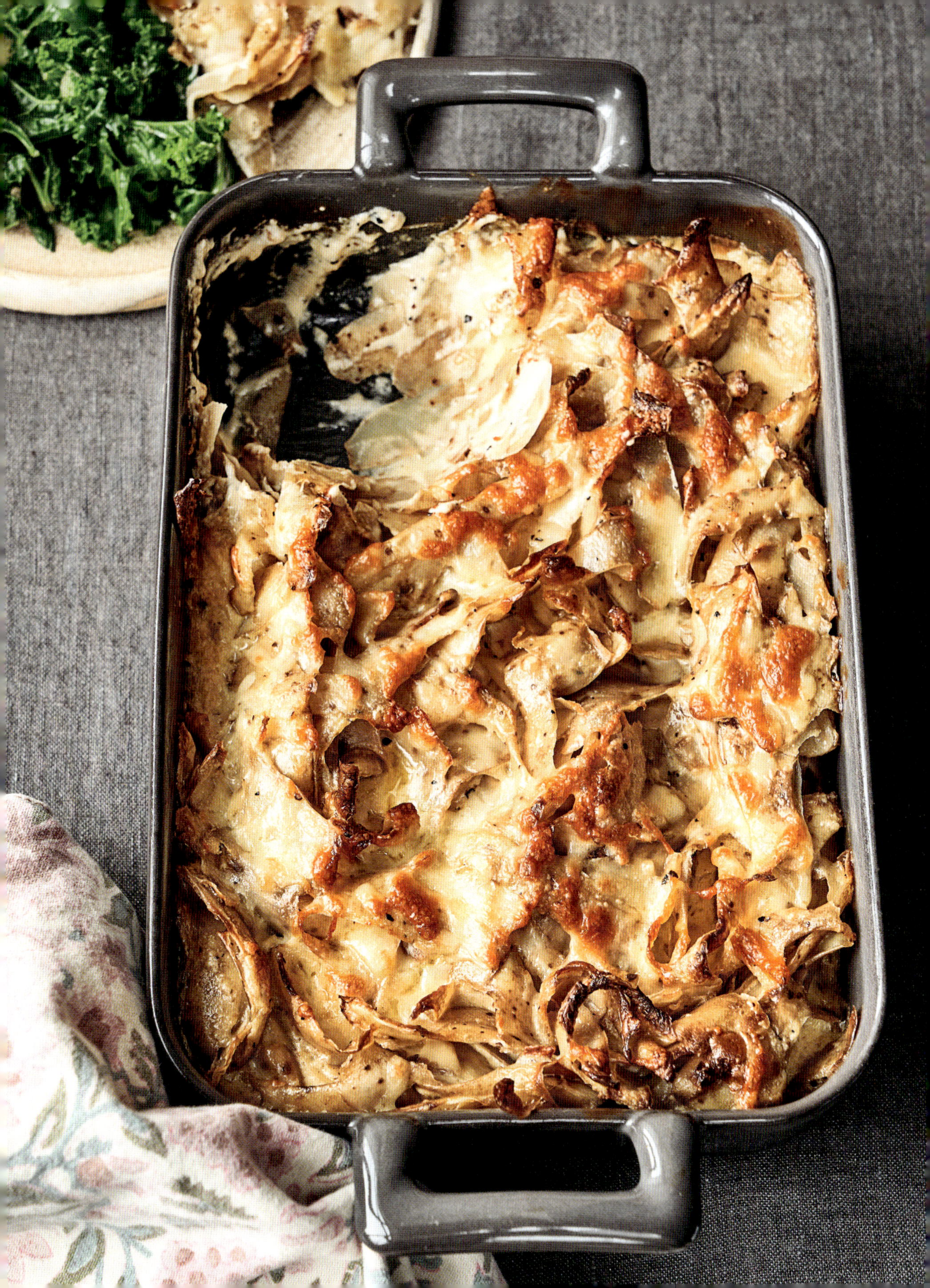

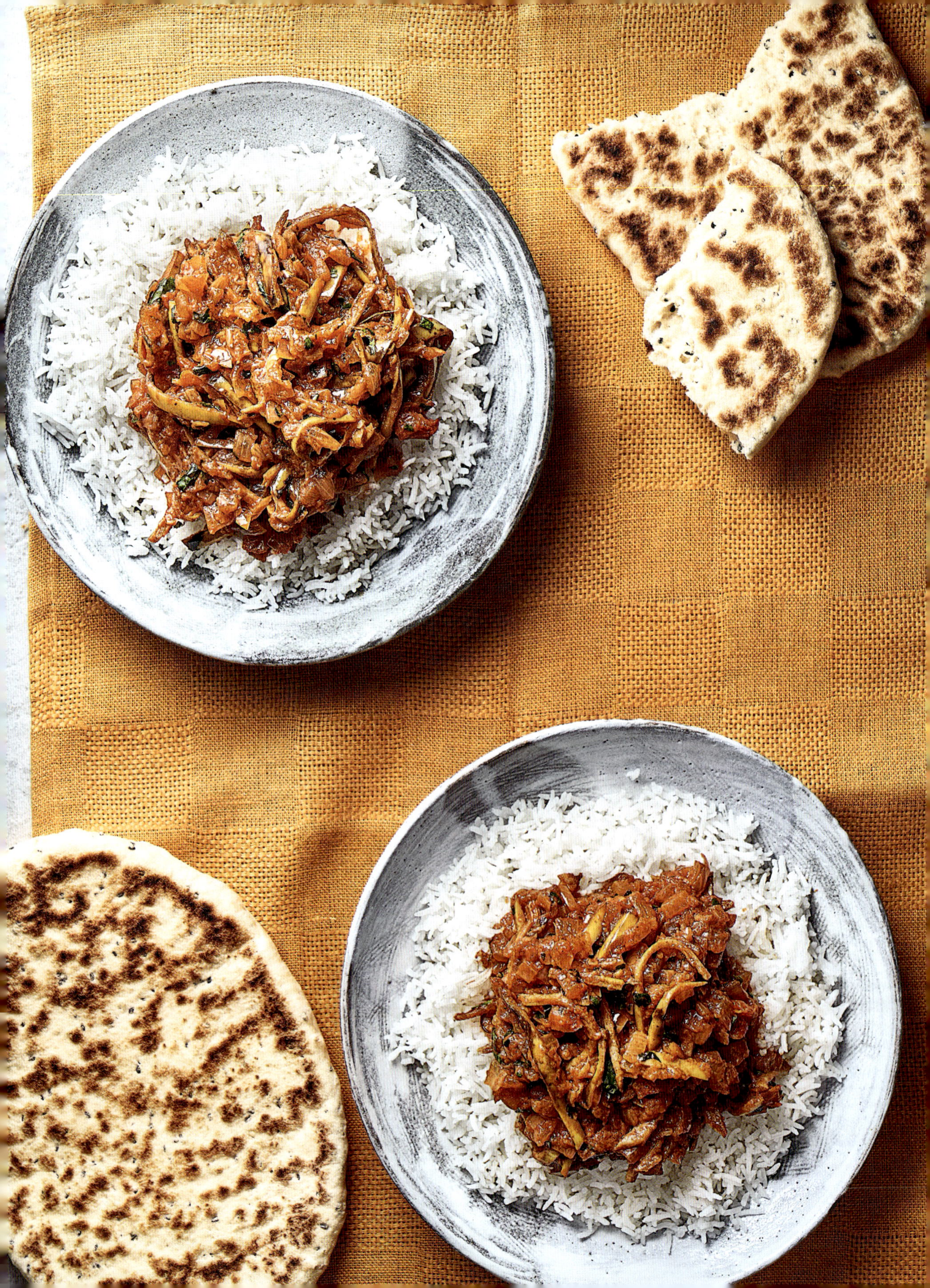

BANANA PEEL CURRY

We have eaten banana peel our whole life, so we are in no way shocked or bamboozled by something like this. I know that is not normal for everyone, but if you are making banana bread or have kids like mine and go through bananas like they are going out of fashion, give this a try. It's so easy and such a great way to use up something that pretty much everyone chucks way.

PREP: 8 MINS
COOK: 1 HOUR 10 MINS
SERVES: 4

Peels of 6 bananas
1 lemon, juice only
5 tablespoons oil
2 onions, diced
1½ teaspoons salt
2 tablespoons ginger paste
2 tablespoons garlic paste
1 tomato, diced
2 tablespoons tomato purée
3 tablespoons garam masala
2 teaspoons chilli powder (optional)
300ml water
Thinly sliced coriander, to serve

Start by thinly slicing your banana peels and squeezing the lemon juice all over to stop the browning process a little. They will brown as soon as they are peeled – they are notorious for it – but that is okay.

Pour the oil into a medium non-stick pan and as soon as the oil is hot, add the onions and salt and cook till browned.

As soon as the onions are soft and brown, add the ginger paste, garlic paste, tomato and tomato purée, cook for a few minutes and then add the garam masala and chilli powder and mix through.

Add the sliced banana peels and cook in the spices over a high heat for a few minutes. Pour in the water and cook over a medium heat, with the lid on, for 30 minutes.

Take off the lid and cook now till the mixture is drier and not watery. Sprinkle over the coriander and serve.

TIP *Don't throw away the lemon halves after squeezing. Fill the cavity with bicarbonate of soda, pop into a bowl and place in the back of your fridge to capture any nasty fridge smells.*

DATE COFFEE

This coffee is naturally caffeine-free because it is made with dates! We go through so many dates because we love them and eat them all year round. So, I collect the seeds to make this every few months. Give it a try – it's a great alternative for a caffeine-free night-time drink.

PREP: 8 MINS **COOK:** 20 MINS

SERVES: 2–4

200g date seeds (or as many as you can gather over a period)

Start by washing your date seeds. Wash them of any of the sticky date flesh residue and leave them to dry naturally. If you leave them on a windowsill, they will dry in no time at all.

Preheat the oven to 180°C.

Put your date seeds onto a baking tray and roast till they are dark. Make sure they are not black or this will give off a more bitter taste, but I know lots of people love that bitter taste, so if that's you, keep at it.

Take them out of the oven and leave to cool on the tray completely.

Use a coffee grinder, spice grinder or smoothie maker with a milling blade to grind the seeds till you have coffee-like granules. It should be a really fine powder.

Now make the coffee as you would in a cafetière. Enjoy it however you normally like your coffee. I love this date coffee black with a squeeze of sweet honey.

TIP *Date grounds also make a great exfoliator. Mix the grounds with coconut oil to make a simple exfoliator that will remove dead skins cells and moisturize.*

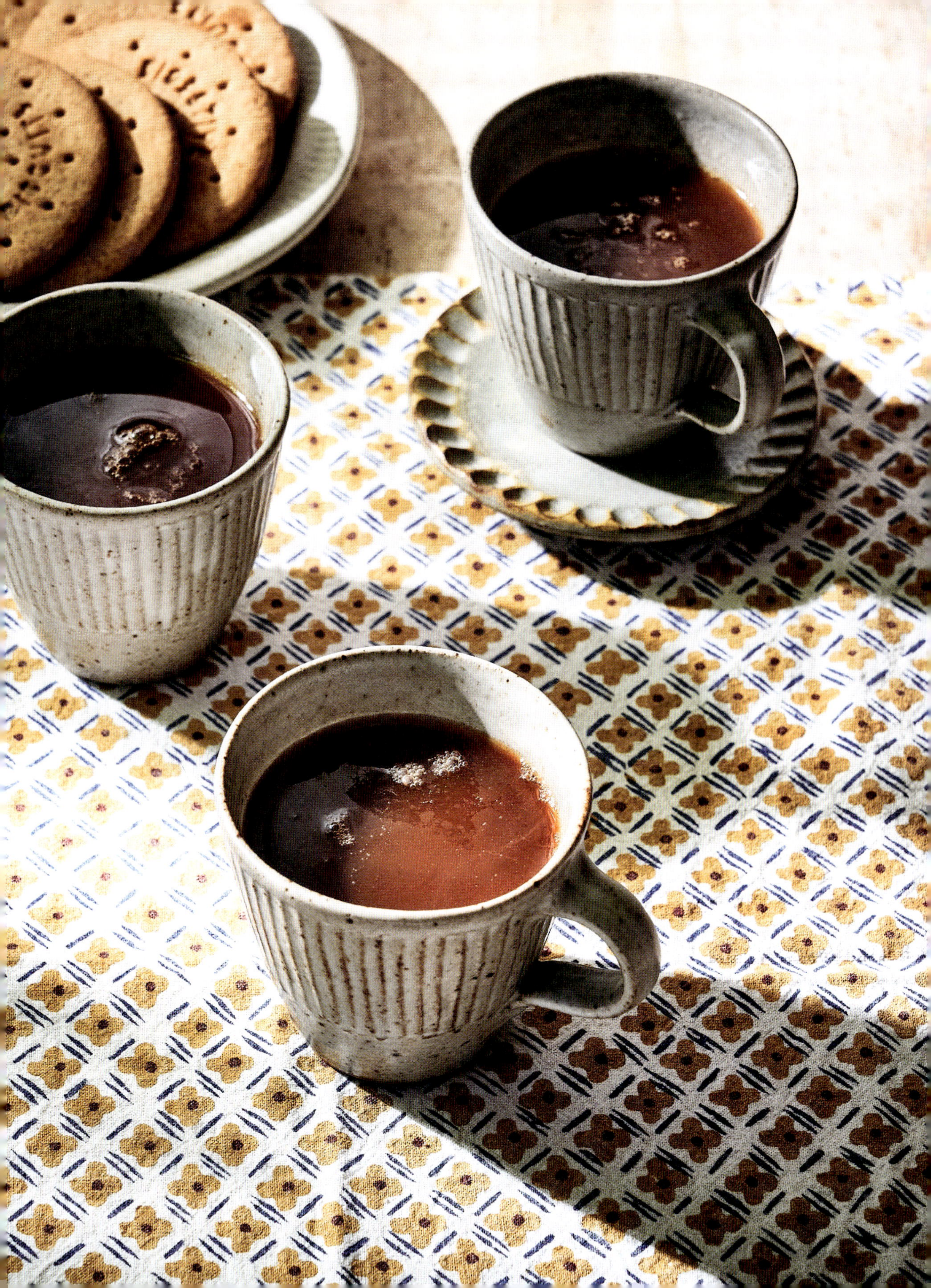

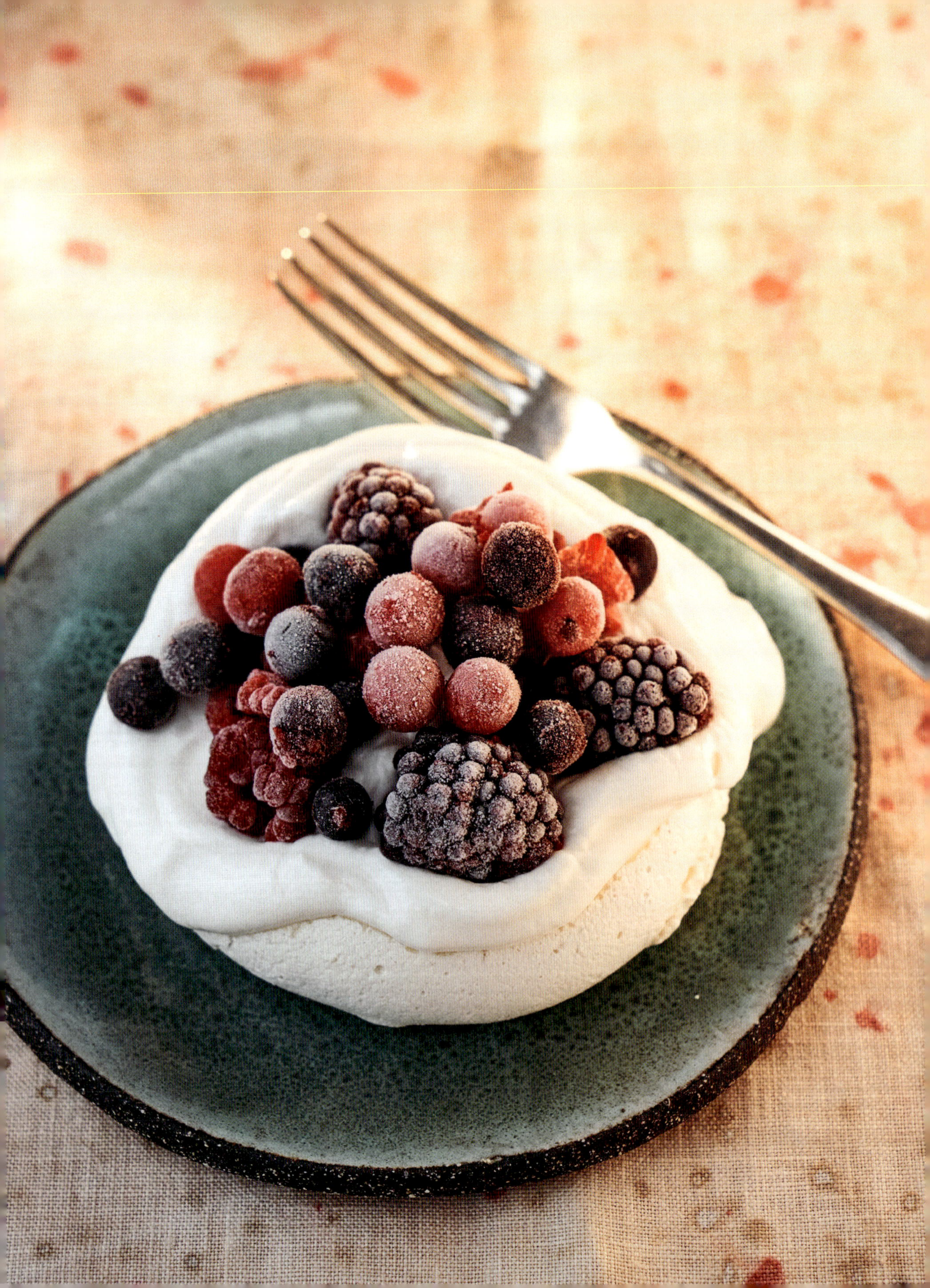

CHICKPEA WATER MERINGUES

This is the best waste product recipe of all time. The chickpea water that we drain when we open a tin of chickpeas is very similar to egg whites and fluffs up like egg whites, making for great vegan meringues. Before anyone asks, no, they do not taste like chickpeas!

PREP: 15 MINS **COOK:** 2 HOURS

MAKES: 20 MEDIUM MERINGUES OR 1 LARGE PAVLOVA

400g tin of chickpeas

225g caster sugar

Preheat the oven to 100°C and have four baking trays ready lined with baking paper (if you are making small meringues) or one tray (if you are making one large one).

Drain the chickpeas and save the water. Don't you worry, they won't go to waste (see my Chickpea and Chicken Traybake on page 81). You should have about 150ml chickpea water.

Start by whisking this and as soon as it starts to get frothier, add the sugar in one spoon at a time, making sure it is incorporated after each addition. Scrape down the edges of the bowl where sugar may have sprayed – we want all the sugar crystals to melt into the meringue mix.

Once you have used up all the sugar, you should have meringue that stands up in stiff peaks.

Spoon the mixture onto the tray(s) and bake for 2 hours. Once the time is up, turn the oven off and leave the meringues to sit and dry in the oven till the oven is cold.

As these are vegan, I like to keep it that way and serve with a coconut yoghurt, sweetened with vanilla and icing sugar, alongside fresh or frozen berries.

TIP *Meringues can be frozen. Just pop into a zip-sealed bag, tightly seal and freeze, then defrost as and when needed.*

INDEX

A
almonds: butternut squash tart **172**
    cinnamon bread granola **184**
    pear and rose tart **204–7**
anchovies: roast butternut squash **171**
apple jam **237**
apricots: bag of salad chutney **175**
aubergines: chickpea and chicken traybake **81**
avocado: poached egg breakfast board **32**

B
bananas: banana and sugar drop doughnuts **191**
    banana bread pancakes **50**
    banana peanut bark **192**
    banana peel curry **241**
    basic banana bread **49**
basil: perfect herby pesto **43**
beans: chilli **142**
    minestrone **122**
    peanut chicken traybake **155**
    potato farls **180**
    tomato bean shakshuka **36**
beef: beef stew and dumplings **101**
    beef stroganoff **137**
    beef suya kebabs **67**
    bolognese **141**
    cheat's birria **68**
    chilli **142**
    cottage pie **113**
    lasagne soup **114**
    Mongolian beef seaweed rice wraps **94**
    Mongolian beef with sticky rice **93**
    stroganoff free-form pie **138**
beetroot: *as alternative ingredient* **238**
    poached egg breakfast board **32**
biscuit spread, caramelized: butternut squash tart **172**
biscuits: lime cheesecake **220**
bolognese **141**
bread: bread and butter pudding **183**
    cheese fest potato bake **28–9**
    cinnamon bread granola **184**
    kulfi ice cream **208**
    loaf of bread **23**
    meatball parathas **90**
    no-nonsense naan **24–5**
    roast butternut squash **171**
    soda bread **188**
broccoli: peanut chicken traybake **155**
brown rice and peas **102**
brownies: white chocolate and caramel brownies **223**
buttermilk pancakes **187**
butternut squash: butternut squash tart **172**
    roast butternut squash **171**

c

cabbage, red pickled: poached egg breakfast board **32**

cakes: basic banana bread **49**
    espresso chocolate cake **203**
    filo crinkle cake **211**
    sherbet lemon loaf **212**

caramel: white chocolate and caramel brownies **223**

caramelized biscuit spread: butternut squash tart **172**

carrots: *as alternative ingredient* **238**
    beef stew and dumplings **101**
    carcass risotto **57**
    carrot and cod curry **152**
    carrot soup **149**
    lasagne soup **114**
    minestrone **122**

celery: chicken cacciatore **107**
    carcass risotto **57**
    minestrone **122**
    rice paper chips and dips **72**

cheat's birria **68**

cheat's pilau **40**

cheese: cheese and lamb samosas **78**
    carcass risotto **57**
    cheese and onion pancake **196**
    cheese fest potato bake **28–9**
    cheese fondue **195**

cod mornay **111**
corn chowder individual pies **164**
courgette spaghetti **63**
courgette spaghetti frittata **64**
lasagne soup **114**
macaroni cheese **129**
meatball marinara **118**
minestrone **122**
paneer karahi **126**
perfect herby pesto **43**
potato farls **180**
potato skin gratin **238**
scissor cut pesto pasta **44**

chicken: chicken and orzo **146**
    carcass risotto **57**
    chicken and prawn koftas **71**
    chicken cacciatore **107**
    chicken curry **145**
    chicken sausage mushroom casserole **85**
    chicken tikka masala and rice **108**
    chickpea and chicken traybake **81**
    just roast chicken **52–5**
    noodle soup **156**
    peanut chicken traybake **155**
    rice paper chips and dips **72**
    smoky chicken burritos **125**
    spiced chicken-topped hummus **82**

INDEX / 247

Swedish-style meatballs **89**
chickpeas: chickpea and chicken traybake **81**
    chickpea water meringues **245**
    just roast chicken variation **55**
    spiced chicken-topped hummus **82**
chilli **142**
chilli oil, crispy: home made **32**
chocolate: banana peanut bark **192**
    easy raspberry pudding pots **215**
    espresso chocolate cake **203**
    hazelnut chocolate cookies **224**
    white chocolate and caramel brownies **223**
chocolate spread: bread and butter pudding **183**
chutney, bag of salad **175**
cinnamon bread granola **184**
clementine sugar **234**
cocoa powder: chilli **142**
coconut, dessiccated: cinnamon bread granola **184**
cod: carrot and cod curry **152**
    cod mornay **111**
coffee: date coffee **242**
    espresso chocolate cake **203**
condensed milk: kulfi ice cream **208**
cookies: hazelnut chocolate cookies **224**
corn chowder **163**
corn chowder individual pies **164**
cottage pie **113**
courgettes: courgette spaghetti **63**
    courgette spaghetti frittata **64**
couscous: tabbouleh **176**

cream: beef stroganoff **137**
    cheese fest potato bake **28–9**
    easy raspberry pudding pots **215**
    kulfi ice cream **208**
    lime cheesecake **220**
    potato skin gratin **238**
    strawberry lemonade trifle **216**
    ultimate mashed potato **27**
cream cheese: lime cheesecake **220**
crème fraîche: chicken sausage mushroom casserole **85**
    poached egg breakfast board **32**
crispy chilli oil: home made **32**
crumble, peach pecan **219**
cucumber: chicken and prawn koftas **71**
    Mongolian beef seaweed rice wraps **94**
    peanut chicken traybake **155**
curry: banana peel curry **241**
    carrot and cod curry **152**
    chicken curry **145**
    chicken tikka masala and rice **108**
    lime pickle lamb **117**
    paneer karahi **126**
custard: filo crinkle cake **211**
    strawberry lemonade trifle **216**

D

date coffee **242**
dates: cinnamon bread granola **184**
defrosting **16**
digestive biscuits: lime cheesecake **220**
doughnuts: banana and sugar drop doughnuts **191**

E

eggs: courgette spaghetti frittata **64**
    fresh test **64**
    poached egg breakfast board **32**
    poached eggs made simple **31**
    tomato bean shakshuka **36**
eggs, pickled: sloppy joes **75**
    tabbouleh **176**
equipment **14**
espresso chocolate cake **203**

F

filo crinkle cake **211**
fish: carrot and cod curry **152**
    cod mornay **111**
    teriyaki salmon and sticky rice **130**
freezers **16**

G

garlic powder salt **232**
granola: cinnamon bread granola **184**
green beans: peanut chicken traybake **155**

H

hazelnut chocolate cookies **224**
honey: filo crinkle cake **211**
    honey mustard toad-in-the-hole **159**
    peanut chicken traybake **155**
    poached egg breakfast board **32**
hummus, spiced chicken-topped **82**

I

ice cream, kulfi **208**

J

jam: apple jam **237**
    bread and butter pudding **183**
    pear and rose tart **204–7**
jelly: strawberry lemonade trifle **216**

K

kale: minestrone **122**
kidney beans: chilli **142**
kulfi ice cream **208**

L

lamb: bolognese **141**
    cheese and lamb samosas **78**
    chilli **142**
    lasagne soup **114**
    lime pickle lamb **117**
    meatball marinara **118**
    sloppy joes **75**
lasagne soup **114**
lemons: banana peel curry **241**
    beef suya kebabs **67**
    chicken and orzo **146**
    chickpea and chicken traybake **81**
    easy raspberry pudding pots **215**
    just roast chicken variation **55**
    minestrone **122**
    perfect herby pesto **43**
    sherbet lemon loaf **212**
    spiced chicken-topped hummus **82**
    strawberry lemonade trifle **216**
    tabbouleh **176**

INDEX **/ 249**

lime pickle lamb 117
limes: chicken and prawn koftas 71
    lime cheesecake 220
    smoky chicken burritos 125

M
macaroni cheese 129
mango pickle: lime pickle lamb 117
marmalade: lime cheesecake 220
marzipan: peach pecan crumble 219
mayonnaise: cheese fest potato bake 28–9
    Mongolian beef seaweed rice wraps 94
    ultimate mashed potato 27
meatball marinara 118
meatball parathas 90
meatballs: meatball marinara 118
    meatball parathas 90
    Swedish-style meatballs 89
meringues, chickpea water 245
milk *see also* pancakes: bread and butter pudding 183
    cod mornay 111
    corn chowder 163
    macaroni cheese 129
    potato skin gratin 238
    soda bread 188
minestrone 122
mint: tabbouleh 176
Mongolian beef seaweed rice wraps 94
Mongolian beef with sticky rice 93
mushrooms: beef stroganoff 137
    chicken cacciatore 107
    chicken sausage mushroom casserole 85
mustard: *as alternative ingredient* 94
    beef stroganoff 137
    honey mustard toad-in-the-hole 159
    sausage, mash and mustard gravy 121

N
naan, no-nonsense 24–5
noodle soup 156

O
oats: cinnamon bread granola 184
    peach pecan crumble 219
onions: banana peel curry 241
    beef stew and dumplings 101
    beef stroganoff 137
    beef suya kebabs 67
    bolognese 141
    brown rice and peas 102
    carcass risotto 57
    carrot soup 149
    cheat's birria 68
    cheese and onion pancake 196
    chicken and prawn koftas 71
    chicken cacciatore 107
    chicken curry 145
    chicken sausage mushroom casserole 85
    chickpea and chicken traybake 81
    corn chowder 163
    just roast chicken variation 55

lime pickle lamb 117
minestrone 122
paneer karahi 126
roast butternut squash 171
sloppy joes 75
smoky chicken burritos 125
Swedish-style meatballs 89
tabbouleh 176
onions, crispy fried: cod mornay 111
rice paper chips and dips 72
oranges: cinnamon bread granola 184
filo crinkle cake 211

P

pancakes: banana bread pancakes 50
buttermilk pancakes 187
cheese and onion pancake 196
paneer karahi 126
parathas: meatball parathas 90
pasta: chicken and orzo 146
courgette spaghetti 63
courgette spaghetti frittata 64
freezing 47
lasagne soup 114
macaroni cheese 129
minestrone 122
scissor cut pesto pasta 44, 47
peach pecan crumble 219
peanut butter: banana peanut bark 192
beef suya kebabs 67
bread and butter pudding 183

peanut chicken traybake 155
peanuts: banana peanut bark 192
peanut chicken traybake 155
pear and rose tart 204–7
peas: brown rice and peas 102
cod mornay 111
pecans: banana bread pancakes 50
basic banana bread 49
peach pecan crumble 219
peppers: chicken cacciatore 107
meatball marinara 118
perfect herby pesto 43
pesto: perfect herby pesto 43
scissor cut pesto pasta 44, 47
pickled red cabbage: poached egg breakfast board 32
pies: corn chowder individual pies 164
cottage pie 113
creamy sausage handheld pies 86
stroganoff free-form pie 138
pilau, cheat's 40
pine nuts: perfect herby pesto 43
pistachios: filo crinkle cake 211
kulfi ice cream 208
poached egg breakfast board 32
poached eggs made simple 31
pomegranate: tabbouleh 176
potatoes: carrot soup 149
cheese and onion pancake 196
cheese fest potato bake 28–9
cottage pie 113

crispy fried roasties **179**
just roast chicken variation **55**
potato farls **180**
potato skin gratin **238**
sausage, mash and mustard gravy **121**
ultimate mashed potato **27**
prawns: chicken and prawn koftas **71**
cod mornay **111**
prawn shell oil **231**
rice paper chips and dips **72**
puddings: bread and butter pudding **183**
easy raspberry pudding pots **215**
peach pecan crumble **219**
strawberry lemonade trifle **216**

R

raspberries: easy raspberry pudding pots **215**
rice: brown rice and peas **102**
carcass risotto **57**
cheat's pilau **40**
Mongolian beef seaweed rice wraps **94**
Mongolian beef with sticky rice **93**
simple rice **39**
smoky chicken burritos **125**
teriyaki salmon and sticky rice **130**
rice paper chips and dips **72**
roses: pear and rose tart **204–7**

S

salad: bag of salad chutney **175**
tabbouleh **176**
salmon: teriyaki salmon and sticky rice **130**
samosas, cheese and lamb **78**
sausages: chicken sausage mushroom casserole **85**
creamy sausage handheld pies **86**
honey mustard toad-in-the-hole **159**
sausage, mash and mustard gravy **121**
toad burgers **160**
scissor cut pesto pasta **44**, **47**
seaweed: Mongolian beef seaweed rice wraps **94**
sherbet lemon loaf **212**
shopping **12**
sloppy joes **75**
soda bread **188**
soups: carrot soup **149**
corn chowder **163**
lasagne soup **114**
minestrone **122**
noodle soup **156**
soured cream: chicken and prawn koftas **71**
spinach: paneer karahi **126**
spring onions: carrot and cod curry **152**
chicken and prawn koftas **71**
Mongolian beef with sticky rice **93**
potato farls **180**
smoky chicken burritos **125**
sriracha: Mongolian beef seaweed rice wraps **94**
strawberries: strawberry lemonade trifle **216**
strawberry vinegar **233**

stroganoff free-form pie **138**
sunflower seeds: cinnamon bread granola **184**
Swedish-style meatballs **89**
sweetcorn: corn chowder **163**
    corn chowder individual pies **164**

T
tabbouleh **176**
tacos: cheat's birria **68**
tahini: spiced chicken-topped hummus **82**
tarts: butternut squash tart **172**
    pear and rose tart **204–7**
teriyaki salmon and sticky rice **130**
toad burgers **160**
tomato soup (canned): bolognese **141**
    chicken tikka masala and rice **108**
    everything tomato sauce **35**
    lasagne soup **114**
    sloppy joes **75**
tomatoes: banana peel curry **241**
    cheat's birria **68**
    chicken cacciatore **107**
    chicken curry **145**
    lime pickle lamb **117**
    meatball marinara **118**
    minestrone **122**
    paneer karahi **126**
    scissor cut pesto pasta **44**
    tabbouleh **176**
    tomato bean shakshuka **36**
tortillas: cheat's birria **68**

cheese and lamb samosas **78**
    smoky chicken burritos **125**
trifle, strawberry lemonade **216**
turkey: Swedish-style meatballs **89**

V
vinegar, strawberry **233**

W
walnuts: tabbouleh **176**
wasabi paste: Mongolian beef seaweed rice wraps **94**
waste reduction tips: date seed exfoliator **242**
    egg freshness test **64**
    peach stones **219**
    plant watering with potato water **27**
    tap cleanming with limes **220**
white chocolate: lime cheesecake **220**
    white chocolate and caramel brownies **223**

Y
yoghurt: bag of salad chutney **175**
    chicken and orzo **146**
    rice paper chips and dips **72**
Yorkshire pudding: honey mustard toad-in-the-hole **159**
    toad burgers **160**

THANKS

To get an opportunity to thank everyone on paper is priceless. Writing books is hard, but most of all it is a ton of fun.

Fun times, fun recipes, fun people and so many laughs it hardly ever feels like work.

Thanks to the delivery driver who's been delivering the food to our door every few days for months, he is probably deeply concerned for our cholesterol levels, based on how many eggs I get through while testing.

Thank you, Anne, for all of the hundreds of meetings we do. You know all I wait for is the green light. To be able to do what I love the most, write recipes, make lives easier and make people confident in the kitchen. Thank you for helping me get to the green light.

Thank you to Abdal and to my kids, Musa, Dawud and Maryam, for wading through the messy kitchen to find dinner. But mostly thank, for being teenagers that are eating me out of house and home. This makes testing recipes so much easier; I make, they eat and so on. Long may the cycle continue.

Thank you, Ione, for playing email tennis with me. For going back and forth, for discussing for just entertaining my insecurities, listening to my worries and being available to hear me out, all the time.

Thank you, Dan, for always believing that every book is a great book, for always being sure and always being around to taste food, eat food and just enjoy food as it should be enjoyed.

Thank you, Georgia, these recipes cannot go anywhere till they are tested, thank you for cooking, testing and being so complimentary.

Thank you, Roya, for always just getting the vision on point every single time, may your fabric collection broaden and your props cupboard be forever spilling over.

Thank you, Chris, for showing up year after year and not getting fed up with my face or my food. You capture everything as it should be, but most importantly you listen.

Thank you, Aggie, so much for being available and just rattling through the sheer number of recipes that get sent through. Thank you being a part of the team.

Thank you, Heather, Annie and Martha, for putting me together, for making me feel nice.

Thank you, Sarah, for jig-sawing this book together to create something wonderful and unique each and every time.

Thank you, Rob and Hollie, without you guys, there would be no pictures to photograph. I appreciate you both more than you know.

Thank you to the entire MJ team that work tirelessly to put it all together. Thank you Bea, Gaby, Ciara, Alice and Hattie.

Biggest thank you to everyone who has supported me up to this point. Thank you to anyone who buys this book. I hope it makes you more confident in the kitchen and most of all I hope it makes you happier in the kitchen.

Nadiya x

MICHAEL JOSEPH

UK | USA | Canada | Ireland | Australia
India | New Zealand | South Africa

Michael Joseph is part of the Penguin Random House group of companies whose addresses can be found at global.penguinrandomhouse.com.

Penguin Random House UK

First published in Great Britain by Michael Joseph, 2024
001

Text copyright © Nadiya Hussain, 2024
Photography copyright © Chris Terry, 2024 excet pages 18, 58, 132, 166, 198, 226 © Shutterstock and page 96 © Getty Images

By arrangement with the BBC
BBC Logo copyright © BBC, 1996
The BBC logo is a registered trademark of the British Broadcasting Corporation and is used under licence

The moral right of the author has been asserted

Set in Journal Sans New, TT Chocolates, Qanelas Soft and Winden Alt

Colour reproduction by Altaimage Ltd
Printed and bound in Germany by Mohn Media Mohndruck GmbH

A CIP catalogue record for this book is available from the British Library

ISBN: 9780241620052

www.greenpenguin.co.uk

FSC® C018179 MIX Paper | Supporting responsible forestry

Penguin Random House is committed to a sustainable future for our business, our readers and our planet. This book is made from Forest Stewardship Council® certified paper.